STRATEGIES FOR

TEACHING STUDENTS

with Learning and Behavior Problems

NINTH EDITION

Sharon Vaughn | Candace S. Bos

PEARSON

Boston   Columbus   Indianapolis   New York   San Francisco   Upper Saddle River
Amsterdam   Cape Town   Dubai   London   Madrid   Milan   Munich   Paris   Montréal   Toronto
Delhi   Mexico City   São Paulo   Sydney   Hong Kong   Seoul   Singapore   Taipei   Tokyo

Vice President and Editorial Director: Jeffery W. Johnston
Executive Editor: Ann Castel Davis
Senior Development Editor: Max Effenson Chuck
Editorial Assistant: Andrea Hall
Vice President, Director of Marketing: Margaret Waples
Marketing Manager: Joanna Sabella
Project Manager: Kerry Rubadue
Operations Specialist: Michelle Klein
Senior Art Director: Diane Lorenzo
Text Designer: Studio Montage
Creative Director: Blair Brown

Cover Art: Hero Images/Corbis
Media Producer: Autumn Benson
Media Project Manager: Noelle Chun
Full-Service Project Management: S4Carlisle Publishing Services
Composition: S4Carlisle Publishing Services
Printer/Binder: Courier/Kendallville
Cover Printer: Courier/Kendallville
Text Font: 9.5/12.5 ITC Garamond Std

Credits and acknowledgments for materials borrowed from other sources and reproduced, with permission, in this textbook appear on the appropriate page within the text.

Every effort has been made to provide accurate and current Internet information in this book. However, the Internet and information posted on it are constantly changing, so it is inevitable that some of the Internet addresses listed in this textbook will change.

Photo Credits: p. v, Pearson Education; p. 1, Tyler Olson/Shutterstock; p. 27, Goodluz/Shutterstock; p. 47, MShieldsPhotos/Alamy; p. 71, Scott Griessel/Fotolia; p. 113, Laura Bolesta/Merrill; p. 141, William87/Fotolia; p. 175, Monkey Business Images/Shutterstock; p. 219, Lisa F. Young/Shutterstock; p. 275, Monkey Business Images/Fotolia; p. 313, Tanya Constantine/Blend Images/Alamy; p. 405, Jacky Chapman/Janine Wiedel Photolibrary/Alamy

Library of Congress Cataloging-in-Publication Data
Vaughn, Sharon,
    Strategies for teaching students with learning and behavior problems / Sharon Vaughn, University of Texas-Austin, Candace S. Bos, Late of University of Texas-Austin.—Ninth edition.
        pages cm
    ISBN-13: 978-0-13-357106-6
    ISBN-10: 0-13-357106-8
    1. Learning disabled children—Education—United States. 2. Problem children—Education—United States. 3. Remedial teaching—United States. I. Bos, Candace S., 1950 II. Title.

    LC4705.B67 2015
    371.9—dc23
                                        2013035885

10 9 8 7 6 5 4 3 2 1
V011

ISBN 13: 978-0-13-357106-6
ISBN 10:   0-13-357106-8

To Jane Vaughn and Lucy Vaughn, who practiced progress monitoring by asking me regularly how far I was and whether I would finish the book on time.

SHARON VAUGHN (Ph.D., University of Arizona) holds the H. E. Hartfelder/Southland Corporation Regents Chair in Human Development and is the Executive Director of the Meadows Center for Preventing Educational Risk at the University of Texas. She is a recipient of the CEC Research Award and the AERA Special Education SIG distinguished researcher award. She was the editor-in-chief of the *Journal of Learning Disabilities* and the coeditor of *Learning Disabilities Research and Practice*. Dr. Vaughn is the author of numerous books and research articles that address the reading and social outcomes of students with learning difficulties including *Teaching Students Who Are Exceptional, Diverse, and At Risk in the General Education Classroom* with Jeanne Schumm and Candace Bos (5th ed., Allyn & Bacon). Currently she is the principal or coprincipal investigator on several Institute for Education Science, National Institute for Child Health and Human Development, and Office of Special Education Programs research grants investigating effective interventions for students with learning disabilities and behavior problems as well as students who are English language learners.

Preface

While traveling by car on a typical Arizona scorcher between Phoenix and Tucson after attending a state Association for Children and Adults with Learning Disabilities meeting, Candace Bos and I were discussing the content and assignments for the methods courses we taught at our respective universities. The conversation inevitably drifted to what we would like to do better. Because both of us were responsible for preparing teachers and potential teachers to work effectively with students who have learning and behavior problems, we spent a considerable amount of time discussing the content of our classes. We concluded that we would like the class and the textbook for the class to provide adequate background in procedures for teaching skill and content areas such as reading, math, oral and written expression, and social and study skills. We also would like our students to understand which methods are most effective with what types of students and why.

The first edition of this book was the result of that initial lengthy discussion, which focused on the ideal content that would prepare teachers to meet the needs of elementary and secondary students with learning and behavior problems. Each new edition continues to present fresh ideas and information, always while keeping sight of our original purpose.

New to This Edition

- Emphasis and integration of the Common Core State Standards (CCSS) throughout the text.

- Coverage of response to intervention (RTI) has been updated to include the multitiered system of support.

- All academic areas have been updated to reflect the emphasis on higher-level thinking including reading comprehension and complex texts as well as problem solving, fractions, and algebra.

- Increased emphasis on classroom management and positive behavior support, both in the target chapters as well as throughout the book.

- Key research and practice opportunities have been updated and enhanced.

- The strategies infused throughout the text remain and have been extended, based on current knowledge.

you will see in this chapter, Mary Jo and her principal provided Tier 2 interventions by hiring and training teaching assistants and provided Tier 3 interventions using Mary Jo and the reading specialist. In this chapter, you will learn more about RTI and multi-tier systems of support and how you might facilitate implementation in your school.

Response to Intervention and Multi-Tier Systems of Support

How did we come to RTI and multi-tier systems of support? Why is implementation of these models a productive way to prevent academic and behavior problems as well as contribute to identification of students with disabilities? Many educators perceive that although special education may be available to serve students with disabilities, many other students with learning needs do not qualify for special education. What are some possible solutions to this dilemma? One solution that is recommended in the reauthorization of IDEA (IDEA 2004) is to provide RTI as a means of preventing learning and behavior difficulties. RTI is the most current model for screening students and using their responses to intervention as a data source to facilitate identifying students who need special education services (Brown-Chidsey & Steege, 2011; Glover & Vaughn, 2010).

Students with learning disabilities have most often been identified by determining their potential or ability, usually with an intelligence test, and comparing that with their achievement, as measured by reading or math tests. The idea of this approach is to determine if students have significant differences between their potential or ability and their academic achievement in reading or math. Students who assessed as being low in both ability and achievement could often not qualify for special education services. This process had many difficulties, including (a) overreliance on IQ measures and (b) the requirement to wait for a discrepancy between IQ and achievement (e.g., math or reading performance), which might have meant that students would not be provided services until too late. The reason for the waiting period for most students is because students in the early grades (kindergarten through third grade) have had limited exposure to school achievement opportunities and therefore have a difficult time showing a discrepancy between their IQ and achievement. RTI was conceptualized as a potential solution to these problems. First, it provides a universal screening (schoolwide) whereby educators can readily identify students with potential learning or behavior problems and implement research-based practices. Second, teachers monitor students' academic or behavioral responses and use the response data as a means of determining students' success and thus subsequent

needs. Students who respond well to interventions do not require subsequent support, whereas students whose response to interventions (e.g., supplemental reading instruction for 30 minutes a day) is low may receive additional supplemental instruction. In addition, educators use the data gathered as a result of monitoring student progress, or *progress monitoring*, to assist in the referral and identification for special education.

As a result of the recommended use of RTI, eligibility and identification criteria for learning disability are described as follows (IDEIA 2004; reauthorization (614(b) (6)(A)-(B)]):

When determining whether a child has a specific learning disability:

- The LEA [local education agency] is not required to consider a severe discrepancy between achievement and intellectual ability.
- The LEA may use a process that determines if a student responds to scientific, research-based intervention as part of the evaluation.

While the example provided in the law is specific to learning disabilities, it is also appropriate to provide a similar approach for students with behavior problems. Therefore, RTI may help identify students with learning disabilities by replacing discrepancy criteria and using students' responses to intervention as data to facilitate decision making and assessment process. By replacing discrepancy criteria and using students' responses to intervention as data to facilitate decision making, the RTI model may help identify students with learning disabilities while providing instruction and opportunities for learning as critical elements in the assessment process. RTI may help students with behavior problems by providing schoolwide approaches to preventing behavior problems and specific interventions for students with significant problems.

How does multi-tier system of support fit in within RTI? States like Kansas prefer using a term like *multi-tier system of support* because they view this term as being more inclusive and addressing learning and behavior as well as providing opportunities to implement individual student problem-solving approaches as well as more standardized approaches to intervention. The intention is that there is a systemic approach to change

48   Chapter 3

Chapter-by-Chapter Revisions

Chapter 1: Monitoring and Teaching for Understanding

- Streamlined to ensure that the essential information is highlighted.
- A new *Web Resources* replaces the old *Tech Tips*.

Chapter 2: Approaches to Learning and Teaching

- Significant changes ensure that only the most relevant approaches to teaching students with learning and behavior problems are addressed.
- Revised to increase emphasis on how teachers can implement effective instruction for students with learning and behavior problems.

Chapter 3: Response to Intervention and Multi-Tier System of Support

- Updated with the most relevant research on RTI and with additional information on multi-tiered levels of support.

Chapter 4: Managing Behavior

- Updated to emphasize classroom management practices including how to effectively manage behavior problems as well as increasing on-task behavior to improve learning.

Chapter 5: Coteaching and Collaborating: Working with Professionals and Families

- Revised to reflect special education teachers' increasing co-teaching and collaboration with other professionals.
- Updated practices and strategies to ensure success in coteaching and collaboration.

Chapter 6: Assessing and Teaching Oral Language

- Updated with new practice ideas as well as videos to improve oral language instruction.

Chapter 7: Assessing and Teaching Reading: Phonological Awareness, Phonics, and Word Recognition

- Updated research and content to demonstrate the latest practices in assessing and teaching reading

Chapter 8: Assessing and Teaching Reading: Fluency and Comprehension

- Updated with increasing emphasis on comprehension and content area reading
- Updated with increasing emphasis on reading after grade 3.

Chapter 9: Assessing and Teaching Writing and Spelling

- Updated with instructional practices in writing that are associated with improved outcomes and that can be readily applied in both the general education and special education setting.

Chapter 10: Assessing and Teaching Content Area Learning and Vocabulary

- Revised to provide additional coverage of vocabulary instruction.

Chapter 11: Assessing and Teaching Mathematics

- Updated to reflect CCSS and emphasis on fractions and algebra.

Text Organization and Special Features

From that conversation many years ago, we determined three important goals for this text:

1. *Foundations.* To provide information about general approaches to learning and teaching so that the foundation for the methods and procedures for teaching all learners can be better understood.

2. *Detailed methods.* To supply descriptions of methods and procedures that include sufficient detail so that teachers and other professionals know how to use them.

3. *Organization and planning.* To present information about classroom and behavior management, consultation, and collaboration with families and professionals so that beginning teachers can develop a plan of action for the school year and experienced teachers can refine these skills.

To help meet these goals, a number of special features have been developed. *Apply the Concept* and *Evidence-Based Practice* features, for example, give special educators hands-on classroom implementations in reading, writing, content areas, and mathematics that are proven successful for all students, including those with learning and behavior problems.

Enhanced eText

One of the exciting developments in this edition is inclusion of its digital features. The eText for this *Strategies for Teaching Students with Learning and Behavior Problems* (Ninth Edition) is an affordable, interactive version of the print text that includes videos, interactive links to helpful Web sites, and interactive chapter assessment quizzes.

To learn more about the enhanced Pearson eText, go to **www.pearsonhighered.com/etextbooks**.

- *Video marginal notes with reflective questions* ▶ link to videos that show classroom footage and experts in the field elucidating concepts and strategies discussed in the text. Approximately 50 of these clips are interspersed throughout the text.

- *Via links to YouTube videos* within this eText, students will find occasional YouTube video clips that illustrate strategies discussed in the text.

- *End-of-chapter assessments* give students the opportunity to test their understanding of concepts and strategies that they have learned in that chapter. Questions are aligned with the chapter's learning outcomes, and feedback for incorrect answers is provided.

- *IRIS Center Resource links* provide readers access to The IRIS Center at Vanderbilt University, founded by the U.S. Department of Education's Office of Special Education Programs (OSEP), which develops training enhancements material for pre-service and in-service teachers. The Center works with experts from across the country to create challenge-based interactive modules, case study units, and podcasts that provide research-validated information about working with students in inclusive settings. This content has been integrated throughout the text, where appropriate.

> In this **video** ▶, you will see children engaged in partner reading. How do they respond to this strategy? What are some advantages and disadvantages? How does the teacher support the students while they are partner reading?

- *Web Resources* marginal notes, available throughout the chapters, encourage further exploration of chapter topics. You will find the URLs for these resources on the pages of your text.

- *Weblinks* in each chapter provides links to Web sites of organizations, institutions, and government resources that reflect the rich community and depth of assets that await students as they further their educational pursuits.

Support Materials for Instructors

The following resources are available for instructors to download on www.pearsonhighered.com/educators. Instructors enter the author or title of this book, select this particular edition of the book, and then click on the "Resources" tab to log in and download textbook supplements.

Instructor's Resource Manual and Test Bank (0133571157)

The Instructor's Resource Manual and Test Bank includes key topics for mastery, lecture-discussion outlines, invitation for learning activities, and think-and-apply questions for the basis for class discussions or use in exams. Some items (lower-level questions) simply ask students to identify or explain concepts and principles they have learned. But many others (higher-level questions) ask students to apply those same concepts and principles to specific classroom situations—to actual student behaviors and teaching strategies.

PowerPoint™ Slides (0133801322)

The PowerPoint™ slides include key concept summarizations, to enhance learning. They are designed to help students understand, organize, and remember core concepts, skills, and strategies.

TestGen (0133801330)

Test Gen is a powerful test generator available exclusively from Pearson Education publishers. You install TestGen on your personal computer (Windows or Macintosh) and create your own tests for classroom testing and for other specialized delivery options, such as over a local area network or on the Web. A test bank, which is also called a Test Item File (TIF), typically contains a large set of test items, organized by chapter and ready for your use in creating a test, based on the associated textbook material. Assessments—including equations, graphs, and scientific notation—may be created for both print and testing online.

The tests can be downloaded in the following formats:

TestGen Testbank file: PC

TestGen Testbank file: MAC

TestGen Testbank: Blackboard 9 TIF

TestGen Testbank: Blackboard CE/Vista (WebCT) TIF

Angel Test Bank (zip)

D2L Test Bank (zip)

Moodle Test Bank

Sakai Test Bank (zip)

Acknowledgments

Candace S. Bos and I launched this book together as junior faculty 30 years ago. Since her death, I have done one of the most challenging things of my professional career, writing and revising the book without my dear friend and colleague. I knew what an outstanding writer and teacher–educator she was; I know even better now. Working on this book is a clear reminder of how much she taught me and how hard it is to work without her. Ann Davis, editor, provided more than her usual excellent support and good ideas. Max Chuck, developmental editor, provided valuable suggestions and advice. Max is so capable and supportive that her assistance has made this the best edition yet. I would also like to thank Dr. Amory Cable for her careful and thoughtful work.

Many people deserve a great deal more acknowledgment than their names appearing here will provide. I wish to acknowledge and thank the teachers whom Candy and I have written about in this book. The time we have spent in their classrooms— observing, discussing, and teaching—has afforded us the ability to write a book that is grounded in classroom experiences and practices. These teachers include Juan Caberra, Judy Cohen, Joan Downing, Mary Lou Duffy, Joyce Duryea, Jane Eddy, Louise Fournia, Joan Gervasi, Sally Gotch, Linda Jones, Sharon Kutok, Tom Lebasseur, Tiffany Royal, Marynell Schlegel, Mary Thalgott, and Nina Zaragoza.

I also thank Janette Klingner of the University of Colorado at Boulder for her support on the RTI chapter, and Terry L. Weaver of Union University for contributing and revising the math chapter. I would also like to thank several individuals whose expert support and assistance in previous editions remain in this edition: Dr. Ae-hwa Kim and Dr. Jeannie Wanzek. A special thank you to Kim Shumake for all of her support.

I especially wish to acknowledge the following individuals for their reviews of the ninth edition: JoBeth DeSoto, Wayland Baptist University; Roger Kent Hamilton, Florida State University; Barry E. McNamara, Dowling College; Amy Shearer Lingo, University of Louisville; and Stephen W. Wills, Georgia College and State University.

A special thank you for the contributions of Dr. Alison Gould Boardman, and Katie Klingler Tackett, who all provided outstanding suggestions and practical ideas.

Special thanks also to my husband, Jim, and to my brother, Jim, and his wife, Meg, who provided me with a gorgeous place to write revisions of the book in Geneva, Switzerland, and to their children Jane and Lucy who practiced progress monitoring by asking me regularly how far I was and whether I would finish the book on time.

Most important of all, we would like to thank the teacher whose observations, research, and thinking has done more to guide our development and the field of special education than any other: Samuel A. Kirk.

Brief Contents

Contents

Part 2   Instructing Students with Learning and Behavior Problems

Special Features

Apply the Concept

Evidence-Based Practice

Monitoring and Teaching for Understanding

1

LEARNING OUTCOMES

1. Recognize characteristics of students with learning disabilities as well as those with behavior disorders.
2. Learn the multiple ways in which individuals with learning disabilities are identified.
3. Be able to complete an individualized education program (IEP) on a target student with disabilities.
4. Summarize the critical components related to effectively teaching students with learning and behavior problems.

This book is about children and adolescents who have difficulty learning and interacting appropriately in school. If you saw these children in school, it is very likely that you would not be able to readily identify them until they were engaged in an academic activity that challenged them (e.g., writing, reading) or they were exhibiting extreme behaviors (e.g., screaming out of control). What are these students like? Teachers describe them this way:

Servio is extremely sensitive and gets upset at the least little thing. For example, yesterday Jo'Jame walked by his desk and bumped into him, and he jumped up and starting screaming at him. He got very aggressive, and if I had not intervened I strongly suspect there would have been a fight. He used to throw things at school, but he doesn't do that anymore. He doesn't have any friends in the class, and most of the other students don't want him around them. Sometimes he is very quiet and almost cooperative, but these times only last until someone does or says something he doesn't like.

Dana has a great deal of difficulty with her work. She appears to have trouble remembering. Well, not always. Sometimes she remembers how to read a word; other days she looks at the same word, and it's like she has to scan all of the information in her head to try to locate the name of the word. I know she is trying, but it is very frustrating because her progress is so slow. She is also very easily distracted. Even when the instructional assistant is working with her alone, she will look up and stop working at the littlest things. Something like the air-conditioning going on and off will distract her from her work. I know she is bright enough, but she seems to have serious problems learning.

Tina is more work for me than the rest of my class put together. She has both academic problems and behavior problems. For example, after I have explained an assignment to the class, Tina always asks me several questions about the assignment. It's like I have to do everything twice, once for the class and then again for Tina. She has a terrible time with reading. She reads so slowly, and she often reads the wrong word. For example, she will say "carrot" for "circus" and "monster" for "mister." She often doesn't know what she's read after she's finished reading it. Also, she can never sit still. She is always moving around the room, sharpening her pencil, getting a book, looking out the window. It is hard for her to do the same thing for more than a few minutes. She's always bugging the other students. She's not really a bad kid, it's just that she is always doing something she's not supposed to be doing, and she takes a lot of my time.

The purpose of this book is to acquaint you with the teaching skills and strategies necessary to understand and teach students like Servio, Dana, and Tina. This chapter provides background information on students with learning and behavior problems and an overview of the teaching–learning process. This chapter also introduces response to intervention (RTI) as a framework for facilitating identification of students with learning and behavior problems.

As you read this book, we encourage you to reflect on how the information presented can be interwoven into your thoughts about the teaching–learning process. We encourage you to seek opportunities to work with students with learning and behavior problems and to use the research-based practices presented in this book in seeking supervision and feedback from well-prepared professionals. We also encourage you to use a reflective, problem-solving orientation to teaching. This model of teaching and learning serves as a framework for reflecting on what you do, consulting with others to seek better information and practices, and making adjustments to improve outcomes for students with learning and behavior problems.

Students with Learning and Behavior Problems

Most educators can recognize with little difficulty those students who have learning and behavior problems. They are students who call attention to themselves in the classroom because they have difficulty learning and interacting appropriately. Students with learning and/or behavior problems manifest one or more of the following behaviors:

- *Poor academic performance.* Students display significant problems in one or more academic areas such as spelling, reading, and mathematics. The key to understanding students with learning disabilities is that they display unexpected underachievement. What do we mean by unexpected underachievement? This means that students have the cognitive processes to succeed academically and perform well in one or more other academic areas but have a significant difficulty in one or more areas such as spelling, writing, reading, and/or math.

- *Attention problems.* Many students seem to have difficulty working for extended periods of time on a task. They may have trouble focusing on the teacher's directions. These students are often described by teachers as being easily distracted. They have a difficult time completing tasks, and because their mind wanders, they miss critical information.

- *Hyperactivity.* Some students are overactive and have a difficult time staying in their seats and completing assigned tasks. They move from task to task, and often from location to location in the classroom. When working on an assignment, the least little noise will distract them.

- *Memory.* Many students have a hard time remembering what they were taught. Often their difficulty remembering is associated with symbols such as letters and numbers. These students may remember something one day but not the next.

- *Poor language abilities.* Many students with learning disabilities have language difficulties that are manifested in a number of ways. As toddlers, these students may have taken longer in learning to talk. Often these language problems can be corrected through speech therapy. Many also have difficulty developing phonological awareness skills—hearing the sounds of language separately and being able to blend and segment them (e.g., hearing /b/, /a/, /t/ separately and then blending to say, "bat"). Students may have difficulty with vocabulary, understanding the concept, using language to adequately express themselves orally or in writing, or developing age-appropriate math skills.

- *Aggressive behavior.* Some students are physically or verbally assaultive. They may hit, kick, get into fights, and/or verbally threaten or insult others. These children are easily upset and cope with being upset by acting out.

- *Withdrawn behavior.* Some students seldom interact with others. Unlike shy students, who may have one or two friends, these students are real loners who avoid involvement with others.

- *Bizarre behavior.* Some students display unusual patterns of behavior. They may stare for long periods of time at objects that they hold in the light, they may sit and rock, or they may display aggressive behaviors at times and withdrawn behaviors at other times.

Students with learning and/or behavior problems often exhibit more than one of these behaviors. Yet some students exhibit these behaviors and are not identified as having learning or behavior problems. There are other factors that teachers consider when determining how serious a learning and behavior problem is.

Factors in Determining the Severity of a Learning or Behavior Problem

From 15% to 25% of all students have some type of learning or behavior problem; however, students with learning disabilities and behavior problems that are identified as special education represent a much smaller percentage of the student population (typically less than 6%). Students with learning disabilities are five times more prevalent than those with behavior disorders. Of course, this could be because teachers and parents are not inclined to identify students as having a significant behavior problem that constitutes a disability. There are several factors to consider when you are determining how serious a problem is:

1. *Persistence of the problem.* Sometimes a student has a learning or behavior problem for a short period of time, perhaps while there is some type of crisis in the family, and then it disappears. These behaviors and feeling states are not considered problems if they occur occasionally. Other students display persistent learning and behavior problems throughout their schooling experience. These problems have more serious consequences for the students.

2. *Severity of the problem.* Is the student's learning or behavior problem mild, moderate, or severe? Is the student performing slightly below or significantly below what would normally be expected of him or her? Is the behavior slightly different or substantially different from that of the student's peers?

3. *Speed of progress.* Does the student appear to be making steady progress in the classroom despite the learning or behavior problem? We do not expect all students to learn at the same rate. In fact, in an average fourth-grade classroom, the range of performance varies from second-grade level to seventh-grade level. However, a critical question is whether the student is responding appropriately to classroom instruction and making at least 1 year's growth academically every year.

4. *Motivation.* Is the student interested in learning? Does the student persist at tasks and attempt to learn? Does the student initiate and complete tasks without continual praise and encouragement?

5. *Parental response.* How do family members feel about a child's academic and/or behavioral progress? How do they think it compares with the child's progress in the past? Are they concerned about how their child's abilities compare with those of other children the same age? How have siblings performed in school?

6. *Other teachers' responses.* How did the student perform in previous classes? What do previous or other teachers say about the student's learning style, academic abilities, and behavior?

7. *Relationship with the teacher.* What type of relationship does the student have with his or her present teacher? Sometimes a poor interpersonal match between the student and the teacher may interfere with the student's academic performance and/or behavior.

8. *Instructional modifications.* What attempts has the teacher made to modify the student's academic and/or behavioral program? Does the student seem responsive to attempts at intervention? If the student is not performing well in a traditional reading program, has the teacher tried other instructional approaches to reading? Has the student had opportunities to work with different students in the class? If the problem is behavior, what behavior change programs have been implemented? Have any been successful?

Is there a good match between the student and the classroom setting? Some children function best in a highly structured classroom where the rules, expectations, and assignments are very clearly stated. Other children function better in a learning environment where there is more flexibility.

9. *Adequate instruction.* Has the student had adequate exposure to the material and enough time to learn? Some students have little experience with formal learning situations before coming to school. Other students have multiple experiences, including preschool programs that teach letters and letter sounds. Students who have less exposure to school learning situations or whose parents provide few school-like learning experiences may need more time and exposure to the learning environment before they make gains. Determine what prerequisite skills are missing and how they can be acquired.

10. *Behavior–age discrepancy.* Does the student display problems that are unusual or deviant for the student's

age? What types of behaviors is the student exhibiting that are or are not age appropriate?

11. *Other factors.* Are there other factors that might be contributing to the student's learning and/or behavior problems? For example, how closely do the student's background experiences, culture, and language match those of the teacher and other students in the class? Are there any health-related factors that might be interfering with the student's learning or behavior? Have the student's vision and hearing been adequately assessed to determine whether they might be affecting the student's learning or behavior?

Considering these factors will help you to identify the severity of the student's problems and determine whether the student needs additional classroom supports.

The Defining Features of Special Education

How does special education for students with learning and behavior problems differ from a good general education? Consider the following six features of instruction that, according to Heward (2013), define effective instruction for students with learning and behavior problems:

1. *Individually planned.* Instruction, materials, and setting of instruction are selected or adapted on the basis of student needs.

2. *Specialized.* Instruction and adaptations include related services and assistive technology that are not often a part of the general education curriculum.

3. *Intensive.* Precise, targeted instruction is designed to assist students in making efficient progress toward gaining necessary skills and strategies.

4. *Goal-directed.* Instruction focuses on individual goals and objectives necessary for student success.

5. *Employ research-based methods.* Selection and application of effective teaching methods are supported by research.

6. *Guided by student performance.* Student response to instruction is continually assessed for use in evaluating the effectiveness of instruction and adjusting instruction when necessary.

Heward (2013) further states that teachers may hold misunderstandings about teaching and learning that interfere with successful delivery of special education for students with disabilities. For example, many educators and administrators are taught that a structured curriculum including instruction and practice in individual skills is unnecessary and harmful to students' general learning. Contrary to this belief, students with learning and behavior problems often need academic tasks broken down into smaller, obtainable skills in order to progress.

A guiding principle of special education is that it is goal directed and guided by student performance.

Evidence-based instruction is the ongoing alignment of appropriate instruction based on an ongoing system of measuring students' progress. Therefore, assessment of student outcomes is needed to guide appropriate instruction and to move students as quickly as possible to ensure student success in academics and related areas. This means that instruction must be focused and provided with a sense of urgency. Unstructured lessons and activities without regard for effectiveness can be detrimental to students with learning and behavior problems. These students need the very best instruction using research-supported techniques to ensure that time is not wasted and teachers are providing opportunities for students to gain the necessary abilities and obtain the motivating experience of success. One of the primary goals of a special education is to accelerate the positive behavior and educational outcomes of students with learning disabilities and behavior problems. Throughout this book, we will demonstrate effective instructional techniques in reading, written expression, math, and other content areas for students with learning and behavior problems.

Learning and Educational Environments for Students with Learning and Behavior Problems

Most students with learning and behavior problems are educated in the general education classroom. But students who have severe learning and behavior problems may receive a range of support services, including reading or math support, counseling, individualized instruction with a teaching assistant, and special education.

In many schools, reading or math specialists assist students with learning problems. These specialists typically provide supplemental instruction to the regular reading or math instruction the students receive in the general education classroom. Such additional instruction can help students with learning problems make sufficient progress in reaching expected performance levels. Often, specialists and classroom teachers collaborate to ensure that the instruction they provide is consistent and follows a similar sequence of skills.

Some classroom teachers have a teaching assistant who provides supplemental instruction for students with significant learning or behavior disorders. You may find yourself in a situation where you are supervising one or more teaching assistants. Teaching assistants often do not have the instructional background that specialists do. Therefore, it is imperative that teachers provide teaching assistants with sufficient guidance. This includes planning lessons, training in effective instruction for students with learning problems, and monitoring instruction. When teaching assistants are given appropriate instructional tools for teaching students with learning problems, the supplemental help they provide often helps students to make the necessary progress to learn at expected levels.

Students with disabilities receive services through special education. PL 94-142, reauthorized in 2004 as the Individuals with Disabilities Education Act (IDEA), ensures that a continuum of placements is available for students. This continuum is conceptualized as proceeding from the least to the most restrictive. The term *restrictive*, in an educational sense, refers to the extent to which students are educated with nondisabled peers. A more restrictive setting is one in which students spend no part of their educational program with nondisabled peers. In a less restrictive setting, students may spend part of their educational day with nondisabled peers. IDEA mandates that all students should be educated in the least restrictive educational environment possible (IDEA, 2004).

Including Students with Learning and Behavior Problems

When students with special needs are included in the general education classroom, either their specialized services are provided within the general education class, or they are pulled out of the classroom for a portion of the day to receive the services. How do schools and teachers decide if a student should be included for all or part of the school day?

The decision to include a student with special needs is made by an individual educational planning and placement committee. This committee is typically made up of one or both of the child's guardians, the special education teacher, the general education teacher, relevant professionals such as the school psychologist, and the administrator who supervises the special education program in which the student participates. At the recommendation of the special education and general education teachers and the professionals who evaluate the student's progress, the committee collectively decides whether the student's social and educational needs would best be met in the general education classroom and writes up the individualized education program (IEP) accordingly. What types of information do special education teachers use to determine inclusion in general education? The answer varies by district and school, and several essential information sources are helpful:

> In this **video** ▶, a 4th grader with learning disabilities shares his experiences in the general education classroom. Do you feel the supports and services that were put in place for him were successful and, if so, how is this demonstrated?

- Based on classroom observations, how is the target student performing in the general education classroom? What supports does the student need to ensure success?
- Based on progress monitoring and other assessment data, how effectively is the student learning in the general education classroom? What supports does the student need to ensure success?
- Has the target student been provided intensive interventions? If yes, how has the student responded to these interventions?
- What types of classroom-based interventions have been provided, and how effective have they been?
- What views and insights do the parents hold about the student's performance and inclusion in the general education classroom?
- What views do previous teachers and educational specialists hold about the student's performance in the general education classroom?

The goal is to provide students with an appropriate education with access to the general education classroom. For students to receive special education that is outside of the general education classroom, evidence that the students' educational and social needs are better met in the special education classroom is required. Most students with emotional and learning disabilities spend at least some of their school day in general education classrooms with their nondisabled peers. Therefore, both general education and special education teachers are often responsible for the instruction and outcomes of students with disabilities.

In 1975, Public Law 94-142 was passed, providing an opportunity for all students with disabilities to achieve an appropriate education. Thirty-five years later, The Department of Education reported on the national impact of IDEA, including the following key impacts from the report, *Thirty-Five Years of Progress in Educating Children with Disabilities Through IDEA, 2004*:

- More young children with disabilities receive high-quality early intervention.
- More children with disabilities are attending neighborhood schools and receiving access to the general education curriculum.
- More youth with disabilities are graduating from high school.
- More youths with disabilities are enrolled in post-secondary programs.
- More young adults with disabilities are employed.

For students between the ages of 3 and 5 years, 49% spent 80% or more of their time with typical achieving peers. Where were students with learning disabilities and behavior disorders educated? Almost 59% of students identified as having specific learning disabilities spent 80% of their time in general education classrooms, whereas only 37% of students identified as emotionally disturbed were in general classrooms for that same amount of time. It is quite likely that fewer students identified as seriously emotionally disturbed are in general education because their behavior interferes significantly with the academic progress of others in the classroom.

IDEA introduced the concept of a continuum of placements, including the *least restrictive environment* (LRE). Since its passage in 1997, there has been a growing interest in educating students with disabilities with their peers who are nondisabled. IDEA contained a strong mandate to provide greater access to the general education curriculum. As more students with special needs are placed in general education classrooms, with special education teachers consulting or collaborating with classroom teachers, the emphasis on consultation/collaborative models has grown.

> See Chapter 5 on coordinating instruction with families and other professionals.

Why is inclusion important for students with learning and behavior problems? Students want to succeed in the general education classroom with age-similar peers. The vast majority of students with learning disabilities and behavior problems profit from extensive time in the general education classroom when instructional and behavioral supports meet their needs. Because students with learning disabilities exhibit significant difficulties in one or more academic areas (e.g., reading, math, writing), it is likely that they will also require more intensive academic support in their areas of need.

Lawmakers intended for students with special needs who are included in the general education classroom to receive accommodations for their learning and/or emotional needs within the classroom. The special education teacher, as consultant/collaborator with the general education classroom teacher, is to facilitate the implementation of the student's IEP and then promote effective practices and planning to ensure appropriate instruction is given. Working cooperatively with the special education teacher, the general classroom teacher is responsible for planning, monitoring, and delivering the instruction or intervention the student needs.

Most secondary-level (middle and high school) classroom teachers stated that they had not used IEPs or psychological reports to guide their planning for special education students. They had, however, gathered information from the families and former teachers of students with special needs. Some teachers said that they had very little contact with the special education teacher who monitored their students with special needs, and they were not aware that the students had IEPs. A few teachers had no contact with a special education teacher and were unaware that they even had a student with special needs in their class. In such cases, there was clearly a lack of communication between the special education teacher responsible for monitoring the progress of the students with special needs and the general classroom teacher.

WEB RESOURCES

For further information on inclusion issues and activities that may be helpful in the classroom, take a look at The National Dissemination Center for Children with Disabilities at www.nichcy.org.

Identifying Students with Learning Disabilities

What issues relate to appropriate identification of students with learning disabilities? Individuals with learning disabilities have typically been identified through referral by classroom teachers or families, followed by a complete battery of assessments designed to identify whether the students meet criteria as learning disabled. Typically, these assessments include an IQ and an achievement test. If students' IQ scores are a certain number of points above their achievement scores (i.e., a large discrepancy between the IQ and achievement scores), the students are identified as having a learning disability because of their "unexpected underachievement." There has been considerable concern about the appropriateness of administering IQ tests to students, particularly minority students. Additionally, there may be no justification for administration of IQ tests because the extent to which the IQ–achievement discrepancy is an appropriate measure for identification of learning disabilities has been questioned (Bradley, Danielson, & Hallahan, 2002; Branum-Martin, Fletcher, & Stuebing, 2012; Stuebing et al., 2002).

WEB RESOURCES

The International Dyslexia Association provides excellent background information on students with reading disabilities: http://www.interdys.org.

What is IQ–achievement discrepancy, and what are the concerns about using it? IQ–achievement discrepancy is the common practice by which the IQ test (e.g., a cognitive or intelligence test that is typically individually administered and provides an estimate of overall ability) and standardized achievement scores (e.g., an individually administered test of reading or math that typically is norm referenced) of students are compared, in the belief that a significant discrepancy (higher IQ scores than achievement scores on one or more relevant outcomes) is a strong indicator of learning disabilities. The four specific concerns about this practice are as follows:

1. The discrepancy is difficult to determine with young children and may unnecessarily postpone identification until second grade or later; this concern highlights why some refer to the IQ–achievement discrepancy as the "wait to fail" model.

2. Many young children aged 5 to 7 benefit greatly from prevention programs, particularly in reading, that could keep them from developing greater difficulties in reading or math.

3. Formal IQ and achievement tests are expensive to administer and interpret, and the money might be better used to provide instruction.

4. IQ tests provide little information to teachers to assist them in improving or modifying their instruction.

What alternatives are there to traditional IQ–achievement discrepancy approaches for identifying students with learning disabilities? The most frequently suggested alternative is RTI. Though the exact use and application of RTI vary somewhat depending on who is describing it, RTI typically involves a multitiered system of interventions, a data collection system that informs decision making, and ongoing progress monitoring. The number of tiers, what data are collected, and the measures used to determine if a child is "responding" to an intervention might differ depending on the school and content area. RTI can also be conceptualized as a systematic application of data-based decision making to enhance outcomes for all children (D. Fuchs, Fuchs, & Compton, 2012; Vaughn & Fletcher, 2012). RTI provides a preventive approach to special education and promotes early screening and interventions so that students at risk for academic or behavior difficulties are provided with timely and appropriate services.

> Further information about RTI is presented in Chapter 3.

RTI addresses concerns about the IQ–achievement discrepancy because students begin to receive help as soon as they start demonstrating academic or behavior difficulties, regardless of what grade they are in. In addition, many students need only an "extra boost" in order to succeed in the general education classroom. For those students, future reading difficulties may be prevented by early intervention. Students who respond adequately to the intervention and can make appropriate progress in the classroom are considered high responders to the intervention; typically, they do not need further intervention and are unlikely to require special education. Students whose response to the intervention is low may be referred for further evaluations and considered for special education (L. S. Fuchs & Vaughn, 2012; Vaughn & Fuchs, 2006). To determine if a student has responded to an intervention, the measures used for screening and progress monitoring are typically quick and easy to administer and are directly related to skills needed for academic or behavior success in the classroom. Therefore, these measures help teachers pinpoint where a student is having difficulties and alter or improve their instruction accordingly (see Apply the Concept 1-1).

The National Association of State Directors of Special Education (NASDSE) has developed readily accessible guides to RTI that are available on its web site, as well as the publication *Response to Intervention: Policy Considerations and Implementation* (National Association of State Directors of Special Education, 2006). Also, the National Center on RTI, provides numerous resources related to assessment and identification as well as RTI.

Developing an Individualized Education Program

What is an IEP, and what is the process for developing and updating an IEP? Procedures for setting goals and planning instruction are designated by law for students who have been identified as requiring special education services (including students with learning or emotional disabilities). IDEA requires that an IEP be developed for each student with special educational needs. A multidisciplinary team develops, implements, and reviews the IEP, which is both a process and a document. The process involves a group of individuals, often referred to as the IEP team, using assessment information, eligibility, and the needs of the student to establish an appropriate specialized educational program for a student with disabilities. The document is a record of the decisions that have been agreed upon by the team and a guide for improving student outcomes. The IEP must be reviewed annually and can be revised at any time to address lack of expected progress, the results of any reevaluations, or other relevant information provided by either the school or family members. Figure 1-1 presents a sample IEP completed for John, a fifth grader with learning disabilities.

The members of the multidisciplinary team include the following people:

- A representative of the local education agency— an administrator who is qualified to supervise services to students with disabilities and who is knowledgeable about the general education curriculum as well as resources and services available.

- Parent(s) or guardian(s).

- Special education teacher.

- At least one general education teacher if the student is participating or is likely to participate in general education classes.

- Evaluator—someone who can interpret the results from the student's educational, psychological, and/ or behavioral evaluations.

- Student, if the teachers and parents determine that it is appropriate for the student to attend the IEP meeting. If transition services are being discussed, the student must be invited to participate.

Adopting an RTI Model to Identify Students with Learning Disabilities

The 2004 reauthorization of IDEA recommends that states and schools abandon the IQ–achievement discrepancy to identify students with learning disabilities and instead use an RTI approach. However, IDEA does not require that schools use RTI. Your principal asks your opinion on what your school should do to identify students with learning disabilities.

What are the pros and cons of the IQ–achievement discrepancy and RTI? Which model do you recommend that your school use in determining special education eligibility?

In August 2006, regulatory guidelines for implementing RTI were published (U.S. Department of Education, 2006a, 2006b). Key aspects of the guidelines include the following:

- State criteria must not *require* but may *permit* school districts to use a severe discrepancy between intellectual ability and achievement to identify students as learning disabled.

- State criteria must permit the use of a process based on children's responses to scientific, research-based intervention, that is, an appropriate RTI model.

- When determining specific learning disabilities (SLDs), personnel must determine whether children are making age-appropriate progress or making progress to meet state-approved grade-level standards.

- Lack of achievement may not be due to lack of appropriate instruction in reading or math. Thus, if the student has had inadequate or inappropriate instruction in the general education classroom, significant and intensive supplemental instruction is required before placement in special education.

- There are many models or frameworks for implementing RTI. To illustrate, some districts use a problem-solving model in which they implement research-based practices by using a team of professionals to make ongoing decisions, whereas other school districts use a standardized approach in which research-based interventions are provided routinely by well-trained professionals.

- Though specific procedures are not described, the importance of timelines and structured communication with family members is emphasized.

- Frequent and ongoing assessments to determine response to intervention can be determined by the state.

- RTI as a means for identifying students with learning disabilities is not a substitute for a comprehensive evaluation.

- No single procedure can be relied on to determine whether a student qualifies for special education.

- Other professionals as appropriate. Parents or the school may invite others who can provide information or assistance, such as an interpreter, therapists or other personnel who work with the student, or a student advocate such as parents' friends or lawyers.

What should be included in the IEP? According to Section 514(*d*)(1)(A) of IDEA (2004), as of July 1, 2005, the IEP must include the following nine elements:

1. The student's current levels of educational performance and social-emotional functioning, including how the student's disability affects the student's involvement and progress in general education settings.

2. Measurable annual goals that address the student's individual learning needs and that, to the extent possible, enable the student to participate in and progress in the general education classroom.

3. Special education, related services, and supplementary aids and services to be provided to the student, including program modifications or supports for school personnel that will be provided for the student.

4. An explanation of the extent to which the student will not participate in general education classes.

5. A statement indicating how the student will participate in state- or districtwide assessments and outlining any modifications and accommodations to be provided during testing. If the student will not participate in state or district assessments, the IEP must include an explanation of why the student will not participate and how the student will be assessed.

6. When special education services will begin, as well as the frequency, location, and duration of services and modifications.

7. How progress toward annual goals will be measured and how the family will be regularly informed of progress toward these goals. IDEA mandates that parents/guardians be updated on their children's progress toward IEP goals and objectives when report cards are issued for all students.

8. Explanation of transition services at age 16, including measurable postsecondary goals, to help the student prepare for a job or college by taking appropriate classes and/or accessing services outside of school.

9. A list and signatures of the committee members present.

FIGURE 1-1 Sample Individualized Education Program

Individualized Education Program

I. Demographic Information

Last	First	M.I.	Date
Smith	John	E.	May 12, 2014

Student I.D.	Address	Home Phone	Work Phone
2211100	23 Lakeview St. Collier, MN 32346	(459)555-5555	(459)555-5000

Age	Grade Level	Home School	Program Eligibility
11	5	Lakeview Elementary	Learning Disabilities

Reason for Conference: ❑ Staffing ☑ Review

II. Conference

Parent Notification

Attempt #1:	Attempt #2:	Attempt #3:
Letter: 3-02-14	Phone call: 3-13-14	Notice sent home with student: 3-22-14

Parent Response: Will attend as per phone call on 3-13-14

III. Present Levels of Educational Performance

John is a 5th grade student whose disability inhibits his ability to read required material. John can read 35/100 in two minutes from a 4.0 grade level paragraph and 45/100 in two minutes from a 3.0 grade level paragraph. John can answer 8/10 literal questions and 4/10 inference questions from a 4.0 grade level passage read to him.

IV. Annual Goals and Short-Term Benchmarks

1. John will increase reading fluency to the 4.0 grade level.

   John will read orally a passage at the 4.0 grade level in 2 minutes with 50 or more words correct.

   John will use correct intonation and prosody when reading orally a passage at the 4.0 grade level 50% of the time.

2. John will improve the percentage of accuracy when responding to literal and inferential questions.

   John will answer literal questions from a 4.0 grade level passage read to him with 75% accuracy.

   John will answer inferential questions from a 4.0 grade level passage read to him with 90-100% accuracy.

Describe the extent to which the student will not participate in general education settings and explain why the student cannot be placed in general education settings.

John will not participate in general education settings for language arts, science, and social studies instruction. John requires close supervision when completing tasks, high levels of assistance, and intensive, systematic instruction.

V. Related Services

Type of Service, Aid or Modification			Location	Time per day/week
Assistive Technology:	❑ Yes	☑ No		
Adaptive PE:	❑ Yes	☑ No		
Audiology Services:	❑ Yes	☑ No		
Counseling:	❑ Yes	☑ No		
Interpreter:	❑ Yes	☑ No		
Medical Services:	❑ Yes	☑ No		
Occupational Therapy:	❑ Yes	☑ No		
Orientation/Mobility:	❑ Yes	☑ No		
Physical Therapy:	❑ Yes	☑ No		
Psychological Services:	❑ Yes	☑ No		
Special Transportation:	❑ Yes	☑ No		
Speech/Lang. Therapy:	☑ Yes	❑ No	Self-contained class, 30 min./wk	

(continued)

FIGURE 1-1 Continued

VI. Assessment Participation

Will the student participate in state and district assessments: ☑ Yes ☐ No

If yes, what accommodations or modifications will be provided?

☐ None ☑ Flexible Setting ☐ Flexible Presentation ☑ Flexible Scheduling
☐ Flexible Responding

If no, indicate why state and district assessments are inappropriate:

VII. Transition Planning/Statement

☑ Under 14: Transition planning not needed.

☐ 14–15 years old: Statement of transition services needed that focuses on student's course of study.

☐ 16 years old: Outcome statement that describes a direction and plan for the student's post–high school years from the perspective of student, parent, and team members.

VIII. Scheduled Report to Parents/Guardians

John's parents will be informed of progress toward his annual goals via parent/teacher conferences and interim report cards (4 times per year). Parents will be notified of goals that have been met and the rate of progress toward meeting all of the annual goals.

IX. Initiation/Duration Dates

Special education and related services will initiate ___September 2014___ , through ___June 2015___
(MM/YY) (MM/YY)

IX. Persons Attending Conference

Signature	Position	Date
Mary Smith	Parent	May 12, 2014
Jonathan Smith	Parent	May 12, 2014
Laura Jones	Special Education Teacher	May 12, 2014
Rafael Gonzalez	General Education Teacher	May 12, 2014
Larry Brick	LEA Representative	May 12, 2014
Harrison Washington	School Psychologist	May 12, 2014
John Smith	Student	May 12, 2014

Writing Effective IEP Goals

A major part of the IEP involves the annual goals. An annual goal usually covers an entire school year. According to IDEA (2004), short-term objectives are also included for students who take alternate assessments aligned to alternate achievement standards. Short-term objectives are smaller steps that help the student reach the annual goal. Completion of related sets of short-term objectives should lead to accomplishment of the annual goals developed by the multidisciplinary team. Figure 1-2 shows an example of an annual goal and short-term objectives. Goals can address academic, social-emotional, or functional needs. The written statements of annual goals

FIGURE 1-2 Sample Goal and Short-Term Objectives in an IEP

Annual Goal:

Lisa Mckinney will achieve a math score at the fourth-grade level or above on the Mathematics Achievement Assessment.

Short-Term Objectives

1. Lisa will demonstrate mastery of multiplication and division facts (0-10) by completing weekly one-minute timed multiplication and division fact math tests with 90% accuracy.
2. Given 10 three-digit-by-two-digit multiplication problems, Lisa will solve the problems with 90% accuracy.
3. Given 10 two-digit-by-one-digit division problems, Lisa will use long division to solve the problems with 90% accuracy.
4. Given 10 one-step word problems, Lisa will identify the operation (addition, subtraction, multiplication, or division) and solve with 90% accuracy.
5. After correctly solving five one-step word problems, Lisa will describe with 80% accuracy (either orally to the teacher or in writing) how she got her answers.
6. Given daily teacher-prepared "problem-of-the-day" assignments, Lisa will copy each problem into her math notebook and work cooperatively with a partner to solve it, showing work and the correct solution four out of five times.

must meet certain requirements. According to Gibb and Dyches (2000), annual goals must

- Be measurable.
- Tell what the student can reasonably achieve in a year.
- Relate to helping the student succeed in general education settings and/or address other educational needs ensuing from the disability.
- Include short-term objectives.

Consider SMART as a guideline for writing IEP goals:

- **S**pecific. Be sure the goals that you write are very specific about the academic and social/behavioral expectations you have for the target student.
- **M**easurable. Write goals in ways that you can measure whether student has achieved them. For example, "student will be referred to the office for inappropriate behavior 2 or fewer times each month."
- **A**chievable. Establish goals that reflect high expectations but are also reasonable for the student to achieve.
- **R**elevant. Determine goals that are relevant to the student and reflect the school context and future goals.
- **T**ime Limited. Specify the time frame in which the goal will be achieved, and identify the time frame as 1 year or less.

For IEPs that also include short-term objectives, Gibb and Dyches (2000) suggest the following:

- Describe the behavior in an observable, measurable way (e.g., "Luis will add two-digit numbers").
- Include the circumstances under which the behavior will take place (e.g., "given manipulatives and peer assistance").
- State the criterion for mastery (e.g., "with 85% accuracy").

During the IEP conference, family members and professionals work together to identify appropriate accommodations and modifications that will assist the student in learning skills in class. It is important to include teachers in the decisions about accommodations and modifications because they are the ones responsible for implementing these in the classroom. For example, if the IEP team decides that a student needs a highlighted textbook in science, someone must be available to do the highlighting, or the accommodation cannot be carried out. Furthermore, effective communication systems must be in place so that all teachers and support personnel who will work with the student are aware of the accommodations and modifications that will be implemented. The processes involved in designing and implementing effective accommodations and modifications are discussed further in this chapter as well as in following chapters.

Writing IEPs can be challenging, and many teachers use software and Web sites to facilitate their development. The most useful IEP software programs allow a teacher to select from skill sequences and write long-term and short-term objectives, freely customizing skills and objectives to meet individual needs.

Often school systems or special education units adopt one particular IEP software application for use by its entire staff. You may find that to be the case in your school district. Some programs are installed in individual computers; others are Web based. Web-based systems are especially useful because you can access the data from any online computer. It is also easier to transfer records as the child moves along in his or her education, from teacher to teacher and school to school.

WEB RESOURCES

Because the IEP-writing process is complicated, several software programs are available to help teachers. Following is a list of IEP management software names along with their primary Web addresses:

- IEPMaker Pro, by Chalkware Education Solutions at www.iepware.com.
- Class/Bridge IEP Program, by Class/Bridge at www.classplus.com.
- IEP Writer Supreme II, by Super School Software at www.superschoolsoftware.com.

Family Involvement

The IEP meeting is a way for family members and school personnel to communicate about the education of a student with disabilities. According to IDEA, "parents are considered equal partners with school personnel" in the IEP process. The IEP serves as a safeguard not only for students but also for families and the education team. All reasonable attempts to ensure the participation of family members in the IEP process should be taken:

- Schedule IEP meetings at times that are convenient for families, checking with them in advance to determine a suitable date, time, and location.

- Notify families well in advance of the meeting. Include in the notice the purpose, time, and location of the meeting and the names and positions of the people who will be in attendance. Parents/guardians should be involved in the decision about whether the student will attend.

- If family members choose not to attend even after reasonable efforts have been made to accommodate their schedules, the school should use other methods to involve them, including telephone calls or home visits. The school must document its attempts to involve family members.

- The school must take measures to ensure that families understand IEP proceedings, including providing an interpreter if English is not their first language.

- Family involvement in the development of the IEP should be documented, and parents/guardians should receive a copy of the IEP.

Remember that often too much emphasis is placed on compliance rather than on genuine communication with family members (Harry, 2008; L. Lo, 2012; Seligman & Darling, 2007). Educators are more effective when they consider the following:

- Educators and parents are working as a team for a common goal—the student's success.

- Pay attention to when and why defensive behavior arises. Put your feelings aside, and help others, including family members, to build positive relationships. If the team is unable to act positively, postpone interactions until the defensiveness can be handled.

- Understand and consider the needs and interests of parents/guardians and their child. Consider what the issues and goals are from their perspective.

> In this **video** ▶, several professionals and parents discuss the importance of involving parents in their children's education. How would you, as an educator, communicate with and involve the parents of students with disabilities in every aspect of their children's education?

- Remember that most families are doing the best that they can under the circumstances of their lives.

Student Involvement and Self-Determination

The self-directed IEP is designed to facilitate students' participation in IEP meetings (Arndt, Konrad, & Test, 2006). By law, students need to attend IEP meetings only if appropriate. In practice, many students with learning and emotional disabilities do not attend these meetings, even when the students are in secondary-level settings and can provide information and contribute to decision making about their education. The benefits to involving students with disabilities in the IEP decision-making process include helping them develop a commitment to learning and a sense of responsibility and control over the decisions made regarding their learning.

> Chapter 5 describes strategies you can use for actively involving families in their children's education, including planning and implementing programs.

Why do many students not attend the conferences? The primary reason is that they are not provided an opportunity. Providing students who are age appropriate with an opportunity to influence their educational program is an essential first step in ensuring that the program will succeed. J. E. Martin and colleagues (2006) describe a typical IEP process for secondary students with disabilities. The special education teacher at this meeting does most of the talking and directing (51%), with families doing considerably less (15%), and students the least (3%). Yet a student-directed IEP is likely to have considerable benefit both in terms of identifying appropriate goals as well as successfully motivating students to achieve those goals. What are some ways in which students might be successfully included in the IEP meeting?

- Have the student start the meeting and introduce self and others.

- Allow the student to direct the meeting, including telling the purpose of the meeting.

- With necessary supports, ask the student to review his or her progress on previous goals.

- Provide ample support for teachers and parents to ask questions and provide information.

- Identify future goals and mechanisms for successfully reaching them.

- Consider asking the student the following questions:

  What are your goals in school?

  How successful have you been in meeting them?

  Are you working hard to meet goals?

What are you doing well? What would you like to do better?

- Prompt students to ask others at the meeting what they think of stated goals, progress, and future goals.
- Ask students to specify the support needed to meet the agreed-upon goals.
- Encourage the student to summarize and close the meeting.

Including students in their IEP meeting can be an important step in enhancing students' self-determination—the opportunity to make important decisions about their own lives and to be actively involved in decisions about their own learning. Self-determination is important because students who engage in self-determination have improved academic performance. Teachers can improve the self-determination of students in the IEP process by actively engaging students in the IEP development and the monitoring of their progress toward meeting IEP goals.

Key Elements of the Transition Planning Process

The primary objectives of the transition process for individuals with disabilities is the same as it is for all of us—as seamless a transition as possible to postsecondary settings and being able to function successfully in adult life (i.e., dealing reasonably well with the demands of adulthood). All of this is within the context of knowing that each of us struggles at times with the realities of everyday life.

As the classroom teacher, how can you ensure that this happens? The vehicle for documenting transition is the IEP.

The key elements of the transition planning process include proactive transition education, opportunities to dream about who you want to be and how you will achieve it, assessment of critical areas to help with decision making, transition planning, and opportunities to receive feedback about how you are performing and what you need to do to meet your goals.

The formal phase of the transition-planning process begins with the comprehensive assessment of a student's transition needs. The general areas in which a transition-needs assessment should focus include a range of transition domains. The key transition areas that are identified by different states vary greatly; some of the more common transition planning areas are as follows:

- Community participation
- Daily living
- Employment
- Financial and income management
- Health

- Independent living (includes living arrangements)
- Leisure and recreation
- Postsecondary education
- Relationships and social skills
- Transportation and mobility
- Vocational training

It is important that a comprehensive transition-needs assessment consider all of these areas. If a needs assessment is conducted effectively, the results should lead to the development of transition-related goals. In some cases, the results will lead to the recognition that more in-depth information is needed.

The actual transition-planning phase comprises goal development highlighting two types of goals and a number of activities that are needed to accomplish these goals. One type of goal is *instructional*, in that it focuses on knowledge and skill needs in academic, social, behavioral, and other functional areas. Goals that are instructional should be written into a student's IEP. The other type of goal emphasizes *linkage* to needed services and supports. These goals may be quick action items (e.g., a phone call to place one's name on a waiting list), or they may be more elaborate activities (e.g., going through the process of selecting an appropriate postschool training program). Most students will not require both types of goals for every transition area that is assessed.

The reauthorization of IDEA in 2004 introduced a new component to the transition process. IDEA regulations state:

> For a child whose eligibility terminates under circumstances described in paragraph (e)(2) of this section, a public agency must provide the child with a summary of the child's academic achievement and functional performance, which shall include recommendations on how to assist the child in meeting the child's postsecondary goals. (Section 300.305(e)(3))

This new feature is designed to provide students, and their families, with a document that should be useful in a variety of adult settings (workplace, postsecondary education). The key features of the summary of performance document include generation of information on both academic and functional levels; a revisiting of "measurable" postsecondary goals; and a list of recommendations that will be helpful in settings related to the goals.

Aside from the implications that are stated in the federal definition of transition services, certain principles should guide the transition planning process. The Apply the Concept 1-2 highlights the four key guiding principles.

Instructional goals relate to knowledge and skills needs and should be written in the IEP as academic or social goals. *Linkage goals*—the types of goals that are typically associated with transition planning—focus on

Guiding Principles for the Transition Planning Process

- The more that is known about the receiving settings and about the student's levels of competence to deal with these settings, the more likely a seamless transition can be achieved.

- The more comprehensive the transition-needs assessment is, the easier it is to develop useful and meaningful transition plans.

- Effective transition assessment and plans can be achieved only when school-based transition personnel know the students or have ways to inquire about the student.

- Student involvement in the transition-planning process is not only highly desirable but also required by law (i.e., based on the student's preferences and interests).

Useful linkage-type goal statements should include the following four components, all of which contribute to development of an effective plan of action:

1. Present level of performance
2. Specific activities to be performed to accomplish the goal
3. Anticipated date of completion of activities
4. Person(s) responsible

---

making connections to the supports and services that will be needed in postsecondary settings and are written in the section of the IEP that deals with transition services.

In the past, some states required another document, an individual transition plan (ITP), which was a separate document from the IEP, as the principal vehicle for guiding transition activities. Most states simply included transition goals as part of the existing IEP under a section typically called "Statement of Transition Services." Historically, the focus of transition planning was primarily on goals that we defined previously as *linkage type*. The emerging practice is to include all transition-planning information on the IEP. The critical issue is the importance of considering both instructional and linkage goal statements for areas of need. In this IRIS Module, you can explore strategies to support students with disabilities as they transition out of high school and into the adult world.

For example, Sheila is a high school student with significant learning disabilities and behavior disorders. Her situation illustrates why two different types of goals often need to be developed. To develop an effective transition plan, information from key stakeholders, particularly the students, are needed. The following goals need to be developed for Sheila based on numerous data sources, including findings from her transition planning inventory indicating that school personnel and the student perceived that she would have considerable challenges in succeeding in a postsecondary program. They agreed that Sheila needed:

- Assistance in understanding print materials including materials from the Web, written directions, and other text sources necessary for postsecondary transition.

- Guidelines in supporting test taking.

- To acquire skills for time management and organization.

- Help understanding the purpose of the Students with Disabilities Office on campus.

- Assistance in organizing documentation of disability status.

- To develop a resource for obtaining tutoring and other supports.

- To develop a resource list for counseling and other supportive services.

Teaching Students with Learning and Behavior Problems

What goes into teaching students with learning and behavior problems? In the beginning of this chapter, we introduced three students, Servio, Dana, and Tina. Instruction for these students needs to be carefully orchestrated to take into account the interactive nature of their instructional needs within an effective teaching–learning process. The *teaching–learning process* is a model of teaching and learning that takes into account the complexity of the learning environment or context, the knowledge and skills of the teacher and the learner, and the instructional cycle the teacher implements to facilitate learning. An effective teaching–learning process for students with learning and/or behavior problems is based on *individual programming*. Although students may be instructed in groups, the teacher plans and designs instruction for each student's needs, realizing that students have both common and unique needs. The teaching–learning process

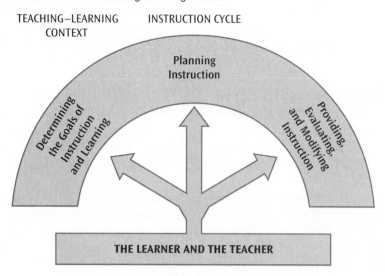

FIGURE 1-3 The Teaching–Learning Process

TEACHING–LEARNING CONTEXT   INSTRUCTION CYCLE

Planning Instruction

Determining the Goals of Instruction and Learning

Providing, Evaluating, and Modifying Instruction

THE LEARNER AND THE TEACHER

is shown in Figure 1-3. It presents a reflective, problem-solving approach to teaching students with learning and behavior problems. Let us look first at the key players in this process: the learner and the teacher.

The Learner

The learner brings to school knowledge and experiences on which to build, and strategies to assist in the learning process. Our assessment process focuses on determining the skills and knowledge the student has and needs to have to succeed at grade level.

Skills and knowledge not only play an important role in learning, but also influence the learner's attitudes and efforts toward learning. Randy and Tamara illustrate this point. In fifth grade, Randy was determined to learn how to read, although at the time he was struggling with beginning reading books. He worked all year on his reading, and at the end of the year, he had grown in his reading skill by about one grade level. Still, he carried with him the attitude that reading was important and that he should continue to struggle with a process that for him was quite difficult. Tamara, on the other hand, was a sixth grader who was reading at about the third-grade level. For her, learning to read was a much easier process, yet she finished the year making only marginal gains. Why? She believed that reading simply was not necessary for her life and that her future goal, being a mother, just didn't require her to be a good reader. It is likely that these students' attitudes influenced their rate of learning.

A student's strategies for learning also affect the teaching–learning process. When you are told to read a chapter in a textbook and study for a test, what strategies do you employ? Do you preview the chapter before reading? Do you ask questions as you read to check your comprehension? Do you underline or take notes? Do you review your notes before the test, rehearsing the

important points? These are all strategies that make you a more effective student.

The Teacher

The teacher brings to the learning situation teaching knowledge and skills; beliefs and attitudes about teaching, learning, and the world; and practices for influencing students' learning and engagement.

As you read this section, reflect on your beliefs and attitudes about teaching, learning, and students who experience learning and behavior problems. What is the nature of learning, and what is the role of the teacher?

Learning can be perceived as changes in behavior that result in students' demonstrating new knowledge and skills. The role of the teacher is that of an educational technician who engineers instruction or arranges the environment so that the probability of learning and improved behavior is increased. This is accomplished by providing students with effective instruction and rewards for learning. An effective teacher conveys knowledge and skills in a systematic, explicit manner. This perception of learning and teaching is probably best reflected in applied behavior analysis. It is also reflected in instructional strategies and materials that are based on systematic ordering and teaching of skills.

Learning can also be perceived as a dynamic process in which students play an active role, constantly interacting with the environment and people around them. Not only do students' notions, ideas, and skills change in the learning process, but so does the environment in which learning takes place. Thus, learning is not merely the accumulation of knowledge and skills, but it is also the active construction and transformation of ideas based on observations and experiences. This perception of learning is represented in schema theory. The teacher creates an environment in which students can take risks and develop flexible learning and thinking strategies as they acquire skills and knowledge.

For example, Ms. Kranowski, a special education teacher who works with students who have learning and behavior problems, has 11 students—fourth through sixth grade—in her self-contained class. Each day after lunch, they practice writing. Ms. Kranowski uses a process approach to teaching writing in which students select their own topics and write about them, sometimes taking several weeks to complete a piece. Students usually write multiple drafts, sharing their work with other students and the teacher.

At first, the learners in Ms. Kranowski's class needed to develop a process for writing. They needed to develop purposes for their writing other than to please the teacher or to complete the worksheets. As the students became more confident of their drafts, they needed to learn skills such as how to organize a descriptive paragraph and a story and how to use dialogue and quotation marks. Although Ms. Kranowski continues with this process approach to writing, she now also spends time teaching skills to small groups. She uses systematic skill lessons, modeling a skill, then having the students practice it in their own writing and in published and teacher-made materials. Whereas the first approach to teaching represents an interactive model of teaching and learning, during skill lessons Ms. Kranowski serves as the conveyor of knowledge by explicitly teaching systematic skill sequences. Ms. Kranowski's instruction shifts to reflect the needs of the students in her class.

How does Ms. Kranowski explain her simultaneous use of these different approaches to the teaching–learning process?

Well, when I first began using a process approach to teaching writing, I found that the students really learned to like writing. For me, that was a big accomplishment, since most of these kids had previously hated writing. But I also found that because these students have so many learning problems and take so much practice to learn a new skill, they just weren't getting enough opportunities to practice intensely a new writing skill when they were first trying to learn it. Consequently, they never learned the skills very well. Now, 2 days a week, we take about 20 minutes for a skill lesson. I select the skill according to the needs of the students as a group. Right now we are working on dialogue and quotation marks. I introduce the skill and show how I use it in my writing. Then several of the students demonstrate how they can use it in their writing. We use an overhead projector, and they project their writing on the screen. We talk about how to add quotation marks, and they add them right then. For the next several weeks when they are writing their pieces, I encourage them to use dialogue, and we make an effort to compliment each other when the quotation marks are right. If the students need additional practice, I provide them with stories in which they have to add quotation marks to the

writing. We also take turns reading stories and books that have lots of dialogue, and the students identify the dialogue and tell where the quotes go. I realize that this is really mixing two philosophies of teaching and learning, but for me it's the best way to get the job done.

The Instructional Cycle

Within the teaching–learning process, the *instructional cycle* helps to shape and sequence teaching and learning (refer to Figure 1-3 again). Based on progress monitoring relating to students' learning and behavior, Ms. Kranowski sets instructional goals; plans instruction; and provides, evaluates, and modifies instruction based on students' progress, which she monitors through ongoing assessment. She uses this cycle in a flexible way, taking into account the *characteristics of the learner*, her *teaching beliefs and attitudes*, and the *context* in which the teaching and learning are happening. Sometimes she changes her instructional goals on the basis of input from the students or feedback about rate of learning. Sometimes she modifies her plans and the way in which she instructs to reach her instructional goals more effectively. When Ms. Kranowski added skill lessons to the writing curriculum, she changed her plans, which resulted in changes in instruction. The features of effective instruction should be considered in developing and implementing each part of the instructional cycle.

Features of Effective Instruction

Effective instruction is tantamount to a balancing act. Some teachers appear to be magicians because they seem to effortlessly balance the various features of effective instruction. However, keeping this balance requires a clear understanding of each feature as well as knowledge about how and when to implement them. Following are some of the features of effective instruction that should be present in all teaching:

1. Assessing progress
2. Designing instruction
   - Determining goals of instruction
   - Flexible grouping
   - Adaptations
   - Scaffolding
   - Careful use of instructional time
3. Delivering instruction
   - Quick pacing
   - Sufficient opportunities for student response
   - Error feedback

These features will benefit all the students in a classroom, but they are particularly helpful for students with learning and behavior problems.

Assessing Progress

The goal of ongoing progress monitoring is to determine whether the instruction is effective and should be continued as currently implemented or whether adjustments are needed. Progress monitoring is a form of assessment that is linked directly to instruction. Assessing progress means continually examining data from both formal and informal assessments to determine students' knowledge and skills. Teachers who use a variety of assessment tools to determine what students know and don't know are more likely to adjust their instruction to meet students' needs and have improved outcomes for students. You can obtain information from reading inventories, standardized tests, observations, and student work samples to assist you in monitoring students' progress and to guide planning and instruction. Monitoring students' learning will help you to determine when students require extra assistance, and you will be able to adjust instruction accordingly. Monitoring of student progress should be frequent (one to three times per week) and ongoing.

Progress Monitoring According to the instructional cycle (Figure 1-3), instruction is implemented after learning and instructional goals have been established and instruction has been planned. However, instruction is more effective and efficient if at the same time the instruction is being implemented, it is also being evaluated and—based on the evaluation—modified.

As we evaluate, it is crucial to keep a written record of student progress. The written record provides a means for objectively reflecting on the data to determine whether progress is evident (e.g., Deno et al., 2009; Berkeley, Bender, Peaster, & Saunders, 2009). While progress monitoring is a useful tool, some teachers find classroom management challenges and time demands interfere with effective implementation of progress monitoring. When used effectively, progress monitoring provides a written record for communicating with others regarding student progress. Sharing progress with parents, principals, other teachers, and—most important—the student provides a sense of accomplishment and satisfaction for all involved.

> In this **video**, the teacher is demonstrating the use of a progress monitoring program (DIBELS) to monitor her students' progress. What types of data were collected? How was that data used? How was technology used to assist the assessment process?

Having students monitor their own progress can increase their motivation for learning and pride in their accomplishments. Self-monitoring procedures have been used successfully with students who have learning and behavior problems, using the following procedures (see for more details, Heward, 2009, pp. 428–429):

* With students, identify the academic and/or social behaviors that they will monitor. Specify them in terms that the student understands.
* Use procedures that make record keeping with self-monitoring easy: for example, a simple paper-pencil form, wrist counter, tally counter, or a software program.
* Provide prompts to remind the student to self-monitor. These prompts can be from the teacher, another student, or check marks on a paper that lists the cues for the student to monitor.
* Model the self-monitor. Show the student how to monitor, and model the monitoring for them.
* Encourage the student to self-monitor. Provide frequent feedback and support to students when they self-monitor. Observe changes in their behavior, and report these observations to the student as well as the parents.

Types of Evaluation Measures

Although a teacher or student can use many methods to evaluate progress, generally one or more of three basic types are used: progress graphs and charts, performance records, and process records. Progress graphs are frequently used for measuring daily progress on individual skills or knowledge.

> In this **video**, watch this science lesson and notice how the teacher involves students in monitoring their growth and progress. What similar methods could you use in other content areas?

Performance records are usually used for measuring progress across time (e.g., grading period, semester, and year). Curriculum-based measurement (www.studentprogress.org) is an example of a performance record that is closely tied to the curriculum being taught. Curriculum-based measures not only focus on the progress that is evident in the curriculum, but also document progress in the learning process. Using a weekly assessment, teachers chart the progress students are making toward a goal and then adjust instruction to ensure adequate progress toward meeting that goal. Portfolios, learning logs, and dialogue journals can supplement the use of curriculum-based measures.

Progress Graphs and Charts Progress graphs and charts are generally used to measure progress on one behavior or skill. Graphs seem particularly well suited for self-monitoring because the results are displayed

FIGURE 1-4 Timing Chart Using a Line Graph

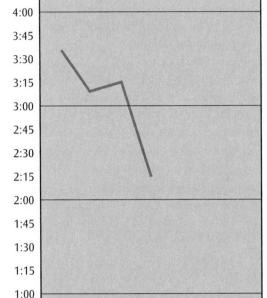

Student Name: _Hector_

Task: _x facts, 50 facts_

Minutes

Dates

FIGURE 1-5 Timing Chart Using a Bar Graph

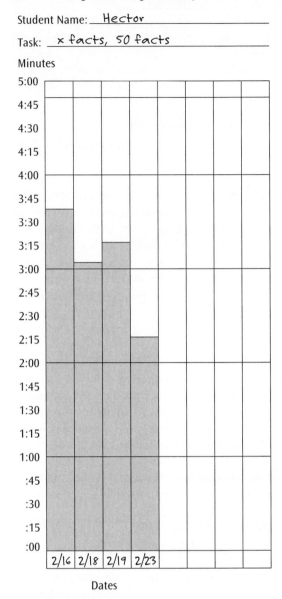

Student Name: _Hector_

Task: _x facts, 50 facts_

Minutes

Dates

in such a manner that they are easy to interpret (see Figures 1-4 and 1-5). To be suitable for a progress graph, the behavior, skill, or knowledge must be quantifiable, either by time or by occurrence. For example, Ms. Shiller, a junior high teacher for a self-contained classroom of students with emotional disabilities, uses progress graphs for the following activities:

- Silent reading rate
- Speed in completing math facts
- Percentage of questions answered correctly for the social studies assignment
- Number of times the student disrupted other students during the morning independent learning activity
- Student and teacher rating of written pieces, based on interest and readability

With a progress graph, the measurement unit is marked on the vertical axis. For example, _time_ for graphing silent reading rate, _speed_ for graphing math facts completed, and _percent_ for graphing the percentage of social studies questions answered correctly would be marked on the vertical axis. On the horizontal axis, the occurrence unit is marked (e.g., date, teaching session, social studies assignment number). It is relatively easy to plot progress data on either a line graph, as depicted in Figure 1-4, or a bar graph, as shown in Figure 1-5.

Progress charts are usually used in the same manner as progress graphs: to measure progress on one skill or behavior. The difference between a progress chart and a progress graph is that with a chart, the score is reported but is not presented in a relational manner (see Figure 1-6). Although progress charts are generally more efficient in the use of space, they do not provide the clear

FIGURE 1-6 Progress Chart for Sight Words

Name: Lisa	3/12	3/14	3/15	3/18
sometimes	+ + +	+ + +	+ + +	+ + +
everyone	– – o	– o +	o + +	+ + +
when	– – –	o o +	– o +	o + +
themselves	– o +	o + +	o + +	+ + +
mystery	– o o	o o +	+ o +	+ o +
hurry	o o +	+ + +	+ + +	+ + +
their	– o –	o + o	+ o +	+ + +
friend	+ o +	+ + +	+ + +	+ + +
mountain	– o o	o o +	+ + o	+ + +
trail	– + –	– o –	– + +	+ o +
route	– – o	o + o	o + o	o o +

+ Correct and automatic

o Correct but not automatic

– Incorrect

visual representation of student performance; therefore, student progress or lack of it is not so readily apparent. Consequently, graphing is generally recommended over charting for student self-monitoring.

Performance Records Performance records are often used to record student progress across a set of skills or knowledge and for a significant length of time. An IEP is a performance record in that annual goals and short-term objectives are written, and evaluation of the goals and objectives is recorded in the IEP (see Figure 1-1). Many school districts have developed skill and knowledge competencies or objectives that students need to attain at various grade levels. These are often arranged on an individual student performance record so that as a student becomes proficient in a listed competency, it can be noted (see Figure 1-7). Many commercial reading, math, writing, and other content area programs publish performance records so student progress can be recorded. One caution in using such performance records is that although most of them measure proficiency, they do not measure maintenance, generalization, or application. Consequently, a teacher may receive a performance record on a student and find that the student cannot perform some of the skills that are listed as mastered.

In addition to collecting permanent products, the teacher and/or the students may want to keep a progress journal. Usually, this journal accompanies the

FIGURE 1-7 Competency-Based Performance Record

Student: Karen

Competency Area and Skill	Mastery
Early Reading	
Identifies letters of alphabet	10/00
Names letters of alphabet	12/00
Holds book, turns pages one at a time	9/00
Looks first at left page, then at right	9/00
Distinguishes print from pictures	9/00
Scans left to right, top to bottom	9/00
Reads along listening to a familiar book	9/00
Rhymes words	11/00
Identifies words in a familiar book	10/00
Beginning Reading	
Reads simple stories (preprimer/primer)	3/01
Identifies consonant sounds	2/01
Identifies short vowel sounds	2/01
Identifies long vowel sounds	4/01
Identifies simple sight words in isolation	2/01
Recognizes that "s" makes words plural etc.	4/01

performance record or progress graphs and charts, and provides the student or teacher with space in which each can write comments about progress. Ms. Shiller found that progress journals were particularly helpful for documenting progress regarding students' behavior. She used this method in combination with graphs to evaluate several students' progress. She found that her dated journal entries provided insights into how she might modify the instructional context and the instruction.

Curriculum-based measurement (CBM) is one system of performance records that highlights the close tie between curriculum and student performance, using frequent samplings from curriculum materials to assess students' academic performance (e.g., Christ & Ardoin, 2009; Espin et al., 2008; www.studentprogress.org). CBM has been used successfully for students who have learning and behavior problems to improve reading fluency, reading comprehension, spelling, and arithmetic computation in both general education and special education classrooms (e.g., Keller-Margulis, Shapiro, & Hintze, 2008). For example, reading fluency in a third-grade class can be measured each week by having each student read 100-word passages from the reading curriculum and graphing fluency rates across time. This type of measurement provides ongoing data for making instructional decisions. Teachers can assess changes in student performance over time by considering level of performance as affected by instructional change, rate of learning (as reflected by changes in the slope of the trend line) compared to the goal or aim rate, and variability in the consistency of the performance.

When a teacher approaches instruction with a plan of action, it is important to remember that the plan will need to be modified. Effective instruction takes place when the instructional procedures and content match the overall teaching–learning process. Because the teaching–learning process is dynamic and flexible, the instructional process must also be dynamic and flexible.

Designing Instruction

Once objectives have been set and students' skills have been assessed, instructional design and adaptation is next (see IRIS resources). Designing instruction refers to using student data to plan for effective instruction (University of Texas Center for Reading and Language Arts, 2000a, 2000b). When teachers systematically adjust instruction in response to assessment information, students' rate of learning increases (L. S. Fuchs, Fuchs, Hamlett, Phillips, & Karns, 1995).

How can teachers design instruction so that the needs of all the students in a classroom are met? Many teachers find it difficult to teach the wide range of skills their students require. Because the students' deficits are so many and so varied in level, it seems impossible to cover them all. The steps to designing instruction are as follows:

1. Use the information gathered from various assessment tools. Curriculum-based measurements are particularly suited for this purpose because they are ongoing and closely aligned with *curricular goals* (University of Texas Center for Reading and Language Arts, 2000a, 2000b).

2. Group students with similar instructional needs.

3. Set specific instructional targets that focus on particular concepts, using curricular objectives and annual goals as a guideline.

4. Prepare a schedule, and choose and sequence appropriate activities and tasks.

5. Set up a group management system that is specifically designed to provide instruction in a variety of grouping patterns.

6. Identify students who need additional, more intensive instruction.

Determining Goals of Instruction Setting goals for instruction helps a teacher know where he or she is going. Several questions a teacher may ask in setting goals for instruction and learning are as follows:

- Have I used the information I have about the characteristics of the learner?
- Have I taken into account my beliefs and attitudes?
- Have I involved the students in setting the goals?
- Have I set goals that are realistic yet challenging to both the learner and me?
- How do these goals fit within the larger teaching–learning context (e.g., goals of the school, curriculum, long-range career goals of the student)?

When Ms. Kranowski (the special education teacher described earlier who has 11 students in fourth through sixth grade who have learning and behavior problems) set her instructional goals for writing, she decided that she had two major objectives: to have the students experience successful writing in a variety of forms and to have the students develop writing skills that would help them in school and later in life. She wanted very much to involve the students in setting goals, believing that the students would then have a greater commitment to reaching those goals. She began the year by telling the students about "the way that writing works" in the classroom. She shared the importance of supporting each other, for she wanted students to set a goal of working together. As they worked together, shared their writing, and got to know each other better, Ms. Kranowski sat down with each one of the students and helped them select skills for improvement. By analyzing the students' written products, observing the students as they wrote, talking with the students about their writing, and using her knowledge about the scope and sequence of writing skills, she felt comfortable working with students in selecting goals. In this way, Ms. Kranowski's instructional goals were interwoven with her students' learning goals.

Flexible Grouping Deciding what type of grouping pattern to use is also part of designing instruction. Because of the large range of abilities, interests, and background knowledge in most classrooms, it is best to use flexible grouping. Flexible grouping, another component of effective instruction, refers to the use of a variety of grouping practices that change depending on the goals and objectives for the lesson. Mixed-ability groups, same-ability groups, whole groups, pairs, and individualized instruction can be used to meet different student and instructional needs. Groups should be flexible, and students should be regrouped on a regular basis.

Adaptations The purpose of making instructional adaptations is to ensure that students can participate in instruction, activities, homework, and assessment to the extent possible in the general education classroom. The use of adaptations enhances learning for all students, not only those with learning and behavior problems. Adaptations can be divided into three categories:

1. Instructional design (e.g., accessing resources, collaborating with other professionals, having a plan for adaptations, and integrating technology)

2. Instructional and curricular (e.g., making learning visible and explicit; using clear, simple language; breaking a task or activity into steps; and providing multiple ways of demonstrating learning)

3. Behavioral support (e.g., teaching alternative behaviors, being consistent, providing structure, and being proactive)

Using adaptations provides for differentiated instruction, which maximizes learning for all students. When determining whether adaptations are necessary, consider the demands of the lesson and the skills of the learner. If there is a mismatch between the abilities required by the lesson and the student's skills, adaptations may be necessary. The adaptations that are used should create a better match between the student's skills and the task. For example, if a lesson on main ideas will require students to write the main idea of a story but a student with a reading disability has difficulty writing letters or words quickly, there may be a mismatch between the demands of the lesson and the student's abilities. If the instruction on main ideas is at the correct level for the student, adaptations to the lesson can allow the student to benefit more from the instruction. One adaptation may be to give the student extra time to write the main idea sentence. A second possible adaptation may be to have the student work with a partner to develop a main idea sentence. In this case, the student with the reading disability can be fully involved in creating the main idea sentence, but the partner can write the sentence.

Scaffolding An essential element of effective instruction is the use of scaffolding (Alfieri et al., 2011). *Scaffolding*

means adjusting and extending instruction so that students are challenged and able to develop new skills. The teacher provides supports that give students opportunities to meet objectives and to explain their learning. The teacher can scaffold instruction to meet students' needs by manipulating the task, materials, group size, pace, presentation, and so on. The metaphor of a scaffold captures the idea of an adjustable and temporary support that can be removed when it is no longer needed. Vygotsky (1978) describes learning as occurring in the *zone of proximal development*: "the distance between the actual developmental level as described by independent problem solving and the level of potential development as determined through problem solving under adult guidance or in collaboration with more capable peers" (p. 86). Important to promoting development within the students' zones of proximal development is the teacher's ability to relinquish control of the strategies to the students. To scaffold instruction effectively, teachers must teach new content in manageable steps; use explicit, systematic instruction for each step; and provide practice and review until students are independent and confident (see Apply the Concept 1-3).

Teaching in manageable steps involves breaking complex tasks into smaller steps to allow students to master each step of the task. Each step should be slightly more difficult than the previous one and should lead up to the full, complex skill the students are to learn. Providing specific instruction for each step of a complex task not only allows student success, but also creates a clear picture of what subskills students have mastered and what still needs further instruction or practice.

In addition to teaching in small segments, each step must be taught by using explicit, systematic instruction. *Explicit instruction* includes modeling, guided and independent practice, and use of consistent instructional procedures. *Systematic instruction* refers to sequencing instruction from easier to more difficult and teaching the easier skills to mastery before introducing more complex skills. Many reading strategies require complex thought processes and quick decision making. Students with reading difficulties or disabilities often do not automatically infer the thought processes that good readers use. Therefore, strategies for reading words and comprehending text must be taught in an overt way. Modeling strategies and guiding students through new tasks assist them in acquiring new skills without frustration. As they master each step, students become more independent in their ability to perform the skill or strategy.

Scaffolding reading instruction is analogous to the process many parents use when teaching their child to ride a bike. Although most children have seen many models of other adults and children riding bikes, a model of the whole bike-riding process by itself is probably not enough for a child to understand all the tasks that go into riding a bike successfully. Consequently, many parents

Scaffolding Instruction

Use the following guidelines to scaffold instruction for students with learning and behavior problems:

- Break the task into small steps.
- Teach easier skills first, then more difficult skills.
- Slow the pace of new skill introduction to allow for more practice of a task.
- Use a small group size.
- Make thought processes for accomplishing tasks overt by talking to students about what you are thinking when you engage in the task. Have students share what they are thinking when they practice the task.
- Teach strategies for completing complex skills.
- Model all steps involved in completing tasks.
- Provide teacher assistance during the first student attempts at skills.
- Praise the accomplishment of each small step.
- Use concrete materials during initial skill instruction.
- Vary the materials used.

divide riding a bike into smaller steps and teach each step explicitly, while allowing the child sufficient opportunities to practice and master each step. For example, as a first step, a parent may model and provide guided practice for sitting on the bike. The parent may provide explicit instruction by telling the child where to place feet and hands and how to work the pedals for moving forward and braking. Second, the materials may be scaffolded by attaching training wheels. This allows the child to practice what the parent has taught about sitting and pedal movement without having to deal with balancing the bike too. After the child has mastered riding with training wheels, the next step may be for the parent to take the training wheels off and hold the bike while running with the child as the child rides the bike. This allows the child to begin getting a feel for the balance needed to ride the bike independently. Parents can also assist the child in the thought processes for bike riding— look straight ahead, don't lean to one side, and so on. This explicit instruction helps the child learn techniques for balancing on the bike. The next step may be to slowly remove the scaffold by holding the bike less and less tightly, and finally letting go while the child rides. The final step for the child is to balance and pedal without the parent holding on to get the bike started.

Dividing bike riding into manageable steps not only helps the child learn a new, complex skill with less frustration (or in this case less injury), but also allows faster learning because the steps of the process are made explicit and practiced to mastery. Reading instruction should be similarly broken down into manageable steps, and each step should be taught explicitly and practiced to mastery. Independent reading is the ultimate result, but independent reading requires many, many steps and thought processes. For students with reading difficulties or disabilities to succeed, all of these must be taught explicitly and effectively.

Time Management One of the most powerful tools for improving learning is *careful use of instructional time*. Ideally, students with the greatest instructional needs would receive the most time in effective instruction, but this often not the case (Phelps et al., 2012). For teachers working with students who are performing below grade level, effective time management becomes an essential part of designing and providing effective instruction. In addition to avoiding wasting time, teachers must decide how much time to give to each activity or concept. When deciding how to sequence activities and how much time to spend on each, the teacher must think about the learner, the materials, and the task (Kame'enui & Carnine, 1998). As discussed earlier, the features of effective instruction must be balanced carefully, and their implementation must be ongoing. Assessment is a necessary step in designing instruction; similarly, instruction is an integral part of assessment and student monitoring.

Instructional Process: Modifying Instruction Ms. Kranowski watched and listened to the students and analyzed their written products over time. She used curriculum-based measures to gauge skills in capitalization, punctuation, spelling, and grammar. All these evaluative measures led her to the same conclusion: Her students' writing skills were not improving at a rate that she considered adequate. Ms. Kranowski decided to compile all the data using a class summary sheet. She then examined the data to find similar needs among her students. Estrella, Aileen, Luther, Jacqueline, and Sally were having difficulty capitalizing proper nouns. While the rest of the class completed a first draft of a story, Ms. Kranowski spent 10 minutes with these students, providing direct and explicit instruction on the rules of capitalization. She had prepared several examples of proper nouns, which she used to monitor her students' understanding by asking them to think aloud about why the nouns were or were not capitalized.

In determining how to modify her instruction, Ms. Kranowski thought about the ideas presented in Apply the Concept 1-4. She felt that she had adequately addressed the first four questions. Student motivation, attention, encouragement, and modeling had been good. She did not feel as comfortable about her answers to the next three questions: prior knowledge, manner of presentation, and practice. Sometimes she thought she wasn't focusing enough on one or two writing skills. She tended to present too much and not allow for enough practice and feedback. Ms. Kranowski decided that her modifications had to alleviate the problems with presentation, practice, and feedback. Her solution was the skill lessons that focused on teaching specific writing skills twice a week. For Ms. Kranowski and her students, this solution was successful. Her students began acquiring and maintaining the targeted writing skills. Now she is asking questions and planning for generalization and application.

Delivering Instruction

In addition to planning and designing effective instruction for students with reading problems, teachers must consider the delivery of the instruction. Several features occur during the delivery of effective instruction, including effective pacing, providing sufficient opportunities for students to respond, and feedback. Many of these same instructional practices benefit students who are English language learners (ELLs) and also have learning problems. See Apply the Concept 1-5 for a description.

Quick Pacing *Quick pacing* refers to instruction and student response that move at a manageable pace for students while taking full advantage of every minute of instruction. A quick pace eliminates unnecessary teacher talk and minimizes the amount of time between activities, allowing for more instructional time. A quick pace also keeps students alert and provide lots of opportunities for students to participate. For students who are behind in their reading skills, increased instructional time is essential. To catch up to expected levels of reading, students with reading problems have to make more progress than an average reader. A quick pace also keeps students actively engaged in the lesson. This, in turn, increases their instructional time. When teachers effectively use the scaffolding techniques discussed earlier, students can succeed, and the lesson can move at a quick pace.

1-4 APPLY THE CONCEPT

Questions for Evaluating the Instructional Process

- *Student motivation.* Am I creating a context in which learning is valued? Am I providing students appropriate choices about tasks and materials?

- *Student attention.* Am I creating an environment in which students can and are encouraged to attend to the learning task? Am I providing opportunities for students to work in settings that promote their attention?

- *Encouragement.* Am I creating a setting in which students are encouraged to take risks and be challenged by learning? Do I provide adequate feedback to each student regarding learning and social behavior?

- *Modeling.* When teaching a new task, do I first model what I want students to do? Do I use "think-alouds" to show students how I manage a task? Are the students given the opportunity to watch, listen, and talk to others so that they can see how the knowledge or skill is learned?

- *Activating prior knowledge.* Am I getting the students to think about what they already know about a skill or topic, and are they given the opportunity to build on that information in an organized fashion?

- *Rate, amount, and manner of presentation.* Are the new skills and knowledge being presented at a rate and amount that allow the students time to learn, and in a manner that gives them enough information yet does not overload them.

- *Practice.* Are the students given ample opportunity to practice? How much time do I provide students to practice and learn from each other?

- *Feedback.* Are the students given feedback on their work so they know how and what they are learning?

- *Acquisition.* Are the students given the opportunity to learn skills and knowledge until know something almost automatically?

- *Maintenance.* Are the students given the opportunity to continue to use their skills and knowledge so that they can serve as tools for further learning?

- *Generalization.* Are the students generalizing the skills and knowledge to other tasks, settings, and situations? Are the students, other teachers, or parents seeing the learning?

- *Application.* Are the students given the opportunity to apply their skills and knowledge in new and novel situations, thereby adapting their skills to meet the new learning experiences?

Designing Instruction for English Language Learners with Learning Disabilities

Students with learning disabilities who are English language learners (ELLs) benefit from many of the same instructional practices associated with improved outcomes for monolingual students, when teachers consider the language demands of the activities. Effective teachers adjust their instruction to consider the language and concept demands of their instruction. These teachers realize that ELL students' understanding of new concepts may be enhanced through instruction that uses routines, embeds redundancy of language use in lessons, and provides explicit discussion of vocabulary and the structure of language required to complete the task. Furthermore, teachers who are effective with ELL students present lessons that are organized to teach students to be aware of what they are learning and where they are confused. Haager and colleagues (Graves, Gersten, & Haager, 2004; Haager, Gersten, Baker, & Graves, 2003) conducted an observational study in 14 classrooms that included students who were ELLs, representing more than 10 different language groups. They identified effective teachers based on students' academic outcomes. They then looked at the instructional practices of these teachers and found that effective teachers of ELLs

- Use explicit teaching.
- Monitor student progress.
- Provide opportunities to practice new learning.
- Incorporate strategies that support student acquisition of English language skills.

Which instructional practices should you use in your teaching to ensure that English language learners have opportunities to learn? Providing clear, specific, and easy-to-follow procedures helps students learn new skills and strategies. It is also important to provide opportunities for students to acquire the language associated with these new skills and strategies. Teaching explicitly assists students; this includes identifying and using the structural and visual cues present in words, making relationships among concepts, words, or ideas visible and connected.

Sufficient Opportunities for Student Response When delivering a lesson, teacher routines should provide for maximum opportunities for students to respond with teacher feedback. For new instruction, teachers model the expected response and then give students an opportunity to practice. For activities previously taught, students practice and review skills taught and also generalize to more difficult tasks. Therefore, lessons should be filled with opportunities for students to respond and demonstrate what they are learning. There are several ways to increase the number of opportunities to respond within a lesson:

1. *Limit teacher talk.* Limiting the length of teacher talk can be accomplished by breaking up teacher modeling or explanations of concepts with questions for the students. Students can replicate teacher models or respond to related questions as each step of a process or strategy is taught.

2. *Use choral and individual responding.* Choral responding permits all students participating in the lesson to answer at the same time. Its use, followed by individual responses of students, increases the number of opportunities a particular student has to practice skills within a lesson.

3. *Use a variety of grouping formats.* Teaching students in small groups or using structuring lessons for pairs of students gives each student more turns to practice new skills. Students who have reading difficulties or disabilities often need extensive practice to learn new concepts. Providing additional practice opportunities within the lesson is an effective way to increase student skill levels.

Feedback *Feedback* refers to the teacher assistance that is provided when students respond during a lesson, while reading a passage, or working independently. Students with academic difficulties or disabilities need teachers to assist them with errors immediately and to provide additional opportunities to practice the skill correctly after assistance.

When students read or answer questions incorrectly without immediate error feedback, they practice the skill incorrectly. The effects of inaccurate practice can add up quickly, allowing the student to learn the skill incorrectly. This means that the student will have to spend a significant amount of time relearning the skill in the future. Also, students who respond correctly benefit from positive and specific feedback about the aspects of the task they performed well. Examples of feedback include: "You added the numbers correctly in all of the problems in the first line, however, there are two errors in problem #3. Can you find them?"; "I like the way you read this paragraph with expression. Read the next paragraph the same way, but I would like you to pause at the end of each sentence. Let me read one sentence for you to show you what I mean."

- Students with learning and behavior problems exhibit one or more of the following: consistent poor academic performance, attention problems, hyperactivity, memory problems, poor language, and behavior problems. The problems are characterized as persistent, severe, and the speed of recovery is slow.

- Typically, students are identified as having learning disabilities through their classroom teachers, a number of assessments, and by taking IQ tests. However, recently, there has been concern over the accuracy and fairness of IQ. Some refer to these tests as the "wait to fail" model because of a discrepancy between expectations and low achievement of some students—especially minorities. Response to intervention (RTI) addresses concerns about IQ achievement issues because it involves providing help to students as soon as they need it. RTI typically involves a multitiered system of interventions, a data collection system that informs decision making, and ongoing progress monitoring.

- The individualized education program (IEP) is both a process and a document. The process involves a group of individuals who establish an appropriate specialized educational program. At the IEP meeting, the team determines and documents whether a student is eligible for special education services; which services will be provided, the amount of services, and where they will occur; the goals and objectives, adaptations needed; and additional considerations as necessary, such as accommodations to statewide assessments. Data from the screening, progress monitoring, and interventions can be used to determine whether students have a learning disability or a severe behavior problem.

- Both the teacher and the student bring into the classroom knowledge and skills, as well as beliefs about school and about the world. Therefore, learning involves the accumulation of knowledge and skills, but it is also the active construction and transformation of ideas based on observations and experiences. Research has been conducted that supports the use of the following instructional features to meet the needs of students with learning and behavior problems: assessing progress, designing instruction, delivering instruction, and error feedback.

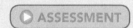

After completing this chapter, test your knowledge of the concepts by completing the Assessment.

Approaches to Learning and Teaching

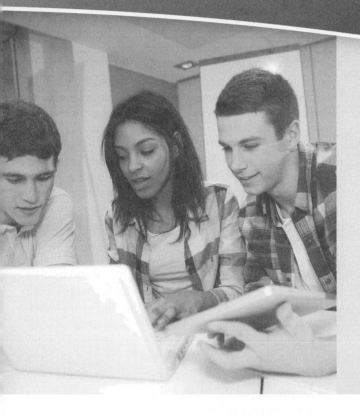

LEARNING OUTCOMES

1. Explain applied behavioral analysis and how teachers can use it in classrooms to increase desirable behaviors and decrease undesirable behaviors.

2. Provide an overview of how teachers can use cognitive strategy instruction (CSI) to teach academic, cognitive, or social skills.

3. Describe social learning practices and executive functioning, then list several practices that might influence both executive processing as well as academic outcomes.

Meaghan knew by the time she was a senior in college that she wanted to be a special education teacher, but was close to finishing her psychology degree and did not want to change majors. Instead, Meaghan completed her undergraduate degree in psychology and then returned to school part-time to pursue a degree with certification in special education. While going to school part-time, she was also working as a teaching assistant in a middle school. Fortunately, much of what she learned in psychology was directly applicable to the work she was doing with a team of special education teachers. She had learned a great deal about various learning theories as a psychology major and, in particular, how to use applied behavior analysis. Now, much of what she was asked to implement as schoolwide behavior support was based on the applied behavior analysis she had learned as an undergraduate. She understood the importance of looking for positive behaviors and providing reinforcement to students when they exhibited them. She also understood how to be consistent in her application of rules. Furthermore, her coursework that addressed cognitive behavioral theories also assisted her in effectively implementing many of the cognitively based math and reading strategies that she was encouraged to use by the special education teachers. All in all, the longer she worked as a special education teaching assistant, the more she appreciated her strong background in learning theory.

This chapter highlights some of the critical features of learning as they relate to delivering effective instruction and providing classroom management. We link specific models such as applied behavior analysis to practices in the classroom to facilitate understanding and designing effective behavioral and academic learning practices. These practices guide teachers in modifying their teaching to promote effective and efficient learning. The chapter is sequenced to move from less to more cognitively oriented models. Many of the general principles that are presented in this chapter will be applied to specific content areas in subsequent chapters. As you read this chapter, we encourage you to think about students who you know are not succeeding in school and who have learning and behavior problems. How are their learning patterns and habits explained by the various approaches to learning described in this chapter? What general teaching principles do the different approaches suggest to help such students? How can technology assist in the teaching–learning process?

Applied Behavior Analysis

What is applied behavioral analysis, and how can teachers use it to improve the behavior of their students? Teachers and other professionals who use applied behavior analysis understand that many of the behaviors of their students are learned and therefore they can be taught new behaviors. Using applied behavior analysis, the focus is on identifying observable behaviors and manipulating the antecedents and consequences of these behaviors to change behavior.

Manipulating Antecedents

An *antecedent* is an environmental event or stimulus that precedes a behavior and influences the probability that the behavior will recur in the future. For example, students learn that when the teacher pulls the cart with the video machine on it to the front of the room, that behavior serves as an antecedent to watching a film. Teachers learn that a change in their classroom structure might be an antecedent for students' exhibiting higher levels of classroom behavior problems. Antecedents influence desirable and undesirable behaviors. It is relatively easy for teachers to manipulate antecedents to change student behaviors. Teachers can do this by analyzing the environment and identifying factors that contribute to desirable and undesirable behaviors. By identifying and changing these factors, teachers can increase student learning and minimize or eliminate antecedents that interfere with successful learning. In observing antecedent behaviors, the teacher usually considers instructional content, classroom schedule, classroom rules, classroom arrangement, and peer interactions.

Instructional Content   Teachers can consider a number of ways to manipulate instructional content to control behavior: make activities more interesting, incorporate student preferences, reduce task difficulties

or length, provide choices, and develop functional or age-appropriate activities. By modifying educational programs, teachers can prevent students' inappropriate or undesirable behavior and establish a pleasant classroom environment. For example, Blair (1996) found that incorporating the students' activity preferences into circle time and academic activities in a preschool/kindergarten essentially eliminated the undesirable behavior of young students who had significant behavior problems. Another example is the teacher who realized that students would begin fooling around when waiting in line to transition to recess or lunch. She decided to give students a question related to their work that they would have to solve with a partner while waiting in line.

Classroom Schedule   A well-designed schedule allows everyone to predict what will occur during the school day and assist with the allocation of instructional time. Teachers can involve students in planning the daily schedule. In addition, it is important to avoid revising a schedule because changes can be disruptive, undermining students' ability to predict what will happen during the day. If there are changes to the schedule, posting them in a visible place is useful.

> Watch this **video** ▶, and listen to the numerous suggestions given by a sixth-grade teacher to help you establish a consistent classroom schedule and why it is beneficial to do so.

Classroom Rules   When properly developed and stated, carefully selected rules can contribute to a positive classroom atmosphere. They help students understand what will and will not be accepted in the

> In this **video** ▶, watch as a veteran teacher explains how her school developed a schoolwide rule system with clear expectations and consequences for all students. What advantages have occurred since they implemented these changes?

classroom. It is important to select a limited number of rules to make it easier for students to remember them. Seek the class's input on the rules to increase students' commitment to following them. State rules positively to help students identify the acceptable behavior, and post the rules so students can refer to them.

Classroom Arrangement Noises and crowding in a classroom sometimes increase undesirable behaviors. Arranging the furniture in the classroom to partition some areas can reduce noise levels, and limiting the number of students in any area can reduce crowding.

> See Chapter 4 for additional information on classroom arrangement and sample room arrangements.

Peer Interactions The classroom and the school are important social communities, and peer interactions play a significant role in determining the levels of desirable and undesirable behaviors. Teachers can facilitate peer interaction by pairing students who have good social skills with students who have more difficulty in prosocial skills, encouraging interaction between students with and without disabilities, and teaching prosocial skills to decrease inappropriate behaviors and to increase appropriate behaviors.

> For more information on teaching prosocial skills, refer to Chapter 4.

Increasing Desirable Behaviors Through Consequences

During the past few weeks, Ms. Glenn has focused on teaching Marjorie, Sheila, and Ali subtraction with regrouping. During this time, she demonstrated many of the principles by using 10 packs of sticks. Today, the students apply the principles on the chalkboard. Ms. Glenn then asks the students to practice the skills independently by completing a math sheet with 12 subtraction-with-regrouping problems. She watches them complete the first problem correctly. Now she needs to teach another group, yet she wants to be sure that these three students will continue to work on their math.

Progress Monitoring According to principles of applied behavior analysis, behavior is influenced by the consequences that follow it. Ms. Glenn needs to decide what consequences will follow appropriate math performance to maintain or increase its occurrence. She tells Marjorie, Sheila, and Ali, "If you get nine or more problems correct on this math sheet, I will let you have 5 minutes of free time in the Fun Corner." Free time in the Fun Corner is a big reinforcement for all three students,

and they accurately complete the math sheet while she works with other students.

There are four principles to apply in attempting to maintain or increase behavior:

1. The behavior must already be in the student's repertoire. In the preceding example, Ms. Glenn's students knew how to perform the math task. To maintain or increase social or academic behaviors, the teacher must first be sure that the student knows how to perform the target behaviors.

2. A consequence must follow the precise behavior to be changed or must be linked to the behavior through language. For example, the teacher may say, "Because you completed all of your math assignments this week, I'll let you select a movie to watch."

3. A reinforcer is whatever follows a behavior and maintains or increases the rate of the behavior.

4. To be most powerful, reinforcement should occur immediately following the behavior.

Thus, to increase the frequency of a behavior, we can manipulate the consequence that follows the behavior.

> **WEB RESOURCES**
> See the following Web site for an overview of applied behavior analysis from the Association for Behavior Analysis International at www.abainternational.org.

Reinforcement Reinforcement is the most significant way to increase desirable behavior. There are two types of reinforcement: positive and negative; both increase responding. How do they differ? The major difference between positive and negative reinforcement is that *positive reinforcement* is the *presentation* of a stimulus to increase responding, whereas *negative reinforcement* is the *removal* of a stimulus to increase responding.

> In this **video**, watch the children participate in their art lesson. Identify the individual and group methods the teacher uses to reinforce the students' learning and behavior.

Positive reinforcement increases responding by following the behavior with activities, objects, food, and social rewards that are associated with increasing the behavior. Toys, games, and privileges such as helping the teacher or having extra recess time are examples of positive reinforcers. Negative reinforcement increases responding by removing a stimulus. For example, if the teacher turned off the music in the classroom and students' work activity increased, then removing the noise of the music would have served as a negative reinforcement for the class.

The practice of negative reinforcement is often misused because the term *negative* is misinterpreted to mean harmful or bad, and therefore, the implication is that positive reinforcement is good and negative reinforcement is bad. Negative reinforcement simply means taking away something unpleasant if a specific behavior is exhibited. If a teacher scowls at a student until the student works, removing the scowl is negative reinforcement. The learning that takes place through negative reinforcement is avoidance learning. A common use in schools is the completion of work assignments to avoid staying after school. Students often use negative reinforcement with adults. An example is a child who throws a temper tantrum until he or she gets what he or she wants.

The effectiveness of a reinforcement program depends on selecting reinforcers that actually increase the target behavior. One way teachers can make sure that they use appropriate reinforcers for each student is to develop a reinforcer preference checklist for identifying reinforcers. Activities and events that a student selected when given a wide choice are more likely to be strongly reinforcing. To prevent students from being satiated with the reinforcer, reinforcement menus are recommended. Instead of providing one reinforcer over time, giving a choice of reinforcers increases their value and prevents satiation.

Many teachers are concerned that using reinforcers can prepare students for being "bribed" or "paid" to exhibit the behaviors that they are supposed to do. However, for students with behavior disorders, many of them have little experience using appropriate behaviors, so reinforcers can serve as a means to motivate them to practice appropriate behaviors. In using reinforcers with your students, it is important to start with more *intrinsic reinforcers* such as using activities that are reinforcing to the student (e.g., listening to music, coloring) and move to more *tangible reinforcers* such as tokens and food only as necessary. For example, a hierarchy of reinforcers, ranging from internal self-reinforcement ("I did a good job") to more extrinsic or tangible reinforcers such as choosing from a toy store, are presented in Apply the Concept 2-1.

How do you decide which reinforcers you should use? Selecting reinforcers is a critical decision because it influences their effectiveness. Consider the following suggestions when selecting reinforcers:

- Observe and record behaviors and events that are reinforcing to the student. For example, some students like to have their hands or face touched with a feather, other students like verbal praise, and some students like to have time with their friends.
- Consider the age and interests of the person whose behavior you want to improve, and consider what is reinforcing to them.
- After you consider what you know about the person, his or her age, interests, and what he or she likes and dislikes, identify a list of potential reinforcers.
- Use the behaviors that the person likes to engage in as reinforcers for the behaviors that he or she likes less.
- Interview the person about the things that he or she likes and would be reinforcing to that person.
- Try something new as a reinforcer.
- Consider using reinforcers that occur naturally in the environment.
- Be sure to keep a record of the target behavior and the extent to which it is influenced by the reinforcers.

2-1 APPLY THE CONCEPT

Classroom Reinforcers: Intrinsic (Internal) to Extrinsic (Concrete, Tangible)

Reinforcer	Examples
Self-managed reinforcers	Checks for raising hand, stars for not fighting at lunch, charting behavior
Positive recognition by student	I did a good job; I'm working hard; I'm listening to the teacher
Positive contact from teacher or students	Standing near student, patting student's desk, providing opportunities for student's friends to sit near student
Positive feedback from teacher	"You are working hard." "You are focusing on the lesson." "I really like the way you cooperated."
Privileges related to the target behavior	Student who is reducing fighting at recess is given more recess time for not fighting. Student who is focusing on completing work is given less homework for completing work.
Privileges not related to target behavior	Running errands for the teacher, free time, opportunities to socialize with friends
Tangible rewards including food, tokens, materials	Raisins, crackers, school materials such as pencils or paper, tokens to exchange for toys or other items of value

Secondary Reinforcers A *secondary reinforcer* is a previously neutral behavior that is paired with a reinforcer and therefore takes on reinforcing properties of its own. Thus, if the teacher always calls a student up to the teacher's desk before rewarding the student, then being called to the teacher's desk becomes a secondary reinforcer.

Sincere praise and attention are the most frequently used secondary reinforcers. Teachers are often quite skillful at using such subtle but effective secondary reinforcers as a hand on the shoulder, a pat on the head, a smile, or a wink. Many teachers position themselves carefully in the room to be near students whose behavior they want to reinforce with their attention. Apply the Concept 2-2 provides options for letting students know you value their good work and behavior.

Recall earlier when we talked about reinforcers, we discussed that ideally teachers use the least intrusive, or intrinsic, reinforcers (e.g., teaching students to recognize their achievements). However, there are often times when special education teachers need to use more extrinsic reinforcers (e.g., toys, privileges). Sometimes teachers manage these externalizing reinforcers by initiating a token reinforcement system. A *token system* is one in which the teacher gives coupons, chips, points, or stars to students if they exhibit target behaviors. For example, the teacher may give tokens for students who are listening and not disrupting others, for doing homework, for completing work on time, and for working well with others. Tokens are symbols in that they usually have little inherent value but can be exchanged for valuable things or privileges. Token systems can be simple, such as receiving stars for completing writing assignments, with each star worth 3 minutes of extra recess. Figure 2-1 presents several cards that teachers can use with younger students to record points. Token economies can also be quite complicated, as in a level system with rewards and privileges that vary according to the level of behavioral control the student exhibits. Students are assigned to levels contingent on their behavior. Being raised or lowered to a different level occurs as students accumulate points. Points are awarded and deducted for a full range of behaviors. More complicated token systems are typically used to manage aggressive behaviors displayed by severely disturbed students.

Shaping If reinforcement increases the rate of behavior, what does a teacher do if a target behavior is occurring at a very low rate or not at all?

For example, Mr. Kladder's goal is to shape Rhonda's behavior so that she is performing multiplication facts quickly and automatically. During the initial teaching phase, Mr. Kladder rewards Rhonda for computing 3×5 by adding five 3s. After Rhonda demonstrates that she can perform this behavior with a high degree of accuracy, Mr. Kladder no longer reinforces her for adding the numbers but reinforces her only for skip-counting 5, 10, 15, and then writing the answer. After Rhonda is successfully able to skip-count, she is reinforced for computing the answer in her head and writing it down. Now Mr. Kladder begins to give Rhonda timed tests in which she is reinforced only for beating her best time. Mr. Kladder is *shaping* Rhonda's behavior by reinforcing responses that more and more closely approximate the target response.

The Premack Principle If one activity occurs more frequently than another, the more frequently occurring activity can be used as a reinforcer to increase the rate of the less frequently occurring activity (Premack, 1959). For example, Adam more frequently participates in outdoor play than in writing stories. His teacher can make outdoor play contingent on completing writing assignments.

2-2 APPLY THE CONCEPT

33 Ways to Say "Very Good"

1. Exactly right.
2. Keep working on it, you're getting better.
3. You outdid yourself today.
4. Great!
5. You figured that out fast!
6. Good work!
7. You really make my job fun.
8. Fantastic!
9. I knew you could do it!
10. You are doing much better today.
11. Way to go!
12. Perfect!
13. That's the way to do it!
14. You are good.
15. Congratulations!
16. You got that down pat.
17. Wow!
18. That's right!
19. That's much better.
20. Wonderful!
21. That's quite an improvement!
22. That's great!
23. One more time and you will have it.
24. Tremendous!
25. You did it that time.
26. You've got your brain in gear today.
27. Nothing can stop you now.
28. Terrific!
29. Now you have it!
30. You make it look easy.
31. Sensational!
32. Good for you!
33. You are learning fast.

FIGURE 2-1 Forms for Recording Points Earned in a Token Economy

Source: P. Kaplan, J. Kohfeldt, and K. Sturla, *It's Positively Fun: Techniques for Managing the Learning Environment* (Love, 1975), pp. 15–16. Reproduced by permission of Love Publishing Company.

Using the Premack principle has several advantages for teachers, including ease of use and relying on events that are already occurring in the classroom. For example, a teacher might determine that a student with learning problems really likes reading, sort of likes math, and really does not like spelling. The teacher could then use reading as contingent on completing spelling. A more appropriate list for most students with learning and behavior problems might include 5 minutes of free time contingent on completing spelling. Reinforcing activities such as talking quietly with friends or listening to music can be used to increase the rate of less desirable activities such as completing a book report.

Group Contingencies Group contingencies can be used to increase desirable behavior or decrease undesirable behavior. When *group contingencies* are used, a group of students is either reinforced or loses reinforcement, contingent on the behavior of the entire group or of a target student in the group. For example, a teacher could establish a 20-minute block of free time at the end of the school day. Every time the noise level in the classroom exceeds the teacher's limits, she subtracts 1 minute from the allocated free time. Group contingencies can also be used to change the behavior of a particular student in the class. For instance, Carla is a 12-year-old student with behavior problems who has been mainstreamed into a sixth-grade class. During Carla's first couple of weeks in the class, she continually got into fights with her classmates during recess. The teacher told the class that she would extend their recess by 10 minutes if Carla did not get into any fights

during recess. The class included Carla in their group play, and fighting was eliminated. However, there are dangers in group contingencies being dependent on the behavior of an individual. The individual could use his or her position to manipulate the behavior of others in the class. It is also possible that the individual will view himself or herself negatively because of this position.

Axelrod (1998) defines group contingencies by identifying a 10-step program for their use:

1. Select only one behavior to change.
2. Carefully specify in a written format the behavior that you want to change.
3. Determine through careful observation how often and when the behavior occurs.
4. Think about what might be reinforcing to all members of the group.
5. Decide what the group contingency will be that will cause the reinforcer to be used.
6. Be sure to identify a behavior that everyone in the group can perform.
7. Provide the reinforcer contingent on a reasonable improvement in the target behavior.
8. Let each member of the group as well as the group as a whole know when they are behaving appropriately.
9. Monitor the progress of the group and each member of the group.
10. Revise the program as needed.

FIGURE 2-2 Sample Contingency Contract Form

I've Got An Offer You Can't Refuse

If_____

_____ by _____

Then_____

_____

_____

| date | student |
| witness | Teacher |

Source: P. Kaplan, J. Kohfeldt, and K. Sturla, *It's Positively Fun: Techniques for Managing the Learning Environment* (Love, 1975), pp. 21. Reproduced by permission of Love Publishing Company.

Contingency Contracting *Contingency contracting* is an agreement between two or more persons that specifies their behaviors and consequences. A common example of a contingency contract is the agreement between parent and child regarding an allowance. The child agrees to perform certain behaviors in return for a specified amount of money each week. The contingency contract should specify who is to do what, when, under what conditions, and for what consequences (see Figure 2-2).

Decreasing Undesirable Behaviors Through Consequences

Unfortunately, some students manifest behaviors that interfere with their learning or the learning of others. Techniques for decreasing these undesirable behaviors include extinction, differential reinforcement, response cost, punishment, and time-out.

Extinction *Extinction* is the removal of reinforcement following a behavior. For example, a teacher wants to extinguish a student's shouting out answers in class. She determines that telling the student to raise his hand is reinforcing the shouting behavior. She knows this because the shouting out continues, and she recognizes that the student finds her attention (commenting on his shouting out) is reinforcing to him. To extinguish shouting out, the teacher removes the reinforcer (saying, "Raise your hand" to the student) and ignores the student's shouting out.

Extinction can be an effective means of decreasing undesirable behaviors, but it is often slow and can be impractical for many behaviors that occur within the classroom because the reinforcers for the undesirable behavior are often difficult for the teacher to control. For example, the student who continually shouted out in class was being reinforced not only by the classroom teacher's attention ("Raise your hand"), but also by other students who attended to him when he shouted out. A teacher who wants to reduce this behavior through extinction has to eliminate both the teacher's reinforcement and the reinforcement of others in the class. To compound the difficulty, slipups by a teacher or students intermittently reinforces the behavior and maintains it for a long time.

Another characteristic of extinction is its effect on the rate at which the target behavior continues to occur. During extinction, the target behavior will increase in rate or intensity before decreasing. Thus, a teacher who is attempting to eliminate tantrums through extinction will observe the tantrums occurring more frequently at first, lasting longer, and perhaps even being louder and more intense than before extinction. If the teacher continues to withhold reinforcement, usually attention, the rate and intensity will decrease, and tantrums can be eliminated. For this reason, it is extremely important to chart behavior when using extinction. To document behavior change, take *baseline data*, a record of the frequency and/or duration of the behavior before implementing the intervention, and continue to record data after intervention is implemented.

Although extinction can be an effective way to decrease undesirable behaviors, it requires patience and the ability to control all of the reinforcers. Ignoring, the most frequently applied form of extinction in the classroom, is an important skill for teachers to learn. Three points to remember about using ignoring as a means of decreasing undesirable behavior are:

1. Ignoring can be effective when the behavior is being reinforced by teachers or students who are willing to discontinue reinforcement.

2. If a teacher attempts to eliminate a behavior through ignoring, the behavior must be ignored *every* time it occurs.

3. Ignoring will not be effective if the behavior is being maintained by other reinforcers, such as the attention of selected classmates.

Differential Reinforcement *Differential reinforcement* involves strengthening one set of responses in contrast to another. It is an effective procedure for developing a positive behavior management plan. The main advantage of differential reinforcement is that positive consequences are used to reduce the strength of undesirable behavior. Therefore, negative side effects associated with punishment procedures are avoided. There are several forms of differential reinforcement.

Differential Reinforcement of Incompatible Behaviors and Alternative Behaviors Differential reinforcement of incompatible behaviors (DRI) involves identifying desirable behaviors. Reinforcement is then provided contingent on the occurrence of the targeted desirable behaviors. For example, while ignoring the out-of-seat behavior of a student, the teacher targets and reinforces the desirable behavior that is incompatible with it—in this case, in-seat behavior. Therefore, when Scott is sitting in his seat, the teacher is quick to catch his appropriate behavior and reinforce it. In addition, the teacher would intermittently reinforce Scott for being in his seat. In the case of DRI, the new response (incompatible behavior) is selected because it represents an incompatible alternative to the disruptive behavior; the two behaviors cannot occur simultaneously. In differential reinforcement of alternative behaviors (DRA), the alternative behavior is not necessarily incompatible with the disruptive response, and it can occur at the same time as the undesirable behavior. The goal of using DRA is to strengthen a range of appropriate behaviors that teachers will attend to naturally, thereby reinforcing a broad repertoire of appropriate behavior. Careful planning should ensure that the reinforcers selected are sufficiently attractive and delivered with sufficient frequency to motivate student performance while removing reinforcers from the undesirable behavior. Both DRI and DRA ensure that new behaviors are fostered at the same time that undesirable behaviors are being diminished.

Differential Reinforcement of Other Behaviors Differential reinforcement of other behaviors (DRO) is the reinforcement of the nonoccurrence of target behavior during a specified time period; reinforcers are delivered following time intervals when the target behavior does not occur. For example, a teacher may allow a student free time at the end of each 30-minute scheduled period when no target behavior occurred. Therefore, determining the length of the reinforcement period before using DRO is important. Brief intervals of 1 to 10 minutes may be selected for high-rate behaviors, and intervals up to a day in length may be used for low-rate behaviors. DRO may be most effective when used in combination with a DRA procedure by reinforcing occurrences of alternative behavior as well as providing reinforcement for intervals when a zero rate of the target behavior occurred. When combined with other methods, DRO can be a powerful procedure.

Regardless of the type of differential reinforcement, reinforcing behavior through consequences requires the teacher to do four things:

1. Identify the behavior that is to change (interfering behavior).
2. Identify the desirable behavior that is incompatible with the interfering behavior.
3. Stop reinforcing the interfering behavior.
4. Reinforce the desirable behavior.

Response Cost *Response cost* is a procedure in which a specified amount of a reinforcer is removed after each occurrence of the target behavior. Withdrawal of favored activities and tangible reinforcers are common response strategies for young children. For example, a student is not allowed to play during free-choice session because of his or her aggression toward peers. One of the most common response-cost strategies for older students is the withdrawal of tokens following a target behavior. For example, say students earn 20 points for completing each assignment throughout the day. Points can be exchanged for primary reinforcers at the end of the day. Engaging in a target behavior may result in a response cost of 30 points. Response cost is an aversive procedure that should be used carefully because it can inadvertently be used to punish positive behaviors. For example, teachers may be tempted to ask students to complete additional work if assignments are completed before the end of the class period, but additional work requirements may act as a response cost for early assignment completion.

Punishment *Punishment,* the opposite of reinforcement, is following a behavior with a consequence that decreases the strength of the behavior or reduces the likelihood that the behavior will continue to occur. Unfortunately, punishment does not ensure that desired behavior will occur. For example, a student who is punished for talking in class might stop talking but may not attend to his or her studies for the remainder of the day.

There are many significant arguments against the use of punishment:

- Punishment is ineffective in the long run.
- Punishment often causes undesirable emotional side effects, such as fear, aggression, and resentment.
- Punishment provides little information about what to do, teaching the individual only what not to do.
- The person who administers the punishment is often associated with it and also becomes aversive.
- Punishment frequently does not generalize across settings, thus it needs to be readministered.
- Fear of punishment often leads to escape behavior.

If there are so many arguments against using punishment, why is it so often chosen as a means for changing behavior? There are many explanations, including lack of familiarity with the consequences of punishment and the inability to effectively use a more positive approach. Also, punishment is often reinforcing to the punisher, reducing the occurrence of the undesirable behavior, therefore reinforcing its use.

The use of punishment is not suggested, and instead teachers are encouraged to identify ways of reinforcing appropriate behaviors.

Time-Out *Time-out* involves removing a student from the opportunity to receive any reinforcement. For example, to impose a time-out, the teacher asks a student to sit in the hall during the remainder of a lesson, or asks a young child to leave a group, or asks a student to sit in a quiet chair until he or she is ready to join the group.

Unfortunately, time-out is frequently used inappropriately. The underlying principle behind the successful use of time-out is that the environment the student is leaving must be reinforcing and the time-out environment must be without reinforcement. This is not as easy to achieve as one might think. For example, when Elizabeth was talking and interfering with others during a science lesson, her teacher thought she would decrease Elizabeth's behavior by sending her to time-out, which was a workstation in the back of the room away from the group. The teacher became discouraged when Elizabeth's inappropriate behavior during science class increased in subsequent lessons rather than decreased. A likely explanation is that Elizabeth did not enjoy science class and found sitting in the back of the room looking at books reinforcing. The efficacy of time-out is strongly influenced by environmental factors. If the environment the student is leaving is unrewarding, then time-out is not an effective means of changing the student's behavior.

Teachers who use secluded time-out areas or contingent restraint (holding the student down plus withdrawal, exclusion, and seclusion) should be aware of the legal implications of such intervention and should obtain the necessary authorization from school administrators and from parents or guardians. Contingent restraint is considered a last option procedure and is typically used to decrease self-injurious behavior or aggressive behavior in individuals with autism or cognitive disabilities (Hersen et al., 2005).

A position paper on the use of behavior reduction strategies has been issued by the Council for Children with Behavior Disorders (CCBD, 2002). Recommended procedures for successfully implementing time-out are listed in Apply the Concept 2-3.

Stages of Learning

One way to apply the principles of learning is through stages of learning. The *stages of learning* (see Figure 2-3) are the levels a student moves through in acquiring proficiency in learning (Bryant, Smith, & Bryant, 2007). For example, the first stage of learning, *entry*, is the level of performance the student is currently exhibiting. During the second stage, *acquisition*, the components of the target behavior are sequenced into teachable elements. Each teachable element is taught to mastery through a high rate of reinforcement, shaping, and consistent use of cues. When the behavior is occurring at a high level of accuracy, the focus of the learning is on *proficiency*. During this stage, the teacher's goal is to increase the student's accuracy and fluency in performing the behavior. At the next stage, *maintenance*, the goal is for the behavior to be maintained at the target level of accuracy and proficiency with intermittent reinforcement and a reduction in teacher assistance and cues. The next stage is *generalization*, in which the target behavior transfers across settings, persons, and materials. Generalization may be a separate skill that needs to be taught. Apply the Concept 2-4 provides further information on how to teach for generalization. At the final stage, *application*, the learner is required to extend and use the learning in new situations. Application is a difficult skill for special learners, and the teacher's role is to demonstrate and provide a range of opportunities for applying the newly acquired skill.

2-3 APPLY THE CONCEPT

Guidelines for Implementing Time-Out

Time-out, like punishment, should be used as a last resort. Teachers should discuss this intervention with school administrators and parents before implementing it, and follow these steps:

1. Students should be told in advance which behaviors will result in time-out.
2. The amount of time students will be in time-out should be specified ahead of time.
3. The amount of time students are in time-out should be brief (1 to 5 minutes).
4. Students should be told once to go to time-out. If a student does not comply, the teacher should unemotionally place the student in time-out.
5. Time-out must occur every time an undesirable behavior occurs.
6. Contingencies should be set in advance for students who fail to comply with time-out rules.
7. The time-out area should be constantly monitored.
8. When time-out is over, a student should return to the group.
9. Positive behaviors that occur after time-out should be reinforced.

FIGURE 2-3 Stages of Learning

Source: Based on Rivera, D. P., and Smith, D. D. (1997). *Teaching Students with Learning and Behavior Problems,* 3rd ed. Boston, MA: Allyn & Bacon.

Hall and Hall (1998) provide helpful suggestions about how to handle the potential problems that occur with time-out. Several of their suggestions follow:

- Add time to a student's time-out for refusing to go to time-out or displaying other inappropriate behaviors such as screaming, yelling, and kicking.

- Students should be required to clean up any mess made during time-out before they return from time-out.

- Be sure to have a backup consequence if a student refuses to go to time-out and the amount of time added reaches 30 minutes (usually considered the maximum amount).

- Do not argue with individuals when they either try to talk you out of time-out or indicate that you have no right to put them in time-out. Ignore their comments.

- If the inappropriate behavior involves two students and it is not possible to determine the source of the problem, do not argue; put both students in time-out.

- If the student displays the behavior in a place where it is not possible to use time-out, indicate that time-out will be provided when you return to the classroom.

- Be sure to chart the effects of time-out so that you can determine whether it is working.

Cognitive Strategy Instruction

How is cognitive strategy instruction (CSI) used to teach academic, cognitive, or social skills? CSI integrates ideas from behavioral, social, and cognitive learning theories and assumes that cognitive behavior (thinking processes), like observable behaviors, can be changed. This model of instruction is based on the earlier work from social learning theory (Bandura, 1977, 1986) and cognitive behavior approaches (Meichenbaum, 1977; see National Association of Cognitive-Behavioral Therapists). CSI incorporates principles of behavioral learning but adds principles from social learning theory and cognitive theory that are important to consider when the goal of instruction is to

---

2-4 APPLY THE CONCEPT

Teaching to Generalize

Assuming that most students will need to "generalize" the strategies learned to other settings, what can teachers do to ensure generalization occurs?

1. Increase students' knowledge of how to "reinforce" themselves for using the instructional strategies or practices in other settings. For example, ask students to keep a log of when they practice independently, and provide reinforcement.

2. Teach students how to develop and apply their own reinforcers for using strategies

appropriately. For example, "I remembered to use my cue cards. I now remember better what I read and am more likely to get a good grade."

3. Provide opportunities for students to practice the instructional practices within the materials needed to generalize their use. For example, students who have learned to complete math problems with support in the resource room are asked to apply the same problem-solving practices to math problems in the general education classroom.

4. Observe students in other settings where use of the strategies would be valuable. Provide cues for use, and reinforce appropriate practices.

change the way the student thinks. In numerous research studies, CSI has been shown to be particularly effective with students who have learning and behavior problems (Swanson, 1999a, 1999b).

Let's look at how Ms. Neal helps Marlow and his classmates better understand the science concepts and textbook she is using in her seventh-grade resource science class. Even though Marlow, a student with behavior disorders, can identify most of the words in the text, he remembers only a few details from what he reads. Ms. Neal wants to teach Marlow and his classmates how to understand and remember the major points of a reading. She decides that if she wants to teach the students this cognitive behavior, she will have to give them a consistent set of steps to use in completing the process, in much the same way that we use a consistent set of steps to tie shoes. She also knows that for the students to learn what to do, they need to observe someone else. But how can she do this?

First, she selects the steps she wants to teach Marlow and the other students to use when they read their science text. Next, she and the students discuss the strategies the students currently use and their effectiveness. They also discuss the importance of improving their skills and the payoff for improvement. Ms. Neal then tells the students about the steps she uses when she reads. To model these steps, she reads and explains what she is thinking (i.e., cognitive modeling). Then she talks them through the steps as the students try them. Finally, Ms. Neal gives the students lots of opportunities to practice the steps when reading their textbooks, encouraging them at first to say the steps aloud as they work through them. She provides feedback on how they are doing, and she teaches them how to evaluate their own performance.

Using these systematic techniques, Ms. Neal finds that in several weeks Marlow and his classmates are improving in their ability to remember the important information from their science text. In addition, they are beginning not to rely so much on the strategy she taught them. It is almost as if they are using it automatically, without having to consciously remember to use it. Ms. Neal believes that she has taught her students a good strategy for thinking about what they are reading and that she has changed their cognitive behavior (thinking processes). To promote generalization, Ms. Neal discusses with Marlow and his classmates other opportunities they have for using the strategy. The students begin keeping a list, on the board, of occasions when the strategy can be used. They also begin using the strategy on these different occasions (e.g., reading the newspaper during current events, reading other textbooks, editing each others' stories and essays) and discussing how useful the strategy was in helping them.

Common Features of Cognitive Strategy Instruction

CSI has been used to develop a range of academic and social skills. Common features of CSI include strategy steps, modeling, self-regulation, verbalization, and reflective thinking.

Strategy Steps   A series of steps are usually identified for the student to work through when solving a problem or completing a task. These steps are based on an analysis of the cognitive and observable behaviors needed to complete the task. Before Ms. Neal began teaching, she determined the steps in the reading strategy she wanted to teach Marlow and his classmates.

Modeling   In CSI, modeling is used as a primary means of instruction. Modeling can be a very effective teaching technique. With CSI, students are asked not only to watch observable behaviors as the instructor performs a task, but also to listen to the teacher's self-talk.

> Watch the think-aloud procedure in this video ▶, as modeled by a fourth-grade teacher during a reading lesson. How does she explain the importance of the modeling strategy?

In this way, the teacher models both observable behaviors and the unobservable thinking processes associated with those behaviors. Being able to model thinking processes is an important component for teaching such cognitive skills as verbal math problem solving, finding the main idea in a paragraph, editing written work, and solving social problems. In most instances, the person who does the modeling is the teacher or a peer, but video and puppets have also been used.

Self-Regulation   Self-regulation refers to learners monitoring their thinking and actions through language mediation. Students first use language to mediate their actions by overtly engaging in self-instruction and self-monitoring. Later, this language mediation becomes covert.

Using self-regulation, students act as their own teachers. Students are expected to take active roles in the learning process and to be responsible for their own learning. Although they work under the guidance of a teacher, students are expected to monitor their learning, change or modify strategies when difficulties arise, evaluate their performance, and in some cases provide self-reinforcement.

Self-regulation implies that students develop organizing, planning, evaluating, and goal-setting behaviors that help them regulate their academic learning and/or their behavior. For example, related to academic tasks such as math and reading, students effectively organize their learning tasks and goals, set timelines for accomplishing these goals, establish procedures for evaluating their progress, and have mechanisms for applying strategies to help them learn and meet their goals. Similarly, related to behavior, students who use self-regulation are aware of the behaviors that they are monitoring (e.g., shouting out in class) and identify practices for ensuring that they can meet these goals (e.g., holding up a red card so the teacher knows that they have something very important to say) and practices for monitoring their success. Students may monitor their own behavior and establish either independently or with support from the teacher mechanisms for reinforcing themselves as they achieve goals.

Peer monitoring and support can be extremely useful in increasing appropriate behavior. For example, peers can be taught to help students monitor their behavior and record it (D. H. Anderson, Fisher, Marchant, Young, & Smith, 2006). Peers can be exceedingly helpful in group support and as reinforcers to maintain appropriate behaviors.

In reviewing self-regulation outcome research conducted with students with behavior disorders, numerous studies indicate that self-regulation procedures can be extremely effective in enhancing both the academic and social behavior of students (J. R. Nelson, Smith, Young, & Dodd, 1991; Vohs & Baumeister, 2010).

Verbalization Verbalization is typically a component of self-instruction and self-monitoring in which overt verbalization or self-talk is faded to covert verbalization. Many CSI programs rely on a talk-aloud or think-aloud technique (e.g., Rosenzweig et al., 2011; Swanson, 1999b). After listening to the teacher think aloud as he or she performs the targeted processes and task, students are encouraged to talk aloud as they initially learn the strategy. For example, Ramon might say the following as he completes a two-digit subtraction problem without regrouping: "Start at the ones place, and take the bottom number away from the top. Write the answer in the ones place. Now go to the tens place. Do the same thing." Usually, these overt verbalizations occur only during the initial stages of learning. As the strategy becomes more automatic, students are encouraged to think to themselves instead of thinking aloud.

In addition to verbalization about the learning processes, students are also encouraged to make self-statements about their performance. For example, "That part is done. Now go to the next part" or "I'm getting much faster at this" or "I need to think about all my choices before I decide."

Learning to think aloud as a mechanism to support students' understanding of how to think about their learning and behavior is a difficult task. Try the following practices to facilitate thinking aloud with your students:

1. Model self-talk and self-statements as you perform the tasks.

2. Start with tasks in which the students are somewhat proficient. Later, as students become comfortable with self-talk, you can switch to tasks in which you want them to acquire more proficiency.

3. Develop and use cue cards to help students remember the steps they are to talk through.

As an example of the third method, see Figure 2-4 for the cue cards that teachers can use to guide students through reading comprehension practices. The cue cards can be reminders about what to think about when students are reading complex texts.

Reflective Thinking Reflective thinking requires students to take the time to think about what they are doing. Teaching students who have learning and behavior problems to stop and think is an important skill to include in instruction. Many students with learning and behavior problems act without considering the consequences and demonstrate limited and ineffective strategies for approaching academic tasks and social situations. They approach these tasks and situations in a disorganized, haphazard way, often without thinking about the consequence of their actions. In using cognitive strategy instruction, teachers assist students in using reflective thinking.

The specificity of the questions and cues can be important for success. For example, teachers can cue students about behavior before going to lunch (e.g., What are the three things we do at lunch?) or cue them about writing (e.g., remember to reread what you wrote, and circle the words that you need help spelling).

Teaching Implications of Cognitive Strategy Instruction

CSI is designed to actively involve students in learning. General guidelines to consider for actively engaging students in learning include the following:

- Analyze the target behavior you want to see students using, and be sure that you model or describe it carefully to students.

- Determine what strategies students are already using, and encourage them to continue or describe how to apply them to the expected task.

FIGURE 2-4 Cue Cards Used for Teaching Reading Comprehension

Card #1.

> Sometimes kids disagree and no one knows about it. They keep it between themselves. However, that was certainly not the case with Melodee and Monika. Everybody knew that they could not be in the same place at the same time and not wrangle with each other. Even their parents knew about what they were like when they were together. It wasn't just competitions either. It was a deeper problem.
>
> *Stop at the end of each paragraph. Ask yourself, "What's happening?" If you need to reread to refine your answer, do so.*

Card #2.

> Sometimes kids disagree and no one knows about it. They keep it between themselves. However, that was certainly not the case with Melodee and Monika. Everybody knew that they could not be in the same place at the same time and not wrangle with each other. Even their parents knew about what they were like when they were together. It wasn't just competitions either. It was a deeper problem.
>
> *Write or underline words that you do not know. Reread sentences around the word to see if you can figure it out.*

Card #3.

> Sometimes kids disagree and no one knows about it. They keep it between themselves. However, that was certainly not the case with Melodee and Monika. Everybody knew that they could not be in the same place at the same time and not wrangle with each other. Even their parents knew about what they were like when they were together. It wasn't just competitions either. It was a deeper problem.
>
> *Stop at the end of the reading and ask yourself, "What are the big ideas of what I've read?"*

- Select strategy steps that are as similar as possible to the strategy steps that good problem solvers use. Make them simple and easy to remember.
- Work with students to develop strategy steps that they can and will use.
- Teach prerequisite skills.
- Teach strategy steps, using modeling, self-instruction, and self-regulation.
- Give explicit feedback.
- Teach strategy generalization.
- Help students maintain the strategy.

Guidelines for monitoring the effects of instruction (see Apply the Concept 2-5) reflect an increasing observation that students with learning and behavior problems benefit from applying practices that assist them in focusing their attention and thinking on the task. In particular, success has been documented in applying self-regulation practices in three areas: improving social behavior, reading comprehension, and writing. For example, in writing, students who think aloud as they write and set goals for how they will improve their writing make better progress in writing (Mason, Reid, & Hagaman, 2012). As discussed in Apply the Concept 2-6, researchers at the Center for Research on Learning at the University of Kansas have

2-5 APPLY THE CONCEPT

Guidelines for Assessing Strategy Effectiveness

1. Does the student use the strategy independently?
2. Does the student perceive that the strategy helps him or her succeed?
3. Has the student modified the strategy for his or her own use?
4. Does the student use the strategy in other settings?
5. How likely is the student to continue using the strategy?

Application of Cognitive Strategy Instruction: The Learning Strategies Curriculum

Can the principles of CSI be applied to academic tasks in such a way that adolescents with learning disabilities can succeed in performing the skills required for secondary school settings? The Strategies Intervention Model (Bulgren, Deshler, & Lenz, 2007; Deshler, Ellis, & Lenz, 1996) is a comprehensive example of a series of research-based instructional practices based on CSI.

The goal of the Strategies Intervention Model is "to teach learning disabled adolescents strategies that will facilitate their acquisition, organization, storage, and retrieval of information, thus allowing them to cope with the demands of social interaction" (Alley & Deshler, 1979, p. 8). Learning strategies are techniques, principles, or routines that enable students to learn to solve problems and complete tasks independently. Strategies include how a person thinks and acts when planning, executing, and evaluating performance on a task and its outcomes. Broadly, a learning strategy (1) includes a general approach to solving a set of problems, (2) promotes goal-directed behavior, (3) teaches selection of appropriate procedures, (4) guides implementation of a procedure, (5) shows how to monitor progress, (6) can be controlled, and (7) provides and focuses on cues to take action. Learning strategies instruction focuses on how to learn and how to use what has been learned.

The Learning Strategies Curriculum (Lenz, 2006) contains three strands of academic, task-specific strategies. The Acquisition Strand enables students to gain information from written materials and includes such strategies as the Word Identification Strategy (Lenz, Schumaker, Deshler, & Beals, 1993) and the Paraphrasing Strategy (Schumaker, Denton, & Deshler, 1993). The Storage Strand consists of strategies to assist students in organizing, storing, and retrieving information. The First-Letter Mnemonic Strategy (Nagel, Schumaker, & Deshler, 1994) is an example of a Storage Strategy. The Expression and Demonstration of Competence Strand contains strategies that enable students to complete assignments, express themselves, and take tests. The Test Taking Strategy (Hughes, Schumaker, Deshler, & Mercer, 1993), the Paragraph Writing Strategy (Lyerla, Schumaker, & Deshler, 1994), and the Error Monitoring Strategy (Schumaker, Nolan, & Deshler, 1994) are examples of strategies that assist students in taking tests, writing cohesive paragraphs, and editing written work.

Each strategy uses a teaching model that incorporates principles of cognitive behavior modification. The stages in the model are:

Acquisition

Stage 1 Pretest and Make Commitments

Obtain measure(s) of current functioning.

Make students aware of inefficient/ineffective habits.

Obtain students' commitments to learn.

Stage 2 Describe the Strategy

Ensure that students have rationales for strategy use.

Ensure that students know characteristics of situations for when and where to use the strategy.

Describe results that can be expected.

Supervise goal setting.

Describe and explain the strategy steps.

Present the remembering system.

Stage 3 Model the Strategy

Demonstrate the entire strategy, thinking aloud.

Involve the students in a demonstration.

Stage 4 Elaboration and Verbal Rehearsal

Assist students to verbally rehearse the strategy steps and what each step means.

Require students to memorize the strategy.

Stage 5 Controlled Practice and Feedback

Supervise practice in easy materials.

Provide positive and corrective feedback.

Move from guided practice to independent practice.

Require mastery.

Stage 6 Advanced Practice and Feedback

Supervise practice in materials from regular coursework.

Provide positive and corrective feedback.

Fade prompts and cues for strategy use and evaluation.

Move from guided practice to independent practice.

Require mastery.

Stage 7 Confirm Acquisition, and Make Generalization Commitments

Obtain measure(s) of progress.

Make students aware of progress.

Obtain the students' commitment to generalize.

Phase I: Orientation

Discuss situations, settings, and materials in which the strategy can be used.

Evaluate appropriateness of strategy in various settings and materials.

Identify helpful aspects of the strategy and adjustments.

Make students aware of cues for using the strategy.

Phase II: Activation

Program the students' use of the strategy in a variety of situations.

Provide feedback.

Reinforce progress and success.

Phase III: Adaptation

Identify cognitive processes.

Discuss how the strategy can be modified to meet differing demands.

Assist students in applying the modifications.

Phase IV: Maintenance

Set goals related to long-term use.

Conduct periodic reviews.

Identify self-reinforcers and self-rewards.

Provide feedback.

---

developed a learning strategy curriculum as well as a number of task-specific strategies (e.g., finding the main idea, decoding unknown words, test taking, listening, and taking notes) that employ CSI.

Social Learning and Interactive Dialogue

Learning is a social event in which language plays an important role. Applying this concept, teachers and students discuss what they are learning and how they are going about learning. Such interactive dialogue or instructional conversations between teachers and learners provide language models and tools for guiding one's inner talk about learning (Moll, 2010). Initially, a more expert person may model the self-talk and vocabulary related to the cognitive processes. However, this gives way to a collaborative or interactive dialogue in which the learner assumes increasing responsibility. This type of teaching allows for the instruction of cognitive and metacognitive strategies within purposeful, meaningful discussions and provides a means for selecting, organizing, and relating the content matter being discussed. For example, in reciprocal teaching (Oczkus, 2010; Palincsar & Brown, 1984), a technique designed to foster comprehension and comprehension monitoring, the teacher and students take turns leading dialogues that focus on their knowledge of the information they are studying and on the processes they are using for understanding and for checking their understanding.

A synthesis of the most productive conversations (Soter et al., 2008) reveals that both teacher- and student-led discussions benefit when

- Students occupy the "talk-time" for extended periods of time.

> See Chapter 8 for more on processes students can use to check their understanding.

- Teachers prompt students to discuss texts by asking open-ended questions (i.e., questions that do not have a *yes* or *no* answer) that are related closely to the text and are engaging.

- Teachers ask authentic questions that are linked to the text, resulting in greater elaboration of talk by students, which results in higher-level thinking about the text.

- Teachers promote discussions that highlight a more analytic approach rather than provide extensive opportunities for students to express themselves in less analytic ways.

Scaffolded Instruction

As the expert, the role of the teacher is to provide temporary and adjustable support as students' develop new skills, strategies, and knowledge. The instruction is referred to as *scaffolded instruction* (Archer & Hughes, 2011).

The concepts of scaffolding and zones of proximal development were explained in Chapter 1.

Actively engaging students in the process of solving problems rather than as passive members of the instructional classroom is associated with improved outcomes (Gallimore et al., 2009). For example, in a 5-year study conducted by Gallimore et al., teachers who used an inquiry-focused protocol (students were actively engaged in solving problems related to literacy and numeracy) had several key outcomes including improved student performance and greater perceptions of accountability on the part of the teachers. These outcomes were

> The middle school teacher in this **video** shares methods to scaffold the learning of students at various learning levels in his classroom. What strategies does he suggest using to scaffold learning, especially through the use of technology?

more likely to occur when teachers worked in teams with shared interests in outcomes.

What are some of the key practices for scaffolding instruction? Though scaffolding instruction varies by age and content, some of the following practices are useful (van De Pol, Volman, & Beishuizen, 2010):

- Initially provide more teacher support and then fade support as a student's proficiency increases.
- Increase transfer of independent learning.
- Use diagnostic strategies to inform instruction.
- Provide adequate explaining, modeling, and feedback.
- Use questions to guide instruction and feedback.

The University of Kansas Center for Research on Learning requires that persons planning to implement the Learning Strategies Curriculum obtain training. Also, the Iris Modules provide an in-depth description of learning strategies. This teaching model relies heavily on modeling, self-instruction, and self-regulation. It encourages students to assume an active and collaborative role in learning.

There are many instructional implications, but the following four are particularly important:

1. Instruction is designed to facilitate scaffolding and cooperative knowledge sharing among students and teachers within a context of mutual respect and critical acceptance of others' knowledge and experiences.

2. Learning and teaching should be meaningful, socially embedded activities.

3. Instruction should provide opportunities for mediated learning, with the teacher or expert guiding instruction within the students' zones of proximal development.

4. Students' experiences, backgrounds, and knowledge can provide the basis on which learning is built.

Executive Functioning, or Metacognition

The specific processes in the information-processing system (i.e., attention, perception, working memory, and long-term memory) are controlled or coordinated by what has been referred to as *executive functioning* (see Figure 2-5). For example, as learners, we must decide which stimuli to attend to (e.g., the book we are reading and/or the smell of the apple pie baking), whether to rely more on feature analysis or context and prior knowledge when perceiving information, what memory strategies are most effective for keeping the information active in working memory, and what is an effective and efficient way to store the information so we can retrieve

it later. Making decisions allows us to control the learning process.

This executive functioning has also been referred to as *metacognition* (Flavell, 1976). Metacognition is generally considered to have two components:

1. An awareness of what skills, strategies, and resources are needed to perform a cognitive task

2. The ability to use self-regulatory strategies to monitor the thinking processes and to undertake fix-up strategies when processing is not going smoothly

In many ways, metacognition is similar to the concepts of self-evaluation and self-regulation that we presented in the previous section on CSI. Metacognition requires learners to monitor the effectiveness of their learning and, on the basis of feedback, regulate learning by activating task-appropriate strategies. Read the short essay in Apply the Concept 2-7, and see how you use your metacognition.

Students with learning and behavior problems certainly have potential for difficulties with metacognition. For example, the essay that you read in Apply the Concept 2-7 was also read by groups of seventh graders, some of whom had reading disabilities and others who were average achievers. They were asked to read the essay and decide whether it made sense. Although most of the average-achieving students recognized the inconsistency, most of the students with learning disabilities reported that there was nothing wrong with the essay (Bos & Filip, 1984). Teaching students to monitor their reading comprehension and to ask themselves questions while they read to ensure understanding is an important part of engaging executive processing.

Executive Functioning: Implications for Instruction

When teaching, think about how you can modify your teaching and the learning environment to facilitate directing students' attention to relevant stimuli and their perception of incoming information. How can you teach students to use executive functioning to coordinate the various learning and memory strategies?

Several general implications follow:

1. *Provide cues to students so that they can be guided to the relevant task(s) or salient features of the task.* For instance, when giving a lecture, provide cues to assist students in attending to the key points by giving an overview of the lecture, writing important concepts on the board, providing students with a written outline of the lecture, or teaching students how to listen and look for

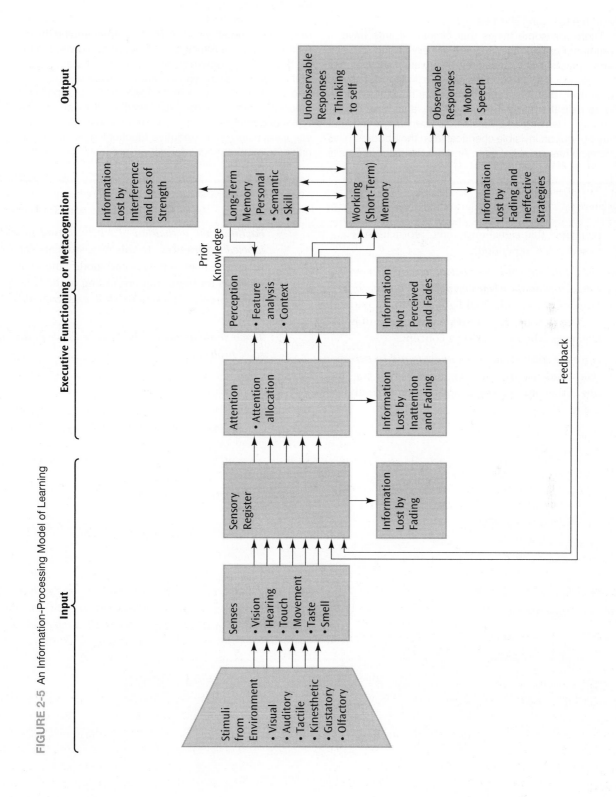

FIGURE 2-5 An Information-Processing Model of Learning

Comprehension Monitoring

Read the following short essay:

There are some things that almost all ants have in common. For example, they are all very strong and can carry objects many times their own weight. Sometimes they go very, very far from their nest to find food. They go so far away that they cannot remember how to go home. So, to help them find their way home, ants have a special way of leaving an invisible trail. Everywhere they go, they put out an invisible chemical from their bodies. This chemical has a special odor. Another thing about ants is they do not have noses to smell with. Ants never get lost. (Bos & Filip, 1984, p. 230)

As you read the first part of this essay, you probably read along smoothly and quickly, comprehending the information and confirming that in fact what you were reading made sense. However, when you read the last couple of lines of the essay, you probably slowed your reading rate, possibly went back and reread, and/or stopped and thought about what you were reading. If these are the types of cognitive strategies in which you engaged, then you were using your executive functioning, or metacognition, to monitor your information-processing system.

behaviors that signal important information (e.g., raised voice, repetition).

2. *Have students study the critical feature differences between stimuli when trying to perceive differences.* For example, highlight the "stick" part of the letters *b* and *d*, or provide instances and noninstances when discussing a concept.

3. *Have the students use the context to aid in perception.* Students are not likely to substitute *bog* for *dog* if they are reading a story or sentence about a dog.

4. *Facilitate the activation of schemas, and provide labeled experiences.* In this way, students can develop adequate schemas and modify their current schemas for better understanding of the concepts being presented in both skill and content-area subjects.

5. *Teach students how to be flexible thinkers and to solve problems.*

Summary

- Applied behavior analysis is based on the notion that behaviors are learned. In this way, individuals can either unlearn undesirable behaviors or be taught new behaviors. The first step to helping students learn and use appropriate behaviors is to manipulate antecedents, or to attend to the events or stimuli that precede certain behaviors. When undesirable behaviors do occur, using consequences can help students to unlearn or replace selected behaviors.

- Cognitive strategy instruction (CSI) is a systematic method that teachers use to change thinking processes by organizing the teaching and monitoring of task completion or skill development and by actively involving students in learning. Examples of strategies or skills that are taught in CSI are finding the main idea, decoding unknown words, and taking notes. In brief, the teacher selects a target strategy, works with the student to develop the strategy steps, and gives feedback. Social learning practices are based on the notion that learning occurs through interactions between the student and the teacher and the student and other students. Therefore, an emphasis is placed on language as a teaching tool and the instructional conversations that occur between teachers and students (as well as between students). There is also a focus on students' resources or background knowledge, language, and culture.

- Social learning and executive functioning recognizes that learning is related to such processes as memory and cognition; thus, how we understand, recall, and organize information is relevant to our retention and understanding. Examples of instructional features that incorporate these theories are activating prior knowledge; relating new learning to existing schemas; and teaching and monitoring the use of metacognitive strategies to organize task completion and to check for understanding.

 ASSESSMENT

After completing this chapter, test your knowledge of the concepts by completing the Assessment.

Response to Intervention and Multi-Tier System of Supports

Mary Jo Meneke is the special education teacher at Birdseye elementary school. She serves all students with both learning disabilities and behavior disorders at her school. Mary Jo has been a special education teacher for 8 years, and her role has changed considerably. Initially, her primary role at the school was as a resource teacher who provided pullout academic support to students with identified learning disabilities, as well as an inclusion support teacher for students who were mainstreamed for most of the school day. Three years ago, the district special education director met with all of the elementary special education teachers and asked them to work with her in implementing an RTI model that included multi-tier systems of support in their school.

The school was already implementing several components of an RTI model including screening for reading and math difficulties twice a year in kindergarten and first grade, but decided to enhance the screening procedures through fifth grade. They also were providing reading intervention support in first grade, but decided to identify appropriate interventions for students in first through fifth grades in reading and in first through third grade in math. The school principal asked Mary Jo to work with the other special education teachers to design their implementation of RTI schoolwide.

This provided several professional development opportunities. Mary Jo decided that she could assist in selecting research-based interventions in reading and math. It also allowed her to facilitate training of key personnel to provide these interventions. As you will see in this chapter, Mary Jo and her principal provided Tier 2 interventions by hiring and training teaching assistants and provided Tier 3 interventions using Mary Jo and the reading specialist. In this chapter, you will learn more about RTI and multi-tier systems of support and how you might facilitate implementation in your school.

Response to Intervention and Multi-Tier Systems of Support

How did we come to RTI and multi-tier systems of support? Why is implementation of these models a productive way to prevent academic and behavior problems as well as contribute to identification of students with disabilities? Many educators perceive that although special education may be available to serve students with disabilities, many other students with learning needs do not qualify for special education. What are some possible solutions to this dilemma? One solution that is recommended in the reauthorization of IDEA (IDEIA 2004) is to provide RTI as a means of preventing learning and behavior difficulties. RTI is the most current model for screening students and using their responses to intervention as a data source to facilitate identifying students who need special education services (Brown-Chidsey & Steege, 2011; Glover & Vaughn, 2010).

Students with learning disabilities have most often been identified by determining their potential or ability, usually with an intelligence test, and comparing that with their achievement, as measured by reading or math tests. The idea of this approach is to determine if students have significant differences between their potential or ability and their academic achievement in reading or math. Students who assessed as being low in both ability and achievement could often not qualify for special education services. This process had many difficulties, including (a) overreliance on IQ measures and (b) the requirement to wait for a discrepancy between IQ and achievement (e.g., math or reading performance), which might have meant that students would not be provided services until too late. The reason for the waiting period for most students is because students in the early grades (kindergarten through third grade) have had limited exposure to school achievement opportunities and therefore have a difficult time showing a discrepancy between their IQ and achievement. RTI was conceptualized as a potential solution to these problems. First, it provides a universal screening (schoolwide) whereby educators can readily identify students with potential learning or behavior problems and implement research-based practices. Second, teachers monitor students' academic or behavioral responses and use the response data as a means of determining students' success and thus subsequent

needs. Students who respond well to interventions do not require subsequent support, whereas students whose response to interventions (e.g., supplemental reading instruction for 30 minutes a day) is low may receive additional supplemental instruction. In addition, educators use the data gathered as a result of monitoring student progress, or *progress monitoring*, to assist in the referral and identification for special education.

As a result of the recommended use of RTI, eligibility and identification criteria for learning disability are described as follows (IDEIA 2004; reauthorization [614(b) (6)(A)-(B)]):

> When determining whether a child has a specific learning disability:
> *   The LEA [local education agency] is not required to consider a severe discrepancy between achievement and intellectual ability.
> *   The LEA may use a process that determines if a student responds to scientific, research-based intervention as part of the evaluation.

While the example provided in the law is specific to learning disabilities, it is also appropriate to provide a similar approach for students with behavior problems. Therefore, RTI may help identify students with learning disabilities by replacing discrepancy criteria and using students' responses to intervention as data to facilitate decision making and provide instruction and learning as critical elements in the assessment process. By replacing discrepancy criteria and using students' responses to intervention as data to facilitate decision making, the RTI model may help identify students with learning disabilities while providing instruction and opportunities for learning as critical elements in the assessment process. RTI may help students with behavior problems by providing schoolwide approaches to preventing behavior problems and specific interventions for students with significant problems.

How does multi-tier system of support fit in within RTI? States like Kansas prefer using a term like *multi-tier system of support* because they view this term as being more inclusive and addressing learning and behavior as well as providing opportunities to implement individual student problem-solving approaches as well as more standardized approaches to intervention. The intention is that there is a systemic approach to change that provides rapid implementation of necessary support services at the level of intensity needed by the student.

Past and Present Challenges

In this book we use RTI and multi-tier system of supports synonymously, realizing that their implementation in practice may vary based on state, district, or even school guidelines. One of the goals of RTI and multi-tier system of supports is to change a prevailing view related to "waiting for students to fail." Too often, when students first showed signs of struggling academically or behaviorally, the prevailing approach was to wait and hope that their progress would improve over time. The idea was that students might simply be slow to achieve academically because of normal developmental or experiential differences and that it would be a disservice to assess them prematurely and place them in special education. Yet students who struggled were provided with few avenues for extra support. Also, as described earlier, young students who were evaluated for possible special education placement sometimes had not yet exhibited enough of a discrepancy between their ability and their achievement to qualify for special education services. For these reasons, this approach was often referred to as the "wait to fail" model.

RTI is different. All students are screened early, often as early as kindergarten, and their progress is assessed frequently so that those students who do not seem to be making adequate progress are provided with timely interventions, before they have a chance to fall further behind. Thus, RTI is a *prevention and intervention model.* As you read this chapter, think about what these changes mean for special educators—and for students.

Previous Identification Procedures Since inception, the field of learning disabilities has struggled with numerous challenges related to its definition and identification procedures. Vaughn and Klingner (2007) note that these challenges include

- An increase of more than 200% of students identified as having a learning disability since the category was established
- Questionable procedures for determining learning disabilities through emphasis on an IQ–achievement discrepancy and processing disorders
- Students identified using a "wait to fail" model rather than a prevention–early intervention model
- Subjectivity in student referral for services, with teachers' and others' perceptions sometimes weighing too heavily in the process
- Students' opportunities to learn not adequately considered during the referral and identification process

- Considerable variation from state to state concerning identification procedures and prevalence rates for learning disabilities
- An identification process that provides little information to guide instructional decision making
- Problematic assessment practices, particularly for culturally and linguistically diverse students
- Disproportionate numbers of culturally and linguistically diverse students inappropriately identified for and served in special education

These challenges to the traditional model for identifying students with learning disabilities illustrate the importance of adopting the RTI model, also referred to as multi-tier system of supports. RTI provides early and ongoing screening of students with early intervention and uses data to facilitate decision making for identification. This resolves many previous issues at the early grades of waiting for students to have the IQ–achievement discrepancy, waiting to provide the intensity of interventions needed, assuring that students were provided research-based approaches, and documenting progress monitoring and other assessment approaches as students progressed.

Challenges to Implementing an RTI Approach Whether schools are implementing RTI or multi-tier system of supports, there are challenges to assuring that personnel are adequately prepared, that there are appropriate resources for screening and progress monitoring, that increasingly intensive interventions are available, and that a decision-making process is in place to assist key decision makers. Possible difficulties with implementing an RTI approach include questions about who provides the more intensive secondary and tertiary interventions (a paraprofessional, general education teacher, special education teacher, or other specialist) and the extent to which validated instructional practices exist in academic areas other than reading, such as math or writing. For many schools and teachers, a significant challenge is determining what constitutes progress. For example, if a student's reading skills are improving, how do you know if the student is improving rapidly enough? How do you decide if a more intensive intervention is appropriate? Establishing procedures to help special and general educators with decisions provides for a more efficient and effective implementation of RTI.

Challenges that you may need to consider when implementing RTI within your school include:

1. **Determining responders from nonresponders.** When do we determine that students are making either adequate progress and no longer need interventions or inadequate progress and require more intensive interventions?

2. **Providing the necessary professional development for practicing professionals.** This is particularly challenging because the professional development is required for all key stakeholders including principals, school psychologists, teachers, and instructional support personnel.

3. **Implementing effective and appropriate roles for families.** Ensuring family involvement in RTI can be challenging initially, because it may require adjustments to new practices.

Other challenges to effective implementation of RTI and multi-tier system of supports have been addressed by many schools and districts and include:

- Personnel may require additional professional development to implement selected components of RTI (e.g., screening, intervention) and may also require specific professional development on how to use RTI the way the school or district has in mind. Because RTI is a framework and not a set of prescribed procedures, educators who are new to the school district may not know the procedures used by that school or district and will require additional training to effectively implement RTI.

- High-quality instruction in early reading and math has developed a solid basis in research; however, research-based practices for implementing instruction in other domains (e.g., writing) and in all domains with older students (grade 4 and higher) are less well delineated. Thus, some schools decide to implement RTI only in grades kindergarten through third grade and only in selected areas such as reading and behavior or reading, math, and behavior.

- Although there has been extensive learning by school leaders about implementing RTI practices in their schools, many principals are still learning about screening, progress monitoring, and implementation of tiers of intervention for effective implementation of RTI models.

- Many perceive RTI as a special education initiative rather than a combined general and special education initiative. Thus, classroom teachers may be disinclined to take leadership roles within the implementation of RTI if they perceive that it is really a special education initiative.

- Inadequate local- and state-level policies and resources may compromise effective implementation of RTI. School districts may not have the materials, professional development, or other resources to support implementation of RTI.

- Some schools have elected to implement RTI at the middle and high school level, but models for effective implementation of RTI at the secondary level are less well developed and require consideration about screening, progress monitoring, and interventions that are considerably different than at the early elementary level (Reed, Wexler, & Vaughn, 2012).

The overview in Table 3-1 compares identification of students with learning disabilities before IDEIA 2004 to the identification process with RTI.

Initiatives Influencing RTI

Four major initiatives set the stage for changes in how we think about students with disabilities and RTI. First, in August 2001, the Office of Special Education Programs brought together leading researchers to discuss numerous issues related to identifying learning disabilities (R. Bradley, Danielson, & Hallahan, 2002). The team reached consensus on principles related to learning disabilities and the eventual use of RTI to facilitate more appropriate identification of students with learning disabilities (L. S. Fuchs & Vaughn, 2012; Vaughn & Klingner, 2007):

- *Learning disabilities* is a valid construct that represents a life-span disorder.

- Individuals with learning disabilities require a special education.

- The exact prevalence of learning disabilities is unknown; however, the rate is likely between 2% and 5%.

- The use of IQ–achievement discrepancy is not adequate for identifying students with learning disabilities.

- Linking processing disabilities to learning disabilities has not been adequately established; also, most processing disabilities are difficult to measure and link to treatment.

- The use of reliable and valid data from progress monitoring is a promising addition to identifying individuals with learning disabilities.

- Much is known about effective interventions for students with learning disabilities, and yet ineffective interventions continue to be used.

Second, the President's Commission on Excellence in Special Education held public hearings throughout the United States and received hundreds of written comments (President's Commission on Excellence in Special Education, 2002) about the state of special education in the nation's education system. The commission concluded that special educators were spending too much time on paperwork and not enough time teaching. The commission also noted that general education and

TABLE 3-1 Identifying Students with Learning Disabilities: Before IDEIA 2004 and with RTI

Before IDEIA 2004	RTI
No universal academic screening.	All students are screened.
Little progress monitoring.	Progress monitoring assesses whether students are reaching goals—multiple data points are collected over an extended period of time across different tiers of intervention.
"Wait to fail" model—students frequently not provided with interventions until they have qualified for special education.	Students are provided with interventions at the first sign they are struggling; there is an increased focus on proactive responses to students' difficulties.
Focus on within-child problems or deficits.	Ecological focus. Systems approach to problem solving, focused on instruction and interventions varied in time, intensity, and focus.
Clear eligibility criteria (i.e., a child either did or did not qualify for special education services). Categorical approach—targeted, intensive interventions typically not provided unless a student was found eligible for special education.	Tiered model of service delivery with interventions provided to all students who demonstrate a need for support, regardless of whether they have a disability.
Multidisciplinary team mostly made up of special education professionals; individual students typically referred by classroom teachers with academic and/or behavioral concerns.	Problem-solving (or intervention) teams include general and special educators; teams consider progress-monitoring data and all students who are not reaching benchmarks.
Reliance on assessments, particularly standardized tests.	Collaborative educational decisions based on ongoing school, classroom, and individual student data; adjustments to instruction/intervention based on data.
Assessment data collected during a limited number of sessions.	Multiple data points collected over time and in direct relationship to the intervention provided.
"Comprehensive evaluation" consisting mainly of formal assessments conducted by individual members of the multidisciplinary team, often the same battery of tests administered to all referred children.	"Full and individualized evaluation" relies heavily on existing data collected throughout the RTI process; evaluation includes a student's response to specific validated interventions and other data gathered through observations, teacher and parent checklists, and diagnostic assessments.
Learning disability construct of "unexpected underachievement" indicated by low achievement as compared to a measure of the child's ability (i.e., IQ–achievement discrepancy).	Learning disability construct of "unexpected underachievement" indicated by low achievement and insufficient response to validated interventions that work with most students ("true peers"), even struggling ones.

Source: Based on Response to Intervention, by J. K. Klingner, 2009, in S. Vaughn & C. S. Bos, *Strategies for Teaching Students with Learning and Behavior Problems* (7th ed.). Columbus, OH: Pearson. Reprinted with permission.

special education seemed to be operating as two separate systems rather than as a coherent whole. In the report, the commission recommended shifting to a prevention model that takes into account the fact that students with disabilities are also part of general education and that requires special and general educators to work together more closely.

Third, the National Research Council report on the disproportionate representation of culturally and linguistically diverse students in special education provided similar recommendations to those proposed by the Office of Special Education (Donovan & Cross, 2002). The council promoted widespread use of early screening and intervention practices and RTI models. The council's premise was that if schoolwide behavior and early reading programs help culturally and linguistically diverse students receive the support they need and improve their opportunities to learn, then the number of students who exhibit ongoing problems will decrease and the students who continue to struggle will more likely be those who require a special education.

Based on these initiatives, Congress passed the Individuals with Disabilities Education Improvement Act (IDEIA 2004). The new law promoted RTI as a means for preventing learning difficulties and furthering accurate identification of students with learning disabilities. Furthermore, Congress urged the use of early intervening services (EIS) to provide students with support as soon as they show signs of struggling.

Fourth, the National Research Council report on the disproportionate representation of culturally and linguistically diverse students in special education provided similar recommendations to those proposed by the Office of Special Education (Donovan & Cross, 2002). The council promoted widespread use of early screening and intervention practices and RTI models. The council's premise was that if schoolwide behavior and early reading programs help culturally and linguistically diverse students receive the support they need and improve their opportunities to learn, then the number of students who exhibit ongoing problems will decrease and the students who continue to struggle will more likely be those who require a special education. The National Research Council's recommendations (Donovan & Cross, 2002) follow:

- Recommends using alternative approaches to identifying students with learning disabilities, but does not require abandoning use of the IQ–achievement discrepancy criterion.

- Urges early screening and early intervention so that students who show signs of struggling do not fall further behind.

- Recommends a multi-tiered intervention strategy. A *multi-tiered intervention strategy* is a set of layers of instruction that increase in intensity (e.g., increase amount of instruction, decrease group size) based on how well students are succeeding in a less intensive instructional format.

  1. The first tier in a multi-tiered intervention approach is typically the classroom instruction.

  2. The second tier is often additional instruction that is provided by the classroom teacher.

  3. The third tier of instruction is even more instruction, often provided by a trained person or a specialist such as the special education teacher.

- Asks districts to review practices to accelerate learning so that students make adequate progress in special education.

- Recommends ongoing systematic progress monitoring of students' responses to high-quality, research-based interventions. Progress monitoring provides frequent assessments of how students are learning target knowledge or skills, to determine if their response to instruction is adequate.

- Requires better integration of services between general and special education.

- Emphasizes the role of context when referring, identifying, and serving students in special education.

Figure 3-1 provides an overview of the practices related to RTI that are used by states.

A strong rationale supports RTI practices for several reasons, not the least of which is the attempt to better integrate support and services for individuals with disabilities. For example, a student with a learning disability who is included in the general education classroom may also have a speech and language specialist, be taught in reading and math by the special education teacher, have opportunities during the day to work with the Title I reading teacher, and also meet with the school psychologist once or twice a month. One of the goals of RTI is to integrate services and to eliminate settings in which general education teachers do "their thing" and special education teachers are quite separate and disconnected.

Components of Response to Intervention and Multi-Tier System of Supports

What are the components and implementation practices in an RTI or a multi-tier system of supports approach? Because the conceptual components of both RTI and multi-tier system of supports are more alike than different, we describe the common elements and refer to these components as being part of RTI; and that is the terminology currently used in the law. RTI is considered an instructional model for preventing learning and behavior problems and providing data-based evidence of students' performance in research-based interventions. Educators use this data in conjunction with assessment and classroom-based observations to facilitate referral and placement in special education, when needed. RTI provides a framework for monitoring the progress of all students, particularly those with difficulties.

What are the critical elements that are part of RTI? Fundamentally, there are many frameworks for implementing RTI, not just one. However, within these multiple frameworks, there are critical components including:

- Screening and progress monitoring.

- Implementation of effective classroom instructional practices so that all students have an opportunity to learn (Tier 1).

- Implementation of a multi-tiered system of supports when students fall behind; initially with less intensive intervention (Tier 2) and then later with more intensive intervention if students' progress is not adequately accelerated so that they reach grade-level expectations.

- Provision of a more intensive individualized intervention (Tier 3) for students for whom a less intensive intervention is inadequate (Tier 3). Students who are considered special education may be provided services within Tier 3 or within a fourth tier of intervention, depending on the instructional framework used by the school or district.

- Access to increasingly intensive interventions and more systemic support is provided based on students' needs. The timing of when students are referred for special education can be determined by the model's application (some after Tier 2, some after Tiers 3 or 4) or can be based on more traditional approaches where the teacher makes a referral and uses data from the progress monitoring and intervention as additional sources of evidence.

RTI is a schoolwide model that typically starts with students in kindergarten and may continue throughout the elementary grades or even into middle school in some districts. Go to **IRIS Module: RTI: Considerations**

FIGURE 3-1 Response to Intervention (RTI) Model Recommended by State

Guidance on RTI	State Model Developed	Developing Model	No Model Specified
California	Arizona	Alabama	Alaska
Illinois	Delaware	Arkansas	New Jersey
Maine	Florida	Colorado	South Carolina
Maryland	Georgia	Connecticut	
Massachusetts	Iowa	Hawaii	
Missouri	Kansas	Idaho	
North Dakota	Louisiana	Indiana	
Tennessee	Nebraska	Kentucky	
Texas	North Carolina	Michigan	
Virginia	Ohio	Minnesota	
	Oregon	Mississippi	
	Pennsylvania	Montana	
	Utah	Nevada	
	Washington	New Hampshire	
	West Virginia	New Mexico	
		New York	
		Oklahoma	
		Rhode Island	
		South Dakota	
		Vermont	
		Wisconsin	
		Wyoming	

Source: Based on Implementation of Response to Intervention: A Snapshot of Progress, by S. Berkeley, W. N. Bender, L. G. Peaster, & L. Saunders, 2009, *Journal of Learning Disabilities, 42,* pp. 85–95.

for School Leaders to learn about some of the considerations school leaders make when implementing RTI in their schools. Although no one single model is accepted as the "gold standard," RTI models commonly include four key components (Glover & Vaughn, 2010; D. Fuchs, L. S. Fuchs, & Vaughn, 2008; L. S. Fuchs & Vaughn, 2012):

1. *Implement high-quality, research-based instruction matched to the needs of students throughout all of the multi-tier levels of support.* Only instructional practices that generally produce high learning rates for students are used, as demonstrated by scientific research. The implementation of high-quality instructional practices as interventions is intended to increase the probability of positive student responses. Whether you are teaching reading or math at the elementary or secondary level, the instructional programs, materials, and practices you use should be selected based on the best research available rather than your own ideology or perspective. When students are provided typically effective intervention, students' response is easier to interpret. For example, students who respond well to this instruction eventually meet learning goals. Students whose response yields lower academic progress require a more intensive intervention.

2. *Provide universal screening to identify students at risk and monitor students' learning over time, to determine their level and rate of performance (for ongoing*

decision making). Educators assess all students' learning to determine if they are making progress toward meeting expected benchmarks at a rate commensurate with that of peers. Educators provide students who do not seem to be progressing with extra assistance in the form of interventions targeted to their needs. What does this mean for you as an educator? Consider your expectations and goals for learning each week. Create a brief assessment that will help you determine what students know about what you are teaching that week. At the end of the week (or two), use the assessment again to determine how much students have learned. Use this information for reteaching and/or making decisions about additional intervention.

3. *Provide interventions of increasing intensity when students continue to struggle.* The intensity of instruction can be enhanced by reducing group size, increasing time, and/or making sure that interventions are even more carefully tailored to the students' instructional needs. Determine what options for providing intervention are available. Typically, schools provide additional interventions for elementary students in math and reading. It may also be possible to provide additional supports in spelling and writing. For older students, additional reading classes or after-school tutoring may be available. As another option, consider how you might restructure and regroup students so that you can provide additional instruction to those students with the highest needs by decreasing their group size, increasing the time they are provided instruction, or increasing opportunities to practice with feedback.

4. *Make important educational decisions based on data.* Decisions about selecting instructional interventions, the intensity of the interventions (e.g., how much time each day and in what group size the intervention is provided), and the duration of the interventions (e.g., 2 weeks, 8 weeks) are based on students' responses to the interventions. As you examine students' performance based on data (e.g., weekly or biweekly assessments), consider instructional adjustments that you could make to ensure that all students have improved outcomes. Also consider whether selected students would benefit from additional instruction.

To learn about useful software and online assessment tools, see Tech Tips. These tools will help you better understand and implement an RTI model.

Screening and Progress Monitoring

Screening involves providing a reliable and valid measure that can be easily and quickly administered to large numbers of students to determine whether these students have academic difficulties. For example, in kindergarten, students may be screened for reading problems by asking them to identify letters. With older students, screening may ask them to read a passage at grade level and then respond to questions. These data sources allow teachers to identify students with difficulties and then to provide them additional instruction as needed. Within an RTI model, screening is typically conducted at the beginning and middle of the year. Screening may be provided in reading or math or for behavior.

Progress monitoring involves frequent and ongoing measurement of student knowledge and skills *and* the examination of student data to evaluate instruction. Used with a few students or the entire class, progress monitoring is essential to effective implementation of RTI because it allows key stakeholders, such as the special education and classroom teachers as well as other specialists (e.g., speech and language teacher), to determine the rate of growth students are achieving and to determine whether additional intervention is needed. Go to IRIS Module: RTI (Part 2) Assessment, where you will learn assessment procedures related to RTI and how to use the student data from this progress monitoring to make decisions about instructional planning. Use these case studies to enhance your progress-monitoring skills. To better understand why progress monitoring is used and how to use it, see Apply the Concept 3-1.

Universal Screening

How does universal screening fit into the RTI model? *Universal screening* in reading and math is an essential component of RTI models at the Tier 1 level. This process involves administering a brief test to all students to determine who is likely to be at risk for academic difficulties. In the same way that schools have checked children's vision for years to screen students for potential problems, screening for math and reading problems helps identify students who need treatment. In many schools, screening is carried out two times a year (beginning of school and middle of school year), and in others screening occurs three times a year (beginning, near middle, and toward the end of the school year).

Screening instruments usually have few items and are short in duration. Screening is used to determine whether additional testing is needed. Schoolwide academic screening was rarely implemented with previous models. Instead, it was typically the classroom teacher who first noticed that students were struggling and referred them for an evaluation. Invariably some students were overlooked. With universal screening, however, everyone is tested.

As an example of universal screening, Texas provides universal screening in reading for all students in kindergarten through second grade. The classroom teacher conducts the screening, and the most frequently used screening measure

Using Progress Monitoring in the Classroom

Why Use Progress Monitoring?

- To keep track of student learning
- To identify students who need additional help
- To assist in arranging small-group instruction
- To design instruction that meets individual student needs
- To refer and identify students for special education based on data gathered during progress monitoring

How Do I Monitor Student Progress?

- Assess all students at the beginning of the year in the critical areas that predict success in reading and math for their grade level. Most screening instruments specify what the predictor skills are for reading and math for each grade level (e.g., see www.aimsweb.com).
- Use assessments to identify students who need extra help and to create goals for learning. Once you determine which students require extra help, you can plan small-group instruction.
- Monitor the progress of students in small groups more frequently (weekly or monthly) in the specific skill or area being worked on.
- Assess progress by comparing learning goals with actual student progress. Students who are making adequate progress should still be assessed approximately three times a year to ensure that they are learning and continue to achieve at grade level.

What Are the Benefits of Progress Monitoring?

- According to the National Center on Monitoring Student Progress, the following are benefits of progress monitoring:
- Increased learning because instructional decisions are based on student data
- Improved accountability
- Better communication about student progress with family and other professionals
- Higher expectations for low-achieving students
- Fewer special education referrals

is the Texas Primary Reading Inventory (TPRI). The TPRI was developed and used to screen Texas students; this diagnostic instrument provides information on a student's reading/language arts development (from kindergarten through third grade). The quick screening takes just a few minutes and is individually administered by the classroom teacher. Students' performance on the quick screen assists teachers in deciding whether a more diagnostic assessment would provide the necessary information to help teachers design instruction. The screening and assessment tool helps teachers decide in which of the critical elements of reading (e.g., phonics, fluency, and comprehension) the student needs additional instruction; it even provides lessons to facilitate decision making about what instruction should be provided.

Universal screening is also a quick way to identify general performance levels and determine whether students are on track to developing proficiency in the fundamental skills of reading and math. We know much more than we used to about how to predict future reading levels, for example, using phonological awareness and rapid naming tasks. Thus, we can determine with some accuracy which students are at risk and require additional intervention. Foorman and Ciancio (2005) point out that "the purpose of early screening could be identifying students *not* at risk so that instructional objectives can be established for students potentially at risk" (p. 494).

Screening also provides valuable information about class performance and identifies teachers who might need further professional development. Once students have been identified as needing additional assistance using a screening measure, interventions are provided.

Numerous assessments can be used as screening instruments (see Table 3-2 for a list of possible reading screeners).

Some tests assess only one or two elements of reading (such as the C-TOPP, which tests only phonological processing), whereas others tap into several reading components. Some are quick to administer, such as the Test of Word Reading Efficiency (TOWRE), and others take much longer, such as the QRI-4 (Rathvon, 2004).

Using Screening to Make Educational Decisions

Screening is useful for providing quick information at the classroom or group level as well as at the student level. When all of the students in a school are screened, school administrators can examine assessment results for patterns across, as well as within, classrooms. Problems that are widespread across classrooms call for schoolwide interventions. Or it could be that most of the students in the majority of classrooms do well, whereas in one or two classrooms

TABLE 3-2 Possible Screening Measures for Reading

Assessment	Publisher and Web Site	Grades or Ages	Oral Lang.	PA	Phon.	Word ID	Flu.	Voc.	Comp.	Comments
AIMSweb Curriculum-Based Measurement (CBM)	Edformation http://www.aimsweb.com	K–12	No	Yes	Yes	No	Yes	No	Yes	Offers Web-based data management
Basic Early Assessment of Reading (BEAR)	Riverside http://www.riverpub.com	K–3								Pencil–paper and computerized versions
Comprehensive Test of Phonological Processing (CTOPP)	PRO-ED http://www.proedinc.com	K–3								Phonological processing only
Dynamic Indicators of Basic Early Literacy Skills (DIBELS)	Sopris West/Cambium http://www.dibelsassessment.com	K–3, 4–6							Yes (4–6 only)	Grade 4–6 students assessed only in fluency and comprehension
Fox in a Box-2	CTB McGraw-Hill http://www.ctb.com	PreK–3								Includes PreK
Qualitative Reading Inventory-4 (QRI-4)	Allyn & Bacon/Longman http://www.ablongman.com	K–12								Informal assessment instrument
Scholastic Reading Inventory (SRI)	Scholastic teacher	K–12								Computer adaptive; includes data management system
Slosson Oral Reading Test (SORT-R3)	Slosson http://www.slosson.com	K–12								Word ID only
Test of Early Reading Ability (TERA-3)	Pearson http://ags.pearsonassessments.com PRO-ED http://www.proedinc.com	Ages 3.6–8.6								Assesses letter knowledge and environmental print
Test of Word Reading Efficiency (TOWRE)	Pearson http://ags.pearsonassessments.com	Ages 6.0–24.11								Pseudo-word reading and Word ID only
Texas Primary Reading Inventory (TPRI)	Texas Education Agency http://www.tpri.org	K–2	Yes							Includes screening section and inventory section

Note. Lang. = language; PA = phonological awareness; Phon. = phonics; ID = identification; Flu. = fluency; Voc. = vocabulary; Comp. = comprehension.

a lot of students seem to be struggling. When this is the case, data indicate a classwide problem for which it may be most appropriate to provide interventions at the class level. When only a few students are struggling relative to their peers, then problems seem to be at an individual level, and individual interventions are warranted.

Using Progress Monitoring to Assess Student's Response to Intervention

Whereas screening is used to assess *all* students to determine who might need additional support, progress monitoring is applied to individual students to assess their response to interventions. Like screening measures, progress-monitoring instruments are quick to administer and focus on targeted skills in the core curriculum. The purposes of progress monitoring are to closely monitor students' progress, to develop profiles of students' learning, and to assess the effectiveness of interventions so that changes can be made if necessary. These data can be quite useful if children continue to struggle and the decision is made to conduct a comprehensive evaluation of their strengths and needs. Progress-monitoring measures are administered frequently, perhaps once a month, or as often as once a week in some cases.

> **WEB RESOURCES**
>
> For more information on progress-monitoring measures and procedures specific to reading and mathematics, see the following Web sites: http://www.rtinetwork.org and http://www.centeroninstruction.org.

For a list of steps to follow in using progress monitoring, see Apply the Concept 3-2.

Multi-Tier Systems of Support: Implementing Increasingly Intensive Intervention

RTI models often discuss instruction or intervention in terms of tiers of support or tiers of instruction. Typically, *tiers* represent the level of intensity of instruction provided to a student or group of students (see Figure 3-2). The expectation is that the vast majority of students will receive Tier 1, which is research-based classroom instruction. Only students for whom this instruction is inadequately meeting their needs will receive additional "tiers" of instruction, either less intensive, Tier 2, or more intensive, Tiers 3 or even 4.

As students move through the tiers, the intensity of the interventions they receive increases. How do you increase intensity?

- Intensity typically refers to *altering group size* (e.g., students in Tier 2 may be in a group of six, whereas students in Tier 3 are in a group of three).

- Intensity may also be provided by increasing *instructional time* (e.g., students are provided an additional 30 to 45 minutes of instruction in reading).

- Another way to increase intensity is to change the instructional practices or materials so that they are more directly aligned with students' learning

3-2 APPLY THE CONCEPT

Steps in Conducting Progress Monitoring

When screening students and conducting progress monitoring,

- Screen all students in the fall.
- Rank students by grade level and by classroom. In other words, compile assessment results so that patterns of achievement within classrooms and across classrooms at every grade level can be examined. Be sure to determine if there are normative findings to determine how students' performance compares with others outside the class, school, and district.
- Identify lower achieving students in each grade or classroom.
- Set goals for individual students.

- Use frequent progress monitoring with students identified as low achievers. Progress monitoring might occur monthly or as often as every week, particularly with the lowest students, on targeted skills (e.g., oral reading fluency).
- Assess students who score at adequate levels or higher on the screening instrument less frequently, for example, three times a year (i.e., in the fall, winter, and spring).
- Create graphs that provide visual displays of students' progress.
- Evaluate progress-monitoring data regularly using a systematic set of decision rules to determine whether interventions seem to be effective for individual students.
- Revise interventions as necessary in response to the data.

FIGURE 3-2 Three-Tier Model of Response to Intervention

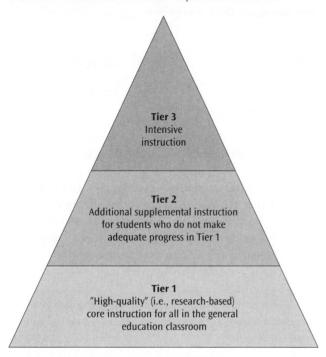

The concept of universal design can be applied to instructional materials to meet the varied needs of all learners. We need materials that increase the usability for everyone, appealing to different learners' needs, methods of input, learner backgrounds, and abilities and disabilities. Such classroom materials may have varying levels of difficulty, multiple means of input, various modes of presentation, and features to customize pace and feedback. Following are some programs that use the concept of universal design:

- *The Early Learning Series,* from Marblesoft Simtech. The programs feature multiple difficulty levels, include a built-in record-keeping system, and allow teachers to customize the learning environment to meet the specific needs of each individual child.
- *Measures of Academic Progress (MAPS),* by Northwest Evaluation Association (NWEA). This research-based, state-aligned assessment tool helps teachers monitor students' growth and progress by having students take adaptive tests in mathematics, reading, science, and language use. Teachers can then use this information to guide their instruction.

needs. For example, perhaps students in the classroom are using a grade-level reading program; students in Tier 3 may be provided a direct-instruction approach to reading.

Some RTI models include three tiers, and others include a fourth tier. In reading, for example, approximately 80% of all learners make adequate progress in Tier 1, 15% to 20% may require some supplemental instruction in Tier 2, and about 5% to 6% need the intensive intervention implemented in Tier 3. As the special education teacher, your role may be to facilitate inclusion of students with disabilities in Tier 1, identify effective treatments for Tiers 2 and 3, and perhaps train teachers and other personnel to implement these interventions. Within a multi-tier system of support, you may work with teachers and other school personnel to make accommodations and adaptations to instruction to assure students' success. You may also assist them in using evidence-based decision making, relying on data collection to influence their instruction.

Using Technology to Implement RTI or Multi-Tier Systems of Support

A key objective of RTI, as well as multi-tier systems of support, is to select an instructional strategy to match a student's specific needs. Universal design, authoring software, and assessment software are aspects of technology that can facilitate RTI. Universal design is a growing movement toward designing products and environments to accommodate the diverse needs and abilities of all people.

Tier 1: Classroom Instruction   What distinguishes Tier 1 from all of the other tiers of instruction? The primary distinction is that Tier 1 involves all students in the classroom with an intention of providing them with the most effective instruction or behavior supports. For example, in a fourth-grade math or reading class, the math or reading instruction provided to all of the students in the class is referred to as Tier 1 instruction. Ideally, the instructional practices and materials meet the highest standards based on our current research and provide every student with the opportunity to maximize their success.

In Tier 1, general education teachers provide evidence-based instruction to all students in the class. The instruction must be evidenced-based so that when students are not making adequate progress and additional instructional intervention is provided (e.g., Tier 2), we know that the students have had an adequate opportunity to learn. We do not want students provided Tier 2 and Tier 3 intervention because they were not provided adequate Tier 1 instruction. For example, in schools where Tier 1 instruction has not been thoughtfully planned to align with research, many students are not making adequate progress, and supplemental interventions (Tiers 2 and 3) are required for an extensive number of students. What happens in schools where Tier 1 instruction aligns with research? Fewer students require more intensive tiers of instruction.

What do classroom teachers do during Tier 1 instruction? Classroom teachers or support personnel screen students using easy-to-administer screening measures that are selected for the grade level they are teaching. Typically, screening takes less than 10 minutes per student for each content area (e.g., reading, math) and can be done at the beginning and middle of the year. Students who are having difficulty in reading or math are administered progress-monitoring measures regularly to determine their progress. Teachers differentiate instruction as needed and strive to provide appropriate, effective instruction for their students.

Tier 2 Intervention   Tier 2 intervention is provided for those students who are not making adequate progress in Tier 1—in other words, those who are not responding to instruction. Tier 2 interventions are typically provided in small groups, with the intention of providing additional instruction that will allow the student to make adequate progress in Tier 1 instruction without further intervention. Tier 2 interventions *supplement* rather than supplant the core curriculum taught in Tier 1 general education classrooms and are intended to reinforce the concepts and skills taught there. What is meant by *supplement?* Students who are provided Tier 2 intervention continue to receive their classroom-based Tier 1 instruction that is differentiated to meet their learning needs.

Is Tier 2 intervention part of special education? No, Tier 2 intervention is still under the domain of general education; however, in your school or district, the special education teacher may assist with identifying Tier 2 intervention approaches and may assist with preparing school personnel to provide instruction. Yet the support that students receive in Tier 2 is still under the domain of general education. It is *not* special education. All children who appear to be struggling, as evidenced by their slow rate of progress and low assessment scores, are entitled to this support. Researchers refer to both the slow rate of progress and low levels of overall learning as a *dual discrepancy* (Burns & Senesac, 2005; L. S. Fuchs, Fuchs, & Speece, 2002).

Teachers continue to monitor the progress of students while they are receiving Tier 2 support. Tier 2 interventions are provided for a fixed duration (e.g., 10 weeks).

After this time, educators examine progress-monitoring and other data to answer the following questions:

- Is the student making good progress, and should he or she return to Tier 1–only instruction?
- Is the student making some but not sufficient progress to move to Tier 1, thereby necessitating that he or she receive another dose of Tier 2 intervention?
- Is the student making very little progress, thereby requiring him or her to be moved to Tier 3?

Tier 3 Intervention   Tier 3 intervention is provided to those students who continue to experience difficulties and show minimal progress during secondary, or Tier 2, interventions. Typically, the majority of students who require intervention benefit from the combination of Tier 1 and Tier 2 intervention and do not require more intensive interventions (Tier 3). Tier 3 intervention is typically provided for a longer time period and more frequently than secondary intervention. It is expected that the instructional materials may be changed or adjusted from those used in Tier 2. Depending on the number of tiers in the RTI model, this tier may or may not be special education. Tier 3 students receive explicit instruction individually or in small groups of two or three students. (See Figure 3-3 for a description of how Tiers 2 and 3 compare.) See the National Center on Intensive Interventions for a description of intensive interventions and sample lessons in reading and math.

> In this **video** ▶, the teacher describes how to use data and the problem solving model within the RTI framework to make instructional decisions for students who receive Tier 3 support. What responsibilities does she identify for each professional involved in the process?

Implementing Interventions

Not everyone agrees on who should decide which interventions to implement in an RTI model, or how these decisions should be made. Most people agree on who should provide Tier 1 instruction—the classroom teacher.

FIGURE 3-3 How Do Tier 2 and Tier 3 Differ?

	Tier 2 Instruction	Tier 3 Instruction
Daily instruction	30 minutes per day **(plus Tier 1)**	50 minutes per day
Duration	10 to 12 week **(1 or 2 rounds)**	10 to 12 weeks **(possibly several rounds)**
Group size	Small group/individual	Smallest group possible/individual
Ongoing progress monitoring	Weekly	Weekly

But what about interventions for Tier 2 and Tier 3? Can the classroom teacher find time in her busy schedule to provide additional intervention to students who need it? Can this intervention be provided by well-prepared paraprofessionals? These issues are typically determined at the district and school level for you.

When students require an intervention (Tier 2, 3), how should this intervention be selected and provided? Some researchers recommend a standard treatment protocol model (D. Fuchs & L. S. Fuchs, 2006; Vaughn et al., 2011). Others prefer a problem-solving model (Marston, Muyskens, Lau, & Canter, 2003). Still others favor a hybrid model that is a combination of these two approaches (Glover & Vaughn, 2010; Vaughn, Linan-Thompson, & Hickman, 2003). As the National Association of State Directors of Special Education noted that selecting between a standardized or individualized approach is an artificial decision and that RTI systems integrate the best features from each of them (Batsche et al., 2005). The National Center on Intensive Interventions for Students with Disabilities provides guidelines for using a data-based individualization approach that uses a standardized intervention as a framework for modifying instruction appropriately for students with significant academic and behavioral needs. Using ongoing assessment as a guide to progress and student response, teachers learn to make adjustments in instruction to meet the learning needs of students.

Standard Treatment Protocol   Ms. Cable was a fourth-grade teacher working in a school that used an RTI framework. During her first year in the school, the principal provided training for all of the kindergarten through fifth-grade teachers on a secondary reading intervention that had been selected by the school district to be used with students who demonstrated reading difficulties. Ms. Cable was informed that because all students who were at risk for reading problems were using the same intervention (variation within grade level), the school was using a standard protocol model.

With the *standard treatment protocol model*, the same empirically validated treatments are used for all children with similar problems. The standard treatment protocol does not differ from child to child. The interventions are chosen from those that have an evidence base, and instructional decisions follow a standard protocol. Possible approaches might include explicit instruction in phonological awareness or in phonics skills, fluency or comprehension interventions, or computer programs. Specific research-based interventions for students with similar difficulties are provided in a standardized format to ensure conformity of implementation. Proponents argue that the standard treatment protocol is the most research-based of the approaches to RTI and leaves less room for error in professional judgment (D. Fuchs & L. S. Fuchs, 2006).

Problem-Solving Model   The problem-solving model is a more individualized approach. For each child who is not progressing, a problem-solving team—composed of the classroom teacher, school psychologist, special education teacher, and any other key educational stakeholders (e.g., parent, speech and language therapist)—meets to consider all of the data available so that they can come up with an intervention plan for the child. Interventions are planned specifically for the targeted student and are provided over a reasonable period of time. The process typically follows these steps:

1. *Define the problem.* Ms. Chung, a fourth-grade teacher, indicated that Thomas was not making progress in math. He seemed easily distracted, did not complete his math work during class, did not participate in team problem solving during math, and had incomplete math homework consistently. She was confident that Thomas was going to fail fourth-grade math. The problem-solving team suggested that the school psychologist observe Thomas during class and meet with him afterward.

2. *Analyze the problem.* After viewing Thomas in the class, the school psychologist asked Ms. Chung to provide samples of Thomas's work over the past month. Both agreed that Thomas would benefit from small-group instruction in math for about 30 minutes every day. They thought that Thomas was making some progress, but it was too slow, and they identified that when he was working in a small group he paid more attention.

3. *Develop a plan.* Several other fourth-grade students lacked progress in math, so they were assembled in a group that met every day with one of the fourth-grade teachers.

4. *Implement the plan.* Thomas started the additional math instruction the following week and received supplemental math instruction daily. His progress in math was monitored every week and this data was retained in a file.

5. *Evaluate the plan.* After 10 weeks, the problem-solving team determined that Thomas was making very good progress, and they attributed it to the additional instruction he was receiving. They projected that after about 10 more weeks of supplemental intervention he would be caught up with his classmates.

This approach maximizes problem-solving opportunities by allowing teams to be flexible. Ms. Chung appreciated that her professional expertise was valued but realized that it took considerable time to attend meetings with other professionals and design effective interventions for the students in her class who were behind in reading and math. Ms. Chung appreciated the contributions of the problem-solving team and their recommendation to involve the school psychologist. Together, she felt that they had come up with a successful strategy for Thomas.

Differences between the Standard Protocol and Problem-Solving Models Ms. Cable and Ms. Chung taught at schools that were implementing RTI frameworks, yet Ms. Cable was implementing a standard protocol intervention, and Ms. Chung was implementing a problem-solving intervention for the students in her class requiring secondary (Tier 2) interventions. Research suggests that both of the models can be effective, and in fact, most sites implement a hybrid in which aspects of each model are used (Tackett, 2009).

What is the main difference between standard treatment protocol and problem-solving approach? The fundamental difference between the standards protocol and the problem-solving model is the extent to which decision-making teams engage in analyzing individual student data before selecting and implementing interventions (Christ, Burns, & Ysseldyke, 2005). With a standard treatment protocol, there is little examination of the reasons for a child's struggles. The rationale is that for secondary interventions, considerable evidence shows which interventions are effective, and the best strategy is to implement an effective intervention. In contrast, the problem-solving model is more flexible. The emphasis is on individualized, targeted interventions based on an analysis of the learning context, environmental conditions, and instructional variables as well as on the progress-monitoring data and other assessment data for a student (Glover & Vaughn, 2010).

Decision-Making Team or Multi-Tier System of Support Team How is the RTI (or multi-tier systems of support) model implemented within schools? Who takes the leadership role for directing RTI? The answers to these questions vary by school and district. It is common to have a team of professionals who work together to guide the RTI process at the school level. Schools might have one or more decision-making teams, and membership might be flexible, depending on the expertise needed for a given situation. You may be asked to be a member of the team to provide insights into curriculum expectations and suggestions for what interventions might be effective with students, or you may be asked only to attend team meetings that are relevant to students you teach.

Decision-making teams should include members with relevant expertise. One team member must have expertise in learning disabilities. Another should be an expert in the targeted area of concern (e.g., reading, mathematics, behavior). If the student is an English language learner (ELL), it is critical that someone on the team have expertise in language acquisition, and if relevant, bilingual education.

The overall purpose of the team is to ensure that the RTI model in the school is implemented effectively and that all students who need additional support are identified early, provided appropriate interventions, and monitored over time. See Apply the Concept 3-3 for more about how team members facilitate the RTI process.

Mr. Chan works in an elementary school in California. He describes how his decision-making team works:

> When the majority of a class is progressing and about 20% or fewer of the students differ from their peers in rate of progress, then the role of the team is to determine which Tier 2 interventions to implement with students who are slower to respond. When students who are receiving Tier 2 interventions continue to experience difficulty, the decision-making team convenes to determine which steps to take next. The team might decide to try different Tier 2 interventions, or perhaps more intensive Tier 3 interventions. The team might decide to initiate a more comprehensive evaluation for possible special education identification.

Mr. Chan's experience is similar to other teachers who are in schools using an RTI framework. Even within the RTI model, however, due-process safeguards apply. Families must provide permission for an evaluation to take place. As before the passage of IDEIA 2004, families may request an evaluation for their child.

Responders and Nonresponders to Intervention One of the important contributions of using a multi-tier system

---

3-3 APPLY THE CONCEPT

How Team Members Facilitate RTI and Multi-tier System of Supports

Members of the decision-making team facilitate the RTI process in several ways, including the following:

- Review progress-monitoring data of students in interventions and for grade levels and the school as a whole.
- Observe classroom instruction to ensure that research-based instruction is occurring.

- Provide professional development to teachers and other key educators.
- Assist with data collection and monitoring.
- Facilitate instructional decision making.
- Organize intervention groups, and monitor their effectiveness.
- Communicate with parents and professionals.

of supports in which students are provided primary (Tier 1), secondary (Tier 2), and tertiary (Tier 3) interventions is that it is possible to quickly identify when students are falling behind and provide additional intervention that is targeted to meet their needs. Fortunately, the majority of students respond well when provided additional intervention (Tier 2). We refer to students who respond well to intervention as *responders*. These students may need additional intervention in the future but are generally able to maintain grade-level performance or near grade-level performance with occasional Tier 2 intervention. An example of a good response is when the gap narrows between a student's academic performance in the target area (e.g., reading, math) and the progress of her or his peers. In other words, the student seems to be catching up. On the other hand, students who make minimal or no gains after being taught with high-quality, validated interventions are considered to be inadequately responding to intervention; in other words, they are *nonresponders*. For these students, the gap keeps growing between them and their peers. These students may need more intensive long-term interventions, most likely through special education services.

> **WEB RESOURCES**
>
> Go to the National Center for Learning Disabilities (NCLD) Web site at http://www.ncld.org to expand your understanding of RTI.

Nonresponders do not seem to make adequate progress even when instructed with a research-based approach. It is important to evaluate "adequate progress" both in terms of how the student's performance compares with grade-level peers as well as how the student's performance compares with previous performance by the student. Why? Not all students can readily achieve grade-level expectations, but they can close the gap between their current performance and grade-level expectations. When students do not seem to be responding to an instructional method, it is important to try a different approach. RTI researcher Amanda VanDerHeyden defines nonresponders as "students for

whom we have not yet found the right intervention" (personal communication, February 2006). See Apply the Concept 3-4 for help in identifying why children may not respond to instruction.

Role of Teachers

What is the role of the teacher within an RTI model? At a professional development session designed to improve teachers' knowledge of the RTI model at Sunset Elementary School, Mrs. Jacobs, a 20-year veteran teacher who had taught all grades from second through fifth grade, said, "I think I understand the basic principles of the RTI model, but I just don't understand what I'm supposed to do to facilitate implementation. What is my role?" Amanda VanDerHeyden (2009) indicates that teachers and other school personnel need to establish procedures to accomplish the following:

- Identify students who need intervention. This is typically done using a schoolwide screening in which students who fail the screening at their grade level are considered at risk and provided secondary or tertiary intervention.
- Provide evidence-based interventions that effectively improve learning for the vast majority of students receiving the intervention. Typically, the classroom teacher provides the secondary intervention (Tier 2). This may occur in small groups or individually. Sometimes teachers coordinate their Tier 2 instruction by working cooperatively with teachers in their same grade to provide intervention to a small group of students while the other teacher provides a large-class activity.
- Monitor the effects of the intervention to ensure that it positively influences learning. If the classroom teacher is providing the intervention, and if students in Tier 2 intervention are not making adequate progress, the teacher should consult with the special education teacher or school psychologist.
- Make decisions, in consultation with other key professionals, about the need for more or less

3-4 APPLY THE CONCEPT

Identifying Why Students May Not Respond to Instruction

Before concluding that a student is a nonresponder who needs more intensive services, consider that the student may not be responding to instruction for many reasons, such as:

- The method is not an effective one with this student, and a different approach would yield better results.
- The level of instruction might not be a good match for the student.
- The environment might not be conducive to learning.

intensive intervention so that monitoring students' progress through the tiers is possible.

- Meet regularly with interested stakeholders including parents, other teachers, and school psychologists to facilitate successful interventions and identification of students who need special services.

The teacher plays the most important role in implementing an RTI model. Because the primary focus of the RTI model is early identification of students who need additional assistance, the teacher is a critical link in ensuring that this happens.

Once a student has been identified as needing additional assistance, the special education teacher may be consulted. The special education teacher plays several important roles in a multi-tiered RTI model, which include the following:

- Collaborate with general education teachers, and provide consultation services.
- Help to identify children with disabilities.
- Offer intensive interventions to Tier 3 students.
- Help Tier 3 students access the general education curriculum.

Special educators may work with struggling students who have not been labeled as having disabilities. In some ways these are similar to the roles special education teachers assumed in the past, and in other ways they are quite different. These shifting roles will require some fundamental changes in the way general education and special education personnel do their work (Burns, Griffiths, Parson, Tilly, & VanDerHeyden, 2007; Clough & Lindsay, 2012).

Collaborating and Consulting

As with previous models, particularly coteaching and inclusion, teachers in an RTI model collaborate with other teachers (e.g., English language development teacher, reading specialist) to provide students who have instructional or special needs with a seamless set of services. Special education teachers may still spend part of

In this **video** ▶, a teacher is meeting with a case manager and special education teacher about one of his struggling students. What suggestions did the teacher pick up from this conversation about different ways to present information for students who might struggle with vocabulary and spelling?

their day coteaching or meeting with general education teachers to meet the special education students' instructional needs. The purpose of these efforts is to ensure that students with disabilities receive accommodations and adaptations so they have access to the general education curriculum and can participate in the general education program to the extent they are able.

Another way that teachers collaborate is by serving on RTI problem-solving (or intervention) teams that consider progress-monitoring data and other data and make decisions about teacher and student needs. Teachers provide their expertise when planning interventions or assessments. They are most likely the team members with the greatest expertise about learning difficulties and can offer insights about individual cases.

Using RTI Data to Identify Students with Disabilities

As you recall from the beginning of the chapter, one of the reasons congress recommended using an RTI approach is that there was considerable concern about the validity of traditional practices for identifying students with learning disabilities (e.g., IQ–achievement discrepancy practice). For this reason, you are likely to work in a school or district that uses data from screening, progress monitoring, and other records related to students' progress in primary and secondary interventions to influence decision making about identifying students with learning disabilities.

How might this work? There is no uniform procedure used in all states; however, many states are using data they accrue during progress monitoring of students in interventions to facilitate referral and decision making about whether students do or do not have a learning disability. When students have participated in targeted interventions at the Tier 2 level and still do not seem to progress, the decision-making team may conclude that a comprehensive evaluation is needed to determine whether the students have learning disabilities. Not all researchers agree about how much and what kind of additional data are needed to make this determination. The National Association of School Psychologists emphasizes that RTI requires a "shift from a within-child deficit paradigm to an eco-behavioral perspective" (Canter, 2006). In other words, the data collected should include information about the instructional environment as well as within-child factors. For example, *within-child factors* that have traditionally been the focus of determining whether a student has special needs include cognitive functioning, which can be measured by an IQ test; academic functioning, often assessed by individually administered tests in reading, math, writing, and spelling; or functioning on such processing measures as auditory and visual tasks. The change in perspective provides less emphasis on these within-child factors and more emphasis on how students are performing in the classroom, whether students are meeting the academic and social demands of their grade level, and whether the classroom environment is conducive to learning.

Most experts agree that RTI data may not be sufficient to identify learning disabilities but that RTI data should serve as the core of a comprehensive evaluation. It is likely that comprehensive formal and informal measures of the child's academic skills will be administered in addition to the screening measures, progress monitoring, and other assessment data already collected. The focus should be to develop a profile that includes information about the student's strengths as well as areas of need. The special education teacher and/or other members of the team would observe the child in different contexts to better understand the instructional environment and how appropriate it seems, as well as under what conditions the student seems to thrive or struggle. Observations should include a focus on how well the child is doing in comparison with similar peers.

A psychologist may or may not conduct an evaluation of the student's intellectual ability and cognitive functioning. Just how this is done depends on the state's and district's policies and what the problem-solving team decides is useful data. If the team has concerns about the child's mental and emotional health, the psychologist also conducts assessments in these areas. A social worker interviews the parents about the child's background and developmental milestones. The team collects additional information, such as about the child's attendance patterns. The family members are involved in the process as valued team members.

The teacher then works with the team to review and analyze all relevant data to make decisions about the best course of action for the child. They develop an intervention plan and set learning and, if appropriate, behavioral goals. If the team determines that the student has a disability, then they develop an individualized education program.

See Chapter 1 to review the IEP process.

Providing Interventions

Using a research-based approach to instruction means that the vast majority of students (typically 80%) will be meeting grade-level expectations. These students will not need additional interventions. However, in some schools 20% to 40% of students will require secondary (Tier 2) or tertiary (Tier 3) interventions. What does this mean for the classroom teacher?

Depending on how your school is organized, the classroom teacher is likely to be involved in the provision of the Tier 2 interventions. This means that a subgroup of students will require additional instruction three to five times per week for 20 minutes or more. Typically, this instruction is provided in small groups by the classroom teacher, a paraprofessional, a reading teacher, or other educators trained to provide interventions. Because these students may need instruction that is closely aligned with their instructional needs, the teacher providing the additional instruction uses the data from progress monitoring to guide instruction. Teachers will adjust the pacing of the lesson, provide adequate differentiation, select appropriate materials, provide students with

In this video ▶ , the teacher discusses methods to provide interventions within the classroom. How do using these methods improve teacher instruction and enhance student learning?

3-5 APPLY THE CONCEPT

How to Provide Appropriate Feedback

Following are examples of how to provide feedback to students that will result in an effective intervention:

- Nod, make eye contact with students, smile, and indicate approval.
- Use verbal praise providing specific feedback about what the student did well.
- Pat the student on the arm to indicate that he or she answered a question correctly.
- Repeat the students' response, adjusting it to indicate the needed change; then ask the student to repeat the answer correctly.
- Write the student's response, and then elaborate to extend or expand.
- Ask students to write a response, and then give specific feedback on what aspects are correct.

- Describe why the answer or work was correct.
- Describe what the student could say or do to make the answer more correct.
- Summarize the key ideas.
- Summarize what students should have learned.
- Ask students to identify what they learned.
- Advise students to start the task again.
- Ask another student to build on what a different student has said.
- Show students how to make specific corrections.
- Ask students to explain how their work is correct or incorrect.
- Ask students to show you where in the text their answer was drawn.

ongoing feedback, and allow students adequate opportunities to respond with guided feedback. Providing students with appropriate feedback is essential to effective interventions. Apply the Concept 3-5 provides some examples of how to provide this feedback.

There are several helpful resources to help you with interventions. Apply the Concept 3-6 identifies considerations for implementing effective interventions.

In addition to the instruction provided by the general education teacher, the special education teacher works

3-6 APPLY THE CONCEPT

Guidelines for Implementing Effective Tier 2 Interventions

- *Implement universal screening to identify students at risk for reading problems.* Develop procedures for screening all students at least twice a year (beginning of year and middle of year) to determine students at risk for reading or math problems. Provide students at risk with appropriate interventions.

- *Determine students' instructional needs.* Determine students' knowledge and skills related to relevant reading or math skills/knowledge expected at their grade level. For example, for reading, the instructional needs may be several of the following elements: phonemic awareness, alphabet knowledge, phonics, word reading, word or text fluency, vocabulary, spelling, and comprehension.

- *Form small same-ability groups.* For secondary intervention, form groups of students with similar learning needs. Group sizes should be as small as local resources will allow.

- *Provide daily, targeted instruction that is explicit, is systematic, and provides ample practice opportunities with immediate feedback.* Divide the instructional content into small instructional units (e.g., 3 to 5 minutes per unit) for each lesson.

- *Focus on the reading or math skills that have the highest impact on learning, based on students' current performance.* Provide modeled examples before student practice. Scaffold instruction, and make adaptations to instruction in response to students' needs and to how quickly or slowly students are learning.

- *Follow a systematic routine.* Use clear, explicit, easy-to-follow procedures, and sequence instruction so that easier skills are introduced before more complex ones.

- *Pace instruction quickly so students are engaged and content is covered.* Maximize student engagement, including many opportunities for students to respond.

- *Provide ample opportunities for guided initial practice and independent practice.* Monitor student understanding and mastery of instruction frequently. Adapt instruction so that items are more difficult for some students and easier for other students.

- *Include frequent and cumulative reviews of previously learned material.* Reteach, when necessary.

- *Ensure that students are reading texts at the appropriate level of difficulty.* When students are reading text independently without teacher (or peer) guidance and support, levels of accuracy need to be very high. When students are reading text with teacher guidance and support, lower levels of accuracy may be appropriate. Reading accuracy levels vary from source to source. To calculate reading accuracy, divide the number of words read correctly by the total number of words read. Take into consideration:

  - *Independent level:* Texts in which no more than approximately 1 in 20 words is read incorrectly (accuracy level: 95% to 100%).

  - *Instructional level:* Texts in which no more than approximately 1 in 10 words is read incorrectly. Students need instructional support from the teacher (accuracy level: 90% to 94%).

  - *Frustration level:* Texts in which more than 1 in 10 words is read incorrectly (accuracy level: less than 90%).

- *Provide many opportunities for struggling readers to apply phonics and word study learning to reading words, word lists, and connected texts.*

  - Have students practice reading words and texts at the appropriate level of difficulty (usually, instructional level under the direction of the teacher).

  - Include the reading of word cards or words in phrases or sentences to increase word-recognition fluency (often used with high-frequency and irregular words and words that contain previously taught letter–sound correspondences or spelling patterns).

  - Include comprehension instruction that introduces new vocabulary words, incorporates graphic organizers, and teaches comprehension strategies explicitly.

- *Include writing to support reading and spelling.* Have students apply what they are learning about letters and sounds as they write letters, sound units, words, and sentences. Involve parents so they support students' efforts by listening to them read and practice reading skills.

- *Conduct frequent progress monitoring (e.g., every 1 to 2 weeks) to track student progress and inform instruction and grouping.*

Using Intensive Interventions

Marla is teaching a 30-minute lesson to a group of second- and third-grade students who are all reading at an upper-first- or a second-grade level. Progress-monitoring data indicate that all four students need to build their word study skills. During their first activity, the teacher asks students to review a previously taught word study component—words that end in *ide* or *ike*. She asks students to take 1 minute to write all of the words they can think of that have the -ide or -ike rime, or, in other words, are in the same word families. Marla lets them know when time is up, and they count up all of the words they have listed. The student with the most words reads them aloud, while other students check their lists to see if they have written down any words not stated by the first student, and read these aloud. This is a quick warm-up activity that also serves as a review of previously learned material.

Next Marla introduces two-syllable words that have an open vowel–silent e pattern: be-side, a-like, lo-cate, fe-male, e-rase, do-nate, re-tire, ro-tate, pro-vide, and mi-grate. The last two are "challenge" words because they include blends. Before the lesson began, Marla had written the words on the whiteboard at the front of the classroom, each with a hyphen between syllables. Each student also has a list of the words at his or her desk, one row with the hyphens in each word and another without them. Marla directs students to count how many syllables they see in each word. Next she has them mark vowels and consonants. She asks the students what they notice about the first syllable in each word, and then what they notice about the second syllable in each word (i.e., that all have the open vowel–silent e pattern). She points out that they have learned the syllables before and probably recognize most of them. She asks them to look for syllables they know. Then together the students read the words.

Marla explains and demonstrates what the words mean. For example, for the word *erase*, she erases a word on the board, and for *retire*, she reminds the students that one of their previous teachers has retired. Students practice reading the words, first with the entire group, and then taking turns with a partner. Marla then asks students to look at the story they are reading today. She reminds them of key words previously introduced that they will see in the story. She also asks them to look at the title and the key words and pictures and to make predictions about what they will read or learn. She continues with the lesson, providing students opportunities to read silently and aloud and to ask and answer questions about what they are reading.

---

one-on-one or with small groups of students in reading, math, or other content areas (Vaughn et al., 2012; Vaughn & Linan-Thompson, 2003). Instruction is intense, frequent, and of longer duration than at previous tiers in the RTI model. The special education teacher controls task difficulty and provides ongoing systematic and corrective feedback; progress monitoring continues. See Apply the Concept 3-7 for an example of how Marla conducts intensive interventions in her reading class.

What RTI and Multi-Tier Systems of Support Can and Cannot Do

Recently, researchers worked with an entire team of elementary special education teachers who were responsible for RTI implementation in their schools (Swanson, Solis, Ciullo, & McKenna, 2012). They provided very interesting data through observation and interview. Overall, the teachers were positively impressed with many of the changes provided through implementing RTI, including the fact that students were provided interventions earlier in their schooling, smaller group instruction, more information about student progress, and opportunities to work with a range of professionals. Teachers also recognized that there were challenges with implementing RTI including additional paper work and meetings, and strains with scheduling interventions.

Here are three key points about what RTI can and cannot do:

- RTI neither creates nor fixes learning disabilities. However, models such as 3-Tier Reading provide a safety net for students who might end up in special education simply because they have not been provided adequate instruction or appropriate interventions before referral for special education services (see Meadows Center for a description of the 3-Tier Reading framework).
- RTI is a dynamic model that allows students to move between levels of interventions, depending on results of ongoing progress monitoring and benchmark assessments.
- The key to the 3-Tier model and other RTI models is to provide effective instruction early to ensure that students are provided with the resources and support they need to become proficient learners.

Teachers vary a great deal in how they apply different instructional approaches. How well a teacher implements a practice influences how well students learn. This commonsense finding has important implications for anyone implementing RTI. Determining whether a program is well implemented and appropriate for students requires observing in classrooms. The program being implemented

Determining Whether Interventions Are Needed

To determine whether teachers should provide interventions,

- Examine the program to determine whether it has been validated with students like those in the class. Some students may not be responding adequately to instruction because the instruction is not based on empirical findings.

- Determine whether instruction is at an appropriate level for students and the program is well implemented. Students may be low responders because they are getting inadequate amounts of instruction.

- Establish whether teachers are sufficiently differentiating instruction to meet diverse student needs.

---

by the classroom teacher may be appropriate, but the teacher may not be using it effectively. Maybe the teacher is struggling with classroom management and needs assistance in this area before being able to focus more on instruction. In any case, it is important to explore what can be done to improve instruction and to provide group interventions before providing individual interventions (see Apply the Concept 3-8).

RTI for Students Who Are Culturally and Linguistically Diverse

RTI has the potential to improve outcomes for students who are culturally and linguistically diverse and to more accurately determine which students need special education services (Klingner & Edwards, 2006; Thorius & Sullivan, 2013). RTI practices that are responsive to the cultural and linguistic needs of students can assist teachers in determining whether students' progress is related to what they are being taught, their background experiences, or how they are being taught. The quality of RTI depends on the quality of the RTI team involved. Without sufficient knowledge about cultural and linguistic diversity, for example, educators implementing RTI may presume that a child who does not make progress at a certain pace must have a disability, rather than recognize that the child may need additional time and support while learning English. Educators may also equate cultural differences with cultural deficits, which may influence their interpretations of their diverse students' behaviors (Klingner & Solano-Flores, 2007).

Working with Families

Family involvement has been a required part of identifying and monitoring students with disabilities since the earliest version of the IDEA. Explore this IRIS Module: Collaborating with Families, and you will learn to collaborate with families through videos and strategies to build the home–school connection and support student learning. Family involvement is required in all aspects of

identifying students with disabilities—regardless of the model used. If schools are using RTI models, families must be informed and involved in the process. Just as before, families can request a formal evaluation for a disability at any time. A family should also be notified early in the RTI process that a child seems to be struggling and that the school plans to try specific interventions to help. The Council for Exceptional Children suggests that schools let families know about their child's participation in the RTI process at least by Tier 2. Schools should

- Describe the RTI process and the multi-tier system of supports.
- Provide families with written intervention plans that are clearly explained.
- Obtain families' consent.
- Provide families with regular updates about their child's progress.

The NCLD has developed a guide for parents that provides a complete description of RTI and all of the components using language that parents can readily understand. The guide, *A Parent's Guide to Response to Intervention (RTI),* by Candace Cortiella, is a marvellous asset for parents and teachers and includes an overview of RTI for parents, a glossary of key terms related to RTI, an overview of tiered instruction referred to as *tiered intervention 101,* a sample intervention plan, and many checklists and worksheets to help parents untangle where students might be in the RTI process. Among many beneficial ideas provided, the guide advises that parents understand the following information about intervention plans:

- A description of the specific intervention
- The length of time (such as the number of weeks) that will be allowed for the intervention to have a positive effect
- The number of minutes per day the intervention will be implemented (such as 30 to 45 minutes)

- The persons responsible for providing the intervention
- The location where the intervention will be provided
- The factors for judging whether the student is experiencing success
- A description of the progress-monitoring strategy or approach, such as curriculum-based measurement (CBM), that will be used
- A progress-monitoring schedule
- How frequently (the parents) will receive reports about (their) child's response to the intervention

Several states have developed documents for parents, to assist them in understanding RTI and are available on their state Web sites.

Using RTI Models in Middle Schools and High Schools

Because RTI was designed as a prevention approach, it is typically provided at the elementary grades. However, there are districts and school sites that are using RTI models with older students, particularly in grades 6 to 8.

Mr. Morris is one such teacher who worked at a middle school that is implementing an RTI model. As the science teacher, he was unsure what his role would be. He learned that all of the content teachers would be participating in professional development to enhance their knowledge and skills at providing vocabulary and comprehension learning to their students. This was part of the school's Tier 1 instruction, and all content-area teachers (e.g., math, science, social studies, language arts) were participating.

His class consists of study groups supplemented with in-class modeling and coaching. Reading coaches, who are part of the research team, facilitate monthly study groups with content-area teachers, focus on effective practices for teaching students to read and comprehend academic (content area) text, including research-validated instructional practices targeting vocabulary (e.g., providing examples and nonexamples of words, semantic feature analysis) and comprehension (e.g., question generation, summarization strategy instruction, strategic use of graphic organizers). Mr. Morris said, "At first I was skeptical but then I learned some very practical strategies that were actually helpful to me in teaching all of the students. The emphasis is not on preparing content area teachers to teach reading, but on giving them evidence-based instructional approaches to teach students vocabulary and comprehension in their specific content domain."

Mr. Morris went on to explain how their school uses RTI to provide secondary interventions for students identified as at risk for reading problems based on their low scores on the state assessment of reading. Selected teachers provide a standardized reading intervention to students who were at risk for reading problems but scored very close to grade-level expectations. Other teachers provided a more individualized approach to students who had more significant difficulties. Figure 3-4 compares the differences between the standardized and individualized approaches. For a summary of reading interventions for older students with reading difficulties, see the review by Reed and Vaughn (2010).

FIGURE 3-4 Comparison between Standardized and Individualized Interventions

Standardized	Individualized
Reduced instructional decision making	Increased instructional decision making based on assessment results
High control of materials used for instruction	Lower control of materials used for instruction
Highly specified curriculum	Low-to-moderate specification of curricula
Use of time specified	Flexibility in use of time to address specific student needs
High levels of fidelity to a single approach	Responsive to needs of students
Motivation results from success	Motivation considered in text selection
Systematic and explicit instruction	Systematic and explicit instruction
Fast-paced instruction	Fast-paced instruction
Ongoing progress monitoring	Ongoing progress monitoring

Source: Based on Response to Intervention with Older Students with Reading Difficulties, by S. Vaughn, J. M. Fletcher, D. J. Francis, C. A. Denton, J. Wanzek, & J. Wexler et al. (2008), *Learning and Individual Differences, 18*, pp. 338–345.

- RTI and multi-tiered systems of support address numerous challenges associated with past procedures for supporting student learning and identifying students with learning disabilities. Previous identification criteria focused on establishing a discrepancy between achievement and potential as measured with an IQ test. Yet this way of determining who qualified for special education turned out to be problematic for multiple reasons. Not all students who struggle and need special education demonstrate an IQ–achievement discrepancy.

- Universal screening and progress monitoring are essential components of RTI. Through these assessment procedures, data-based decisions can be made about which research-based instructional practices educators should use to teach students. Screening is done as part of the first tier of an RTI model. All students are screened. Progress monitoring can also be part of the first tier, but it is an essential component of Tiers 2 and 3. The progress of all students who receive interventions targeted to their instructional needs is monitored frequently. The purposes of progress monitoring are to assess the effectiveness of the interventions so that changes can be made if necessary and also to develop a profile of the student's learning. These data can be quite useful when determining whether a student has a learning disability.

- The multi-tier systems of support include several key components: Tier 1, Tier 2, and Tier 3. With each tier, the amount of support provided the student becomes more intense. For each tier, research-based instruction is well matched to students' needs and implemented with fidelity by skilled, caring teachers. This entails coordinating screening, instruction, intervention, assessment, and progress monitoring, as well as providing ongoing professional development.

- Teachers play several important roles in an RTI model. The most important role they play is to provide high-quality, research-based instruction so that when students demonstrate low reading or math skills, it is because they need additional instruction and not because their current instruction is inadequate. Teachers may also assist with screening, progress monitoring, and providing interventions. They collaborate with other educators (e.g., special education teacher, English language development teacher, school psychologist) and other service providers, offering consultation services and helping to identify children with disabilities. They also provide intensive interventions to special education students to help them reach learning objectives in targeted areas, such as in reading and/or math. In addition, they help special education students access the general education curriculum.

After completing this chapter, test your knowledge of the concepts by completing the Assessment.

Managing Behavior

LEARNING OUTCOMES

1. Describe the classroom management and positive behavioral support (PBS) teachers can effectively implement to promote prosocial behavior.

2. Summarize the purpose and procedures of developing an effective functional behavioral assessment (FBA).

3. Identify students with social difficulties, and classify the students who need intervention.

4. Describe procedures for arranging the instructional environment of the classroom to promote appropriate behavior.

As Donna Douglas listened to her son, Jeff, playing with a classmate in his room, she closed her eyes and flinched when Jeff said, "That's not how you do it. I know how to do it. Give it to me." She hoped that the classmate would understand Jeff and not find her son's difficulty in interacting with others so disagreeable that the classmate would not return. Donna knew that Jeff was not mean or cruel, but he had a difficult time controlling his impulses and communicating with others.

At their weekly meeting, Malik's special education teacher's first comment to the school counselor was, "I feel let down. Malik and I had an agreement that I would give him free time at the end of the day if he brought a signed note from his regular classroom teachers that indicated his behavior was appropriate in class. After 3 days of signed notes and free time, I checked with his regular classroom teachers only to find out that Malik had his friends forge the teachers' initials. The teachers had not seen the note. Though this experience is discouraging, I remind myself that 2 years ago, Malik was incapable of spending even 30 minutes in a regular classroom without creating havoc. He has improved, and he even has a friend in the regular classroom. It is comforting to know that despite periodic setbacks, he's making progress."

Jeff and Malik, like many students with learning and behavior problems have a hard time in school, at home, and at work because of how they interact with others. This chapter will help you to understand how to promote more effective behavior in students who have learning and behavior problems. We describe interventions that you can use to improve student behaviors, along with programs and activities that can assist in teaching interpersonal social skills. First we discuss how teachers can use effective classroom management practices as well as positive behavioral support (PBS) approaches to promote success in their classrooms.

Classroom Management and Positive Behavioral Supports

How can teachers use classroom management and PBS to promote prosocial behavior? When someone mentions classroom management, most teachers think of discipline and classroom management rules. In fact, many special education teachers most dread the part of their job that addresses students' behaviors, largely because teachers think of classroom management as what one does *after* a student has a behavior problem. Another way to think about classroom management is to consider what one can do to establish a school and classroom climate that promotes desirable behaviors and reduces inappropriate behaviors. Thus, the majority of a teacher's classroom management efforts take place *before* any behavior problems. Students are taught to have expectations for the behaviors and routines of the classroom. Effective classroom management works very hard to prevent behavior problems. Take a look at the Web site Positive Behavioral Interventions & Supports, designed to assist teachers in preventing behavior problems as well as solving them.

It is important to establish processes and procedures early in the year that provide students with a clear understanding of the routines and the behaviors that are acceptable. Organizing these acceptable practices as a group and establishing them early is a critical first step for successful classroom management. One way to inform and get "buy in" from students about the classroom rules is to discuss the rules and possible consequences with them. The more specifically a teacher defines what he or she wants students to do and not do, the more likely the teacher is to see those behaviors. For example, teachers should consider providing clear expectations about the following:

- When it is acceptable to talk with peers and when it is not
- When it is acceptable to move around the classroom and when it is not
- How students are expected to move from the classroom to other settings in the school
- Behaviors expected during typical class routines such as group work, whole-class instruction, and individual study time
- When and how assignments should be submitted

- What students should do when they have a conflict with another student

As new children enter the class during the year, assigning a veteran student as a guide or mentor can help the new student to understand the rule system of the classroom.

The purpose of some classroom rules is to regulate student behaviors that are likely to disrupt learning and teacher activities or cause damage or injury to property or others. Sharing the explicit conduct rules and demonstrating the rewards of working within the rule system is particularly important for students with behavior problems. Making rewards contingent on full class participation can also assist a teacher because students will encourage each other to work within the rule system.

Ms. Schiller works with junior high students with emotional disorders in a self-contained setting. Establishing conduct rules early in the year and setting up a reward system for "good behavior" is an important part of her program. Ms. Schiller comments:

As far as I know, all of the students in this class are here primarily because they cannot cope with the rule systems in regular classrooms. This happens for a variety of reasons, and as a part of our social skills program, we discuss some of the reasons and how to cope with them. But the majority of the day is focused on academic learning. To accomplish effective learning, we have a set of written and unwritten rules that the students and I are willing to operate under. We establish these rules at the beginning of the year during class meetings. In these meetings, we talk about how the school operates and the rules under which it operates, and then we decide what rules we want the classroom to function under. Usually it takes several days to establish these rules. The rules we generally decide on are these:

- During discussions, one person talks at a time.
- When a person is talking, it is the responsibility of the rest of us to listen.
- Work quietly so you won't bother others.
- No hitting, shoving, kicking, etc.
- No screaming.
- Do not take other people's possessions without asking.
- Treat classmates and teachers with respect and consideration.
- When outside the classroom, follow the rules of the school or those established by the supervisor.

Each day when we have a class meeting, we discuss the rules, our success with using these rules, and how the rules have operated. Sometimes we add new rules based on our discussions. I involve the students in this evaluation and decision making. We also discuss what we think are reasonable consequences when students have difficulty with the room. Typically, we agree that it is reasonable for student's to have a warning that they are breaking a rule. After one warning, students are given a small consequence, typically loss of 1 minute of free time. After the second warning, we have a consequence that is more significant. Having all of the students knowing the rules and consequences increases the likelihood they buy into them.

Eventually, we begin to decide when the rules can be made more flexible. In this way, I hope that I am helping the students assume more responsibility for their own behavior while at the same time maintaining a learning environment that is conducive to academic as well as social growth.

I think there are three main reasons this rule system works in my classroom. First, the students feel like they own the system and have a responsibility to make it work. We have opportunities to discuss the system and to make changes. Second, we also establish a token system for appropriate behavior and learning. Third, I communicate regularly with the parents, letting them know how their child is performing.

See Chapter 2 for more on token systems.

The classroom rules that a teacher establishes depend on the social context of the school and the classroom and the teaching–learning process. Some guidelines to use in developing and implementing classroom rules and management systems follow:

* Have the students help in selecting rules for the classroom.
* Select the fewest number of rules possible.
* Check with the principal or appropriate administrative personnel to determine whether the rules are within the school guidelines.
* Select rules that are enforceable.
* Select rules that are reasonable.
* Determine consistent consequences for rule infractions.
* Have students evaluate their behavior in relation to the rules.
* Modify rules only when necessary.
* Have frequent group meetings in which students provide self-feedback as well as feedback to others about their behavior.
* Allow students to provide solutions to nagging class or school issues through problem solving.

* Consider rules that are consistently broken, and determine ways to provide time each day for students to appropriately break the rule. For example, if students are talking during class, tell them that if they are respectful to others for 45 minutes you will provide them 5 minutes at the end of class to talk with each other.

Classroom Management and Student Behavior

Lisa Rosario is a first-year, middle school resource-room teacher in a suburban school district. She is not happy with the behavior of the students who come to the resource room. She told an experienced special education teacher in her school, "I feel like I know what to teach and how to teach, but I just can't seem to get the students to behave so that they can learn. What can I do to make the students change?" The experienced teacher suggested that Ms. Rosario first look at her own behavior to change the behavior of the students in her classroom. Figure 4-1 provides a checklist for teachers to evaluate the effectiveness of their interventions.

In this video ▶, several teachers share specific methods they have used to control minor behavior issues and disruptions within their classrooms. Why is it beneficial to deal with these small issues in positive, proactive ways?

Ms. Rosario is not alone. Teachers identify classroom management as a cause of stress and frequently cite it as the reason they leave the teaching profession. Following

FIGURE 4-1 Implementation Checklist

If your intervention is not working, consider the following:

* Have you adequately identified and defined the target behavior?
* Have you selected the right kind of reinforcer? (What you decided on may not be reinforcing to the student.)
* Are you providing reinforcement soon enough?
* Are you providing too much reinforcement?
* Are you giving too little reinforcement?
* Are you being consistent in your implementation of the intervention program?
* Have you made the intervention program more complicated than it needs to be?
* Are others involved following through (e.g., principal, parent, "buddy")?
* Is the social reinforcement by peers outweighing your contracted reinforcement?
* Did you fail to give reinforcers promised or earned?

are some guidelines for Ms. Rosario to consider when facilitating more appropriate behavior among her students:

1. *Look for the positive behavior, and let students know you recognize it.* Most teachers indicate that they provide a lot of positive reinforcement to their students. However, observations in special and general education teachers' classes indicate relatively low levels of positive reinforcement (McIntosh, Vaughn, Schumm, Haager, & Lee, 1993; E. A. Swanson & Vaughn, 2010). Teachers need to provide a lot more positive feedback than they think is necessary. Start by trying to track how many positive things you say each day to each of your students. Remember, they need to reflect accurately your academic or behavioral expectations. Look for at least five positive things you can say to each student each day.

One of the fundamental rules about positive feedback is that it needs to be both specific and immediate. "Carla's homework is completed exactly the way I asked for it to be done. She has numbered the problems, left space between answers so that they are easy to read, and written the appropriate heading at the top of the paper." A second fundamental rule about positive feedback is that teachers need to be clear about what behaviors are desirable and undesirable.

A clear list of class rules and consequences is an important step in making classroom management expectations understandable. Procedures that are part of the classroom routines need to be taught to students. Rules outline the behaviors that are acceptable and unacceptable. Teachers' criteria for what constitutes a behavior problem are the basis for classroom rules (Emmer, Evertson, & Worsham, 2009). For example, Lisa Rosario, who indicated that she had difficulty with classroom management, engaged in further discussion with the experienced teacher and realized she had difficulty establishing and enforcing classroom procedures. Once the experienced teacher observed in her classroom and assisted her in establishing routines, Ms. Rosario experienced significantly fewer difficulties with classroom management.

Positive reinforcement with elementary and secondary students needs to be considered differently. Elementary students find public recognition in front of the entire class more rewarding than do older students, who prefer to receive individual feedback.

2. *Reinforcers can be used to encourage positive behavior.* Both positive reinforcement and negative reinforcement increase behavior. Most people think that negative reinforcement means something harmful or "negative," but that is not the case. Positive reinforcement is the presentation of a stimulus (verbal response, physical response such as touching, or a tangible response such as a reward) following the target behavior, intended to increase a target

See Chapter 2 for more on reinforcement.

behavior. Figure 4-2 lists reinforcers that teachers may want to consider for use in their classrooms.

3. *Use a token economy.* A token economy is a structured plan for delivering reinforcers (tokens) following the display of target students' behaviors and/or the absence of undesirable student behaviors. Token economies can be adapted for use in a variety of settings and have been used extensively in special education. For example, teachers can post in the classroom a list of desirable behaviors (e.g., raising a hand and waiting to be called on by the teacher before talking) as well as undesirable behaviors (e.g., hitting classmates). Posted along with the behaviors are the corresponding number of tokens (e.g., points, chips, tickets) that students can earn for exhibiting target behaviors and eliminating noxious behaviors. Teachers can award tokens as target behaviors occur and/or deliver tokens after a specific period of time has elapsed (e.g., Terrell receives one token at the start of each hour, provided that he has not hit a peer during the previous 60 minutes). Teachers can award tokens to individuals as in the previous example, or award the entire class. Either way, the underlying principle is that students will be motivated to earn tokens that are collected and exchanged for previously determined privileges (e.g., a class pizza party or first choice of equipment at recess).

4. *Change inappropriate behavior.* Behaviors that are interfering are the ones that teachers can most easily identify. It is much easier for teachers to list the behaviors they would like to see reduced than to identify behaviors that they would like to see increased. What are some guiding principles to assist in changing inappropriate behavior?

- Do not use threats. Consider carefully the consequences that you intend to use. Do not threaten students with a consequence that you are actually unwilling to use or that will force you to back down.

- Review class rules and consequences. Follow through consistently on the rules you make and with the consequences you have predetermined.

- Do not establish so many rules that you spend too much time applying consequences. You will find yourself continually at war with the students.

- Do not establish consequences that are punishing to you. If you are stressed or inconvenienced by the consequence, you may eventually begin to resent the student, which would interfere with your relationship.

- Listen and talk to the student, but avoid disagreements or arguments. If you are tempted to argue, set another time to continue the discussion.

- Use logic, principles, and effective guidelines to make decisions. Avoid using your power to make students do something without connecting it to a logical principle.

- Do not focus on minor or personal peeves. Focus on the problems that are the most interfering.

Student Provides Self-Reinforcers
- Students give themselves points for behaving well.
- Students say positive things to themselves, "I'm working hard and doing well."
- Students monitor their own behavior.

Adult Approval
- Verbal recognition from the teacher that a student is behaving appropriately, "Juan you are following directions on this assignment."
- Physical recognition from the teacher that students are behaving appropriately. Teacher moves around the classroom and touches students on the shoulder who are behaving appropriately.
- Teacher informs family or other professionals of the appropriate behavior of a student. This can be accomplished with "good news notes" or verbally.

Peer Recognition
- Teacher informs other students of the appropriate behavior of a student. "The award for Student of the Day goes to the outstanding improvement in behavior demonstrated by [student's name]."
- Peers can put the names of students who have demonstrated appropriate behavior into a designated box. These names can be read at the end of the week.
- A designated period of time is allocated at the end of the class period (high school) or day (elementary school) to ask students to recognize their fellow classmates who have demonstrated outstanding behavior.

Privileges
- Students are awarded free time after displaying appropriate behavior.
- Students are allowed to serve in key classroom roles after demonstrating outstanding behavior.
- Students are awarded passes that they can trade in for a night without homework.

Activities
- Students can perform an activity they like (e.g., drawing) after they complete the desired activity (e.g., the activity during that class period).
- Students can perform their tasks on the computer.
- Students can perform their tasks with a partner they select.

Tokens
- Tokens are items (e.g., chips, play money, points) that can be exchanged for something of value.
- Use tokens to reward groups or teams who are behaving appropriately.
- Allow groups of individuals to accumulate tokens that they can "spend" on privileges such as no homework, or free time.

Tangibles
- Tangibles are rewards that are desirable objects to students but usually not objects that they can consume (e.g., toys, pencils, erasers, paper, crayons).
- Tokens can be exchanged for tangible reinforcers.
- Tangible reinforcers can be used to reward the class for meeting a class goal.
- Tangible reinforcers may be needed to maintain the behavior of a student with severe behavior problems.

Consumables
- Consumables are rewards that are desirable objects to students that they consume (e.g., raisins, pieces of cereal, candy).
- Tokens can be exchanged for consumable reinforcers.
- Consumable reinforcers can be used to reward the class for meeting a class goal.
- Consumable reinforcers may be needed to maintain the behavior of a student with severe behavior problems.

Source: Based on *Teaching Students Who Are Exceptional, Diverse, and at Risk,* by S. Vaughn, C. S. Bos, and J. S. Schumm, 2014, Boston: Allyn & Bacon. Copyright 2014 by Allyn & Bacon. Adapted with permission.

- Treat each student as an individual with unique problems and abilities. Avoid comparing students' behaviors or abilities, because this does not assist students in self-understanding or in better understanding the problems and abilities of others.

- Remember that students' problems belong to them. Although their problems may interfere with your work, they are not *your* problems. Students with behavior or emotional problems are often successful at transferring their problems to others. Students need to learn to resolve their own conflicts.

- Students often say or do things that are upsetting to teachers. Recognize your feelings, and do not let them control your behavior. Do not respond to the upsetting behavior of a student by striking back, humiliating, embarrassing, or berating the student.

- Solicit the assistance of families and students in putting any problem in writing to ensure that everyone agrees on what needs to be changed.

- Get student and family input on the behavior problem and suggestions for what might reduce it.

- Set up a plan that identifies the problem, consequence, and/or rewards for changes in behavior. See Figure 4-3 for a sample behavior contract and Figure 4-4 for a self-management plan.

Positive Behavioral Support

In recent years, the principles of behavior management have been applied in various community settings (e.g., school, family) with supports to reduce problem behaviors and develop appropriate behaviors that lead to enhanced

FIGURE 4-3 Sample Behavior Contract

Date: _____

Mr. Wangiri will give one point to Joleen when she exhibits any of the following in his classroom:

1. She raises her hand appropriately and waits for the teacher to call on her before responding to a question or seeking information.
2. She sits appropriately (in chair with all four legs on the ground).
3. When annoyed by other students, she ignores them or informs the teacher instead of yelling at and/or hitting others.

After Joleen has earned 10 points, she may select one of the following:

1. She may obtain a 20-minute coupon to be used at any time to work on the computer.
2. She may serve as the teacher's assistant for a day.
3. She may obtain a 15-minute coupon for free time.
4. She may have lunch with the teacher and brought by the teacher.

Joleen may continue to select awards for every 10 points earned. New awards may be decided upon by the teacher and Joleen, and added to the list. I, Joleen Moore, agree to the conditions stated above, and understand that I will not be allowed any of the rewards until I have earned 10 points following the above stated guidelines.

_____
(student's signature)

I, Mr. Wangiri, agree to the conditions stated above. I will give Joleen one of the aforementioned rewards only after she has earned 10 points.

_____
(teacher's signature)

FIGURE 4-4 Self-Management Plan

Name: Kiernen Smathers

Target Behavior: Submit completed homework to the teacher on time or meet with teacher before the assignment is due to agree on an alternative date and time.

Where Behavior Occurs: Mathematics and Science

Goals:

1. Kiernen will use an assignment book and write down the assignments, guidelines, and due dates. The teacher will initial these to ensure that he understands them and has written them correctly.
2. Kiernen will interpret what he needs to do for each assignment and ask questions as needed.
3. Kiernen will discuss any assignments with the teacher ahead of time if he anticipates not having them ready on time.

Time Line: Meet each Friday to review progress and assignments. Revise plan as needed.

Reinforcer: Kiernen will receive 15 minutes of extra time to work on the computer each day his assignments are completed.

Evaluation: Kiernen will write a brief description of the program's success.

---

social relations. This modification of behavior management principles is called *positive behavioral support* (*PBS*). Recently, schoolwide positive behavioral supports have been expanded to include positive behavioral intervention and supports (PBIS). Many schools find that they are coping with increasing numbers of behavior problems, fighting, bullying, discontent among students, and general lack of discipline. This situation does not exist because teachers or administrators are not caring or lack concern about the issue. It occurs because a schoolwide adoption of a consistent and fluent model needs to occur. PBIS is a proven model for establishing a positive schoolwide community (Horner, Sugai, et al., 2009).

The focus of PBIS is to develop individualized interventions that stress prevention of problem behaviors through effective educational programming to improve an individual's quality of life (Janney & Snell, 2000; Sugai, O'Keefe, & Fallon, 2012). Because behavior is a form of communication and is often related to the context, PBIS involves careful observation of circumstances and the purpose of a problem behavior. A significant number of negative behaviors can be dealt with by modifying the environment (e.g., altering seating arrangements). PBIS also emphasizes teaching appropriate behaviors to replace the inappropriate behavior through readily implemented practices such as the "Good Behavior Game" (Wright & McCurdy, 2012).

Applied Behavior Analysis   Applied behavior analysis is based on identifying observable behaviors and manipulating antecedents and consequences of these behaviors to change behavior. The application of these principles to change maladaptive behaviors is referred to as *behavioral therapy*. The three major components of applied behavior analysis are as follows:

1. *Target behaviors are defined operationally.* For example, a teacher described a behaviorally disturbed child

in her classroom as "emotional." Although most of us know what *emotional* means, each of us probably imagines a somewhat different behavioral repertoire when we think of a student as behaving in an emotional way. In the same way, if asked to chart the emotional behavior of a student, it is unlikely that any two observers will offer the same observations. For this reason, teachers are asked to describe the behaviors that they observe when a student is acting emotionally. "*When I ask her to turn in her work, she puts her head down on her desk, sighs, and then crumples her paper.*" Identifying specific behaviors students exhibit assists teachers in clarifying what is disturbing them, and it also assists in the second step, measurement.

2. *Target behaviors are measured.* To determine a student's present level of functioning and to determine if a selected intervention is effective, target behaviors must be measured before and during intervention. Some behaviors are easy to identify and measure. For example, the number of times Val completes his arithmetic assignment is relatively easy to tabulate. However, behaviors such as "out of seat" and "off task" require more elaborate measurement procedures.

The three types of measurement procedures most frequently used are event, duration, and interval sampling. *Event sampling* measures the number of times a behavior occurs in a designated amount of time. Sample behaviors include the number of times the bus driver reports a student's misconduct, the number of times a student is late for class, or the number of times a student does not turn in a homework assignment. *Duration sampling* measures the length of time a behavior occurs, for example, the amount of time a student is not seated, how long a student cries, or the amount of time a student is off task. It is possible to use event and duration samplings for the same behavior. The teacher might want to use both measurements or select the measurement procedure that will give the most information about the behavior. *Interval sampling* explores whether a behavior occurs during a specific interval of time. For example, a teacher may record whether a student is reported for fighting during recess periods. Interval sampling is used when it is difficult to tell when a behavior begins or ends and when a behavior occurs very frequently.

In addition to the measurement of the target behavior, it is helpful to identify the antecedents and consequences of the target behavior. Knowing what occurs before a problem behavior and what occurs immediately after gives important information that assists in developing an intervention. If every time a student cries, the teacher talks to the student for a few minutes, it could be the teacher's attention that is maintaining the behavior. Listing antecedents can provide information about the environment, events, or people who trigger the target behavior. An analysis of antecedents and consequences facilitates the establishment of a successful intervention procedure.

3. *Goals and treatment intervention are established.* On the basis of observation and measurement data and an analysis of antecedents and consequences, goals for changing behavior and intervention strategies are established. The purpose of establishing goals is to specify the desired frequency or duration of the behavior. Goal setting is most effective when the person exhibiting the target behavior is involved in establishing the goals. For example, Dukas is aware that he gets into too many fights and wants to reduce this behavior. After the target behavior has been identified and measured, the teacher and student examine the data and identify that the only time Dukas fights is during the lunchtime recess. They set up a contract in which the teacher agrees to give Dukas 10 minutes of free time at the end of each day when he does not fight. The student agrees with the contract. The teacher continues to measure the student's behavior to determine whether the suggested treatment plan is effective.

There are many treatment strategies in behavior support that teachers can use to effect change. For example, teachers can use reinforcers to shape new behaviors, reinforce incompatible behaviors, or maintain or increase desired behavior. Teachers can use extinction, punishment, or time-out to eliminate undesired behaviors. Figure 4-5 presents guidelines for using time-out. Teachers may use contracts or token economies to change behavior.

These strategies are discussed in the section on applied behavior analysis in Chapter 2.

With these intervention strategies, consequences are controlled by another (e.g., the teacher). Self-management is a procedure in which the individual controls the consequences. Self-management is particularly effective with older children, adolescents, and adults because the control and responsibility for change are placed in their hands. With assistance from a teacher, counselor, or other influential adult, the adolescent implements a self-management program by following three steps:

1. Identify the behavior the person wants to change (e.g., being late for school).
2. Identify the antecedents and consequences associated with the behavior. For example, Kamala says, "When the alarm rings, I continue to lie in bed. I also wait until the last minute to run to the bus stop, and I frequently miss the bus."
3. Develop a plan that alters the antecedents and provides consequences that will maintain the desired behavior. For example, Kamala decides to get up as soon as the alarm rings and to leave for the bus stop without waiting until the last minute. She arranges with her parents to have the car on Friday nights if she has arrived at school on time every day that week.

FIGURE 4-5 Time-Out: Guidelines for Effective Implementation

Using time-out can help reduce problem behaviors, but it can also be misused. What is time-out? Time-out is when students are informed of the negative behaviors for which they will be denied access to opportunities for positive reinforcement (Alberto & Troutman, 2006). Some examples of time-out practices outlined by Ryan, Sanders, Katsiyannis, and Yell (2007) include the following:

- *Planned Ignoring*—This occurs when the teacher allows the student to remain in the setting, however, all attention from the teacher and peers is removed for a designated period of time.
- *Withdrawal of Materials*—All materials related to the behavior are removed for a specified period of time. For example, if a student throws a ball at another student in an aggressive manner, he or she is not allowed access to the ball for a specified period of time.
- *Contingent Observation*—Students are removed from the setting but are able to observe. For example, on the playground a student who exhibits inappropriate behavior watches from the sidelines for a specified period of time.
- *Seclusion Time-Out*—The student is removed from the setting and placed in isolation for a specified period of time.

When using time-out practices, remember the following guidelines:

- Use time-out as a last resort.
- Discuss time-out procedures with school administrators and parents before implementation.
- Put time-out procedures in writing, and file them with school rules.
- Provide students with information in advance about what behaviors will result in time-out.
- Place students in time-out only for brief time periods (15–20 minutes).
- Before placing the student in time-out, specify the amount of time he or she will be in time-out.
- Tell the student to go to time-out. If the student does not comply, the teacher should unemotionally place the student in time-out.
- Use time-out *immediately* following the inappropriate behavior.
- Establish contingencies in advance for the student who fails to comply with time-out rules.
- Always monitor the time-out area.
- When the time specified for time-out is over, the student should join his or her classmates.
- Provide reinforcement for appropriate behavior after time-out.

An obvious disadvantage of a self-control model of behavior change is that it relies on the student's motivation for success. Students who are not interested in changing behaviors and who are not willing to analyze antecedents and consequences and develop potentially successful intervention strategies will be unsuccessful with self-determined behavior-change plans.

Rick is a fourth-grade student who has learning disabilities (LD), poor social skills, and difficulty interacting with peers. He was seen hitting other students and is known to get into fights for no apparent reason. A careful observation of Rick's interactions with peers and his behaviors suggested that hitting was Rick's way of saying, "Get off my back." Rick was taught to say, "Get off my back" and walk away instead of hitting. All the teachers in the school reminded Rick to "use his words instead of his hands" to communicate. He was taught other specific skills necessary for successful social interactions such as joining a group and initiating and maintaining a conversation. Teachers tried to pair Rick with other students during classroom activities to provide him with opportunities to practice his new skills.

In this case, Rick's behavior and the environment in which target behaviors occurred were observed. Once the causes, circumstances, and purposes of the behaviors had been identified, the classroom teacher met with other teachers to discuss and enlist their help in providing Rick

with the support he would need. The teachers also developed a list of specific social skills to teach Rick. Over time, Rick's problem behaviors decreased, his social skills improved, and he made friends with a few students.

Kasim is a first-grade student with behavior problems. He gets in trouble for taking materials from his neighbors without requesting their permission. His teacher moved Kasim's desk closer to the end of the row so that he would have only three neighbors. She also taught Kasim to think and take out all the materials he needed to do a particular assignment—for example, completing a worksheet requires the worksheet, pencil, and eraser. She even placed a small box labeled "materials needed" on his table so that Kasim could place all the materials he needed for a particular task in his box and not have to borrow from his neighbors. The teacher also taught Kasim appropriate ways of asking others to lend him their materials.

In this case, Kasim's target behaviors and the environment in which they occurred were observed, and then the causes, circumstances, and purposes of the behavior were determined. The teacher then decided to alter the physical environment (by moving Kasim's desk) to reduce the circumstances in which Kasim could intrude on his neighbors. She also taught him alternative behaviors (organizing his materials) to replace his inappropriate behaviors (taking materials from neighbors).

Schoolwide Positive Behavior Support Models   What does a schoolwide PBS model look like? The first step is to establish a primary prevention model in which the focus is on preventing behavior problems schoolwide (OSEP Technical Assistance Center on Positive Behavioral Interventions and Supports, 2009; Sugai, Horner, & Gresham, 2002). This requires ensuring that most school goals (80% or more) are stated in positive terms. The use of punishment is severely restricted to only emergency and very severe cases. This means that all school personnel know the positive rules that are established and that a concerted effort is made to ensure that all students are aware of positive school behavior and rules. School administrators are also actively involved in knowing and supporting implementation of the rules. This requires establishing contracts with students who have ongoing behavior problems to identify their needs and establish peer and adult support for changing their behaviors. Thus, ongoing progress monitoring is also an important feature. Though initially time-consuming to establish, PBS yields significant results over time, reduces behavior problems, and improves the school climate. For students with disabilities whose behavior problems are so profound that they interfere with their learning or that of their classmates, an FBA is required.

Considerable evidence shows that PBS can be taught to and used by parents/guardians very effectively (Blair, Lee, Cho, & Dunlap, 2011). Parents and other family members have successfully engaged students with severe problem behaviors in alternative behaviors and modified contexts that no longer support their behavior problems. How can this be done? Much like the procedures used by general and special education teachers with students with extreme behavior problems, family members can identify the behavior problems through assessment and then alter their feedback so that the child's behavior problems are no longer supported and thus become ineffective (Janney & Snell, 2006). This yields more positive and constructive parent–child interactions.

Developing a Functional Behavioral Assessment

What is the purpose of an FBA, and what are the procedures for developing an effective FBA? According to the Individuals with Disabilities Education Act (IDEA), students with disabilities who have significant behavior problems that interfere with their own learning or with the learning of other students must have an FBA. An FBA and a behavioral improvement plan (BIP) are designed to identify behavior problems of students and to develop an intervention plan to treat these behavior problems. The procedures and practices for developing a BIP are not nearly as well defined as are those for an IEP, and many school personnel still are unclear about how and when to conduct FBAs and design BIPs. Because it is much more likely that an FBA and a BIP will assist a student than interfere, it is always a good idea to conduct an FBA and develop a BIP.

Steps in conducting an effective FBA include:

1. Define the target behavior in behavioral terms. Clearly specify the behavior(s) you would like to see the student perform in observational terms that can be recorded and monitored.

2. Collect and monitor the target behaviors through ongoing data collection that considers frequency, intensity, and rate.

3. Record the events and behaviors that precede and follow the target behavior. In this way, the antecedent, behavior, and consequences are noted.

4. Develop a hypothesis of the conditions under which the target behavior occurs. This hypothesis guides the intervention plan.

5. Develop an intervention plan that considers the antecedents and reinforcers and is built to test the hypothesis.

Figure 4-6 provides an example of an FBA.

Response to Intervention and Classroom Behavioral Support

Many of the fundamental principles of RTI have been used to support appropriate schoolwide behavior. For example, Sugai and colleagues (Fairbanks, Sugai, Guardino, & Lathrop, 2007; Sugai & Simonsen, 2012) emphasized graduated levels of support as a means of improving schoolwide behavior as well as for addressing the social and behavioral problems of individual students. What does RTI mean with respect to social behavior issues?

* *Tier I:* As part of a schoolwide behavioral support program, a school might screen for behavior problems and introduce increasingly intensive interventions to meet school, teacher, and student needs. Schoolwide expectations establish appropriate consequences and procedures for reviewing progress toward schoolwide goals. Practices at the classroom level include opportunities for students to participate and be engaged in classroom activities; positive support for appropriate behavior; minimizing transition time between activities; and providing ongoing feedback and support for academics and social behavior.

* *Tier II:* In a behavioral support model, students who display similar behavior problems might be provided with an intervention that provides additional

FIGURE 4-6 A Sample Functional Behavioral Assessment

Target Behavior I: _____

Baseline Assessment Method: *Baseline Frequency of Target Behavior:*
   parent interview   _____
   teacher interview   _____
   checklists   _____
   systematic observation   _____
   frequency counts of target behaviors _____
   sequence analysis (required)   _____
   norm-referenced assessments   _____

Target Behavior II: _____

Baseline Assessment Method: *Baseline Frequency of Target Behavior:*
   parent interview   _____
   teacher interview   _____
   checklists   _____
   systematic observation   _____
   frequency counts of target behaviors _____
   sequence analysis (required)   _____
   norm-referenced assessments   _____

Target Behavior III: _____

Baseline Assessment Method: *Baseline Frequency of Target Behavior:*
   parent interview   _____
   teacher interview   _____
   checklists   _____
   systematic observation   _____
   frequency counts of target behaviors _____
   sequence analysis (required)   _____
   norm-referenced assessments   _____

Purpose of Target Behavior I:

1. To obtain something?   yes   no   what?   _____
2. To escape/avoid something?   yes   no   what?   _____
3. Other factors?   yes   no   what?   _____
Hypothesis: _____
Replacement Behavioral Goal: _____
Necessary Skills?   yes   no, needs additional instruction in _____

Purpose of Target Behavior II:

1. To obtain something?   yes   no   what?   _____
2. To escape/avoid something?   yes   no   what?   _____
3. Other factors?   yes   no   what?   _____
Hypothesis: _____
Replacement Behavioral Goal: _____
Necessary Skills?   yes   no, needs additional instruction in _____

Purpose of Target Behavior III:

1. To obtain something?   yes   no   what?   _____
2. To escape/avoid something?   yes   no   what?   _____
3. Other factors?   yes   no   what?   _____
Hypothesis: _____
Replacement Behavioral Goal: _____
Necessary Skills?   yes   no, needs additional instruction in _____

FIGURE 4-6 Continued

Student Name:_____ School: _____ Meeting Date: _____

Submitting Teacher: _____ Beginning Date: _____ Review/End Date: _____

Functional Behavioral Assessment Worksheet
(Sequence Analysis)

Antecedent	Behavior of Concern	Consequence

I. Committee Determined Target Behaviors

1. _____

2. _____

3. _____

The following persons attended and participated in the FBA meeting:

Name:	Position:	Date:
_____	Parent	_____
_____	LEA Representative	_____
_____	Special Education Teacher	_____
_____	Student	_____
_____	General Education Teacher	_____
_____	_____	_____
_____	_____	_____
_____	_____	_____
_____	_____	_____

Method for Reporting Progress to Parent:

☐ progress report

☐ parent confernce

☐ other

Frequency for Reporting Progress to Parent:

_____

_____

_____

Source: M. E. Shippen, R. G. Simpson, & S. A. Crites (2003, May/June), A practical guide to functional behavioral assessment, *Teaching Exceptional Children, 35,* pp. 43–44. Copyright © 2003 by the Council for Exceptional Children. Reprinted with permission.

supports, prompts, feedback, and acknowledgment to ensure that behavioral changes occur.

- *Tier III:* If the combination of a schoolwide behavioral support model and group interventions is not associated with improved behavioral outcomes, then more specific and intensive interventions focused at the student level are introduced and monitored.

Remember, consistent with a response to intervention approach, PBIS is characterized by the implementation of a continuum of behavior support with a set of practices that includes universal screening, continuous progress monitoring, team-based decision-making rules and procedures, explicit monitoring of implementation fidelity, and ongoing professional development (Sugai & Simonsen, 2012).

Social Difficulties

In addition to the types of behavior problems that call attention to themselves such as acting out and not obeying rules, many students with learning and behavior problems also exhibit problem in social interactions that negatively influence their success.

In discussing the social skills of students with LD and how others perceive them, it is important to realize that not all students with LD have social difficulties. Many of them are socially competent, making and maintaining friends and struggling to please their teachers and parents. Many adults with LD who are participating in postsecondary education programs identify their social skills as their strengths.

Internalizing and Externalizing Behaviors

The social behaviors of students with learning and behavior problems is often described as having two dimensions: externalizing and internalizing (P. Cooper & Bilton, 2002). Externalizing behaviors are those that are extremely disturbing or intolerable to others (e.g., aggression, hyperactivity, delinquency). Conversely, internalizing behaviors are those that are more likely to adversely affect the student who displays them than other people (e.g., depression, immaturity, obsessive–compulsive behavior, shyness).

Students with behavior disorders who exhibit externalizing behaviors appear to be experts at identifying and performing the behaviors that are most disturbing to others. Donald, in the following example, is a student who exhibits externalizing behaviors.

When Mr. Kline discovered that Donald was to be placed in his fourth-grade class next year, his stomach did a flip-flop. "Any student but Donald," thought Mr. Kline, "he's the terror of the school." Every teacher who had had Donald in class had come to the teachers' lounge at the end of the day exhausted and discouraged. The real catastrophe was the effect Donald seemed to have on the rest of the class. Mild behavior problems in other students seemed to worsen with Donald's encouragement. Donald's hot temper and foul language left him continually fighting with other students. This year, he had hit his teacher in the chest when she had tried to prevent him from running out of the classroom. While escaping, he shouted, "I'll sue you if you touch me." Mr. Kline had once seen Donald running at full speed down the hall, knocking over students along the way, and screeching as though he were putting on brakes as he swerved into his classroom. Mr. Kline knew that next year was going to be a difficult one.

Students like Donald are frequently avoided by more socially competent students in class and are disliked and feared by other class members. They are loners who move from one group to the next after alienating group members, or they develop friendships with other students whose behavior is also disturbing to others. These students present extremely difficult classroom management problems.

Students with behavior disorders who exhibit internalizing behaviors are often less disturbing to others but frequently create concern because of their bizarre behavior. Elisa, in the following example, is a student who exhibits internalizing behaviors.

Elisa, a fifth grader, had just moved to the area. Her mother brought Elisa to register for school but refused to speak with the school secretary. Instead, she demanded that she be allowed to register Elisa with the school principal. Elisa's mother told the school principal that Elisa would sometimes act "funny" to get attention and should be told to stop as soon as she tried it. The principal noted that Elisa had not said one word. In fact, she had sat in a chair next to her mother looking down and rocking gently. Elisa's mother said that Elisa had been receiving special education services during part of the day and was in a regular classroom most of the day. In the regular classroom, Elisa was a loner. She spoke to no one. When another student approached her, Elisa reared back and scratched into the air with her long fingernails, imitating a cat. If other children said something to her, Elisa would "hiss" at them. She would sit in the room, usually completing her assignments and, whenever possible, practicing writing elaborate cursive letters with her multicolored pen. She spent most of the day rocking. She even rocked while she worked.

Problems like Elisa's are usually thought of as being internal and resulting from a unique pathology. Other classmates, recognizing that these children are very different, may attempt to interact, but they are usually rebuffed. Students with internalizing behaviors are easy victims for students whose problem behaviors are more externalizing.

It is important to note that not all youngsters with behavior problems demonstrate either externalizing or internalizing problems. Many youngsters with behavior disorders display both externalizing and internalizing problems. This is not difficult to understand if one imagines a child who is often shy and withdrawn who, when frustrated or forced to interact with others, becomes aggressive and acts out.

Characteristics of Students with Social Disabilities

We expect students with behavior disorders to have difficulty in successfully interacting with others. Students with behavior disorders are identified and placed in special programs because their social problems are so interfering that these students are unable to function adequately with only the services provided within the general education classroom.

Social Interaction   The type and quality of interactions that students with LD engage in are different from those of their peers.

Communication Difficulties   Expressing one's ideas and feelings and understanding the ideas and feelings of others are integral parts of socialization. Adults and children who have good social skills can communicate effectively with others, whereas students with learning and behavior problems frequently have trouble in this area, known as *pragmatic communication*. Children with LD often have poor pragmatic skills, such as eye contact, turn taking, initiative, interaction, sharing, requesting, and responding (Abudarham, 2002).

The student with LD is often a difficult communication partner. For example, verbal disagreements during a learning task between students with mild intellectual disabilities and normal-achieving students were examined in one study (Okrainec & Hughes, 1996). Students with mild intellectual disabilities initiated conflicts less often, thus taking on a respondent role, and used higher-level conflict-initiating strategies, such as justification, delay/distractions, and question/challenges, less often. Initiating conflicts less often can prevent the exchanges of ideas that promote intellectual development as well as moral development and social development for students with mild intellectual disabilities. In addition, justifications can be a useful verbal skill for averting conflicts that may result in aggressive or violent acts.

Aggression   Perhaps the behavior with which teachers are least able to cope is aggression. Aggressive behaviors include assaulting others, fighting, bullying, having temper tantrums, quarreling, ignoring the rights of others, using a negative tone of voice, threatening, and demanding immediate compliance. Many students with behavior problems display these types of aggressive behaviors.

> **WEB RESOURCES**
>
> For more information about meeting the needs of students with destructive behaviors, consider viewing the Web site from the Institution on Violence and Destructive Behavior, pages.uoregon.edu/ivdb/.

In a study conducted by Lancelotta and Vaughn (1989), five types of aggressive behaviors and their relation to peer social acceptance were examined:

1. *Provoked physical aggression:* Attacks or fights back following provocation from another.

2. *Outburst aggression:* Has uncontrollable outbursts without apparent provocation that may or may not be directed at another person. An example is a student who gets angry and throws a fit for no apparent reason.

3. *Unprovoked physical aggression:* Attacks or acts aggressively toward another person without provocation. An example is a student who starts a fight for no reason.

4. *Verbal aggression:* Says aggressive things to another person to attack or intimidate him or her. An example is a student who threatens to beat up another student.

5. *Indirect aggression:* Attacks or attempts to hurt another indirectly so that it is not likely to be obvious who did it. An example is a student who tells the teacher that another student does bad things.

The study demonstrated that girls are less tolerant of all types of aggression than are boys. Also, all types of aggression resulted in lower peer ratings by their fellow students, with the exception of provoked aggression for boys. This means that boys who fight back when they are attacked first by other boys are not more likely to be poorly accepted. This, however, is not true for girls who fight back when they are attacked. All of the other subtypes of aggression are related to poor peer acceptance.

Aggression does not go away without treatment and is correlated with such negative outcomes as alcoholism, unpopularity, aggressive responses from others, academic failure, and adult antisocial behaviors. Specific skills for teaching students to deal more effectively with their aggressive responses are an important component of social skills programs for students with behavior disorders.

Following are some ways in which teachers can address aggression and bullying in the classroom:

- All students must understand what types of behaviors are considered aggressive. Teachers can hold class discussions about which examples of aggressive behavior are identified and listed to ensure that all students know what is meant by *aggression*.

- Teachers can establish a no-tolerance rule regarding aggressive behavior and have a schoolwide plan for how every adult and child will handle aggression from others. *No tolerance* means that the school has a policy (other than expulsion) for responding to aggressive behavior.

- The teacher can establish relationships with students and families that provide support.

- The teacher can provide preemptive techniques to prevent fights. This can include stopping heated arguments and monitoring students who do not usually get along.

- The teacher and other school staff can stop aggressive behavior immediately.

- The teacher can identify when and where the student is aggressive and attempt to eliminate those situations.

- The teacher can teach students to resolve their own conflicts and mediate difficulties between other students.

- The teacher can establish practices that allow students to describe what happened before and during an aggressive act.

- As a schoolwide model, the school staff can establish a caring and supportive environment for students and adults.

Apply the Concept 4-1 discusses the problem of bullying and teasing students with disabilities.

Attention Problems/Hyperactivity Attention deficits and hyperactivity are characteristics that are often observed in students with learning and behavior disorders. Families report that 3.7% of children have both attention deficit hyperactivity disorder (ADHD) and LD (T. J. Smith & Adams, 2006). Students with attention deficits frequently display a pattern of inattention, and students with hyperactivity often exhibit patterns of impulsivity; these patterns are evident in a variety of contexts, including home and school.

You may be asked, what is the difference between attention deficit hyperactivity disorder (ADHD) and attention deficit disorder (ADD)? Technically the terminology for diagnosis is ADHD. However, you will notice that many parents and even professional use the term ADD as a general term for ADHD. Typically, people are referring to the same sets of behaviors when they use the terms ADHD and ADD. What are the most common characteristics of ADHD? Typically students are described as being easily distracted with difficulty demonstrating sustained attention to tasks. They are also observed as demonstrating impulsivity, which can be described as having difficulty with impulse control or delay of gratification. The third common characteristic is hyperactivity, which refers to excessive activity and restlessness. It is important to note that almost everyone demonstrates one or more of these characteristics some of the time. ADHD is characterized by excessive, long-term, and pervasive demonstration of these behaviors.

Students with attention deficits and/or hyperactivity may be treated with medication. Some children experience unpleasant physical symptoms and are affected by the drugs in some settings but not in others. Most children who receive medication for hyperactivity are under the care of a physician whom they see infrequently. Thus, monitoring the effectiveness of the drug is often the responsibility of family members and teachers. Perhaps the most effective technique for monitoring the effects of drugs is observing the student's behavior and determining whether there have been significant changes, either positive or negative, and report them to the school nurse and/or parents.

4-1 APPLY THE CONCEPT

Preventing Bullying and Teasing of Individuals with Disabilities

Have you ever worried about a school bully or excessive teasing? If you have, you are not alone. Schools and educators have reported that bullying and excessive teasing are a serious school problem, one that is exacerbated when students are perceived as different. Thus, students with learning and behavior problems may be particularly susceptible to harassment and bullying. When students are isolated from their peers or do not participate in mainstream programs, they are at increased risk for bullying (J. H. Hoover & Salk, 2003).

Following are some facts about bullying (J. Hoover & Stenhjem, 2003; Sullivan, 2010):

- Bullying is the most common form of aggression among youths.
- Males are more likely to bully and be bullied.

- Many teachers (as many as 25%) do not perceive that bullying is wrong and therefore rarely intervene. Be sure you work to change this view and stop bullying as soon as you see it.
- Most students perceive that schools do little to respond to bullying.
- Physical bullying peaks in middle school.

A schoolwide intervention program was designed and used in Finnish schools with a goal to reducing school bullying and victimization (Kärnä et al., 2010, 2011). The program aims to: (1) increase awareness of the role of the group in maintaining bullying, (2) increase empathy toward victims, (3) improve strategic use of practices to support self-efficacy, and (4) increase student's coping skills when victimized. The program entails 10 lessons over a 20-hour time period implemented by teachers. At the end, students sign a contract about reducing victimization and bullying. The program also identifies a team to identify students who are bullied.

When students demonstrate attention problems, teachers can do the following:

- Use clear ways of cueing students to obtain their attention (Shore, 2003). For example, say, "I'm counting backward to one, and then I want all eyes on me. Five, four, three, two, one." Some teachers use chimes or other instruments to obtain students' attention. Another idea is to tell students that you are going to clap a pattern and then you want them to "clap the same pattern and then look at me."

- Develop a signaling system with a student or selected students to cue them to pay attention. The signal could be a slight touch on the shoulder or passing the student a colored card to indicate that he or she is not paying attention.

- Look for times when students are attending and focusing, and also establish a system for cueing them when they are doing well.

- Consider where in the classroom and near whom students work, and make adjustments to promote better focus on assignments.

- Shorten the work periods and assignments. Focus on understanding and getting a few items right rather than completing all aspects of tasks.

- Provide clear and limited directions that are easier to follow.

- Assist students in making effective transitions.

- If a student is taking medication, monitor his or her behavior to note the effects of the medication and possible changes in behavior (Shore, 2003).

- Use computer-assisted learning.

- Check out the following organizations and their Web sites for additional information: Attention Deficit Disorder Association, and Children and Adults with Attention-Deficit/Hyperactivity Disorder.

Self-Concept Ask parents what they most want for their children, and many of them will mention that they want their children to be happy and to be successful—they want them to be proud of themselves. In many ways, they are hoping that their children have a healthy and positive self-concept, or self-perception. How we view ourselves is highly related to our comparison group. Therefore, it is not surprising that students with learning and behavior difficulties often have poor self-concepts. These students are aware of how their learning performance compares with that of others.

What can teachers do to improve the self-concept of students with LD or behavior problems? The most important development for self-concept is success. It does not have to be success in school, though there may be

school-related activities that provide opportunities for success. In a large-scale evaluation of the relation between self-concept and academically achievement, self-concept of students with disabilities was an excellent predictor of their achievement (Ju, Zhang, & Katsiyannis, 2013). It may be useful to involve students in extracurricular activities such as sports or music, because students with LD who participate in these activities have a similar self-concept as average-achieving students (Kloomok & Cosden, 1994). Teachers and parents can provide opportunities for students to demonstrate what they do well and provide encouragement in the areas of difficulty. One parent described it this way:

> The best thing that happened to my son is swimming. We knew from the time Kevin was an infant that he was different from our other two children. We were not surprised when he had difficulties in school and was later identified as learning-disabled. His visual/motor problems made it difficult for him to play ball sports, so we encouraged his interest in swimming. He joined a swim team when he was six, and all his friends know he has won many swimming awards. No matter how discouraged he feels about school, he has one area in which he is successful.

Apply the Concept 4-2 describes what teachers might do to support self-regulation in students.

Social Difficulties That Are Prevalent During Adolescence

In addition to the characteristics of students with learning and behavior disorders that we discussed earlier, several difficulties are prevalent during adolescence that can affect students with special needs. These are the mental health issues of social alienation, suicide, anorexia nervosa, and alcohol and other drug abuse. Why might special education teachers need to consider these difficulties as well as other variables related to social adjustment in adolescents with learning and behavior problems? Perhaps the most important reason is that teachers are often the first to be aware of mental health problems and can be valuable resources for identification and support.

> In this **video** ▶, listen as several teens describe their experiences with cliques. Do you recall similar groups from your high school? How can identification with a particular group help and/or be harmful to adolescents as they develop into adulthood?

Social Alienation Social alienation arises from the extent to which youngsters feel that they are not part of or do not have an affinity for the school or the people in the school. Social alienation has been interpreted to refer

How Teachers Can Promote Students' Self-Regulation

Self-regulation is the development of mechanisms for monitoring our own behavior and regulating our thinking and emotions (Galinsky, 2010). To promote self-regulation consider the following:

1. Consider using "think-alouds" as a mechanism to model self-regulation. "Let's see. I am really getting tired of doing these word problems, and there are still 2 more to do. I'm going to take a 30-second break and rest my head and then I'm going to finish the next two problems." Model for students the think-aloud processes that you would like them to use to regulate their behavior.

2. Teach students mechanisms for changing "what they think" as a means of changing what they do. For example, by modeling, "I'm pretending that I'm standing in line and someone cuts in front of me. My first thought is, 'they can't do that. I'm going to push them'. Then I think to myself, 'I bet I can use my words rather than my hands to change this.' I say, 'Would you move behind me? I was standing here.'

3. Offer process-directed praise or criticism to students (Dweck & Kamins, 1999) such as, "This paper is clearly written," or, "You really concentrated and finished this biology assignment." Focus on the activity the students are engaged in, such as reading, writing, or art, and avoid person-directed praise or comments such as, "You are good in biology." This will help reduce the amount of external reinforcement needed and instead reinforce student performance.

4. Reduce the amount of external reinforcement and focus on reinforcing student performance. Rather than saying, "Good work" or "Excellent job," focus on the behaviors, such as, "You really concentrated and finished this biology assignment. You needed to ask for help, but you got it done. How do you feel about it?"

5. Link students' behaviors to outcomes. "You spent 10 minutes working hard on this worksheet, and you finished it."

6. Provide encouragement. Because they experience continued failure, many students are discouraged from attempting tasks they are capable of performing.

7. Discuss academic tasks and social activities in which the student experiences success.

8. Discuss your own failures or difficulties, and express what you do to cope with these. Be sure to provide examples of when you persist and examples of when you give up.

9. Encourage students to take responsibility for their successes. "You received a B on your biology test. How do you think you got such a good grade?" Encourage students to describe what they did (e.g., how they studied). Discourage students from saying, "I was lucky" or "It was an easy test."

10. Encourage students to take responsibility for their failures. For example, in response to the question "Why do you think you are staying after school?" encourage students to take responsibility for what got them there. "Yes, I am sure Jason's behavior was hard to ignore. I am aware that you did some things to get you here. What did you do?"

11. Structure learning and social activities to reduce failure.

12. Teach students how to learn information and how to demonstrate their control of their learning task.

13. Teach students to use procedures and techniques to monitor their own gains in academic areas.

14. Show students how to use timers to increase the amount of time that they spend on a task. Also provide them with the mechanisms for giving themselves rewards such as time to not do work as a reward for completing tasks.

---

to alienation from teachers or peers (Seidel & Vaughn, 1991). Not surprisingly, social alienation begins early in a youngster's school career but is most obvious during adolescence. In a study by Seidel and Vaughn (1991), students with LD who dropped out of school differed from those who did not when they rated how they felt about teachers and classmates. Not surprisingly, students with LD who drop out do not perceive their teachers as friends. Furthermore, these students are more likely to state, "The thing I hated most about school was my teachers." Students with LD who dropped out also felt that their classmates "would not have missed them if they moved away," and they did not look forward to seeing their friends at school. Interestingly, these students did not differ on their academic achievement scores but did differ on the extent to which they felt that they were socially accepted and liked by their teachers and classmates.

Different school environments trigger feelings of loneliness in students depending on the individual student's temperament. Thus, it is important for teachers to realize that students who are more withdrawn need additional support to be comfortable in less structured settings. It may be useful to rehearse with them what they can do or to assist them in establishing routines with which they are comfortable in these settings.

To help students feel less socially alienated, teachers can do the following:

- Provide opportunities for students to work in small groups that encourage all students to participate.
- Set the tone in the class that all students are valuable and have something important to contribute.
- Take a moment between classes to ask about students, and demonstrate that you care.
- Allow students to participate in decision making regarding class rules and management.
- Identify youngsters who are uninvolved and/or detached, and refer them to the counselor.
- Encourage students to participate in school-related extracurricular activities.
- Ask students who are lonely whether there is a person in the class they like, and seat them nearby.
- Try grouping students into small groups or pairing students during activities.
- Provide students with activities to engage in with peers (e.g., hide and go seek) during less structured times such as recess and lunch. Encourage students to play together.

Suicide Two Leominster, Massachusetts, teenagers died in a shotgun suicide pact next to an empty bottle of champagne after writing farewell notes that included "I love to die I'd be happier I know it! So please let me go. No hard feelings" (*Boston Herald,* November 10, 1984, p. 1). Although the autopsy showed high levels of alcohol in the girls' bloodstreams, there were no indications that either girl was involved with other drugs or was pregnant. It appeared as though both girls willingly participated in the suicide act. In another note, one of the girls wrote, "I know it was for the best. I can't handle this sucky world any longer" (*Boston Herald,* November 10, 1984, p. 7). The cause of the suicide pact is unknown.

A suicidologist/psychiatrist who asked to be anonymous gathered suicide notes left at coroners' offices. The text of each letter plus the age and sex of the person who left the suicide note are real. According to his analysis at least half of the notes indicated some doubt about wanting to commit suicide. This suggests that monitoring individuals at risk for suicide may have some prevention success.

Any suicide is shocking, but the suicide of a child or adolescent is particularly tragic. Suicides between birth and the age of 15 are termed *childhood suicides.* Between ages 15 and 19, they are referred to as *adolescent suicides.* Suicide is one of the top three causes of death for people under 24 years of age; 5,000 adolescents each year take their own lives in the United States (Centers for Disease Control and Prevention; www.cdc.gov).

Suicide attempts by adolescents are frequently made to accomplish one or more of the following four goals:

1. To escape stress or stressful situations
2. To demonstrate to others how desperate they are
3. To hurt or get back at others
4. To get others to change

The National Institute of Mental Health addresses the following questions about suicide.

What are the factors that make individuals more at risk to commit suicide?

- Depression and other mental health problems
- Substance abuse
- Prior suicide attempt
- Family history of suicide
- Family violence including physical and sexual abuse
- Firearms in the home
- Incarceration

It is important to note that individuals at risk for suicide have been found to have decreased levels of serotonin and impulsive disorders. The National Institute of Mental Health reports that men and women differ in the methods used for suicide. See Table 4-1 for a summary of suicide methods for males and females.

"Suicidal patients are often very difficult because they so frequently deny the seriousness of their attempts" (Toolan, 1981, p. 320). They often make comments such as, "It was all a mistake. I am much better now." Even if they attempt to discount the attempt, it should be treated with extreme seriousness.

Early detection of students who are at risk for suicide can help in providing services and reducing that risk. Students who are contemplating suicide may provide subtle verbal clues such as, "Don't bother grading my test,

TABLE 4-1 Suicide Methods for Males and Females

Suicide by	Males (%)	Females (%)
Firearms	56	30
Suffocation	24	21
Poisoning	13	40

because by tomorrow it really won't matter what I got on it" (American Academy of Child and Adolescent Psychology, 2009; American Foundation for Suicide Prevention, 2009). Signs that may be related to suicide include depression, flat affect, an emotion-laden event (e.g., parental divorce), and isolation. Teachers of students with learning and behavior problems should be particularly knowledgeable about these symptoms because these students, particularly those in special education classrooms, are considered by their counselors to be more at risk for depression (Howard & Tryon, 2002). Also, students with severe reading problems are significantly more likely to experience suicidal ideation or suicide attempts and are also more likely to drop out of school (Daniel et al., 2007). Apply the Concept 4-3 presents some warning signs of suicide.

Sheras (1983) offers six general considerations for dealing with adolescent suicide attempts:

1. All suicide attempts must be taken seriously. Do not interpret the behavior as merely a plea for attention. Do not try to decide whether the attempt is real. The National Mental Health Association (2003) indicates that four out of five suicidal adolescents provide clear signs that they are considering suicide, including the following:

   - Direct and indirect threat
   - Obsession with death
   - Writing that refers to death
   - Dramatic changes in appearance or personality (e.g., changes in eating and/or sleeping habits)
   - Giving away possessions
   - Change in school behavior

2. Develop or reestablish communication with the person. Suicide is a form of communication from a person who feels that he or she has no other way to communicate.

3. Reestablish emotional or interpersonal support. Suicide is an expression of alienation, and the person needs to be reconnected with significant others.

4. Involve the adolescent in individual and/or family therapy. Often, the adolescent feels unable to establish communication with a significant person (e.g., a parent) and needs assistance from another to do so.

4-3 APPLY THE CONCEPT

What Are Some of the Suicide Warning Signs?

These warning signs should be taken very seriously and never ignored. Teach adolescents and young adults these signs so that they can respond appropriately to their peers.

- *Suicide Notes*—If you find, read, or are told about a suicide note that has been written, do not consider it silly or funny. Take it very seriously and report it.
- *Threats*—All threats to do harm to oneself should be taken very seriously.
- *Previous Attempts*—Pay particular attention to students who have attempted suicide in the past.
- *Depression*—When depression includes signs of helplessness or hopelessness, be very concerned about risk for suicide.
- *Final Arrangements*—Consider efforts to make final arrangements such as giving away valuable objects and preparing goodbyes as serious risk signs for suicide.
- *Self-Injurious Behavior*—Treat attempts at injuring oneself such as jumping out of a car and cutting as risk signs for suicide.

- *Sudden Changes in Appearance, Personality, Friends, and Behavior*—Observe dramatic changes in appearance (neat to sloppy), excessive changes in personality, and other significant changes as potential signs for risk of suicide.
- *Death and Suicide Themes*—Students may exhibit unusual and peculiar preoccupation with death themes that they demonstrate in their drawings and writings.

There are a variety of online resources that you can access for more information:

American Academy for Child and Adolescent Psychiatry

American Association of Suicidology

Depression and Bipolar Support Alliance (DBSA)

Light for Life Program

National Institute of Mental Health Suicide Prevention Resources

National Mental Health Association

U.S. Department of Health and Human Services

Source: Save a *Friend: Tips for Teens to Prevent Suicide,* from R. Lieberman and K. C. Cowan, 2006, Bethesda, MD: National Association of School Psychologists. Retrieved from http://www.nasponline.org.

5. Work with the youngster to identify the problem or problems and to provide realistic practical solutions to the problems.

6. Devise a "no-kill" contract that requires a student to promise in writing not to inflict harm on himself or herself. Students who have agreed to such a contract tend to find it more difficult to follow through with plans of suicide (Pfeffer, 1986).

What should you do if you think someone is suicidal? The National Institute of Mental Health recommends the following if you think someone is suicidal.

- Do not leave the person alone.
- Try to get the person to seek immediate help from his or her doctor or the nearest hospital emergency room, or call 911.
- Eliminate access to firearms or other potential tools for suicide, including unsupervised access to medications.

Social Interventions

Understanding and using different interventions to affect the social skills of students with LD and behavior disorders is extremely important. Using a particular intervention may be effective with one student but considerably less effective with another student or another problem. The best way to determine whether an intervention is working is to target specific social skills and to measure their progress over time. Though immediate improvement is unlikely, there should be some improvement in 4 to 6 weeks; if there is no improvement, the teacher may consider trying another intervention.

A range of intervention strategies can assist in teaching appropriate social skills to students with LD and behavior disorders. The purpose of social skills training is to teach the students a complex response set that allows them to adapt to the numerous problems that occur in social situations. Common goals of social skills training programs include the ability to do the following:

- Solve problems and make decisions quickly.
- Adapt to situations that are new or unexpected.
- Use coping strategies for responding to emotional upsets.
- Communicate effectively with others.
- Make and maintain friends.
- Reduce anxiety.
- Reduce problem behaviors.

Interpersonal Problem Solving

Most people spend an extraordinary amount of time preventing and solving interpersonal problems. Whether we are concerned about what to say to our neighbor whose dog barks loudly in the middle of the night, how to handle an irate customer at work, or our relationships with our parents and siblings, interpersonal problems are an ongoing part of life. Some people seem to acquire the skills necessary for interpersonal problem solving easily and with little or no direct instruction; others, particularly students with learning and behavior disorders, need more direct instruction in how to prevent and resolve difficulties with others.

The goal of interpersonal problem-solving (IPS) training is to empower students with a wide range of strategies that allow them to develop and maintain positive relationships with others, cope effectively with others, solve their own problems, and resolve conflict with others. The problem-solving approach attempts to provide the student with a process for solving conflicts.

Four skills appear to be particularly important for successful problem resolution (Bell & D'Zurilla, 2009; D'Zurilla & Nezu, 2010). First, the student must be able to identify and define the problem. Second, the student must be able to generate a variety of alternative solutions to any given problem. Third, the student must be able to identify and evaluate the possible consequences of each alternative. Finally, the student must be able to implement the solution and determine the effects of the solution implementation. This may require rehearsal and modeling.

Whereas these four components are characteristic of most interpersonal problem-solving programs, programs often incorporate additional components and procedures. For example, a social problem-solving intervention was conducted with 50 students with serious emotional disturbances by Amish, Gesten, Smith, Clark, and Stark (1988). The intervention consisted of 15 structured lessons that occurred for 40 minutes once each week. The following problem-solving steps were taught:

1. Say what the problem is and how you feel.
2. Decide on a goal.
3. Stop and think before you decide what to do.
4. Think of many possible solutions to the problem.
5. Think about what will happen next after each possible solution.
6. When you find a good solution, try it.

The results of the intervention indicated that students with serious emotional disturbances who participated in the intervention improved their social problem-solving skills and were able to generate more alternatives to interviewing and role-playing measures.

The following sections describe several IPS programs that have been developed, implemented, and evaluated with students who have learning and behavior disorders.

Fast

PROCEDURES: FAST is a strategy that is taught as part of an IPS program to second-, third-, and fourth-grade students with LD who have been identified as having social skills problems (Vaughn & Lancelotta, 1990; Vaughn, Lancelotta, & Minnis 1988; Vaughn et al., 1991). The purpose of FAST is to teach students to consider problems carefully before responding to them and to consider alternatives and their consequences. Figure 4-7 presents the FAST strategy. In step 1, Freeze and Think, students are taught to identify the problem. In step 2, Alternatives, students are taught to consider possible ways of solving the problem. In step 3, Solution Evaluation, students are asked to prepare a solution or course of action for solving the problem that is both safe and fair. The idea is to get students to consider solutions that will be effective in the long run. Step 4, Try It, asks students to rehearse and implement the solution. If they are unsuccessful at implementing the solution, students are taught to go back to alternatives. Students with LD practiced this strategy by using real problems generated by themselves and their peers. Following is a description of the procedures used in the problem-solving study.

1. In each classroom, ask students to rate all same-sex classmates on the extent to which they would like to be friends with them. Students who receive few friendship votes and many no-friendship votes are identified as not well accepted. Students who receive many friendship votes and few no-friendship votes are identified as very well accepted.

2. Students with LD who are not well accepted are paired with a same-sex popular classmate, and the

FIGURE 4-7 FAST: An Interpersonal Problem-Solving Strategy

> **Freeze and think!**
>   What is the problem?
>
> **Alternatives?**
>   What are my possible solutions?
>
> **Solution evaluation**
>   Choose the best solution:
>   safe?
>   fair?
>
> **Try it!**
>   Slowly and carefully
>   Does it work?

pairs become the IPS skills trainers for the class and school.

3. Children who are selected as IPS skills trainers are removed from the classroom two to three times a week and are taught problem-solving strategies for approximately 30 minutes each session.

4. These students who are the "class trainers" are taught the FAST strategy (see above) such as accepting negative feedback, receiving positive feedback, and making friendship overtures.

5. Classmates record problems they have at home and at school and place their lists in the classroom problem-solving box. Trainers use these lists as they learn the strategies outside of class as well as for in-class discussion.

6. After the IPS trainers have learned a strategy, such as FAST, they teach it to the entire class, with backup and support from the classroom teacher.

7. During subsequent weeks, the trainers leave the room for only one session per week and practice the FAST strategy as well as other strategies with classmates at least one time per week. These reviews include large-group explanations and small-group problem-solving exercises.

8. Students who are selected as trainers are recognized by their teacher for their special skills. Other students are asked to consult the problem-solving trainer when they have difficulties.

Apply the Concept 4-4 shows an activity sheet used as part of a homework assignment for students participating in the training.

ASSET: A Social Skills Program for Adolescents

PROCEDURES: The purpose of ASSET is to teach adolescents the social skills they need to interact successfully with peers and adults (Hazel, Schumaker, Sherman, & Sheldon-Wildgen, 1981). Eight social skills are considered fundamental to successful relationships:

1. *Giving positive feedback.* This skill teaches students how to thank someone and how to give a compliment.

2. *Giving negative feedback.* This skill teaches students to give correction and feedback in a way that is not threatening.

3. *Accepting negative feedback.* This skill teaches students the all-important ability to receive negative feedback without walking away, showing hostility, or other inappropriate emotional reactions.

Activity Sheet for FAST

This activity sheet can be used to give children written practice in using the FAST strategy.

You are in the cafeteria. Another student keeps bugging you. He hits you, pokes you, tries to steal your food, and will not stop bullying you. You start to get angry. What would you do? Use FAST to help you solve the problem.

1. *Freeze and think.* What is the problem?

   _____
   _____

2. *Alternatives.* What are your possible solutions?

   _____
   _____
   _____

3. *Solution evaluation.* Choose the best one. Remember: Safe and fair works in the long run.

   _____
   _____

4. *Try it.* Do you think this will work?

   _____
   _____

A friend of yours is upset. She is teased a lot, especially by a boy named Kenny. She told you that she wants to run away from school. What could you tell your friend to help her solve the problem? Use FAST to help you.

1. _____
   _____
   _____
   _____

2. _____
   _____
   _____

3. _____
   _____

4. _____
   _____

---

4. *Resisting peer pressure.* This skill teaches students to refuse their friends who are trying to seduce them into some form of delinquent behavior.

5. *Problem solving.* This skill teaches students a process for solving their own interpersonal difficulties.

6. *Negotiation.* This skill teaches students to use their problem-solving skills with another person to come to a mutually acceptable resolution.

7. *Following instructions.* This skill teaches students to listen and respond to instructions.

8. *Conversation.* This skill teaches students to initiate and maintain a conversation.

PROCEDURES: The Leader's Guide (Hazel et al., 1981) that comes with the ASSET program provides instructions for running the groups and teaching the skills. Eight teaching sessions are provided on videotapes that demonstrate the skills. Program materials include skill sheets, home notes, and criterion checklists. See Apply the Concept 4-5 for a description of the procedures for implementing ASSET.

Circle of Friends Circle of Friends is a friendship-enhancement program that has been evaluated with 6- to 12-year-old students with emotional and behavioral disorders (Frederickson, 2010; Frederickson & Turner, 2003). The primary purpose of Circle of Friends is to establish a supportive meeting each week (for about 1 hour) to provide opportunities for peers to learn to interact with and support their fellow students with emotional or behavior problems.

Circle of Friends

PROCEDURES: Circles of Friends are run by the counselor or school psychologist with the classroom teacher as a participant. The focus child is a student whom the teacher has identified as having significant behavior problems and peer interaction difficulties that would improve if peers in the classroom provided the appropriate interactions and supports. An outside leader (usually the school psychologist or counselor) conducts the Circle of Friends group. Students from the target student's class are included in the Circle of Friends. Typically, the target student is not present during the meetings.

ASSET—A Social Skills Program for Adolescents

Procedures

Each lesson is taught to a small group of adolescents. There are nine basic steps to each lesson:

1. Review homework and previously learned social skills.
2. Explain the new skill for the day's lesson.
3. Explain why the skill is important and should be learned and practiced.
4. Give a realistic and specific example to illustrate the use of the skill.
5. Examine each of the skill steps that are necessary to carry out the new social skill.
6. Model the skill, and provide opportunities for students and others to demonstrate correct and incorrect use of the skills.
7. Use verbal rehearsal to familiarize the students with the sequence of steps in each social skill, and provide a procedure for students to be automatic with their knowledge of the skill steps.
8. Use behavioral rehearsal to allow each student to practice and demonstrate the skill steps until they reach criterion.
9. Assign homework that provides opportunities for the students to practice the skills in other settings.

These nine steps are followed for each of the eight specific social skills listed here.

Comments

The ASSET program has been evaluated with eight students with LD (Hazel, Schumaker, Sherman, & Sheldon, 1982). That evaluation demonstrated that the students with LD involved in the intervention increased in the use of social skills in role-play settings. The curriculum guide provides specific teaching procedures and is particularly relevant to teachers working with adolescents. A DVD that includes video vignettes of the social skills, a leader's guide, and program materials are available from Research Press (www.researchpress.com).

Following are the main features in using Circle of Friends in the classroom:

1. During the first meeting, the leader explains to the group why the target student is not present and solicits the cooperation and support of the peers. Students who are participating are first asked to identify only the strengths and positive behaviors of the target student.

2. After the target student's positive behaviors have been identified, the leader asks students to identify the challenging behaviors that the target student exhibits. The leader makes links between the target student's difficult behaviors and the types of responses and supports that students could provide. Then the leader requests that six to eight students volunteer to serve as the Circle of Friends. The rest of the students are dismissed.

3. The Circle of Friends meets approximately eight times with the leader and the target student. During these meetings, students are reminded to follow the basic ground rules of confidentiality, seeking adult help if they are worried, and listening carefully to each person.

4. The leader and students identify a target behavior and roles that each of them will play to ensure that the target student can maintain the target behavior. Students role-play and set goals for the forthcoming week. Each week, they review and describe their success and establish new behavioral goals.

COMMENTS: Students with emotional and behavior disorders who participated in the Circle of Friends (Frederickson, 2010; Frederickson & Turner, 2003) were better accepted by their peers in the classroom after participation than were similar students who had not participated in such a program. Although the Circle of Friends did not influence students' overall perceptions of the climate of the classroom, it did (positively) influence their perceptions of the target student.

Skillstreaming: Structured Learning Structured learning is a psychoeducational and behavioral approach to teaching prosocial skills to students both with and without disabilities (Goldstein, Sprafkin, Gershaw, & Klein, 1980). Skillstreaming can be implemented by teachers, social workers, psychologists, or school counselors. The program is available for young children (McGinnis & Goldstein, 2003), elementary-age children (McGinnis & Goldstein), as well as adolescents (Goldstein, McGinnis, Sprafkin, Gershaw, & Klein, 1997). Skillstreaming continues to be implemented with positive outcomes for youngsters (e.g., Sheridan et al., 2011).

The first component, *modeling,* involves a verbal and behavioral description of the target skill as well as the steps that compose the target skill. At this point, the teacher might role-play the steps in the skill, and other models may also role-play, exhibiting the target skill itself. During the second step, students are encouraged to enact role-plays based on actual life experiences. These role-plays are facilitated by coaching and cues from the teacher. Next, the teacher and other observers provide feedback. Specific attention is paid to elements of each role-play that were effective and appropriate. Skills that were not role-played effectively are modeled by the teacher. In the final step, students are provided with opportunities to practice the steps and skills in the real world (e.g., outside the classroom).

The structured learning procedure for elementary students offers 60 prosocial skills and their constituent steps, arranged into five groups: classroom survival skills, friendship-making skills, skills for dealing with feelings, skill alternatives to aggression, and skills for dealing with stress. The structured learning procedure for adolescents also has 60 prosocial skills. It differs from the program for elementary students by including skills related to planning and decision making.

Principles for Teaching Social Skills

Teachers need to consider a number of points relevant to teaching social skills, no matter what social skills program they use:

1. *Develop cooperative learning.* Classrooms can be structured so that there is a win–lose atmosphere in which children compete with each other for grades and teacher attention, or structured so that children work on their own with little interaction among classmates, or structured for cooperative learning so children work alone, with pairs, and with groups, helping each other master the assigned material. Teachers can structure learning activities so that they involve cooperative learning and teach students techniques for working with pairs or in a group. The following four elements need to be present for cooperative learning to occur in small groups (D. W. Johnson & Johnson, 2009; R. T. Johnson & Johnson, 1986):

> In this **video** ▶, you will watch a numerous strategies that support students' appropriate social skill instruction within the context of an academic lesson. What methods does the teacher suggest to use? How do they benefit the students?

a. Students must perceive that they cannot succeed at the required task unless all members of the group succeed. This may require appropriate division of labor and giving a single grade for the entire group's performance.

b. There must be individual accountability so that each member of the group is assessed and realizes that his or her performance is critical for group success.

c. Students must have the necessary collaborative skills to function effectively in a group. This may include managing conflicts, active listening, leadership skill, and problem solving.

d. Sufficient time for group process must be allowed, including discussing how well the group is performing, developing a plan of action, and identifying what needs to happen.

2. *Students benefit from working with peers in supportive and academically structured activities.* Students not only benefit academically when interventions focus on reading and math outcomes; there is also a small effect for social, self-concept, and behavioral outcomes (Ginsburg-Block, Rohrbeck, & Fantuzzo, 2006). Thus, there are benefits academically as well as socially.

3. *Use principles of effective instruction.* Many teachers claim that they do not know how to teach social skills. Considering the social skills difficulties of special education students, methods of teaching social skills to students may need to become part of teacher training programs.

Teaching social skills requires implementing principles of effective instruction. These are used and explained throughout this text and include obtaining student commitment, identifying target behavior, pretesting, teaching, modeling, rehearsing, role-playing, providing feedback, practicing in controlled settings, practicing in other settings, posttesting, and follow-up. Following are social skills that learning- and behavior-disordered students frequently need to be taught:

- *Body language.* This includes how students walk, where they stand during a conversation, what their body language "says," gestures, eye contact, and appropriate facial reactions.

- *Greetings.* Teaching greetings may include expanding students' repertoire of greetings, selecting appropriate greetings for different people, and interpreting and responding to the greetings of others.

- *Initiating and maintaining a conversation.* This includes a wide range of behaviors such as knowing when to approach someone; knowing how to ask inviting, open questions; knowing how to respond to comments made by others; and maintaining a conversation with a range of people, including those who are too talkative and those who volunteer little conversation.

- *Giving positive feedback.* Knowing how and when to give sincere, genuine, positive feedback and comments.

- *Accepting positive feedback.* Knowing how to accept positive feedback from others.

- *Giving negative feedback.* Knowing how and when to give specific negative feedback.

- *Accepting negative feedback.* Knowing how to accept negative feedback from others.

- *Identifying feelings in self and others.* Through the ability to recognize feelings in both self and others, students are able to predict how they will feel in a given situation and prepare for responding appropriately to one's own and others' feelings.

- *Problem solving and conflict resolution.* Knowing and using problem-solving skills to prevent and solve difficulties.

4. *Teach for transfer of learning.* For social skills to transfer or generalize to other settings, the program must require the rehearsal and implementation of target skills across settings. Social skills training programs need to ensure that learned skills are systematically demonstrated in the classroom, on the playground, and at home.

5. *Empower students.* Many students with learning difficulties feel discouraged and unable to influence their learning. They turn the responsibility for learning over to the teacher and become passive learners. How can we empower students?

- *Choice.* Students need to feel that they are actively involved in their learning.

- *Consequences.* Students will learn from the natural and logical consequences of their choices.

- *Documented progress.* In addition to teacher documentation of progress made, students need to learn procedures for monitoring and assessing their progress.

- *Control.* Students need to feel as though they can exercise control over what happens to them. Some students feel as though their learning is in someone else's hands and therefore is someone else's responsibility.

6. *Identify strengths.* When developing social skills interventions for students with special needs, be sure to consider their strengths as well as their needs. Because appearance and athletic ability relate to social acceptance, these areas need to be considered when determining the type of social intervention needed. For example, if a youngster's physical appearance is a strength, the teacher can compliment the student on his or her hair, what the student is wearing, or how neat and sharp the student looks. Also, knowing something about the students' areas of strength can be helpful in identifying social contexts that may be promising for promoting positive peer interactions. For example, a student with LD who is a particularly good swimmer and a member of a swim team may find it easier to make friends on the swim team than in the academic setting. Students with LD who acquire strengths in appearance and athletic activities may have areas of strength from which to build their social skills. However, many children with LD do not have the motor ability or eye–hand coordination to succeed in the athletic area. Other areas, such as hobbies or special interests, can be presented in the classroom so that the student with LD has an opportunity to be perceived as one who is knowledgeable. Students with learning and behavior disorders who are not well accepted by their classmates may have friends in the neighborhood or within their families (e.g., cousins). Perhaps the most important point to remember is that if a child is not well accepted by peers at school, this does not necessarily mean that the child does not have effective social relationships outside of the school setting.

7. *Reciprocal friendships.* Reciprocal friendship is the mutual identification as "best friend" by two students; that is, a student who identifies another student as his or her best friend is also identified by that same youngster as a best friend. It has been hypothesized that reciprocal friendships play an important role in reducing the negative effects of low peer acceptance (Vaughn, McIntosh, et al., 1993). From this perspective, it may be less important to increase the overall acceptance of a student in the classroom and more effective to concentrate on the development of a mutual best friend. Because it is quite unlikely that all students in the classroom are going to like all of the other youngsters equally, development of a reciprocal friendship is a more realistic goal for most youngsters with learning and behavior problems.

Preparing the Instructional Environment

How should teachers arrange the instructional environment of the classroom to promote appropriate behavior? As she completed her first year of teaching as a junior high special education teacher, Ms. Habib commented,

I'm really looking forward to next year. The first year of teaching has to be the hardest. There is so much to get organized at the beginning of the year, so many decisions to be made, and so many new routines and procedures to learn. You need to determine how to arrange the room to facilitate learning, what materials to select or develop, and how to organize the materials so that the students can find them easily. You must decide how to group the students and how to schedule them into the room. In comparison to this year, next year should be a breeze. I'll be able to spend much more time refining my teaching skills, focusing on the students, and strengthening the program.

In many ways, Ms. Habib is a manager, as are all teachers. We will explore some of the decisions that teachers have to consider in getting started, and look at some options they might consider in making those decisions. Many of the important decisions that you will be making will influence the classroom management and behavior of your students.

Arranging the Environment

The teaching–learning process takes place within a specific context. Making this context or environment pleasant and conducive to learning can facilitate the teaching–learning process. Furthermore, considering how the environment may be arranged to "prevent" behavior problems is an important consideration.

> In this **video** ▶, the important features of a functional and flexible classroom environment are described. What methods can you use when arranging your future classroom? What problems could occur if teachers do not consider these factors?

Instructional Arrangement

The term *instructional arrangement* refers to the manner in which a teacher organizes instructional groups to promote learning and behavior. Inclusive settings require arranging grouping instruction with general education teachers. Generally, there are six instructional arrangements: large-group instruction, small-group instruction, one-to-one instruction, independent learning, cooperative learning, peer teaching, and classwide peer tutoring. Effective instruction and management of behavior require aligning the instructional arrangement with the learning needs of students with consideration of how it might also promote effective behavior.

Large-Group Instruction In large-group instruction, a teacher usually provides support or explicit instruction to a group of six or more students. Large-group instruction is appropriate when the goal of instruction is similar for all students. Teachers often use this type of instructional arrangement when there are particular instructional practices or content knowledge that it is helpful for all students to acquire at the same time. This arrangement is also useful when the teacher is providing a "model" (e.g., demonstrating how to effectively solve a math problem) or when the teacher is promoting discussion (e.g., the teacher asks students to discuss the factors that contributed to a social studies event). Large-group instruction can be used both for didactic instruction (i.e., instruction in which one person, usually the teacher, provides information) and for interactive instruction (i.e., when students and teachers discuss and share information). In large-group instruction, students generally have less opportunity to get feedback about their performance and less opportunity to receive corrective feedback. Because large-group instruction is the most frequently used arrangement in general education classrooms, students can benefit from opportunities

to learn in other grouping formats, particularly small-group instruction.

Following are some activities that teachers can implement to make large-group instruction as effective as possible:

- Ask all students a comprehension question, and then ask them to discuss their answer with a partner. This gives all students in the group an opportunity to reflect and comment on the question.

- Provide a whiteboard and a marker or paper and pencil to all students in the large group. Ask them to write words, sentences, letters, or answers as you instruct the group as a whole.

- Use informal member checks to determine whether students in the group agree, disagree, or have a question about what they are learning.

- Ask selected students to provide in their own words a summary of points of view that have been expressed by several different students in the group.

- Distribute lesson reminder sheets that provide students with a structure for answering questions about what they learned from a lesson, what they liked about what they learned, and what else they would like to learn. This increases the likelihood that students will attend to lessons and learn more.

- Model how to solve a math problem, and then provide students an opportunity to solve a similar problem with feedback from other students and the teacher.

What are some of the ways teachers can promote positive behavior within a large-group setting? First, establish guidelines for appropriate responding in the large group. "As I explain how to do the math problem, I'm going to stop and review. I will call on students to respond. Please wait for me to call your name before responding." Second, provide multiple opportunities for group response and individual response with feedback. Large-group instruction that involves too much teacher talk and modeling without adequate time for students to respond with feedback is less likely to be successful. Third, tell students frequently what you like about their behavior. For example, "all of you are listening while I'm explaining this," "thank you for raising your hands to respond."

Small-Group Instruction Small-group instruction usually consists of groups of more than two students but fewer than six. Small-group instruction is effective when the teacher wants to provide specific instruction to target students that allows for feedback and support. Teachers form small groups of students who either are at different ability levels (heterogeneous groups) or have similar abilities in a particular curriculum area (homogeneous groups).

One benefit of using small groups is that a teacher can individualize instruction to meet each group's specific needs. For example, during a cooperative learning activity in which students are grouped heterogeneously, the teacher is able to give a mini lesson to a group that is having difficulty working together.

Same-ability, or homogeneous, groups are often used for teaching those specific elements of instruction that are specifically needed by the target students either because they need additional practice or need to learn prerequisite skills not needed by other students. In using small-group instruction, a teacher usually involves one group of students while the remaining students participate in independent learning, cooperative learning, or peer tutoring. Sometimes teachers who work in resource rooms schedule students so that only two to five students come at one time; thus, all the students can participate in small-group instruction at once. Many teachers prefer using a horseshoe table arrangement for small-group instruction because it allows them to easily reach their instructional materials and to closely interact with students.

Following are some of the activities that teachers can implement to make small-group instruction as effective as possible:

- Arrange your instructional schedule to allow for daily small-group instruction for students who are behind in reading and several times a week for all other students.
- Provide flexible small-group instruction that addresses the specific skills and instructional needs of students.
- Use student-led small groups to reteach or practice previously taught information, reread stories, develop and answer questions, and provide feedback on writing pieces.

What are some ways teachers can promote appropriate behavior during small-group instruction? First, teachers can establish and review expectations during small-group behavior. For example, explaining to students, "I am going to review how to write a summary of text, and then I am going to do a text summary with the group while you write on your white boards. Next I'm going to ask each of you to work individually to complete a summary of a new text, and I'll give you feedback while you are reading and writing." Second, ensure that students in the group are provided work that they can do or that is modified to meet their instructional needs. Third, provide students an opportunity to practice with feedback that both facilitates learning and keeps them motivated and interested.

One-to-One Instruction One-to-one instruction occurs when a teacher works individually with a student. This instructional arrangement allows the teacher to provide intensive instruction, closely monitoring student progress and modifying and adapting procedures to match the student's learning patterns. The Fernald (1943) visual-auditory-kinesthetic-tactile (VAKT) method of teaching word identification and Reading Recovery, discussed in Chapter 7, recommends a one-to-one instructional arrangement. At least some one-to-one instruction is recommended for students with learning and behavior problems because it provides them with some time each day to ask questions and receive assistance from the teacher. The major drawback of one-to-one instruction is that while one student is working with the teacher, the other students need to be actively engaged in learning. To accomplish this, independent learning, cooperative learning, peer teaching, and classwide peer tutoring are frequently used. Managing student behavior in one-on-one teaching is typically not challenging, but many of the practices about establishing routines, providing feedback and encouragement, and aligning instruction to students' learning needs apply.

Independent Learning Independent learning is one way to enable students to practice skills about which they have already received instruction and have acquired some proficiency. Teachers frequently associate independent learning with individual worksheets, but computer activities or various assignments such as listening to an audio book, writing a story, reading a library book, or making a map for a social studies unit can also be independent learning activities. The key to successful independent learning is to ensure that the assignments and activities are ones that students have had significant practice in and have demonstrated that they can complete or initiate with little teacher guidance or feedback.

Ensuring that a student can complete an independent learning activity can be accomplished through questioning activities. For example, when Miriam selects library books, Ms. Martino asks Miriam to read about 100 words to her, and then she asks Miriam several questions. If Miriam misses 5 or fewer words and can answer the questions easily, then Ms. Martino encourages her to read the book on her own. If Miriam misses 5 to 10 words, then Ms. Martino arranges for her to read the book using cooperative learning or peer tutoring. If Miriam misses more than 10 words and struggles to answer the questions, then Ms. Martino may encourage her to select another book. In fact, Ms. Martino has taught Miriam and the rest of the students in her self-contained classroom for students with behavior disorders the Five-Finger Rule: "If in reading the first couple of pages of a book, you know the words except for about five and you can ask yourself and answer five questions about what you have read, then this book is probably a good one for you to read."

How can teachers support appropriate student behavior during independent learning tasks? The first thing to consider is expectations for students during independent learning. Typically, the teacher is working with another group of students and is hoping for minimal interruptions. Providing a mechanism for students to alert you that they have a question without interrupting you is valuable. One way to do this is to have several question cards in a central location in the room. These cards can look like large question marks. If a student has a question, they can take a card and put it at their learning station. When you have a good time to stop with the group you are instructing, you can go to the learning stations of the students with questions and address them.

Cooperative Learning Cooperative learning, sometimes considered team-based learning, occurs when students work together and use each other as resources for learning. Four basic elements need to be included for small-group learning to be cooperative: interdependence, collaborative skills, individual accountability, and group processing (D. W. Johnson, Johnson, & Smith, 2007; Michaelsen & Sweet, 2008). How can teachers establish interdependence with their students working in cooperative groups?

- Create a learning environment in which students perceive that the goal of the group is for all members to learn, that is, interdependence; everyone sees that it is to their advantage for all members of the group to succeed.
- Consequences are based, at least in part, on group performance rather than individual performance; thus better learners are motivated to support students with learning needs.
- All members of the group receive the materials needed to complete the task.
- Students have complementary roles that foster the division of labor. For example, one student may serve in the role of the group leader, another as the recorder of the ideas, and another as the team spokesperson.

Collaborative skills are required for a group to work together effectively. These collaborative skills can be taught to students explicitly by defining skills and their importance, modeling how the skills are used, allowing students to practice skills in cooperative groups, and providing students with corrective feedback. Individual accountability ensures that each student is responsible for learning the required material and contributing to the group. Teacher evaluations (e.g., of quizzes, individual products) can help to determine whether each student has learned the material. Students can also use progress-monitoring forms to track their own behavior and progress. Progress-monitoring forms might include questions such as, "How did I contribute to the learning of the group today?" and "In what way did I help or not help my group to complete our work?" Providing opportunities for the group to evaluate how well they did and how they might improve their performance in the future may be useful.

Apply the Concept 4-6 provides additional guidelines for including students with disabilities in cooperative learning groups.

Two basic formats for cooperative learning are often used in general or special education classrooms. In a *group project,* students pool their knowledge and skills to create a project or complete an assignment. All students in the group participate in the decisions and tasks that ensure completion of the project. Using the *jigsaw format,* each student in a group is assigned a task that must be completed for the group to reach its goal. For example, in completing a fact-finding sheet on fossils, each student might be assigned to read a different source to obtain information for the different facts required on the sheet.

What considerations might teachers have when managing student behavior during cooperative groups?

- Consider establishing guidelines for how members of the group interact including providing opportunities for each member of the group to contribute.
- Consider how you might evaluate both individual performance and group performance.
- Provide a mechanism for members of the group to evaluate their own performance and that of the group as a whole.
- Provide a mechanism for members of the group to help each other.
- Consider how to prevent group members from dominating decisions and progress.
- Ensure that all members of the group take responsibility for the product.

Cooperative learning has been integrated into several approaches to teaching reading, math, writing, and even content area learning such as social studies and science. In future chapters you will learn about cooperative learning practices specifically applied to these instructional areas.

Opportunities to participate in cooperative learning experiences are particularly important for students with learning and behavior problems. As well as supporting development of targeted academic skills, cooperative learning helps students experience positive interactions with peers and develop strategies for supporting others. In orchestrating cooperative learning, it is important to provide students with sufficient directions that they understand the purpose of the activity and the general rules

Guidelines for Including Students with Special Needs in Cooperative Learning Activities

When students with disabilities are included in a cooperative group lesson in the general education classroom, teachers may consider the following to facilitate their success:

- Adjust group size, and create heterogeneous groups of students who are likely to work well together. Would some students benefit from three students in a group instead of four or five? Are there target students in the class who work particularly well with students with special needs?

- Identify the strengths of the students with special needs, and provide them opportunities to serve in roles in their groups that maximize what they do well and still provide them opportunities to learn. For example, if a student is a good public speaker, allow him or her to be the group spokesperson.

- Consider each student's individualized education program (IEP) goals and academic strengths and weaknesses when assigning roles. For example, modifications in materials may be necessary if a student with below-grade-level reading skills is assigned the role of reading directions.

- Arrange the room to ensure face-to-face interaction between students and to make groups easily accessible to the teacher. Round tables work well, but chairs clustered together or open floor areas can also be used.

- Inform students of criteria for both academic and interpersonal success. Some teachers hand out a grading rubric with an outline of specific criteria for grading in each area of evaluation (e.g., creativity, neatness, group work, correct information, quiz).

- Provide mini lessons before and/or during the cooperative group activity to teach academic or cooperative skills. Students need to know what group work "looks like," and many teachers conduct several lessons on how to work in cooperative groups before beginning the learning activities. Teachers can also provide small doses of instruction to individual groups during the activity, as needed.

- Monitor and evaluate both individual achievement and group work. Many teachers carry a clipboard with students' names and lesson objectives so that they can record student progress as they monitor groups.

- Reflect on the cooperative learning activity, and note changes for future lessons. Did the lesson go as well as you would have liked? Did students learn the required material?

for working in groups. Initially, a teacher may want to participate as a collaborator, modeling such behaviors as asking what the other people think, not ridiculing other collaborators for what they think, and helping other collaborators and accepting help from others. As students become comfortable in collaborating, they can work cooperatively in teams without the teacher's input.

Peer Teaching In the peer-teaching instructional arrangement, one student who has learned the targeted skills (the tutor) assists another student in learning those skills. This type of teaching takes place under a teacher's supervision. When using peer teaching, the teacher needs to plan the instruction and demonstrate the task to student pairs. The tutor then works with the learner, providing assistance and feedback. One advantage of peer teaching is that it increases opportunities for the student learning the skills to practice and get feedback, thus peer teaching is most beneficial for practicing acquiring skills.

One important aspect of peer teaching is preparing the students to serve as peer tutors by teaching them specific instructional and feedback routines to ensure success (D. Fuchs, Fuchs, Mathes, & Simmons, 1997).

Students benefit from learning basic instructional procedures for providing reinforcement and corrective feedback and for knowing when to ask the teacher for assistance. For example, in Mr. Hyde's seventh-grade social studies class, students learned to work with peers to practice talking about the meaning of key concepts and terms. Each week, the key persons, places, and concepts are provided to pairs of students. As they are taught these key ideas, they record them in their social studies folders. Students are then given 10 minutes to turn to their partner and review the key ideas related to these key concepts.

Remember that poor readers show academic and social gains in both the tutor and tutee roles (Elbaum, Vaughn, Hughes, & Moody, 1999). Therefore, it is important to alternate roles so that students get the chance to benefit from serving as both the tutor and the tutee. You may wonder how you might effectively integrate students with learning and behavior problems as tutors in your classroom. Research focusing on peer tutoring with special education students has most frequently been used to teach or monitor basic skills such as letter–sound connections, oral reading, answering reading comprehension questions, and practicing spelling words, math facts, and new sight-word vocabulary (e.g., Rafdal, McMaster, McConnell, Fuchs, & Fuchs, 2011). In these cases, students with disabilities can be taught procedures for leading the peer-pairing practice (e.g., reading the sight words on the card and then showing them to their partner to read), thus serving in the role of tutor. Peer tutoring improves a broad array of social and academic outcomes for students with severe disabilities, as well as increasing their access to the general education curriculum (Carter & Kennedy, 2006).

Another important type of peer teaching is cross-age tutoring, in which older students instruct younger ones. Cross-age tutoring has many advantages, including the fact that older students are supposed to know more than younger students, so there is less stigma about being tutored. Also, both the tutor and the tutee enjoy the opportunity to meet someone of a different age. Another aspect of cross-age tutoring that can be effective is allowing students with LD or behavior disorders to tutor younger students who also demonstrate LD or behavior disorders.

Classwide Peer Tutoring Classwide peer tutoring is a structured technique for improving students' reading abilities. Students of different reading levels are paired (e.g., a high or average reader is paired with a low reader) and work together on a sequence of organized activities such as oral reading, story retelling, and summarization. The reading material can be a basal reader, a trade book or magazine, or other appropriate material. The criterion is that the lower reader in each pair must be able to easily read the materials assigned to his or her dyad. Peer pairing can occur within class, across classes but within grade, and across grades. This teaching takes place under a teacher's supervision. Peer teaching increases the opportunities for a student to respond by allowing peers to supervise, model reading, ask questions, and generally support their classmates' participation in reading. When using peer teaching, the teacher needs to plan the instruction and demonstrate the task to the pair. The tutor then works with the learner, providing assistance and feedback.

Extensive research on classwide peer tutoring reveals that students with disabilities as early as kindergarten (e.g., D. Fuchs et al., 2003), as well as secondary students (Calhoon & Fuchs, 2003), benefit when the procedure is implemented consistently (e.g., 30-minute sessions conducted three times per week for at least 16 weeks). Students of all ability levels demonstrate improved reading fluency and comprehension.

Partner learning is not limited to elementary school or only as a means to enhance reading fluency. Studies have demonstrated that partner learning can also improve students' outcomes in world history, reading, math,

and across academic areas (Maheady, Harper, & Mallette, 2001; Mastropieri, Scruggs, Spencer, & Fontana, 2003).

WEB RESOURCES

For further information on two related peer-tutoring practices, view the following Web site: Peer-Assisted Learning Strategies (PALS) (What Works Clearing House, Intervention: Peer-Assisted Learning Strategies, http://ies.ed.gov/ncee/wwc/interventionreport .aspx?sid=364.

Physical Arrangement The physical layout of a classroom should be flexible enough to allow for different instructional arrangements. For example, the individual learning area can be reorganized into a large-group instructional area by rearranging the desks. The small-group instructional area can also be used for a cooperative learning project.

Following are eight ideas to keep in mind when developing the room arrangement:

1. To the extent possible, place the recreational and audiovisual/computer areas away from the teaching area. These areas will naturally be somewhat noisier than the other areas.

2. Place student materials in an area where students can easily get to the materials without bothering other students or the teacher.

3. Place your teaching materials directly behind where you teach so that you can reach materials without having to leave the instructional area.

4. If there is a time-out area, place it out of the direct line of traffic and use partitions that keep a student in the time-out area from having visual contact with other students.

   See Chapter 2 for principles governing the use of time-out.

5. Make the recreational area comfortable, with a carpet, comfortable reading chairs, pillows, and a small game table, if possible.

6. Place all the materials needed for a learning center in the learning center area. In this way, students will not be moving around the room to collect needed materials.

7. Instruct several students as to where materials and supplies are kept so that when students cannot find something, they do not ask you, but ask other students.

8. Establish procedures and settings for students who have completed tasks and/or are waiting for the teacher.

Instructional Materials and Equipment

Selecting, developing, and organizing instructional materials and equipment are important aspects of classroom management. Whether selecting or developing materials, there are several factors to consider:

- What evidence is there that these materials or curricula have been effective with students with learning and behavior problems?
- What curricular areas (e.g., reading, English, math, social skills) will I be responsible for teaching?
- What are the academic levels of the students I will be teaching?
- In what instructional arrangement(s) do I plan to teach each curricular area?
- How can the materials be used across the stages of learning (i.e., acquisition, proficiency, maintenance, generalization, and application)?
- Will the materials provide a means for measuring learning?
- Are the materials designed for teacher-directed learning, student-to-student learning, or individual learning?
- Will materials need to be replaced, and do I have a budget to replace them?

Selecting Published Materials Besides considering the factors just mentioned, it is important to think of the cost, durability, consumability, and quality of published materials. Before materials are purchased, it is advantageous to evaluate them. Sample materials can generally be obtained from publishers or found at educational conferences or districtwide instructional centers. Teachers should read research reports that provide information about the effectiveness of materials. When research is not available, it is often useful to talk with other teachers who use materials to determine when and with whom they are effective. Sometimes it is possible to borrow the materials and have the students try them and evaluate them.

Publishers may be interested in how their materials work with low-achieving students and students with learning and behavior problems. They may be willing to provide a set of materials if the teacher is willing to evaluate the materials and provide feedback about how the materials work with target students.

Selecting and Using Instructional Equipment In addition to selecting instructional materials, teachers will want to choose equipment to facilitate learning. Along with various software programs, such equipment is becoming an increasingly important part of a teacher's toolkit. In addition to a computer in the classroom and/or the use of a computer lab in the school, other equipment can facilitate learning in your classroom.

Digital Recorders Digital recorders are relatively inexpensive and can be used in a variety of ways in the classroom. Headphones allow students to listen without disturbing others. Following are 10 instructional applications for recorders:

1. A teacher can record reading books so that students can follow along during recreational reading or use for repeated reading.

2. One way to adapt textbooks is to record them.

3. It is helpful for some students to record what they want to write before they begin writing. They can record their ideas and then listen to them as they write their first drafts.

4. Students can record their reading every 2 to 4 weeks to hear their progress. After a student records his or her reading, it is important that the teacher and the student discuss the reading, identifying strengths and areas that need improvement. This recording can also be shared with parents to demonstrate progress and document continuing needs.

5. Spelling tests can be recorded so that students can take them independently. The teacher first records the words to be tested, allowing time for the students to spell the words. After the test is recorded, the teacher spells each word so that the student can self-check.

6. When working on specific social or pragmatic language skills (e.g., answering the telephone, asking for directions, introducing someone), record the students so that they can listen to and evaluate themselves. Sims 3 by Electronic Arts Inc.

   Children can create and be part of communities that they and others create. These programs continue to be creative, engaging, and highly entertaining.

7. At the secondary level, class lectures can be recorded. Students can then listen to review the material and complete unfinished notes.

8. Students can practice taking notes by listening to recordings of lectures. By using recordings, students can regulate the rate at which the material is presented.

9. Oral directions for independent learning activities can be recorded for students. This can be particularly helpful when a teacher is trying to conduct small-group or one-to-one instruction while other students are working on independent learning activities.

10. Many instructional materials contain prerecorded resources.

Using LCD Projectors or Smart Boards These excellent teaching tools allow users to display the images and to develop them while teaching.

The following are suggestions that may be helpful:

1. Keep the amount of information presented relatively limited.

2. Use a different-colored pen to highlight important points.

3. Have extra markers available.

4. Use the tools to develop language experience stories.

5. Use the tools to demonstrate editing and revisions in writing.

6. Use the tools along with a think-aloud procedure (e.g., teacher talks-aloud what they are thinking while they perform math problem) to demonstrate math procedures such as how to work long division.

7. These tools can record students' responses to your questions and then display them for the entire group/class to review.

Other Small Equipment Several other pieces of small equipment should be considered in selecting equipment for either a resource room or a self-contained classroom.

• A stopwatch can serve as an instructional tool and a motivator. For some tasks, it is important that students learn to respond at an automatic level (e.g., sight words, math facts). Students can use a stopwatch to time themselves or their classmates. These times can then be recorded on a time chart (see Figure 4-8). Using these charts, students can set goals, record their times, and try to improve on previous times.

• An individual writing board is an excellent tool for obtaining individual written responses during small group and large group discussions. Mr. Howell uses these boards during review sessions in his resource high school history class. During the review sessions, he asks students questions, and they write their answers on the writing boards. He then asks them to display their boards. In this way, each student responds to each question in writing instead of one student orally responding to one question. Mr. Howell and the students believe that this is a better way to review because it requires them to think about and answer every question and to write the answers. Writing is important because it is generally required when the students take tests. Although small chalkboards can be used as individual writing boards, white boards and dry-erase markers are now readily available.

Developing Instructional Materials In addition to purchasing published materials and equipment, most teachers find the need to develop their own instructional materials to supplement commercial materials. For

FIGURE 4-8 Time Chart

example, some teachers make sentence strips containing the sentences from each story in a beginning reader. Many teachers develop materials to provide students with additional practice in skills they are learning. Developing self-correcting materials and/or materials in a game format can be advantageous.

Self-Correcting Materials Self-correcting materials provide students with immediate feedback. Students with learning and behavior problems frequently have a history of failure and are reluctant to take risks when others are watching or listening. Self-correcting materials allow them to check themselves without sharing the information with others. Many computer programs and electronic learning games incorporate self-correction. Figure 4-9 presents an example of a self-correcting activity that teachers can easily make.

FIGURE 4-9 Self-Correcting Activity

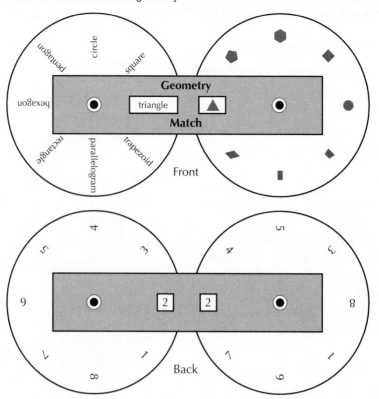

One key to self-correcting materials is immediate feedback (Mercer, Mercer, & Bott, 1984). The materials should be simple enough that students can learn to use them easily and check their answers quickly. The materials should be varied so that the interest and novelty level remain relatively high.

Another key to developing self-correcting materials is to make them durable so that they can be reused. Using heavy cardboard can increase the durability of materials. Laminating or covering the materials with clear contact paper are good ways to make materials more durable. Special markers or grease pencils can then be used.

Instructional Games Students with learning and behavior problems often need numerous opportunities to practice an academic skill. Instructional games can provide this practice in a format that is interesting to students.

The first step in designing an instructional game is to determine the purpose of the game. For example, the purpose might be to provide practice in the following:

- Forming word families (e.g., -at: *fat, sat, cat, rat*)
- Identifying sight words associated with a specific piece of reading material being used in the classroom
- Using semantic and syntactic clues by using the cloze procedure (e.g., "For dessert Brian wanted an icecone.")

- Recalling multiplication facts
- Reviewing information (e.g., identifying the parts of a flower)

The second step is to select and adapt a game that can be used to practice a skill or review knowledge. For example, commercial games such as Monopoly®, Chutes and Ladders®, Candyland®, Clue®, Sorry®, and Parcheesi® can be adapted for classroom use. A generic game board can also be used (see Figure 4-10). Generic game boards can be purchased from some publishing companies. The key in selecting and adapting a game is to require the students to complete the instructional task as part of the turn-taking procedure. For example, when Candyland is adapted to practice sight words, students select a sight word card and a Candyland card. If they can correctly read the sight word, then they can use their Candyland card to move as indicated. When Monopoly is adapted for math facts, students first have to select and answer a math fact. If they answer it correctly, they earn the opportunity to throw the dice and take a turn.

When the same skills are being practiced by many students in a class, the teacher may want to develop a specific game for the skill. Math Marathon® is a specific game in which students move forward on a game board, depicting a race, by answering math word problems. Different sets of math word problem game cards can be developed, depending on the students' problem-solving ability levels.

FIGURE 4-10 Generic Board Game

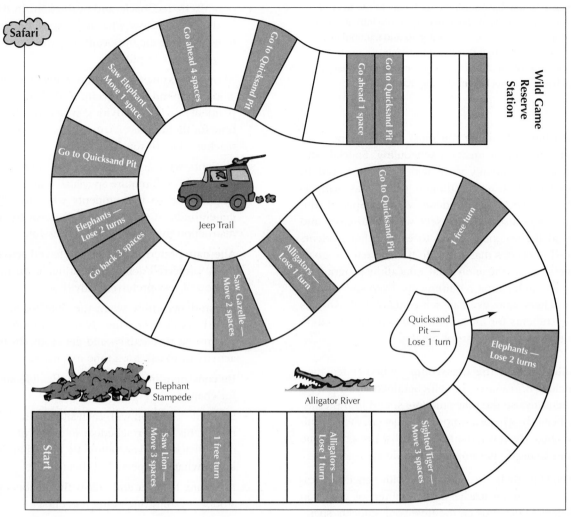

1. You are on a safari, trying to get to the Wild Game Reserve Station.
2. Begin at Start.
3. Each player rolls a die. The player with the highest number goes first.
4. Roll the die and draw a Game Card. If you answer the Game Card correctly, move the number shown on the die. If you do not answer the Game Card correctly, do not take a turn.
5. The first player to get to the Wild Game Reserve Station wins.

The third step is to write the directions and develop the materials. With a manila folder, the name of the game can be written on the tab, and the board can be stored so that the students can scan the tabs to find the game. The materials for the game can be kept in an envelope inside the folder. The directions for the game and a list of materials that should be found inside can be written on the envelope.

The fourth step is to demonstrate the game to the students so that they can learn to play it independently.

Organizing and Managing Materials Selecting and developing materials make up only one part of effective materials management. Classroom materials need to be organized in such a manner that the teacher and

students have easy access to the materials without bothering other students.

Ms. Beyar coteaches in a language arts classroom for 1 hour each day, during which the class is divided into either mixed-ability or same-ability groups, depending on the lesson. Ms. Beyar has several suggestions regarding managing materials in the general education classroom:

> The first thing Ms. Casey [the general education teacher] and I did was expand the student library. We purchased

In this **video** ▶, examine the methods used to guide students in obtaining and using the necessary materials, and classroom space, to successfully complete their projects. What tips can you take from this teacher and his students?

books that represent a wider range of reading levels. We also began to purchase small sets of books to use in reading groups. Finally, we worked together to organize a closet and a file cabinet with adapted materials and manipulatives that we both use. I find that these materials are beneficial with children of all ability levels. I didn't realize that we would benefit so much from sharing materials!

Scheduling

When teachers talk about the most difficult aspects of their jobs, they often mention scheduling. Special education teachers generally work with between 5 and 10 general education teachers (though it can be as many as 25 teachers) to coordinate students' services. Special education teachers also work closely with counselors and teachers at the secondary level to ensure that students are placed in classes that will help them reach the goals and objectives of the individual education program as well as meet graduation requirements. Even special education teachers who work in self-contained classrooms schedule students for integration into general education classroom activities for part of the day.

Scheduling within the Classroom Whether teaching in an inclusion, resource, or self-contained classroom, it is important to use the time students spend in the classroom efficiently. There are no easy answers to scheduling problems. However, the following list presents some guidelines to use in developing a schedule:

- Schedule time to communicate with general education classroom teachers. The amount of time you schedule depends on the time your students spend in the general education classroom. Generally speaking, coteachers should schedule more time for this than resource teachers, and resource teachers should schedule more time than self-contained classroom teachers. While the frequency of such meetings will vary according to your students' needs, it is important that meeting times occur consistently. This time will prove invaluable in assisting students to be successful in regular classrooms.

- Schedule time to observe the classrooms in which your students are placed or are going to be placed. This alerts you to the class demands and schedules of the classroom, and will help you in planning for your students' learning in that classroom.

- Schedule time to meet with other professionals (e.g., speech/language pathologist, school psychologist).

- Alternate instructional arrangements. For example, do not schedule a student to participate in independent learning activities for more than 30 minutes at a time.

- Plan for time to provide the students with advance organizers, feedback, and evaluation. In this way, students will know what is going to happen, and they will have the opportunity to think about what they have accomplished.

- Allow for explicit instruction. Sometimes we have students spend the majority of their time in independent learning activities, which results in little time for them to receive direct instruction from the teacher, aide, or tutor.

- Students who are included in general education classrooms still require specialized instruction. Organize time so that students with disabilities in general education classrooms receive the explicit instruction they need to be successful.

- Alternate preferred and less preferred activities, or make preferred activities contingent on the completion of less preferred activities.

- Let students know when the time for an activity is just about over. This gives them time to reach closure on this activity and get ready for the next activity or to ask for a time extension.

- Be consistent in scheduling, yet flexible and ready for change.

- Schedule a session with each student in which you review his or her schedule in your room and in other teachers' classrooms. Be sure that students know what is expected of them.

- Plan time to meet and talk with members of your student's family, including parents.

Figures 4-11 and 4-12 present sample schedules for a resource room and a special education program. For the resource room, the schedule for one group of students is presented, whereas for the special education program, the entire day's schedule is presented.

Developing an Overall Schedule for a Resource Consultant Program Scheduling students' time while in the special education classroom is one issue, but the overall schedule for teaching in a resource or inclusion setting presents significant scheduling issues and requires that the teacher work closely with other teachers and professionals in the school. Teachers who assume roles as special education resource or inclusion teachers must first clarify and decide what their job responsibilities will be. Generally, these responsibilities can be divided into six general areas:

1. Providing direct instruction to the students, either in the general education classroom or in a separate classroom

2. Providing indirect instruction to the students by consulting with general education teachers and parents

FIGURE 4-11 Schedule for Fourth- Through Sixth-Grade Students

Date: 4/15

Time	José	Amelia	Scott	Todd	Carmen	Frank
10:00	Small Group Inferential Reading	Comprehension Computer Activity	Small Group Instruction Reading	Social Studies Text Using Request Procedure with Carmen	Social Studies Text Using Request Procedure with Todd	Small Group Instruction Reading
10:20	Inferential Comprehension Activity on Computer	Small Group Instruction Reading	Social Studies Text with Self-Questioning	Small Group Instruction Reading	Small Group Instruction Reading	Word Drill Social Studies Text with Self-Questioning
10:40	Writing Process	Writing Process	Writing Process (Computer)	Writing Process	Writing Process	Writing Process (Computer)
	Spelling	Spelling	Spelling	Spelling	Spelling	Spelling
11:15	Practice Computer	Practice Game	Practice Game	Practice Tape Recorder Test	Practice Game	Practice Game

FIGURE 4-12 Sample Schedule for Intermediate-Level Special Education Program

	Activity			
Time	**Group 1**	**Group 2**	**Group 3**	**Group 4**
8:15	Writing Process — Students working on reports			
9:15	Reading: Small group instruction (teacher)	Reading: Independent learning activities	Learning center: Map reading	Reading: Small group instruction (aide)
9:45	Reading: Independent learning activities	Reading: Small group instruction (aide)	Reading: Small group instruction (teacher)	Learning center: Map reading
10:15	Announcements			
10:20	Recess			
10:45	Math: Group instruction (teacher)		Computer lab for Math practice (aide)	
11:15	Computer lab (aide)		Group instruction (teacher)	
11:50	Lunch			
12:40	Recreational Reading/Writing			
1:00	Social Studies: Large group instruction			
1:45	Science: Cooperative learning activities			
2:15	Recess			
2:40	Health—Mon./Art—Tues./P.E.—Wed./Special Activity—Thurs., Fri. (Current: Producing a play)			
3:10	Earned "fun time" or time to complete work			
3:30	Dismissal			

3. Assessing current and referred students
4. Serving as an instructional resource for other teachers and professionals within the school
5. Planning, coteaching, and modifying instructional materials and/or assessments for students
6. Facilitating implementation of response to intervention (RTI) models in their schools

The time a teacher spends in each of these roles will directly influence the schedule he or she develops. For example, if the teacher's major roles are to provide instructional services indirectly to students, to assess current and referred students, and to serve as an instructional resource, then little time will be spent in scheduling groups of students in the resource room. Instead, the teacher will serve primarily as a consultant to others. A sample schedule for a teacher who provides direct and indirect support is presented in Figure 4-13.

By contrast with a teacher who is primarily a consultant, Ms. Beyar provides explicit instruction to most of the students she teaches for an average of 60 minutes per day, 4 days per week. Because she serves 22 students, she has developed a schedule that allows her some time to consult with general education teachers on a consistent

FIGURE 4-13 Coteaching Schedule

Week of: __April 15__

Time	Monday	Tuesday	Wednesday	Thursday	Friday
7:30	IEP Meeting	Instructional Review Meeting (2nd grade)	Child Study Team Meeting	IEP Meeting	Instructional Review Meeting (4th grade)
8:15	Work with 5th-grade low-reading group ———→				———→
9:00	Observe and assist LD/EH students in class-room (1st grade)	Assessment	Observe and assist (2nd grade, kindergarten)	3rd grade 4th grade	5th grade 6th grade
11:30	Meet with individual teachers	Planning and material development ———→		Meet with individual teachers	Planning and material development
12:30	Lunch ——————————————————————————→				———→
1:00	Work with 2nd-grade low-reading group ———→				———→
1:30	Conduct study skills class for selected 4th–6th graders	Conduct social skills class for group of EH students	Conduct study skills class	Conduct social skills class	Conduct study skills class
2:00	Work with Ms. Jones on implementing writing process ———→			Work with Mr. Peters on using semantic feature analysis for teaching vocabulary	Assessment
2:30	Provide direct instruction in reading to 5 students with learning disabilities ———→			———→	
3:30	Dismissal (check with teachers as needed) ———→				———→
3:45	End of day				

basis, but she has also allocated time to teach and assess current and referred students. To facilitate her scheduling, she has for the most part grouped students according to grade level, with the older students attending in the morning and the younger students in the afternoon.

She explains her schedule as follows:

I have arranged for the older students to come in the morning because I feel that I can take over the responsibility for teaching these students reading and writing—the content that is usually taught in the morning in many general education classrooms. I have developed a strong program in teaching reading comprehension, and I am using a process approach to teaching writing. Currently I am using content area textbooks, trade books, and literature for teaching reading comprehension, and the students are working on writing reports, literature critiques, and short stories on topics of their choice. Because I am responsible for these students' reading and writing, I am accountable for grading the students in these areas. Using this schedule, these students for the most part are in the general education classroom for content area subjects and math. I feel that this is important. When they go to junior high, they will probably be taking general math, science, social studies, and other content area classes. If they have been missing these classes in the general education classroom during the fourth through sixth grades, they will really have trouble catching up. It's hard enough for these students—we want to give them every advantage possible.

I often provide their reading instruction in content areas such as social studies and science. Thus, while the emphasis is on reading rather than knowledge acquisition, I feel that I am extending their background knowledge of concepts they will be taught in social studies and science.

I have the younger students come after lunch, because I feel that many of these students need two doses of reading, writing, and math. These students get instruction in these areas in the morning in the general education classroom, and then I give them additional instruction in the afternoon. With this arrangement, it is important that I communicate with the general education classroom teachers so that we each know what the other is doing. We don't want to confuse the students by giving them conflicting information or approaches to reading.

I also have one day a week that I use for assessment, consulting with classroom teachers, checking on the students in the general education classroom, and meeting and planning with my teaching assistant. I feel that this time is very important. All of my students spend most of the school day in the regular classroom. If they are really struggling in those settings, I need to know so that I can provide additional support.

There are always some exceptions to the general guidelines I use for scheduling. I have three students whom I monitor only in the general classroom. These students see me as a group on my assessment/consulting day. We talk about how it is going and discuss what is working for them and what frustrates them. I feel that this time is critical for their successful inclusion. I also have two fifth-grade students who have good oral language skills but are reading on the first-grade level. They come for an additional 30 minutes late in the day, and we use the Fernald VAKT method to learn sight words.

I also developed a special schedule for my teachers' aide. She works directly with students to supplement and enhance skills they have initiated with me. She also provides supports to students with learning and behavior problems in the general education classroom by providing modified assignments, homework, and assessments.

Special Considerations for Scheduling in Secondary Settings Scheduling in resource and consultant programs in secondary settings generally is less flexible than in elementary-level programs. Teachers must work within the confines of the instructional periods and the curricular units that students must complete for high school graduation. One of the major responsibilities for resource/ consultant teachers in secondary settings is to determine subject areas in which students need special classes and areas in which they can succeed in general education classes without instructional support. These decisions about scheduling must be made on an individual basis and should be made with the involvement and commitment of the student as well as the teachers involved.

With the greater use of learning and study strategies in secondary special education programs, secondary special education teachers may want to consider their role as that of learning and behavior specialists. As learning and behavior specialists at the secondary level, teachers spend part of their day consulting with the content area teachers/specialists, coteaching, discussing progress-monitoring measures and how to administer and use data, and approaches to successfully transitioning students to postsecondary experiences (e.g., 2- or 4-year college, work, or other professional training).

INSTRUCTIONAL ACTIVITIES

This section provides instructional activities related to developing socialization skills. Some of the activities teach new skills; others are best suited for practice and reinforcement of already acquired skills. For each activity, the objective, materials, and teaching procedures are described.

Please Help

OBJECTIVE: To teach students a process for asking for help when needed and yet continuing to work until assistance is given; to have a record-keeping system that allows the teacher to monitor how many times each day he or she assists each student.

GRADES: Primary and intermediate

MATERIALS: A 6- to 8-inch card that states "Please Help _____ [student's name]" and provides a place to list the date and comments

PLEASE HELP JENNIFER		
DATE	TIME	COMMENTS

TEACHING PROCEDURES: Construct the Please Help card for each student, including a place to mark the date and comments. Give all the students a card, and inform them that they are to place the card on their desks when they need help. They are to continue working until the teacher or someone else is able to provide assistance.

When you or your assistant is able to provide help, mark the date and time on the card and any appropriate comments such as "We needed to review the rules for long division," or "She could not remember the difference between long and short vowels," or "He solved the problem himself before I arrived."

Problem Box

OBJECTIVE: To give students an opportunity to identify problems they are having with others and to feel that their problems will be heard and attended to.

GRADES: All grades

MATERIALS: Shoebox decorated and labeled as "Problem Box"

TEACHING PROCEDURES: Show the students the box that is decorated and identified as the Problem Box. Place the box in a prominent location in the classroom. Tell the students that when they have problems with other students, teachers, or even at home, they can write the problems down and put them in the box. At the end of every day, you and the students will spend a designated amount of time (e.g., 15 minutes) reading problems and trying to solve them as a class. Be sure to tell students that they do not need to identify themselves or their notes.

During the designated time, open the Problem Box and read a selected note. Solicit assistance from the class in solving the note. Direct students' attention to identifying the problem, suggesting solutions, evaluating the consequences of the solutions, identifying a solution, and describing how it might be implemented.

A Date by Telephone

OBJECTIVE: To give students structured skills for obtaining a date by telephone.

GRADES: Secondary

MATERIALS: Two nonworking telephones

TEACHING PROCEDURES: Discuss with the students why preplanning a telephone call with a prospective date might be advantageous. Tell them that you are going to teach them some points to remember when calling to ask for a date. After you describe each of the following points, role-play them so that the students can observe their appropriate use:

1. Telephone at an *appropriate time.*
2. Use an *icebreaker,* such as recalling a mutually shared experience or a recent event in school.
3. *State what you would like to do, and ask him or her to do it.* Ask the person whether he or she likes to go to the movies. When there is an initial lull in the conversation, mention a particular movie that you would like to take her or him to, and state when you would like to go. Then ask the person whether he or she would like to go with you.
4. If yes, *make appropriate arrangements* for day, time, and transportation. If no, ask whether you can call again.

Be sure that each student has an opportunity to role-play.

Making and Keeping Friends

OBJECTIVE: To have students identify the characteristics of peers who are successful at making and keeping friends and, after identifying these characteristics, to evaluate themselves in how well they perform.

GRADES: Intermediate and secondary

MATERIALS: Writing materials

TEACHING PROCEDURES: Ask the students to think of children they know who are good at making and keeping friends. Brainstorm what these children do that makes them successful at making and keeping friends. On an overhead projector or chalkboard, write the student-generated responses about the characteristics of children who are good at making and keeping friends. Then select the most agreed-on characteristics, and write them on a sheet of paper with smiley faces, neutral faces, and frowning faces so that students can circle the face that is most like them in response to that characteristic. Finally, ask students to identify one characteristic that they would like to target to improve their skills at making and maintaining friends.

How Good Are You at Making and Keeping Friends?

Next to each item, circle the face that best describes how well you do.

1. I tell friends the truth.

2. I call friends on the phone.

3. I share my favorite toys and games with friends.

Identifying Feelings

OBJECTIVE: 77

GRADES: Primary and intermediate

MATERIALS: Cards with pictures of people in situations in which their feelings can be observed or deduced

TEACHING PROCEDURES: Select pictures that elicit feeling words such as *happy, angry, jealous, hurt, sad,* and *mad.* Show the pictures to the students, and ask them to identify the feelings of the people in the pictures. Discuss what information in the picture cued them to the emotional states of the people. Then ask the students to draw a picture of a time when they felt as the person in the picture feels. Conclude by asking students to discuss their pictures.

I'm New Here (and Scared)

By Sandra Stroud*

OBJECTIVE: To help students who are new to your community and school make a positive adjustment. For many students, moving to a new school can be an especially traumatic experience.

GRADES: K–12

MATERIALS: The *goodwill* of a group of socially competent student volunteers and their adult leader—a teacher, guidance counselor, or school administrator

TEACHING PROCEDURES: The adult in charge organizes a school service club whose purpose is to take new students under its wing and help them feel welcome at their school. Students in this organization can be given sensitivity training to help them understand how new students feel when they move to a new area of the country and enter a new school. The group can discuss and decide on the many strategies they can use to help new students feel at home. One of their functions could be to speak to whole classes about how it feels to be a new student at a school and to suggest how each student at this school can help new students when they arrive.

For a new student, nothing is quite as traumatic when entering a new school as having no friend or group with whom to sit when the students go to the cafeteria for lunch. Therefore, one of a new student's greatest needs is for someone to invite him or her to have lunch with them. This should be the number-one priority of the members of the welcoming club. New students may eventually become members of this club, joining in the effort of welcoming and helping the new students who follow them.

I'm in My Own Little House

By Sandra Stroud

OBJECTIVE: To help young children acquire a sense of personal space as well as an understanding of other people's space. Many young children have not acquired an inner sense of space—of their own space and of space that belongs to others. As a result, the more active of these youngsters, usually little boys, tend to intrude on other children's space and, in the process, annoy the other children. As a result, they may not be well liked by their classmates. The problem is made worse by the fact that many primary school children sit at long tables where the space of one student often overlaps the space of others.

*Note: This instructional activity was written by a mother who would have been so grateful if her son's middle school had had such a program when he entered the eighth grade there. As it was, things were pretty rough for him until his band teacher realized that he was skipping lunch. She paved the way for him to begin eating lunch with a group of boys who became his best friends.

GRADES: Primary

MATERIALS: Individual student desks, and colored masking tape

TEACHING PROCEDURES: The teacher arranges the room so that each student desk sits in a 3-square-foot area. The desks are just close enough to each other to make it possible for students to pass materials from one student to another without leaving their seats. On the floor around each desk, the teacher outlines the 3-square-foot block with colored masking tape.

The teacher explains the taped areas, or blocks, by telling a story about a child who wanted a little house that was all her own where no one would bother her or her belongings. This was "her" house. Just as her house was hers, she knew that the other children needed their houses and that she shouldn't bother them or their houses either. (The teacher makes up the story according to his or her imagination or to fit the situation in the classroom.)

Introducing People
By Dheepa Sridhar

OBJECTIVE: To teach students to introduce friends to one another appropriately.

GRADES: Intermediate and secondary

MATERIALS: None required

TEACHING PROCEDURES: Discuss the importance of introducing people. Allow students to share experiences such as when they were with a friend who was either good at or had difficulty in introducing them to his or her other friends. Tell students that you are going to teach them some points to remember when they introduce people to each other. After describing each of the following points, ask students to role-play to demonstrate their use:

- Provide additional information about the person being introduced such as "This is R. J.; he's new to our town," or "This is R. J.; he's good at baseball."
- Provide additional information about people in the group who have common interests with the new person such as "Steve plays basketball."
- Talk about those common interests.

Invitation to Play
By Dheepa Sridhar

OBJECTIVE: To teach students to invite a classmate to play with them.

GRADES: Primary

MATERIALS: Toys

TEACHING PROCEDURES: Tell students that they should take the following steps when requesting a classmate to join them in play:

1. Decide what you want to play (e.g., jump rope, building with Legos®).
2. Check to see whether you have the materials (rope or Legos).
3. Check to see what the person you want to play with is doing.
4. Wait for a lull in the activity that the person is engaging in.
5. Ask the person whether he or she would like to play (rope or Legos).
6. If the person refuses, ask what else he or she would like to play.
7. Have students role-play and provide feedback.

In Your Shoes
By Dheepa Sridhar

OBJECTIVE: To facilitate students in taking a different perspective.

GRADES: Intermediate and high school

MATERIALS: Cardboard cutouts of two pairs of shoes of different colors, masking tape, index cards with social problems written on them (e.g., "Jake was supposed to go to a baseball game with Ashraf over the weekend. He has been looking forward to this event all week. On Friday, Ashraf says that he would rather go to a movie instead of the game.")

TEACHING PROCEDURES: Discuss the importance of taking the other person's perspective. Tell the students this activity will help them see a different perspective.

1. Tape a line on the floor with the masking tape. Write the name of a character (e.g., Jake and Ashraf) on each pair of shoes. Place each pair of shoes on either side of the line.
2. Have two students volunteer to be Jake or Ashraf.
3. Ask one student to stand on Jake's shoes and the other student to stand on Ashraf's shoes.
4. Let them talk about the problem.
5. Ask the students to exchange places and discuss the problem.
6. Help the students to reach a solution that is acceptable to both parties.

This activity can also be used with students who are experiencing problems with each other instead of hypothetical situations. Although only two students can participate at a time, the rest of the class can help by generating solutions and discussing the consequences of those solutions.

Summary

The use of classroom management strategies is important because it creates an environment with structure and routine so that learning can occur. Teachers should develop procedures, rules, consequences, and reinforcers so that both they and the students know how to navigate the classroom and what to expect if something goes wrong. Teachers who implement effective classroom management recognize and reinforce positive behavior as well as identify and change inappropriate behaviors. PBS is a classroom management system that focuses on prevention of problem behaviors through attention to the learning environment.

An FBA is designed to identify behavior problems of students, and a BIP is used to develop an intervention plan to treat these behavior problems. An FBA is required if students' behavior is interfering with their learning or the learning of other students.

Students with behavior and learning difficulties often lack the social competence necessary to engage in effective interactions with others. Although students with behavior disorders by definition lack social competence and generally have severe emotional and behavioral difficulties, many individuals with LD also struggle to make and maintain positive interpersonal relationships with others. Individuals with LD often (but not always) have poor conversational skills; may have difficulty perceiving, interpreting, and processing social information; may exhibit aggressive behaviors or attention problems; and may display atypical appearance.

Teachers must pay attention to the physical space in which they teach. They should keep books and resources organized and clearly marked, and they should use a variety of instructional arrangements depending on student needs and learning activities.

 ASSESSMENT

After completing this chapter, test your knowledge of the concepts by completing the Assessment.

Coteaching and Collaborating: Working with Professionals and Families

5

LEARNING OUTCOMES

1. Identify some of the challenges of working in inclusive settings.
2. Distinguish among the three major models for consultation and collaboration.
3. Describe the principles of communication, and give examples of how teachers can communicate with parents and professionals.
4. Analyze the role of the special education teacher's role as a consultant to general education teachers, and identify potential barriers to successful inclusion.
5. Summarize the teacher's role in addressing the needs of the entire family.

Mrs. Tupa works in a hospital emergency room, so she is accustomed to talking to people who are grieving. Mrs. Tupa states:

I often speak to parents about the recovery of their children. Fortunately, most of the children have injuries or illnesses from which they will recover completely. I've been trained in the importance of telling the parents as quickly and completely as possible all we know about their child's condition. The only reason I'm telling you this is that I want you to understand that I am accustomed to dealing with difficulties. But I was unprepared for the inconsistent information I would receive about our son.

When our third child, Chad, was born, my husband and I couldn't have been happier. Our first two children were girls, whom we enjoy immensely, but both of us were hoping for a boy. Chad walked and talked later than the girls, but I knew that boys are often developmentally slower than girls, so we were not concerned. When Chad was a preschooler, he often had difficulty thinking of the right word for an object and his language was often difficult to follow. When the girls told stories about events that happened to them, we could understand clearly what they were communicating. This was often not the case with Chad. When we spoke with his pediatrician, the doctor informed us that this was not uncommon.

When Chad entered kindergarten, he did not know all of his colors and showed little ability to remember the names of the letters in the alphabet. He was just not very interested in the school part of kindergarten though he enjoyed the playing part. His kindergarten teacher said that she had seen a number of students like Chad, often boys, and suggested that we keep Chad in kindergarten another year. Our neighbor, who is a teacher, thought this might not be a good idea, since Chad was already large for his age. We spoke with the principal, who seemed very busy and thought we should take the advice of the kindergarten teacher. We retained Chad. Spending another year in kindergarten seemed to do little good, however. Chad was still unable to identify letters, though he was very popular because of his size and knowledge of the kindergarten routine.

First grade was worse yet. Chad showed no signs of reading and was confusing letters. His writing resembled that of a much younger child. By now we were very concerned and made several appointments with his first-grade teacher. She was very responsive and suggested that we have Chad tutored during the summer. The tutor said that Chad had an attention problem and was having trouble with letter and word reversals. She suggested that we have him tested for learning disabilities. The school psychologist agreed to do the testing, and it was late in the fall before we were called and given the results.

Though both my husband and I are professionals, we felt somewhat intimidated by the number of school personnel at the meeting. On our way home, as we tried to reconstruct what we heard, we realized that we had misunderstood and missed a lot of information. I heard the school personnel say Chad's intelligence was normal, but my husband thought that it couldn't be normal because his verbal intelligence was low. We decided to make a list of questions to ask at our next meeting. We felt that we had made a major stride forward, since Chad would now be receiving special instruction for 1 hour each day from a learning disabilities specialist; however, we still felt we understood very little about his problems. I only wish we had been told more completely and quickly about Chad's problem.

Many parents have had similar experiences. They have noticed that their child is different in some areas from other children of the same age. These parents seek advice from friends, medical professionals, and school professionals and often feel confused and frustrated. When the child is identified as having learning disabilities or emotional disorders, many parents at first feel relieved, hoping that this identification will lead to solutions that will eliminate the child's learning or behavior problem. The difficult adjustments are that the child will probably always have learning or behavior problems and that the special education teacher will be unable to provide any magic cures, and certainly no quick solutions.

Learning disabilities and emotional disorders are complex phenomena, and knowledge of all the factors that they involve is incomplete. Special education teachers work effectively with parents when they are sensitive to parental concerns about identification and intervention, yet speak honestly about what they know and do not know. Families need educators to provide them with encouragement about what they can do at home and about an effective plan for providing instructional supports for their child. Families need to know about the educators' best knowledge of their child's learning and behavior problem and also need to be informed of what educators are less sure of.

This chapter focuses on the special education teacher as a coteacher and an effective communicator. One of the essential roles of special education teachers is coteaching and working with other professionals (e.g., general education teacher, school psychologist), as well as communicating with family members and between special education teachers and other school-related professionals. This chapter deals with the issue of the special education teacher as a manager, communicator, and collaborator.

Successful Inclusion and Coteaching

What are some of the challenges and opportunities of working in an inclusive classroom and working with general education teachers? Considering the many complexities of teaching and the increasing demands for high performance and preparing students for postsecondary success, classroom teachers are required to provide instruction for increasingly diverse student populations and are still held accountable for covering the prescribed curriculum in a manner that ensures most students learn that content. Classroom teachers sometimes feel that they must choose between covering the content adequately and differentiating instruction appropriately for the range of special learners in their classroom. One of the significant roles of the special education teacher is to support general education teachers in meeting content goals and common core state standards while also providing appropriate instruction for students with special needs.

Many special education students need more time to master new concepts and skills, and they master those concepts and skills only if instruction is presented to them in a manner that enables them to grasp the new material. Teachers must know and use a variety of instructional strategies to ensure that all students have an opportunity to learn. This takes time and planning.

In general, teachers at the middle and high school levels indicate that it is often not feasible for them to plan specifically for students with special needs (Isherwood & Barger-Anderson, 2007; Schumm et al., 1995 a, b). Furthermore, when coteaching has been compared to other models such as resource-room settings, the findings for students are mixed (Solis et al., 2012). This suggests that the model of service delivery may not be the issue; rather, the quality of instruction provided to students is what makes the difference (Zigmond, 2003). General education teachers are willing to work with special education professionals to make accommodations for students with special needs as they teach—particularly when those accommodations are useful to other learners in the classroom. There are many opportunities for special and general education teachers to align their knowledge and skills and improve outcomes for students with disabilities.

Challenges to Special Education Teachers

Two special education teachers at different schools had very different points of view about their experiences working as coteachers with general education teachers to improve learning for students with disabilities. One teacher said, "It was the best year of my teaching career. Ms. Walberg was terrific and taught me so much about what to expect from general education. I think all of the students benefited because we worked so well together and shared so much of the teaching." Another teacher at a different school said, "This year was enough to get me to leave education. I never really felt like I was an equal partner in the classroom. I always felt like I was the teaching assistant. Furthermore, it was so painful to watch how practices were implemented for students who needed help and weren't getting it. Yet I never really felt anyone was listening to me."

Ms. Peres, a special education teacher, states it this way:

> I am convinced that students with disabilities need to be in general education classrooms if at all possible. However, I have learned that we need to prepare them both socially and academically. Much of what we do in special education classrooms does not prepare them for general education. They are used to individual and small-group instruction, receiving lots of feedback and lots of reinforcement, and being relatively free to ask for and receive assistance. This does not reflect what happens in the general education classrooms in this school. Although the teachers are great, they have 28 to 32 students in each class. Large-group instruction and cooperative and independent learning are the most frequently used instructional arrangements.

The first key to making inclusion work is to cooperate with the general classroom teacher and to observe that classroom to determine the learning and social demands.

The second key is to gain a commitment from the student. He or she has to want to work toward the goal. I always describe the classroom demands to the student, and sometimes he or she goes to observe. Then we plan how we're going to get ready for "going to Mrs. Fereira's class for math."

The third key is to begin simulating those learning and social demands in my classroom. I start gradually. Usually, I begin by decreasing the feedback and reinforcement. Next I focus on the academic demands. I get the lessons and textbooks from the classroom teacher, and I begin to assign the lessons. At first, the rate of learning is matched to the student's learning rate. But once the student is succeeding with the assignments, I begin to increase the rate until it matches that of the general education classroom. As this procedure continues, I gradually reduce the amount of reinforcement and feedback and work with the student to become a more independent learner.

The fourth key is to monitor the student and to continue to work with the classroom teacher to modify and

> In this **video** ▶, a sixth-grade special education teacher shares his memories, experiences, and professional growth during his 11-year career. What aspects does he identify as the benefits and challenges of his position?

Adaptations General Education Teachers Are Willing to Make

Teachers identified the following as *highly* feasible to implement:

1. Provide reinforcement and encouragement to assist students with learning.
2. Establish a personal relationship with included students.
3. Involve included students in whole-class activities.
4. Establish routines that are appropriate for included students.
5. Establish expectations for learning and behavior.

Teachers identified the following as not likely to be implemented:

1. Adapt long-range plans to meet the needs of included students.
2. Adjust the physical arrangement of the room to meet the needs of included students.
3. Use alternative materials or adapt current materials for students with special needs.
4. Adapt scoring and grading criteria for students with special needs.
5. Provide individualizing instruction to meet students' special needs.

adapt materials, methods, and the teaching–learning environment as needed.

I have developed this strategy through experience. Many times, I have found that my test scores, informal assessments, and student progress data indicate that the student is reading at grade level. In the past, I would jump to the conclusion that the student was ready to perform without assistance in the general education classroom. Yet too often I would find the student in difficulties within 3 weeks. I was really setting the students up for failure. I had attended only to their reading level, not to the social and academic demands.

I've been very successful with this strategy. I have all but 4 of my 14 students included for most of the school day.

Ms. Peres's discussion of how she provides effective instruction and behavioral support for her students in the general education classroom demonstrates that she values communication, collaboration, and consultation with the general education classroom teachers.

WEB RESOURCES

What you need to know about special education is described on the Office of Special Education Programs Web site http://www2.ed.gov/about/offices/list/osers/osep/index.html.

Understanding the Challenges of General Education Classrooms

Special education teachers need to understand what students with special needs can reasonably expect in general education classrooms so that they can provide the support and skills necessary for success. Although expectations vary considerably by teacher, there are some common expectations:

- General education teachers report that they are willing to make adaptations and accommodations that do not require preplanning and can occur during the instructional process. If additional modifications are required (e.g., assignments or tests), then the special education teacher can provide them (see Apply the Concept 5-1).
- Teachers are not willing to provide significant modifications for students with disabilities, particularly at the middle and high school levels.
- Students with disabilities participate infrequently during class and rarely respond to teachers' questions (McIntosh, Vaughn, et al., 1993).
- Undifferentiated large group instruction is representative of what occurs in general education classrooms; yet one-on-one or small-group instruction is better for students with learning difficulties.

WEB RESOURCES

For more information about meeting the needs of all students in inclusive classrooms, see the IRIS Web site on inclusive education resources and collaboration http://iris.peabody.vanderbilt.edu/.

Consultation and Collaboration

What are three major models for consultation and collaboration? Although both terms—*consultation* and *collaboration*—are often used to describe the role of many special education teachers, teachers prefer the term *collaboration*. Why?

Teachers indicate that they prefer collaborative modes of working on student problems rather than handing over problems to experts or working on them independently (Arguelles, Vaughn, & Schumm, 1996). Teachers perceive that the term *collaboration* more accurately describes the nature of their relationships. As one special education teacher noted, "We actually work together to solve problems. It's not like I have all of the answers or she has all of the problems. We really help each other come up with ideas that work." We have found that general education teachers feel much the same way.

What is collaboration? *Collaboration* refers to the interaction that occurs between two professionals, often between special education teachers and general education teachers, and to the roles that they play as equal partners in problem-solving endeavors. When teachers collaborate, they

- Work together to solve problems and generate feasible solutions that they implement and evaluate.
- Reflect on their own instructional practices and are eager to make changes that improve outcomes for students.

What are some of the ways in which special education teachers might expect to collaborate with other professionals? A significant part of their role is to collaborate with parents and any other specialist who is associated with the teacher's students with special needs. Whether working as a resource room teacher, a self-contained special education teacher, or a coteacher, special education teachers also have considerable opportunities to collaborate with general education teachers. They may also work in a program in which most of the workday involves collaboration with other teachers.

One important way in which special education teachers collaborate with general education professionals is in developing ways to make curricula more accessible to students with special needs. Curriculum planning can address such important issues as identifying changes in curriculum that are forecast by national boards and professional groups, identifying the ways in which these new trends will affect the curriculum and students with special needs, examining the scope and sequence of the present curriculum and determining where changes best fit, identifying new goals and discussing the prerequisite skills needed for students with special needs, and identifying areas of mismatch or in which new curriculum is inappropriate for target students.

Additional ways in which special education teachers collaborate with general education teachers include:

- *Coteaching*—Working with classroom teachers to provide instruction together in general education classrooms. For example, a special education teacher might coteach with an English teacher at the secondary level who has several students with disabilities in his class. The goal would be for the special education teacher to provide access to the general education curriculum for the students with disabilities. The special education teacher might provide small-group instruction within the classroom, modify homework assignments, and assist with test preparation and other accommodations for students with disabilities as needed.

- *Consultant teaching*—Working with classroom teachers to solve problems for students with disabilities who will be included in general education classrooms. For example, the special education teacher may be asked to observe the student with disabilities in the general education classroom as a means to identifying behavioral or instructional practices that might facilitate success for the target student. Another example may be that the special education teacher modifies particular tests or assignments to promote access to the general education curriculum for the student with disabilities. Consultant teaching differs from coteaching in that the special education teacher observes, assesses, and helps plan for instruction but typically does not provide direct instruction in the general education classroom.

- *Coordination of paraprofessionals*—Working with classroom teachers to coordinate and support the activities of paraprofessionals who assist students with disabilities in the general education classroom. For example, the special education teacher may have a paraprofessional assigned to a student with severe behavior problems during science and math in the general education classroom. The student may have the knowledge and skills to benefit from the general education classroom but may not have the appropriate behaviors. The special education teacher could provide the paraprofessional with the guidelines for positive behavioral support to enhance the student's success in the classroom.

- *Teacher assistance teams (TATs)*—Participating in school-based teams of professionals, classroom teachers, and administrators that assist classroom teachers in meeting the instructional and behavior needs of individual students. For example, the special education teacher might organize grade-level meetings at the elementary level (e.g., all fourth-grade teachers meet at the same time) or content area meetings at the middle school level (e.g., all social studies teachers meet at the same time) to discuss ways to promote successful learning and behavior for students with learning and behavior problems.

Collaboration within a Response to Intervention Framework

What is the role of the special education teacher within a response to intervention (RTI) framework? RTI has provided new opportunities and expectations for cooperation between special education teachers and general education teachers. Special education teachers may meet and plan with general education teachers about the Tier 2 interventions provided in math and reading and may also play a significant role in providing interventions for students in Tier 3. What are some of the collaborative activities that special education teachers may engage in within an RTI framework? A few considerations follow (Haager & Mahdavi, 2007; J. J. Hoover & Patton, 2008):

- Organize screening and progress-monitoring measures, and determine cut points for which students will be provided reading and math intervention.
- Determine how interventions should be implemented and organized.
- Develop a checklist for high-quality implementation of interventions.
- Develop training for teachers and paraprofessionals to provide high-quality intervention.
- Determine how to adjust interventions to meet the needs of students performing at a range of grade levels and with varying instructional needs.
- Determine how to adjust instruction when students make minimal progress in interventions.

In summary, the critical role for the special education teacher is to collaborate with all key stakeholders in the school, including school psychologists, speech and language specialists, general education teachers, and school leaders, to make critical decisions about (1) determining and implementing research-based practices, (2) collecting and using ongoing data to make effective decisions for students with learning and behavioral problems, (3) identifying appropriate practices for differentiating instruction within the classroom and interventions, and (4) communicating effectively with all key stakeholders so that appropriate instruction is provided to all students with learning and behavior problems. Check out the National Association of State Directors of Special Education Web site for interesting resources on collaboration and response to intervention.

Resources Needed for Collaboration

No resource impedes successful collaboration more than time. Special and general education teachers confirm the difficulties of finding adequate time to effectively collaborate during the workday (Friend, 2000; Stivers, 2008). If time is not built into teachers' schedules, collaboration is unlikely to occur on a regular basis. Furthermore, if it is not part of the schedule, then teachers come to resent having to collaborate because it means taking time from their personal schedules. Another critical aspect of time management for special education teachers is finding mutually available time when they can collaborate with

the many teachers with whom they work. Time management is especially challenging at the secondary level. Following are some ways in which collaborative time can be arranged (Vaughn, Bos, & Schumm, 2013):

- Administrators designate a common time for collaborating professionals (e.g., all fifth-grade team members) to work together.
- School boards pay professionals for one extra time period each week that can be used to collaborate or meet with families.
- School districts provide early dismissal for students one day a week so that team members have a common planning time.
- Teachers meet for brief but focused planning periods on a regularly scheduled basis.
- Resources such as administrators, families, volunteers, and university students are used to help cover classes. For example, short planning sessions may be scheduled during recess when larger groups of students can be monitored by a teacher and a volunteer.

Space for meeting is another necessary resource. Special education teachers are often fortunate because they have an office or a small classroom for their materials. But finding a quiet place to meet is particularly challenging in schools where overcrowding is the norm.

Additionally, participants in collaborative models need to be familiar with procedures for successful collaboration. An orientation that addresses basic questions about their roles and responsibilities is helpful to all personnel who are involved in collaboration. Administrative support can be crucial to ensuring that teachers are given appropriate time, space, and knowledge of procedures to implement an effective collaborative model.

Like other educational approaches, consultation and collaboration models have the potential for benefit as well as misuse and misunderstanding. Apply the Concept 5-2 describes potential benefits and misuses.

Collaboration Issues and Dilemmas

All special education teachers work collaboratively with general education teachers, and many special education teachers work with general education teachers at least 50% of the time. Consequently, special education teachers need to recognize several issues and dilemmas to perform their job effectively.

1. *Student ownership.* Traditionally, special education students have been the responsibility of the special education teacher, even if they were placed in a general education classroom for part of the day. This perspective is no longer feasible or desirable. The new perspective is one of

Benefits and Misuses of Consultation and Collaboration

Consultation and collaboration models have several potential benefits and misuses (Zigmond, 2003).

Potential Benefits

1. Reduction of stigma
2. Better understanding across education disciplines
3. On-the-job training for general education teachers in skills for effectively meeting the needs of special education students
4. Reduced mislabeling of students as disabled
5. Suitability in meeting the needs of secondary school students
6. Spillover benefits to general education students from working cooperatively with special education teacher

Potential Misuses/Problems

1. Excessive caseload management for special education teachers
2. Unrealistic expectations from viewing the consulting model as a panacea and/or under-training and overloading the special education teacher
3. Inadequate support and cooperation from classroom teachers
4. Converting the model to a tutoring or aide approach
5. Providing inadequate funding
6. Faulty assumptions about cost savings
7. Faulty assumptions about program effectiveness
8. Unrealistic expectations for changes in academic success and social acceptance
9. Inadequate preparation for vocational experiences after school
10. Inadequate time to plan, communicate, and effectively instruct target students

Overall, the most important question to address is whether students with learning and behavior problems are having their needs met through a consultation and collaborative model. The model may be highly effective for some students and less so for others.

---

shared ownership whereby all educators feel responsible for the success of the student with special needs.

2. Individual versus class focus. General education teachers have the responsibility for all students in their class. Particularly at the upper elementary and secondary grade levels, general education teachers focus on teaching the content and less on teaching individual students. This contrasts with the focus of special education teachers, whose planning and instruction aim at the needs of individual students. These differing perspectives may mean that general and special education teachers need to develop solutions that promote content support within a model that provides the necessary instructional support for students with special needs. Mrs. Vermillion put it this way, "I am a special education teacher, and so the direction of my interest is always with the individual student and how the educational setting can be altered to meet his or her needs. During the last few years, I realize that I've needed to adjust my perspective if I am to work effectively with classroom teachers. When they think about planning for students, they think about the class as a whole." What are some of the changes Mrs. Vermillion has instituted so that she can have a more successful connection with the general education teacher?

• Develop materials including assessments and homework that are content appropriate, enhance learning for all students, and meet the needs of students with disabilities.

• Spend additional time learning the content so that she can provide appropriate accommodations for students.

• Look for resources for the general education teacher (e.g., books, charts, videos) that provide content instruction but also support learning of students with disabilities.

3. Content versus accommodation. When classroom teachers discuss their planning and instruction, one of the most consistent themes is content coverage (Kloo & Zigmond, 2008; Schumm et al., 1995 a, b). Classroom teachers recognize that state and national laws pressure them to cover more content. Jon Lau, a ninth-grade science teacher, says, "Waiting until the students understand would result in lack of adequate coverage of material. It is my responsibility to cover the content in the time I am allocated."

This notion of content coverage as the horse leading the instructional wagon is a consistent and pervasive problem in general education and now directly influences the instruction of students with special needs. There is some consensus that "less is more" and that a reduced focus on content coverage would enhance the quality of instruction for all learners.

You can imagine the difficulty for classroom teachers who feel pressured to cover extensive amounts of content when special education teachers make suggestions that slow down the pace or require them to make adaptations for students' special learning needs. This issue is not insolvable. Teachers are willing to make adaptations and accommodations they believe will help students and do not require extensive amounts of preparation.

4. *New roles for special education teachers.* Perhaps one of the greatest challenges for teachers who are learning to work collaboratively with other teachers is that they assume different roles than those they previously had. These roles can include supporting special education students in the general education classroom; teaching with another teacher in a content area in which they have little or no background knowledge, particularly at the secondary level; helping students with assignments; and engaging in disciplining and classroom management of a range of students. A veteran special education teacher tells of the changing roles and responsibilities of moving from her own classroom to coteaching with other teachers. She discusses this role shift with the kind of nostalgia that shows that she misses many of the comforts of her own classroom and routines, yet realizes that many students are benefiting from her engagement in the general education classroom (Klingner & Vaughn, 2002).

What are some of the activities of special education teachers who are working more collaboratively with general education teachers? They spend the majority of their time in general education classrooms either monitoring the learning and behavior of target students or teaching a large group of students (six or more but not the entire class) (Harbort et al., 2007). Less frequently occurring activities include responding to students' comments or questions, small-group instruction (fewer than six students), extended individual student interaction, and managing behavior.

5. *Real world versus the student's world.* Another dichotomy between general and special education teachers is the purpose of education. Classroom teachers feel that they are preparing students for the "real world." From their perspective, people in the real world do not make accommodations for different learning styles. Fundamentally, they view the real world as expecting the same thing from everybody and therefore, to best prepare youngsters, their role as teachers is to expect the same thing from every student.

Ms. McDowell, a secondary special education teacher, handles the problem this way: "When classroom teachers talk to me about the real world, I'm prepared. First, I present them with the idea that students are never going to be successful in the real world if they do not have an opportunity to learn and experience success in their present world. Their present world is that teacher's

classroom. Second, I present them with the fact that employers are required by law to make reasonable accommodations for individuals with disabilities. Also, I never ask general education teachers to make adaptations or accommodations that aren't useful to most students in the classroom." In fact, instructional interventions that are used to improve learning for students with disabilities are at least as effective—and sometimes more effective—for students without disabilities (Vaughn, Gersten, & Chard, 2000; Vaughn, Wanzek, et al., 2009).

Problem-Solving Models Problem-solving models are ways in which teams of educators (e.g., special education teacher, general education teacher, speech and language therapist, school counselor, reading specialist) at each school implement a prevention approach to meeting the needs of students at risk for special needs and with special needs. These approaches provide instructional, behavioral, and assessment support to teachers at the school-building level so that early services can be provided to students to ensure their needs are met. Problem-solving approaches have as goals early prevention of learning and behavior problems, use of student data to influence decision making about placement in special education, and replacing more traditional approaches to assessing and identifying students with disabilities.

How do you implement a problem-solving approach in your school? The problem-solving model is systematic and involves frequent and ongoing student-data collection. In most cases, students are screened using relatively easy to administer reading and/or math screening measures.

WEB RESOURCES

See Student Progress http://www.studentprogress .org for descriptions of screening and progress-monitoring measures.

When students are identified as having difficulties, they are provided evidence-based interventions using ongoing student-progress-monitoring measures to ensure that students are closing the gap between their current performance and expected performance. Students who make adequate progress are no longer provided intervention, and those who need additional supports may be provided more extensive interventions. These interventions can be provided by personnel trained by the special education teacher or other educational personnel; or in some schools, certified teachers provide the instructional support.

Problem-solving models are considered necessary because many students' needs are not met early, and they fall behind academically. In a traditional special education model, students are often not referred for special education support until third or fourth grade, when their learning needs are significant and are not readily remediated. The intention of problem-solving models is that students' needs will be met early and based on students' responses to these early interventions, better information about which students have special needs can be determined.

Problem-solving approaches are used in several states, including Minnesota, Iowa, and North Carolina to name a few, and typically involve variations on the following four-step process:

1. Define the problem. Specifically designate what the student's need is academically or behaviorally (e.g., Marcus is reading two grade levels behind his peers and is reading 40 words correctly per minute when the school average for his grade is 97 words per minute).

2. Plan an intervention. The team decides what the appropriate intervention for Marcus would be. In this case, Marcus is provided 30 minutes daily of additional instruction in a small group that is instructed by the reading specialist.

3. Implement the intervention. The team decides that Marcus would continue in the intervention for 12 weeks with progress monitoring using oral reading fluency obtained every other week.

4. Evaluate the student's progress. Based on student progress after 12 weeks, the team would decide if Marcus is making adequate progress but needs to continue in the intervention, is making adequate progress and can discontinue participation in the intervention, or is making inadequate progress and needs another more intensive intervention.

Interventions are usually selected from a bank of research-based interventions that have been identified by the school or district (Berkeley, Bender, Peaster, & Saunders, 2009).

Coteaching

Coteaching, or cooperative teaching, occurs when general and special education teachers work cooperatively to ensure that all students in the classroom, including students with disabilities, are provided appropriate instruction. Coteaching can be conducted in several ways but typically involves the general and special education teachers' sharing planning, presentation, assessment, and classroom management to promote successful outcomes. Villa, Thousand, and Nevin (2008) also remind us what coteaching is not. Coteaching is not one person teaching while another prepares materials, not one person's views dominating instructional decision making, not tutoring, and not one person watching while another teaches.

What are some of the models for coteaching and collaborative instruction between general and special education teachers? Table 5-1 provides a description of several approaches and the roles of teachers in their implementation (Solis, et al., 2012). It is important to note that it is likely that each of these approaches would be used while coteaching, depending on instructional goals and students' needs.

TABLE 5-1 Coteaching Approaches

Type of Coteaching	Description	General Education Teacher Role	Special Education Teacher Role
Classroom Teacher Instructs	Classroom teacher is primarily responsible for instruction. Special education teacher monitors students' work and provides instruction individually and in small groups as needed, targeting students with disabilities.	Lead teacher	Support
General and Special Education Teacher Instructs	Both the general and special education teacher are responsible for teaching groups of students with an aim for providing more targeted instruction to heterogeneous groups of students.	Lead teacher	Lead teacher
Station Teaching	Students work in small groups and either move from learning activity to learning activity or stay in one place and teachers move to them.	Lead teacher	Lead teacher
Homogeneous Groups	Students who understand key ideas and concepts are provided extended instruction by classroom teacher, while students with additional learning needs are provided instruction by special education teacher.	Extends teaching	Addresses students learning needs
Whole-Class Team Teaching	Teachers work together cooperatively to teach a whole-class lesson. One teacher may take the lead role, while the other interjects information or questions, makes clarifications, or restates information to increase understanding among all students.	Lead teacher	Lead teacher

Coteaching Perceptions

Consider asking and answering these questions with your coteacher as a means for determining areas of strength and potential areas to focus on within your coteaching setting:

1. We both have equal access to all information about general education students in the class?
2. We both have equal access to all information about special education students in the class?
3. We both are perceived by key administrators as appropriate contacts for issues about the class?
4. We both are perceived by parents as appropriate contacts for issues about the class?
5. If a problem with a student arises, we are both comfortable addressing it and communicating with each other about it?
6. We have adequate time to plan?
7. We both have access to materials in the classroom?
8. The desks and chairs for both teachers are equivalent?
9. Decisions about what to teach are shared?
10. Decisions about how to teach are discussed and agreed upon?
11. Decisions about adaptations to meet the special learning needs of students are discussed and agreed upon?
12. Decisions about adaptations to tests and other evaluations are discussed and agreed upon?
13. We provide each other with feedback that is useful and improves our instruction?
14. We coteach effectively and with few difficulties?
15. We respect the contributions of our coteacher?
16. We communicate and problem solve problems effectively?

See Apply the Concept 5-3 for a description of questions to ask to promote a successful coteaching experience.

Although there is some debate over the effectiveness of coteaching as a way to meet the needs of students with disabilities (Isherwood & Barger-Anderson, 2007; Zigmond, 2001), limited data indicate that coteaching can have a positive impact on student achievement (Scruggs, Mastropieri, & McDuffie, 2007). Of course, the effectiveness of coteaching is related to what students need to learn and whether they can learn it well within a coteaching setting. Generally, teachers report that they benefited professionally from coteaching. They also report increased cooperation among students within their class and additional time and attention for students with disabilities. Teachers did consistently express concerns that many of the students with disabilities demonstrated significantly low academic skills with learning needs that were difficult to meet in the general education classroom (Scruggs et al., 2007).

Villa and coworkers (2008) indicate that coteaching is likely to be beneficial when:

- Teacher use of collaborative skills increases teacher responsiveness. When teachers share ideas, work together, and promote each other's successes in the classroom, all students are provided improved instruction. When collaboration is effective, a broader range of students has access to the curriculum.

- Teachers support and identify the use of research-based practices. In coteaching settings, teachers can structure classrooms to use various grouping practices, reducing the prevailing use of whole-class instruction and increasing small-group and peer teaching. Coteaching also provides opportunities for teachers to identify research-based practices and inform each other of ways to more effectively implement these practices.

- Teachers use problem solving to provide individualized learning and meet all students' needs. Teachers who identify learning and behavior problems in their class and solve problems to more effectively meet the needs of students are likely to yield beneficial learning outcomes.

- Teachers empower each other through coteaching. Teachers who effectively coteach can empower each other through collaborative decision making, confirming effective practices, and sharing difficult situations.

How Coteaching Works

When coteaching, special and general education teachers plan broad, overall goals and desired outcomes for the class as a whole as well as for specific students in the class. Both special and general classroom teachers lead instruction during the same instructional period. Although one teacher may provide some instruction to the group as a whole, most of the instructional time involves both teachers working with small groups or with individual students. Because students are frequently grouped heterogeneously, the special education teacher works with many students, including those who are identified as benefiting from special education. Complementary instruction and supportive learning activities are part of the teachers' coplanning and instruction.

Coteaching Models Coteaching involves much more than just putting a special and a general education teacher in the same classroom. For example, Weiss and Lloyd (2002, 2003) found that in coteaching situations it was often difficult for special education teachers to provide the type of focused, explicit instruction that they used in special education classrooms. Therefore, to be successful, both teachers must carefully plan what role each will take and the type of instruction they will each provide.

Teachers can implement a variety of coteaching models. Many teachers select a coteaching model based on both overall instructional goals and the individual needs of students in the classroom. Before choosing a coteaching model, the general and special education teachers need to decide what lesson or unit will be taught, being careful to consider general education curriculum requirements as well as the individual needs of students with disabilities specified on their individualized education program (IEP). Most teachers find that they use more than one model during a week and even during a day. Following are several coteaching models that teachers have found useful (Conderman, Bresnahan, & Pedersen, 2009; Vaughn, Schumm, & Arguelles, 1997). For further information on coteaching, check out the Web site of the National Dissemination Center for Children with Disabilities.

Model A: One Group; One Lead Teacher, One Teacher "Teaching on Purpose" Many teachers in coteaching situations end up spending their time grazing, that is, going from student to student, to make sure they are following along, but without a specific plan or goal in mind. "Teaching on purpose" is a method of checking for understanding and providing short installments of explicit instruction that are related to key ideas, concepts, or vocabulary from the main lesson. When teaching on purpose, one of the teachers gives short lessons to individuals, pairs, or small groups of students during or as a follow-up to whole-group instruction. In 1 or 2 minutes, the teacher who is teaching on purpose might approach a student after instruction by

In this **video** ▶, you will hear one teacher describe different coteaching methods she and her coteacher have used as they have learned to collaborate during their first year as coteachers. What methods have they found to be successful?

the lead teacher to follow up on key ideas and concepts, encourage participation, answer questions, or review directions. In about 5 minutes, the teacher can review concepts and vocabulary or check for understanding. If further instruction is needed, the teacher can take a bit longer to provide a mini lesson that is related to the main lesson (e.g., how to find the main idea). When coteaching is used effectively, the teacher has a specific objective in mind and targets particular students to ensure that they are learning specified material. Some examples of what coteachers can do when they teach on purpose include:

* Reinforce big ideas of the lesson to one or two students.
* Ask a student a question related to the overall instruction to see if they are learning.
* Ask students to write the key word or words about what they are learning.
* Connect what students are currently learning to previous learning.
* Check written work, and provide specific feedback and suggestions.

Model B: Two Mixed-Ability Groups; Two Teachers Teach the Same Content In Model B, the class is divided into two mixed-ability groups, and each teacher instructs one group. The purpose of this coteaching model is to reduce the group size to increase the number of opportunities for students to participate and interact with one another and to have their responses and knowledge monitored by a teacher. This format is often used when difficult new content is introduced or when smaller groups are beneficial for certain instructional activities, such as discussion. For example, the coteachers may divide the class into two heterogeneous groups during the discussion of a book that has been read as a whole group. At the end of the lesson, the two groups come together to summarize what they learned and to integrate information between groups. Some other examples of when you might use this grouping format include:

* One teacher is doing a science lab experiment with half of the class while the other teacher is reviewing key ideas related to learning from the experiment.
* One teacher is teaching about a controversial issue in social studies (e.g., socialism versus capitalism), and the other teacher is teaching the same content, but the small groups allow students more opportunities for discussion.
* One teacher is reviewing key grammatical functions related to paragraph writing with half of the students who need the lesson, while the other teacher is working on composing five-paragraph essays.

Model C: Two Same-Ability Groups; Teachers Teach Different Content Students are divided into two groups on the basis of their skill level in the topic area. One teacher reteaches, while the other teacher provides alternative information or extension activities to the second group. For example, during a unit on fractions, one teacher can lead a reteaching activity on dividing the parts of a whole, while the other teacher facilitates an activity on creating story problems using fractions. In effective coteaching, the general education teacher does not always assume the role of lead teacher, nor does the special education teacher always reteach. Teachers share responsibilities and alter roles from one lesson to the next.

Model D: Multiple Groups; Teachers Monitor/Teach Model D is often used during cooperative learning activities and in reading groups and learning centers. One option for Model D is to have several heterogeneous groups and one or two homogeneous groups based on skill level. One or both teachers work with groups for the entire period. For example, during reading in Ms. Chamber's fifth-grade class, the special education teacher, Mrs. Scholar, provides reading instruction to a group of students with low reading ability that includes several students with disabilities. The classroom teacher has two other groups who rotate between working in centers and working with her in a group. Another example is Mr. Young's third-grade math class in which Mrs. Scholar and he arrange for four groups of students to rotate between them and two centers during a 50-minute period. This allows each teacher to work with a relatively small group of students (approximate five to seven) for 25 minutes every day. Another possibility during social studies or science is to have students move in small groups through four or five centers. Two centers are teacher-assisted, and the remaining centers have activities that can be done independently by groups. Students might also work in cooperative groups or pairs while both teachers provide mini lessons and monitor progress.

Model E: Whole Class; Two Teachers Teach Together In this model, teachers work cooperatively to teach a lesson. One teacher may lead the whole-class lesson, while the other teacher interjects to clarify the material. Often the general education teacher provides curriculum material, and the special education teacher adds strategies to help students with disabilities remember key ideas and organize information. For example, teachers might spend 10 minutes modeling problem-solving techniques and explaining directions for a science lesson on observation in which students will work cooperatively to record observations and make predictions about a "mystery matter." One teacher lists the steps of the activity, while the other points to a flowchart indicating the correct sequence to follow. In the next section on coteaching with secondary students, there is a description of activities that Mr. Prudhi (a special education teacher) might use to support instruction. These examples are very relevant for the model of two teachers teaching together.

To learn more about coteaching, look for the www.youtube: Successful Co-Teaching: Keys to Team Development for great coteaching ideas.

Coteaching with Secondary Students Coteaching varies necessarily between elementary and secondary levels. At the elementary level it is not uncommon for coteaching to occur for as much as half of the day. In these settings, the special education teacher may have as many as six to eight students in two target classrooms for most or all of the day. The special education teacher could then spend several hours a day in each of those classrooms coteaching with the general education teacher. For example, the special education teacher, Ms. Gentry, coteaches with the fourth-grade teacher, Mr. Marcus, and the fifth-grade teacher, Ms. Lau. She teaches reading and math in the morning with Mr. Marcus and then again with Ms. Lau in the afternoon. The special education teacher coplans reading and math activities with the general education teacher, and both decide how to target and support the learning of the students with disabilities.

At the secondary level, coteaching is different for the special education teacher, Mr. Prudhi. He would describe his role as more of a supportive teacher (Villa et al., 2008), meaning that the content area teacher for math, social studies, and science take primary responsibility for designing and delivering the lesson, and his role is to support instruction for students with disabilities. What are some of the activities that Mr. Prudhi might perform within the supportive teaching role?

He might

- Determine the big idea of the instructional unit that week, and make it clear to the students with special needs.

- Identify the key academic vocabulary and concepts related to learning the unit, and teach those to students with special needs to ensure that they can learn the content.

- Identify resources that would facilitate learning for students with special needs, such as supportive texts written at levels the student can read, technology that would provide access to visual images or other information to promote learning, and/or a video that would make some of the key concepts more accessible.

- Conduct a pretest on the material to be taught that week to determine what students know and what they need to know to successfully master the information that week.

- Provide modifications to assignments, homework, or assessments so that they are accessible to students with disabilities.
- Communicate with key personnel at the school to facilitate learning for target students.
- Communicate with parents to facilitate learning for target students.
- Develop resources, such as overheads, PowerPoint slides, graphs, and other learning devices, to facilitate learning for all students.
- Provide 60-second lessons to key students to reinforce ideas taught and ensure learning.
- Provide small-group lessons to key students as needed.
- Follow up with students to ensure learning is sustained and connected to previous learning.

Apply the Concept 5-4 provides guidelines for effective coteaching in elementary school classes for students with learning and behavior problems.

Coplanning Special education teachers often coplan with general education teachers for the students with special needs who are in their classrooms. Sometimes special education teachers also coteach in those classrooms; at other times, they assist the teacher in planning and making adaptations for students with special needs to lessons that will be taught without their assistance or facilitate development of appropriate evaluations or homework assignments.

In long-range coplanning, special education and general education teachers plan broad overall goals and outcomes for a class and the specific students with disabilities who are in that class. This coplanning of broad goals occurs quarterly or more frequently as needed, and accommodates the IEPs of students with disabilities.

Special education and general education teachers may also coplan specific lessons and outcomes for a unit of study or for a designated period of time (e.g., weekly). The planning pyramid (Schumm, Vaughn, & Harris, 1997) provides a process for coplanning by special and general education teachers to meet the needs of students with disabilities in general education classrooms. As can be seen in Figure 5-1, a form for unit planning, and in Figures 5-2 and 5-3, forms for lesson planning, forms can be used to facilitate the process. Working together, teachers complete the forms to identify their objectives, materials needed, and their roles and responsibilities in delivering the instruction. While planning, the special education teacher can provide ideas for adaptations, clarification, scaffolding, and use of materials to facilitate

5-4 APPLY THE CONCEPT

Guidelines for Effective Coteaching

Effective coteaching involves the following:

1. *Voluntary participants.* Teachers should choose to work together and should not be forced into a collaborative teaching situation (Scruggs et al., 2007). Ms. Andrews is a special education teacher who has been coteaching in three fourth-grade classrooms for several years to assist children with learning and behavior problems. She began collaborating after attending a workshop on coteaching with the fourth-grade team from her school. She says the reason she and her team are successful is because "we enjoy working together, have compatible teaching styles, and feel comfortable discussing differences."

2. *Shared responsibility.* Teachers combine their knowledge and resources to plan instruction. Therefore, they also share the accountability for the outcomes of those decisions.

3. *Reciprocity of ideas.* While the amount and nature of input will vary by teacher, both teachers must accept each other's contributions as integral to the collaborative process.

4. *Problem solving.* Not only must teachers collaborate to identify and find solutions to meet student needs, they also must accept that problems will arise when two professionals work together to coordinate instruction. Dealing with problems that arise during collaboration is not so different from finding solutions to student problems. To solve a problem it is helpful to identify concerns, share information regarding the problem, brainstorm possible solutions, evaluate the ideas, create a solution plan, try the solution, and evaluate its success (Villa et al., 2008).

5. *Interactive communication.* Effective communication occurs when teachers trust each other and are not afraid to voice either their agreement or disagreement, when they communicate accurately and directly, and when they remain sensitive to differences (Villa et al., 2008).

6. *Conflict resolution.* Disagreements and even arguments are inevitable in any collaborative process. Implementing a plan to resolve conflicts can lead to better solutions than if the problem is ignored (Idol et al., 2000).

FIGURE 5-1 Unit-Planning Form

What some students will learn.	Date: _____ Class Period: _____
	Unit Title: _____
	Materials/Resources:
	_____
	_____
	_____
What most students will learn.	_____
	Instructional Strategies/Adaptations:
	_____
	_____
	_____
What *all* students should learn.	_____
	Evaluation/Products:
	_____
	_____
	_____
	_____

FIGURE 5-2 Weekly Coplanning Form

Time Period: _____   Week Of: _____   Content Area: _____

	GE	SE
Goals:		
Activities:	GE	SE
Monday		
Tuesday		
Wednesday		
Thursday		
Friday		
Material(s):	GE	SE
Monday		
Tuesday		
Wednesday		
Thursday		
Friday		
Groups/Students:	GE	SE
Monday		
Tuesday		
Wednesday		
Thursday		
Friday		
Evaluation:		**Other:**

FIGURE 5-3 Example Elementary Coteaching Lesson Plan

General Educator: _Ms. Marco_   Special Educator: _Ms. Sanders_   Grade: _5_

Date	Coteaching Technique	Specific Teacher Tasks	Materials	Evaluation	Individual Student Needs
2/8	Model B: Two mixed-ability groups	Literary Discussion: Both teachers lead discussions on the class reading of *The Cay*. In each group, teacher and students write comprehension questions. Students call on volunteers to respond to their questions. Teacher interjects throughout the discussion, making sure all students have a chance to ask and answer questions.	Student copies of *The Cay* Discussion journals	Evaluate discussion journals Monitor participation	Assist Roger in formulating a response to share with class; remind Sam to pause first to organize thoughts before responding; Joe completes journal on computer
2/9	Model D: Five same-ability groups	Literacy Groups: Teachers each work with one of the two lower groups to provide explicit instruction in word analysis. The other three student groups work independently to complete reading and literacy assignments.	Student books Reading log	Chart number of words decoded correctly Evaluate reading logs	Ms. M: Mini lesson on *r*-controlled vowels Ms. S: Reteach syllabication strategy for decoding
2/10	Model D: Six mixed-ability groups	Survival Centers: Ms. S works at the Vocabulary center with Roger's group. She then follows his group to the Survival Word Game station and provides a word-building mini lesson. Ms. S remains at the Word Building station and provides a building words mini lesson to Sandy's group. Ms. M monitors the remaining groups.	Center activities	Monitor group work Evaluate student work in word building	Roger works in a pair instead of in a foursome; Sandy brings behavior contract to stations
2/11	Model A: One group: Teaching on purpose	Research Reports: Ms. S gives directions for research report. Ms. M monitors work while Ms. S sees three small skill-level groups (10–12 minutes each) to work on fluency/decoding.	Step-by-step research planners	Record fluency progress on student charts Evaluate planners	Roger uses modified research planner; Joe and Pedro complete work on computer
2/12	Model C: Two groups: One reteach	Research Reports: Ms. S works with students who are ready to begin research while Ms. M reteaches students who need assistance to develop a plan for their individual research projects.	Step-by-step research planners Research materials	Evaluate planners	Julie and Sam paraphrase steps before writing; Joe and Pedro complete work on computer

learning. Essential to the success of the planning pyramid is the identification of core ideas, concepts, vocabulary, and/or principles that the teachers determine to be essential for all students to learn. This information is entered at the base of the pyramid. Information that the teacher deems important for most students to learn is written in the middle of the pyramid. Information for a few students to learn is written at the top of the pyramid. Teachers who implement the planning pyramid find that it not only facilitates the organization of the material they intend to teach, but also provides guidelines for instruction (Schumm et al., 1997).

Successful Coteaching Joyce Duryea is an elementary special education teacher who has worked as a resource room teacher for 9 years (Klingner & Vaughn, 2002, provide a case study of Joyce if you would like to read more about her). She was asked to work collaboratively with three general education teachers who had approximately five students with disabilities in each of their classrooms. Joyce said, "When I was preparing to be a special education teacher, it never occurred to me that I would need to know how to coteach in a general education classroom. I always thought I would have my group of students with special needs and that is the way it would be." However, she has found her new role exciting and challenging. Joyce puts it this way: "I think I'm a better teacher now, and I definitely have a much better understanding of what goes on in the general education classroom and what kinds of expectations I need to have for my students."

Several core issues must be addressed if coteaching partnerships are likely to succeed (Pugach & Winn, 2011; Scruggs et al., 2007):

- *Who gives grades, and how do we grade?* Perhaps the issue that warrants the most discussion before coteaching is grading. Special education teachers are accustomed to grading based on the effort, motivation, and abilities of their students. General education teachers consider grades from the perspective of a uniform set of expectations. Communicating about grading procedures for in-class assignments, tests, and homework will reduce the friction that is frequently associated with grading students with disabilities in the general education classroom. Grading can be particularly challenging at the secondary level, where grades can be used to make high-stakes decisions about access to postsecondary education, rank in class, and graduation.
- *Whose classroom management rules do we use, and who enforces them?* Most general and special education teachers know the types of academic and social behaviors they find acceptable and unacceptable. Rarely is there disagreement between teachers about the more extreme behaviors; however, the subtle classroom management issues that are part of the ongoing routines of running a classroom can cause concerns for teachers. It is beneficial for teachers to discuss their classroom management styles and their expectations for each other in maintaining a smoothly running classroom. Critical to success is determining when and with whom the special education teacher should intervene for discipline purposes.
- *What space do I get?* When a special education teacher spends part of his or her day instructing in another teacher's classroom, it is extremely useful to have a designated area for the special education teacher to keep materials. Special education teachers who coteach for part of the school day in another teacher's classroom feel more at home and are better accepted by the students when they have a legitimate claim on space, including a designated desk and chair.
- *What do we tell the students?* Teachers often wonder whether students should be told that they have two teachers or whether they should reveal that one of the teachers is a special education teacher. We think that it is a good idea to inform the students that they will be having two teachers and to introduce the special teacher as a "learning abilities" specialist. Students both accept and like the idea of having two teachers. In interviews with elementary students who had two teachers (special education and general education), the students revealed that they very much liked having two teachers in the classroom (Klingner, Vaughn, & Schumm, 1998). Similarly, early in the school year, inform parents that their child will have two teachers and that both will be responsible for their child's learning.
- *How can we find time to coplan and coordinate?* The most pervasive concern of both general and special education teachers who coteach is finding enough time during the school day to plan and discuss their instruction and the learning of their students. This is of particular concern for special education teachers who are working with more than one general education teacher. Teachers need a minimum of 45 minutes of uninterrupted planning time each week if they are to have a successful coteaching experience. One suggestion that has been made by several of the teacher teams with whom we have worked is to designate a day or a half-day every 6 to 8 weeks when teachers meet exclusively to plan and discuss the progress of students as well as changes in their instructional practices.
- *How do we ensure parity between teachers?* Teachers consistently report that having equal footing in the classroom is the preferred working arrangement for successful coteaching. There may be occasional examples of a teacher having considerably more knowledge and expertise and thus serving as the mentor for the coteacher, but typically when teachers view themselves and each other as having skills and knowledge to benefit the coteaching situation, success is more likely.
- *How do we know if it's working?* Many teachers work so hard to make coteaching work that they overlook the most important goal: ensuring that students learn. Teachers must collect and evaluate student data to determine whether instruction is effective. A general rule to follow if students are not making adequate progress is to increase the intensity of instruction and decrease the teacher–student ratio. In addition to student learning, it is important that coteachers take time to evaluate the

coteaching process. Dieker (2001) found that effective coteachers discussed their roles and responsibilities on an ongoing basis and made adjustments as needed.

Collaboration with Paraprofessionals and Families

In addition to working closely with general educators, special education teachers must also collaborate frequently with paraprofessionals and families. While some of the same principles for collaborating with general educators apply when collaborating with paraprofessionals and families, it is important to keep in mind that the differences in roles and expertise between you and the paraprofessionals and families will influence how you communicate and collaborate. However, you all should share a common goal: student success. Check out Reading Rockets for excellent information about working with parents and other educational professionals:

Collaborating with Paraprofessionals Schools often rely on paraprofessionals to provide support to general and special education teachers and students. Often, the special education teacher is in charge of supervising paraprofessionals. Many exceptional education specialists work closely with paraprofessional teaching assistants. Although teaching assistants never have complete responsibility for planning, implementing, or evaluating a student's program, they often participate in all of these areas. It is important that paraprofessionals not be assigned to students whom the teacher then spends little time seeing. Paraprofessionals need to have their teaching responsibilities rotated among many students so that the teacher spends frequent intervals teaching and evaluating all students. Because paraprofessionals are often responsible for implementing class rules, they need to be completely familiar with class and school rules and their consequences. Many paraprofessionals comment that they are successful in their roles when they have confidence that they understand what is expected of them. Suggestions for working with paraprofessionals are provided in Apply the Concept 5-5.

What skills are important in working with paraprofessionals? Competencies that administrators, teachers, and paraprofessionals identified as important for teachers to have when working with paraprofessionals (Ashbaker & Morgan, 2006; Wallace, Shin, Bartholomay, & Stahl, 2001) include:

- *Open communication.* Teachers should share student-related information and explain the role of the paraprofessional to the paraprofessional and to all other personnel.
- *Planning and scheduling.* Coordinating the paraprofessionals' schedules is the responsibility of the special education teacher at most schools. It may be helpful to have a written schedule that is evaluated and revised based on students' needs and observation of effective practices.
- *Instructional support.* Teachers should provide regular feedback to paraprofessionals about their instruction. Schedule time frequently initially, and then less often as paraprofessionals' skills are established, to observe instruction, provide feedback, and then model the instructional practices that you need the paraprofessional to implement.
- *Modeling for paraprofessionals.* Modeling instructional strategies and a professional manner of interacting with students are part of a teacher's responsibility when supervising paraprofessionals.
- *Training.* Special education teachers are often responsible for providing on-the-job training for paraprofessionals. This includes expectations about communicating with others, communicating with students, managing student behavior, and completing appropriate paperwork.
- *Providing support for RTI.* Many paraprofessionals are asked to serve key roles in the implementation of RTI models. These roles include screening students, scoring screening and progress-monitoring measures, and providing interventions to individual students or small groups. Paraprofessionals work much more successfully when they are fully and adequately prepared for these roles and provided ongoing support and feedback from the special education teacher.
- *Responding to students, teachers, and families in ethically responsible ways.* One of the critical roles of the special education teacher is to adequately prepare paraprofessionals for their ethical responsibilities related to confidential student and family information as well as grades and student behavior. The Council for Exceptional Children (CEC) provides guidelines for paraprofessionals on ethical practices). Ethical practice skills recommended by CEC for paraprofessionals include (1) respond to professionals, students, and family members in ways that are consistent with laws and policies; (2) demonstrate problem solving, flexible thinking, conflict management techniques, and analysis of personal strengths and preference; (3) act as a role model for students with disabilities; (4) demonstrate a commitment to supporting learners in achieving their potential; (5) demonstrate that they can separate personal and professional issues as a paraeducator; (6) maintain a high level of competence and integrity; (7) use prudent judgment;

Working with Paraprofessionals

Jamie DeFraites is a first-grade teacher in New Orleans. Her multicultural classroom of 22 students includes 11 Vietnamese children and 2 Hispanic students who are English-language learners. Jamie explains, "I love my class and was actually asked to loop to second grade—so I'll have the same students next year!"

Jamie is fortunate enough to work with two paraprofessionals, who join her classroom at different times during the day. Here are Jamie's tips for working with paraprofessionals:

1. It's important to have mutual respect and trust. I let the paraprofessionals know how fortunate I feel to have additional adults in the classroom and how important their job is in helping all students learn. I also thank them every chance I get—in the presence of the principal, parents, and students.

2. At the beginning of the year, I talk with the paraprofessionals individually about their interests and skills and try to match their duties with their strengths. Both paraprofessionals are bilingual (one in Vietnamese and one in Spanish), so assisting me with parent communication is very important. One of the paraprofessionals is very creative and helps me design learning centers. The other is very interested in math and helps me with review and extra practice for students with challenges in that area.

3. Each of the paraprofessionals is eager to learn new skills and strategies. It is worth my time to explain instructional strategies to them so that they can do more than grade papers—they can actually interact with children in small groups or individually. It took me a long time to learn to teach—I'm still learning. I don't assume that the paraprofessionals automatically know how to teach. If I can share some of my training, the payoff is big for my students.

4. At the beginning of the year, we also clarify roles, responsibilities, classroom routines, and expectations for student learning and behavior. Spending that time in planning and communicating is time well spent. We're on the same page.

5. The paraprofessionals both work with several other teachers, so their time in my class is very limited. We have to make each minute count. Their tasks have to be well defined. I also plan a backup—what to do when there is nothing to do.

6. Finally, I encourage the paraprofessionals to get additional professional training. I let them know about workshops and other opportunities to learn. The more they learn, the more my students benefit!

Jamie admits that she would like to have a regular planning time with the paraprofessionals. As she says, "Often, we have to plan on the run." Also, her school district does not require periodic feedback or performance review sessions. This is something Jamie definitely recommends. "Fortunately, I have not run into problems with either paraprofessional, but if I did, it would be a good idea to have a system for giving feedback in a systematic way."

Source: Sharon Vaughn, Candace S. Bos, & Jeanne Shay Schumm, *Teaching Exceptional, Diverse, and At-Risk Students in the General Education Classroom*, 6th ed. (Boston: Allyn & Bacon, 2013). Copyright © by Pearson Education. Reprinted by permission of the publisher.

(8) demonstrate proficiency in oral and written communication as well as other academic skills as needed; (9) engage in activities to increase their own knowledge and skills; (10) engage in self-assessment; and (11) accept and use constructive feedback.

- *Management.* Teachers need to maintain regular and positive interactions with paraprofessionals and support their skill improvements.

Collaborating with Families Family involvement and collaboration are fundamental to student success. What can you do to help increase family and school collaboration? Dettmer, Thurston, and Selberg (2004) provide some key ideas:

- Place the focus of any discussion on the needs and wants of the family and the students, not on their values.

- Accept the family and the student as they are. Stop wishing that they were different.

- Remember that most family members are not trying to provide poor parenting. Rather, they are often doing the best they can in their given circumstances.

- Respect the family's right to have different values than you do.

In addition, remember that family members are often experts on their child. In most circumstances, they know their child much better than you do. Approach them with this

> In this **video** ▶, you can observe a meeting between John's teachers and his mother to discuss his academic and behavior issues. How do they collaborate to make decisions to help John at school and at home?

knowledge in mind. Do your best not to talk down to parents; treat them as you would like to be treated if your roles were reversed. By establishing a collaborative relationship with parents, you may obtain insights about your students that you would not be able to get in any other manner.

When working with families from diverse cultural and linguistic backgrounds, it is important to learn as much as you can about your students' backgrounds. A minimal but important step is to learn the correct pronunciation of the family's name and a few words in their native language. Enlist the support of a translator, if possible. Ideally, the translator should be trained in special education.

Matuszny, Banda, and Coleman (2007) developed a four-step plan for collaborating with culturally and linguistically diverse families. The plan is designed to aid teachers in better understanding a particular family's needs as well as to strengthen the trust between the family and the teacher. The steps are as follows:

1. The first phase is *initiation*. During this phase, which preferably occurs before the school year begins, the family members and teacher get to know each other. This contact should be informal and fun. True collaboration is difficult if the relationship between a family and teacher remains impersonal and/or uncomfortable.

2. During *building the foundation*, the second phase, teachers establish trust with families by providing them with choices (e.g., how they would like to be involved in the classroom or how they would like to receive information from the teacher) and asking for input on certain classroom routines or behavioral procedures.

3. The third phase, *maintenance and support*, involves positive communication, which is delivered according to the families' preferences about how they would like to be contacted.

4. *Wrap-up and reflection* is the last phase of collaboration. The teacher and the family reflect on what worked and did not work in terms of their collaboration. This information can be used to plan for the next year or passed on to the next teacher.

Communication with Other Professionals

What are the principles of communication, and how can teachers communicate with parents and professionals? In addition to assessment, intervention, curriculum development, and classroom management, a major role for the teacher of students with learning and behavior problems is communication. Effective special education teachers communicate regularly with general education and other special education teachers, school administrators, and other educational and psychological professionals such as the school psychologist, speech/language therapist, and so on. Ability to communicate effectively is a skill that significantly affects an educator's job success. Despite the importance of this skill, most teachers finish school with no formal training in communication.

Principles of Communication

Successful communication with parents, teachers, and other professionals is built on certain principles. Particularly within inclusion models and frameworks that emphasize RTI, teachers' success with communication influences positively their success as professionals and the learning outcomes of their students.

Mutual Respect and Trust Building mutual respect and trust is essential for successful communication. As a special education teacher, you are likely to work cooperatively with the school psychologist in several important ways including screening students and evaluating students who are referred for special education or who have been placed in special education for several years and require another evaluation. You may also work with the speech and language specialist, because many of the students with disabilities also demonstrate speech or language problems currently, or have done so previously. It is very likely you will be coteaching, coplanning, or cooperating on an ongoing basis with several general education teachers. All of these individuals will have more confidence in you and be more willing to work with you to benefit students with disabilities if you establish a relationship of respect and trust with them.

Acceptance People know if you do not accept them or do not value what they have to say. Parents/guardians are aware when teachers do not really want to see them during conferences but are merely fulfilling a responsibility. Acceptance is communicated by how you listen, look, respond, and interact with others.

Pointers for communicating acceptance include the following:

- Demonstrate respect for the knowledge and needs of each of the professionals with whom you work. Often special education teachers assume that general education teachers do not "understand" the needs of the target student with disabilities.
- Demonstrate respect for the diverse languages and cultures that families and their children represent.
- Introduce professionals to other members of the education team in a way that sets the tone for acceptance.

- Give each professional working with the student an opportunity to speak and be heard.
- Ensure that a language of acceptance is used by all professionals and families.

Listening Effective listening is more than waiting politely for the person to finish. It requires hearing the message the person is sending. Effective listeners listen for the real content of the message as well as for the feelings in the message. Often this requires restating the message to ensure understanding.

Mrs. Garcia, the mother of 12-year-old Felipe, telephoned his special education resource room teacher, Mr. Sanchez.

Mrs. Garcia: Felipe has been complaining for the past couple of weeks that he has too much work to do in his biology and math classes and that he is falling behind. He says he is flunking biology.

Mr. Sanchez: How much would you say he is studying each night?

Mrs. Garcia: It's hard to say. He stays out with his friends until dinner, and then after dinner, he starts talking about all his homework. Sometimes he sits in front of the TV with his books, and sometimes he goes to his room.

Mr. Sanchez: He has mentioned in my class how much work he has to do. I wonder if he is feeling a lot of pressure from different teachers, including me?

Mrs. Garcia: Well, he has said he thinks you are working him too hard. I know sometimes he is lazy, but maybe you could talk to him.

Mr. Sanchez: Felipe works very hard in my class, and I expect a great deal from him. I will talk with him after school and arrange a meeting with his other teachers as well.

Mrs. Garcia: Thank you, and please do not tell Felipe I called. He would be very upset with me.

Questioning Knowing what type of questions to ask can help individuals to obtain the information they need. Questions can be open or closed. An *open question* is a question that allows the respondent a full range of responses and discourages short yes-or-no answers. Open questions begin with *how, what, tell me about,* and similar phrases.

Mrs. Lishenko suspected that Matt, one of her students, was staying up very late at night, because he was coming to school very tired and seemed to drag all day. He was also resting his head on his desk in the afternoon. She decided to call Matt's father to discuss the problem. She started the conversation by giving Matt's father some information about a meeting of family members that was going to be held in the school district that she thought would be of particular interest to him. She

then proceeded to describe Matt's behavior in class. Finally, Mrs. Lishenko asked, "What do you think might be happening?" Matt's father began to confide that he was not paying much attention to Matt's bedtime and that Matt was staying up late watching movies on the new DVD player. Mrs. Lishenko's question gave Matt's father the opportunity to explain what he thought was happening. Rather than posing several possibilities or telling Matt's father that Matt was staying up too late at night, Mrs. Lishenko asked an open question, which allowed Matt's father to interpret the situation. Matt's father suggested that he would establish a firm bedtime. In this situation, asking an open question allowed Matt's father both to indicate how he felt and to offer a solution.

Involving people in identifying problems increases the likelihood that they will not feel threatened and that they will be willing to make necessary changes.

Staying Directed Follow the lead of professionals, paraprofessionals, and parents whenever they are talking about a student. A skillful consultant can respond to others and still keep the discussion focused. It is not uncommon for families to mention other related home factors that may be influencing their child's progress in school, such as marital difficulties, financial problems, or other personal problems. When professionals or parents discuss serious problems that are beyond our reach as educators, we need to assist them in finding other resources to help them with their problems. Ms. Lopez, a special education teacher at the middle school, keeps the name and telephone number of the school counselor as well as other community outreach resources near her telephone. She is ready to refer parents and other professionals for assistance when needed.

Apply the Concept 5-6 provides a list of tips for effective communication with professionals and families.

Developing Interviewing Skills

Interviews are the key to open communication and effective intervention. Special education teachers often work as consultants to paraprofessionals, general education classroom teachers, other educational and psychological specialists, and families. These interviewing skills help to meet the need to ask questions that inform and to follow up appropriately on information provided. There are five steps to good interviewing:

1. *Ask open questions.* Open questions permit respondents a full range of answers, allowing them to bring up a topic or problem they have on their mind. Open questions are generally followed by questions that require more specificity. Mr. Schwab, the special education resource room teacher, began his interview with Mrs. Francosa, the fourth-grade teacher, by asking an open question: "How is Yusuf's behavior lately?"

Facilitating Effective Communication with Professionals and Families

1. Indicate respect for their knowledge and understanding of the child.

2. Demonstrate respect for the diverse languages and cultures families and their children represent.

3. Introduce them to other members of the education team in a way that sets the tone for acceptance.

4. Give each person an opportunity to speak and be heard.

5. Ensure that a language of acceptance is used by all professionals and family members.

6. Even when you are busy, take the time to let professionals and family members know that you value them, and that you are just unable to meet with them at this time.

7. Avoid giving advice unless it is requested. This does not mean that you can never give suggestions; however, the suggestions should be given with the expectation that the person may or may not choose to implement them.

8. Avoid providing false reassurances to colleagues or families. False reassurances may make them and you feel better in the short run but in the long run are harmful. When things do not work out as you predicted, everyone can become disappointed and potentially lose trust.

9. Ask specific questions. Using unfocused questions makes it difficult to conduct a consistent, purposeful conversation.

10. Avoid changing topics too often; this requires that you monitor the topic and direct others to return to the topic.

11. Avoid interrupting others or being interrupted, which disturbs the conversation and makes effective collaboration difficult.

12. Avoid using clichés. A cliché as a response to a problem situation makes the other person feel as though you are trivializing the problem.

13. Respond to colleagues and family members in ways that attend to both the content of their message and their feelings.

14. Avoid jumping too quickly to a solution. Listening carefully and fully to the message will help you get at the root of the problem.

Source: S. Vaughn, C. S. Bos, & J. S. Schumm, *Teaching Students Who Are Exceptional, Diverse, and At-Risk in the General Education* Classroom (Boston: Allyn & Bacon, 2013). Reprinted with permission.

---

2. *Obtain specificity.* This requires asking questions or making restatements that identify or document the problem. After Mrs. Francosa describes Yusuf's behavior in the general education classroom, Mr. Schwab attempts to identify key points and to obtain specificity in describing the behavior: "You said Yusuf's behavior is better in the classroom but worse on the playground. Can you identify which behaviors in the classroom are better and which behaviors on the playground are worse?" Without drilling the interviewee, an attempt is made to identify the problem and provide documentation for its occurrence so that an appropriate intervention can be constructed.

3. *Identify the problem.* Problem identification can be based on information obtained, or problems can be identified by the person being interviewed, often in the process of answering questions: "It seems like there is good progress in terms of completing classroom work. Let's figure out a way of reinforcing that behavior. There's a problem with Yusuf's responding to teasing on the playground. His response has been to fight, which is getting him in more trouble. Any thoughts about how we might change that behavior?"

After listening to suggestions from the teacher, Mr. Schwab might add, "Let me provide some suggestions that have been effective in the past with other students."

4. *Solve problems.* Suggestions for solving identified problems and implementing the solutions are generated. Both the professional being interviewed and the consultant contribute suggestions to solving the problem. Often, other professionals are included in the suggestions: "Perhaps we could discuss Yusuf's problem with his counselor and ask her to teach him some strategies for coping with teasing. We could also identify the students who are teasing him and reinforce them for not teasing."

The tone for problem solving should be one of flexibility. There are often many possible solutions but only a few that will work with a particular student. The goal is to find a solution the teacher is willing to implement that is effective for the student.

5. *Summarize and give feedback.* Summarize the problem and the plan of action. Be sure to indicate who is responsible for what. Whenever possible, establish a timeline for completing the tasks: "You will send home notes to Yusuf's parents, informing them of his progress in seatwork in the classroom. I will meet with the

counselor about his problem on the playground, and you will talk with his peers and arrange a system for reinforcing them for not teasing. I'll check back with you during lunch this week to see how things are going. I'm very pleased with this progress, and I am sure much of it is due to your hard work and follow-up."

Working with Other Professionals

What is the role of the special education teacher as a consultant to general education teachers, and what are the considerations and barriers for successful inclusion? Consulting and communicating with professionals is an important task for teachers of students with learning and behavior problems. Teachers need to develop and maintain contact with the school psychologist, counselor, speech/language therapist, physical therapist, occupational therapist, principal, and other related professionals. Because 90% of all students with learning and behavior disorders are included for all or part of the day, a positive, cooperative working relationship with general classroom teachers may be most important of all.

Communication with General Education Teachers

When a student with a learning or behavior problem is placed in the general education classroom, the special education teacher can take several steps to communicate effectively with the general education teacher:

> In this **video** ▶, you will learn the many ways that general education teachers collaborate with parents, administrators, special education teachers, related service providers, and others in order to best meet their students' needs. What methods did the general education teachers model that facilitate collaboration and communication?

1. Describe the type of learning or behavior problem the child has and some general guidelines for how to deal with it in the general classroom.

2. Provide a copy of the child's IEP to the classroom teacher, and discuss the goals, objectives, special materials, and procedures needed.

3. Describe the progress reports you will be providing to the home and putting in your files.

4. Develop a schedule for regular meetings, and discuss other times that both the classroom teacher and special teacher are available for meetings.

5. Ask the classroom teacher how you can help, and describe the special accommodations that are needed.

Even when special education teachers develop and maintain an effective communication program with general education teachers, there are still a number of potential barriers to successful inclusion:

1. *The general education teacher may feel unable to meet the needs of the included student with disabilities.* Ms. Huang has been teaching second grade for 2 years. When she was informed that Omar, a student who has been identified as having an emotional disorder, was going to be included in her general education classroom for several hours each morning, she panicked. She explained to the principal that she had not taken any coursework in special education and did not feel able to meet the needs of the new student. The special education teacher met with Ms. Huang to describe Omar's behavior and explain the progress he was making. She assured Ms. Huang that Omar would be carefully monitored and that she would check with Omar and Ms. Huang daily at first and then less frequently as he adapted to the new setting and schedule. She asked Ms. Huang to explain what types of activities usually occurred during the time Omar would be in her room, and she identified ways for Ms. Huang to succeed with Omar. The special education teacher took careful notes and asked many questions about Ms. Huang's expectations so that she could prepare Omar before his transition to the general education classroom. In this situation, communication that provided specific information about the student's learning problems and what the classroom teacher could do to ensure a successful learning environment proved most helpful. In addition, the special education teacher obtained expectations about the general education classroom so that she could best prepare the student for the transition.

2. *The general education classroom teacher may not want to work with the included student with disabilities.* Mr. Caruffe, a seventh-grade science teacher, expected all students to perform the same work at the same time, with no exceptions. He was particularly opposed to having special education students in his classroom because he felt that they required modifications to his core program. His philosophy was, "If students need modifications, they don't belong in the general education classroom, they belong in special education." Dealing with teachers like Mr. Caruffe can be particularly challenging for special education teachers. Despite continuous attempts to work out a collaborative effort, educational philosophies can be sufficiently different that special education teachers feel it is hopeless to attempt inclusion in certain classrooms. Problems arise when alternative classrooms are not available without reducing the content areas available to special students. If there are multiple teachers for each content area, students may be included into classes where teachers are more accepting. Principals can help by setting a school policy that rewards teachers for working appropriately with pupils who have learning and behavior problems.

3. *Finding time to meet regularly with all classroom teachers is difficult.* At the elementary level, special education teachers meet regularly with all classroom teachers who have students included for all or part of the day. This consultation includes discussing students' progress, planning students' programs, adapting instruction in the general classroom, and solving immediate academic and social problems with students. It is better to meet weekly with classroom teachers for a short period of time (10 to 15 minutes) than to meet less often for longer periods of time.

At the secondary level, continued involvement with all classroom teachers is a challenge. In large schools, the exceptional students' general education classroom teachers vary within content area and by year. It is possible for special education teachers to have over 25 teachers with whom they consult. Special education teachers manage this by meeting with teachers in small groups. Sometimes they organize these groups by content area to discuss successful adaptations made within a common content. Sometimes meetings are organized to focus on the needs of a particular student, and all teachers who work with this student meet at the same time. Finding time and maintaining contact with general education teachers requires creativity and persistence.

4. *Students may not be accepted socially by peers in the general education classroom.* This problem occurs not just with students who have behavior problems, but also with students who have learning disabilities. Following is a list of behaviors that are considered important by both general education and special educators for success in general education classrooms:

- Follows directions
- Asks for help when appropriate
- Begins an assignment after the teacher gives the assignment to the class
- Demonstrates adequate attention
- Obeys class rules
- Tries to complete a task before giving up
- Doesn't speak when others are talking
- Works well with others
- Respects the feelings of others
- Refrains from cursing and swearing
- Avoids getting in fights with other students
- Interacts cooperatively with others
- Respects the property of others
- Shares materials and property with others
- Refrains from stealing the property of others
- Tells the truth

Special education teachers may want to focus on teaching these behaviors before and during a student's transition to inclusion.

Collaboration in an RTI Model

Collaboration among the various personnel involved in a school's RTI model is essential for a number of reasons. First, remember that using an RTI framework can help a school identify what supplemental instruction or intervention students may need to "catch up" to their grade-level peers. To ensure that a student is receiving appropriate intervention, communication among the classroom teacher, intervention provider, and other school personnel (e.g., the reading coach, special education teacher, or school psychologist) needs to be consistent and frequent. Many schools implementing RTI set aside regular weekly or monthly meeting times and space for teachers and specialists to discuss student data and make instructional changes, if necessary.

Collaboration between professionals also helps schools address what several administrators have identified as the number-one challenge to successful implementation of RTI: scheduling. By having teachers work collaboratively in creating schedules conducive to providing interventions, schools are better able to offer interventions on a consistent basis. Mrs. Middlestock, an elementary special education teacher, works with teachers at each grade level before the beginning of the school year to help teachers identify a common time across grade levels when students can be pulled out for interventions. By working collaboratively with her colleagues to identify intervention times, Mrs. Middlestock feels that she achieves greater teacher buy-in in terms of support for RTI and that teachers are more likely not to forget to send their students to her for Tier II interventions.

In some schools, particularly at the middle school level, Tier II interventions are used to preteach or reteach concepts from the general education curriculum. Therefore, it is crucial that classroom teachers and intervention teachers collaborate on pacing and content so that students are pretaught vocabulary and concepts and/or given additional practice on concepts or skills in a timely and appropriate manner. In addition, collaboration can be used to ensure that intervention teachers are delivering interventions with fidelity. In schools using RTI to identify students with learning disabilities, it is necessary to ensure that the interventions the students receive are delivered as they were designed to be taught. Mrs. Middlestock collaborates frequently with the other intervention providers and when possible observes them to make certain that all of the interventions are being delivered with fidelity.

Working with Families

What is the teacher's role in addressing the needs of the entire family? This section highlights the teacher's interaction with families. We first discuss family adjustment, including sibling adjustment, to a child with learning and behavior problems. We also describe family-centered practice and explore families' involvement with the schools and their role in planning their child's educational program.

Family Adjustment

The family is an important force in a child's learning and development. From a systems perspective, many mental health professionals recommend an integrated approach to working with students with learning disabilities and behavior disorders. This integrated approach typically involves all or part of the family in the program, including an initial meeting with the entire family; involvement of selected family members; or ongoing clinical help that involves the family at certain times. Not all families who have children with learning and behavior problems need therapeutic assistance. For example, a family-centered approach to positive behavioral supports has been heralded for families of children with severe behavior and emotional difficulties (Carr et al., 2002; Dempsey & Keen, 2008).

Adjusting to a child with learning and behavior disorders is often difficult, resulting in stress (Lessenberry & Rehfeldt, 2004), with greater stress for those families who have children with signification social and behavioral disabilities, particularly those that are disruptive (Hastings, Daley, Burns, & Beck, 2006; Orsmond, Seltzer, Greenberg, & Krauss, 2006). Understanding how families adjust and interact with the child on the basis of their interpretation of the child's needs is an important role for the special education teacher. However, several key findings about families of children with disabilities have positive implications in working with these families (Ferguson, 2002):

- Overall patterns of adjustment and well-being are similar across families with children with and without disabilities. Thus, families who have a child with a disability are probably more like other families than they are different.

- Significant numbers of parents and siblings report that there are perceived benefits and positive outcomes from having a child or sibling with disabilities. This does not suggest that all aspects are easy but that many aspects are viewed positively.

- Having a family member with disabilities is stressful to all members of the family, but engaging the family in meaningful and functional ways is beneficial.

Siblings In addition to how parents respond to a child with learning or behavior problems, the responses of other siblings is important. Lardieri, Blacher, and Swanson (2000) conducted a study to determine whether the presence of a child with learning disabilities, with or without reported behavior problems, affects the psychological well-being and self-concept of the child's siblings.

Although sibling relationships in families of children with and without learning disabilities differed in their perception of the quality of their sibling relationships and self-reports of their own behavior, the difference was not significant enough to render a clinical diagnosis of sibling maladjustment. Not surprisingly, some siblings appear to be affected very little, whereas others are affected more seriously. Some siblings may have concerns about causes of the difficulty; explanations for the unusual behaviors of their sibling; adjustments in parenting that may be interpreted as more time, attention, or leniency toward their sibling (Gallagher, Powell, & Rhodes, 2006).

Many families are concerned because their child with learning disabilities or behavior disorders takes more of their time and consideration than do the other children in the family. Siblings may feel as though the child with special needs is getting all of the family's attention and special privileges. It is important for parents/guardians to develop schedules in which they assign special time for each of their children. A sibling of a child with learning disabilities commented:

> Everything always seems to center around Scott. He always seems to be the focus of the conversation and whom my parents are concerned about. I do pretty well in school and don't seem to have many problems, so sometimes I feel left out. It really meant a lot to me when my mother and father both scheduled time during the week for me to be alone with them. Usually my dad and I would go to the park, and sometimes we would go on an errand. Often my mom and I would work together in the kitchen, making my favorite dessert, chocolate chip cookies. The best part was that it was just me and them. I really think it helped me be more understanding of Scott. Somehow, I just didn't resent him so much anymore.

Apply the Concept 5-7 describes what families generally want from professionals.

Family Involvement in Planning and Placement Conferences Families provide consent for evaluation, participate in the program and educational plan, and are kept involved in all decisions regarding a child's educational program. Why are families so involved in special education?

First, it ensures cooperation between home and school. Families can provide information about the child to which the schools may not have access, and family members can follow up on educational goals in the home. Second, it ensures that families will have access to information about student evaluations and records and can better monitor appropriate placement and programming by the school. One area that holds significant potential benefits is involving family members in the planning and placement conference for the child.

What Families of Students with Learning Disabilities Want from Professionals

In a survey of over 200 families of children with learning disabilities, families indicated what they really wanted from professionals (Dembinski & Mauser, 1977). A summary of the findings follows:

1. Families want professionals to communicate without the use of jargon. When technical terms are necessary, they would like to have the terms explained so that they can understand.

2. Whenever possible, they would like conferences to be held so that all family members can attend.

3. They would like to receive written materials that provide information that will assist them in understanding their child's problem.

4. They would like to receive a copy of a written report about their child.

5. They would like specific advice on how to manage specific behavior problems of their child or how to teach needed skills.

6. They would like information on their child's social as well as academic behavior.

The information that is obtained about the child's learning and behavior problems can increase family members' understanding, which in turn can lead to changes in family behavior toward the child. In addition, family members learn about the focus of the child's school program and can reinforce those learning and behavior efforts in the home. Unfortunately, this is more the ideal than a description of the real world. Despite the best intentions of school personnel and parents, cooperative and extensive family involvement in the placement and planning process is minimal.

There are many explanations for lack of family involvement in educational planning. One is that school personnel do not have adequate time to meet with families and fully explain the child's program or do not know how to take advantage of family members' knowledge and preferences (Harry, 2008). In a recent review of research on parent involvement for students with disabilities from different cultural groups, Harry's (2008) review of the literature concludes that there are several barriers to widespread use of ideal practices, including a deficit view of families, cross-cultural misunderstandings related to the meanings of disability, and culturally different views of the roles of parents and caregivers.

Often families can attend meetings only early in the morning before going to work or in the evening on their way home. These times usually conflict with the schedules of school personnel and require them to meet with families outside of their required work time. Because of their dedication and interest in children, professionals are often willing to meet at these times, but they are not motivated to meet for extended periods of time.

Families may perceive the professionals as responsible for appropriate decisions in their child's best interest and do not want to be coparticipants in the educational program. Rather than a lack of interest in the child's program, this may actually indicate less confidence in their own ability to participate effectively.

It could be that families would like to be more involved but feel intimidated by the number of professionals and the uncommon terminology. Many parents are not comfortable in a setting in which there are numerous professionals such as teachers, the principal, psychologist, counselor, or speech and language therapist, who are providing views on the parent's child. These parents may feel these professionals have information to offer, but worry that it isn't the right information for the decision making that is happening. Parents may be unfamiliar with new terminology and may not be comfortable asking questions.

During conferences, special education teachers need to be sensitive to family members' feelings and needs. They can serve as advocates for the parents, asking questions of the classroom teacher or other professionals that they feel the family member may have wanted to ask but did not.

The Spotlight on Diversity feature provides considerations for working with families from culturally and linguistically diverse groups. Apply the Concept 5-8 addresses involvement of all families in the special education process.

Conferences with Family Members: Planned and Unplanned Planned conferences with family members occur frequently and include multidisciplinary team meetings, annual parent–student meetings, or regularly scheduled meetings to report on academic and behavioral progress. Conferences provide teachers with the opportunity to do the following:

- Review the student's materials, grades, and work progress.
- Meet with other professionals to provide an overall review and report on student progress.

Spotlight *on Diversity*

Considerations for Families Who Are Culturally and Linguistically Diverse

1. Assume that families want to help their children.

2. Consider your language when talking with parents, and be thoughtful about not using language that suggests a deficit model of considering the child.

3. Provide materials in a range of formats including orally, in writing (family's language), through videotape, and through formal and informal presentations.

4. For parents who are interested, provide opportunities for families to learn the skills and activities the students are learning so they can reinforce them in the home.

5. Provide opportunities for families to influence their child's educational program.

6. Provide workshops that include role-playing and rehearsing situations between families and school personnel to increase families' confidence in working with school personnel.

7. Involve families from the community who are familiar with the culture and speak the home language of the children's families in work at the school.

8. Provide an informal meeting with families so they can exchange experiences and learn tips from each other.

9. Invite families to school, and ask them to share their backgrounds or activities with other students and families.

10. Provide ongoing professional development for teachers and other educators so that they are familiar with linguistic and cultural practices and respond sensitively with this knowledge to parents and other family members.

The law provides for early intervention services that meet the developmental needs of children from birth to the age of 3 and their families, including physical development, cognition, language, social, and self-help skills. Parents and families play an important role, and an individualized program plan must be designed to meet their needs. This program plan, called the individualized family service plan (IFSP), should provide a coordinated array of services, including the following:

- Screening and assessment

- Psychological assessment and intervention

- Occupational and physical therapy

- Speech, language, and audiology

- Family involvement, training, and home visits

- Specialized instruction for parents and the target student

- Case management

- Health services that may be needed to allow the student to benefit from the intervention service

See Apply the Concept 5-8 for an overview of family involvement in special education.

Criteria for Establishing an IFSP

The IFSP is a family-oriented approach to designing an effective management plan for infants and toddlers with disabilities (birth to age 3). The IFSP must be developed by a multidisciplinary team and should include the following elements:

- A description of the child's level of functioning across the developmental areas: physical, cognitive, communication, social or emotional, and adaptive

- An assessment of the family, including a description of the family's strengths and needs as they relate to enhancing the development of the child with disabilities

- A description of the major goals or outcomes expected for the child with disabilities and the family (as they relate to providing opportunities for the student)

- Procedures for measuring progress, including a timeline, objectives, and evaluation procedures

- A description of natural environments in which the early intervention services will be provided

- A description of the early intervention services needed to provide appropriate help for the child and family

- Specifically when the specialized intervention will begin and how long it will last

- A designated case manager

- A specific transition plan from the birth-to-three program into the preschool program

Response to Intervention and Family Involvement

Families have an important role to play when schools implement response to intervention (RTI). This model provides new challenges and opportunities for engaging and communicating with families about their children's progress. Technically, most of what occurs within an RTI model occurs within general education, so questions can arise about when and how to communicate effectively with families.

First, many families may neither know what RTI is nor understand why their child is being screened for learning difficulties. Second, families value knowing if their child is receiving secondary or tertiary interventions and having access to the findings from progress monitoring. Third, teachers can assist families by providing them with a list of sample questions they might want to ask about RTI. An excellent source of information for parents about RTI is the National Center for Learning Disabilities.

5-8 APPLY THE CONCEPT

Family Involvement in the Special Education Process

Response to Intervention: Ten Questions Parents Should Ask

As states and school districts work to implement an RTI process that provides early help to struggling students, families need to understand the components essential to the appropriate implementation of RTI. Here are 10 questions to ask about RTI to help guide you through the process:

1. Is the school district currently using an RTI process to provide additional support to struggling students? If not, do they plan to?

2. What screening procedures are used to identify students in need of intervention?

3. What are the interventions and instructional programs being used? What research supports their effectiveness?

4. What process is used to determine the intervention that will be provided?

5. What length of time is allowed for an intervention before determining if the student is making adequate progress?

6. What strategy is being used to monitor student progress? What are the types of data that will be collected, and how will student progress be conveyed to parents?

7. Is a written intervention plan provided to parents as part of the RTI process?

8. Is the teacher or other person responsible for providing the interventions trained in using them?

9. When and how will information about a student's performance and progress be provided?

10. At what point in the RTI process are students who are suspected of having a learning disability referred for formal evaluation?

- Review the student's portfolio, assessment information, and progress reports.
- Provide samples of the student's most recent work.
- Establish and review goals and criteria for academic and behavioral work.

Sometimes conferences with families are unplanned. Family members may phone, stop by the school, or schedule a conference with little notice. When this occurs, remember these procedures: Listen carefully until the family members have expressed the purpose of their visit, paraphrase what you understand to be their question or issues, and respond to the question and issue as completely as possible. Often family members stop by with a simple question or concern that is a disguise for a larger issue; that is why it is important to listen carefully and wait until family members are finished.

Individuals with Disabilities Education Act and Family Involvement

The Individuals with Disabilities Education Act (IDEA) was passed in 1990 and amended in 2004. This law ensures that all youngsters with disabilities receive a free, appropriate public education, which emphasizes special education and related services designed to meet their unique needs. All students between the ages of 3 and 21 are eligible for a program of special education and related services under Part B of the IDEA; children with disabilities from birth to age 3 are eligible for special education and related services under Part C. Part C, which is a subchapter of the IDEA, is about infants and toddlers with disabilities.

In this video ▶, two special education teachers discuss the special education laws that guide educational practices for students with disabilities. What benefits and/or drawbacks do they mention?

◢ Successful inclusion requires cooperation among professionals, particularly the general and special education teachers. Inclusion also requires willingness to adapt and accommodate instruction and materials to meet the learning and behavaior needs of students. General education teachers have different levels of experience in working with other teachers and students with learning and behavioral problems. Furthermore, many students are not prepared for general education classrooms. Potential problems can be avoided if general education teachers know and use a variety of instructional strategies. This effort takes time and planning, and it can result in less content coverage within a given time frame. Special education teachers can facilitate inclusion by working closely with general education teachers; observing general education classrooms; simulating the academic and social demands of general education classrooms in the special education classroom; and assisting classroom teachers in adapting materials, instruction, and the instructional environment.

◢ Special education teachers work with other professionals to develop systems that meet the needs of students with learning and behavioral problems within an individual school setting. Coteaching occurs when special education and classroom teachers provide instruction together in the general education classroom. Consultant teaching occurs when the special educator works with the classroom teacher to solve problems for students with disabilities in the general education classroom. Special education teachers also coordinate paraprofessionals who assist students with disabilities in the general education classroom. TATs are school-based teams (including support professionals, classroom teachers, and administrators) that assist the classroom teacher in meeting individual students' instructional and behavior needs.

◢ Teachers are effective when they take the time to build mutual trust, to accept others' points of view, to really listen to what families and other professionals say, to provide encouragement to family members and personnel who work with students with special needs, and to use straightforward language to explain information. In addition, teachers can learn more from personal communication by asking open-ended questions that solicit thorough responses. Balancing listening and responding to family members provides teachers with a mechanism of ensuring they are meeting parents' goals while also communicating relevant school-related information. In this way, teachers develop a working alliance in which all members of the group have a common goal of developing an appropriate program for the student.

◢ Consultants who provide special education services must work with the general education teachers. Communication and collaboration are key to successful inclusion, and finding time to work with the general education teacher is a challenge and a necessity. It is also important that the special education teacher work within the RTI framework

◢ Families have different issues and concerns, so the first step is to listen carefully to parents to ensure that you know their questions, challenges, and goals for their child. Identifying and addressing the needs of the entire family are essential to assisting a student. Teachers can also assist families by addressing their issues, providing appropriate and accurate information about their child's performance, and providing resources such as information about summer activities, guidelines for assisting students with homework or academic skills, and accessing support systems with other parents or organizations. By valuing the parents' role in their child's education and by using the parents' knowledge about their child, teachers and families can work together to develop an appropriate educational program. RTI practices provide a unique opportunity for schools and families to communicate and collaborate before referral, during screening and assessment, when secondary interventions are provided, and through examining the collected data.

After completing this chapter, test your knowledge of the concepts by completing the Assessment.

Assessing and Teaching Oral Language

LEARNING OUTCOMES

1. Describe the components of language including the main areas of language delays, as well as how they manifest in the development of content, form, and use of language.

2. Identify guidelines for teaching oral language, content, form, and use.

3. Detail the strategies and considerations on which teachers should focus when teaching culturally and linguistically diverse learners.

4. Explain practices teachers can use for working with families to develop students' language skills.

5. List the procedures special education teachers might implement with language specialists to implement response to intervention (RTI).

Malik is a second grader who is good at sports—especially soccer. He seems like such a capable young boy until he talks. Whether he is having a conversation or trying to read, he has difficulty thinking of the right words. Yesterday he was trying to describe the work that he and his dad had done on his go-cart. He could not think of the words *screwdriver, hammer, sandpaper, wheels, axle, steering wheel,* and *engine.* Sometimes he tried to describe what he wanted to say; for example, when he could not think of *screwdriver,* he said, "It's the thing you use to put in things that are kind of like nails." Sometimes he can only think of a word that is similar to the word he is trying to say; for example, he said, "I was using the hitter to hit some nails." Malik also has trouble remembering words when he reads. He does not remember simple sight words and consequently has to resort to attempting to sound out the words. Often, the words he cannot remember are not phonetic (e.g., *come, are, was, very*), so his strategy is only somewhat useful. Malik is in a second-grade classroom, but he receives speech and language therapy for his language problems, and in addition to his core reading program, he receives tutoring support for his reading difficulties.

Monica is in fifth grade. If you just listen to her, you would not necessarily recognize that she has a language problem. Her vocabulary is adequate for a student her age, and she uses fairly sophisticated sentences. But Monica's language frequently seems to get her in trouble. Monica is growing up in a tough neighborhood, but she goes to school in a middle-class neighborhood across town. She has difficulty switching her language style to match the new context of the school. She continues to use the language she uses with friends, resulting in the interpretation that she is both arrogant and disrespectful to teachers. Monica also has other problems using language effectively. She has difficulty determining when a listener is not understanding what she is trying to explain. Instead of restating her point in another way, she continues with her description or explanation. When the listener asks her to clarify a point, Monica implies that the listener is stupid. She also does not take turns easily during conversations. She either monopolizes the conversation or expects the other person to do all the talking while she gives little feedback to indicate that she is listening. Consequently, Monica is perceived as a student with behavior problems, although there is no indication of any serious emotional problems. She sees her counselor once a week. However, this is really not enough. She has difficulty with reading and writing, and this influences her learning in social studies and science as well. In the last several months, the speech-language pathologist has been consulting with the counselor and Monica's teachers. They are working with Monica to help her use language more effectively and to vary it across contexts. Perhaps with all professionals working together, they will be able to eliminate some of the learning and behavior problems Monica is currently experiencing.

Antoine is a third grader with language delays. He started talking at age 3½, and his language now seems more like that of a first grader. He began receiving speech and language therapy at age 4. Although he is currently in a class for students with mild-to-moderate disabilities, he receives speech and language therapy for 30 minutes, 4 days a week. Antoine is delayed in all aspects of language. His vocabulary is limited, he uses simple sentence patterns, and he uses language primarily to obtain information and attention and to inform others of his needs. He rarely initiates a conversation, but he will carry on a conversation if the other person takes the lead. Mrs. Borman, his teacher, works closely with the speech-language pathologist to help ensure that Antoine is receiving the structured language programming he needs throughout the school day. One of Mrs. Borman's roles in this programming is to provide Antoine with many opportunities to practice and receive feedback on the skills he is learning in speech-language therapy.

As teachers, we will undoubtedly work with students like Malik, Monica, and Antoine. To assist these students in developing effective language and communication skills, we need to understand the *content of language instruction* and *strategies for teaching language*.

Components of Language

We now know more about the importance of language development in facilitating access to learning than ever before. Did you know that language development is an excellent predictor of reading outcomes, particularly as they relate to reading comprehension? Furthermore, students who have underdeveloped language have difficulties in all areas of learning including math, social studies, and science. Language is the foundation for learning, and ensuring that students have at minimum an adequate language foundation is essential. One of the ways teachers can promote students' language development is to improve their own knowledge about language and how to integrate principles and practice throughout the school day. The Common Core State Standards provide guidance about language standards that are necessary (www.corestandards.org). Figure 6-1 describes some common core oral language standards.

Within the Common Core State Standards there is an overarching goal that represents the standards for language development from second through twelfth grade. That primary goal is: Use knowledge of language and its conventions when writing, speaking, reading, or listening.

As an educator, this is a very big goal and difficult to consider with respect to the instructional implications at each grade level. The common core further specifies goals for each grade level, starting at grade 2, that are summarized below:

- Compares formal and informal use of English (second grade)
- Chooses words and phrases for affect (third grade)

FIGURE 6-1 Common Core Standards for Language Progressive Skills

Standard	Grade 3	Grade 4	Grade 5	Grade 6	Grade 7	Grade 8	Grades 9–10	Grade 11–12
L.3.1f. Ensure subject-verb and pronoun-antecedent agreement.								
L.3.a. Choose words and phrases for effect.								
L.3.3a. Produce complete sentences, recognizing and correcting inappropriate fragments and run-ons.								
L.4.1g. Correctly use frequently confused words (e.g., *to/too/two; there/their*).								
L.4.3a. Choose words and phrases to convey ideas precisely.[1]								
L.4.3b. Choose punctuation for effect.								
L.5.1d. Recognize and correct inappropriate shifts in verb tense.								
L.5.2a. Use punctuation to separate items in a series.[2]								
L.6.1c. Recognize and correct inappropriate shifts in pronoun number and person.								
L.6.1d. Recognize and correct vague pronouns (i.e., ones with unclear or ambiguous antecedents).								
L.6.1e. Recognize variations from standard English in their own and others' writing and speaking, and identify and use strategies to improve expression in conventional language.								
L.6.2a. Use punctuation (commas, parentheses, dashes) to set off nonrestrictive/parenthetical elements.								
L.6.3a. Vary sentence patterns for meaning, reader/listener interest, and style.[3]								
L.6.3b. Maintain consistency in style and tone.								
L.7.1c. Place phrases and clauses within a sentence, recognizing and correcting misplaced and dangling modifiers.								
L.7.3a. Choose language that expresses ideas precisely and concisely, recognizing and eliminating wordiness and redundancy.								
L.8.1d. Recognize and correct inappropriate shifts in verb voice and mood.								
L.9–10.1a. Use parallel structure.								

The following Language Progressive Skills were identified within the Common Core Standards for Language as likely to require instructional attention across grade levels (www.corestandards.org)

Source: Common Core Standards, retrieved from http://www.corestandards.org

- Recognizes and observes differences between the conventions of spoken and written standard English (third grade)

FIGURE 6-2 Components of Language from a Functionalist Perspective

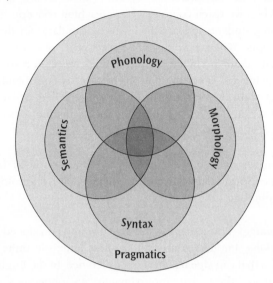

- Chooses words and phrases to convey ideas precisely (fourth grade)
- Chooses punctuation for effect (fourth grade)
- Differentiates between contexts for formal English and informal discourse (fourth grade)
- Expands, combines, and reduces sentences for meaning, reader/listener interest, and style (fifth grade)
- Compares and contrasts varieties of English in stories, dramas, or poems (fifth grade)
- Varies sentence patterns for meaning, interest, and style (sixth grade)
- Maintains consistency in style and tone (sixth grade)
- Chooses language that expresses ideas precisely, consistently, recognizing and eliminating wordiness and redundancy (seventh grade)

The Content of Language Instruction

The content of language instruction for students with learning or language problems focuses on teaching the language code, the rules of the code, and how to use the code to communicate. To help us understand language so that we can more effectively plan the content of language instruction, we will consider several components of language (see Figure 6-2).

Content Content, also called *semantics,* refers to the ideas or concepts we are communicating. Keiko can communicate her desire for two chocolate-chip cookies in numerous ways. For example, she can say, "I want two chocolate-chip cookies," or "Me want choc-chip cookies" (while pointing to the cookie jar and then holding up two fingers). In both cases, the content or ideas are the same.

When we teach content, we are teaching concepts and helping students to learn the labels (vocabulary) for those concepts. When a young child asks such questions as "What's that?" or "What are you doing?" we often respond by giving the label for the object (e.g., spoon, blanket, shirt) or the action (i.e., stirring, making the bed, ironing). In this way, we are teaching the labels for the ideas or concepts.

Form   *Form* refers to the structure and sound of language. Form is usually further divided into phonology, morphology, and syntax.

Phonology Phonemes are the actual sounds produced by speakers. Phonemes are the smallest linguistic units of sound that can signal a meaning difference. In the English language, there are approximately 45 phonemes, or speech sounds, that are classified as either vowels or consonants (e.g., /a/, /k/, /ch/). Learning speech sounds and their relationships to the written letters can help students to identify unknown words when they read and spell (Blachman, 2013; Foorman, Arndt, & Crawford, 2011).

Phonology refers to the rules for combining and patterning phonemes within the language. Phonology also includes the control of vocal features (timing, frequency, duration) that influence the meaning we express when talking. Without changing any words, we can vary the underlying meaning of a sentence simply by the way we change our voice (e.g., intonation, pitch, and stress). For example, try saying, "I like that?" and "I like that." Depending on the intonation, stress, and pitch, the first statement can mean "I don't like that," and the second one can mean "I do like that."

Morphology Whereas phonology focuses on sounds, morphology focuses on the rule system that governs the structure of words and word forms. Whereas phonemes are the smallest sound units, morphemes are the smallest units of language that conveys meaning. There are two different kinds of morphemes: root words, or words that can stand alone (e.g., *cat, run, pretty, small, form*), and affixes (prefixes, suffixes, and inflectional endings), which are added to words and change the meaning of the words (e.g., *cats, rerun, smallest, transformation*).

Helping elementary and secondary students learn the various affixes and their meanings can assist them in decoding words, determining the meaning of words, and spelling. For example, students who do not recognize or know the meaning of the word *predetermination* can break it into the root word *determine* (to decide), the prefix *pre-* (before), and the suffix *-tion* (denoting action in a noun). Then the students can decode or spell the word and generate the meaning of *predetermination* as a decision made in advance.

Developmentally, inflectional endings are the easiest to learn, followed by suffixes and then prefixes (Owens, 2007). The most frequently used prefixes in American English are un-, in-, dis-, and non-. Table 6-1 presents some common prefixes, suffixes, and inflectional endings, along with their meanings and several examples. As you can see from the table, definitions of prefixes and suffixes are sometimes vague. Although only one or two definitions are provided in the table, some affixes have four or more definitions (Gunning, 2010a, b). Teaching this information (or a simplified list for elementary-age students) can assist students in understanding and learning new vocabulary and in decoding unknown words. To give students a sense of the meanings, provide experiences with several examples.

Syntax Syntax refers to the order of words in sentences and the rules for determining that order. Just as phonemes combine to form words, words combine to form phrases and sentences. In the same way that rules determine how phonemes can be combined, rules also determine how words can be combined. The basic syntactical structure for English is subject + verb + object (e.g., "Mike eats cereal").

The rules for combining words vary across languages. For example, in English, adjectives almost always precede the noun they modify (e.g., a delicious apple), whereas in Spanish, adjectives generally follow the noun they modify (e.g., *una manzana deliciosa*—an apple delicious).

Use   *Pragmatics* refers to the purposes or functions of communication, or how we use language to communicate (Owens, 2009). Language use, or pragmatics, grows significantly during the school years (Owens, 2009). During the later school years, students use language proficiently with multiple meanings, employing figurative language, sarcasm, and jokes. Students also learn to vary their communication style, or *register,* on the basis of a listener's characteristics and knowledge concerning the topic. By the age of 13, students can switch from peer register to adult register, depending on the person with whom they are talking, and from formal register to an informal register, depending on the setting and circumstances (Nippold & Sun, 2008; Owens, 2007). Pragmatics for students in middle grades is important for connecting well with peers.

The way a speaker uses language will also be influenced by the knowledge the speaker thinks the listener has about the topic being discussed. If you are describing how to hang a picture on a wall, the language you use will depend on whether you think the listener is familiar

TABLE 6-1 Common Inflectional Endings, Prefixes, and Suffixes

Common Forms	Meanings	Examples
Inflectional Endings		
-ed	notes past tense on verbs	helped, studied
-ing	notes present progressive on verbs	helping, studying
-s/-es	notes third person singular on verbs	he helps, she studies
-s/-es	notes plurals on nouns	cats, parties
-'s	notes possessive	Juan's, cat's
Prefixes		
ante-	before, front	antecedent, anterior
anti-	against	antifreeze, antitoxin
bi-	two	bicycle, bisect
co-	with, together	coworker, cooperate
de-	down, remove, reduce do the opposite	descent, dethrone, devalue, deactivate
dis-	opposite	distrust, distaste
en-	to cover, to cause to be	encompass, enslave
ex-	former, from	expatriate, explain
hyper-	above, more, excessive	hyperactive, hyperventilate
hypo-	below, less	hypoactive, hypodermic
il-	not	illogical
im-	not, in, into	impatient
in-	not, in, into	incomplete, inclusion
inter-	between, together	interact, intervene
ir-	not, into	irreversible
mis-	wrong	miscalculate
non-	not	nonstop
out-	beyond, exceeds	outlast, outside
pre-	before, in front of	preface, precaution
pro-	before, in front of, in favor of	proceed, proactive
re-	again, backward motion	repeat, rewind
semi-	half	semifinalist
sub-	under, less than	subordinate, subtitle
super-	above, superior	superordinate
trans-	across, beyond	transportation
un-	not	unlucky, unclear
Suffixes		
-able	capable of, tendency to	dependable
-age	result of action or place	breakage, orphanage
-al	pertaining to	personal
-ance	changing an action to a state	hindrance
-ation	changing an action to a state	determination
-ant	one who (occupation)	accountant, attendant
-en	noting action from an adjective	harden, loosen
-ence	changing an action to a state	dependence, reference
-er/or	notes occupation or type of person	lawyer, writer, sculptor
-er	notes comparative (between two)	larger, younger
-est	notes superlative (among more than two)	largest, youngest
-ful	full of	bountiful, joyful
-fy	to make	magnify, identify
-ible	capable of, tendency to	credible, collectible
-ion/-tion	changing an action to a state	confusion, transformation
-ish	belonging to, characteristic of	Finnish, greenish
-ist	one who (occupation)	artist, biologist
-ive	changes action to characteristic or tendency	creative, active
-less	unable to, without	harmless, thoughtless
-ly	denotes adverbs	loudly, friendly
-ment	result of an action (noun)	entertainment, excitement
-ness	quality, state of being	happiness, deafness
-ous	full of, having	victorious, harmonious
-some	quality or state	handsome, bothersome
-ward	turning to	homeward, wayward
-y	characterized by, inclined to	dirty, sleepy

with a plastic anchor and screw. The manner in which a topic is introduced, maintained, and changes, as well as how we reference topics, is governed by rules of pragmatics. Students who are learning English as a second language and bilingual students with communication disorders may need explicit instruction in pragmatics.

School-Age Language Development and Difficulties

Knowing how language develops during the school years and what difficulties students with learning or language problems demonstrate during these years will help us make decisions concerning the content and focus of language instruction.

Growing evidence suggests that many students with reading problems have mild-to-moderate language problems; the largest subgroup of students with learning disabilities are those who experience language difficulties (Catts, Bridges, Little, & Tomblin, 2008).

Let's examine the development of content, form, and use at the school-age level and the difficulties that students with learning or language problems demonstrate.

Content   During the school years, children increase the size of their vocabularies and their ability to understand and talk about abstract concepts.

Vocabulary Growth During the school years, one of the areas in which students demonstrate the greatest amount of growth is vocabulary. When students enter school, their estimated speaking vocabulary is about 2,500 words (Owens, 2007). School provides students with opportunities to listen, read, and learn, thus increasing their vocabularies. Even math, which is often considered less language-based than social studies and science, contains a significant number of concepts and words to learn (e.g., *subtract, estimate, rational number, trapezoid*).

Schoolchildren also experience an increase in the breadth and specificity of meanings. For example, for a preschooler, the word *bird* may refer to any animal that flies. However, most children later learn a whole set of specific vocabulary that defines different types of birds and their characteristics.

During the school years, students improve considerably in their understanding and organization of abstract concepts. Some examples of this include students' organization of words and ability to group them by such features as animate or inanimate, spatial (location) or temporal (time) relationships, and real or imaginary. For example, in learning about fossils, students learn to simultaneously classify different types of fossils (e.g., trilobites, crinoids, brachiopods) according to plant/animal, extinct/not extinct, and location (e.g., sea, lake, or land).

As students become more proficient word and concept learners, they also learn the multiple meanings of many common words. For example, the word *bank* has several meanings and can function as a noun or a verb:

> Lou sat on the *bank* fishing.
>
> You can *bank* on him to be there.
>
> Put your money in the *bank* for now.
>
> He was able to *bank* the ball to make the basket.

Students with language problems generally have vocabularies that are more limited than average, and their word meanings are generally more concrete and less flexible (Catts & Kahmi, 2005; Owens, 2010). For example, students with learning disabilities may have difficulty understanding the multiple meanings and applications of key words such as *cell* and *factor*.

Many students with reading and language disabilities have greater difficulty understanding that words can have multiple meanings and knowing which meaning to apply. For example, in the question "Was the *fare* that you paid for your taxi ride to the *fair* a *fair* price?" students are required to know and use three different meanings for the word *fair/fare*.

Figurative Language During the school years, students also develop a greater understanding of and ability to use figurative language. Figurative language represents abstract concepts and usually requires an inferential rather than literal interpretation. Figurative language allows students to use language in truly creative ways (Owens, 2007). The primary types of figurative language include the following:

- Idioms (e.g., "It's raining cats and dogs.")
- Metaphors (e.g., "She had her eagle-eye watching for him.")
- Similes (e.g., "He ran like a frightened rabbit.")
- Proverbs (e.g., "The early bird catches the worm.")

Students with language disorders and other disabilities and students who are from other cultures or who have English as their second language tend to have difficulty with figurative language. Yet figurative language, particularly idioms, is used frequently in the classroom. Discussing and using these idioms and adding to the list can assist students with language disorders and second-language learners in improving their understanding and use of the English language. Learning idioms can be particularly helpful to English language learners in better understanding English language. A Web site that provides a list of American English idiom in alphabetical order is Learning English Feels Goods. A sample of items includes:

- About time
- Act one's age
- Actions speak louder than words
- All set
- Add fuel to the fire
- Bark up the wrong tree
- Bank on something
- Be in one's element
- Be a fan of something
- Be up to no good
- Call it a day
- Die of boredom
- Downer
- Earful
- Face the music
- Fall flat
- Get carried away
- Get a move on
- Half-baked
- Hand me down
- Make a bundle
- Make a long story short
- Neck and neck
- Neither here nor there
- Pain in the butt
- Pass the buck
- Read between the lines
- Rain or shine

Word Retrieval Some students with learning or language problems also experience difficulties with word retrieval or word finding (Nippold, 1998; Owens, 2010). A word-retrieval problem is like having the word on the tip of your tongue but not quite being able to think of it. The following dialogue presents a conversation between two third-grade students—one with typical language and the other with word-retrieval problems:

WEB RESOURCES

For additional information on word-finding difficulties, check out Word Finding Difficulties at http://www.wordfinding.com.

Setting: Third-grade classroom
Topic: Discussion about how to make an Easter basket

Susan: Are you going to make, uh, make, uh . . . one of these things [pointing to the Easter basket on the bookshelf]?
Cori: Oh, you mean an Easter basket?
Susan: Yeah, an Easter basket.
Cori: Sure, I'd like to, but I'm not sure how to do it. Can you help me?
Susan: Yeah, first you'll need some, uh, some, uh, the things you cut with, you know. . .
Cori: Scissors.
Susan: Yeah, and some paper and the thing you use to stick things together with.
Cori: Tape?
Susan: No, uh, uh, sticky stuff.
Cori: Oh, well let's get the stuff we need.
Susan: Let's go to, uh, uh, the shelf, uh, where you get, you know, the stuff to cut up.
Cori: Yeah, the paper, and let's also get the glue.

It is obvious from the conversation that both students were frustrated by the communication process. Susan's language is filled with indefinite words (*thing, stuff*), circumlocutions ("The things you cut with"), and fillers ("Let's go to, uh, the shelf, um, where you get, you know, the stuff to cut up"). At first, students like Susan may seem very talkative because of their overuse of descriptions, circumlocutions, and fillers; however, after one listens to them for a while, their language seems empty of information.

Word-retrieval or word-finding problems can occur because students cannot recall the word although they know it or because they have an underdeveloped understanding of the meaning of the word. For example, when a student's semantic network for the concept *bird* is well developed, it will be easier to retrieve the word than if the semantic network is limited and the word has been learned in isolation. Therefore, in assisting students, it is important to help them develop more elaborate understandings of concepts. A second source of word-finding problems is with the retrieval, or search and recovery of the word. In this case, teaching and providing cues (e.g., it's something you ride; peanut butter and _____; it's a type of bird) can assist in retrieval. The Web site speech-language-therapy dot com provides helpful activities to do with youngsters who have word-retrieval difficulties.

Form During the school years, students continue to learn more complex sentence structures. Although by age 5 most students understand and generate basic sentences, first graders do not consistently produce sentences that reflect the syntactical complexities of the

TABLE 6-2   Developmental Sequence for Comprehension of Sentence Types

Syntactic Structure	Sentence	Age of Comprehension By 75%		Age of Comprehension By 90%
Simple imperative	Go!	4–6*	to	6–0 years
Negative imperative	Don't cross!	5–6	to	7–0+ years
Active declarative				
Regular noun and present progressive	The girl is jumping.	3–0	to	3–0 years
Irregular noun and present progressive	The sheep is eating.	6–6	to	7–0 years
Past tense	The man painted the house.	5–6	to	7–0+ years
Past participle	The lion has eaten.	6–0	to	7–0+ years
Future	He will hit the ball.	7–0	to	7–0+ years
Reversible	The car bumps the train.	6–6	to	7–0+ years
Perfective	The man has been cutting trees.	7–0+	to	7–0+ years
Interrogative				
Who . . .	Who is by the table?	3–0	to	3–0 years
What . . .	What do we eat?	3–6	to	5–0 years
When . . .	When do you sleep?	3–6	to	5–6 years
Negation				
Explicit	The girl isn't running.	5–6	to	7–0+ years
Inherent	These two are different.	6–6	to	7–0+ years
Reversible passive	The boy is chased by the dog.	5–6	to	6–0 years
Conjunction				
If . . .	If you're the teacher, point to the dog; if not, point to the bear.	7–0+	to	7–0+ years
. . . then	Look at the third picture; then point to the baby of his animal.	7–0+	to	7–0+ years
neither . . . nor	Find the one that is neither the ball nor the table.	7–0+	to	7–0+ years

Source: E. H. Wiig & E. Semel, *Language Assessment & Intervention for the Learning Disabled*, 2nd ed. (Columbus, OH: C. E. Merrill, 1984). Reprinted with permission of the senior author, Elizabeth H. Wiig, Ph.D., Knowledge Research Institute, Inc.
*4–6 = 4 years, 6 months.

English language. Table 6-2 presents the sequence for selected syntactical structures. Some of the most difficult structures require the use of complex sentences and cohesive devices such as causals (*because*), conditionals (*if*), and enabling relationships (*so that*).

As sentence complexity increases, so does the average length of sentences. Yet it is important to know that mature language still has some grammatical errors, false starts, hesitations, and revisions. Table 6-3 demonstrates the growth in the number of words per sentence or communication unit. As is evident in Table 6-3, spoken sentence length matches chronological age (i.e., an 8-year-old student's sentences are, on the average, eight words long) until the age of approximately 9 years, when the growth curve begins to slow. By high school, adolescents' conversational utterances average 10 to 12 words. Average sentence length, however, is consistently shorter in conversational discourse than in narrative discourse. Youngsters also continue to increase use of inflectional endings, suffixes, prefixes, and irregular verbs. Students with language problems are slower to develop advanced syntactic structures; these delays are most evident in the

elementary grades (Owens, 2007). Table 6-4 lists the age ranges for the development of various word formations and irregular verb usages.

Use   The area of most important linguistic growth during the school years is language use, or pragmatics, as discussed earlier in this chapter. Throughout the school years, students become more empathetic toward the listener and able to understand a variety of perspectives. Older children can vary their communication style, or register, as we discussed earlier.

Young school-age children use language to, for example,

- Gain and hold attention in a socially acceptable manner.
- Use others, when appropriate, as resources for assistance or information.
- Express affection or hostility and anger appropriately.
- Direct and follow peers.
- Compete with peers in storytelling and boasts.

TABLE 6-3 Average Number of Words per Communication Unit (mean)

Grade	High Group	Random Group	Low Group
1	7.91	6.88	5.91
2	8.10	7.56	6.65
3	8.38	7.62	7.08
4	9.28	9.00	7.55
5	9.59	8.82	7.90
6	10.32	9.82	8.57
7	11.14	9.75	9.01
8	11.59	10.71	9.52
9	11.73	10.96	9.26
10	12.34	10.68	9.41
11	13.00	11.17	10.18
12	12.84	11.70	10.65

Source: W. Loban, *Language Development: Kindergarten through Grade Twelve,* Res. Report #18 (Urbana, IL: National Council of Teachers of English, 1976), p. 27. Reprinted by permission of the publisher.

- Express pride in themselves and in personal accomplishments.
- Role-play.

By adolescence, students can do the following:

- Express positive and negative feelings and reactions to others.
- Present, understand, and respond to information in spoken messages related to persons, objects, events, or processes that are not immediately visible.
- Take the role of another person.
- Understand and present complex messages.
- Adapt messages to the needs of others.
- On the basis of prior experience, approach verbal interactions with expectations of what to say and how to say it.
- Select different forms for their messages on the basis of the age, status, and reactions of the listeners.
- Use sarcasm and double meanings.
- Make deliberate use of metaphors.

Some students with learning or language problems also experience difficulties with language *use,* or pragmatics (Owens, 2007). The following dialogue demonstrates how Brice, an adolescent with behavior disorders and subsequent learning problems, has difficulty using language effectively in a conversation with a peer. He tends to switch topics (lack of topic maintenance), does not provide enough context for his listener, does not provide adequate referents for his pronouns, and does not

TABLE 6-4 Development of Word Formation Rules and Irregular Verbs

Word Formation Rules and Irregular Verbs	Age Range (In Years–Months)
Regular noun plurals (balls, chairs)	3–6 to 7–0+
Present progressive tense (running)	3–0 to 3–6
Present progressive tense (going)	3–6 to 5–6
Adjective forms	
Comparative (smaller, taller)	4–0 to 5–0
Superlative (shortest, tallest)	3–0 to 3–6
Noun derivation	
-er (hitter, painter, farmer)	3–6 to 6–6
-man (fisherman)	5–6 to 6–0
-ist (artist, bicyclist)	6–6 to 7–0+
Adverbial derivation (easily, gently)	7–0+
Irregular verbs	
went	4–6 to 5–0
broke, fell, took, came, made, sat, threw	5–0 to 6–0
bit, cut, drive, fed, ran, wrote, read, rode	6–0 to 7–0
drank, drew, hid, rang, slept, swam	7–0 to 8–0
caught, hung, left, built, sent, shook	8–0 to 9–0

Source: Adapted from E. Carrow, *Test of Auditory Comprehension of Language* (San Antonio, TX: Pearson, 2009); K. Shipley, M. Maddox, & J. Driver (1991), Children's development of irregular past tense verb forms, *Language, Speech, and Hearing Services in Schools, 22,* pp. 115–112; E. H. Wiig & E. Semel, *Language Assessment and Intervention for the Learning Disabled,* 2nd ed. (Columbus, OH: C. E. Merrill, 1984).

respond to his listener's requests for clarification. In addition, Brice is unaware of his failure to communicate effectively and blames his conversational partner for communication breakdowns.

Setting: Computer lab

Topic: Brice is explaining to Reid how to play a computer game.

Brice: Did you get in trouble for last night?

Reid: What do you mean for last night?

Brice: You know, for what you did.

Reid: I'm not sure what you're talking about.

Brice: Want to learn how to play Chopperlifter?

Reid: Yeah, I guess, but what about last night?

Brice: Well, one thing you do is put it in the slot and turn on the computer.

Reid: What thing? Do you mean the CD?

Brice: Sure I do. Now watch. *Brice boots the CD and selects Chopperlifter from a game menu.* You got to take it and go pick up the men.

Reid: You mean the helicopter?

Brice: Yeah, aren't you listening?

Reid: Yeah, but you're not telling me enough about the game.

Brice: Yes I am. You're just like my brother, you don't listen.

Reid: I'm not going to put up with this. I'll see you around.

Although this is not reflected in the language sample, Brice also has difficulty varying his language for different audiences. He sometimes sounds disrespectful to adults because he does not vary his language to suit different speakers or contexts. Finally, Brice and other students with pragmatic language difficulties, including students with behavior disorders, tend to misinterpret emotions or meanings indicated by nonverbal communication, including facial expressions and body language, more frequently than their normal peers do. These students may not be classified as having speech and language problems because they have fluent, complex, and clear articulation.

It is important to remember that content, form, and use are related. Sometimes students who appear to have difficulties with language use have them because of limited content and form. For these students, it is important to focus instruction in the areas of content and form and find out whether language use automatically improves

Guidelines for Teaching Language

What guidelines can assist in teaching oral language, content, form, and use? In teaching students with learning or language problems, teachers have traditionally focused on teaching academic skills and have placed less emphasis on the development of oral language skills. However, it is clear that language continues to develop during the school years and that students with reading problems show difficulties in oral language that affect oral as well as written communication (Catts, Compton, Tomblin, & Bridges, 2012). Let's look at some general principles and procedures for teaching oral language skills to these students.

General Guidelines for Teaching Oral Language

Opportunities for teaching oral language abound in the school setting. When we teach students new concepts and vocabulary in content area subjects, we are teaching oral language. When students learn how to give oral reports or retell a story, how to introduce themselves, or how to use irregular verbs, they are learning language. A list of general procedures or guidelines for teaching language is presented in Apply the Concept 6-1 and discussed in this section. These principles not only are important for students with learning problems but also

can benefit other students in the classroom. The speech-language pathologist is a good source for additional guidelines, techniques, and teaching ideas.

Teach Language in Purposeful Contexts   Whether a teacher is teaching a student to use causal relationships (form), to categorize fossils (content), or how to use the telephone to request information (use), it is important to teach language in context. It is difficult to imagine teaching someone how to use a hammer, drill, or saw without using nails, boards, and probably the goal of making a simple wood project. The same should apply in teaching students to use language. Rote practice of sentence structures or rehearsal of word definitions will teach the student little unless this is paired with how to use language.

To foster teaching language in context, the teacher should plan activities that highlight the language skill being taught. For example, Mr. Cardoni used the contexts of following a recipe for chocolate-chip cookies and of building bird feeders to teach the vocabulary related to fractions (e.g., half, one quarter, two thirds, part, whole, fraction). During the activities, the students measured and compared the different fractional parts (e.g., determining what fraction one teaspoon is of one tablespoon). This allowed Mr. Cardoni and his students to talk about the concepts of fractions in a situation in which fractions played an important role in the project and to demonstrate with concrete examples the differences between fractions.

> In this **video** ▶, a teacher is modeling and guiding different language skills during snack time, which is a highly purposeful instructional context. What methods does she use to support the children's oral, written, and spoken language skills in purposeful, meaningful, and fun ways?

In Most Cases, Follow the Sequence of Normal Language Development   Determining the content of instruction is a major part of the teaching–learning process, whether in language, academics, content areas, or social areas. Students with language difficulties may need additional instruction in one of the areas of language development, such as content, form, or use. For example, Susan, the third grader with word-finding problems, has difficulty primarily in the area of content. On the other hand, Brice appears to have adequate content and form in his language but has difficulty with use. Therefore, in planning a language program, begin by determining what knowledge and skills a student has already acquired in the areas of content, form, and use, and then target the subsequent areas in the development process. For instance, if the student is already using past tense ("The boy ate the cake"), you might next focus on past participle ("The boy has

General Principles for Teaching Language

- Teach language in purposeful contexts.
- In most cases, follow the sequence of normal language development.
- Teach comprehension and production.
- Use conversations to promote language development.
- Adjust pacing, chunk information, and check for understanding to promote comprehension.
- Increase wait time to promote production.
- Use effective teaching strategies when presenting a new concept or skill.
- Use self-talk and parallel talk to describe what you and others are doing or thinking.
- Use modeling to demonstrate language.
- Use expansion and elaboration.
- Use structured language programs to provide intensive practice and feedback.
- Use language as an intrinsic motivator.
- Systematically plan and instruct for generalization.

eaten the cake") (see Table 6-2 earlier in the chapter). A speech-language pathologist can be an excellent resource for helping to determine what to teach next.

Teach Comprehension and Production Give students opportunities to develop both their understanding (comprehension) and their ability to express (production) the new knowledge or skill you are teaching. For example, when teaching students to comprehend the past participle, a teacher should label examples of events that have already happened (e.g., "Juan has sharpened his pencil" or "Kim has finished her math assignment"). When providing intensive practice and feedback, the teacher shows students picture-sequence cards (see Figure 6-3) and asks students to identify the picture that demonstrates that something "has happened." To teach production, ask students to explain what has happened by using the past participle form. For example, the teacher could ask, "What have you just done?" When teaching the concepts and vocabulary associated with a new unit or piece of literature, the teacher provides students with opportunities not only to listen to explanations but also to discuss their knowledge of the concepts. Using the pause procedure (Ruhl & Suritsky, 1995), whereby the teacher pauses at logical breaks in the lecture so students can discuss what they are learning with a partner, provides such opportunities. Vaughn and colleagues used the pause procedure of asking students to turn and discuss key concepts and ideas during social studies instruction to enhance vocabulary and comprehension (Vaughn, Martinez, et al., 2009).

Use Conversations to Promote Language Development Students with language problems need opportunities to engage in conversations. Plan opportunities for students to engage in conversations with you and other students

as they work, think, and play. Using discussion groups or promoting "turning and talking" with a peer rather than a question–answer format for reviewing a book or current event is an example of how conversations can be integrated into the classroom. These conversations need not be long, and in secondary settings, they can be accomplished as students enter the room. Apply the Concept 6-2 provides more ideas that you can use and share with teachers and parents about how to promote language through the use of conversations.

Adjust Pacing, Chunk Information, and Check for Understanding to Promote Comprehension Second-language learners and students with language problems often have difficulty comprehending what is being said during class, particularly in content area classes. To promote language comprehension, preteach proper nouns to ensure understanding for all students. Also, use multiple opportunities including oral language, print, and pictures. Whenever possible, state key information in multiple ways.

FIGURE 6-3 Sequence Cards to Help Students Comprehend and Produce Tenses

Promoting Language Through Conversations

- Talk about things in which the child/adolescent is interested.
- Follow their lead in the conversation. Reply to their initiations and comments. Share their excitement.
- Don't ask too many questions. If you must, use questions such as how did/do . . ., why did/do . . ., and what happened . . . that result in longer explanatory answers.
- Encourage the child/adolescent to ask questions. Respond by using information the student has provided as well as integrating new information.
- Use a pleasant tone of voice. You can be light and humorous. Children love it when adults are a little silly.

- Don't be judgmental or make fun of a child's language. If you try to catch and correct all errors, the child will stop talking to you. Rather than correct language or state what is wrong, repeat their statements using correct language.
- Allow enough time for the child to respond.
- Treat the child with courtesy by not interrupting when the child is talking.
- Provide opportunities for the child to use language and to have that language work to accomplish his or her goals.
- Include the child in family and classroom discussions. Encourage participation and listen to his/her ideas.
- Be accepting of the child and of the child's language. Hugs and acceptance go a long way.

Source: Adapted from R. E. Owens, Jr., *Language Disorders: A Functional Approach to Assessment and Intervention* (Boston: Allyn & Bacon, 2010).

It is also helpful if the amount of information that is provided in each segment is reduced. Consequently, information can be chunked or segmented into smaller amounts. For example, observing his students in Mr. Hunt's fifth-grade science class, Mr. Fong noticed that his students usually listened to Mr. Hunt present the first 5 of 15 vocabulary words for a new chapter and recorded about 3 of the words in their science notebooks. After Mr. Fong shared this information with Mr. Hunt, Mr. Hunt decided to chunk the vocabulary into groups of 3 to 5 words and introduce each group only when they were needed rather than all of them at the beginning of a new chapter.

Checking for understanding is also important for facilitating language comprehension. Having a student repeat directions or tell another student what was just discussed are ways to check for understanding other than asking questions.

Increase Wait Time to Promote Production When Marilyn Fantell, a speech-language pathologist, talks about the most important principles for teachers to use when teaching students with language and learning problems, the first one she mentions is wait time. Some students need time to understand what has just been said and to construct a response. These students may have particular difficulty with form (e.g., syntax) and need the extra time to think about the form they should use in constructing their response. Therefore, when a response is required from these students, a teacher should give students extra time to formulate their answer before giving an additional prompt or calling on another student.

Use Effective Teaching Strategies in Presenting a New Concept or Skill As students progress in school, the demands to learn new content and concepts increase exponentially. Particularly for older students, concept knowledge in math, science, and social studies represents a lot of their growth in concept development. Using effective teaching strategies helps students with language difficulties to gain the concepts and content that they need for success in contentarea classes. Based on the teaching–learning process, a number of effective teaching strategies should be incorporated into language instruction. Apply the Concept 6-3 lists key strategies that can be used in teaching a new concept.

> As you watch this video ▶, watch for the teacher to use the effective language intervention strategies identified in Apply the Concept 6-3. Are there any other strategies she could have used to support the student's language development?

Use Self-Talk and Parallel Talk to Describe What You and Others Are Doing or Thinking Using self-talk and parallel talk demonstrates how language is connected to activities. Self-talk describes what the teacher is doing or thinking; parallel talk describes what the student is doing or thinking. Ms. Baraka, a special education teacher who is coteaching in a first-grade classroom, uses parallel talk and self-talk when she joins the students at the different learning centers. She explains, "When I join a center, I try to sit down and join in the activities rather than asking

Effective Teaching Strategies for Language Intervention

Gillam and Loeb (2010) identify principles for proving language intervention to school-age children:

1. *Intensity.* Intensive remediation is essential to progress for students with language impairments. If there is not adequate time during the day for highly focused language intervention, then summers and after-school time is needed.

2. *Active Attention.* Students are more likely to benefit from language interventions when they are interested and engaged in what they are being presented. Signaling students to make sure that they are attending and ready to learn, cueing them when they are paying attention, and providing them with feedback that is engaging about their learning will help ensure that the language intervention is effective.

3. *Feedback.* Receiving feedback about whether responses are correct and then elaborating on this feedback to enhance learning is essential to remediating language difficulties. Direct and not indirect feedback is needed. "That's right, you remembered to sequence your story" is an example of direct feedback.

4. *Rewards.* Supporting internal motivation and recognizing learning and achievement through rewards is an essential feature of effective language intervention programs.

Source: From "Insights from a Randomized Controlled Trial," by R. B. Gillam & D. F. Loeb, January 19, 2010. *American Speech-Language Association Leader.*

---

students questions. I describe what I am doing and what other students in the group are doing. For example, I might say, 'Voytek is making a clay animal. It's blue, and right now he is putting a ferocious snarl on the animal's face. I wonder what kind of animal it is. I think I'll ask Voytek.'" In this way, the students get to hear how words can describe what someone is doing and thinking, and it focuses the attention on the student and the ongoing activities.

Use Modeling to Demonstrate Language Modeling plays an important role in learning language. Whether for learning a new sentence structure, new vocabulary, or a new function or use for language, modeling is a powerful tool. For example, Ms. Simons and her eighth-grade students in resource English class were working on improving discussion skills during literature discussion groups. Ms. Simon was concerned about the number of students who did not clarify what they were saying when it was obvious that other students were not understanding.

To teach clarification skills, Ms. Simons initiated a discussion about clarifying ideas and then modeled how not clarifying ideas and not asking for clarification can lead to confusion. She exaggerated the examples, and the students seemed to enjoy this. Next, Ms. Simons modeled clarification skills as she participated with the students in their literature discussions. As individual students used effective clarifying skills, she commented on this, so that peers were also serving as models. Use of computers with speech recognition and synthetic speech capability also provides for language models and systematic practice such as Laureate Learning Systems.

Use Expansion and Elaboration Language expansion is a technique that is used to facilitate the development of more complex language form and content. By repeating what students say in a slightly more complex manner, the teacher demonstrates how their thoughts can be more fully expressed. For example, Ms. Lee, an elementary teacher, is working to get Rob to connect his ideas and to use adverbs to describe his actions. As he finished several math problems, Rob reported, "I got the first one easy. The second one was hard." Ms. Lee replied, "Oh, you got the first one easily, but the second one was hard." The teacher does not want to imply that she is correcting the student; she is simply showing him a more complex way of expressing the thought. Also, the teacher should expand only one or two elements at once, or the expansion will be too complex for the student to profit from it.

Language elaboration is used to build on the content of a student's language and provide additional information on the topic. For example, Chris, a fourth-grade student with language disabilities, was explaining that snakes have smooth skin. Mr. Anderson elaborated on Chris's idea by commenting, "Snakes have smooth skin and so do lizards. Are there other animals in the desert that have smooth skin?"

Use Structured Language Programs to Provide Intensive Practice and Feedback Teaching in context is critical for learning and generalization. However, sometimes by teaching in context, we do not provide the students with adequate opportunities to practice a new skill. Students who have learning problems need the practice and feedback provided in many language programs and activities to gain mastery of the skill. For example, *Language for Learning* (Engelmann & Osborn, 2008), designed primarily for early elementary students, and *Figurative Language: A Comprehensive Program* (Gorman-Gard, 1991), designed for older students, provide intensive practice in different language content and forms. However, these programs should not serve as the students' entire language program. Although they provide practice and feedback, they generally do not teach the skill within the relevant contexts that are needed for purposeful learning and generalization. Other examples of language development programs can be viewed at Pro.Ed including programs addressing semantics, pragmatics, grammar, phonology, articulation, fluency, listening, and speech and language remediation.

Systematically Plan and Instruct for Generalization As is the case in teaching other skills, language instruction must incorporate into the instructional sequence a variety of contexts, settings, and people with which students interact so they can generalize language learning outside of the instructional setting.

Because language is part of all of our instruction, generalizing principles of language development across settings is possible. Ms. McDonald, a special education resource teacher; Mrs. Kim, the second-grade teacher; and Ms. Cortez, the speech-language pathologist, are working with Julie, a second-grade child with learning disabilities, on sequencing events and using sequence markers (e.g., *first, second, next, last*). When Julie goes to language and resource classes, Mrs. Kim sends a note that lists, in order, the activities Julie has participated in so far during the day. When Julie returns from language and resource class, Ms. Cortez sends back a note that lists her language activities. Each teacher then converses with Julie about what she did in the other teachers' classes, emphasizing sequence and sequence markers. Other activities also build generalization for Julie. Whenever a teacher or Julie's mother reads Julie a story, Julie retells the story and is asked sequence questions. During the weekly cooking activity, Julie and the other students tell the steps in making the food for the day, and the teacher writes these steps on large chart paper with numbers listed beside them. Julie also arranges picture sequence cards and is then asked to describe them. With these activities, Julie receives numerous opportunities to generalize this language skill to a variety of contexts, persons, and settings.

Teaching Language Development Through Content

We teach language content throughout the day. For example, one of the major goals in teaching a new unit in social studies and science is for the students to understand and use the new vocabulary. What are some of the basic vocabulary categories that we may want to teach? Table 6-5 lists some general categories of words and word relationships. Look at some strategies for teaching content or vocabulary, such as the more general vocabulary listed in Table 6-5 and the specific vocabulary found in content area instruction.

Emphasize Critical Features When teaching new concepts, emphasize the features that are important to the meaning. For example, in teaching the concepts of *mountains* and *hills,* the distinguishing or critical features to emphasize are *size* and *height*. In comparison, the *texture of the land* is not important, because it is not a feature that usually helps us to distinguish between hills and mountains. Comparing and contrasting two concepts using a Venn diagram can help students to see the important characteristics (see Figure 6-4). Students remember vocabulary better if they think about how they can use it. Figure 6-5 presents one way in which students can think about a concept in multiple ways.

Vary Concept Introductions Teachers need to keep in mind that concepts should be introduced in a number of different ways. When teaching the concept of *precipitation,* for instance, the teacher may present pictures of different types of precipitation (e.g., snow, rain, sleet, hail, and mist) and have the students tell about a time when they remember each type of precipitation. The class can discuss what is happening to the water in

FIGURE 6-4 Venn Diagram for Comparing Concepts

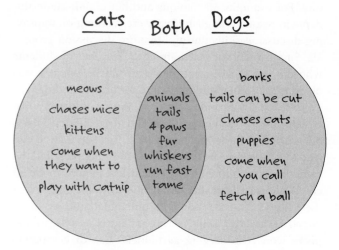

TABLE 6-5 Categories of Words and Word Relationships

Categories	School-Related Examples		
Existence/nouns	science, math, reading, vowels, consonants, sentences, paragraphs		
Actions/verbs	verbs often used in instruction—draw, write, circle, underline, discuss, compare, critique, defend		
Attributes/adjectives	words that describe such attributes as size, shape, texture, weight, position (high/low, first/last), color, age, speed, affect, attractiveness		
Attributes/adverbs	words that describe actions, such as easily, hurriedly, busily, willingly		
Prepositions	locative (in, on, under, beside, in front of, ahead of, behind), directional (off, out of, away from, toward, around, through), temporal (before, after, between), for, from, at, of, to, with, without		
Personal pronouns	*Subjective*	*Objective*	*Possessive*
	I	me	my, mine
	you	you	your
	she, he, it	her, him, it	her, his, its
	we	us	our
	they	them	their
Demonstrative pronouns	this, that, these, those		
Indefinite and negative pronouns	a/an, someone, somebody, something, somewhere, anyone, anybody, anything, anywhere, no one, nobody, nothing, nowhere, the		
Antonyms	full/empty, boiling/freezing, easy/hard, soft/hard		
Synonyms	pants/slacks/trousers/britches		
	laugh/giggle/chuckle		
	happy/glad/pleased/elated/tickled pink		
Homonyms	sail/sale, bear/bare		
Multiple-meaning words	run fast, run in your stockings, go for a run, in the long run		
Comparative relationships	taller than, shorter than		
Spatial relationships	*see* Prepositions		
Temporal-sequential relationships	words connoting measurement, time (days of the week, minutes, seasons), temporal prepositions (first, last, next, then)		
Conditional relationships	if . . . then		
Causal relationships	because, therefore, since		
Conjunctive relationships	and		
Disjunctive relationships	either . . . or		
Contrastive relationships	but, although		
Enabling relationships	in order that, so that		
Figurative language	*Idioms:* catch a plane; hit the road		
	Metaphors: her eagle eye		
	Similes: her eyes twinkled like stars; busy as a beaver		
	Proverbs: The early bird catches the worm.		

the atmosphere when it is precipitating and what the weather is like when precipitation is present.

Present Examples and Nonexamples For example, in learning about cacti, students may generate two lists of plants: one that represents examples of cacti and one that represents nonexamples. Then students can talk about and list the features that make the cacti different from the nonexamples.

Categorize New Concepts A valuable strategy is to categorize new concepts, to ensure students understand how the concepts relate to other concepts. If the concept of *melancholy* is being taught, the students should learn that this is an example of a feeling or emotion. Other feelings are gladness, relief, and hurt. Characteristics of people who are melancholy are "not happy," "quiet," "not talkative," and "somber." These ideas can be depicted in a visual diagram, such as a semantic map, which shows how the different concepts relate to one another (see Figure 6-6).

Present New Vocabulary Simply To help students understand the new material they are learning, present new vocabulary in simple sentences or phrases. It is harder

FIGURE 6-5 Thinking About a Concept in Multiple Ways

Definition	Sentence	Illustration
an oven or furnace for hardening or drying something	a kiln is for rapid drying of lumber.	
Synonym	**Word**	**Antonym**
Microwave	Kiln	Freezer
Create an original sentence using the vocabulary word.	**Create an analogy using the vocabulary word.**	**Where might you hear this word used?**
I used a kiln to dry my lumber for a house.	Kiln is to microwave as icebox is to freezer.	You might find this in a glass blower's shop.

to learn a new concept or idea if the teacher is using difficult language to explain what it means. The rule of thumb is to use simple sentences or phrases to introduce new concepts (i.e., four- to seven-word sentences and two- to four-word phrases).

Reinforce with Games   Use games and other activities to reinforce newly introduced concepts. For example, Twenty Questions is a good game to use to get students to think about the characteristics of a concept and the categories in which the concept falls.

Name That Category is a game that can be played similarly to Name That Tune, except that the object of the game is to earn points by naming the category when examples of a category are given. The sooner the category is named, the more points the player receives.

FIGURE 6-6 Semantic Map of the Concept of *Melancholy*

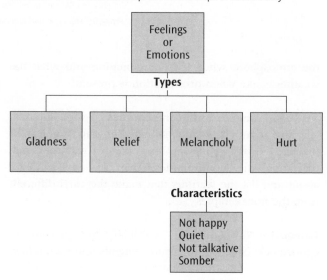

FIGURE 6-7 Sample Cloze Emphasizing Prepositions

Cloze passages can be used either as an oral or written activity, or combined with the oral activity reinforcing the written.

More than anything else, Robert wanted _____ climb _____ the top _____ the mountain. Every day _____ his way home _____ school he looked up _____ the mountain. It was so high that the few trees _____ the top looked very small. He had heard that it would take a day _____ climb _____ the summit, and a day to get back _____ the mountain. One evening when he was looking _____ his window, he saw a campfire burning _____ the top of the mountain. He knew _____ only he practiced hiking, he could make it.

Well, this spring he would start practicing. He and his friend Jim could join the Young Hikers' Club and _____ early summer they would be ready _____ the climb. Robert could hardly wait _____ spring _____ come.

Oral or written *cloze* passages, like that shown in Figure 6-7, can be used to highlight a particular set of concepts being taught.

Idioms, metaphors, similes, and proverbs can be used when playing Charades, with the students acting out the literal meanings of the phrases (e.g., *catch a plane, blow your stack*).

A number of language materials and programs are available for teaching concepts to school-age students. The Instructional Activities feature in this chapter provides selected programs and materials.

Teach Students to Classify and Categorize Words Teaching students to classify and categorize words should improve their long-term memory and thus help them to recall and retrieve specific words. When learning new concepts, students should be encouraged to name the category and then rapidly name the vocabulary in the category. Pictures, written words, and graphic representations such as a semantic map (see Figure 6-6) may help with this activity. When students are having difficulty retrieving a word, provide information about the word to help them retrieve it. For example, if a student is having trouble thinking of the word *eraser,* say to them "it has 3 syllables and begins with this sound, 'e'."

Teach Students to Use Visual Imagery Getting students to "see" in their minds the objects they are trying to retrieve can sometimes help them think of words. To help

In this **video** ⏵, the cloze procedure is described, and you will learn tips to assist teachers in creating and implementing cloze procedures. How can this method be used in different content areas or with different types of texts?

Additional ideas for teaching new concepts and the relationships among those concepts, particularly as they relate to teaching content area subjects (i.e., science, social studies, vocational areas), are discussed in Chapter 10.

students develop these mental images, encourage them to picture new words in their minds. For example, when students are trying to learn the parts of a flower, have them picture a flower in their minds, with the labels for the parts written on the different parts. Have them talk about the kind of flower they pictured, discussing the parts as they describe the flower.

Teach Students to Use Word-Association Clues to Help in Retrieving Words Activities in which students learn and practice word associations (e.g., peanut butter and _____; red, white, and _____) can facilitate word retrieval. These activities may be as broad as asking students to name as many things as they can think of in a given amount of time. But generally, the teacher will want to focus the associations.

Teach Students to Use Synonyms and Antonyms When students cannot recall the precise word they want, they can use an alternative word. Students may be taught to state that the desired word "is the opposite of _____" or "is almost like _____." For example, when struggling to find the word *joyful,* a student can be encouraged to say "It's when you're really happy" or "It's the opposite of feeling sad."

Use Sound, Semantic, or Multiple-Choice Cues to Assist Students in Recalling Words Providing students with cues can assist them in retrieving words. For example, teachers might cue, "It starts with a /k/" (sound cue), "It's not a peach, it's a _____ " (semantic cue), or "It's either a banana, a cat, or a bowl" (multiple-choice cue).

Increase Elaboration in Language Some students with learning disabilities use language that is not very elaborate. When asked to retell stories or events or to give descriptions, these students provide only the most basic information. Teachers can:

1. *Model elaboration by introducing familiar objects or pictured objects and by demonstrating verbal descriptions of their attributes and functions:* In this step, the teacher

describes the object, noting its attributes and functions. In some instances, the teacher may want to contrast it to similar or related objects—for example, describing a cactus and comparing it to a rosebush.

2. *Have students elaborate in response to direct questions:* After modeling, the teacher asks students direct questions about the object that require them to focus on its attributes and functions. For example, the teacher may ask, "What kind of stem does a cactus have? Why does it have such a chunky stem?"

3. *Have students spontaneously describe the object or pictured object:* The teacher asks students to describe the object, using such cues as "Tell me about the cactus. What else can you tell me about it? Are there any other things about it that are important? In what way is a cactus like a rosebush?"

Teaching Form

Form refers to the structure of language. Tables 6-2 and 6-3 (earlier in the chapter) present syntactical and morphological forms that are relevant in teaching school-age students with language and learning problems. This section presents some procedures and activities for teaching these language forms.

Use Developmental Sequences An effective approach to instruction is to teach new sentence structures or prefixes, suffixes, and inflectional endings according to developmental sequences or the order of difficulty. Language programs and activities designed to teach form (see Instructional Activities later in this chapter) can assist teachers in deciding the order in which to teach the various sentence and morphological forms.

Use Familiar Examples When teaching a new structure or form, use familiar, concrete examples and vocabulary. For example, Mrs. Ogbu wants to have her students work on passive sentences. She begins by having her students act out simple events (e.g., Julio tagged Maria during a relay race). Then she asks the students to tell her a sentence about the event. She writes it on the board ("Julio tagged Maria"). Next she shows the students how she can say what had happened in a different way ("Maria was tagged by Julio"). Then the students act out other events and give sentences in the passive voice. In this way, Mrs. Ogbu starts with concrete experiences and uses familiar, simple vocabulary to teach the new sentence structure.

Use Simple Sentences Simplify your language when teaching a new sentence or morphological form. When Mrs. Ogbu initially taught her students passive voice sentences, she used very simple sentences. She could have said, "Julio chased Maria while playing tag," but this sentence would have been much more difficult for the students to put in the passive voice.

Encourage Extension Once the students have learned the new form, have them extend it to situations that need more elaborated and complex sentences and less familiar vocabulary. For example, when teaching the morphological ending -er, move from familiar vocabulary such as *teacher, reader,* and *writer* to less familiar vocabulary such as *painter, plumber, framer,* and *landscaper* in the context of house construction and to the exceptions in this area, such as *mason* and *electrician.*

Use Concrete Objects To make lessons more concrete for learners, use actual objects and events or pictures of them when initially teaching a new structure or form, and pair oral communication with written. Mrs. Ogbu uses the event of playing tag to teach passive voice sentences. She also pairs the oral sentences with the written sentences by writing them on the board. Word and sentence boundaries are clarified by written language, and pictures or actual experiences can assist the students in focusing on the target language pattern. Figure 6-8 demonstrates how pictures and written words can demonstrate possessives.

Vary Introductions New sentence or word forms should be introduced in a variety of ways. For example, when teaching comparative and superlative forms of adjectives during a measuring activity, Ms. Kamulu has the students determine who has the "long/longer/longest" pencils, pens, scissors, shoelaces, hair, and so on. Numerous comparisons can be made by using items found in a classroom, and the various comparisons may be depicted on a chart such as the one shown in Table 6-6. Students can then use the examples and the chart to discuss the comparisons and to practice the targeted language skills.

Teaching Use

According to the American Speech-Language-Hearing Association (ASHA), pragmatics involves three major communication skills:

1. Using language for different *purposes*
   - Greetings (e.g., "Hello.")
   - Informing (e.g., "I am going to school now.")

FIGURE 6-8 Visual Representation Depicting Possessive Marker

Jon's   fishing pole

TABLE 6-6 Comparison Chart

Item	Long	Longer	Longest
red pencils	Susan	Kim	Danny
blue pencils	Susan	Cori	Ken
yellow pencils	Kim	Danny	Ken
white shoelaces	Kim	Danny	Ken
black shoelaces	Cori	Susan	Kim
brown hair	Cori	Kim	Susan
blond hair	Danny	Ken	Stefan

- Demanding (e.g., "I won't go to school.")
- Promising (e.g., "I am going to school in 10 minutes.")
- Requesting (e.g., "Would you take me to school?")
- Asking questions that promote interaction (e.g., "What happened next?" "How did you respond?")

2. Using language *responsively* to *adjust* to the needs of the listener or situation
   - Using different language with friends and parents
   - Providing appropriate background information so listeners can understand what you are saying

3. *Using the rules* for conversations and storytelling that are appropriate for the context and culture
   - Being an effective conversational partner by taking turns, listening, asking questions
   - Interpreting the expressions and facial signals of the other person
   - Providing appropriate cues verbally and nonverbally so your communication is understandable

What do students do who have difficulties with pragmatics, and what can you do to assist them? Students who have pragmatic problems are likely to say inappropriate or unrelated things. For example, another student may be telling a story about a movie they saw, and the student with pragmatic problems may interrupt with an unrelated comment. Sometimes students with pragmatic difficulties do not pick up on social cues and are perceived as inappropriate, making these students less popular and perhaps isolated by peers.

What are some of the things you can do as a teacher to improve language development of students with difficulties with pragmatics?

Use Role-Play Consider role-playing to simulate different situations in which the targeted pragmatic skills are required. Ms. Peterson uses role-playing in her class so that students will have some idea what it will feel like when they are in a situation that requires them to communicate in a certain way or for a specific purpose. Last week the students had to ask each other for directions to their houses during pretend telephone conversations.

This week students are practicing how to ask questions during a simulated science lesson.

Use Pictures or Simulations Some students have difficulty discriminating different nonverbal and verbal communication that accompanies various feelings. By using pantomime or pictures, students can determine what feelings are being expressed and can discuss the cues that helped them determine the feelings. Encourage students to attend to other students' feelings by using such statements as "You look like you're feeling . . ." or "I bet you feel really . . ." or "I can't tell how you're feeling."

Use Conversations Conversations work well as a framework for teaching functional language. Conversations about topics that are familiar to the students or about common experiences can serve as ideal situations for building students' pragmatic skills. Teachers can serve as facilitators by assisting students in using the following conversational skills:

Desired Language Function	Suggested Question or Comment
Comment	"What did you do?"
	"Tell me about . . ."
Request	"Tell your friend . . ."
	"What do you want?"
Question	"Ask me"

Planning Instruction for Students Who Are Culturally and Linguistically Diverse

What are the strategies and considerations on which teachers should focus when teaching culturally and linguistically diverse learners? As a teacher, you will have students from many different cultures and students who are in the process of acquiring English as a second language or second dialect. You may or may not be familiar with the culture and language of these students. Still, it will be important for these students to feel comfortable in your class.

In this **video** ▶, students from different cultural backgrounds share their experiences about what it was like for them when they were first learning to speak English when they arrived in the United States. How would you, as an educator, adapt your teaching style to help students from different cultural and/or linguistic backgrounds to have a positive learning experience?

Diversity

Francisco is a good example of a culturally and linguistically diverse student. He emigrated from Costa Rica to Nebraska at the age of 4 with his parents and siblings. Francisco and his family now live in a Spanish-speaking community within Omaha. Francisco entered school at age 5 with Spanish as his first language and only limited knowledge of English. This situation is common for children who emigrate from countries in Central and South America, Asia and the Pacific Islands, and Eastern Europe. Teachers' knowledge of second-language acquisition and general instructional guidelines can help to make school a success for students like Francisco by helping them view their home language and culture as assets while also learning English (Goldenberg, Reese, & Rezaei, 2011). Effective teachers do the following:

- Have high expectations of their students, and believe that all students are capable of academic success

- See themselves as members of the community, and see teaching as a way to give back to the community

- Believe in diversity, meeting individual student needs, and interacting with other teachers to support shared decision making

- Display a sense of confidence in their ability to succeed with students who are culturally and linguistically diverse

- Honor the languages of the students in their class by recognizing these languages as valuable and acquiring even a few words from each language

- Communicate directions clearly, pace lessons appropriately, involve the students in decisions, monitor students' progress, and provide feedback

Second-Language Acquisition

When students are acquiring a second language, an important variable is the degree of acquisition or proficiency in the first language. A review of research concluded

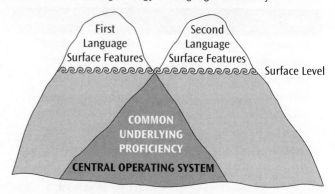

FIGURE 6-9 Iceberg Analogy of Language Proficiency

Source: Adapted from J. Cummins, *Bilingualism and Minority Language Children* (Toronto: Ontario Institute for Studies in Education, 1980). Reprinted with permission of University of Toronto Press. For more information, see Jim Cummins' Second Language Learning and Literacy Development Web (http://www.iteachilearn.com/cummins).

that the better developed the students' first-language proficiency and conceptual foundation, the more likely they were to develop similarly high levels of proficiency and conceptual ability in the second language (August, Shanahan, & Escamilla, 2009).

As can be seen in Figure 6-9, both languages have separate surface features, represented by two different icebergs. However, less visible below the surface is the underlying proficiency that is common to both languages. For example, Table 6-7 compares the phonological, morphological, and syntactical features in Spanish and English, and Table 6-8 highlights some of the grammatical contrasts in African American Vernacular English and Standard American English (SAE). Regardless of the language a person is using, the thoughts that accompany the talking, reading, writing, and listening come from the same language core.

TABLE 6-7 Comparison of Spanish and English Languages

Phonological	Morphological	Syntactical
Fewer vowel sounds: no short *a* (hat), short *i* (fish), short *u* (up), short double *o* (took), or schwa (sofa) *Fewer consonant sounds:* no /j/ (jump), /v/ (vase), /z/ (zipper), /sh/ (shoe), /ʃ/ (sing), /hw/ (when), /zh/ (beige) Some possible confusions: /b/ pronounced /p/: *cab* becomes *cap* /j/ pronounced /y/: *jet* becomes *yet* /ʃ/ pronounced as /n/: *thing* becomes *thin* /v/ pronounced as /b/: *vote* becomes *boat* /y/ pronounced as /j/: *yes* becomes *jes* /sk/, /sp/, /st/ pronounced as /esk/, /esp/, /est/: *speak* becomes *espeak* /a/ pronounced as /e/: *bat* becomes *bet* /i/ pronounced as /ē/: *hit* becomes *heat* /ē/ pronounced as /i/: *heal* becomes *hill* /u/ pronounced as /o/: *hut* becomes *hot* /o͝o/ pronounced as /o͞o/: *look* becomes *Luke*	*de* (of) used to show possession: *Joe's pen* becomes *the pen of Joe* *más* (more) used to show comparison: *faster* becomes *more fast*	use of *no* for *not:* He no do his homework. no auxiliary verbs: She no play soccer. adjectives after nouns: the car blue agreement of adjectives: the elephants bigs no inversion of question: Anna is here? articles with professional titles: I went to the Dr. Rodriguez.

Source: Adapted from C. A. O'Brien, *Teaching the Language-Different Child to Read* (Columbus, OH: C. E. Merrill, 1973).

TABLE 6-8 Grammatical Contrasts Between African American English and Standard American English

African American English Grammatical Structure	SAE Grammatical Structure
Possessive -'s	
Nonobligatory word where word position expresses possession	Obligatory regardless of position
Get *mother* coat.	Get *mother's* coat
It be mother's.	It's mother's.
Plural –s	
Nonobligatory with numerical quantifier	Obligatory regardless of numerical quantifier
He got ten *dollar*.	He has ten *dollars*.
Look at the cat.	Look at the cats.
Regular past –ed	
Nonobligatory; reduced as consonant cluster	Obligatory
Yesterday, I *walk* to school.	Yesterday, I *walked* to school.
Irregular past	
Case by case, some verbs inflected, others not	All irregular verbs inflected
I *see* him last week.	I *saw* him last week.
Regular present-tense, third-person singular -s	
Nonobligatory	Obligatory
She *eat* too much.	She *eats* too much.
Irregular present-tense, third-person singular –s	
Nonobligatory	Obligatory
He *do* my job.	He *does* my job.
Indefinite an	
Use of indefinite a [change "a" to italics]	Use of *an* before nouns beginning with a vowel
He ride in a airplane.	He rode in *an* airplane.
Pronouns	
Pronominal apposition: pronoun immediately follows noun	Pronoun used elsewhere in sentence or in other sentence; not in apposition
Momma *she* mad. She . . .	Momma is mad. *She* . . .
Future tense	
More frequent use of *be going to* (gonna)	More frequent use of *will*
I *be going to* dance tonight.	I *will* dance tonight.
I gonna dance tonight.	I *am going to* dance tonight.
Omit *will* preceding *be*	Obligatory use of *will*
I *be* home late*r*.	I *will* (I'll) *be* home later.
Negation	
Triple negative	Absence of triple negative
Nobody don't never like me.	*No* one ever likes me.
Use of *ain't*.	*Ain't* is unacceptable form
I *ain't* going.	*I'm not* going.
Modals	
Double modals for such forms as *might, could*, and *should*	Single modal use
I *might could* go.	I *might be able to* go.
Questions	
Same form for direct and indirect	Different forms for direct and indirect
What *it is?*	What *is it?*
Do you know what *it is?*	*Do you* know what *it is?*
Relative pronouns	
Nonobligatory in most cases	Nonobligatory with *that* only
He the one stole it.	He's the one *who* stole it.
It the one you like.	It's the one (that) you like.

(continued)

TABLE 6-8 Continued

African American English Grammatical Structure	SAE Grammatical Structure
Conditional if	
Use of *do* for conditional *if*	Use of *if*
I ask *did* she go.	I asked *if* she went.
Perfect construction	
Been used for action in the distant past	*Been* not used
He *been* gone.	He left a long time ago.
Copula	
Nonobligatory when contractible	Obligatory in contractible and noncontractible forms
He sick.	He's sick.
Habitual or *general state*	
Marked with uninflected *be*	Nonuse of *be;* verb inflected
She *be* workin'.	She's *working* now.

Source: Robert E. Owens, Jr., *Language Disorders: A Functional Approach to Assessment and Intervention* (Boston: Pearson/Allyn & Bacon, 2010). Copyright © 2010 by Pearson Education. Reprinted by permission of the publisher. Data drawn from Baratz (1968); Fasold & Wolfram (1970); R. Williams & Wolfram (1977).

Teachers may assume that students who can converse easily in their second language are ready to learn new concepts, strategies, and skills in that language, but this is not necessarily the case. For example, when Jong Hoon entered Ms. Dembrow's third-grade class, she immediately noticed that he conversed easily with the other students in the class and with her. Jong Hoon had emigrated from Korea 2 years earlier and had begun learning English through the school's English as a Second Language (ESL) program. His parents are also studying English in a night course and feel that learning English is important for their economic and personal success in America. Still, Korean is the language that the family speaks primarily in the home. Jong Hoon's language acquisition experiences illustrate the four components described by Ovander and Collier (1998): language development, academic development, cognitive development, and sociocultural processes.

Other teaching strategies and accommodations include the following:

- Simplify your language, but continue to use more complex language as the students' understanding progresses.
- Repeat important phrases, and emphasize key vocabulary.
- Demonstrate concepts; use manipulatives.
- Adapt the materials; don't water down the content.
- Include both language development and content vocabulary development.
- Brainstorm with the whole group.

- Provide direct experiences (e.g., read sources, watch videos).
- Increase wait time.
- Respond to the *message,* not to the correctness of the pronunciation or grammar.
- Don't force reluctant students to speak.
- Pair or group native speakers together.
- Use cooperative learning and peer-group strategies.
- Learn as much as you can about your students' languages and cultures.
- Build on the students' prior knowledge.
- Bring the students' home languages and cultures into the classroom and curriculum.
- Use photos, pictures, and videos to illustrate key ideas and concepts.
- Provide advanced organizers of the "big ideas" of what you are teaching—review these ideas.
- Provide language objectives for every lesson.
- Provide students with opportunities to turn and talk with a partner to express their ideas with one other student.
- Allow students to provide key word answers rather than complete sentences.
- Teach key vocabulary and concepts.
- Monitor students' progress to ensure success.

For example, as Ms. Dembrow became familiar with Jong Hoon, she realized that while his conversational skills made him a comfortable member of the classroom community (*language development*), he was not proficient in academic tasks such as reading and writing in English (*academic development*). She also found that in social studies and science, it was important for her to provide lots of context for teaching new concepts (*cognitive development*). When Ms. Dembrow referred Jong Hoon for possible special education services because of his difficulty with academics, she was not aware of typical patterns of second-language acquisition difficulties. But in problem-solving discussions with the bilingual speech-language pathologist and ESL teacher, she learned that different timelines for developing academic knowledge and skills are to be expected and should not be confused with reading disabilities (*sociocultural processes*).

Working with Families to Extend Language Concepts

How can teachers work with families to develop students' language skills? Children are more likely to learn new vocabulary and language structures when they are active participants in their learning and can practice new concepts in different contexts (home and school). Keep all language activities short and fun so that parents/guardians do not view communication as homework. In planning language activities, it is also important to be aware of cultural and linguistic differences in the home. If a family does not speak English, encourage the student to complete these activities in the language used at home. The following are some suggestions for using newly learned language concepts in a variety of environments:

- Send home a short description or picture of a recent classroom activity or field trip. Encourage parents/guardians to ask open-ended rather than closed questions about the activity. For example, a parent might say, "I understand that you made a papier-mâché vase today. How did you do that?"

- Inform parents/guardians of new vocabulary that children are learning. Have children write a note to their families about what they learned. A child might say, "I learned the word *notorious* today."

- Have children bring new words to class that they have heard at home. Create a word "treasure chest," and encourage the children to be vocabulary "hunters."

- Inform parents of new social language concepts that their children have practiced in class. Have children describe the concept to their families. For instance, a child might say, "I learned what to say if someone is bullying me." Encourage families to practice similar role-plays with the child at home.

- When possible, have students ask their parents questions about topics that they are learning in class. For example, if the class is discussing the food pyramid, have the children ask their families about favorite foods, and set aside a time for them to report to the class on their findings.

- To practice figurative language, have children tell jokes or word puns to their families at home.

- To practice asking questions and listening skills, have students ask their families about hypothetical situations discussed in class. Themes may come from journal topics such as "What would you do if you had a million dollars?"

- Encourage families to discuss books that they read with their children. Send home some tips to encourage discussion around a book (e.g., talk about the pictures, relate the story to the child's own experiences).

Response to Intervention: Working with the Speech-Language Teacher

How can special education teachers work with language specialists to implement RTI? The role of the school-based speech-language teacher has changed significantly in the past decades because of legislative changes in special education. Traditionally, the speech-language teacher has used a clinical/medical model of assessment and intervention, treating students individually or in small groups in a separate resource room.

In this **video** ▶, a speech therapist is working with a child who has difficulty saying certain sounds, which may indicate the presence of an articulation disorder. What methods does the speech and language therapist use to support her student's language development?

However, educational reforms have increased participation of students with disabilities in the general education classroom. In particular, RTI has provided opportunities for increasing interaction among classroom teachers, special education teachers, and speech-language personnel.

RTI models have provided many speech-language teachers opportunities to work closely with other school professionals and parents in a team model, using a combination of direct and indirect service methods to promote language development and assist students with communication disorders. In addition to providing individual or group therapy, these teachers may also collaborate with classroom teachers to develop modifications and strategies for students within the classroom. The role of the speech-language teacher may vary owing to differences in caseload, state or district regulations, and staffing needs. ASHA (www.asha.org) recognizes that RTI provides interesting and valuable new roles and responsibilities for the speech-language educator and also new challenges. With respect to assessment, as districts move from more formal models of assessment to ongoing assessments, speech-language therapists will need to shift their assessment procedures as well so that they think about assessment as it contributes to decision making about student progress. This will require educators to administer more instructionally relevant assessments more frequently.

Assessment and Intervention

Speech-language therapists may also engage in expanded roles related to prevention and intervention. For example, they may assist in schoolwide screening to identify students with early literacy and oral language problems, may assist in developing and/or delivering appropriate prevention practices schoolwide, and may provide interventions to students with communication difficulties.

Speech-language teachers may help students with language difficulties within the school setting in a variety of ways. For students with literacy and language difficulties, they may

- Collaborate with classroom teachers to implement developmentally appropriate language arts and literacy programs.
- Assist in modifying and selecting language and instructional strategies that integrate oral and written communication skills.
- Provide information and training to school personnel regarding the linguistic bases of reading and writing.

- Provide information and support for parents of at-risk children regarding language and literacy activities in the home environment.
- Collaborate with reading professionals and classroom teachers to augment the success of students with language and reading impairments.

For students with difficulties with social–emotional communication skills, speech-language teachers may

- Provide information regarding the link between social–emotional problems and social communication skills (pragmatics).
- Assist in training school staff to use effective verbal and nonverbal communication strategies in conflict resolution.
- Demonstrate lessons to enhance pragmatic communication skills (problem solving, social communication).

What can speech and language therapists do to promote RTI in their schools? Several suggestions include (Ehren, Montgomery, Rudebusch, & Whitmire, 2006; Fletcher & Vaughn, 2009):

- Explain the role of language in curriculum and instruction.
- Provide research-based knowledge on language screening and assessment.
- Provide research-based knowledge on effective language interventions.
- Assist in identifying screening measures.
- Provide professional development on language.
- Interpret the school-level progress in addressing intervention needs of students.
- Participate in the development and implementation of progress monitoring.
- Consult with teachers on issues related to RTI and language intervention.
- Provide supportive language instruction in both Tier 1 (classroom) and Tier 2 (intervention) groupings.
- Help families understand the language basis of literacy and learning.

Involving speech-language therapists in the RTI model implemented schoolwide involves communication and collaboration, but the benefits for teachers, students, and parents are significant.

INSTRUCTIONAL ACTIVITIES

This section provides instructional activities related to oral language. Some of the activities teach new skills; others are best suited for practice and reinforcement of already acquired skills. For each activity, the objective, materials, and teaching procedures are described. When possible, use these activities to reinforce the oral language within the curriculum content (current vocabulary or class topic). See Figure 6-10 for a description of selected materials addressing critical components of language development.

Partner Talk

OBJECTIVE: To provide students with opportunities to produce and orally share ideas and thoughts about a topic (including responses to comprehension questions).

GRADES: Primary

MATERIALS: Two or three questions prepared beforehand by the teacher for discussion. These may be comprehension questions (literal and interpretive) or any type of questions for discussion.

TEACHING PROCEDURES: Have all students find a partner and sit knee to knee, facing each other. Tell the students you would like them to respond to the question you are going to ask. Ask the question, then allow 2 to 3 minutes for students to think of their individual responses. Instruct each member of the pair to take a turn responding to the question, and then to discuss their responses together. For example, if using story comprehension questions, students might discuss what each thinks will happen next in the story, what each thinks is the story problem, or what each might have done differently if he or she were the main character. After 3 to 5 minutes, ask students to return to the larger group, and invite them to share their responses.

ADAPTATIONS: This activity can be adapted for older students by having them write responses or new endings to stories together.

Chef for a Day

OBJECTIVE: To provide students with opportunities to provide a detailed explanation while using ordinal words (*first, second, next*, etc.).

GRADES: Primary

MATERIALS: 8½ × 11-inch card stock, about five sheets per student

TEACHING PROCEDURES: Tell students that they will be explaining to their classmates how to make their favorite meal or snack. Students should draw pictures of the ingredients and steps in the process on separate sheets of card stock (ingredients on one sheet, each step in the process on a separate, additional sheet) and should number their sheets of paper to correspond with the order of steps in the process. Students then share their recipes with their classmates.

Younger students may only provide two or three steps in the process, whereas older students may have more than five steps. Monitor student progress, and suggest adding or combining steps on the sheets of paper as needed. Encourage the students to use specific vocabulary (e.g., *mix, stir, pour, combine,* and *spread*) rather than general vocabulary (e.g., *put*) in their explanations. The recipes should not be too simple (with too few steps to adequately create the snack) or too complicated (so many details that the process is not well understood).

ADAPTATIONS: Have students work in pairs or groups to create the recipe. Have students write some or all of the words in their recipe (this is a good activity for practicing the command form of verbs). If more than one student chooses the same snack, have them compare their recipes to notice similarities and differences in the ways each makes the same snack. Try to make the food item following one of the student's directions.

Creature from Outer Space

OBJECTIVE: To provide students with opportunities for elaboration in response to "wh-" questions regarding concrete, everyday objects and actions (not in response to a story).

GRADES: 2 to 5

MATERIALS: Everyday classroom objects

TEACHING PROCEDURES: Tell the class that you are a space creature who has just landed on planet Earth. You are trying to gather information about life on Earth to take back to share with scientists on your planet. Then ask about anything in the room, and follow up student responses with additional questions that require further elaboration or definition. For example:

Teacher: What is this?
Student: It's a pair of scissors.
Teacher: What are scissors?
Student: You use them to cut paper.

FIGURE 6-10 Selected Materials for Teaching Language

Programs and Games for Global Language Development

HELP (2004) by Andrea M. Lazzari and Patricia M. Peters. East Moline, IL: LinguiSystems, Inc.

Activities include practice on linguistic concepts, paraphrasing activities, thinking and problem-solving tasks, and pragmatic skills as well as language in daily life. Exercises include describing objects and defining words, reading and listening, and applying language skills.

Language Lessons in the Classroom (2003) by Susan Diamond. Phoenix, AZ: ECL Publications.

This book contains over 140 reproducible language activities designed for use in the classroom or by parents at home and designed to stimulate language development and facilitate effective communication skills.

Each language lesson includes: language objectives, materials needed (if any), appropriate grade levels, activity procedure, and consultation ideas. Focuses primarily on students in grades K–5.

Peabody Language Development Kits (copyright 2009) by L. M. Dunn, J. O. Smith, K. B. Horton, and D. D. Smith. San Antonio, TX: Pearson.

This program consists of lessons and materials in a kit that includes lesson manuals, picture cards grouped by categories, puppets to demonstrate concepts, posters depicting scenes and stories, sound books of sound and song activities, and colored chips for manipulation activities such as counting, sequencing, and grouping.

Programs for Auditory Processing

Listen My Children, and You Shall Hear (3rd ed.; 2008) by Betty Lou Kratoville. Austin, TX: Pro-Ed.

This revision of classic stories addresses listening comprehension, vocabulary development, and auditory memory. The third edition improves on the previous edition by combining all of the activities into a single, comprehensive volume. Stories have been updated and a reproducible tracking form for tracking progress is provided at the end of the book.

50 Quick-Play Listening Games (2005) by Kelly Malone, Karen Stontz, and Paul F. Johnson. East Moline, IL: LinguiSystems, Inc.

This book contains ready-to-copy games that reflect classroom listening demands, including phonological awareness, identifying the main ideaand details, and following directions. The games are easy to play and may be used individually or in small groups. Intended for grades K–5.

100% Listening 2-Book Set (2002) by LinguiSystems, Inc. East Moline, IL: LinguiSystems, Inc.

This two-book set targets classroom listening skills necessary at both the primary and intermediate levels. Skills are presented sequentially and mirror daily classroom situations. The books are also sold separately. Targets grades K–5.

Programs and Games for Vocabulary Development and Word Retrieval

Library of Vocabulary Photographs (2010). Austin, TX: Pro-Ed.

One of the essential tools for building vocabulary is to have a collection of pictures to use to demonstrate key words. The complete kit contains more than 600 photographs with the key words on the back. These photographs represent clothing items, community members, appliances, fruits and nuts, parts of the house and the body, tools, toys, recreation, sports, etc. Kits representing each of the areas (e.g., community members), can be purchased separately.

50 Quick-Play Vocabulary Games (2004) by Paul F. Johnson and Patti Halfman. East Moline, IL: LinguiSystems, Inc.

The games included in this resource target thematic vocabulary (such as animals, transportation, and space) and vocabulary skills (such as figurative language, context clues, and abbreviations). The path and card games will help engage your students target vocabulary needs.Intended for grades 1–6.

125 Vocabulary Builders (2000) by Linda Bowers, Rosemary Huisingh, Carolyn LoGiudice, Jane Orman, and Paul F. Johnson. East Moline, IL: LinguiSystems, Inc.

A book of paper-and-pencil tasks for students aged 10–15. These tasks are designed to provide practice with newly acquired vocabulary words.

Concept Builders (2008) by C. Weiner, J. Creighton, and T. S. Lyons. Pearson, Oxford, UK.

These materials are designed to help children explore 43 basic language concepts through active participation in fun activities and conversations. A concept board and pictures for each language concept (e.g., wet/dry) can be copied. Students respond to your questions, such as "Water is ___?" The child chooses which side of the board to place the pictures by asking questions for each picture, for example, "Is this object wet or dry?" Materials are designed to provide interactive dialogue and questioning in conversations with parents, teachers, and/or speech-language teachers.

10 Quick-Play Folder Games: Associations (2005) by Lauri Whiskeyman and Barb Truman. East Moline, IL: LinguiSystems, Inc.

One in a series of folder games (targeting skills such as categories, rhyming, and concepts), this kit contains five double-sided game boards that are ready to play. Targeted skills include describing functions, assigning categories, and reviewing words with multiple meanings. Also available in Spanish. Intended for grades PreK–4.

The Word Book (2010) by E. H. Wilg and E. Freedman. Knowledge Research Institute.

A book of activities designed for teachers or other personnel interested in promoting word and concept learning with youngsters.

FIGURE 6-10 Continued

Rocky's Mountain: A Word-Finding Game (1999) by Gina V. Williamson and Susan S. Shields. East Moline, IL: LinguiSystems, Inc.
   A board game that assists children ages 4–9 with acquiring one of four word-finding strategies. The four strategies are visual imagery, word association, sound/letter cueing, and categorization.

10 Quick-Play Folder Games: Vocabulary (2007) by LinguiSystems. East Moline, IL: LinguiSystems, Inc.
   The games in the set address many skills necessary for vocabulary acquisition. Stimulus items are presented in both Spanish and English. Intended for ages 9–13.

Programs and Games for Grammar

Connect-A-Card (2008). Austin, TX: Pro-Ed.
   Students use cards to build oral sentences, including complex and compound sentences. Using two picture phrase cards and a conjunction card representing 15 of the most commonly used conjunctions including *and, but, although, because*. Designed for all ages; primarily used for ages 6–12.

Teaching Morphology Developmentally (Revised) (2008) by Kenneth G. Shipley and Carolyn J. Banis. Austin, TX: Pro-Ed.
   This program is designed for students aged 2.5 to 10. Activities for teaching bound morphemes include present progressive, plurals, possessives, past tenses, third-person singulars, and superlatives. Includes 552 stimulus cards, a manual, and a reproducible worksheet manual.

Grammar Scramble: A Grammar and Sentence-Building Game (1998) by Rick and Linda Bowers. East Moline, IL: LinguiSystems, Inc.
   A board game with a crossword puzzle format in which students have to intersect sentences. Appropriate for students ages 8 to adult, this program is useful for developing carryover skills for grammar.

100% Grammar (1997) by Mike and Carolyn LoGiudice. East Moline, IL: LinguiSystems, Inc.
   A series of paper-and-pencil activities designed to teach essential grammar components for students aged 9–14. The program includespretests and posttests for each concept, making it helpful for charting progress. Also available in a "LITE" edition with practice items that have fewer contextual demands than the items in the regular edition.

Scissors, Glue, and Grammar, Too! (1996) by Susan Boegler and Debbie Abruzzini. East Moline, IL: LinguiSystems, Inc.
   Cut-and-paste activities for students aged 4–9. Engaging activities to reinforce regular and irregular verbs, comparatives and superlatives, possessive pronouns, "wh-" questions, and more.

Gram's Cracker: A Grammar Game (2000) by Julie Cole. East Moline, IL: LinguiSystems, Inc.
   Students "help" the mouse get to his hole by practicing grammar concepts such as use of pronouns, possessives, past-tense verbs, comparatives, superlatives, copulas, present progressive verbs, and negatives. This game has four levels of difficulty (identification, multiplechoice, sentence completion, and sentence formulation). It is designed for students aged 4–9.

Programs for Pragmatics

Exploring Pragmatic Language (2008) by M. B. Bernarding. Austin, TX: Pro-Ed.
   Two game boards provide opportunities to develop and use pragmatic-language skills with thematic game activities. More than 50 activity-barrier games addressing inferences, guessing, storytelling, and question-and-answer. Designed for students aged 6–14.

Pragmatic Activities for Language Intervention (2008) by Rhea Paul. Austin, TX: Pro-Ed.
   Lessons involve conversational language in a variety of activities including crafts, role-playing, and puppetry. Lessons address developing early words, semantic relations, and word combinations with young children; teaching preschoolers syntax, vocabulary, and concepts needed for communication and school readiness; and assisting older children with the transition from oral language to literacy with metalinguistic activities and complex language forms and concepts.

Conversations: A Framework for Language Intervention (1996) by Barbara Hoskins. Eau Claire, WI: Thinking Publications.
   Offers professionals a framework for facilitating conversational interaction with individuals aged 9 and up who are having difficulty with communication skills. This resource provides the facilitator with plans for helping groups of individuals work together to become more effective conversational partners. Conversations provide many specific activities and suggestions. Professionals may also use them to generate, adapt, and develop other productive ways of working with these varying age groups.

Who? What? When? . . . And More (1999) by Pro-Ed, Inc. Austin, TX: Pro-Ed, Inc.
   This board game requires players to answer a mix of "wh-" questions. Intended for ages 6–12.

Teacher: What is paper?

Student: "It's something you write on."

Teacher: What is writing?

Student: It's making words on paper.

Teacher: Why do you make words on paper?

At some point (before students become frustrated), you can tell them you understand and then move on to the next object (or continue the next day).

ADAPTATIONS: For younger children, use a puppet to represent the alien creature. This activity can be made more difficult by asking more *how* and *why* questions and by selecting things in the classroom that will require higher levels of thought and explanation (e.g., asking about a poem on the wall or about a science experiment). This is also a great activity to check understanding of new vocabulary.

What Did You Say?

OBJECTIVE: To provide students with opportunities to practice saying things in different ways for different purposes.

GRADES: 1 to 5

MATERIALS: None

TEACHING PROCEDURES: This activity helps students understand how the same thing can be said in very different ways (intonation and wording), depending on the context of the situation and the person being spoken to. Have students say the following words, phrases, and sentences using different intonations, given the contexts that follow each:

"Hello"

- To the principal
- To their best friend
- To a baby
- To a person they don't like
- When answering the phone

"Good-bye"

- To their best friend at the end of the day
- To their teacher
- To a friend who is moving away
- To their mom on the phone
- To someone they don't know on the phone

"How are you?"

- As if they were a teacher asking a student at the beginning of the day
- To a friend who is sick

- To a classmate who seems sad
- To someone they just met

ADAPTATIONS: Have students think of different words or expressions they could use instead of the preceding words in quotations. For example, a student may say, "Hi!" or "Hey!" to his or her best friend instead of, "Hello." Use simple puppets (e.g., pictures on popsicle sticks) to assist the students in adopting different roles. For older students, have them practice more complex language tasks in different contexts (making requests, asking for advice, describing a past event).

Which One Doesn't Belong?

OBJECTIVE: To have students identify specific relationships among vocabulary words that they have learned.

GRADES: 1 to 5

MATERIALS: Weekly vocabulary words as a foundation for a list of four words, of which three of the four words are related according to a specific dimension, and one is not. (They do not necessarily need to be written for students.) You may need to use other, related words in the activity to provide relationships to your target vocabulary words. This will vary according to the idea or concept and the students' ability level.

TEACHING PROCEDURES: Tell students that you are going to play a game that will help them think about the main idea you are stressing, for example, colors, animal groups, or important events in state history. You will tell them four words or phrases, and they are to tell you which one of the four does not belong with the others and why. Tell the students the four items. Then have the students tell you which are related and why. Then have them tell you why the fourth is not related to the other three. For example, if one of the weekly vocabulary words is *valley,* the teacher may write *valley, mountain, river,* and *desert* on the board. Students explain why *valley, mountain,* and *desert* are similar and why *river* is different. You may also ask them to generate other words in the same category.

ADAPTATIONS: Have younger students choose from items that can be visualized, such as colors, animals, or objects. The difficulty of the task can be ameliorated by having the actual objects or pictures of the objects for the students to see or by having the students visualize the objects. Older students can choose more successfully from the idea and concept level, although visuals to trigger knowledge may be helpful.

It's for Sale!

OBJECTIVE: To have students use language to elaborate and persuade.

GRADES: 3 to 6 or above (maybe grade 2 at a much simpler level)

MATERIALS: Slips of paper with various products on each one, either written or as pictures from a magazine (e.g., camera, soccer ball, car, perfume or makeup, specific shoes, etc.)

TEACHING PROCEDURES: This can be done in small- or large-group format on one day or with a few students a day across many days. Students should be familiar with skills used in persuasion before undertaking this activity.

Ask students to draw a slip of paper or an item from a jar or hat. Allow them a short but sufficient amount of time to gather their initial thoughts about the item, then give each student 5 minutes to try to "sell" their product to the class or small group. The goal is for students to convince their classmates that they really need or want this product.

After the student is finished, allow classmates 5 minutes to ask him or her questions about the product; the "salesperson" will have to come up with answers to support his or her case and/or further descriptions of the product (these, of course, may be invented).

ADAPTATIONS: Students can be given extra points for including recent idioms or vocabulary in their presentation. After students ask questions of the "salesperson," have them raise their hands to show whether they would want to buy the product. Whoever "sells" the most wins. Students can also work in groups rather than individually to present the product. Have older students try to sell an idea rather than a product. For example, if you have been studying the food pyramid and nutrition, you could write on a piece of paper: "It's important to eat vegetables." The student who draws this paper has to give a persuasive argument to eat vegetables.

Scavenger Hunt

OBJECTIVE: To provide students with opportunities to consider and state relationships between two objects.

GRADES: Kindergarten to 2 (see the Adaptations section for similar activity for students in grades 3 to 5)

MATERIALS: Different items from around the classroom or ones typically found in a house (e.g., envelope, ruler, paintbrush, book, spatula, sponge, cookie cutter)

TEACHING PROCEDURE: Prepare a list of pairs of seemingly unrelated items in advance (e.g., book and paintbrush). Tell each student the pair of items they are to find (or have pictures of the items for younger students; for older students, write the names of the objects). Direct students to look for the items. When they find them, have students talk about the two objects—how they are alike, how they are different, how they are used, and how they might go together. In the example of book and paintbrush, a child might be able to relate the two objects by saying that the illustrator used a paintbrush to make the pictures in the book. For an example, such as pencil and paintbrush, they are alike because both are used to write or draw, but they are different because a paintbrush also needs paint in order to write or draw. For kindergarten students, the comparisons will need to be simpler and more concrete than for older students.

ADAPTATIONS: Adapt this game for students in grades 3 to 5 by having them compare two nouns (or any other types of words or parts of grammar that are being studied). Prepare 30 to 40 word cards with nouns on them (this is great for reviewing and practicing new vocabulary). Divide the class into two groups. Give the first two students in each group a word card each. Direct the two students from each group to work together to create a sentence comparing the two nouns. The first pair to create a sentence wins a point for their team. Continue until one of the teams reaches a predetermined goal and wins the game.

Daydream Chair

OBJECTIVE: To provide students with opportunities to generate ideas about and elaborate on concepts or future story events.

GRADES: 1 to 4

MATERIALS: A special chair in the classroom (e.g., a rocking chair or a director's chair)

TEACHING PROCEDURES: Ask a few students each day to take turns sitting in the "Daydream Chair," describing what each would do if he or she were a certain person or object (or, for older students, in a certain situation).

ADAPTATIONS: For younger students, ask them what they would do if they were a famous person, a tree, a book, a paintbrush, or a similar object. Vary the object or person by student so that each is describing something different. This can also be done in relation to occupations, by having students discuss what people in different occupations do as part of their jobs.

To assist the students in portraying their character, have them hold a picture of the person or object in front of them as they are speaking in the first person (e.g., "I am an astronaut . . ."). Older students can be asked similar questions about what they would do, would have done, or might do in the future if they were a particular character from a story. Vary characters by student.

Find the Way

OBJECTIVE: To provide students with practice in giving and interpreting directions.

GRADES: All grades

MATERIALS: (1) Maps of different areas. For example, use a map of the school for younger students, and use a map of the local area, the state, or the area you are studying in social studies for older students. The map should be labeled. (2) Put the names of places on the map and on small cards so that the cards can be drawn during the game.

TEACHING PROCEDURES: One student is designated as "It." This student is given a map and draws a card that gives the name of the place he or she is to find. The student draws the route on his or her map. The other students are given the same map, but they do not know the destination or the route. Without showing the map to the other students, the student who is "It" must describe, by using words only, how to get to the destination. The other students are allowed to ask three questions to help clarify the directions.

To modify this exercise into a game format, each student can receive a point for each time he or she is successful in directing the other students to the location. After a student has finished, discuss how he or she was effective in giving directions, and make recommendations to improve his or her language abilities.

ADAPTATIONS: A similar format can be used with one student directing the other students on a treasure hunt.

Many Meanings

OBJECTIVE: To give students practice with using homonyms and words with multiple meanings.

GRADES: Intermediate and secondary

MATERIALS: (1) Any generic game board with a die or spinner and pieces to serve as players. (2) A variety of meaning cards and homonyms or words that have multiple meanings (e.g., *heal/heel, meet/meat*) written on one side.

TEACHING PROCEDURES: Have the students set up the game, and clarify the rules. For each turn, a student rolls the die or spins the spinner. The student then picks a card and uses each homonym in a separate sentence to show the difference between the meanings of the words or the multiple meanings. If the student's sentences reflect correct meanings, he or she moves the marker the number of spaces shown on the die or spinner. If the student is unable to make a sentence, other students may help him or her, but the student cannot move the marker. The first student to reach the finish line wins.

ADAPTATIONS: Have the students work in teams, or have the students give definitions of the words rather than using them in sentences.

Surprise Pouches

OBJECTIVE: To give students practice in describing objects.

GRADES: Primary

MATERIALS: (1) A cloth pouch with a drawstring. (2) Small objects that will fit in the pouch.

TEACHING PROCEDURES: Place a small object in the pouch, and have one student in the group feel the object without looking in the pouch. The student cannot give the name of the object but must describe it. The student describes what he or she feels while the rest of the students in the group try to guess what is in the pouch. When the student who is feeling the object thinks the other students have guessed correctly, he or she takes the object out to see whether the students are right. Have the students discuss how the descriptive words helped them guess the object. For example, "Smooth and round made me think it was a ball."

Put a new object in the pouch, and have another student describe the object. Each student should get several turns at describing the objects.

I Spy

OBJECTIVE: To provide students with opportunities to practice and develop descriptive vocabulary.

GRADES: Elementary

MATERIALS: Objects in the surrounding environment or vocabulary words

TEACHING PROCEDURES: Locate an object in the environment. Provide the students with clues that describe the object using the stem "I spy. . . ." For example, "I spy something that has green, narrow leaves." "I spy something that has rough bark." After each clue, the students try to guess what you are spying. The first person to identify the object becomes the next person to select an object and describe it.

ADAPTATIONS: For some students, you may need to assist in picking an object and giving "I spy" clues. If your weekly vocabulary list includes adjectives, give the students extra points for using those words in their descriptions. For older children, place a written list of vocabulary words on the board, and ask them to describe words from that list in the game.

The Add-On Game

OBJECTIVE: To provide students with practice in listening to each other while categorizing and making associations between words within a topic.

GRADES: Primary

MATERIALS: Starter phrases that allow students to develop a list. For example:

- I went to the desert, and I saw . . .
- I went up in space, and I saw . . .
- I went back in time, and I saw . . .

TEACHING PROCEDURES: The students and teacher sit in a circle. Use a topic from social studies, language arts, or science to start your discussion. For example, if you have been studying animals in the rain forest, a student can begin the game by saying, "I went to the rain forest and saw. . . ." This student names one thing that he or she might see in the rain forest. The next student in the circle then repeats the sentence, listing the first item and adding another item. The next student repeats both items and adds a third, and so on. This game can be played in two ways. To play competitively, the student is eliminated from the game when he or she cannot list all the items. The last student to remain in the game wins. To play cooperatively, the object of the game is for the group to beat the number of items remembered in previous games. To keep all students in the game, each student may be allowed two assists from a friend during the game (students are not "out" when incorrect). If a student has already used the two assists, then the number of items the group has correctly remembered is determined and compared to see whether the group beat previous scores.

ADAPTATIONS: This can be adapted to current events or holidays (e.g., gifts for Christmas or treats you got for Halloween).

Round-Robin Stories

OBJECTIVE: To provide students with opportunities to develop story grammar.

GRADES: Elementary

MATERIALS: None required, though a picture of a scene or setting may help students to start the story

TEACHING PROCEDURES: To get students ready to start round-robin stories, tell them that they are going to be telling a story as a group and that each student is to build on the story. Using a picture (if available and needed), tell what the story is going to be about. For example, "This story is about a group of friends who want to earn money to buy something." Have the students identify basic components of the story (names of the characters, setting), and begin telling the story. After several sentences, start a sentence, and have one student in the group finish the sentence. Model a variety of sentence starters. For example:

Subordinate Clauses

- When Jimmy went into the store, he . . .
- After Rita saw the dog in the window, she . . .

Direct Quotations

- Then the father said, ". . ."
- Suddenly, Raul screamed, ". . ."

Causal and Conditional Complex Sentences

- She didn't want to buy the brown dog because . . .
- He felt sad because . . .
- If she spent all of her money, she . . .

On the basis of their ending, start another sentence, and have another student finish it. As students become accustomed to this storytelling process, they should be able to build directly on each other's sentences without your having to start each sentence.

ADAPTATIONS: Use the same procedure, but use wordless picture books to guide students in telling the story.

Barrier Game

OBJECTIVE: To provide students with practice in describing how to make something and to provide practice in listening to directions.

GRADES: Elementary

MATERIALS: (1) Colored blocks for building objects or crayons for drawing objects. (2) Some type of barrier to block the view between the two students or the student and the teacher.

TEACHING PROCEDURES: Divide class into pairs, and explain the directions to the students. Have the students sit so that the barrier is between them. One student draws a simple picture or builds a simple block design. During or after the building or drawing, the student describes to the other student how to make the design. The other student attempts to duplicate the work and can ask questions to get help. When the second student has finished, remove the barrier and have the students compare their work.

ADAPTATIONS: After the students become successful at the activity, the number of questions that can be asked can be limited.

Category Sort

OBJECTIVE: To provide students with practice in sorting objects or word cards by categories.

GRADES: Primary

MATERIALS: (1) Objects or word cards that can be sorted by one or more categories (e.g., colored bears, colored blocks, colored buttons, colored marbles, types of animals, types of food). (2) Word cards that represent categories. (3) Sorting boxes (i.e., small boxes in which the students can sort objects or cards).

TEACHING PROCEDURES: Put a category word card next to each box. Demonstrate how to name each object or word card, and then put all the like objects or cards in the same box. Once the student has sorted the objects or cards, he or she names each category and the objects or cards in each category. The student then talks about what is alike about all the objects or cards in one category. Give older students vocabulary or spelling words to sort. Model how to sort the words in different ways (by meaning, spelling, part of speech, etc.).

Create a Comic

OBJECTIVE: To provide students with practice in using dialogue and telling stories.

GRADES: Intermediate and junior high

MATERIALS: Familiar comic strips or sequences in comic books. Blank out the words in the balloons.

TEACHING PROCEDURES: Present the comic strip to the students, and discuss with them what they know about the comic-strip characters, what is happening, and what could be written in each of the balloons. Have the students write in the different balloons. Take turns reading the comic strip, with different students reading what different characters say. The different comic strips can be put into a comic book that can be shared with other students.

ADAPTATIONS: After students are comfortable with this activity, they can illustrate and dictate their own comic strips.

Play the Part

OBJECTIVE: To provide students with practice in using language during simulations of typical interactions.

GRADES: Intermediate and secondary

MATERIALS: Simulation cards. Each card should describe the situation, the characters, and the goal of the language interaction. Some examples follow:

Situation 1: Two friends meet a third person who is an old friend and known to only one of them. *Characters:* New friend, old friend, person making the introductions. *Goal:* Introduce new friend to old friend and get a conversation started among the three of you.

Situation 2: One person approaches another asking how to find a store about 10 blocks away. *Characters:* Stranger, person giving directions. *Goal:* Give directions that will allow the stranger to find the store.

Situation 3: Two friends are in a store. One tells the other that he or she intends to steal a small item from the store. *Characters:* Friend, person persuading. *Goal:* Convince the friend not to shoplift.

TEACHING PROCEDURES: Explain that each person is to assume the described role and participate as if this were a real situation.

Have the students assume the various characters and discuss what they are going to say in their roles. The students then carry out the role-play. Have the students discuss how effective each person was in using language to accomplish the goal.

Fun with Figurative Language

OBJECTIVE: To provide students with opportunities to enhance proverb and/or idiom understanding.

GRADES: Intermediate and junior high

MATERIALS: Text from class that contains proverbs (e.g., "The early bird catches the worm.") or idioms (e.g., "Keep your head above water.")

TEACHING PROCEDURES: Select a proverb or idiom that is easily explained (e.g., "One rotten apple spoils the barrel"), and model how to interpret the meaning. First, examine the literal meaning, and draw a rough picture if necessary. Then examine the context of the proverb, and consider the character's motivations and feelings. Divide students into small groups. Each group may discuss one or two proverbs within the story using the modeled techniques. In addition, relate the proverb to students' lives and experiences. Discuss when and why a person may use a particular proverb or idiom.

Summary

- Language delays occur either in receptive language (e.g., following directions) or in expressive language (e.g., word finding). Difficulties in either area commonly influence the production and understanding of the content aspect of language, which may lead to difficulty with creative aspects of language, such as understanding and using figurative language. The *form* of language refers to its structure and sound, so for students with language delays, sentences are often shorter and do not progress to contain the same complexity as do the sentences of their peers. *Use*, or pragmatics, is perhaps the most important aspect of language growth. Some students with language difficulties tend to misinterpret meanings and emotions expressed by others and may not be able to express themselves effectively.

- One strategy that promotes *oral* language development includes providing opportunities for students to engage in meaningful conversations. *Content* teaching involves vocabulary development and understanding and applying new concepts. Teaching *form* requires teaching and practicing specific language structures such as prefixes and suffixes. To develop pragmatics, use role-plays or pictures to simulate situations such as greetings, question asking, and expressing emotions.

- Effective instruction for culturally and linguistically diverse learners incorporates two key components. Teachers must both develop the student's English-language acquisition and incorporate the student's first language and culture into learning experiences.

- Children are more likely to learn new vocabulary and language structures when they can practice new concepts in different contexts, including home and school. Examples of home activities include informing families of the vocabulary the student is learning at school and encouraging them to discuss these new words with their children; having families ask open-ended questions about activities, books that they are reading at home, or current events; and inviting families and children to play with language by telling jokes or making puns.

- Within RTI frameworks, special education teachers can work with language specialists to promote language and literacy development with at-risk students as well as students with special needs by (1) collaborating and coteaching with the general education teacher to promote appropriate language and literacy activities including modifying and adjusting typical instruction, (2) providing professional development to school personnel regarding the linguistic bases of reading and writing, (3) providing information and support for parents of at-risk children regarding language and literacy activities in the home environment, and (4) demonstrating lessons that promote language and literacy outcomes for at-risk students and students with disabilities.

After completing this chapter, test your knowledge of the concepts by completing the Assessment.

Assessing and Teaching Reading:
Phonological Awareness, Phonics, and Word Recognition

7

LEARNING OUTCOMES

1. Describe the two overarching constructs that guide reading instruction.
2. Define and provide examples of instruction on phonological awareness, letter–sound correspondence, and phonics.
3. List the six main decoding strategies, and describe how each contributes to successful word identification.
4. Compare explicit and implicit code instruction and when you might use each.

S tudents have a variety of strengths and needs in the area of reading; thus targeted reading instruction is often beneficial. Let's look at two students and see what targeted instruction might be for these students.

Kyle is a second grader who is receiving special education services for his learning disability in the area of reading. He reads at a beginning level and can recognize only about 30 words. When he comes to a word he does not recognize, he sometimes attempts to sound out the word. However, he has difficulty remembering common letter–sound correspondences. This means that when he sees letters, he does not automatically know the sound that letter makes. He also struggles with blending the sounds so that he can generate a word that is close enough to the correct word that he can figure it out. For Kyle, reading instruction will focus primarily on building phonological awareness, letter–sound correspondences, decoding strategies, and fluent word identification. The methods for teaching these components of reading that are presented in this chapter could assist in developing the automatic word recognition that would allow him to focus more of his attention on understanding what he reads. However, though the emphasis is placed on these more basic skills, his instructional program should also include repeated reading of independent and instructional-level decodable books (i.e., books that primarily use words that reflect the phonic and word patterns he has already learned) to build fluency. It should also include the listening, supported reading, and discussion of a wide variety of literature and content area materials to support his development of vocabulary and comprehension. Finally, it will be important for Kyle to have writing activities that relate directly to his reading skills. For example, as he is learning the sounds to read *at*, he can also learn to write words that end in -at such as *hat, mat, fat*, and *cat*. Similarly, as he develops his understanding of different types of text and genres (e.g., narratives such as folktales, adventure stories, and mysteries; expositions such as descriptions, comparisons/contrasts, persuasions), he can build skills at writing).

Manuel, the other student, is an eighth grader who is reading at approximately the fourth-grade level. He entered school speaking both Spanish and English. He struggled with learning to read in Spanish because of his limited vocabulary knowledge and comprehension skills (e.g., getting the main idea, comprehension monitoring). He began reading in English during second grade and continued to struggle with vocabulary knowledge and comprehension, and he also had difficulty with decoding in English, because its letter–sound relationships are not as regular as those in Spanish. As an eighth grader, he is taking English/language arts from Ms. Gonzalez, the special education teacher. Ms. Gonzalez described Manuel's instructional reading program as follows:

> Manuel and the other students in his group are working on building their vocabulary, comprehension, and advanced decoding skills. Currently, they are learning to decode multisyllabic words (e.g., *construction, reconsider*) in which they learn to identify and separate the prefixes, suffixes, and endings. Then if they don't recognize the root word, they use the information they know about open and closed syllables to decode the root word. One of the benefits of this strategy is that the students learn the meanings of the prefixes and suffixes, so it really helps them in learning what the word means. They also use the context by rereading the sentence or the surrounding sentences. For Manuel, this helps him build his decoding skills and vocabulary knowledge at the same time. We also take the time to learn related words. For example, if the word is *construction,* we make a "struct" web with words such as *destruction, construct, reconstruction*, and *deconstruct*. For teaching comprehension, Manuel and his classmates are learning to use collaborative strategic reading. It teaches the comprehension strategies previewing, questioning, summarizing, clarifying, and comprehension monitoring. The students work in collaborative learning groups, and we have been focusing on the eighth-grade social studies content, since Manuel and his fellow students are in general education social studies classes. Next semester, the social studies teacher and I are planning to coteach, and we'll use collaborative strategic reading 2 to 3 days a week to build comprehension skills while learning social studies content knowledge.

Like Kyle's, Manuel's reading program contains various components of reading depending on his needs: word identification (this chapter), vocabulary development, and comprehension.

In this chapter, we present specific methods, techniques, and approaches for teaching phonological awareness, letter–sound relationships, and the alphabetic principle as well as strategies for teaching word identification and word study.

What is perhaps the most consistent challenge of students with learning and behavior problems? The vast majority of students with learning and behavior problems (over 80%) display consistent and persistent problems acquiring proficiency in reading. Thus, special education teachers teach many students who have difficulties in learning to read. Whether working as a coteacher with a kindergarten or first-grade teacher; working with a group of students and providing intensive, small-group instruction in an elementary school; or teaching reading through the content area in a middle or high school, special education teachers spend a great deal of their time teaching reading. Why? First, reading is often considered to be the most important area of education. Reading for understanding and learning is necessary for content-area classes such as social studies, science, and vocational education and for successful employment. Second, students with learning and behavior disabilities have reading targeted as an area of need and have individualized education program (IEP) goals related to reading, more than any other academic area. Third, longitudinal research indicates that if students with learning and behavior problems do not learn to read by the end of third grade, their chances of having reading difficulties throughout their schooling and into adulthood are about 50% (Fletcher, Lyon, Fuchs, & Barnes, 2007). Therefore, developing successful readers early is essential.

Although we have divided our discussion of reading and writing instruction into four chapters (Chapters 7 through 10), we stress the importance of the relationships between reading and writing. Critical to successful reading instruction for students with learning and behavior problems are opportunities for them to spell the words they are learning to read, write about what they are reading, and to write stories and essays using structures and conventions similar to the ones they are reading. As you read these four chapters, think about how reading and writing are reciprocal processes and how they can be taught in such a way that each complements and supports the other.

> Think about how the oral language strategies and instructional techniques that were discussed in Chapter 6 are related to reading and writing and could be incorporated into your teaching.

Reading Instruction

How can teachers address the two overarching concepts that guide reading instruction? The goal of reading instruction is to give students the skills, strategies, and knowledge to read fluently and understand various texts for purposes of enjoyment and learning, whether reading a book, magazine, sign, pamphlet, e-mail message, or Internet site. To accomplish this goal, it is important to think about these two overarching concepts.

1. *Reading is a skilled and strategic process in which learning to decode and read words accurately and rapidly is essential.* The average student entering school has a broad command of oral language. However, reading requires students to be able to distinguish the individual sounds that make up words and understand that letters represent sounds in language. Reading entails using the attentional, perceptual, memory, and retrieval processes necessary to automatically identify or decode words.

The process of recognizing words is called *decoding* or *word recognition*. As students become proficient readers, they recognize most words with little effort. But as students are learning to read or when readers encounter an unknown word, they use decoding to segment and then blend the word by sounds and patterns (e.g., individual sounds; spelling patterns such as -at, -ight; prefixes; suffixes; syllables) and use syntax and context (e.g., semantics) to assist in decoding. In developing decoding skills, students develop metalinguistics, that is, knowledge and skills focused on how language operates.

Knowing and demonstrating how to blend and segment words into sounds or phonemes is a key phonological or metalinguistic skill for decoding and one for which

students with learning/reading disabilities have particular difficulty (e.g., Metsala, 2011; Torgesen, 2000). When decoding is fluent, effort can be focused on comprehension. Thus, a goal of reading and reading instruction is to decode effortlessly so that attention is on comprehension.

As emergent readers encounter print in their environment, they ask questions and learn about how language is represented in its written form. They engage in the following:

* Pretending to read favorite print (e.g., books, poems, songs, chants)
* Reading what they have drawn or written, even when no one else can
* Pointing to just one word, the first word in a sentence, one letter, the first letter in the word, the longest word, etc.
* Recognizing some concrete words (e.g., their names, friends' names, words in the environment such as McDonald's)
* Recognizing and generating rhyming words
* Naming many letters and telling you words that begin with the common initial sound

As beginning readers proceed with learning to read, they learn to

* Identify letters by name.
* Say the common sounds of letters.
* Blend the sounds represented by letters into decodable words.
* Read irregular words.
* Read words, then sentences, and then longer text.

2. *Reading entails understanding the text and depends on active engagement and interpretation by the reader.* Understanding is influenced by both the text and the readers' prior knowledge (Perfetti & Adlof, 2012). When readers read, the author does not simply convey ideas to the readers but stimulates readers to actively engage in such strategies as *predicting* to make hypotheses about the meaning, *summarizing* to put in their own words the major points in the text, *questioning* to promote and check for understanding, and *clarifying* when concepts are not clear. Furthermore, effective readers *make connections* between their prior knowledge (background knowledge) and what they are reading while *monitoring* their comprehension to determine whether they understand what they are reading. When they are not sure, they may decide to employ fix-up strategies such as rereading or reading on for further clarification, or they may decide not to worry about the confusion depending on the purpose for reading. Knowing about these strategies and in which situations to apply different strategies is called *metacognition.*

Students who have reading difficulties frequently have difficulty with efficient memory processing. Memory processes play an integral role in reading comprehension (Jerman, Reynolds, & Swanson, 2012) because they facilitate a coherent construction of the text. If memory processes are inadequate, then more active strategic processes come into play to maintain or repair understanding. This is why monitoring your reading comprehension while you read is so important. It allows the reader to stop and activate strategies to repair understanding. Studies with good and poor readers suggest that the poor readers do not automatically monitor their comprehension or engage in strategic behavior to restore meaning when there is a comprehension breakdown (Cataldo & Cornoldi, 2011). For example, when students are provided texts that have inconsistent or inaccurate information, students with reading difficulties are less likely to recognize these inaccuracies and continue reading as though the text makes sense.

These two overarching concepts can assist in organizing reading instruction into components or areas, as depicted in Figure 7-1. These components and their integration are important in learning how to read effectively and in using reading as a vehicle for learning and entertainment. Because it is important to emphasize certain components or aspects of reading based on the student's level of development and needs, particularly for students with learning/reading disabilities, instruction should integrate these components. For example, while Kyle's reading program emphasized developing phonological awareness, letter–sound correspondences, and word-recognition skills, he also engaged in activities to promote fluency and listening/reading comprehension. In contrast, Manuel's reading program focused on advanced decoding skills, fluency, and comprehension. In this chapter, we turn our attention to the first two components of reading and reading instruction.

FIGURE 7-1 Components of Reading and Reading Instruction

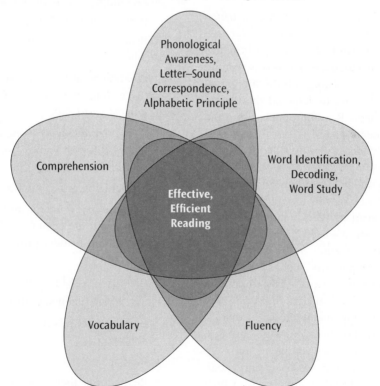

Phonological Awareness, Letter–Sound Correspondence, and Phonics

What are the definitions and examples of instruction of phonological awareness, letter–sound correspondence, and phonics? What is phonological awareness? *Phonological awareness* is knowing and demonstrating that spoken language can be broken down into smaller units (words, syllables, phonemes), which can be manipulated within the alphabetic system or orthography (Vaughn, Bos, & Schumm, 2014). Phonological awareness encompasses the discrimination, counting, rhyming, alliteration, blending, segmentation, and manipulating of syllables, onset-rimes, and phonemes. Examples of activities that support these skills are presented in Apply the Concept 7-1.

Phonemic awareness is the most complex part of a phonological awareness continuum that includes rhyming and segmenting words and sentences. Phonemic awareness is the ability to recognize the smallest sound units of spoken language and how these units of sound, or *phonemes*, can be separated (pulled apart or segmented), blended (put back together), and manipulated (added, deleted, and substituted). The phoneme is the smallest sound in spoken language that makes a difference in words. For instructional purposes related to reading, a phoneme is a single sound that maps to print—sometimes to one letter and sometimes to more than one letter.

Phonological awareness engages students in oral language activities. However, before students can apply these skills to reading, they need to understand phonics. *Phonics* is the way in which the sounds of our language (not the letters) map to print. It is knowing how letter names and sounds relate to each other, referred to as *letter–sound correspondence*. Let's see how a teacher applies these concepts.

Ms. Hernandez, the special education teacher, works for 30 minutes, three times a week in Ms. Harry's kindergarten class. She works with a small group of students who have the most difficulty learning to make letter–sound correspondences and who have difficulty separating words into their individual phonemes and blending and segmenting phonemes. With these kindergartners, Ms. Hernandez reinforces the key words that Ms. Harry is teaching with each letter–sound (e.g., *b*, *ball*, /b/), and has students participate in listening activities in which they have to count the number of syllables in words and sounds in simple words (e.g., *me* and *sit*) and create word families (e.g., *it*, *sit*, *mitt*, *bit*, *fit*, *hit*). At first, she has the students listen when working on these activities. Then she uses letters to demonstrate how the syllables and sounds are related to print.

Ms. Hernandez also works with a small group of six students in Ms. Yu's first-grade class who have difficulty learning to read. Ms. Hernandez engages these students in such activities as listening and clapping the number of sounds in words to help them segment the sounds; saying each sound in a word slowly and then saying them fast to practice blending. When writing the sound, she has them say the word, then say the sounds, then say the first sound and write it, then say the first two sounds and write the second sound, and so on until they have written the word. She consistently pairs speech and print.

Ms. Hernandez is directly teaching phonological awareness, letter–sound relationships, and phonics, all of which are associated with successful reading and spelling. Evidence from research provides consistent support for the

---

7-1 APPLY THE CONCEPT

Phonological Skills and Example Activities

- *Discrimination:* Students listen to determine whether two words begin or end with the same sound.
- *Counting:* Students clap the number word in a sentence, and syllables in a word (e.g., *cowboy*, *carrot*), sounds in a word (e.g., *me*, *jump*).
- *Rhyming:* Students create word families with rhyming words (e.g., *all*, *call*, *fall*, *ball*).
- *Alliteration:* Students create tongue twisters (e.g., Sally's silly shoe sank slowly in the slime).
- *Blending:* Students say the sounds in a word and then say them fast while the teacher pushes blocks or letters together to demonstrate blending.

- *Segmenting:* Students say the word and then clap and say each syllable or sound (e.g., *running* is /run/ /ing/ or /r/ /u/ /n/ /i/ /ng/).
- *Manipulating:* Deleting, adding, substituting, and transposing.

  Deleting: Students listen to words and say them without the first sound (e.g., *bat* becomes *at*).

  Adding: Students listen to words and add syllables (e.g., *run* becomes *running*, *come* becomes *coming*).

  Substituting: Students listen and change sounds (e.g., change /r/ in *run* to /b/ and make *bun*).

  Transposing: Students reverse the sounds (e.g., *nat* becomes *tan*).

---

important role that phonological awareness and processing play in learning to read (National Reading Panel, 2000; Nithart et al., 2011). The skills associated with phonological processing, particularly blending and segmenting individual phonemes, have been one of the most consistent predictors of difficulties in learning to read. Children who lack this metalinguistic insight are likely to be among the poorest readers and, because of their poor reading, to be identified as having a learning or reading disability (e.g., Blachman, 2000; Tunmer, Nesdale, & Wright, 2011). Hence, Ms. Hernandez is working with students in kindergarten and first grade to help prevent or lessen later reading disabilities.

If you would like to learn more about phonemic awareness, check out www.youtube: Phonemic Awareness. Also, if you would like to share with parents a video on phonemic awareness, suggest www.youtube: How to Read: What Is Phonemic Awareness?

Development of Phonological Awareness and Phonics

In general, children's awareness of the phonological structure of language develops from larger units of sounds (e.g., words in a sentence, syllables in a word) to smaller units (e.g., onset-rimes, phonemes). Skills such as rhyming and alliteration develop earlier, and skills such as sound blending, segmenting, and manipulation of phonemes develop later. Activities related to blending, segmenting, and manipulating phonemes are the most important for improving reading. Table 7-1 presents a continuum for the development of phonological awareness with definitions. While phonological awareness encompasses the entire continuum, activities that focus on individual sounds in words describe *phonemic awareness.*

The more advanced skills of phoneme blending, segmenting, and manipulation are most related to success in learning to read (Hulme et al., 2012). This is an important point for teachers to remember because it should guide their instruction. The primary focus of phonemic awareness with young children is not rhyming; rather, it is increasing their awareness of the individual sounds in language and how each of these sounds can be represented by a letter or combination of letters. Remember, linking sounds to print is the most immediate goal.

The sequence for teaching phonemic awareness usually starts with teaching segmenting and blending words and syllables before teaching segmenting and blending onset-rimes and phonemes. However, some children vary in the acquisition of these skills. Therefore, instruction at the phoneme level should never be delayed until students understand rhyme or any other phonological awareness skill on the continuum.

Teaching Phonological Awareness and Phonics

The majority of students at risk for reading difficulties have poor phonological awareness and can profit from explicit instruction in blending, segmenting, and manipulating sounds and mapping these sounds to letters as early as possible. As students learn the letter–sound correspondences, phonological tasks such as oral blending and segmenting of onset-rimes and phonemes can be paired with graphemes (letters), thereby explicitly teaching the relationship of speech to print—the alphabetic principle (Fricke et al., 2012).

Teaching phonological awareness includes such activities as the following:

- Listening for words that begin with the same sound (e.g., having all the students whose name begins with /b/ line up)
- Clapping the number of syllables in words and phonemes in words (e.g., for *monument,* students clap 3 times for 3 syllables; or "p/a/t," clap 3 times for 3 phonemes)

TABLE 7-1   Phonological Awareness Continuum

Later Developing	
Skill	**Example**
Phoneme blending, segmentation, and manipulations	Blending phonemes into words, segmenting words into individual phonemes, and manipulating phonemes (e.g., deleting, adding, substituting, transposing) in spoken words
Onset-rime blending and segmentation	Blending/segmenting the initial consonant or consonant cluster (onset) from the vowel and consonant sounds spoken after it (rime)
Syllable blending and segmentation	Blending syllables to say words or segmenting spoken words into syllables
Sentence segmentation	Segmenting sentences into spoken words
Rhyme/alliteration	Matching the ending sounds of words/producing groups of words that begin with the same initial sound
Early Developing	

Source: Based on *First Grade Teacher Reading Academy* (Austin: University of Texas, Texas Center for Reading and Language Arts, 2009).

- Blending and segmenting words by syllables and sounds (e.g., blend these syllables together to make a word, "fab/u/lous," blend these sounds to make a word, s/t/o/p).

- Segmenting and manipulating sounds and syllables (e.g., break the word *butterfly* into syllables – but/ter/fly; break the word *chair* into phonemes (or sounds) ch/ai/r).

To build blending and segmenting skills, a frequently used technique that assists students in learning to separate and blend sounds is the use of the Elkonin procedure, often referred to as Elkonin boxes (Elkonin, 1973). To watch a demonstration of how to use Elkonin boxes, check out **www.youtube: Using Elkonin Sound Boxes: Beach.** As a phonological task, students listen to a word and push a marker, block, or other small object into a printed square for each sound they hear (see Figure 7-2). As students gain knowledge about the letter–sound relationships, they can push or write letters in the boxes. It is one way in which an oral language activity can be made more visible and kinesthetic. Other ways are tapping one finger to the thumb for each sound or watching your mouth in a mirror and feeling the facial movements by placing your fingers on your cheeks and concentrating on how your mouth changes when different sounds are made.

In teaching phonological awareness to students who are having difficulty learning to read, it is important to determine the tasks that are difficult for the student and then to focus instruction according to the students' level of development and needs. For example, Emilia is a second-semester first grader who can segment and blend syllables and onset-rimes (e.g., s-it, f-at, r-un) but has great difficulty segmenting and blending individual phonemes. She has been using manipulatives and counting on her fingers to assist herself, but she is still having difficulty hearing the individual sounds. Emilia may benefit from instruction that demonstrates how the rime

is further divided into individual sounds. Emilia could also watch and feel her mouth as she says each sound to see how it changes as when saying the /a/ and then /t/, the sounds in the word *at*. For Emilia, who has learned the letter–sound correspondences for about six consonant sounds and the short vowel /a/, using letters in the boxes can help her understand how speech maps to print and to read words.

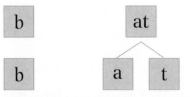

Students may also need assistance in learning how to blend sounds. Figure 7-3 presents a simple procedure for teaching sound blending. The same procedure can be used for teaching how to segment words, except that the teacher would begin with the sounds separated and then gradually present them closer together until they are blended into a word.

General guidelines for teaching phonological awareness activities include the following:

- Consider the students' levels of development and tasks that need to be mastered.

- Model each activity.

- Use manipulatives and movement to make auditory or oral tasks more visible.

- Move from easier to more difficult tasks, considering level of development (syllables, onset-rimes, phonemes), phoneme position (initial, final, medial), number of sounds in a word (*cat* is easier than *split*), and phonological features of the words (e.g., continuant consonants /m/, /n/, /s/ are easier than stops or clipped sounds /t/, /b/, /d/).

- Provide feedback and opportunities for practice and review.

- Make learning fun.

A number of programs and resources are available for teaching phonological awareness and phonics (see Figure 7-4 for a selected list), and a number of sources provide lists of children's books focused on different aspects of phonological awareness (Strickland & Schickedanz, 2009; Yopp & Yopp, 2009).

There are several interesting YouTube presentations of phonics instruction, including one that demonstrates how to sound out a word. Go to **www.youtube: Teaching Reading, Phonics Lessons, and Sounding out Words.** Another demonstration shows kindergarten students reading using a phonics approach, **www.youtube: Phonics Instruction.**

FIGURE 7-2 Using the Elkonin Procedure to Support Phonemic Awareness

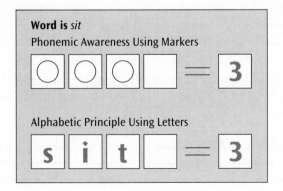

FIGURE 7-3 Procedure for Teaching Sound Blending

To train a child in sound blending, use the following procedure.

Teacher:	Say *shoe*.
Child:	Shoe.
Teacher:	Now, what am I saying? /**sh-sh-sh/oo-oo-oo**/. [Say it with prolonged sounds, but no break between the sounds. If the child responds correctly, say:] Good. Now what am I saying? [Give a little break between the sounds.] /**Sh/oe**/. [Then say it with the child.] Shoe. Now what am I saying? [Give a quarter-second break between the sounds.] /**Sh/oe**/.
Child:	Shoe.
Teacher:	Shoe. Good. What am I saying now? [with a half-second break between the sounds] /**Sh/oe**/.
Child:	Shoe.
Teacher:	Now what am I saying? [Give a one-second break between the sounds.] /**Sh/oe**/.

At each step, if the child does not respond with "shoe," repeat the previous step and then again stretch out the sounds, confirming or prompting at each step. Proceed by increasing the duration until the child can say "shoe" in response to the sounds with approximately one second between them.

Repeat this experience with the word *me*.

The main task for the teacher is to give a word with two sounds, increasing the duration of time between them until the child gets the idea of putting the sounds together. Then the child is presented with three-sound words such as /**f/a/t**/, and then with four-sound words such as /**s/a/n/d**/. It is important to recognize that the number of sounds in a word may not correspond to the number of letters in a word. For example, the word *shoe* has four letters, but only two sounds. The teacher must be careful to present the sounds correctly and use the correct timing.

Source: S. A. Kirk, W. D. Kirk, & E. H. Minskoff, *Phonic Remedial Reading Lessons* (Novato, CA: Academic Therapy Publications, 1985), pp. 12–13. Reprinted by permission.

FIGURE 7-4 Selected Programs and Resources for Teaching Phonological Awareness and Phonics

A Basic Guide to Understanding, Assessing, and Teaching Phonological Awareness by Torgesen, J. K., and Mathes, P. G., 2000, Austin, TX: PRO-ED.

Interventions for Reading Success by Haager, D., Domino, J. A., and Windmueller, M. P., 2006, Baltimore: Brookes.

Ladders to Literacy: A Kindergarten Activity Book, 2nd ed., by O'Connor, R. E., Notari-Syverson, A., and Vadasy, P. F., 2005, Baltimore: Brookes.

The Lindamood Phoneme Sequencing Program for Reading, Spelling, and Speech by Lindamood, P. A., and Lindamood, P., 1998, Austin, TX: PRO-ED.

Phonemic Awareness in Young Children: A Classroom Curriculum by Adams, M. J., Foorman, B. G., Lundberg, I., and Beeler, T., 1998, Baltimore: Brookes.

Phonological Awareness and Primary Phonics by Gunning, T. G., 2000, Boston: Allyn & Bacon.

Phonological Awareness Assessment and Instruction: A Sound Beginning by Lane, H. B., and Pullen, P. C., 2004, Boston: Allyn & Bacon.

The Phonological Awareness Book by Robertson, C., and Salter, W., 1995, East Moline, IL: LinguiSystems.

Phonological Awareness Training for Reading by Torgesen, J. K., and Bryant, B. R., 1994, Austin, TX: PRO-ED.

Road to the Code: A Program of Early Literacy Activities to Develop Phonological Awareness by Blachman, B. A., Ball, E. W., Black, R., and Tangel, D. M., 2000, Baltimore: Brookes.

Sounds Abound by Catts, H., and Olsen, T., 1993, East Moline, IL: LinguiSystems.

The Sounds Abound Program: Teaching Phonological Awareness in the Classroom (formerly Sounds Start) by Lechner, O., and Podhajski, B., 1998, East Moline, IL: LinguiSystems.

Response to Intervention and Progress Monitoring: Phonological Awareness and Phonics

Successfully preventing reading disabilities and appropriately serving students with reading disabilities requires an understanding of how response to intervention (RTI) and progress monitoring can be coordinated at the early grades to address phonological awareness and phonics.

Response to Intervention How do we know if students are responding to instruction in phonemic awareness and phonics? The answers to several questions can provide valuable information for determining students' responses to instruction:

- Have students received scientifically based reading instruction in phonemic awareness and phonics from their classroom teacher?

- Have students received adequate opportunities to respond, obtain feedback, and see modeling to scaffold their learning?

- How does the performance of students with low response compare to the performance of other students in the class?

- Have students with low phonemic awareness received instructional opportunities in small groups to acquire phonemic awareness and phonics?

- Is progress monitoring data available to show the scope of the student's progress?

Answering these questions can help us determine whether students have received adequate instruction and thus whether their low response is a function of exceptional needs in the target area. Knowing the opportunities students have to learn helps us discern the severity of the problem.

How do we know when students are responding adequately to instruction in phonics and word study? If students are receiving scientifically based reading instruction in phonics and word study, we can determine whether they are low or high responders based on two essential criteria: (1) How do they respond relative to others in their class and others in the same grade in other classes in the school? and (2) What is the slope of their progress based on progress-monitoring measures acquired at least every 2 weeks? If a student's progress is significantly below other students in the class and/or his slope for his progress based on progress monitoring of phonics and word study is lower than expected, then the student may not be responding adequately to phonics and word-study instruction.

Progress Monitoring Determining students' performance in each of the building blocks of reading (e.g., phonemic awareness, phonics, word reading) is an essential first step in designing an effective intervention program. Teachers using progress monitoring can determine what students can do and what they need to learn. Thus, teachers can design an instructional program that is targeted to the needs of the students. Assessments that tell the teacher specifically how a student is performing

In this **video** , a teacher describes how she assesses her students' early literacy skills and how she uses the data to make appropriate instructional decisions. What instructional strategies are recommended to improve children's phonological and reading skills?

and what else the student needs to know are referred to as *diagnostic assessments*. Using appropriate assessments, teachers can determine how the student's performance compares with those of other students of that same age or in that grade. These assessments are referred to as *norm-based assessments*. Appropriate assessments allow the teacher to monitor the progress of students and determine whether their progress is on track or whether the teacher needs to alter instruction to improve their performance. These assessments are referred to as *progress-monitoring assessment* or *curriculum-based measures*.

Progress monitoring of students' knowledge and skills in phonological awareness and the alphabetic principle provides teachers with necessary data to inform decision making about grouping and instruction. A good progress-monitoring system will also allow teachers to determine whether any of the three important aspects of phonemic awareness are problematic: deletion, segmenting, and/or blending.

Progress monitoring in phonemic awareness assists teachers in identifying students who are at risk for failing to acquire phonemic awareness skills, and in monitoring the progress that students make in response to phonemic awareness instruction. There are two important aspects of phonemic progress-monitoring measures: They should be predictive of later reading ability, and they need to guide instruction. The following brief descriptions of tests and progress-monitoring measures may be useful for teachers as they make decisions about what methods they will use to monitor students' progress in phonemic awareness:

- *STAR: Early Literacy (SEL)*. SEL is a computer-adaptive procedure that provides for ongoing assessment of early literacy skills including general readiness to read, graphophonemic knowledge, phonemic awareness, phonics, comprehension, structural analysis, and vocabulary. The test takes approximately 10 minutes and can be used with students in grades kindergarten through 3. The program is available through Renaissance Learning.

- *AIMSweb Systems*. These systems offer progress-monitoring tools for letter-naming fluency, letter–sound fluency, phoneme segmentation fluency, and nonsense-word fluency. There are 23 to 33 alternative forms available for each grade, and ongoing technical support is provided. The program is available from Edformation, Inc.

- *Phoneme Segmentation Fluency*. There are 20 forms of this measure, with 20 words for each form. All forms have two to five phonemes for each of the 20 words. This measure is also individually administered; however, unlike the Yopp–Singer Test of Phoneme Segmentation, this measure is timed. Students are given 60 seconds to get as many phonemes correct as possible. Students receive points for each phoneme (word part) correct, even if the entire word is not correct. Also, students are not provided corrective feedback for errors.

WEB RESOURCES

For a complete description of this phoneme segmentation fluency measure as well as information on technical adequacy, a video clip on administration and scoring, and examples of how to administer and score, see the following Web site: https://dibels.uoregon.edu/.

• *Comprehensive Test of Phonological Processing (CTOPP).* The CTOPP is administered individually to students to determine their skill in phonological awareness and to guide the teacher in designing appropriate instruction. The test is designed for individuals between the ages of 5 and 24 and assesses three areas: phonological awareness, phonological memory, and rapid naming ability. If teachers are interested in assessing more specific areas of phonological awareness, additional subtests are available.

WEB RESOURCES

For further information on the CTOPP see http://www.proedinc.com.

When selecting a measure, teachers consider the following:

- Does it accurately predict which students will have later difficulties in reading?

- Does it differentiate current high, average, and low performers?

- Does it determine which phonemic awareness skills they need to teach?

- Does it provide multiple forms so that they can administer it multiple times per year?

- Is it matched with the needs of the population of students they teach?

If the teacher can answer yes to all of these questions, the measure will serve well.

Teaching Letter–Sound Correspondences

As students learn letter–sound correspondences and move to higher phonological awareness skills such as blending, segmenting, and manipulating sounds, it is important that they associate speech with print (Moats, 2009; Shaywitz, Morris, & Shaywitz, 2008), thereby teaching the alphabetic principle or understanding that the sequence of letters in written words represents the sequence of sounds in spoken words. In Figure 7-2, while the task in the first row involves asking the students to segment words into sounds by moving a marker into a box for each sound (phonemic awareness), in the second row the students pair the sounds with letters by writing the letters in the boxes (alphabetic principle). Sometimes a phoneme is represented by more than one letter (e.g., consonant digraphs such as /sh/, /ch/, /ph/). One way to note this is by using a dotted line between the letters in the digraphs.

Knowledge of individual speech sounds is not particularly important when using oral language to converse. However, in learning to read and write and in developing a second language, this knowledge can be quite valuable and is accentuated by these tasks. Expert estimates of the number of speech sounds or phonemes in English vary from 40 to 52. For purposes of teaching students, most estimates are about 44 (Owens, 2010). In learning to read and write, students learn more than 100 spellings (graphemes) for these phonemes.

The largest division of phonemes is consonants (C) or vowels (V). Table 7-2 presents the 25 consonant sounds with their typical spellings and representative words that use these sounds. The table groups the sounds according to the manner in which they are articulated and highlights how the sounds are related. For example, there are eight sound pairs in which the only difference between the two sounds in each pair is whether the sounds are produced with a resonance in the throat (voiced) or without resonance (voiceless):

Voiced	Voiceless
/b/ bat	/p/ pat
/d/ dig	/t/ tack
/g/ gate	/k/ kite
/v/ vase	/f/ fit
/th/ this	/th/ think
/z/ zip	/s/ sat
/zh/ buzz	/sh/ ship
/j/ jump	/ch/ chip

For students who consistently confuse voiced or voiceless sounds, it is helpful to teach whether the sounds are voiced or unvoiced. They can distinguish the difference by placing their fingers on their throat to feel the vibrations in their larynxes or by covering both of their ears

TABLE 7-2   Consonant Sounds, Typical Spellings, and Manner of Articulation

Consonant Sounds	Typical Spellings	Initial	Middle, Final	Manner of Articulation
/p/	p	pot, pick	stop	voiceless stop @ lips
/b/	b	bat, barn	cab, robe	voiced stop @ lips
/t/	t, -ed	time, tap	pot, messed	voiceless stop @ tongue behind teeth
/d/	d, -ed	deer, dinner	bad, ride, cried	voiced stop @ tongue behind teeth
/k/	c, k, ck, qu	kiss, can, quick	back, critique	voiceless stop @ back of mouth
/g/	g	gate, girl	rag	voiced stop @ back of mouth
/f/	f, ph	first, fit	graph, off, rough	voiceless fricative @ lip/teeth
/v/	v	very, vase	love	voiced fricative @ lip/teeth
/th/	th	think, thin	mother, either	voiceless fricative @ tongue between teeth
/th/	th	the, then	both, ether	voiced fricative @ tongue between teeth
/s/	s,	sap, cent, psychology	less, piece	voiceless fricative @ tongue behind teeth
/z/	z, -es, -s, x	zip, xerox	has, dogs, messes, lazy	voiced fricative @ tongue behind teeth
/sh/	sh	ship, sure, chef	push, mission, ration	voiceless fricative @ roof of mouth
/zh/	z, s		azure, measure, beige	voiced fricative @ roof of mouth
/ch/	ch, tch	chip, chase	much, hatch	voiceless affricate @ roof of mouth
/j/	j, g	jump, gist	judge, soldier	voiced affricate @ roof of mouth
/m/	m	me, mom	him, autumn, comb	nasal @ lips
/n/	n, kn, gn, pn, mn	now, know, gnat, pneumonia, mnemonics	pan, sign	nasal @ tongue behind teeth
/ng/	ng		sing, english	nasal @ back of mouth
/y/	y	you, use	feud	voiced glide @ roof of mouth
/wh/	wh	where, whale		voiceless glide @ back of mouth with rounding of lips
/w/	w	we, witch	sewer	voiced glide @ back of mouth with rounding of lips
/h/	h	happy, who		voiceless glide @ throat
/l/	l	lady, lion	mail, babble	liquid @ tongue behind teeth
/r/	r	ride, write		liquid @ tongue behind teeth

Source: Adapted from V. Fromkin, R. Rodman, & N. Hyams, *Introduction to Language*, 9th ed. (Boston, MD: Wadsworth, 2011); and L. C. Moats, *Speech to Print: Language Essentials for Teachers* (Baltimore: York Press, 2010).

and listening as they say the sound pairs. Having students check whether they can feel the sound may help them to decode or spell a word.

Consonant sounds can also be distinguished by the flow of air as stops or continuants. Stops are aptly named because they are of short duration and the airflow is stopped completely for a short time (Moats, 2000). Stops (or clipped sounds) include /b/, /d/, /g/, /j/, /k/, /p/, /t/, and /ch/. In contrast, continuant sounds can be blended smoothly with the next sound without a break in the air flow (e.g., /f/, /s/, /v/, /w/, /z/, /sh/, /zh/, and /th/). The following are important points to remember when teaching consonants:

- CVC words that begin with continuants and end with stops are generally the easiest for blending the sounds (e.g., *fat, sap*).

- In some programs, when blending stops it is suggested to "bounce the stop sounds," such as /b-b-b-b-a-t-t-t/ for *bat*, so that students do not attach a "schwa" sound to the stop consonants (e.g., /buh/ and /tuh/).

- Nasal sounds are difficult to hear, sound different in the middle of words (e.g., *wet* or *went*), and are often omitted or substituted by emergent readers and writers. One strategy that students can use to check for a nasal is to gently touch their noses while saying the word and feel whether the nose vibrates.

- Students may have problems hearing the difference between /wh/ and /w/ because many Americans pronounce them in the same manner—for example, *witch* and *which* (Moats, 2000).

- The sounds /r/ and /l/ can be difficult for some students because they are some of the last sounds that students learn to articulate and because their pronunciation varies considerably across languages (e.g., in Spanish, they may be trilled or rolled; in Japanese and Cantonese, the sounds of these two phonemes are not differentiated).

This information about consonant sounds is helpful when teachers analyze students' oral reading and spelling.

Students who know the letter–sound correspondences are more likely to substitute similar sounds. For example, it is more likely that students would substitute /n/ or /m/ for /ng/ than other sounds because they are nasals. Similarly, substitutions of /d/ for /b/ and /p/ for /b/ could well be related to the similar manner in which the sounds are articulated (i.e., /d/ and /b/—similar formation of the mouth; /p/ and /b/—same formation of mouth but voiceless and voiced) rather then to visual processing.

The English language also makes use of consonant digraphs and consonant blends. A *consonant digraph* is two consonants that represent one sound (*ph* for /f/). A *consonant blend*, or *consonant cluster*, combines the sounds of two or more consonants so that they are clustered together. Table 7-3 provides a listing of the consonant digraphs and blends. When students omit a letter in a cluster, such as reading *fog* for *frog*, ask questions that lead them to see that the second sound in the blend is missing (e.g., "Listen, what sound do you hear after the /f/ in *frog*, /f-r-o-g/?" "What two sounds does the word *frog* begin with?"). It may also be helpful to have the students compare the words in written form or use boxes to assist students in seeing the missing letter.

TABLE 7-3 Common Consonant Digraphs and Clusters

Common Consonant Digraphs		Common Initial Consonant Clusters			
Correspondence	Example Words	With *l*	Example Words	With *s*	Example Words
ch = /ch/	chair, church	Bl	blanket, black	sc	score, scale
gh = /f/	rough, tough	Cl	clock, clothes	sch	school, schedule
kn = /n/	knot, knob	Fl	flag, fly	scr	scream, scrub
ng = /˜/	thing, sing	Gl	glove, glue	sk	sky, skin
ph = /f/	phone, photograph	Pl	plum, place	sl	sled, sleep
sc = /s/	scissors, scientist	Sl	slide, show	sm	smoke, smile
sh = /sh/	shoe, shop			sn	snake, sneakers
th = /th/	there, them	**With *r***	**Example Words**	sp	spider, spot
th = /th/	thumb, thunder	Br	broom, bread	st	star, stop
wh = /w/	wheel, where	Cr	crow, crash	str	street, stream
wr = /r/	wrench, wrestle	Dr	dress, drink	sw	sweater, swim
		Fr	frog, from		
		Gr	green, ground		
		Pr	prince, prepare		

Common Final Consonant Clusters			
With *n*	Example Words	With *l*	Example Words
Nce	prince, chance	Ld	field, old
Nch	lunch, bunch	Lf	wolf, self
Nd	hand, wind	Lk	milk, silk
Nk	tank, wink	Lm	film
Nt	tent, sent	Lp	help
Other	**Example Words**	Lt	salt, belt
Ct	fact, effect	Lve	twelve, solve
Mp	jump, camp		
Sp	wasp, grasp		
St	nest, best		

Source: Based on T. G. Gunning, *Creating Literacy Instruction for All Students*, 8th ed. (Boston, MA: Pearson/Allyn & Bacon, 2012).

The second category of sounds is vowels. In general, there must be a vowel in every English syllable, and consonants are formed around the vowel. Vowel sounds can be ordered on the basis of the open or closed position of the mouth. Say each of the vowels in the vowel circle, and note how your mouth moves from a closed, smiling position (e) to an open position (oo).

As with the consonants, we can analyze students' oral reading and spelling to learn about their knowledge of vowels sounds. For example, substituting an /e/ for /a/ would be more likely than substituting an /e/ for /o/ because of the closeness of the sounds. It is also obvious why students often confuse /ir/, /er/, and /ur/ in spelling, because these three spellings represent the same sound. Thus, *bird* can be spelled *bird*, *burd*, and *berd*, and the student must use visual memory to remember that it is *bird*. The vowel sounds have different spelling patterns, as demonstrated in Table 7-4.

Sometimes the same spelling pattern has different sounds (e.g., the "ea" in *beat* and *bread* or the "ou" in *soup*, *could*, and *shout*). For students with severe difficulties in decoding, it may be helpful to systematically teach

TABLE 7-4 Vowel Spellings

	Vowel Sound	Major Spellings
Short Vowels	/a/	r_ag, h_appen
	/e/	g_et, l_etter, thr_{ea}d
	/i/	w_ig, m_iddle, _event
	/o/	f_ox, pr_oblem, f_ather
	/u/	b_us
Long Vowels	/ā/	n_ame, f_avor, s_ay, s_{ai}l
	/ē/	h_e, _even, _{ea}t, s_{ee}d, b_{ea}n, k_{ey}, th_ese, _{ei}ther, funn_y, s_er_ious
	/ī/	h_ide, t_iny, h_{igh}, l_{ie}, sk_y
	/ō/	v_ote, _open, c_{oa}t, b_{ow}l, _old, th_{ough}
	/ū/	_use, h_uman, f_{ew}
Other Vowels	/aw/	d_{au}ghter, l_{aw}, w_alk, _off, b_{ou}ght
	/oi/	n_{oi}se, t_{oy}
	/o͝o/	w_{oo}d, sh_{ou}ld, p_ush
	/o͞o/	s_{oo}n, n_{ew}, pr_ove, gr_{ou}p, tw_o, fr_{ui}t, tr_uth
	/ow/	t_{ow}er, s_{ou}th
	/@/	_above, _oper_ation, sim_ilar, _opin_{io}n, s_uppose
r Vowels	/ar/	f_{ar}, l_{ar}ge, h_{ear}t
	/air/	h_{air}, c_{are}, wh_{ere}, st_{air}, b_{ear}
	/i(@)r/	d_{ear}, st_{eer}, h_{ere}
	/@r/	h_{er}, s_{ir}, f_{ur}, _{ear}th
	/or/	h_{or}se, d_{oor}, t_{our}, m_{ore}

Source: Based on T. G. Gunning, *Creating Literacy Instruction for All Students*, 8th ed. (Boston, MA: Pearson/Allyn & Bacon, 2012).

TABLE 7-5 Vowel Combinations

Vowel Combination	Order of Frequency for Different Sounds
ea	/e/ as in *eat*, /e/ as in *bread*, /a/ as in *great*
ei	/e/ as in *ceiling*, /a/ as in *vein*
ey	/e/ as in *key*, /a/ as in *grey*
ie	/e/ as in *piece*, /i/ as in *pie*
oo	/oo/ as in *moon*, /oo/ as in *book*
ou	/ou/ as in *house*, /oo/ as in *soup*
ow	/ou/ as in *owl*, /o/ as in *snow*

the frequency of the sounds for a vowel combination so that when decoding an unknown word, they can try the various sounds in a systematic manner and use syntax and semantics (i.e., context of the text) to determine the word. Table 7-5 shows the vowel combinations with order of frequency for the different sounds (Herzog, 1998).

Students who are acquiring English and speak another language may not have developed fluency in all the English sounds. This is because different languages use different speech sounds, and students are most comfortable using the speech sounds of their native language.

Consequently, students may have difficulty not only pronouncing these sounds but also hearing them. Do not be surprised if *chin* is read and spelled as *shin* or *vase* is read and spelled as *base*.

Guidelines for Teaching Letter–Sound Correspondences

Students use letter–sound correspondences to decode words. Struggling readers benefit from learning to blend and segment sounds so that they can decode and spell words. A number of programs have been developed using systematic approaches to introduce the letter–sound relationships and how to blend sounds to read words, for example: *Word Detectives: Benchmark Word Identification Program for Beginning Readers* (Gaskins et al., 2004); SRA: *Corrective Reading*); *Lindamood Phoneme Sequencing Program for Reading, Spelling, and Speech*; *Alphabet Phonics* (Cox, 1992); *Kindergarten and 1st Grade Peer Assisted Learning* (Mathes, Torgesen, & Howard, 2001). These programs have similar features of instruction that include

Before watching the instructional strategies in this **video** ▶, review your textbook's guidelines for teaching letter-sound correspondence. What other methods would you also suggest trying?

- Teaching a core set of frequently used consonants and short vowel sounds that represent clear sounds and nonreversible letter forms (e.g., /a/, /i/, /d/, /f/, /g/, /h/, /l/, /n/, /p/, /s/, and /t/). (See Figure 7-5 for a list of 120 words that can be made using these 11 letter–sound correspondences.)

FIGURE 7-5 Words Using 11 Common Letter–Sound Correspondences

i, t, p, n, s, a, d, l, f, h, g							
1. it	16. sin	31. tan	46. tap	61. slat	76. lint	91. pass	106. pits
2. if	17. fin	32. pan	47. nap	62. flat	77. hint	92. lass	107. sits
3. in	18. lid	33. Dan	48. sap	63. flap	78. past	93. glass	108. fits
4. tip	19. did	34. fan	49. lap	64. flag	79. fast	94. pill	109. hits
5. nip	20. hid	35. pad	50. gap	65. span	80. last	95. hill	110. pats
6. sip	21. dig	36. sad	51. gas	66. snap	81. list	96. gill	111. hats
7. pip	22. fig	37. dad	52. snip	67. plan	82. lisp	97. still	112. taps
8. lip	23. pig	38. lad	53. slip	68. glad	83. gasp	98. stiff	113. naps
9. pit	24. gig	39. fad	54. spit	69. snag	84. stand	99. sniff	114. gaps
10. sit	25. at	40. had	55. slit	70. and	85. gland	100. staff	115. slips
11. fit	26. an	41. tag	56. flit	71. sand	86. plant	101. add	116. slits
12. lit	27. pat	42. nag	57. tilt	72. hand	87. slant	102. tips	117. flips
13. hit	28. sat	43. lag	58. flip	73. land	88. split	103. nips	118. flaps
14. tin	29. fat	44. sag	59. spin	74. sift	89. splat	104. sips	119. snaps
15. pin	30. hat	45. pal	60. slid	75. lift	90. splint	105. lips	120. lifts

Source: Neuhas Education Center, Bellaire, Texas. Based on A. R. Cox, *Foundations for Literacy: Structures and Techniques for Multisensory Teaching of Written English Skills* (Cambridge, MA: Educators Publishing Services, 1992).

- Beginning immediately to blend and segment the sounds to read and spell the words and read the words in decodable text (i.e., text in which most of the words are composed of letter–sound correspondences that have been taught).

- Separating the introduction of letter sounds with similar auditory or visual features (e.g., /e/ and /i/, /m/ and /n/, /b and /d/).

- Using a consistent key word to assist students in hearing and remembering the sound (e.g., *a apple* /a/, *b boy* /b/).

- Teaching that some letters can represent more than one sound. For each letter, first teach the most frequent sound, and then teach other sounds (e.g., in English, /c/ in *cat* then /s/ in *city*, and /g/ in *gate* then /j/ in *Jim*; in Spanish, /g/ in *gato* [cat] then /h/ in *gemelo* [twin]).

- Teaching that different letters can make the same sound, such as the /s/ in *sit* and *city*.

- Teaching that sounds can be represented by a single letter or a combination of letters (e.g., /e/ in *me* and *meet*).

- Adding a kinesthetic component by having students trace or write the letter as they say the sound.

- Having students use mirrors and feel their mouths to see and feel how sounds are different.

- Teaching students how multiple letters can represent one sound (e.g., igh in *tight* represents the long vowel *i*).

Knowing letter–sound correspondences is a key element in understanding the alphabetic principle and learning to decode and spell unknown words. However, programs that focus too heavily on teaching letter–sound relationships and not on putting them to use in reading connected text are likely to be ineffective. Through modeling and discussion, students need to understand that the purpose for learning these relationships is to apply them to their reading and writing activities.

Family Participation in Beginning Reading

Parents/guardians are very interested in having information that will allow them to provide the best support possible to their children as they acquire the important early skills related to reading. Consider demonstrating some of the activities that family members can do at home and encouraging them to engage children in fun and meaningful activities that are associated with improved outcomes in reading. The following are some inexpensive or free materials available to families:

1. *A Child Becomes a Reader: Birth to Preschool.* This 31-page guide is written for parents/guardians and provides excellent ideas to build early language and sound awareness skills in young children. To order copies of this booklet, contact the National Institute for Literacy at EdPubs, P.O. Box 1398, Jessup, MD 20794–1398. Call 800-228-8813, or e-mail edpuborders@edpubs.org.

2. *A Child Becomes a Reader: Kindergarten to Grade 3.* This 63-page guide is written for parents/guardians and provides valuable and exciting ideas and activities that parents can use at home to enhance reading outcomes for their children in kindergarten through third grade. To order copies of this booklet, contact the National Institute for Literacy at EdPubs, P.O. Box 1398, Jessup, MD 20794-1398. Call 800-228-8813, or e-mail edpuborders@edpubs.org.

WEB RESOURCES

Many Web sites also contain valuable information for parents on how to teach young children to read. Some useful sites include the following:

- **The International Reading Association (IRA)** www.reading.org Documents include "Getting Your Child Ready to Read" and "Support Your Beginning Reader."

- **The U.S. Department of Education** www.ed.gov/parents/read Documents include "Helping Your Child Become a Reader," "Reading Tips for Parents," "Put Reading First: Helping Your Child with Reading."

- **The Canadian Department of Education** www.edu.gov.on.ca Documents include "Helping Your Child Learn to Read: A Parent's Guide."

- **The National Association for the Education of Young Children** http://www.NAEYC.org.

Word Identification, Decoding, and Word Study

What are the definitions of the seven main decoding strategies, and how does each contribute to successful word identification? Being able to quickly and easily recognize words is the key to successful reading (Ehri, 2004). Successful readers identify words automatically, and if they do not know a word, they have effective decoding strategies to decipher the word. Successful reading requires students to develop a sight word vocabulary (i.e., words that students recognize without conscious effort) and decoding strategies to support them when they encounter an unknown word.

What Is a Sight Word?

A *sight word* is one that students can read quickly and automatically with little delay. When reading words by sight, the words are accessed from information in memory, that is, from one's storehouse of words. For emergent readers, visual cues assist in recognizing familiar words when they are highly contextualized (e.g., a child recognizes *McDonald's* when it is presented with the golden arches but not when the word is presented without that context).

While watching this video, consider the different strategies the teacher uses to help her students learn to instantly recognize sight words. Why is it essential for young children to automatically identify sight words when they read?

Knowledge of letter–sound relationships serves as a powerful system that ties the written forms of specific words to their pronunciations and allows children to recognize words (e.g., *McDonald's* as an individual word). Students more efficiently store words in memory when they group or consolidate words by multiletter units such as onset-rimes, syllables, suffixes, prefixes, and base words. For example, if readers know -tion, in-, and -ing as multiletter units, then learning longer sight words such as *questioning* and *interesting* is easier. Thus, teaching key spelling patterns, prefixes and suffixes, and major syllable types can assist students in learning to automatically recognize words and read more fluently (Conner et al., 2011).

You can tell when readers are reading words by sight because they read the words as whole units, with no pauses between smaller units (syllables, sounds), and they read the words within 1 second of seeing them. To experience how powerful automatic word recognition is, look at Figure 7-6. Say the name of each picture as quickly as you can, and ignore the words printed on the pictures. Was it almost impossible to ignore the words? This occurs because you are processing the words automatically, in this case despite your intention to ignore them. It is particularly important that readers have multiple opportunities to practice reading and spelling words until they become automatic and have word identification or decoding strategies to assist them in decoding a word when they do not automatically recognize it.

Decoding Strategies for Identifying Words

What decoding or word identification strategies do readers employ to decode words they do not know automatically? Research on teaching struggling readers, including those with specific reading disabilities, would suggest that seven strategies are helpful in teaching these students to decode words (see Apply the Concept 7-2).

FIGURE 7-6 Picture-Naming Task Demonstrating How Words Are Processed Automatically

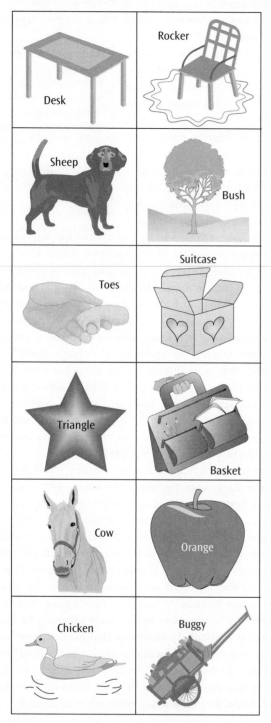

Desk

Rocker

Sheep

Bush

Toes

Suitcase

Triangle

Basket

Cow

Orange

Chicken

Buggy

Source: Adapted from L. Ehri (1987), Learning to read and spell words, *Journal of Reading Behavior, 19,* pp. 5–11.

Phonic Analysis

Identify and Blend Letter–Sound Correspondences into Words This is referred to as *phonic analysis,* or *phonics.* This strategy builds on the alphabetic principle and assumes that the students have basic levels of

phonological awareness and knowledge of some letter–sound correspondences. It entails the process of converting letters into sounds, blending the sounds to form a word, and searching memory to find a known word that resembles those blended sounds. Teachers use many cues to assist students in using phonic analysis to decode words:

- Cue the students to say each sound, and then have them say it fast.
- Demonstrate and have the students point to each letter sound as they say the sound, and then have the students sweep their fingers under the word when they say it fast.
- Place letters apart when saying the sounds, and then push the letters together when you say it fast.
- Begin with simple familiar VC (*in*) and CVC (*him*) words, and then move to more complex sound patterns, such as CCVC (*slim*), CVCC (*duck*), and CVCe (*make*).

Figure 7-7 provides a scope and sequence for teaching phonics.

Onset-Rime

Use Common Spelling Patterns to Decode Words by Blending One salient feature of the English language is the use of spelling patterns, also referred to as *onset-rimes, phonograms,* or *word families.* When using spelling patterns to decode an unknown word, students can segment the word between the onset (/bl/ in the word *blend*) and the rime (end) and then blend the onset and rime to make the word (*blend*). Figure 7-8 presents a list of 37 common rimes that make almost

FIGURE 7-7 Scope and Sequence for Teaching Phonics

Level	Categories	Correspondence	Model Word	Correspondence	Model Word
Preparatory	Letter names, phonemic awareness, rhyming, segmentation, perception of initial consonants				
1	High-frequency initial consonants	s = /s/	sea	r = /r/	rug
		f = /f/	fish	l = /l/	lamp
		m = /m/	men	g = /g/	game
		t = /t/	toy	n = /n/	nine
		d = /d/	dog	h = /h/	hit
	Long vowels: word-ending single-letter vowels and digraphs	e = /ē/	he, me	ee = /ē/	bee, see
		o = /ō/	no, so		
	Lower-frequency initial consonants and *x*	c = /k/	can	c = /s/	city
		fo = /b/	boy	g = /j/	gym
		v = /v/	vase	y = /y/	yo-yo
		j = /j/	jacket	Z = /Z/	zebra
		p = /p/	pot	x = /ks/	box
		w = /w/	wagon	x = /gs/	example
		k = /k/	kite		
	High-frequency initial consonant digraphs	ch = /ch/	church	th = /th/	thumb
		sh = /sh/	ship	wh = /wh/	wheel
		th = /th/	this		
	Short vowels	a = /a/	hat	u = /u/	pup
		i = /i/	fish	o = /o/	pot
		e = /e/	net		
2	Initial consonant clusters	st = /st/	stop	fr = /fr/	free
		pl = /pl/	play	fl = /fl/	flood
		pr = /pr/	print	str = /str/	street
		gr = /gr/	green	cr = /kr/	cry
		tr = /tr/	tree	sm = /sm/	small
		cl = /kl/	clean	sp = /sp/	speak
		br = /br/	bring	bl = /bl/	blur
		dr = /dr/	drive		
	Final consonant clusters	ld = /ld/	cold	mp = /mp	lamp
		lf = /lf/	shelf	nd = /nd/	hand
		sk = /sk/	mask	nt = /nt/	ant
		st = /st/	best	nk = /dk/	think
	Less frequent digraphs and other consonant elements	ck = /k/	lock	ng = /ng/	hang
		dge = /j/	bridge		
	Long vowels: final *e* marker	a-e = /a&/	save	e-e = /e&/	these
		i-e = /&&/	five	u-e = /u&/	use	o-e =
/o&/	hope				
	Digraphs and trigraphs	ee = /e&/	green	ow = /o&/	show
		ai/ay = /a&/	aim, play	igh = /&&/	light	oa =

(continued)

Source: Based on Thomas G. Gunning, *Creating Literacy Instruction for All Students*, 8th ed. (Boston, MA: Pearson/Allyn & Bacon, 2012). Copyright © 2012 by Pearson Education. Reprinted by permission of the publisher.

FIGURE 7-7 Continued

Level	Categories	Correspondence	Model Word	Correspondence	Model Word
/o&/	boat	ea = /e&/	bread		ea =
/e&/	bean				
	Other vowels	ou/ow = /ow/	out, owl	oo = /oo&/	book
	oi/oy = /oi/	oi/oy = /oi/	oil, toy	oo = /oo&&/	tool
/aw/	author, paw				au/aw =
	r vowels	ar = /ar/	car	are = /air/	care
	er = /&r/	er = /&r/	her	air = /air/	hair
/&r/	sir	ear = /i(&)r/	fear		ir =
/&r/	burn	eer = /i(&)r/	steer		ur =
	for				or = /or/
3 /sh/	Consonants mission	ti = /sh/	action	t,ti = /ch/	future question
					ssi =
	Consonant digraphs	ch = /k/	choir	kn = /n/	knee
	ch = /sh/	ch = /sh/	chef	wr = /r/	wrap
	ghost	ph = /f/	photo		gh = /g/
	Vowels	y = /e&/	city	o = /aw/	off
	y = /&&/	why		al = /aw/	ball
	gym	ew = /u&/	few		y = /i/
	father			e = /i/	remain
					a = /o/

500 words (Wylie & Durrell, 1970), and a more complete list of rimes is presented in Figure 7-9. Guidelines for teaching onset-rimes follow the same guidelines as those suggested for teaching phonic analysis except that the word is segmented at the level of onset-rime rather than at the phoneme level. In contrast, Spanish does not use onset-rime to the extent that English does and, consequently, it is generally not taught. However, words that contain rhyming syllables can form word families, such as /sa/ in *masa* (flour), *tasa* (cup), and *casa* (home).

Synthetic and Analytic Phonics

Teaching word analysis by having students learn individual letter–sound correspondences or rime patterns and then blending the sounds together to make the word is referred to as a *synthetic method* for teaching word

FIGURE 7-8 Thirty-Seven Common Rime Patterns from Primary-Grade Texts

-ack	-ail	-ain	-ake	-ale
-ame	-an	-ank	-ap	-ash
-at	-ate	-aw	-ay	
	-ell	-est		
-eat				
-ice	-ick	-ide	-ight	-ill
-in	-ine	-ing	-ink	-ip
-ir				
-ock	-oke	-op	-ore	-or
-uck	-ug	-ump	-unk	

analysis. For example, if the word is *pan*, then the students would say each sound individually (/p/ /a/ /n/) or the onset-rime (/p/ /an/) and then blend them together to make the word *pan*. Using this method, the students are saying the individual sounds or onset-rime and then *synthesizing* or combining them to make the word.

Teachers can also use an *analogy method* for teaching word analysis, thereby providing students with a means of decoding a word other than sounding it out or blending the sounds into a word. When teaching onset-rime, teachers cue the students to look at the unknown word to determine the spelling pattern (e.g., /an/). Then they think of the key word (e.g., *pan*) or other words with the same spelling pattern (*ran, than, tan*). The students then substitute the initial sound(s) of the unknown word for the initial sound(s) of the key word (*fat*). Cues that students can use to promote decoding by analogy are as follows:

"What words do I know that look the same?"

"What words do I know that end (or begin) with the same letters?"

Structural Analysis

Use Knowledge of Word Structures Such as Compound Words, Root Words, Suffixes, Prefixes, and Inflectional Endings to Decode Words and Assist with Meaning Between the third and seventh grades, children learn from 3,000 to 26,000 words. Most of these words are encountered through reading and learning to be aware of words you don't know the meaning of (word consciousness), and

FIGURE 7-9 Common Rime/Spelling Patterns

		Vowel Sound	Major Spellings	Model Word
Short Vowels		/a/	rag, happen, have	cat
		/e/	get, letter, thread	bed
		/i/	wig, middle, event	fish
		/o/	fox, problem, father	mop
		/u/	bus	cup
Long Vowels		/ā/	name, favor, say, sail	rake
		/ē/	he, even, eat, seed, bean, key, these, either, funny, serious	wheel
		/ī/	hide, tiny, high, lie, sky	nine
		/ō/	vote, open, coat, bowl, old, though	nose
		/ū/	use, human	cube
Other Vowels		/aw/	daughter, law, walk, off, bought	saw
		/oi/	noise, toy	boy
		/ŏo/	wood, should, push	foot
		/ōo/	soon, new, prove, group, two, fruit, truth	school
		/ow/	tower, south	cow
		/ə/	above, operation, similar, opinion, suppose	banana
r Vowels		/ar/	far, large, heart	car
		/air/	hair, care, where, stair, bear	chair
		/i(ə)r/	dear, steer, here	deer
		/ər/	her, sir, fur, earth	bird
		/i(ə)r/	fire, wire	tire
		/or/	horse, door, tour, more	four

Source: Thomas G. Gunning, *Creating Literacy Instruction for All Students*, 8th ed. (Boston, MA: Pearson/Allyn & Bacon, 2012). Copyright © 2012 by Pearson Education. Reprinted by permission of the publisher *of Reading* Behavior, 19, pp. 5–11.

only a limited number are taught directly (M. F. Graves, 2006; Kame'enui & Bauman, 2012). Teach students, including secondary students, to analyze words for compound words, root words, prefixes, suffixes, and inflectional endings (Lin et al., 2012; Reed, 2008) for the following reasons:

- It provides students with ways to segment longer, multisyllabic words into decodable (and meaningful) parts.
- It assists students in determining the meaning of words.

For example, the word *unbelievable* can be segmented into three parts, un-believe-able. Not only does chunking make the word easier to decode, it also tells us about the meaning. In the case of *unbelievable*, *un-* means "not," and *-able* means "is or can be." Hence, *unbelievable* means "something that is not to be believed."

Teaching students to divide words into meaning parts (morphemes) is often first begun by analyzing compound words. Then high-frequency prefixes (e.g., dis-, re-, in-, un-),

Table 6-1 provides a list of common prefixes, suffixes, and inflectional endings and their meanings.

suffixes (e.g., -er/-or, -ly, -tion/-ion, -ness), and inflectional endings (e.g., -s, -es, -ing, -ed) can be taught. See Apply the Concept 7-3 to learn more about what prefixes, suffixes, and inflectional endings to teach.

Ideas and guidelines for teaching and reinforcing structural analysis include the following:

- Teach meanings along with recognition of the meaning parts.
- Explain and demonstrate how many big words are just smaller words with prefixes, suffixes, and endings.
- Write words on word cards, and cut the cards by meaning parts. Have students say each part and then put the word together and blend the parts together to say the word. Discuss the meaning of each part.

Pre-(Before)	In (Not)	Re-(Again)	Super-(Superior)
precaution	incomplete	replace	supermarket
prevent	incompatible	return	superintendent
precede	insignificant	redo	superman

Which Prefixes, Suffixes, and Inflectional Endings Should You Teach?

How many prefixes do you need to teach? Four prefixes, un-, re-, in- (and im-, ir-, il- meaning *not*), and dis-, account for 58% of all prefixed words. If you add 14 more prefixes (en-/em-, non-, in-/im- (meaning *in*), mis-, sub-, pre-, inter-, fore-, de-, trans-, super-, semi-, anti-, and mid-), you will have accounted for about 95% of words with prefixes (White, Sowell, & Yanagihara, 1989). The inflectional endings of -s/-es, -ed, and -ing account for about 65% of words that have inflectional endings and suffixes. If you add the suffixes -ly, -er/or, -ion/-tion, -ible/-able, -al, -y, -ness, -ity, and -ment, you have accounted for over 85%. Other suffixes that are used frequently include -er/est (comparative), -ic, -ous, -en, -ive, -ful, and -less (White et al., 1989). Remember, it is important to teach the meanings along with how to decode them.

Demonstrate how adding the *e* to the end of CVC words makes the short vowel change to a long sound (*cap* becomes *cape*, *kit* becomes *kite*). For younger students, teachers may want to generate a story about how the *e* bosses the vowel and makes it a long vowel sound—hence, "The Bossy E." Books such as *Market Day for Mrs. Wordy* also demonstrate the concept.

- Ask students to sort or generate words by meaning parts. Following is an example:

People Who Do	Things That Do	More	Words That Have -er
reporter	computer	fatter	cover
geographer	heater	greater	master
runner	dishwasher	shorter	never

- Present words that have the same prefix or suffix but in which the prefix or suffix has different meanings. Ask students to sort words by their meanings. If students are sorting, leave space so that they can add more words. Following is an example:

  - Ask students to decode words they do not know, by covering all but one part of the word and having them identify it, then uncovering the next part and identifying it, and so on. Then have them blend the parts together to read the word.

  - Make a class or student dictionary that has each word part, its meaning, and several example words.

  - Develop word webs or maps that demonstrate how one root word can make a cadre of related words (see Figure 7-10).

Syllabication

Use Common Syllable Types Many students with reading disabilities have particular difficulty decoding multisyllabic words. This skill becomes critical by about third grade. Six basic syllable configurations or types can be identified in English spelling; these are presented in Table 7-6. The syllable types are useful because they encourage students to look for and recognize print patterns across words.

When teaching syllable types, emphasize that each syllable has one vowel sound. However, the vowel sound may be represented by one or more letters (e.g., CVCe, vowel team). Ideas for teaching include dialogues that promote discovering the generalization, word sorts by syllable types, and games to provide practice. For example, in teaching the CVCe (e.g., *cake, lime, pole, tube*), the following dialogue encourages students to induce the generalization:

Teacher: How many vowel sounds do you hear in each of these words? [Say *five, rope, cape, cube, kite, these*.]

Students: One.

Teacher: [Write *five, rope, cape, cube, kite, these*.] How many vowels do you see?

Students: Two.

Teacher: Which vowel sound do you hear? Tell me what is happening with the *e*.

Students: The first vowel is long, and you do not hear the *e*.

Automatic Word Recognition

Automatically Recognize High-Frequency and Less Phonetically Regular Words Regardless of their letter–sound predictability, words need to be taught so that they are automatically recognized. Furthermore, it is not practical to teach students to analyze all words in the English language, because the patterns they follow may not occur frequently enough to teach. Figure 7-11 presents a list of 200 high-frequency words in order of their frequency of occurrence. This list is drawn from a compilation of words that occur in books and other materials read by schoolchildren and make up about 60% of the words found in these texts (Zeno, Ivens, Millard, & Duvvuri, 1995). For example, the most frequently occurring word, *the*, makes up about 2% of words.

FIGURE 7-10 Root Word Map of *Friend*

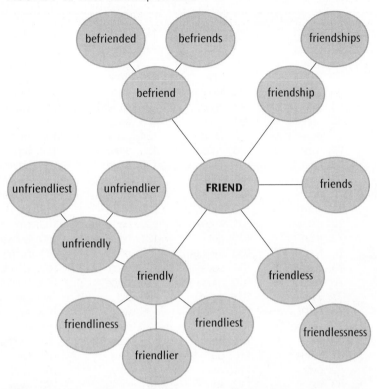

FIGURE 7-10 Root Word Map of *Friend*

Source: Adapted from C. S. Bos, N. Mather, H. Silver-Pacuilla, & R. Friedmann Narr (2000), Learning to teach early literacy skills—collaboratively, *Teaching Exceptional Children, 32* (5), pp. 38–45.

Two factors should be considered in deciding what words to teach as high-frequency words: utility and ease of learning (Gunning, 2010, 2012). The biggest payoff for students will be learning words that occur most frequently. The words *the, of, and, a, to, in, is, you, that,* and *it* account for more than 20% of the words that students will encounter. In considering the ease of learning, nouns and words with a distinctive shape are generally easier to learn. With struggling readers, teachers should first teach the words that the students will encounter most frequently.

The following guidelines can be used for teaching less predictable words (Cunningham, 2008; Gunning, 2010, 2012):

• Teach the most frequently occurring words.

• Check to make sure that students understand word meaning, particularly if they have limited language, a specific language disability, or are English language learners (ELLs).

• Introduce new words before students encounter them in text.

TABLE 7-6 Six Syllable Types

Type	Description/Examples
Closed (CVC)	Ends in at least one consonant; vowel is short: *bed, lost,* and *magnet,* dap- in *dapple,* hos- in *hostel*
Open (CV)	Ends in one vowel; vowel is long: mo- in *moment,* ti- in *tiger,* ta- in *table,* me
Consonant-Vowel-Consonant-e (CVCe)	Ends in one vowel, one consonant, and a final *e;* vowel is long, the final *e* is silent: *name, slope, five,* -pite in *despite,* -pete in *compete*
Vowel Team (CVVC)	Uses two adjacent vowels; sounds of vowel teams vary: *rain, sweet,* -geal in *congeal,* train- in *trainer,* bea- in *beagle*
R-controlled (CV+r)	Vowel is followed by /r/, and vowel pronunciation is affected by /r/: *fern, burn, car, forge, charter*
Consonant-le (C+le)	Unaccented final syllable with a consonant plus /l/ and silent *e:* -dle in *candle,* -tle in *little,* -zle in *puzzle*

FIGURE 7-11 High-Frequency Words

1. the	30. had	59. would	88. find	117. same	146. different	175. am
2. of	31. but	60. other	89. use	118. right	147. numbers	176. us
3. and	32. what	61. into	90. water	119. look	148. away	177. left
4. a	33. all	62. has	91. little	120. think	149. again	178. end
5. to	34. were	63. more	92. long	121. also	150. off	179. along
6. in	35. when	64. two	93. very	122. around	151. went	180. while
7. as	36. we	65. her	94. after	123. another	152. tell	181. sound
8. you	37. there	66. like	95. word	124. came	153. men	182. house
9. that	38. can	67. him	96. called	125. three	154. say	183. might
10. it	39. an	68. time	97. just	126. word	155. small	184. next
11. he	40. your	69. see	98. new	127. come	156. every	185. below
12. for	41. which	70. no	99. where	128. work	157. found	186. saw
13. was	42. their	71. could	100. most	129. must	158. still	187. something
14. on	43. said	72. make	101. know	130. part	159. big	188. thought
15. are	44. if	73. than	102. get	131. because	160. between	189. both
16. as	45. will	74. first	103. through	132. does	161. name	190. few
17. with	46. do	75. been	104. back	133. even	162. should	191. those
18. his	47. each	76. its	105. much	134. place	163. home	192. school
19. they	48. about	77. who	106. good	135. old	164. give	193. show
20. at	49. how	78. now	107. before	136. well	165. air	194. always
21. be	50. up	79. people	108. go	137. such	166. line	195. looked
22. this	51. our	80. my	109. man	138. here	167. mother	196. large
23. from	52. then	81. made	110. our	139. take	168. set	197. often
24. I	53. them	82. over	111. write	140. why	169. world	198. together
25. have	54. she	83. did	112. sat	141. things	170. own	199. ask
26. not	55. many	84. down	113. me	142. great	171. under	200. turn
27. or	56. some	85. way	114. day	143. help	172. last	
28. by	57. so	86. only	115. too	144. put	173. read	
29. one	58. these	87. may	116. any	145. years	174. never	

Sources: Based on Thomas G. Gunning, *Creating Literacy Instruction for All Children*, 8th ed. (Boston, MA: Pearson/Allyn & Bacon, 2012). Copyright © 2012 by Pearson Education. Reprinted by permission of the publisher. Adapted from S. M. Zeno, S. H. Ivens, R. T. Millard, & R. Duvvuri, *The Educator's Word Frequency Guide* (Brewster, NY: Touchstone Applied Science Associates, 1995).

* Limit the number of words that are introduced in a single lesson.

* Reinforce associations by adding a kinesthetic component such as tracing, copying, and writing from memory.

* Introduce visually similar words (e.g., *where* and *were*, *was* and *saw*) in separate lessons to avoid confusion.

* Ask students to compare visually similar words (e.g., *what* with *when*) and highlight the differences between the two words.

* Provide multiple opportunities for students to read words in text and as single words until they automatically recognize the words.

* Review words that have been taught previously, particularly if the students miscall them when reading text.

* Provide opportunities for students to get automatic at recognizing words, such as with games that require quick word recognition or power writing (i.e., writing the words multiple times in a short length of time).

Syntax and Semantics

Use Knowledge of Word Order (Syntax) and Context (Semantics) to Support Pronunciation and Confirm Word Meaning What does it mean to use syntax and context to decode a word? For example, consider the following sentence, "He followed her through the street until she reached the _____ and then turned and left." How might you decide what the word is in the blank using syntax and context if you don't know the word? You might be able to determine that the word is likely a noun because the word *the* precedes it. But what else might you learn with using more alphabetic related clues? It is very difficult to learn how to read a word using syntax and context alone, though they can help confirm the word. Let's assume you are using decoding with semantics and syntax and you know the first letter is a /d/ sound. You might conclude that the word is *door*. However, if you have sophisticated decoding skills, you will look beyond the first letter and use the vowel and final sound d/o/g and understand that the word is *dog*.

Many students with reading difficulties rely too heavily on syntax and context to decode unknown words (Briggs, Austin, & Underwood, 1984). Good readers use syntax and context to cross-check their pronunciation and monitor comprehension (Share & Stanovich, 1995; Torgesen, 1999). Key questions that students can ask are as follows:

"Does that sound right here?"

"Does that make sense?"

"Am I reading 'through' the word and looking at all the parts and sounds?"

Students should first be taught to decode unknown words using phonics, structural analysis, and syllabication. Then teach them to cross-check pronunciation by asking whether words "make sense."

In looking at these seven word-decoding strategies, instruction for students who are having difficulty learning provides systematic instruction in letter–sound correspondences, phonic and structural analysis, and syllabication because they are the powerful strategies for reading text in alphabetic writing systems. In addition, reading instruction should provide numerous and varied opportunities to read and write, with most of the reader's attention focusing on comprehension.

Teaching Phonics, Word Recognition, and Word Study

How can the use of explicit and implicit code instruction be compared? Jamal, a third grader, has the lowest reading level in his class, and he is not making progress in reading. When he reads first-grade-level texts out loud, the teacher assists him in pronouncing about 30% of the words. He reads slowly and cannot remember previously known words. He knows fewer than 30 sight words, and he applies inconsistent strategies to decode words. Sometimes he attempts to sound out a word letter by letter, but he has difficulty with the letter–sound relationships beyond the first several letters, particularly the vowel sounds, as well as difficulty in accurately blending the sounds together. Hence, this strategy rarely results in his pronouncing the words correctly. Even though Jamal struggles in decoding the individual words, he can generally get the meaning of these simple texts. He has good oral language skills, and his life experiences result in his being familiar with much of the content of what he reads (he has adequate background knowledge). His math skills are at a third-grade level, although he has not yet learned his math facts to the automatic level.

Lupita, another third grader, is also struggling to learn to read. Like Jamal, she is reading at the first-grade level, and she has a sight vocabulary of about 40 words in Spanish and 25 in English. When she entered kindergarten, she had limited oral language proficiency in both Spanish and English. She is in a bilingual program that initially taught reading in Spanish but began transitioning her to English in second grade. This year, much of the reading instruction is in English. Like Jamal, she has difficulty remembering words automatically, and her reading, even of very easy text, is slow and laborious. Her decoding strategies rely primarily on sounding out words, but she does not know many of the letter–sound correspondences and has difficulty blending. When she does not recognize a word, her most consistent strategy is to look to the teacher for assistance. Lupita's oral language in both Spanish and English is low. Although she communicates with her friends, she is shy about responding in class and appears to have limited background experiences to assist her understanding what she is reading or learning. Lupita does well in basic math but has difficulty with word problems.

In beginning to work with students who have limited sight words and word identification strategies, like Jamal and Lupita, it is helpful not only to determine the students' current strategies, but also to determine what instructional approaches have been used previously, how consistently, for how long, and with what success. It is also helpful to use the intervention research to inform the teacher's decision making. If the school the student is attending is using an RTI model, data about previous interventions may be available.

Beginning reading approaches that emphasize explicit, direct teaching of phonological awareness, and word identification strategies that rely on using phonics, onset-rime, and structural analysis result in greater gains in word recognition and comprehension than approaches in which phonological awareness and phonics are more implicitly taught (Stuebing et al., 2008). Consequently, explicit code instruction approaches should be a part of a balanced reading approach for most students with special needs.

WEB RESOURCES

For helpful Web sites on learning more about explicit code instruction see:

- **Reading Rockets** http://www.readingrockets.org.
- **International Dyslexia Association** http://www.interdys.org.
- **International Reading Association** http://www.reading.org.
- **Vaughn Gross Center for Reading at the University of Texas** http://www.texasreading.org.
- **Florida Center for Reading at the Florida State University** http://www.fcrr.org.
- **LD Online** http://www.ldonline.org.

Explicit Code Instruction

Explicit code approaches teach phonological awareness; letter–sound correspondences; the alphabetic principle; and the use of phonic analysis, structural analysis, and syllabication to decode unknown words. They emphasize three instructional features:

1. Systematic instruction of letter–sound correspondences and teaching students to blend the sounds to make words and segment sounds to spell words

2. Scaffolded instruction so that modeling, guidance, and positive and corrective feedback are integral features of instruction

3. Multiple opportunities for practice and review in various contexts (e.g., games with words cards, constructing sentences, reading texts)

Typically, the beginning reading materials that are associated with these approaches are controlled for the phonic and structural patterns they use; hence, they are referred to as *decodable text*. See Apply the Concept 7-4 for information about different text types and their purposes related to teaching students beginning reading.

Linguistic Approach: Onset-Rime and Word Families

The linguistic approach uses controlled text and word families (onset-rimes, phonograms, or spelling patterns) such as -at, -ight, and -ent to teach word recognition. This approach is particularly useful for students with reading problems.

Beck (2006) describes word-building sequences in which word types are oganized into four categories.

- The A category addresses CVC words and short vowels with blends and digraphs. Students learn to read simple word combinations with a minimal number of variations in letter–sound combinations and then increasingly more complex letter combinations. Words like *sat, lit, sand* are learned first, progressing to more complex letter combinations such as *pitch, right,* and *fling.*

- The B category addresses instruction in CVCe words (e.g., *rate, bike, tone*). The words are organized based on the complexity of their patterns, and thus teachers can readily determine where students are having difficulty and what to reteach.

- The C category addresses instruction in long-vowel digraphs and vowel pairs that have the same vowel phoneme (e.g., *pail, day*).

- The D category focuses on *r*-controlled vowels such as *car, turn,* and *fern.*

7-4 APPLY THE CONCEPT

Text Types and How They Facilitate Learning to Read

For students with learning and behavior problems, matching the text type with the level and purpose for instruction provides a scaffold that supports students as they learn to read and also provides them with opportunities to practice what they are learning (Palincsar & Duke, 2004). Beginning text can be classified into five general categories, each of which serves a different but complementary purpose for teaching students to read.

Type of Text and Characteristics	Support for Beginning Reading
Predictable/Pattern Language	**Emphasizes Student Use of**
• Repeated language patterns with accompanying pictures that make it easy to predict what the rest of the text says	• Memory
• Control of language pattern, rhyme, rhythm, sentence structure with difficulty increasing gradually across levels of text	• Context and picture clues
	• Repeating language patterns
	• Repeating reading of text
• Example of text: "I have a soccer ball (picture of soccer ball). I have a basketball (picture). I have a baseball (picture). I have a kick ball (picture). I like to play ball."	**Emphasizes Teacher Use of**
Types	• Modeling the concept that print has meaning
• Patterned text with picture/text match	• Modeling how books work (e.g., concept of a sentence, word; directionality)
• Cumulative pattern with information added on each page (e.g., "I ate an apple. I ate an apple and some grapes. I ate an apple, some grapes, and three bananas. I have a stomachache.")	• Developing oral reading fluency and expression
• Familiar poems and songs	

Decodable Text

- Text that introduces sound–symbol relationships, onset-rimes, and sight words in a controlled sequence so that difficulty level increases across levels
- Text that provides opportunities to apply the alphabetic principle and begin reading using the letter–sound correspondences and onset-rimes that have been taught
- Control for words, sound–symbol relationships, onset-rimes, sentence structure
- Example: "Peg had a pet pup. The pup was sad. The pup wanted to get fed, but Peg was in bed. The pup ran to Peg's bed."

Types

- Emphasizes onset-rimes such as "The fat cat sat on the hat." Sometimes called *linguistic readers*.
- Emphasizes systematic introduction of sound–symbol relationships, usually starting with a few consonants and short vowels in CVC words. Sometimes called *phonic readers*.

Emphasizes Student Use of

- Blending sounds and sounding out words to decode them
- Using onset-rimes to make words and using analogy to decode words (e.g., "If I know *pit*, then this word must be *lit.*")
- Learning to recognize less predictable words by sight as whole words (e.g., *was, come*)

Emphasizes Teacher Use of

- Modeling how to blend and segment sounds and providing independent practice in these skills
- Developing students' letter–sound and simple spelling pattern knowledge
- Sounding out words when unknown
- Using onset-rime or word chunks to decode words
- Developing independent, fluent reading of words, sentences, and connected text

Transitional Text

- Integrates predictable and decodable text so that across levels predictability decreases and decodability increases
- Example: "So she said to Grandpa, 'Can you rock Nick for a little while? Maybe you can get him to stop.' 'Sure,' Grandpa said. 'Now I can try.' But Grandpa had no luck. So he said to me. 'Can you play with Nick for a little while? Maybe you can get him to stop.' 'Sure,' I said. 'I will pick him up. It's my turn to try!'" (*Pick Up Nick,* by Kate McGovern, pp. 10–14).

Emphasizes Student Use of

- Diminishing use of memory and context clues to identify words
- Increasing use of blending sounds, sounding out words, and onset-rime to decode unknown words
- Learning to recognize less predictable words by sight

Emphasizes Teacher Use of

- Modeling how to blend and segment sounds
- Modeling how to sound out and use onset-rime to decode unknown words
- Developing independent, fluent reading of words, sentences, and connected text

Easy Reader Text

- Series of books that gradually increase in difficulty across levels but are less controlled than predictable, decodable, or transitional texts
- Less control of words with more difficult high-frequency words, more polysyllabic words, and more complex sentences
- More complex plot and information and more text per page
- Some use of short chapters
- Example: "'And it means that we can begin a whole new year together, Toad. Think of it,' said Frog. 'We will skip through the meadows and run through the woods and swim in the river?'" (*Frog and Toad Are Friends,* by Arnold Lobel, p. 8).

Emphasizes Student Use of

- Using simple syllabication, prefixes/suffixes, and chunking with polysyllabic words (e.g., *unprepared*) and using more complex spelling patterns (e.g., *fright*)
- Using sight word knowledge and working on automaticity and fluency

Emphasizes Teacher Use of

- Modeling more complex decoding strategies using more difficult words
- Developing student's oral reading fluency and expression
- Modeling comprehension strategies while reading aloud

Authentic Literature and Nonfiction

- Text that is written with limited regard for word or sentence difficulty and provides more complex plots and information
- Varies widely in style and genre

Examples:

- *The Tale of Peter Rabbit* by Beatrix Potter
- *Owl Moon* by Jane Yolen
- *Bearman: Exploring the World of Black Bears* by Laurence Pringle

Emphasizes Student Use of

- Listening and reading comprehension strategies
- Developing knowledge of different writing styles and genres
- Applying advanced decoding strategies in less controlled texts

Emphasizes Teacher Use of

- Reading for enjoyment and modeling fluency when reading aloud
- Motivating students and creating interest in reading
- Discussing literature and teaching listening/reading/comprehension strategies

Linguistic Approach—Onset-Rime and Word Families

PROCEDURES: The linguistic approach is built on a salient feature of the English language, that is, onset-rime. Look again at Figure 7-9 the list of 37 common rimes, and at the even more complete list in Figure 7-10. In teaching onset-rime, words are segmented and blended at the onset-rime level rather than the phoneme level, and words are taught in related groups that are often referred to as *word families* (e.g., -at: *cat, fat, bat, sat, rat;* -ight: *right, might, fight*). Sight words or less phonetically regular words are kept to a minimum. Figure 7-12 provides an example of a beginning text from a typical linguistic reader. These readers give the students extensive practice with the word families and systematically introduce onset-rime patterns. Figure 7-13 presents a list of selected linguistic reading programs and linguistic readers.

FIGURE 7-12 Sample Linguistic Reading Story

> ### Nat and the Rat
> Nat is a cat.
> She is a fat cat.
> She likes to sit on her mat.
> Dad likes to pat Nat.
> One day Nat sat on Dad's lap for a pat.
> Nat saw a rat.
> She jumped off Dad's lap and ran after the rat.
> That made Nat tired.
> So Nat sat on her mat.

FIGURE 7-13 Selected Linguistic Reading Programs and Readers

> *The Basic Reading Series*, Rasmussen, D., and Goldberg, L., 2000, Columbus, OH: SRA/McGraw-Hill.
>
> *Foundations*, 2004, Bothell, WA: The Wright Group/McGraw-Hill.
>
> *Let's Read: A Linguistic Reading Program*, Bloomfield, L., and Barnhart, R. K., 1965, 1994–1997, Cambridge, MA: Educators Publishing Service.
>
> *Merrill Reading Program*, Bertin, P. et al., 1999, Columbus, OH: SRA/McGraw-Hill.
>
> *Preventing Academic Failure*, Bertin, P., and Perlman, E., 1999, Columbus, OH: SRA/McGraw-Hill.
>
> *Ready Readers*, 2004, Parsippany, NJ: Modern Curriculum Press/Pearson.
>
> *Sullivan's Programmed Reading* (3rd ed.), Buchanan, C., 1988, Honesdale, PA: Phoenix Learning Resources.
>
> *Sundance Phonic Letters, Sounds, Readers*, 1998–1999, Northborough, MA: Sundance.

When students cannot identify a word family word, one strategy is to use a synthetic method of decoding by having them segment the word at the onset-rime level (e.g., for the word *flat*, cover the /fl/ and have the student read the /at/, then cover the /at/ and have the student give the sound /fl/, and then expose the whole word and have the student blend the two segments together to make the word *flat*). Another strategy is to use an analogy method in which the students think of another word, or the key word, they know with the same rime pattern (e.g., *cat*) and then substitute the initial sound(s) to make the word *flat*. Activities such as word sorts in which students sort words by word families, constructing word walls using onset-rime patterns, making word family houses (see Figure 7-14), and playing games such as Word Family Concentration and Can You Write a Word that Rimes With are all ways of reinforcing onset-rime patterns.

COMMENTS: Teaching students about onset-rime and word families gives them another context for understanding the alphabetic principle and how English sounds map to print. It also reinforces the phonological awareness skill of rhyming. The use of a linguistic approach and linguistic readers provides struggling readers with multiple opportunities to learn and practice onset-rime patterns. Some students benefit from decoding at the phoneme level (e.g., /c-a-t/) in addition to learning decoding at the onset-rime level (e.g., /c-at/). Students with reading problems who are instructed in both these decoding methods make the greatest gains in reading (Carroll, et al., 2011). Several cautions should be mentioned in regard to this approach. First, like other explicit code instruction, the texts often provide limited opportunities for the development

FIGURE 7-14 Word Family House

of comprehension. Therefore, the use of children's narrative and expository literature should be incorporated into the reading program to develop listening comprehension. To demonstrate this point, reread the text given in Figure 7-12, and then try to generate five comprehension questions. Second, some words that are introduced in a family may represent unfamiliar or abstract concepts. For example, when learning the -og family, a student may be asked to read about "the fog in the bog."

Reading Mastery and Corrective Reading   *Reading Mastery Signature Edition* (Engelmann et al., 1995) and *Corrective Reading* (Engelmann et al., 1999) are highly structured, systematic reading programs that use a direct instruction model for teaching and a synthetic method for teaching phonics and structural analysis. These programs directly teach individual sound–symbol relationships, blending of sounds, and how to build these sounds into words. The programs include components in decoding and comprehension, with comprehension focusing on the systematic development of logical reasoning skills and the use of questioning to promote comprehension. Whereas *Reading Mastery* is designed for elementary-level students, *Corrective Reading* is designed for students in grades 4 through 12 who have not mastered decoding and comprehension skills. Both programs are best taught in small- to medium-sized groups.

> In this **video** ▶, you will observe a Corrective Reading lesson. What strategies does the teacher use to encourage his student's progress? How is progress monitored?

Evidence-Based **PRACTICE**

Reading Mastery and Corrective Reading

PROCEDURES: *Reading Mastery* and *Corrective Reading* are built on principles of direct instruction (Carnine et al., 2010), which for reading include the following:

- Design instruction to maximize the amount of time students are engaged (e.g., students work in small groups with teacher; students give responses in unison after adequate wait time so that all students have time to think).
- Teach students to rely on strategies rather than require them to memorize information (e.g., teach several letter sounds such as /m/, /t/, /s/, /f/, /a/, and /i/ and the sounding-out strategy to decode words).
- Teach procedures to generalize knowledge (e.g., have students apply the sounding-out strategy to new sounds to build additional words).
- Use a teaching format that includes an introduction stage, followed by guided practice, independent practice, and review.

- Teach to mastery (specific criterion level).
- Teach one skill or strategy at a time.
- Systematically teach skills and strategies in a cumulative manner.
- Prerequisite knowledge or skills are taught first (e.g., sounds of letters before words).
- Instances that are consistent with the strategy are introduced before exceptions (e.g., teach consistent CVCe words such as *gave* and *made* before exceptions such as *have*).
- High-utility knowledge is introduced before less useful knowledge (e.g., teach frequent irregular words such as *of* and *was* before less frequent ones such as *heir* and *neon*).
- Easy skills are taught before more difficult ones.
- Information and strategies that are likely to be confused are introduced separately (e.g., letters *b* and *d* and words *were* and *where*).
- Systematic review and practice are provided.
- Monitor student performance, and provide corrective feedback.
- Use a reinforcement system that promotes student engagement and learning.

In both programs, students are taught a consistent method of responding to sounds and sounding out words. Using the guide in Figure 7-15, teachers touch the first ball of the arrow and cue as follows:

"Say it with me or sound it out. Get ready."

They touch quickly under each sound, saying each sound: /rrreeed/. They repeat until students are consistent and then cue as follows:

"Say it fast. What sound or what word?"

They repeat until students consistently respond with the sound or word.

In both programs, the teacher is given specific procedures to follow, including scripted lessons. These scripted lessons specify what the teacher is to say and include hand signals. Part of an early lesson from *Corrective Reading: Word Attack Basics—Decoding A* (Engelmann, et al., 1999) is presented in Figure 7-16. Each lesson contains multiple exercises that focus on word-attack skills such as sound identification, pronunciations, say the sounds, word reading, sentence reading, story reading, and spelling from dictation. Lessons are designed to last from 30 to 50 minutes

FIGURE 7-15 Guide for Sounding Out a Word

r e d

FIGURE 7-16 Portion of an Early Lesson from *Corrective Reading*

Exercise 2
Pronunciations

Note: Do not write the words on the board. This is an oral exercise.

Task A
1. Listen. He was mad. [Pause.] **Mad.** Say it. [Signal.] Mad.
2. Next word. Listen. They wrestled on a mat. [Pause.] **Mat.** Say it. [Signal.] *Mat.*
3. Next word: ram. Say it. [Signal.] *Ram.*
4. [Repeat step 3 for *sat*, *reem*, *seem*.]
5. [Repeat all the words until firm.]

Task B Sit, rim, fin
1. I'll say words that have the sound iii. What sound? [Signal.] iii. Yes, iii.
2. [Repeat step 1 until firm.]
3. Listen: **sit, rim, fin.** Your turn: **sit.** Say it. [Signal.] *Sit.* Yes, *sit.*
4. Next word: **rim.** Say it. [Signal.] *Rim.* Yes, *rim.*
5. Next word: **fin.** Say it. [Signal.] *Fin.* Yes, *fin.*
6. [Repeat steps 3-5 until firm.]
7. What's the middle sound in the word rrriiimmm? [Signal.] *iii.* Yes, *iii.*
8. [Repeat step 7 until firm.]

Exercise 3
Say the Sounds

Note: Do not write the words on the board. This is an oral exercise.

1. First you're going to say a word slowly without stopping between the sounds. Then you're going to say the word *fast.*
2. Listen: ssseee. [Hold up a finger for each sound.
3. Say the sounds in [pause] ssseee. Get ready. [Hold up a finger for each sound.] ssseee. [Repeat until the students say the sounds without stopping.]
4. Say it fast. [Signal.] *See.*
5. What word? [Signal.] *See.* Yes, *see.*
6. [Repeat steps 2–5 for *sad, mad, mat, me, seed, in, if, sat, ran, rat.*]

Exercise 4
Sound Introduction

1. [Point to *i*.] One sound this letter makes is iii. What sound? [Touch.] iii.
2. [Point to *d*.] This letter makes the sound d. What sound? [Touch.] d.
3. Say each sound when I touch it.
4. [Point to *i*.] What sound? [Touch under] i. iii.
5. [Repeat step 4 for d, e, d, r, t, s, ă, m.]
   To correct:
   a. [Say the sound loudly as soon as you hear an error.]
   b. [Point to the sound.] This sound is_____. What sound? [Touch.]

c. [Repeat the series of letters until all the students can correctly identify all the sounds in order.]
6. [Point to the circled letters.] The sound for one of these letters is the same as the letter name. That's the name you say when you say the alphabet.
7. [Point to *i*.] Listen: iii. Is that a letter name? [Signal.] No. Right, it isn't.
8. [Point to *a*.] Listen: **ăăă.** Is that a letter name? [Signal.] *No.* Right, it isn't.
9. [Point to *e*.] Listen: **eee.** Is that a letter name? [Signal.] *Yes.* Yes, it is. Remember, the sound you're learning for eee is the same as the letter name.

Individual Test

I'll call on different students to say all the sounds. If everybody I call on can say all the sounds without making a mistake, we'll go on to the next exercise. [Call on two or three students. Touch under each sound. Each student says all the sounds.]

Exercise 6
Word Reading

Task A Sat
1. Say each sound when I touch it.
   [Point to *a*.] What sound?
   [Touch under *s*.] sss.
   [Point to *a*.] What sound?
   [Touch under *a*.] **ăăă**.
   [Point to *t*.] What sound?
   [Touch under *t*.] t.
2. [Touch the ball of the arrow for *sat*.]
   Now I'm going to sound out the word. I won't stop between the sounds.
   [Touch under *s, a, t* as you say.] **sssăăă.t.**
   [Point to *t*.] What sound?
3. [Touch the ball of the arrow.] Do it with me. Sound it out. Get ready.
   [Touch under *s, a, t*.] **sssaaat.** [Repeat until the students say the sounds without pausing.]
4. Again. Sound it out. Get ready. [Touch under *s, a, t*.] **sssaaat.** [Repeat until firm.]
5. All by yourselves. Sound it out. Get ready. [Touch under *s, a, t*.] **sssaaat.** [Repeat until firm.]
6. [Touch the ball of the arrow.] Say it fast. [Slash right, along the arrow. *Sat*.] Yes, you read the word *sat.*

s a t

Source: S. Engelmann, L. Carnine, & G. Johnson, *Corrective Reading: Word-Attack Basics, Teacher Presentation Book I—Decoding A* (Columbus, OH: SRA/McGraw-Hill, 1999), pp. 26–29. Reprinted by permission of the McGraw-Hill Companies.

FIGURE 7-17 Sample from a Story from *Reading Mastery: Rainbow Edition*

thē fat man and his dog had ➤

a car. thē car did not run. ➤

Source: S. Engelmann & E. C. Bruner, *Reading Mastery I: Rainbow Edition—Storybook I* (Columbus, OH: SRA/McGraw-Hill, 1995), pp. 53–54. Reprinted by permission of the McGraw-Hill Companies.

with time provided for direct teaching, group reading, individual reading practice, and monitoring of progress with feedback. Both programs have placement tests.

Whereas *Corrective Reading* uses standard print, the initial levels of *Reading Mastery* (Engelmann & Bruner, 1995) employ modified print that includes marking the long vowel sounds and reducing the size of silent letters (see Figure 7-17). Both programs provide for reading of decodable text, though *Corrective Reading* emphasizes reading expository texts.

Corrective Reading teaches skills in word identification including word attack, decoding strategies, and skill application and skills in comprehension including thinking basics, comprehension skills, and concept applications. The program provides daily feedback and has a built-in reinforcement system.

COMMENTS: Research has demonstrated that these programs are effective for improving the reading skills of students with reading difficulties and students from disadvantaged backgrounds (e.g., Rupley et al., 2009; Weiser & Mathes, 2011). Much of the teaching of phonic analysis skills is conducted in an explicit manner, which has been demonstrated to be advantageous for students with learning and behavior problems (Weiser & Mathes, 2011). Several cautions should be noted. First, these programs rely heavily on oral presentation by the teacher and oral responses and reading by the students. Second, the programs are highly scripted, making modifications difficult. Third, the nonstandard print used with Levels I and II of *Reading Mastery* may limit some students' access to other decodable books. Although other books with the nonstandard print are available, the number is limited.

Phonic Remedial Reading Lessons The *Phonic Remedial Reading Lessons* (Kirk et al., 1985) were developed in the 1930s to teach phonic analysis skills to students with cognitive impairments. The lessons follow principles of systematic direct instruction in that they use such principles as minimal change, one response to one symbol, progress from easy to hard, frequent review and overlearning, corrective feedback, verbal mediation, and multisensory learning. The lessons are designed as an intensive phonics program to be used individually or in groups of no more than two or three students. They

are not recommended as a general technique for teaching beginning reading; rather, they are a technique to use with students who have not yet learned an efficient method of identifying unknown words (Kirk et al., 1985).

Evidence-Based PRACTICE

Phonemic Remedial Reading Lessons

PROCEDURES: The program begins by developing the readiness level for the lessons. Readiness skills include auditory discrimination and auditory sound blending. Return to Figure 7-3, which presents a simple procedure for teaching sound blending. Developing readiness also includes learning the sound–symbol associations for the short *a* sound and 11 consonant sounds (i.e., /c/, /d/, /f/, /g/, /h/, /l/, /m/, /p/, /s/, /t/, /w/).

Once these skills have been learned, the first lesson is introduced (see Figure 7-18). For each lesson, students sound out each word in each line, one letter at a time, and then give the complete word. Each lesson is organized into four parts and is based on the principle of minimal change. In the first part, only the initial consonant changes in each sequence; in the second part, only the final consonant changes; in the third part, both the initial and final consonants change; in the fourth part, the space between letters in a word is normal.

In addition to these drill lessons, high-frequency sight words are introduced, and highly controlled stories are interspersed throughout the program. Frequent review lessons are also provided.

COMMENTS: This program provides a systematic and intensive approach to teaching phonic analysis skills to beginning readers. However, the approach places little emphasis on comprehension and reading for meaning and incorporates limited practice in connected text. We suggest using other books to give students the opportunity to practice their word identification and comprehension skills with other reading materials.

English Language Learners and Reading Difficulties
To what extent are the practices identified for phonological awareness and phonics appropriate for students

FIGURE 7-18 First Lesson from Phonic Remedial Reading Lessons

a

at	sat	mat	hat	fat
am	ham	Sam	Pam	tam
sad	mad	had	lad	dad
wag	sag	tag	lag	hag

sat	sap	Sam	sad
map	mam	mad	mat
hag	ham	hat	had
cat	cap	cad	cam

sat	am	sad	pat	mad
had	mat	tag	fat	ham
lag	ham	wag	hat	sap
sad	tap	cap	dad	at

map	hag	cat	sat	ham	tap
sap	map	hat	sad	tag	am
Pam	mat	had	tap	hat	dad
fat	mad	at	wag	cap	sag

Source: S. A. Kirk, W. D. Kirk, & E. H. Minskoff, *Phonic Remedial Reading Lessons* (Novato, CA: Academic Therapy Publications, 1985), p. 22. Reprinted by permission.

who are ELLs? If they are appropriate, how can teachers facilitate their acquisition of these skills in English? Unfortunately, we know substantially more about teaching students with reading difficulties who are monolingual English students than about teaching students who are ELLs. However, a growing knowledge base informs our instruction in early reading with ELLs (Shanahan & Beck, 2006; Vaughn, Cirino, et al., 2006; Vaughn & Ortiz, 2008). A summary of findings reveals:

- ELLs who were given direct instruction in early reading in English benefited in the number of words read correctly per minute (Gunn et al., 2000).

- Bilingual students with significant reading problems who participated in 22 tutoring sessions in a systematic and explicit approach to phonics and word and sentence reading significantly improved on word identification when compared with controls (Denton et al., 2004).

- Moderate-to-high effect sizes were reported for word attack, passage comprehension, phoneme segmentation, and oral reading fluency among second-grade ELLs at risk for reading disabilities participating in 58 sessions (35 minutes each) of supplemental intervention in group sizes of one to three students (Linan-Thompson, Vaughn, Hickman-Davis, & Kouzekanani, 2003). Only three students made less than 6 months' growth during the 3-month intervention.

- In a study of young children with problems learning to read in English but who spoke Sylheti (a dialect from Bangladesh), students who participated in Jolly Phonics rather than Big Books made significant gains on phonics recognition and recall and writing sounds, as well as on reading words and reading nonwords (Stuart, 1999). Findings indicate that a more structured, systematic approach that includes phonics resulted in better outcomes for ELLs than interventions without these elements.

- Young bilingual students (Spanish/English) with low literacy and oral language skills taught to read in English made considerable gains over their first-grade year and maintained these advantages into second grade (Vaughn, Cirino, et al., 2006; Vaughn, Mathes, et al., 2006). Similarly, young bilingual students (Spanish/English) with low literacy and oral language skills taught to read in Spanish also made considerable gains and outperformed comparison students and maintained these gains into second grade (Vaughn, Cirino, et al., 2006; Vaughn, Linan-Thompson, et al., 2006).

Do you need to teach bilingual readers to learn to read differently than you teach monolingual students to learn to read? Fundamentally, all students learn to read in the same way whether they are bilingual or monolingual. Bilingual students learning English will need additional language and vocabulary supports and mechanisms for linking what they know in their first language to their second language. Good readers—whether they are monolingual English or ELLs—rely primarily on decoding words (understanding the sound-to-print correspondence, or alphabetic principle). They do not rely primarily on context or pictures to identify words. When they use context, it is to confirm word reading or to better understand text meaning. Well-developed phonics instruction helps ELLs develop the skills and strategies they need to effectively and efficiently establish a map for making sense of how English language works in print. As with monolingual students, phonics instruction is a piece of the reading instruction, not the entire program. Good phonics instruction is well integrated into language activities, story time, and small-group support to create a balanced reading program. Learning to read in languages in which the print is less consistently connected to sounds (like English) takes longer than learning to read in languages that have more consistent orthographies, such as Spanish.

Multisensory Structured Language Instruction
Multisensory structured language programs combine systematic explicit teaching of phonemic awareness, the alphabetic principle, phonics and structural analysis, syllabication, and decoding with activities that incorporate the visual, auditory, kinesthetic (movement), and tactile (touch) (VAKT) modalities. Multisensory structured language instruction was developed in the 1930s by Samuel Orton, a neuropathologist, and Anne Gillingham, a school psychologist. They developed reading remediation methods that built associations between the modalities such as "having the child trace [the letter] over a pattern drawn by the teacher, at the same time giving its sound or phonetic equivalent" (Orton, 1937, p. 159) or teaching spelling through analysis and writing of the sequence of sounds in words. The content of multisensory structured language programs includes teaching phonology and phonological awareness; sound–symbol associations that must be mastered in two directions: visual to auditory and auditory to visual; syllable instruction; morphology syntax; and semantics. These programs use the following instructional features or principles (Birsh, 2011):

- Multisensory presentation of VAKT modalities are used simultaneously to enhance memory and learning

- Systematic and cumulative progression that follows the logical order of the language, moves from easy to difficult, and provides systematic review to strengthen memory

- Direct instruction that entails the explicit teaching of all concepts, skills, and strategies

- Systematic practice of decoding and spelling skills at the word, sentence, and text levels in controlled, decodable text

- Diagnostic teaching that requires teachers to be adept at individualizing instruction on the basis of careful and continual assessment of students' learning

- Instruction that incorporates synthetic methods (teaching the parts and how they work together to make a whole) and analytic methods (teaching the whole and how it can be broken down into its component parts)

These programs are designed for students with dyslexia or those who are experiencing substantial difficulty learning to read. Examples of multisensory structured language programs in addition to other structured reading programs are presented in Figure 7-19. The Gillingham-Stillman method (Gillingham & Stillman, 1997) is described in more detail. It is designed to be implemented by highly trained and skilled teachers who develop their lessons using a prescribed format. For more information on training, see Orton Academy.

Daily lessons applying the Orton-Gillingham Approach last between 45 and 60 minutes and typically include the following elements: (1) letter and sound review; (2) instruction in a new phonogram (letter–sound relationship); (3) practice reading selected words that represent previously learned letter–sound relationships (e.g., students were taught the sounds s/p/t/f/m/r/a/e, so students practice reading words *pet, at, map;* (4) students practice writing sounds and sound combinations dictated by the teacher; (5) same as number 4 with words previously taught; and (6) oral reading of controlled text. All of the lessons are responsive to the progress and needs of students.

FIGURE 7-19 Selected Phonics Reading Programs

Alphabetic Phonics and Foundations for Literacy, Cox, A. R., Cambridge, MA: Educators Publishing Service.

Fundations: Wilson Language Basics for K–3, Wilson, B. A., 2005, Millbury, MA: Wilson Language Training Corporation.

The Herman Method for Reversing Reading Failure, Herman, R. D., 1993, Sherman Oaks, CA: Herman Method Institute.

Language! The Comprehensive Literacy Curriculum, Greene, J. F., Longmont, CO: Sopris West.

Lindamood Phoneme Sequencing Program for Reading, Spelling, and Speech: The LiPS Program, Lindamood, P., and Lindamood, P., Austin, TX: PRO-ED.

Project Read, Enfield, M. L., and Greene, V., 2006, Bloomington, MN: Language Circle Enterprise.

Read Well, Sprick, M., Longmont, CO: Sopris West.

Recipe for Reading: A Structured Approach to Linguistics, Traub, N., Bloom, F. et al., 2000, Cambridge, MA: Educators Publishing Service.

Wilson Reading System, Wilson, B. A., 2004, Millbury, MA: Wilson Language Training Corporation.

The Writing Road to Reading, 5th ed., Spalding, R. B. and North, M. E., 2003, Phoenix, AZ: Spalding Educational International.

Teaching Phonic Generalizations

PROCEDURES: This method teaches students how to identify words by teaching phonic generalizations and how to apply these generalizations in reading and spelling. It is designed to be used as the exclusive method for teaching reading, spelling, and penmanship for a 2-year period at minimum.

The method is introduced by discussing the importance of reading and writing, how some children have difficulty learning to read and spell using whole-word methods, and how this method has helped other students. Thereafter, a sequence of lessons is completed, beginning with learning the names of the letters and the letter sounds, learning words through blending sounds, and reading sentences and stories.

Teaching Letters and Sounds. The teaching of letter names and letter sounds employs associations between visual, auditory, and kinesthetic inputs. Each new sound–symbol relationship or phonogram is taught by having the students make three associations:

1. Association I (reading). Students learn to associate the written letter with the letter name and then with the letter sound. The teacher shows the students the letter. The students repeat the name. The students learn the letter sound by using the same procedure.

2. Association II (oral spelling). Students learn to associate the oral sound with the name of the letter. To do this, the teacher says the sound and asks the students to give its corresponding letter.

3. Association III (written spelling). The students learn to write the letter through teacher modeling, tracing, copying, and writing the letter from memory. The students then associate the letter sound with the written letter by the teacher directing them to write the letter that has the _____ sound.

The following six features are important to note in teaching these associations:

1. Cursive writing is preferred and suggested over manuscript.

2. Letters are always introduced by a key word.

3. Vowels and consonants are differentiated by different-colored drill cards (e.g., white for consonants, salmon for vowels).

4. The first letters introduced (i.e., *a, b, f, h, i, j, k, m, p,* and *t*) represent clear sounds and nonreversible letter forms.

5. Drill cards are used to introduce each letter and to provide practice in sound and letter identification.

6. The writing procedure is applied to learning all new letters. The procedure for writing is as follows:
   a. The teacher makes the letter.
   b. The students trace the letter.
   c. The students copy it.
   d. The students write it from memory.

Teaching Words. After the first 10 letters and sounds have been learned by using the associations, students begin blending them together into words. Words that can be made from the 10 letters are written on yellow word cards and are kept in student word boxes (jewel cases). Students are taught to read and spell words.

To teach blending and reading, the letter drill cards that form a word (e.g., *b—a—t*) are laid out on the table or put in a pocket chart. The students are asked to give the sounds of the letters in succession, repeating the series of sounds again and again with increasing speed and smoothness until they are saying the word. This procedure is used to learn new words. Timed activities are used to give the students practice reading the words.

To teach spelling, the analysis of words into their component sounds should begin a few days after blending is started. To teach this method of spelling, the teacher pronounces a word the students can read, first quickly and then slowly. The teacher then asks the students, "What sound did you hear first?" and then asks, "What letter says /b/?" The students then find the *b* card. When all cards have been found, the students write the word. Gillingham and Stillman (1973) stress the importance of using this procedure for spelling. After the teacher pronounces /bat/:

1. Students repeat.

2. Students name letters *b-a-t*.

3. Student write, naming each letter while forming it /*b-a-t*/.

4. Students read *bat*.

This procedure is referred to as *simultaneous oral spelling (SOS)*. Gillingham and Stillman comment that after a few days of practice in blending and SOS, it should be an almost invariable routine to have students check their own errors. When a word is read incorrectly, students should be asked to spell what they have just said and match it against the original word. When a word is misspelled orally, the teacher may write the offered spelling and say, "Read this [e.g., *bit*]." The students would respond, "Bit." The teacher would say, "Correct, but I dictated the word /bat/."

As the students continue to learn and practice new words, they also continue to learn new sound–symbol associations or phonograms. As new phonograms are introduced, more and more words are practiced and added to the word boxes. An example of a daily lesson might be the following:

1. Practice Association I with learned phonograms.
2. Practice Association II with learned phonograms.
3. Practice Association III with learned phonograms.
4. Practice timed word reading for automaticity and accuracy.
5. Practice timed spelling and writing words for automaticity and accuracy.

Sentences and Stories. When students can read and write three-letter phonetic words, sentence and story reading is begun. This begins with reading simple, highly structured stories called "Little Stories." These stories are first practiced silently until the students think they can read them perfectly. Students may ask the teacher for assistance. The teacher pronounces nonphonetic words and cues the student to sound out phonetically regular words. Then the students read the sentence or story orally. The story is to be read perfectly with proper inflection. Later, the stories are dictated to the students. An example of a story follows:

> Sam hit Ann.
> Then Ann hit Sam.
> Sam ran and Ann ran.
> Ann had a tan mitten.
> This is Ann's tan mitten.
> Ann lost it.
> Sam got the mitten.
> Sam sent the mitten to Ann.

Evidence-Based PRACTICE

Multisensory Structured Language Instruction

COMMENTS: For the most part, multisensory structured language programs have been designed and used as remedial programs for students who have not learned to read successfully. They are often used with students identified as "dyslexic." Much of the original research that supports their use was clinical case studies summarized in a review by McIntyre and Pickering (1995) and more recently analyzed by Ritchey and Goeke (2006). The efficacy is limited to case studies, and there is limited research examining their efficacy in a broader way. First, they are best employed by teachers who have been trained in multisensory procedures.

The International Multisensory language education (IMSLEC) www.imslec.org was developed to provide quality training courses for teachers interested in accreditation as a multisensory language specialist. Second, in general, these programs emphasize decoding skills and strategies and use text with such controlled vocabulary

that it can be difficult to build comprehension skills. Hence, a number of the programs suggest simultaneously building listening comprehension until students can read more conventional text.

Word Study: Making Words, Word Building, and Word Walls   Both reading and special educators have stressed the importance of word study as a way of learning the relationships between speech sounds and print, of building word recognition and spelling skills, and of developing vocabulary (Bear, Invernizzi, Templeton, & Johnston, 2012; Cunningham, 2008; Gunning, 2010a, 2010b, 2012). For students with learning and behavior problems, opportunities to construct words using magnetic letters, letter tiles, or laminated letters provide experience in manipulating sounds to find out how the words are affected. For example, the teacher might start with the sounds /s/, /t/, /r/, /n/, and /a/ and ask, "What two sounds make the word *at*?" The teacher would then ask the students to add a letter sound to the beginning to make the word *sat*. Then the students would be directed to remove the /s/. The teacher would then say, "What sound would you add to the beginning to make the word *rat?* Now listen. We're going to make a three-letter word. Take off the /t/ sound at the end of the word. Now add the sound that will make the word *ran*."

Evidence-Based PRACTICE

Word Study

PROCEDURES: Many activities can be developed around word sorts, building words, and word walls. A number of resource books are available, including the following:

 In this **video**, experts describe what word study is and then explore strategies that teachers can use in their classroom in order to increase their students' language skills. Which methods do you think will be the most effective for your future students?

- *Building Words: A Resource Manual for Teaching Word Analysis and Spelling Strategies* (2001), by T. Gunning, Boston, MA: Pearson/Allyn & Bacon.

- *Making Words* and *Making Big Words* including *Making Words: Kindergarten; Making Words: 1st Grade;* and *Making Words: 2nd Grade,* by P. Cunningham and D. Hall (2009).

- *Phonics They Use: Words for Reading and Writing* (6th ed., 2013), by P. Cunningham, New York: Pearson.

- *Unlocking Literacy: Effective Decoding and Spelling Instruction* (2003), by Marcia K. Henry, Baltimore, MD: Brookes.

- *Word Journeys: Assessment-Guided Phonics, Spelling, and Vocabulary Instruction* (2000), by K. Ganske, New York: The Guilford Press.
- *Words Their Way: Emergent Sorts for Spanish-Speaking English Learners* (2009), by Helman et al., Upper Saddle River, NJ: Pearson.
- *Words Their Way: Word Study for Phonics, Vocabulary, and Spelling Instruction* (5th ed., 2012), by D. R. Bear, M. R. Invernizzi, S., Templeton, & F. R. Johnston., Upper Saddle River, NJ: Pearson.

Making Words (Cunningham & Hall, 2009) is an approach to inferring phonics use that requires pattern recognition and understanding of rhyme. Using a specific set of letters (e.g., *a, c, h, r, s, t*), students make approximately 15 words beginning with two-letter words (e.g., *at*) and progressing to three-, four-, and five-letter words (e.g., *tar, cart, star, cash*) until the final "mystery word" is made (e.g., *scratch*). To use *Making Words*, each student needs a set of letters, and the teacher needs a large set of letters and a sentence strip chart to hold the cards and words that are constructed. Before the lesson, the teacher puts the letters the students will need during the lesson in plastic bags and gives a bag to each student. The three steps in the activity are as follows:

1. *Making words.* After the students have identified their letters, the teacher writes the numeral on the board for the number of letters the students are to put in their words. Next, the teacher cues the students to make different two-letter words. For example, with the word *scratch,* the teacher might ask the students to construct the word *at.* When working with a class of students, after each word has been constructed, the teacher selects one student who was correct to use the set of large letters and the chart to spell the word for the other students to check their work. Then the teacher might ask the students to add /c/ to the word *at* to make *cat,* or to make the word *art* and then rearrange the letters to make the word *tar.* The teacher continues to guide students through the lesson by directing them to make words with their letters. The last word includes all the letters a student has been given for the lesson.

2. *Word sorting.* The teacher puts up on the sentence strip chart all the words the students have constructed. The teacher then asks the students how some of the words are alike, and students sort the words by spelling patterns. For example, the teacher would take the word *car* and have the students find the other words that begin with c—*cars, cash, cart;* or the teacher would take the word *art* and have the students find the other art words—*cart, chart.* Other students hypothesize why the words are alike, which assists the students in seeing the spelling patterns.

3. *Making words quickly.* Students write as many words as they can using the day's letters, writing the words in a Making Words Log. Students first write the letters from the lesson, and when the teacher says, "Go," they write words for 2 minutes.

COMMENTS: Both special education and general education teachers have found this practice an effective and efficient way to organize word-identification instruction. Students report that they enjoy the activity and manipulating the letters (Schumm & Vaughn, 1995). However, Schumm and Vaughn (1995) found it necessary to develop more structured lessons and to focus more on teaching word families with less able readers.

Implicit Code Instruction

In comparison to explicit code instruction approaches, implicit code instruction in general does the following:

- Places more emphasis on using context clues, including picture clues, in decoding unknown words
- Begins by teaching an initial set of sight words
- Uses known words to discover word patterns and phonic generalizations
- Teaches onset-rime and phonic and structural analysis within the context of meaningful stories and books
- Puts less emphasis on systematically controlling the introduction of letter–sound relationships and spelling patterns
- Uses text in which the language patterns are at the sentence level (e.g., "I see a dog," "I see a cat," "I see a bear"), rather than the word family or phoneme level (e.g., "The fat cat sat on a mat.")

This section presents two implicit code instruction approaches that have been used with students who experience difficulties in developing fluent word-recognition and effective word-identification strategies: modified language experience and the Fernald (VAKT) method.

Modified Language Experience Approach This approach to teaching early reading facilitates the transfer from oral language to written language by capitalizing on children's linguistic, cognitive, social, and cultural knowledge and abilities (Stauffer, 1970; Wanzek & Vaughn, 2009). These approaches use the students' own language, repeated reading, visual configuration, and context clues to identify words. Several methods for teaching language experience approaches have been developed: Allen's Language Experience Approach in Communication (R. V. Allen, 1976; R. V. Allen & Allen, 1966–68, 1982); Ashton-Warner's Organic

Reading (Ashton-Warner, 1958, 1963, 1972); and Stauffer's Language-Experience Approach (Stauffer, 1970). The modified language experience approach that we describe is designed for students who have limited experience or success with reading and little or no sight vocabularies. The six objectives are as follows:

1. To teach the concept that text is talk written down
2. To teach the metalinguistic skills of sentence and word segmentation
3. To teach left-to-right progression
4. To teach use of semantic and syntactic clues
5. To teach recognition of words both within the context of the experience story and in isolation
6. To teach phonic and structural analysis by discovering patterns in known words

The approach is built on the idea that oral and written language are interdependent and that oral language can serve as the base for the development of written language.

Evidence-Based PRACTICE

Modified Language Experience Approach

PROCEDURES: The procedures for this modified language experience approach are similar to those suggested by Stauffer (1970). However, more structure and practice have been incorporated into this modification to provide for the needs of students who experience difficulties in learning to read. It is designed to be used individually or with groups of two to five students. At the heart of this approach is the language experience story, a story the students write about events, persons, or things of their choice (see Figure 7-20).

FIGURE 7-20 Dictated Language Experience Story

Woody Woodpecker was driving a jet to outer space and saw some aliens. And he got on his jet and went to Jupiter and saw some people from outer space and they were driving jets, too.

First Day. For the first day of instruction, guidelines for developing a language experience story are:

1. *Provide or select an experience.* Provide or have the students select an experience that is of interest to them. Sometimes a picture can help to stimulate ideas, but be sure the students have experiences related to the picture. Remember, you are relying on the students' memory of the experience and their memory for the language used to describe the experience.

2. *Explain the procedure to the students.* Explain that the students are going to be dictating a story about the selected experience. This story will then become their reading text or book.

3. *Discuss the experience.* Discuss the experience with students so that they can begin to think about what they want to put in the dictated story. Students with learning and behavior problems sometimes have difficulty organizing their thoughts. The discussion can serve as time for the students to plan what they want to say. To facilitate the planning process, you may want to write notes or construct a map or web.

4. *Write the dictated story.* Have the students tell the story while you write it. Students should watch as you write or type it. If you are working with several students, you may want to write the story on large chart paper. Have each of the students contribute to the story. If you are working with an individual, sit next to the student so that he or she can see what you write. Encourage the students to use natural voices. The language experience story presented in Figure 7-20 was dictated by Sam, a third grader reading at the primer level.

5. *Read the story to the students.* Ask the students to listen to the story to determine whether they want to make any changes. Make changes accordingly.

6. *Have students read the story.* First have the students read the story together with you (choral reading) until they seem comfortable with the story. When you are choral reading, point to the words so that the students focus on the text as they read. Next have the students read individually and pronounce words that they cannot identify. In some cases, a student may give you a lengthy story, yet his or her memory for text is limited. When this occurs, you may work on the story in parts, beginning with only the first several sentences or first paragraph.

7. *Encourage the students to read the story to others.* This is often a very intrinsically reinforcing activity.

8. *Type the story.* If the story has not already been typed, type it, and make one copy for each student. Also make a second copy for each student to keep and use for record keeping.

Second Day. For the second day of instruction, guidelines for reading the story are as follows:

1. *Practice reading the story.* Have the students practice reading the story using choral reading, individual reading, and reading to one another. When the students are reading individually and they come to a word they do not recognize, encourage them to look at the word and think of what word would make sense. Having the students read to the end of the sentence can also help them to think of a word that makes sense. If students cannot recall the word, pronounce it.

2. *Focus on individual words and sentences.* Have the students match, locate, and read individual sentences and words in the story. Discuss what markers are used to denote sentences and words. Finally, have the students read the story to themselves and underline the words they think they know.

3. *Check on known words.* Have each student read the story orally. On your copy of the story, record the words the student knows.

4. *Type the words from the story on word cards.* Type the words each student knows from the story on word cards.

Third Day. Guidelines for the third day are as follows:

1. *Practice reading the story.* Repeat the type of activities described in step 1 of the second day.

2. *Focus on individual sentences and words.* Repeat the type of activities described in step 2 of the second day.

3. *Check on known words.* With the word cards in the *same order* as the words in the text, have each student read the word cards, and record the words the student knows.

4. *Practice reading the story.* Repeat the type of activities described in step 1 of the second day.

5. *Focus on sentences and words.* Repeat the type of activities described in step 2 of the second day.

6. *Check on known words.* With the cards in *random order*, have each student read the words, and record the words each student knows.

Fourth Day. Guidelines for the fourth day are as follows:

1. *Check on known words.* Repeat step 3 from the third day, using only the words the student knows from the previous day.

2. *Enter known words in the student's word bank.* Each student should make word cards (3 × 5 index cards or scraps of posterboard work well) for the words that he or she can identify in step 1. These words should be filed by the student in his or her word bank (index card box). Words that the student cannot identify should not be included.

3. *Read, illustrate, and publish the story.* Have the students read the story and decide whether they want to illustrate it and/or put it into a language experience book.

Books can be developed for individual students, or one book can be made for the group. Students can then share these books with each other and with other interested people and place them in the library.

Once the students have completed at least one story and have developed 15 to 20 words in their word banks, they can begin to use the banks for a variety of activities, such as generating new sentences, locating words with similar parts (i.e., inflectional endings, beginning sounds, shapes), and categorizing words by use (e.g., action words, naming words, describing words).

As the number of sight words continues to increase, students can write their own stories, using the words from the word bank to assist them. More suggestions for developing activities based on the word bank are given in Apply the Concept 7-5.

COMMENTS: The modified language experience approach provides a method for teaching children initial skills in reading, including the recognition of sight words. The approach uses the students' memory, oral language, and background experiences (Robertson, 1999; Wanzek & Vaughn, 2009), as well as visual configuration and context clues. The language experience approach is also useful in bridging languages for students who are ELLs and responding to cultural differences within a class (Landis, Umolu, & Mancha, 2010). Once the initial sight vocabulary has been built to between 30 and 100 words, students should be encouraged to read other books and stories. Having students record their stories during initial reading and reading on the fourth day allows the teacher to monitor growth.

This approach lends itself to the use of computer technology (Duling, 1999), particularly with the use of word processing, desktop publishing, and multimedia software that incorporates voice and graphics, such as *Children's Writing and Publishing Center* (Learning Company), *Kidwriter II* (Davidson and Associates), and *Kid Pix* (Broderbund), or language experience–based software programs such as *Writing to Read* (J. H. Martin & Friedburg, 1986). For example, Stratton, Grindler, and Postell (1992) integrated word processing and photography into a language experience for middle school students.

Activities are incorporated into the approach to encourage the development of the metalinguistic skills of sentence and word segmentation. However, this approach does not present a systematic method for teaching phonic and structural analysis. For students who have difficulty with these skills, a more structured method of teaching phonic and structural analysis may be needed after they have developed an initial sight vocabulary. This approach may not provide some students with enough drill and practice to develop a sight vocabulary. In those cases, it will be necessary to supplement this approach with activities presented in the section on techniques for building sight words. To learn more about the language

Suggested Activities for Word Bank Cards

1. Alphabetize words in word banks.
2. Match the word with the same word as it occurs in newspapers, magazines, etc.
3. Make a poster of the words known.
4. Complete sentences using word banks. Provide students with a stem or incomplete sentences, and have students fill slots with as many different words as possible. Example:

   He ran to the _____. The _____ and _____ ran into the park.

5. Find or categorize words in word banks:

naming words	science words
action words	color words
descriptive words	animal words
words with more than one meaning	names of people
words with the same meaning	interesting words
opposites	funny words
people words	exciting words

6. Locate words beginning the same, ending the same, or meaning the same.
7. Locate words with various endings.
8. Match sentences in stories with words from word bank.
9. Use word bank cards for matching-card games, such as grab and bingo.
10. Organize words into a story. Students might need to borrow words for this use and may wish to illustrate or make a permanent record of it.
11. Delete words from a story. Have students use words from their word banks to complete the story.
12. Scramble the sentences in the story or words in a sentence.
13. Establish class word banks for different classroom centers, such as science words, number words, weather words, house words, or family words.

Source: Based on R. J. Tierney, J. E. Readence, & E.K. Dishner, *Reading Strategies and Practices: Guide for Improving Instruction* (Boston, MA: Pearson/Allyn & Bacon, 2005).

experience approach, check out the videos with the title *Language Experience Approach* at www.youtube.

Fernald (VAKT) Method The Fernald method (Fernald, 1943, 1988) uses a multisensory or VAKT approach to teach students to read and write words. This method was used by Grace Fernald and her associates in the clinic school at the University of California at Los Angeles in the 1920s. It is designed for students who have severe difficulties learning and remembering words when reading, who have a limited sight vocabulary, and for whom other methods have not been successful. It is usually taught on an individual basis.

Evidence-Based **PRACTICE**

Fernald Method (VAKT)

PROCEDURES: The Fernald method consists of four stages through which students progress as they learn to identify unknown words more effectively. The first stage, which is the most laborious, requires a multisensory approach and uses a language experience format. By the final stage, students are reading books and can identify unknown words from the context and their similarity to words or word parts already learned. At this stage, the students are no longer tracing or writing a word to learn it.

Stage One. Guidelines for Stage One are as follows:

1. *Solicit the student's commitment to learn.* Tell the student that you are going to be showing him or her a technique for learning to read unknown words that has been successful with many students who have not learned in other ways. Inform the student that this method will take concentration and effort on his or her part, but it should be successful.

2. *Select a word to learn.* Have the student select a word (regardless of length) that he or she cannot read but would like to learn to read. Discuss the meaning of the word, and listen for the number of syllables.

3. *Write the word.* Sit beside the student, and have him or her watch and listen while you:
   a. Say the word.
   b. Using a broad-tipped marker on a piece of un-lined paper approximately 4 × 11 inches, write

FIGURE 7-21 Sample Word Using Fernald Technique

11 inches

4 inches

license

the word in blackboard-size script, or in print if the student does not write in cursive. Say the word as you write it.

c. Say the word again as you smoothly move your finger underneath the word. See Figure 7-21 for a model.

4. *Model tracing the word.* Model how the student is to trace the word so that he or she might learn it. Do not explain the process, but simply say to the student, "Watch what I do and listen to what I say."

a. Say the word.

b. Trace the word using one or two fingers. The fingers should touch the paper in order to receive the tactile stimulation. As you trace the word, say the word. Fernald (1943) stresses that the student must say each part of the word as he or she traces it. This is necessary to establish the connection between the sound of the word and its form so that the student will eventually recognize the word from the visual stimulus alone. It is important that this vocalization of the word be natural; that is, it should be a repetition of the word as it actually sounds—not a stilted or distorted sounding out of letters or syllables in such a way that the word is lost in the process. The sound for each letter is never given separately or overemphasized. In a longer word, such as *important*, the student says *im* while tracing the first syllable, *por* while tracing the second syllable, and *tant* as he or she traces the last syllable.

c. Say the word again while moving the tracing finger(s) underneath the word in a sweeping motion.

Model this process several times, and then have the student practice the process. If the student does not complete the process correctly, stop the student when he or she makes an error and cue, "Not quite. Watch me do it again." Continue this procedure until the student is completing the three-stage process correctly.

5. *Trace until learned.* Have the student continue tracing the word until the student thinks that he or she can write the word from memory.

6. *Write from memory.* When the student feels ready, remove the model, and have the student write the word from memory, saying the word as he or she writes. Fernald

(1943) stresses that the student should always write the word without looking at the copy. She comments:

> When the child copies the word, looking back and forth from the word he is writing to the copy, he breaks the word up into small and meaningless units. The flow of the hand in writing the word is interrupted and the eye movements are back and forth from the word to the copy instead of those which the eye would make in adjusting to the word as it is being written. This writing of the word without the copy is important at all stages of learning to write and spell. The copying of words is a most serious block to learning to write them correctly and to recognize them after they have been written (p. 37).

7. *File the word.* After the word has been written three times correctly, the student should place it in his or her word bank.

8. *Type the word.* Within an interval of 24 hours, the student should type and read each word learned by using this process. This helps to establish the link between the written and typed word.

The number of words learned per session using this VAKT process depends on the number of tracings a student needs to learn a new word. This number varies greatly among students. We have worked with students who need fewer than five tracings to learn a new word, whereas other students required over 50 tracings when first beginning this approach.

Fernald (1943) reports, "As soon as a child has discovered that he can learn to write words, we let him start 'story writing'" (p. 33). As the student writes a story and comes to a word he or she cannot spell, the tracing process is repeated. These stories should be typed within 24 hours so that the student can read the newly learned words in typed form within the context of the story.

Stage Two. When the student no longer needs to trace words to learn them, he or she moves to Stage Two. In this stage, the teacher writes the requested word in cursive (or manuscript) for the student. The student then simply looks at the word, saying it while looking at it, and then writes it without looking at the copy, saying each part of the word as he or she writes it from memory. As with Stage One, words to be learned are obtained from words the student requests while writing stories. The word bank continues to function as a resource for the student, but a smaller word box can be used, because the teacher is writing the words in ordinary script size.

Stage Three. The student progresses to the third stage when he or she is able to learn directly from the printed word without having it written. In this stage, the student looks at the unknown printed word, and the teacher pronounces it. The student then says the word while looking at it and then writes it from memory. Fernald reports that during this stage, students still read poorly but can recognize quite difficult words almost without exception after having written them.

During this stage, the student is encouraged to read as much as and whatever he or she wants. Unknown words are pronounced, and when the passage is finished, the unknown words are learned by using the technique described in the preceding paragraph.

Stage Four. The student can recognize new words from their similarity to words or parts of words he or she has already learned. At first, a student may need to pronounce the word and write it on a scrap of paper to assist in remembering it, but later this becomes unnecessary. The student continues to read books that interest him or her. When reading scientific or other difficult material, the student is encouraged to scan the paragraph and lightly underline each word he or she does not know. These words are then discussed for recognition and meaning before reading.

COMMENTS: Empirical evidence lends support to this approach for teaching word identification to students with severe reading disabilities (Berres & Eyer, 1970; Coterell, 1972; Fernald, 1943; Kress & Johnson, 1970; Thorpe & Borden, 1985). Although this approach tends to be successful with such readers, the first several stages are very time consuming for both the teacher and the student, and this approach is appropriate only when other approaches have not been successful.

Techniques for Building Sight Words

Students who read fluently recognize individual words automatically or when they are reading text. Students with reading disabilities struggle with automatic word recognition, which is important not only for words that are decodable (e.g., *and, then, it*), but especially for high-frequency words that are less phonetically regular (e.g., *the, you, was, have*). See Figure 7-11 for a list of high-frequency words. This section presents several techniques that teachers can use to assist students in remembering words.

Sight Word Association Procedure The sight word association procedure (SWAP; J. M. Bradley, 1975) uses corrective feedback and drill and practice to assist students in associating spoken words with written form and can also be used in combination with reading game boards (Erbey et al., 2011). The procedure is appropriate to use with students who are beginning to learn to identify words across various contexts or texts, or with students who require more practice of new words than their current reading program provides. It is designed to be used individually or with small groups.

Sight Word Association Procedure

PROCEDURES: Begin by selecting words from the text that the students consistently miscall or do not identify at an automatic level. You can use about 80% of the words as new words the student needs to learn and 20% as words that the student is reviewing. Write each word on a word card. The procedure for teaching these words (usually three to seven words at a time) is as follows:

1. Discuss the words with students to ensure that they understand the meanings of the words as the words are being used in the text.
2. Present the words to the students one word at a time. Each word is exposed for 5 seconds, and the teacher says the word twice.
3. Shuffle the cards, and ask students to identify the word on each card. Provide corrective feedback by verifying the correctly identified words, giving the correct word for any word that is miscalled, and saying the word if students do not respond in 5 seconds.
4. Present all the words again, using the format given in step 2.
5. Have students identify each word, using the format given in step 3. Repeat this step at least two more times or until they can automatically recognize all the words.

If students continue to have difficulty recognizing a word after the seventh exposure to the word, switch from a recall task to a recognition task. To do this, place several word cards on the table, and have the learners point to each word as you say it. If the students still continue to have difficulty learning the words, use a different technique to teach the words, such as picture association techniques, sentence/word association techniques, or a cloze procedure. A record sheet for keeping track of individual student responses is presented in Figure 7-22. Be sure to review words every several days to determine whether the words are being retained; reteach if necessary.

COMMENTS: This procedure provides a technique for systematically practicing unknown words. It uses principles of corrective feedback and mass and distributed practice to teach words. However, there are several important cautions: (1) use in conjunction with an approach to reading that stresses reading text and using other decoding strategies, (2) ensure students know the meanings of the words being taught, (3) give students ample opportunity to read these words in context.

Picture Association Technique Using a key picture to aid in identifying a word can be beneficial (Mastropieri & Scruggs, 1998; Scruggs et al., 2010). This method allows the readers to associate the word with a visual image. It is on this premise that picture association techniques use key pictures to help students associate a spoken word with its written form.

FIGURE 7-22 Sight Word Association Procedure (SWAP) Record Sheet

									✓Correct
									0 Incorrect
Words	Inital Teaching					Retention			Comments
	1	2	3	4	5	1	2	3	

Picture Association Technique

PROCEDURES: Select words that the students are having difficulty identifying when reading. At first, choose words that are easily imaged, such as nouns, verbs, and adjectives. Write each word on a card (usually three to seven words). On a separate card, draw a simple picture, or find a picture and attach it to the card. In some cases, the students may want to draw their own pictures. Use the following procedure to teach the picture–word association:

1. Place each picture in front of the students, labeling each one as you present it. Have the students practice repeating the names of the pictures.

2. Place next to each picture the word it represents, again saying the name of the word. Have students practice saying the names of the words.

3. Have students match the words to the pictures, and say the name of the word while matching it. Repeat this process until students easily match the pictures and words.

4. Place the words in front of the students, and have them identify the words as you say them. If they cannot identify the correct word, have them think of the picture to aid in their recognition. If they still cannot point to the word, show them the picture that goes with the word.

 needle

5. Have students recall the words by showing the word cards one at a time. Again, if students cannot recall a word, have them think of the picture. If they still cannot think of the word, tell them to look at the picture that goes with the word.

6. Continue this procedure until the students can identify all the words at an automatic level. The same record sheet as the one used for SWAP (Figure 7-22) can be used for this procedure.

7. Have students review the words on subsequent days and, most important, give them plenty of opportunities to read the words in text. When a student is reading and cannot identify a word, encourage the student to think of the picture.

COMMENTS: This picture association technique assists students in forming visual images that facilitate their identification of words. As with the SWAP, this procedure should be used only as a supplemental technique, and students should be given ample opportunities to read the words in text.

Sentence–Word Association Technique

This technique encourages students to associate unknown words with a familiar spoken word, phrase, or sentence.

PROCEDURES: Select three to seven words that students are consistently having difficulty recognizing. Discuss these words with the students, and ask them to find the words in the text and read them in a sentence. Tell the students to decide on a key word, phrase, or sentence that will help them to remember the word. For example, for the word *was*, a sentence might be, "Today he is, yesterday he _____." For the word *there*, the sentence might be, "Are you _____?" Put the words to be taught on word cards, and put the associated word, phrase, or sentence on separate cards. Teach the associations between the key word, phrase, or sentence and the unknown word, using the same procedures as were described for the picture association technique. After teaching, when a student is reading and comes to one of the new words and cannot remember it, have the student think of the associated clue. If the student cannot think of the associated clue orally, tell them the clue.

INSTRUCTIONAL ACTIVITIES

This section provides instructional activities that are related to phonological awareness, phonics, and word identification. Some of the activities teach new skills; others are best suited for practice and reinforcement of already acquired skills. For each activity, the objective, materials, and teaching procedures are described.

Web Resources

To see additional lessons including instructional videos demonstrating lesson instruction, check out the following Web sites:

- The Texas Center for Learning Disabilities (www.texasldcenter.org) This Web site has teacher lesson plans for teaching beginning reading to students by grade level. There are also lesson templates and videos.

- The Florida Center for Reading Research (www.fcrr.org) This Web site has an abundance of sample lessons and games that can be readily implemented.

- The Meadows Center for Preventing Educational Risk (www.meadowscenter.org/) Check out the videos and sample lessons on this Web site. Also, go to the library and look at the many resources for teachers on teaching beginning reading and other video resources.

My Sound Book

OBJECTIVE: To provide students with practice in finding pictures that start with a specific consonant or vowel sound.

GRADES: Primary

MATERIALS: (1) A three-ring binder or folder into which "sound pages" can be inserted. (2) Magazines, old books, or workbooks that can be cut up. (3) Stickers, scissors, and glue.

TEACHING PROCEDURES: Explain to the students that each of them will be making a book where they can collect and keep pictures and stickers that start with various sounds. Select one sound that the students are learning, and have them write the letter representing the sound on the top of the page. Then have them look through magazines, old books, and workbooks to find pictures starting with the sound. Once they have selected the pictures, have them say the names to you so that you both can determine whether the pictures represent the designated sound. Then have students glue the pictures on the sound pages, leaving room to add other pictures they find while looking for pictures representing other sounds. Have students put the sound page in the notebook and share their pictures with other students. Continue until the book is complete. As students collect stickers, you may want to encourage them to put them in the sound book.

Vowel Match

OBJECTIVE: To provide students with practice in decoding words that have various vowel sounds.

GRADES: Primary and intermediate

MATERIALS: (1) One file folder that is divided into two playing areas that consist of 10 boxes for each player. In each box, paste a picture that illustrates a vowel sound. (2) Thirty to 40 playing cards with pictures illustrating vowel sounds.

TEACHING PROCEDURES: Explain the game to the students. Shuffle the cards, and place them face down near the players. Each student draws a card and checks to see whether the vowel sound illustrated on the card matches one of the pictures on his or her side of the game folder. If it does, the player places the card over the picture on the game folder. If the picture does not match, the card is discarded. The first player to cover all the boxes wins the game.

ADAPTATIONS: This game is easily adapted to teaching rhyming words and other sounds such as consonant digraphs or blends.

Sight Word Bingo

OBJECTIVE: To provide students with practice in recognizing words.

GRADES: Primary and intermediate

MATERIALS: (1) Posterboard cut into 10 × 8-inch pieces to use for bingo cards. (2) A list of new words students have encountered in their reading. Such lists can be found in the back of basal readers or in books of lists such as *The New Reading Teacher's Book of Lists* (Fry, Fountoukidis, & Polk, 1985). To make the bingo cards, randomly select words from the list, and write them on the card as illustrated. (3) Colored markers.

Word Bingo			
happen	should	night	enough
below	never	complete	thought
grow	where	while	building
every	through	include	were
country	even	important	between

TEACHING PROCEDURES: One student (or the teacher) is designated as the caller. Each of the remaining students gets a bingo card. The caller randomly selects a word from the list and says the word. The students place a colored marker on the square in which the word is written. The first person to cover all the squares in a horizontal, vertical, or diagonal row calls, "Bingo." The caller and the student then verify the words. If they are verified, that student wins.

ADAPTATIONS: Bingo is a generic game that can be adapted to provide practice for a variety of skills. Following are some examples:

- *Consonant bingo:* Put pictures of objects that start with initial consonants, blends, or digraphs on the bingo cards. The caller says the letters, and the students mark the pictures that have the same consonant, blend, or digraph. This can also be adapted for final consonants.
- *Prefix bingo:* Write prefixes on the bingo cards. The caller says a word with a prefix or gives the definition of a prefix, and the students mark the prefix on their cards.
- *Math fact bingo:* Write the answers to math facts on the bingo cards. The caller says a math fact, and the students mark the answer.

Compound Concentration

OBJECTIVE: To give students practice in identifying compound words and to illustrate how words may be combined to form compound words.

GRADES: Intermediate and secondary

MATERIALS: Thirty-six 3 × 5-inch index cards on which the two parts of 18 compound words have been written. Make sure that each part can only be joined with one other part.

TEACHING PROCEDURE: Have a student shuffle the cards, and place the cards face down in six rows with six cards each. Each player takes a turn at turning over two cards. The student then decides whether the two words make a compound word. If the words do not make a compound word, then the cards are again turned face down, and the next player takes a turn. If the words make a compound word, then the player gets those two cards and turns over two more cards. The student continues playing until two cards are turned over that do not make a compound word. The game is over when all the cards are matched. The winner is the player with the most cards.

ADAPTATIONS: Concentration can be adapted for many skills. Students can match synonyms, antonyms, prefixes, suffixes, initial or final consonants, categories, and math facts.

Go Fish for Rimes

OBJECTIVE: To give the students practice in identifying and reading words with rimes.

GRADES: Intermediate and secondary

MATERIALS: Twenty to 30 index cards (3 × 5 inch) on which words with a particular rime pattern (e.g., -ake, -ail, -ime, -ight) are written. Make sure that each word is written on two cards so that students can match them.

TEACHING PROCEDURES: Have students shuffle the cards and deal five cards to each player. The rest of the cards are placed face down in a pile on the table. Each player reads his or her own cards. Any player who has two cards that contain the same word reads the word and places the pair of cards face up in front of himself or herself (provide assistance as necessary). After everyone has laid out their pairs, the first student asks one other student whether he or she has a specific word (e.g., "Do you have *rake*?"). The student who was asked looks at his or her cards. If that student has the card, he or she reads the card and hands it to the first student. That student puts the pair face up in front of him or her and takes another turn. If the student who is being asked for a card does not have the card, he or she says, "Go fish," the first student takes a card from the pile, and the next student takes his or her turn. When a student has laid down all of his or her cards, the game is over. The person with the most pairs wins.

ADAPTATIONS: Go Fish can be adapted for many skills. Students can match synonyms, antonyms, prefixes, suffixes, or compound words.

Summary

Reading instruction involves teaching the basic skills necessary to read words accurately and rapidly. Reading instruction also incorporates strategies to assist readers in understanding what they read by expanding vocabulary and using comprehension strategies. There is a general progression of skills, and instruction should be organized into the essential components, the focus of which is based on individual student needs.

Phonological awareness is knowing and demonstrating that spoken language can be broken down into smaller units (words, syllables, phonemes). Activities in phonological awareness are conducted orally. For example, a teacher says the word *that*, and students clap the number of sounds they hear (three claps). Letter–sound correspondence is knowing how letter names and sounds relate to each other. Phonics is the idea that words are composed of letters that represent sounds, that those sounds are related to each other (letter–sound correspondence), and that they can be used to pronounce or spell words. Activities involving phonics relate sounds to print and may involve direct teaching of letter sounds, phonemes, and activities to practice the letter–sound relationships. For example, a teacher gives students the phoneme /at/, and students add letters to make additional words (e.g., *cat, that, mat, splat*).

Seven main decoding strategies contribute to successful word identification. These include:

1. Phonic analysis involves identifying and blending letter–sound correspondences into words.

2. Onset-rime consists of using common spelling patterns to decode words by blending either individual sounds/patterns or using an analogy method to think of a word with similar sounds/patterns. Knowledge of common rimes assists readers in recognizing a large number of words that contain the core patterns.

3. Synthetic and analytic phonics

4. Structural analysis involves analyzing words to assist with decoding and determining the meanings of words. Structural analysis is particularly effective for decoding longer, multisyllabic words.

5. Knowledge of syllabication assists readers in recognizing similar chunks of print across words.

6. Automatic word recognition is knowing a word without having to decode it. Because certain words are repeated so often (e.g., *the*), reading is made easier when one can automatically recognize high-frequency words that are less phonetically regular.

7. A knowledge of syntax (word order) and semantics (word meaning) can assist readers in cross-checking pronunciation and monitoring comprehension.

Explicit code approaches teach phonological awareness; letter–sound correspondences; the alphabetic principle; and the use of phonic analysis, structural analysis, and syllabication to decode unknown words. Reading materials associated with this technique generally use decodable texts that highlight specific phonic or structural patterns. Implicit code instruction emphasizes the use of context clues, including picture cues, to decode unknown words. Texts are chosen that will be meaningful to readers and not for particular letter–sound relationships or spelling patterns. Implicit code instruction is often used with emergent readers who have had difficulties developing sight vocabulary and word analysis skills.

 ASSESSMENT

After completing this chapter, test your knowledge of the concepts by completing this Assessment.

Assessing and Teaching Reading:
Fluency and Comprehension

LEARNING OUTCOMES

1. Describe the key components of the Common Core Standards as they relate to reading fluency and comprehension. Describe the anchor standards and how they relate to reading for understanding.

2. Identify an assessment that can be used for monitoring students' fluency, and briefly describe procedures for using and interpreting the data. Then list ways in which fluency data assists teachers in monitoring students' progress. Describe two or more approaches to improving fluency with students with reading difficulties.

3. Describe the assessment and instructional components needed in a reading comprehension program?

4. Describe reading comprehension, including several teaching practices associated with improved comprehension?

Jeff is a second grader who continues to sound out many words. He does not yet have automatic word recognition; consequently, his reading is very slow. Because Jeff uses so much of his cognitive effort reading each word, he has little remaining to concentrate on understanding what he reads.

Shoshanna, a fourth grader, had great difficulty learning to read. After several years of failure, she was taught using a multisensory structured language approach and her word reading improved. However, Shoshanna's reading rate is slow, which interferes with her understanding. When asked to define reading, she places emphasis on reading words correctly rather than on understanding what she reads. Though Jeff and Shoshanna have developed systems for identifying words, they are having difficulties reading fluently—that is, quickly and easily with accuracy and expression.

Why is poor fluency performance a problem? Research indicates that students with significant reading disabilities have difficulty developing fluency and continue to be slow readers into adolescence and adulthood (Chard, Vaughn, & Tyler, 2002; Norton & Wolf, 2012). Students who are slow and labored readers (low fluency) may benefit from fluency instruction aimed at improving their automatic word recognition and practices focused on assisting them in allocating more effort to constructing meaning from what they are reading.

This chapter addresses reading-related constructs of fluency and comprehension for students with reading problems. One key to becoming a good reader is to engage in reading for learning and enjoyment. Yet students with reading difficulties often do not have as many opportunities to engage in reading during school and do not choose reading as a leisure-time activity.

Teachers can assist students in becoming fluent readers and provide them with a wide choice of literature and other materials to read and discuss so that reading becomes a source of learning, enjoyment, and satisfaction. To reach this goal, it is important to plan instruction that focuses on strategies for building fluency and promoting active reading comprehension as presented in this chapter. Before discussing these necessary assessment and instructional practices, it is important to link this work to the Common Core State Standards.

Common Core State Standards: Fluency and Comprehension

The Common Core State Standards for English Language Arts and Literacy in History/Social Studies, Science and Technical Subjects (Common Core State Standards Initiative, 2010) outlines the essential literacy skills students should develop at each grade level, K–12. We refer to them as the CCSS. Figure 8-1 provides the list of CCSS that relate to fluency and comprehension instruction and also provides guidelines for teaching the CCSS for students with learning and behavior problems.

The CCSS specify that all students will read increasingly difficult and challenging texts at each grade level until they are ready by the end of high school to meet the demands of reading within college and career settings. The course for this is to increase and build on previous grade-level accomplishments seamlessly across K–12 grades. The readings and materials for accomplishing this are not prescribed; however, there are sample texts to inform educators in selecting reading materials for their own curriculum. An important feature of the CCSS is the increased exposure to informational text; it is expected that by fourth grade 50% of the selections students read are expository or information texts.

Within CCSS, several strands weave throughout the grades. These are *key ideas and details, craft and structure, integration of knowledge and ideas,* and *range of reading and level of text complexity.* A brief summary of each of these strands follows with implications for teaching students with learning disabilities (Haager & Vaughn, 2013).

Students demonstrate that they understand and can express the *key ideas* in text (e.g., about characters, events, or themes). For very beginning readers (kindergarten), an example is that they can ask and answer questions about key text ideas when prompted by the teacher. For students in grade 2, the expectation is that they can demonstrate that they understand the *key ideas and details* of text by both asking and answering various question types (e.g., who, what, when, where, why, how). As students proceed with reading development, the expectations for understanding key ideas and details expands and, by fourth grade, students are expected to refer to details and examples in text when explaining what text says explicitly and inferentially.

Craft and structure refers to acquiring proficiency in text types, interpretation of perspectives and character in text, and understanding of word meanings and use in text. For example, beginning students are expected to recognize common types of text (e.g., storybooks and poem). In second grade, they should be able to recognize differences in points of view of characters including demonstrating voice change when reading the words of characters. By the time students are in fourth grade, they are expected to determine the meaning of words and phrases as they are used in text.

Integration of knowledge and ideas refers to making connections between key ideas across texts. For example, a beginning reader is expected to view an illustration in text and to determine how the illustration relates to the story, whereas a second grader is expected to identify the reasons an author gives for supporting points in text. Older students are expected to use multiple texts (starting with two text types) and compare and contrast the main ideas in each of these text types.

Range of reading and level of text complexity refers to students' reading and understanding increasingly complex texts that address history, social studies, science, and technical topics at their grade level and beyond. For example, beginning readers should read with purpose and understanding, whereas older students should read texts including information texts (e.g., history, social studies, science) at their grade level and above with support.

FIGURE 8-1 Anchor Standards (CCSS) for Reading, Listening, and Speaking

Anchor Standards for Reading

Key Ideas and Details

1. Read closely to determine what the text says explicitly and to make logical inferences from it; cite specific textual evidence when writing or speaking to support conclusions drawn from the text.
2. Determine central ideas or themes of a text and analyze their development; summarize the key supporting details and ideas.
3. Analyze how and why individuals, events, and ideas develop and interact over the course of a text.

Craft and Structure

4. Interpret words and phrases as they are used in a text, including determining technical, connotative, and figurative meanings, and analyze how specific word choices shape meaning or tone.
5. Analyze the structure of texts, including how specific sentences, paragraphs, and larger portions of the text (e.g., a section, chapter, scene, or stanza) relate to each other and the whole.
6. Assess how point of view or purpose shapes the content and style of a text.

Integration of Knowledge and Ideas

7. Integrate and evaluate content presented in diverse media and formats, including visually and quantitatively, as well as in words.
8. Delineate and evaluate the argument and specific claims in a text, including the validity of the reasoning as well as the relevance and sufficiency of the evidence.
9. Analyze how two or more texts address similar themes or topics in order to build knowledge or to compare the approaches the authors take.

Range of Reading and Level of Text Complexity

10. Read and comprehend complex literary and informational texts independently and proficiently

Anchor Standards for Speaking and Listening

Comprehension and Collaboration

1. Prepare for and participate effectively in a range of conversations and collaborations with diverse partners, building on others' ideas and expressing their own clearly and persuasively.
2. Integrate and evaluate information presented in diverse media and formats, including visually, quantitatively, and orally.
3. Evaluate a speaker's point of view, reasoning, and use of evidence and rhetoric.

Presentation of Knowledge and Ideas

4. Present information, findings, and supporting evidence such that listeners can follow the line of reasoning and the organization, development, and style are appropriate to task, purpose, and audience.
5. Make strategic use of digital media and visual displays of data to express information and enhance understanding of presentations.
6. Adapt speech to a variety of contexts and communicative tasks, demonstrating command of formal English when indicated or appropriate.

Anchor Standards for Language

Conventions of Standard English

1. Demonstrate command of the conventions of standard English grammar and usage when writing or speaking.
2. Demonstrate command of the conventions of standard English capitalization, punctuation, and spelling when writing.

Knowledge of Language

3. Apply knowledge of language to understand how language functions in different contexts, to make effective choices for meaning or style, and to comprehend more fully when reading or listening.

Vocabulary Acquisition and Use

4. Determine or clarify the meaning of unknown and multiple-meaning words and phrases by using context clues, analyzing meaningful word parts, and consulting general and specialized reference materials, as appropriate.
5. Demonstrate understanding of figurative language, word relationships, and nuances in word meanings.
6. Acquire and use accurately a range of general academic and domain-specific words and phrases sufficient for reading, writing, speaking, and listening at the college and career readiness level; demonstrate independence in gathering vocabulary knowledge when encountering an unknown term important to comprehension or expression.

Because many students with learning disabilities and behavior disorders are likely to need support to read at their grade level, it is reasonable to expect that these students will need accommodations and intensive interventions.

All of the Common Core State Standards in English Language Arts-Literacy are available on the Common Core Web site.

Assessing Fluency and Monitoring Student Progress

What is reading fluency, and how is progress in fluency monitored? Fluency is the ability to read a text at an appropriate rate, accurately, and with expression (i.e., *prosody*). We often refer to *fluent readers* as individuals who read with automaticity. By *automaticity* we mean the quick, effortless, and accurate reading of words. It is important to note that although there is emphasis on speed of reading, we do not mean that students should race through what they read without enjoyment or without monitoring their understanding. We are referring to a rate of reading that occurs with little focus or emphasis on decoding individual words. In addition to reading accurately and with appropriate speed, fluency also includes prosody, or reading with phrasing, expression, and in a way that communicates understanding.

Of all of the elements of reading (e.g., phonemic awareness, phonics, word study, comprehension), fluency is the one that is most readily assessed and monitored. That is because in relatively little time, teachers can determine whether students are making adequate progress in fluency and how their progress compares to other students in the same grade at that time of year. Fluency has three parts: rate of reading, accuracy of word reading, and prosody. We typically assess rate and accuracy of reading to determine progress in fluency because prosody is not a particularly strong predictor of reading fluency or comprehension, whereas rate and accuracy of word reading are very good predictors of fluency and comprehension (Y. S. Kim et al., 2010, 2011). Also, it is interesting that while silent and oral reading fluency are related they are distinct and that word reading fluency (reading a list of words rather than connected text) is a better predictor of comprehension for average rather than skilled readers (Y. S. Kim et al., 2011).

Remember that the goal of improving children's rate of reading is not that they read faster, but that they read with such automaticity that they can free up their thinking to understand and enjoy text. With the increased emphasis on oral reading fluency as a progress-monitoring measure, there is concern that some teachers may lose touch with the most important aspect of reading: reading to learn and enjoy text.

Monitoring Student Progress in Fluency

Fluency is most frequently measured by the number of words read correctly per minute (WCPM) and through observations of phrasing, smoothness, and pace. An important reference for teachers to know is the number of WCPM in a specified grade-level passage. For example, Michael reads 50 words per minute in mid-first-grade-level passages. Because Michael is a third-grade student, his fluency indicates that he is considerably behind expectations both in the number of words he reads correctly as well as the level of text he reads. Table 8-1 provides an overview of fluency norms and rates by grade level. The table also provides the expected number of words per minute students are expected to improve.

How do you interpret the information in Table 8-1? The first column tells you the grade-level expectation. The second column tells you the normative data at that particular percentile. For example, students in the 75th percentile in the "winter" of first grade read on average 47 words correct per minute. You can see that for students

TABLE 8-1 Reading Fluency Norms Guidelines for Grades 1–8

Grade	Percentile	Fall	Winter	Spring	Average Weekly Improvement
1	75	–	47	82	2.2
1	50	–	23	53	1.9
1	25	–	12	28	1.0
2	75	79	100	117	1.2
2	50	51	72	89	1.2
2	25	25	42	61	1.1
3	75	99	120	137	1.2
3	50	71	92	107	1.1
3	25	44	62	78	1.1
4	75	119	139	152	1.0
4	50	94	112	123	.9
4	25	68	87	98	.9
5	75	139	156	168	.9
5	50	110	127	139	.9
5	25	85	99	109	.8
6	75	153	167	177	.8
6	50	127	140	150	.7
6	25	98	111	122	.8
7	75	156	165	177	.7
7	50	128	136	150	.7
7	25	102	109	123	.7
8	75	161	177	177	.5
8	50	133	151	151	.6
8	25	106	124	124	.5

Source: Based on Hasbrouk and Tindal, 2006. Numbers for Fall, Winter, and Spring represent words correct per minute. Behavioral Research and Reading, 2005.

at the 25th percentile the average normative performance is consistently lower at each grade level than for students at the 50th or 75th percentile. You can also see that oral reading fluency expectations increase developmentally, though the relative growth after fourth grade is lower than before fourth grade. You might also be interested in the information in the last column of Table 8-1 which provides information on the average weekly improvement. If you are monitoring the progress of a student in the third grade who is a low reader (at or below the 25th percentile), you can see from the table that you would expect them to grow less than 1 word correct per week of instruction.

How do you measure WCPM? A teacher selects two to three passages that are unfamiliar to a student and are at a student's instructional reading level, the level at which the student can read with the teacher's support, or independent reading level. Word recognition is around 90% at the instructional level and at or near 100% at the independent level. After selecting the passages, the teacher makes two copies of each passage of text to be used with the targeted student: one for recording errors and one for the student to read. A stopwatch can be used for timing, and it is often helpful to record audio of the student's reading on a monthly basis so that the student can hear as well as see his or her progress. To observe oral reading fluency assessments determining words correct per minute, take a look at these YouTube videos: **DIBELS NEXT: Oral Reading Fluency (DORF)** and **MASI-R Oral Reading Fluency Measures 3rd Grader**.

The teacher tells the student, "When I say 'Begin,' start reading aloud at the top of the page. Do your best reading. If you come to a word that you don't know, I'll tell it to you." If a student does not read a word within 3 seconds, the teacher says the word. The student reads for 1 minute. Following along as the student reads, the teacher marks his or her own copy by putting a slash (/) through words that were read incorrectly. This includes mispronunciations, substitutions, omissions, words pronounced after hesitations of more than 3 seconds, and reversals. Insertions, self-corrections, and repetitions should not be counted. The teacher should also note whether the student is having difficulty with phrasing; is ignoring punctuation; is reading slowly, word by word, or laboriously; and/or has frequent extended pauses, false starts, sound-outs, and repetitions. The teacher notes the last word the student read when the minute is up. If the student is in the middle of a sentence when the time is up, the teacher should have the student finish the sentence but count only the words the student read up to the stop point. If using WCPM infrequently (once every 10 weeks), the teacher should use two passages to ensure accuracy.

The following formula is used to calculate fluency:

$$\text{Number of words read correctly in 1 minute} - \text{Number of errors}$$

For example, if a student reads 83 words during a 1-minute sample and makes 6 errors, then the WCPM would be 83 minus 6, which equals 77. The scores are averaged across at least two passages to get a mean rate. For example, if on the second reading of a different passage at the same grade level, the student read 84 words correctly but made 11 errors, the WCPM would be 73. The average of 73 and 77 is 75, so during this period, the student's WCPM is recorded as 75.

Guidelines for fluency rates for grades 1 through 8 are presented in Table 8-1. You can use this table to determine the relative performance of your students. For example, you have a student in the fifth grade, and at the beginning of the year, she is reading 60 WCPM. You can look at the chart and see that students in fifth grade at the beginning of the year read on average 110 to 139 WCPM—well above the 60 WCPM of your student. Looking at the chart you see that students read about 50 WCPM in the fall of second grade, providing you with a benchmark for necessary improvement.

Teachers should consider several critical points when assessing reading fluency:

- Text passages that are used for assessment should be comparably leveled each time so that when a student's performance is compared over time, the test is at an appropriate level to compare performance. More difficult texts reduce the rate and accuracy of reading, making comparisons with previous fluency checks invalid.

- Words that are pronounced correctly within the context of a passage are considered read correctly. If a student repeats a word or phrase, it is counted as correct. When students make an error but correct themselves within 3 seconds, it is also counted as correct.

- Words that are read incorrectly are counted as errors. Errors include mispronunciations, substitutions, and omissions.

- When students pause for more than 3 seconds, you should tell them the word and then mark it as an error.

Apply the Concept 8-1 offers commercial fluency measures that provide leveled passages.

Published Fluency Assessments

Teachers can use several sources of passages to compare students' fluency rates over time. Each year additional companies and individuals publish fluency assessments. Following is a brief description of some of the more frequently used fluency measures:

- Dynamic Indicators of Basic Early Literacy Skills (DIBELS Next, 2002. DIBELS has leveled reading passages for assessing fluency for kindergarten through sixth grade. The fluency assessment passages are also available for kindergarten through third grade in Spanish (*Indicadores dinámicos del éxito en la lectura*—R. H. Good, Bank, & Watson, 2004). DIBELS is administered to individual students and takes about 2 to 3 minutes per student.

- The Test of Oral Reading Fluency (2005). Like DIBELS, TORF is administered individually and takes about 2 to 3 minutes per student. Curriculum-based measures were developed by Drs. Stan Deno and Doug Marston.

Ed Checkup

- AIMSweb. This group provides multiple passages at each grade level to provide extensive text for monitoring students' progress. They also provide professional development and training as needed. This measure is owned by Pearson publishers.

- Test of Silent Word Reading Fluency (TOSWRF). This group-administered measure is designed to determine whether students can recognize printed words accurately and efficiently and can be administered to students in first grade and above.

PRO-ED

- Easy CBM oral reading fluency (EasyCBM). This is an individually administered oral reading fluency measure across grade levels.

Using Oral Reading Fluency Scores to Establish Fluency Goals

Fluency information can be plotted in graphs such as the one shown in Figure 8-2. Having students record their own progress serves as a motivation for reading, provides immediate feedback, and allows the students to set goals and see concrete evidence of their progress. Generally, for students with fluency problems, the goal is to add one or two more WCPM per week, with fluency increasing more quickly in the earlier grades. Refer back to Table 8-1 so that you can determine the expected growth per week in oral reading fluency word reading for each grade level and at each percentile within the grade level. Audio recordings of readings allow students not only to graph their progress but also to hear their progress over time. Generally, these reading samples are collected every 1 to 2 months and can be kept across the year.

Jeff's fluency instruction and progress, as shown in Figure 8-2, was measured weekly by using beginning second-grade instructional-level reading materials. He was making consistent progress, and his WCPM increased substantially from the third to the fourth week (three words), when he began to rely less on sounding out words and to attempt to read the words automatically. This also resulted in better phrasing and reading with more expression.

Teachers and students can establish baseline fluency scores and then target acceptable rates of growth in fluency on a bimonthly basis. For example, a student in third grade who reads 50 words per minute WCPM in a second-grade passage is below grade level in both

FIGURE 8-2 Fluency Monitoring

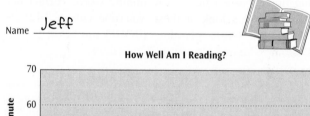

accuracy (the text is below grade level) and speed (the student is reading too slowly). The teacher and student may decide to establish one word per week as the improvement goal. These goals can motivate students

Using Fluency Data

Student Data Show	Instructional Decisions
Student is making steady progress.	Continue in the same level of text.
Student meets goals on first reading.	Move to higher level of text or raise goal.
Student has difficulty achieving goals.	Alter fluency instruction; move to lower-level text or lower fluency goal.

and provide excellent reporting data to parents. Using fluency data can assist teachers in making instructional decisions, as seen in Apply the Concept 8-2.

WEB RESOURCES

For more information on how fluency data can assist teachers in making instructional decisions, see the Web sites at the University of Texas and Florida State University: http://www.meadowscenter.org/vgc/ and http://www.fcrr.org.

The Behavioral Research and Teaching Center at the University of Oregon also provides technical reports and resources on fluency.

Response to Intervention (RTI) and Fluency

Oral reading fluency is frequently used to monitor students' progress in reading. For this reason, it is also used as a means for determining how students with reading difficulties may be responding to interventions. For example, many schools screen students

For a complete description of RTI, see Chapter 3.

in first, second, and third grade using oral reading fluency to determine which students are at risk for reading problems. Teachers provide an intervention to these students four to five times per week for 20 to 40 minutes per day over an 8- to 12-week period. During this intervention, students typically receive an oral reading fluency test every week or two, so that the "slope" of their progress can be charted. Based on students' overall progress and the extent to which they are closing the gap between their oral reading fluency before and during intervention, a decision is made about participation in subsequent interventions. To illustrate, Jeanine, a second grader, was making adequate progress in reading after she was placed in an intervention (more than two words correct per week gain on average) and appeared to be very close to meeting expected reading

performance. Her teachers decided that it would be in her best interest to continue in the intervention for another 10 weeks. Max displayed a different pattern of learning. His overall progress was very low (less than one word correct per week on average), and teachers were concerned that he needed even more intensive intervention. They adjusted his instruction both in the classroom and in the intervention, and provided one-on-one instruction during intervention.

Reading Rockets provides a very interesting Web site with information on reading fluency and response to intervention.

Teaching Fluency

What are effective instructional practices for increasing reading fluency? Fluency instruction is designed to increase automatic word recognition, or the smoothness of the reading; rate, or the pace of reading; and prosody, or expression, appropriate phrasing, and attention to punctuation. According to the theory of automaticity (Samuels, 1997), fluent readers automatically process information at the visual and phonological levels, and therefore can focus most of their attention on the meaning of the text, integrating this information into their existing knowledge. The fluent reader's multitask functioning is made possible by the reduced demands on cognitive resources: The reader no longer has to focus on word recognition and other reading processes, thus freeing cognitive resources for comprehension. Because poor readers take much longer and require more exposures to automatically recognize and recall words, it is important that fluency instruction provide multiple opportunities for practice.

However, it is important to note that fluency may be much more important with beginning readers (students who are reading at the first- and second-grade levels) than it is when students become more mature readers. In the beginning stages of reading, being able to read words automatically and effortlessly is associated with comprehension. As students read better (more than 70 WCPM), fluency may be less important (Stahl, 2004). Also, little compelling evidence suggests that fluency practice with the majority of secondary readers—even those with reading difficulties, is valuable (Wexler, Vaughn, Roberts, & Denton, 2010), and additional research that meets rigorous guidelines is needed (Chard, Ketterlin-Geller, Baker, Doabler, & Apichataburtra, 2009).

Fluency instruction and guided practice reading are important parts of any reading program, particularly for students with learning and behavior problems. Good fluency instruction provides students with repeated practice of reading materials at the student's independent or instructional reading level. In the following section, we examine several proven practices for assisting students in developing fluency in their reading as well as ideas for making difficult text more accessible.

Reading Aloud and Previewing Books

Students develop the concept of fluent reading through listening to and watching others read aloud, through previewing books, and through practice reading materials that are at their instructional to independent reading levels (word recognition from 90% to 100%). There is a growing emphasis on the importance of reading aloud to children and previewing a book as ways not only to develop an enjoyment of literature and books but also to model and build fluent reading (Gunning, 2010a; Whitehurst & Lonigan, 2001). The types of read alouds include repeated reading, story reading with questions, story reading with vocabulary, and other instruction (Swanson, Vaughn, et al., 2011). All of these read-aloud practices are associated with small-to-large effects for young students (preschool through third grade) on outcomes such as language, vocabulary, and phonological awareness.

Guided oral reading is a practice for enhancing fluency. What is guided reading? Guided reading refers to many related approaches of providing support to improve students' fluency. These approaches include reading aloud, modeling fluent reading while students read along, providing opportunities for better readers to serve as models for other students, listening to recorded text read aloud and then reading aloud, and reading poems and other genres after they have been read aloud by the teacher. Guided oral reading promotes the development of reading fluency in a number of ways.

First, it allows a teacher to model fluent reading. In reading aloud to a group of students who are just learning to read, the use of big books can be helpful because it allows the teacher to make the literacy act more visible and creates interest in the story. If a teacher, family member, or volunteer is reading aloud to one child, then sitting close to the child makes it easy for the child to interact with the print and the teacher. When reading aloud, the teacher or volunteer should read with expression, pointing to the words while reading or sweeping the fingers underneath them.

Second, modeling fluent reading by reading aloud provides background knowledge for students so that they can read a book by themselves, with a partner, or while listening to an audio recording. Reading aloud gives the teacher the opportunity to preview difficult words and unfamiliar concepts. Once students have listened to and previewed a book, they have a wealth of knowledge about the book to assist them in reading. In addition, once children have listened to a book, they are more likely to select it as a book they want to read. In a study of kindergartners, Martinez and Teale (1988) found that children chose familiar books (i.e., those read repeatedly by the teacher) to read during free time three times more frequently than they chose unfamiliar books (books the teacher had not read). Rose (1984) compared the effects of teacher-directed previewing and not previewing texts with six students with learning disabilities and found that previewing substantially increased oral reading rates. Other studies have investigated the effects of taped previewing (Rose & Beattie, 1986) and peer previewing (Salend & Nowak, 1988). These procedures also increased fluency of the text but not to the degree that teacher-directed previewing did. Apply the Concept 8-3 presents a procedure for teacher-directed previewing.

Third, modeling fluent reading aloud for students exposes them to books that may be too difficult for them to read. Many students with learning and behavior problems have listening comprehension that is several years more advanced than their reading comprehension. Reading a book aloud affords students the opportunity to talk about literature that is at a more advanced level.

Techniques for building sight words are discussed in Chapter 7.

Fourth, reading aloud can be orchestrated so that older, less adept readers can read books to young children and serve as cross-age tutors. This gives the older students the opportunity to read aloud and to model the role of a good reader, an opportunity that is not often available in the regular or resource classroom.

Reading aloud has the following benefits (Trelease, 2006):

- It provides a positive reading role model.
- It furnishes new information.
- It demonstrates the pleasures of reading.
- It develops vocabulary.
- It provides examples of good sentences and good story grammar.
- It enables students to be exposed to a book to which they might not otherwise be exposed.
- It provides opportunities for discussions concerning the content of the book.

It is important to remember that reading aloud builds vocabulary and comprehension when teachers do the

Guidelines for Implementing Previewing for Promoting Fluency

1. *Decide on an appropriate book or text* (i.e., one that is of interest to the students and at their independent to instructional reading levels). For longer books, preview only a section of the book at a time. Have student copies of the book or text available.

2. *Introduce the book or text* using the title and looking through the text or section. With the students, make predictions about the content. Introduce words that may be difficult for the students to automatically recognize or for which the meaning may be unfamiliar. Students may write these words in a personal dictionary or on word cards.

3. *Have students follow along as you read the book or text orally* at a relatively slow conversational rate (approximately 130 words per minute).

4. *Have students partner and take turns reading* a section after you have read it. Have the stronger partner read first, and as one student reads, have the other student provide support by pronouncing words the student does not know.

5. *Have the students review the difficult words* using techniques for building sight words.

6. *Monitor students' reading fluency* on a regular basis by using the procedures discussed earlier in this chapter in the section titled, "Monitoring Student Progress in Fluency."

---

following (Santoro, Chard, Howard, & Baker, 2008): (1) select texts to encourage "text-to-text" and "text-to-self" connections; (2) identify target words and then ask students to listen for these key words; (3) promote discussions that link students' responses to the text; (4) and preview text, stop while reading, and summarize after reading in ways that promote comprehension. To observe a read-aloud story, go to: www.youtube.com: Reading Aloud: A demonstration (Part 2 of 2).

Initial evidence indicates that when repeated reading is contrasted with continuous reading (e.g., rather than reading the same text more than once, students spend the same amount of time reading text aloud), students do equally well in both conditions (O. E. O'Connor et al., 2007). Thus, teachers may want to provide opportunities for students to read continuously as well as to apply repeated reading procedures. Also, repeated reading along with question generation by students may promote both reading fluency and comprehension (Hua et al., 2012).

Evidence-Based PRACTICE

Repeated Reading

PROCEDURES: Repeated reading consists of rereading short, meaningful passages several times (three to five) until a satisfactory level of fluency is reached. The procedure is then repeated with a new passage. Generally, the student repeatedly reads passages that range from 50 to 200 words in length, until he or she reaches a more fluent reading rate (see Table 8-1) and an adequate word-recognition level (e.g., 90% to 100% word recognition).

When a student reads under the direct supervision of a teacher, the teacher pronounces the words a student does not recognize. To foster comprehension, discussion of the passage follows reading.

Using audio books, students listen to the stories and read and/or follow along with the written text. They listen to and read the same story until they can read the book by themselves. The teacher then listens to students individually read the story and discusses the story with the students. Guidelines for using recorded books, keeping records of students' reading, and using computers are presented in Apply the Concept 8-4.

To view an example of repeated reading, go to: www.youtube.com: The Repeated Reading Method.

COMMENTS: Students reading below grade level who have used repeated reading have consistently demonstrated gains in both fluency and reading comprehension (Chard, Vaughn, & Tyler, 2002):

- Consistently using repeated reading with poor readers increases reading speed, accuracy, expression, and comprehension.

- Text materials should be at the students' independent to instructional reading level (90% to 100% word recognition).

- Passages should be read three to five times.

- Multiple reading of phrases may improve fluency.

- Specific strategies should take into account individual students' characteristics. For more impaired readers, provide more adult guidance during reading, use more decodable texts as reading materials,

Using Recordings, Videos, and E-Books for Repeated Reading

Selecting Books and Passages

Select books and passages that are of interest to the students and for which the students' word recognition is from 85% to 95%. For older readers, high-interest, low-vocabulary stories provide another source.

For more impaired readers, select more easily decodable texts (see Chapter 7). Pattern-language books (see Chapter 7) can be another good source of books because they provide students with frequent repetition of language patterns and words.

Video or Other Means of Recording the Books

Use an audio or video recording device. Audio or video record a book or passage speaking at a conversational rate and with expression. Use appropriate phrasing. Provide the students with cues to assist them in keeping their place in the text while listening to the recording.

- Allow 10 seconds of blank before recording.
- Remind students of any strategies you want them to use (e.g., "Remember to use your finger or a marker as a guide").
- Use a signal to cue turning the page.
- For a new page announce each page number.
- Direct students to put their finger on the first word on the page.

Record about 10 minutes of reading so that it will be easy for students to find their place. Label each recording with the title of the book and the page numbers covered. You can instruct parent volunteers to record books. You can also purchase prerecorded books, but be aware that they may not provide the same level of cueing.

Store the books with their tapes in clear plastic bags. Inside the bag, place the book and tape. If you have multiple copies of the book with a tape, they can be stored together.

Keeping Student Records

Have each student make a reading folder. Staple forms inside the folder on which the student can record the name of the book, the author, the date, how he or she read the book, and with whom he or she discussed the book. In this way, both the teacher and the student have a record of the student's reading.

Computer-Based Reading Practice

Computer software provides another avenue for children to repeatedly read books using the computer. For example, *Living Book Series* (Discus Books) and *Wiggleworks* (Scholastic) both provide opportunities for students to listen to books being read, to read along with the computer, and in the case of *Wiggleworks*, to record their own reading of the book. Reading software provides flexibility; the text can be read in sentences or phrases, or the students can highlight individual words and have them pronounced. Many of these programs easily switch languages (most commonly between English and Spanish) and have built-in record-keeping systems so that teachers know the number of times students read the books and the type of assistance they use.

Using Audio Books at Home to Support English Language Learners

Audio books can also be integrated into a home-reading component. The advantage is that well-recorded books require minimal reading from parents, making them an ideal resource for parents who do not speak or read English. Students can be taught how to use the audio books, and notes can be sent home with the audio books reminding the children and their parents to read and listen to the books two or three times every day.

Name of Book	Author	Dates	Read with				Discussed with	
			Self	Tape	Student	Teacher	Student	Teacher

practice on words and phrases from the text before reading the text, practice reading shorter passages, and model expressive reading.

- Short, frequent sessions of fluency practice (generally 10 to 15 minutes) should be used.

- Transfer of fluency is increased when the overlap of words across passages is substantial (Rashotte & Torgesen, 1985).

- Students should have a way to set goals and record their progress.

Choral Repeated Reading

Choral repeated reading is a technique that combines ideas and procedures from repeated reading and choral reading. We have used the approach with students who have significant reading difficulties in word identification and reading rate.

Choral Repeated Reading

PROCEDURES: Choral repeated reading is designed for students who can comprehend material that is read to them but, because of difficulties in word identification and reading rate, are unable to read material commensurate with their listening comprehension level. Students should have a sight vocabulary of at least 25 words. We suggest the following procedure:

- Explain the technique to the student.
- With the student, select a book of interest that is at a challenging reading level (85% to 90% word recognition) and that has frequent repetition of words and decodable text.
- Establish a purpose for reading by introducing the book and making predictions. Read the book with the student, using the following three-step process:

  1. *Teacher reads:* Start at the beginning of the book, and read a piece of text to the student, ranging from several sentences to a paragraph.

(The length of each section should be short enough that the student can rely on his or her short-term memory as an aid for reading.) Read at a normal rate, and move your finger smoothly along underneath the words as the student watches, making sure that your reading matches your movement from word to word.

  2. *Teacher and student read:* Read the same section together aloud with the student. Continue to point to the words. The two of you may read the section once or several times, rereading until the student feels comfortable reading the section independently.

  3. *Student reads:* Have the student read the section independently. Pronounce any unknown words, and note words that the student consistently has difficulty recognizing. (See Apply the Concept 8-5):

     - Discuss after reading how the story related to your predictions and what you have learned. New predictions and purposes for reading can be set.
     - Repeat the three-step process throughout the book. The length of each section usually increases as the book is read, and the number of times you and the student read together usually decreases. For some students, the first step is discontinued.
     - Write on word cards the words that the student consistently has difficulty identifying

8-5 APPLY THE CONCEPT

Repeated Reading

Have you noticed how young children thoroughly enjoy having the same story read to them over and over again? As the adult sits with the child and reads a familiar book, the child automatically begins to read along. At first, the child joins in on some of the words and phrases. Eventually, the child is reading along for most of the book. With repeated reading of a story, children become so familiar with the text that their memory becomes a great aid to them. Repeated reading as a means of enhancing fluency is based on the idea that as students repeatedly read text, they become fluent and confident in their reading (Chard et al., 2009). And because they are exposed to the same story several times, they have the opportunity to practice identifying unknown words while relying on their memory of the language flow to assist them.

Repeated reading is an empirically based practice that has improved rate of reading in elementary students with reading difficulties (Vadasy & Sanders, 2008). What about the use of repeated reading with secondary students? Considerably fewer studies examine the effectiveness of repeated reading with older students with disabilities, and the studies we have reveal low effects (see Wexler et al., 2008). Another question that teachers may have about repeated reading is whether there are special considerations for students who are English language learners (ELLs). A report on effective instruction for ELLs (Francis, Rivera, Rivera, Lesaux, & Kieffer, 2006) indicates that successful repeated reading includes:

- Oral reading, providing opportunities for students to attend to words and opportunities to practice speaking and reading with expression
- Corrective feedback from adults, drawing students' attention to miscues and pronunciation
- Discussions and questioning about the text read
- Increased exposure to print
- Increased engagement and motivation to read

automatically. Use a variety of activities, for example, discussing the word meanings or locating the words in the text and rereading the sentences, as a means of increasing practice.

- Have the student keep records of his or her progress (see Figure 8-2). Check the student's progress at least every third day when initially using the procedure.

- In this method most of the 10 to 15 minutes allocated is focused on oral reading. As the student becomes more confident in reading ability, use repeated readings with audio books or stories as independent reading activities.

To view an example of choral reading, go to: www.youtube.com and watch some of the videos on choral reading practices.

COMMENTS: Choral repeated reading allows the teacher and student to attend to word-identification skills and comprehension as well as fluency. Using the three-step process also allows the student to read more difficult books. We have found this particularly rewarding for older nonreaders in that the technique quickly gives them success in reading books.

Using Comprehension Cards to Support Summer Reading

Elementary-age students with learning and behavior problems usually do not choose reading as a recreational activity during the summer. John Bittner, a special education teacher, sent home books with the students along with directions on how to read and respond. The students practiced reading a book until they were comfortable. Then he asked the students, with the assistance of their parents, to read the book to him for 3 minutes or to summarize the book. Mr. Bittner also invited parents to leave a message about how the process was going. Parents noted that they liked the summer school connection that made their "sometimes reluctant reader more amenable to reading during vacation."

Recent research supports the work of Mr. Bittner. When students who were poor readers were provided eight books during the summer to read, with postcards providing guidance about what to do with the books, students demonstrated increases in reading achievement over those students who did not participate (J. S. Kim, 2006; J. S. Kim & White, 2008). What types of guidance was provided on the postcards?

- Encourage the students to practice oral and silent reading of the book.

- Ask students to reread parts of the book.

- Guide students to develop questions about the book.

- Ask students to make predictions about what will happen next when reading.

- Ask students to summarize parts of the book while reading.

- Tell students to make connections while reading to the text or to their own response.

- Ask students to read orally with a parent or family member for several minutes.

Peer-Supported Reading

One concern for students with learning and behavior problems is that they read substantially less than high-achieving readers and spend less time engaged in academic behaviors. How can the amount of time devoted to text reading be increased? One strategy is to use peers to support each other when reading for the purpose of building fluency as well as supporting word recognition and comprehension. Techniques such as *assisted reading* (Decker & Buggey, 2012) and *classwide peer tutoring* or *partner reading* (e.g., Berkeley et al., 2010; D. Fuchs, Fuchs, & Burish, 2000) provide opportunities for students to work in pairs and provide support for each other while reading. For the most part, these techniques have been used in general education classrooms to provide more opportunities for students to actively engage in reading. It is important to note that peer-supported reading is an opportunity for supportive practice and not an alternative to instruction provided by teachers. Research suggests that adult instruction to promote fluency is quite important (Kuhn & Stahl, 2003).

In this **video** ▶, you will see children engaged in partner reading. How do they respond to this strategy? What are some advantages and disadvantages? How does the teacher support the students while they are partner reading?

Evidence-Based **PRACTICE**

Peer-Supported Reading

PROCEDURES: Peer-supported reading involves matching higher readers with less able readers to practice rereading text and asking and answering questions about text meaning. How to successfully pair students and select appropriate reading materials are important considerations. One way to pair students is to rank-order the class on the basis of reading fluency and reading level. Then split the class in half, and pair the top-ranked high-performing student with the top-ranked low-performing student, the second-ranked high-performing student with the second-ranked low-performing student, and so on. It is important to check whether there are partners who will not work well together socially, and adjust accordingly.

Maintain the pairings for 3 to 4 weeks. Reading materials should be at the lower performing student's independent-to-instructional reading levels. If peer-supported reading is used three to four times per week, have enough materials selected so that students can work on two new passages per week. As in other fluency techniques, such as repeated reading and repeated choral reading, the reading materials will vary according to the students' needs. At first, it may be advantageous to use short passages or books as students learn the procedures, but high-interest–low-vocabulary chapter books can also be a good source of reading materials.

Teach students how to be both tutors/listeners and tutees/readers, and provide role-play practice and feedback. Give the tutors guidelines for how to correct errors during oral reading (e.g., point out the word, pronounce the word, and have the tutee say the word) and the questions they should ask when the tutee has finished reading (e.g., What is the story about? What is happening in the story now? What do you think will happen next?). Also assist the students in giving positive feedback.

When the students work with their partners, first the stronger reader reads aloud to serve as a model, and then the other reader reads. The teacher should refer to them as *reader one* and *reader two*. Because the lower performing students read what has just been read by the higher performing students, the lower performing students are more likely to read fluently and comfortably. The amount of material read before the students switch roles depends on the material and the readers; it usually ranges from a sentence to a page, or each student reads a specified amount of time (e.g., 5 minutes). Partners can take turns reading a book or passage several times, thus adding a repeated reading component. Copies of guidelines for the tutor and reader can be posted, and each pair can rate themselves on their effort (see Figure 8-3).

COMMENTS: Research consistently indicates that peer-supported reading has positive outcomes for the reading fluency and comprehension of students with learning and behavior problems (Berkeley et al., 2010; Okilwa & Shelby, 2010) even in first-grade classrooms (Mathes, Torgesen, & Howard, 2001). The research results suggest that the strength of the intervention may be related to the additional instructional time and student reading involvement afforded by peer-supported reading. The effects of peer pairing for reading fluency need more research with secondary students (Wexler, Vaughn, Edmonds, & Reutebuch, 2008).

Scaffolded Sustained Silent Reading

A frequently used practice in the general education classroom is to allocate time each day for silent reading of student-selected texts—typically 20 to 30 minutes. Little

FIGURE 8-3 Guidelines for Peer-Supported Reading

Partner Reading Procedures
- First reader reads.
- Second reader reads.
- Students discuss reading with one student asking questions and other student answering.
- Repeat until story is complete.

Tutoring Rules
- Talk only to your partner.
- Talk only about partner reading.
- Be cooperative.

Kinds of Errors
- Saying the word wrong.
- Leaving out a word.
- Adding a word.
- Waiting longer than 4 seconds.

Feedback about Words
- Stop. You missed this word (point to it). Can you figure it out?
- That word is_____. What word? (Reader says word.) Good! Read the sentence again.

research documents the effectiveness of this practice for students with learning or behavior problems; however, a modified version of scaffolded sustained silent reading holds promise (Reutzel, Jones, Fawson, & Smith, 2008).

Evidence-Based PRACTICE

Scaffolded Sustained Silent Reading

PROCEDURES: Most approaches to sustained silent reading involve little interaction between the teacher and the students during the time allocated for reading. Typically both the teacher and the students read for the designated amount of time. Reutzel et al. (2008) recommend a more instructive role for the teacher that involves the following:

- Rather than allowing students to select whatever text they want to read, the teacher assists in identifying appropriate books or texts at their independent reading level.
- The teacher promotes reading across a variety of genres rather than allowing students to consistently read one or two genres (e.g., poetry, fairy tale, biography, information text).
- The teacher scaffolds learning to read for fluency and comprehension.
- The teacher holds brief conferences (5 minutes) to determine students understanding of text.
- The teacher and students record progress in books, read aloud passages for fluency checks, and answer questions.

Readers' Theater: Reading Performance

Although Ms. Sadlowski, the special education teacher, and Ms. Martinez, the fifth-grade teacher, were pleased with the progress students with learning and behavior problems were making in fluency through specific fluency-building activities, they wanted the students to have the opportunity to practice reading for purposes other than to build fluency. They decided to use readers' theater and buddy reading as techniques in which students practice reading a selection until they are fluent and then perform the reading (R. Clark, Morrison, & Wilcox, 2009).

Evidence-Based PRACTICE

Reading Performance

PROCEDURES: In *readers' theater*, students perform a play or a book adapted to script form by reading it aloud to an audience. Because the focus is on reading fluently, students are not expected to memorize the text, and props are minimal. Students with different reading skills can use the same text, because the different parts often vary widely in reading level. Students practice reading their parts with a teacher, tutor, and/or other students who are taking part in the performance. Even simple texts can be adapted to a script form, as Figure 8-4 illustrates.

Buddy reading consists of the students practicing and reading texts to younger students. This provides opportunities for students with learning and behavior problems to practice reading texts that are not at their grade level but are at their independent reading level without the stigma of reading "easy" books. In using buddy reading, it is important to choose books that the students can read easily and that are appropriate for and interesting to younger children.

COMMENTS: Although techniques such as readers' theater and buddy reading do not provide the level of explicit instruction and support that are used with techniques such as repeated choral reading and peer-supported reading, they do give students who have learning and behavior problems opportunities to transfer their reading fluency to tasks other than practicing fluency. Furthermore, they lend themselves to implementation in general education classrooms.

Making Easy Books Acceptable and Difficult Books Accessible

One key to becoming a fluent reader is to read. Yet students with learning and behavior problems who have difficulty reading generally do not have adequate text sources at their reading level.

Fielding and Roller (1992) and Worthy (1996) discuss several strategies for making difficult books more accessible to older readers with disabilities. These strategies include the following:

- Use recorded books or e-books for the computer (see Apply the Concept 8-4).
- Read aloud to the students.
- Use partner reading, in which less able and more able readers are paired.
- Precede difficult books with easier books about the same topic or in the same genre (e.g., books about comets, the solar system, or ghosts; fairy tales; mystery books), thereby familiarizing the child with the vocabulary and text structure in books that are easier to read.
- Use series books to increase students' comfort level. Reading books in a series provides benefits that are similar to those of repeated reading of the same text because of the consistent use of characters, language, and content.

Integrating Fluency Building into a Reading Program

Fluency building is an integral part of a reading program for students who have reading difficulties, and generally represents 15 to 25 minutes of time approximately three times per week (Figure 8-5 describes several

FIGURE 8-4 Example of Adapting a Simple Text to Script Format for Readers' Theater

Original Text	Scripted Text
One day Mrs. Duck went to the pond. It was hot and she wanted a cool drink. Mr. Fox was sitting by the side of the pond. He told Mrs. Duck that she could not get a drink because he was in a bad mood and did not want anyone near his pond. Mrs. Bird heard Mr. Fox say this and she called down sweetly from her branch. . . .	**Mrs. Duck:** I have been working so hard and now I am so thirsty. I need to go to the pond for a nice, cool drink. **Mr. Fox:** Hello, Mrs. Duck. I am in a very bad mood. No one can drink from my pond today. **Mrs. Bird:** This is not your pond. It belongs to everyone.

Source: Based on Texas Center for Reading and Language Arts, *Professional Development Guide: Reading Fluency: Principles of Instruction and Progress Monitoring* (Austin: Texas Center for Reading and Language Arts, University of Texas-Austin, 2000).

FIGURE 8-5 Selected List of Fluency-Building Programs

Peer-Assisted Learning Strategies—Reading (PALS) (Classwide Peer Tutoring)

PALS Reading was developed for students in kindergarten through high school. It is designed primarily for general education classrooms and as supplements to a teacher's more comprehensive reading program. PALS programs target key reading skills including fluency and, because students work with students on these skills, PALS provides students with intensive practice. Evaluative studies indicate that on average PALS accelerates the reading achievement of students with learning disabilities, low-achieving students, and average- and high-achieving students. PALS Math uses a similar format but focuses on math.

Contact: PALS Outreach
        Vanderbilt University
        Peabody Box 328
        230 Appleton Place
        Nashville, TN 37203-5701
        615-343-4782
        e-mail: PALS@vanderbilt.edu

Read Naturally

Students read along while listening to a tape of leveled, recorded high-interest passages and practice until they can read them at a predetermined rate. Students graph WCPM before and after practicing. Comprehension questions provided.

Contact: Read Naturally
        750 S. Plaza Dr. #100
        Saint Paul, MN 55120
        800-788-4085
        Web site: http://www.readnaturally.com
        e-mail: info@readnaturally.com

Great Leaps

Great Leaps addresses fluency at three levels: phonics—students identify sounds and decode simple word patterns; sight phrases—students read phrases with sight words; reading fluency—students read stories. Students graph progress.

Contact: Diarmuid, Inc.
        Box 357580
        Gainesville, FL 32635
        877-GRL-EAPS
        Web site: http://www.greatleaps.com
        e-mail: info@greatleaps.com

Carbo Reading Styles Program

The Carbo reading method has children listen to and repeatedly read along with audiotapes of books that have been recorded at a slow pace but with proper phrasing and intonation until they can read fluently. Books can be recorded by the teacher or can be purchased from the National Reading Styles Institute.

Contact: National Reading Styles Institute, Inc.
        Box 737
        Syosset, NY 11791
        800-331-3117
        Web site: http://www.nrsi.com
        e-mail: readingstyle@nrsi.com

First Grade PALS (Peer-Assisted Literacy Strategies)

This program contains 48 lessons, enough for teachers to use three times a week for 16 weeks as a supplement to their reading program. The emphasis is on peer-interacted learning that addresses phonemic awareness and fluency tasks. The goal is to improve accuracy through repeated practice.

Contact: Sopris West
        4093 Specialty Place
        Longwood, CO 80504-5400
        800-547-6747
        Web site: http://www.sopriswest.com
        e-mail: customerservice@sopriswest.com

The Six-Minute Solution: A Reading Fluency Program

This program has high-interest nonfiction practice passages (approximately 20 for each of the eight levels). The materials include assessment records, charts, word lists, and differentiated instruction through multiple reading levels.

Contact: Sopris West
        4093 Specialty Place
        Longwood, CO 80504-5400
        800-547-6747
        Web site: http://www.sopriswest.com
        e-mail: customerservice@sopriswest.com

QuickReads

This series of program books and materials features short, high-interest nonfiction texts at second- through fourth-grade levels. The materials are designed to improve students' fluency, comprehension, and background knowledge. Each grade level sequentially builds across three books and includes increasingly more difficult high-frequency words and phonics elements. The program includes a pre- and posttest for placement, 12 copies each of the three leveled student books per grade level, a teacher's resource manual, and three read-along audio CDs per grade level. Additional comprehension strategies and extension lessons can be used to support ESL (English as a second language)/ELL students (Hiebert, 2002).

Contact: Modern Curriculum Press
        299 Jefferson Road
        Parsippany, NJ 07054
        800-321-3106
        Web site: http://www.pearsonlearning.com
        e-mail: technical.support@pearson.com

fluency-building programs). In teaching fluency, strategies for improving word-identification skills and comprehension should also be instructional goals. As we mentioned in the discussions of previewing and repeated choral reading, word-recognition and word-extension activities can be

The same activities that we recommend for the word cards generated from language experience stories (see Chapter 7) can be used with word cards generated from these fluency techniques.

developed naturally from the text. Although improving fluency can allow students to allocate more attention to comprehension, not all students will automatically acquire the skills associated with effective comprehension. For some students, methods of teaching comprehension may be required.

Helping Families Improve Their Children's Reading Fluency

Perhaps one of the most necessary tools for improving reading outcomes for children with special needs is wide reading. *Wide reading* refers to both the amount and type of reading in which children are engaged. When students read widely, they read often—at least 20 minutes a day—and they read across many genres. This means that they read different types of books, not just narrative or information books but biographies, history, and technical books. How can teachers increase the wide reading of the students they teach? The best way may be to engage family members in supporting wide reading.

The following are some ideas that teachers can share with families to promote wide reading by their children:

- Establish a time each evening when you read with your child. For beginning readers, this may mean that you take turns reading from a book on his or her level. If your child is a more advanced reader, you may each read different books, but you sit near each other and are engaged in the reading process.

- Determine many ways to access books and print materials. Libraries, bookstores, and online activities are excellent resources to access a wide range of books and print materials. Take advantage of every opportunity to examine and discuss books and other print materials.

- Share what you are reading. Discuss the books and materials that you are reading with your child.

- Ask questions about what your child is reading. The types of questions you ask about what your child is reading can promote continued reading. Children are likely to engage in and extend

reading when family members show interest in what children are reading.

- Read different types of print materials, and share them with your child. Sources that adults read include recipes, newspapers, magazines, reference books, and leisure books. Share these types of reading materials with your child, and engage your child in reading different sources of text. Remember, wide reading is associated with overall improved vocabulary and knowledge.

Assessing Comprehension and Monitoring Progress in Reading Comprehension

What assessments and instructional components should be present in a reading comprehension program? Reading comprehension is the most difficult aspect of reading to assess. Perhaps this is because understanding and interacting with text occurs largely as thinking and is not readily observed. The only access teachers have to knowing whether and how students understand text is to ask students to respond orally or in writing about what they have read. Figure 8-6 lists 12 tests that can assist teachers in making decisions about their students' reading comprehension. These tests can be combined to assess students' comprehension more accurately and completely.

Teachers must consider several critical aspects of a comprehension test before selecting one. First, what is the purpose of the test? Does the teacher want to screen, monitor, diagnose, or evaluate students? Second, what type of information about the students' comprehension is the teacher seeking? Does the teacher want to know whether they can recall what is in the text? Is the teacher interested in whether the students can tell the main idea or make inferences? Third, does the test require a short or long amount of time, is it difficult or easy to score, and will it provide the type of information that will inform instruction?

When children are at the beginning stages of reading (first- or second-grade-level readers) and read fewer than 80 words correctly per minute, it is possible for teachers to monitor their reading comprehension by monitoring the students' oral reading fluency. For early readers, fluency is a good, though not perfect, predictor of reading comprehension. Oral reading fluency is a feasible means for determining whether students understand what they read and whether they are likely to pass high-stakes reading comprehension tests. However, as students develop more mature reading skills, other practices for monitoring their reading comprehension are needed.

One way to monitor students' comprehension is to ask them to retell the most important parts of a text that

FIGURE 8-6 Reading Comprehension Assessments

Title	Ages/Grade Levels	Estimated Testing Time	Key Elements and Strategies	Administration
Clay Observational Survey (Clay, 2002)	Grades K–3	15 minutes	• Oral reading • Reading vocabulary (i.e., words known in reading)	Individual
Comprehensive Reading Assessment Battery	Grades K–6	30–40 minutes	• Fluency • Oral comprehension • Sentence completion	Individual
Gates-MacGinitie Reading Tests (MacGinitie et al., 2000)	Grades K–12 and adult	55–75 minutes	• Word meanings (levels 1 and 2) • Comprehension (short passages of 1–3 sentences for levels 1 and 2; paragraphs for levels 3 and up)	Group
Gray Diagnostic Reading Tests (Bryant, Wiederholt, Bryant, 2004)	Ages 6–13	45–60 minutes	• Letter/word identification • Phonetic analysis • Reading vocabulary • Meaningful reading	Individual
Gray Oral Reading Test 4 (Wiederholt Bryant, 2001)	Ages 6–19	15–45 minutes	• Comprehension (14 separate stories, each followed by 5 multiple-choice questions)	Individual
Gray Silent Reading Test (Wiederholt Blalock, 2000)	Ages 7–26	15–30 minutes	• Comprehension (13 passages with 5 questions each)	Individual, small groups, or entire class
Qualitative Reading Inventory (Leslie Caldwell, 2001)	Emergent to high school	30–40 minutes	• Comprehension • Oral reading • Silent reading • Listening	
Test of Early Reading Ability 3 (Reidetal., 2001)	Preschool-second grade	20 minutes	• Comprehension of words, sentences, and paragraphs • Vocabulary • Understanding of sentence construction • Paraphrasing	Individual
Test of Reading Comprehension (Brown et al., 1995)	Ages 7–18	30–90 minutes	• General vocabulary • Understanding syntactic similarities • Paragraph reading (6 paragraphs with 5 questions each) • Sentence sequencing (5 randomly ordered sentences that need reordering) • Diagnostic supplement: content area vocabulary in math, social studies, and science • Reading directions	Individual, small groups, or entire class
Standardized Reading Inventory 2 (Newcomer, 1999)	Ages 6–14-and-a-half	30–90 minutes	• Vocabulary in context • Passage comprehension	Individual
Woodcock Reading Mastery (Woodcock, 1998)	Ages 5–75	10–30 minutes	• Word comprehension (i.e., antonyms, synonyms, analogies)	Individual
Woodcock-Johnson III Diagnostic Reading Battery (Woodcock, Mather, & Schrank, 2006)	Ages 2–90	5–10 minutes	• Phonemic awareness • Phonics • Fluency • Vocabulary • Reading comprehension	Individual

Source: S. Vaughn & S. Linan-Thompson, *Research-Based Methods of Reading Instruction, Grades K–3* (Alexandria, VA: Association for Supervision and Curriculum Development, 2004), pp. 102–103. Reprinted by permission.

they have just read. Story retelling provides an alternative to traditional questioning techniques for evaluating students' reading comprehension because it involves the integration of many skills that are necessary for reading comprehension. It requires students to sequence and reconstruct key information presented in the text. It also requires students to rely on their memory for factual details and to relate them in an organized meaningful pattern. One advantage to retelling is that the teacher can learn a great deal about what students understand and can determine what additional comprehension skills need to be taught. To observe a teacher using story retelling with a class, go to: www.youtube.com: Story Bits: Retelling Stories to Build Strategies in Read Reading and Real Writing video.

For the purposes of monitoring the progress of comprehension, retelling is administered individually. The following procedures can be applied:

1. Select brief passages (1 to 2 minutes) that are at the students' reading level.

2. Ask younger students to read their passage aloud. Ask older students to read their passage silently.

3. After reading ask students to tell you what it was about or tell you the story.

4. Score the retell on the basis of the depth of information provided. Teachers may want to consider whether students mentioned characters, the story problem, events, problem resolutions, and story quality.

5. You can rate the quality of a students' retell on a 7-point scale, with a higher number indicating a better retell, and use this to monitor their retelling effectiveness over time.

Another way to monitor students' comprehension is by using maze passages. Maze passages provide text written at a range of grade levels and provide students with opportunities to select words from several options that fulfill the meaning of the text where words have been deleted. Read the Spotlight on Diversity for ideas on instructing English language learners with reading difficulties.

> ## WEB RESOURCES
> Sources of maze passages for progress monitoring can be obtained from the National Center on Student Progress Monitoring www.studentprogress.org/.

Response to Intervention and Reading Comprehension

How can teachers use reading comprehension practices to determine students' RTI? Knowing students'

comprehension of text is the single most important outcome of interest when determining their RTI. Several progress-monitoring measures attempt to gauge comprehension. For example, the maze test provides a means for determining whether students can identify the syntactically and semantically correct word that fits in a passage, providing some information about text understanding.

> ## WEB RESOURCES
> For a description of the reliability, validity, and use of maze procedures for monitoring comprehension, see http://www.rti4success.org.

Teaching Comprehension

What is the purpose of comprehension instruction? Comprehension is the essence of reading and the ultimate goal of reading instruction. Reading comprehension is the process of constructing meaning by integrating the information provided by an author with a reader's background knowledge. It consists of three elements: the reader, the text, and the purpose for reading (RAND Reading Study Group, 2002). It involves complex cognitive skills and strategies with which the reader interacts with the text to construct meaning. There are many reasons why students may have difficulty comprehending what they read.

As a fourth grader reading at second-grade level, Amanda would probably better comprehend what she reads if she did not have to allocate so much attention to word identification. On the other hand, Scott is a word caller. He thinks that reading is "reading the words correctly." Even though he can read fluently, he does not attend to the meaning of passages. He frequently has difficulty recalling both the gist and details of a story. Sofia has been diagnosed as having language disabilities, with difficulties in syntax and semantics. These low oral language skills affect her comprehension of what she reads.

Sam can remember what he reads but does not relate it to what he already knows about the topic (schema). Therefore, he has particular difficulty answering questions that require him to use his background knowledge. Paolo, on the other hand, relies too heavily on his background knowledge. This is adversely affecting his reading comprehension because he uses what he knows rather than what the text says when reading.

Kim fails to monitor her comprehension as she reads. She often reports that everything makes sense. Yet when her teacher asks questions, it becomes obvious that Kim has achieved limited comprehension.

All these students are struggling with reading comprehension, although their problems are very different. For

Spotlight *on Diversity*

Instructing English Language Learners Who Are at Risk for Reading Problems

What instructional practices should teachers consider when providing reading instruction to students with reading difficulties who are also ELLs? Teachers might consider the following practices for instruction:

1. *Remember that the quality of instruction is even more important than the language of instruction.* While initial research suggests that students learning to read in their native language perform slightly better, the importance of quality of instruction is even more significant (Cheung & Slavin, 2012).

2. *Consider the commonalities between reading instruction in English and the reading instruction that is provided in the student's native language.* These commonalities can be used to build bridges between languages and apply what is known in one language to the other. Many commonalities exist between reading instruction practices in different languages, even though features of the instructional practices may differ (Linan-Thompson & Vaughn, 2007). For example, oral language instruction, fluency, and reading comprehension are important aspects of learning to read for learners of all languages (Goldenberg, 2008).

3. *Identify procedures for instructing students in all of the critical elements of beginning reading (phonemic awareness, spelling, phonics, vocabulary, language development, fluency, and comprehension).* The following are instructional practices in reading that are effective for beginning ELLs: teaching explicitly; promoting learning of the English language; teaching phonemic decoding and phonics; integrating vocabulary development, use, and extension across the curriculum; maximizing student engagement through interactive teaching and student pairs; and scaffolding learners through instruction that provides opportunities to respond with teacher feedback.

   The foundation skills of phonemic awareness and phonics are more critical in the very beginning stages of reading and less important as students become readers of connected text. Improving vocabulary is an important part of reading and content learning all along. Improving listening comprehension is initially important, and then transferring these comprehension skills to text understanding becomes important.

4. *Recognize that English is the most difficult language of all alphabetic languages to learn to read, and therefore, many of the foundation skills such as spelling and phonics require more explicit and systematic instruction than they might in other alphabetic languages.* A study across 12 alphabetic languages revealed that many of the foundation skills of reading take twice as long for young children to acquire in English than in other alphabetic languages such as Spanish (Seymour, Aro, & Erskine, 2003). Thus, students who know another alphabetic language such as Spanish or Italian will require more time to learn foundation skills such as phonics and spelling to develop fluency and comprehension.

5. *Make connections between the home language and the language of instruction in school.* There are many benefits when teachers make connections between the home language and English. First, it provides students with a ready connection between what they know and what they need to know. Second, it helps students learn more quickly because much of what they know can be used as a foundation for learning a new literacy. Third, it honors the students' home language and background, building language concepts and self-esteem.

6. *Capitalize on every opportunity to use and promote language development during instruction, and give opportunities for students to engage in higher order questions.* ELLs often have limited opportunities to use oral language during instruction and few opportunities to address challenging or higher-order questions. Because students' language development may still be growing, teachers often ask these students questions that allow for one- or two-word responses. These students may have difficulty providing more complex answers, but with structured conversation and opportunities to use academic language, their skills will improve. For example, oral participation can be facilitated by providing scaffolding in the form of sentence stems that offer students a structure for orally responding to challenging questions. To assist students in addressing higher-order questions, teachers may initially model more complex syntactic structures and fade support as students become more proficient in English. Planned discussions can be promoted to encourage academic language, providing small-group or paired cooperative learning activities and development of prior knowledge.

7. *Promote all opportunities to teach and engage in vocabulary and concept building.* Vocabulary development is an essential feature of reading, comprehension, and content learning for ELLs. To fully appreciate and interpret what they are reading, students will be required to learn new words to understand expository and narrative texts (e.g., *civil, equity, molecule*) as well as to learn the meaning of descriptive words (e.g., *worried, marvelous, eagerly*).

Teachers will add to students' vocabulary knowledge by providing highly organized, focused, and repeated opportunities to learn core words well enough to both understand their meaning in context and to apply them in their own language use. Ulanoff and Pucci (1999) suggest that students benefit from previewing important concepts and vocabulary in their primary language before listening to stories read in English and reviewing key concepts in both languages after the reading. For a fun example of all of the ways words and concepts need further explanation for English language learners, go to: www.youtube.com: Lesson 3 – "Kitchen" – English Vocabulary.

8. *Peer pairing and cooperative groups can be used to enhance learning.* Peer pairing and structured group activities are effective practices for improving oral language,

acquisition of higher-level comprehension skills, and interaction for ELLs (Cheung & Slavin, 2012; Saenz, Fuchs, & Fuchs, 2005). Paired learning or cooperative grouping provides intensive individualized instruction for students from varied literacy backgrounds by increasing the amount of time spent in academic engagement and providing immediate feedback (e.g., reading errors, pacing) from peers. For an example of peer pairing with English language learners, go to: www.youtube.com: Supporting ELL Students: Through Partner Word. In the video, students have specific tasks and opportunities to discuss what they are learning, and it may be particularly beneficial for ELLs by presenting opportunities for them to use and learn specific vocabulary related to academic language (August, Branum-Martin, Cardenas-Hagan, & Francis, 2009; Vaughn, Martinez, et al., 2009).

students such as Amanda, word identification difficulties get in the way of comprehension. Focusing on building word-identification skills is probably appropriate for her. However, comprehension skills should not be ignored. This may mean building listening comprehension at her current grade level as well as extending her knowledge of word meanings. For Amanda, it is making sure that reading is perceived as understanding and interacting with the text to construct meaning, not just reading the words correctly. Although word-identification skill development will be important, it needs to be coupled with teaching comprehension.

For Scott, a considerable amount of emphasis in his reading program should be on comprehension. He requires assistance in changing his definition of the reading process. Helping Scott to set comprehension-oriented purposes for reading and teaching him how to ask questions as he reads should assist him in changing his definition of reading.

Sofia's difficulties relate to a language problem that affects her reading comprehension as well as her receptive language. For students such as Sofia, instruction in reading comprehension often parallels instruction in receptive language. Both reading and listening comprehension can be improved simultaneously. For example, when Sofia either listens to or reads a story, she needs to learn to ask and answer such questions as, "Who is the story about?" "Where did it happen?" "What was the problem in the story?" "What happened to solve the problem?" "How did the story end?"

Some students fail to relate what they are reading to what they already know about a topic. This is the case with Sam. Other students have limited background knowledge to bring to the reading process. Teaching strategies that encourage students to activate their knowledge or activities that provide opportunities for

students to enrich their backgrounds before reading can facilitate comprehension.

Although some students do not rely enough on background knowledge, other students rely too much on background knowledge, as is the case with Paolo. Often, these are the same students who tend to overrely on context clues when identifying unknown words. When these students begin reading informational and technical texts that require accurate recall of information, comprehension problems become more evident. Comprehension strategies that encourage self-questioning can encourage such students to pay closer attention to the information presented in the text.

Kim has difficulty monitoring her understanding while reading—the metacognitive skill of comprehension monitoring. Strategies that teach students to ask questions about their comprehension and that require them to paraphrase and summarize what they read should help them to develop metacognitive skills (see Klingner, Vaughn, & Boardman, 2007, for sample reading comprehension practices for students with learning disabilities).

In this section on reading comprehension, we examine a framework for reading comprehension and then focus on instructional strategies for improving reading comprehension. Finally, we discuss approaches used for teaching reading and reading comprehension.

A Framework for Reading Comprehension

One way of guiding reading comprehension instruction is to determine the different reasoning and information-processing skills that are required by readers to construct meaning from what they read. When teaching reading comprehension, we can divide comprehension into types of reasoning according to how readers have to activate their background knowledge to construct the meaning. These three arbitrary categories are as follows:

1. *Textually explicit:* Information is derived directly from the text with minimal input from the readers' background knowledge.

2. *Textually implicit:* Information is derived from the text, but readers are required to use their background knowledge to put together the ideas presented in the text.

3. *Scriptually implicit:* Information is not stated in the text. Readers have to activate and use their background knowledge to obtain the information.

We can also categorize comprehension by the type of information or relationship it represents. For example, a basic question might be something like, "What did Pat do first to get help?" requiring the reader to focus on the sequence of the events in the story. Therefore, it requires a sequencing or temporal relationship. The question "Why was everyone proud of Pat?" requires understanding of a causal relationship. Types of information or relationships can be represented in text in many ways (e.g., main ideas, details, sequence, cause and effect). We can combine types of information with processes required (i.e., textually explicit, textually implicit, and scriptually implicit) to form a matrix for reading comprehension (Figure 8-7).

This matrix can be used in planning comprehension instruction, such as planning activities that will encourage students to engage in all the different facets of comprehension (cells in the matrix). For example, to work on sequencing of ideas, students could retell a story by having each student in the group tell one episode from the story; copy a story onto sentence strips and discuss how to arrange the sentences in a logical order; read an explanation of how to do something and write a list of the steps in order; ask each other sequence questions about a description of how to make something; write a description of how to make something; and then have the other students in the group read the description and make the object. Whereas all of these activities focus on sequencing, both explicit and implicit comprehension are required to complete the various activities.

A matrix rather than a taxonomy is used to depict the various aspects of comprehension because comprehension should not be thought of as a set of hierarchical skills. The comprehension process entails ongoing transactions between a text, the reader, and the author and the active use of comprehension strategies such as predicting, activating background knowledge, asking questions, clarifying, and checking for understanding (D. O. Blachowicz & Ogle, 2008; Klingner et al., 2007).

But comprehension goes further than this. We also read to reflect on and judge the quality of the information. To read critically, students must be able to suspend judgment, consider other viewpoints, and draw logical conclusions. Thus, we engage in *critical reading*, including such skills as the following:

* Recognizing the author's purpose
* Distinguishing between facts and opinions
* Identifying words that signal opinions
* Verifying factual statements
* Detecting assumptions
* Judging sources
* Identifying persuasive language
* Detecting propaganda
* Drawing logical conclusions

FIGURE 8-7 Matrix for Reading Comprehension

Type of Information or Relationship	Type of Reasoning Based on Background Knowledge		
	Textually Explicit	Textually Implicit	Scriptually Implicit
Main idea/summary	X	X	X
Detail	X	X	X
Sequence	X	X	X
Comparative relationship	X	X	X
Cause/effect relationship	X	X	X
Conditional relationship	X	X	X
Vocabulary definition	X	X	X
Vocabulary application	X	X	X
Figurative language definition	X	X	X
Figurative language application	X	X	X
Conclusion	X	X	X
Application		X	X
Analysis		X	X
Synthesis		X	X
Evaluation			X

FIGURE 8-8 Critical and Aesthetic Reading

Critical Reading

Critical reading: The reader reflects on and makes judgments about the content or information in the piece.

Sample Areas of Reflection or Judgment	*Sample Comments*
Reality or Fantasy	I don't think the author expected us to think this could really happen.
Fact or Opinion	You really get the idea they are pushing their point of view.
Adequacy and Validity	Some of this information just isn't right.
Worth	This piece really helped me write my report. I think this article could hurt his political campaign.

Aesthetic Reading

Aesthetic reading: The reader reflects on and makes judgments about the literary style of a piece.

Sample Areas of Reflection or Judgment	*Sample Comments*
Plot	I like the way the author always kept me interested in what was happening.
Characters	I didn't know enough about the witch to really understand why she did it.
Imagery	I could just picture myself being there.
Language	When the author said, "That was one frightened man," I felt a chill in my body.

Critical reading involves thinking about the text in relation to the readers' beliefs. For example, when Ms. Andretti, the intermediate-level inclusion teacher, was working on critical and aesthetic reading in a third-grade classroom, she had the students read a passage about Pat and her father. After reading, she asked the students, "Have you ever had an experience that made you feel like Pat?" Figure 8-8 lists sample areas of critical and aesthetic reading and sample teacher comments.

Guidelines for Teaching Reading Comprehension

If comprehension is the essence of reading, how do teachers go about teaching students with learning and behavior problems to be effective comprehenders? In the late 1970s and early 1980s, observational research indicated that teachers spent little time teaching children how to comprehend (Duffy, Lanier, & Roehler, 1980; Durkin, 1978–79). For example, in Durkin's observational studies of reading instruction in fourth-grade classrooms, only 20 minutes of comprehension instruction was observed in more than 4,000 minutes of reading instruction. Much of what teachers did to "teach" comprehension was ask questions, have students respond, and provide feedback. Furthermore, they provided a steady diet of literal or textually explicit comprehension questions, a ratio of 4:1 literal to inferential, with lower reading groups getting asked even more literal questions than higher-level groups (Guszak, 1972).

Since then, instructional research and practice have focused on how to teach reading comprehension. Even when students have reading comprehension problems, it is important to first determine the factors that may be contributing to these reading difficulties. Before focusing solely on reading comprehension instruction, teachers should answer the following questions:

- Do students have adequate decoding and phonics skills so that they can read words?
- Do students read within the expected rate of reading for their grade level?
- Do students have adequate knowledge of the meaning of words?
- Does students' background knowledge adequately prepare them to understand the text?

For any student who does not meet these criteria, a complete reading comprehension program will require additional emphasis on decoding, fluency, vocabulary, and building background knowledge. It is unlikely that comprehension strategies alone will be sufficient for any student with reading difficulties.

Apply the Concept 8-6 looks at comprehension issues with students who are ELLs.

One of the keys to teaching reading comprehension, particularly for students with learning and behavior problems, is to teach them to use comprehension and comprehension-monitoring strategies (Block, Morrow, & Parris, 2008; Dymock & Nicholson, 2010; Klingner et al., 2007). This includes such strategies as the following:

- *Activating background knowledge:* Thinking about what one already knows about the topic and how one's knowledge relates to what one is reading.
- *Preteaching critical vocabulary and concepts:* Teaching students to prepare to read a text by preteaching essential vocabulary and concepts that facilitate learning and understanding.
- *Generating questions:* Asking relevant questions that promote understanding, such as *who, what, when, where, why*, and *how* questions.

Understanding Reading Comprehension with Students Who Are English Language Learners

For each of the following questions, ask yourself whether you implement the practice: never (1); some of the time, but not enough (2); whenever needed (3). Then, choose several instructional practices that you rated 1 or 2 and begin to implement them more frequently.

Do You

- Ask students to make predictions about what they are going to read by using such features of the text as titles, pictures, and key words?
- Provide students with opportunities to integrate their background knowledge with the critical concepts in the text?
- Identify the language demands of the text they are reading, and preteach related vocabulary and concepts?
- Request that students monitor the words and concepts they do not understand while they're reading, make note of them, and then follow up with them?
- Ask students questions they can answer and then scaffold responses to meet language needs?
- Model and provide opportunities for students to construct mental images that represent text, so they can better remember and understand what they read?
- Provide opportunities for students to seek clarification about confusing aspects of what they read?
- Plan language-related activities that link with comprehending text, and then make these explicit to students?
- Give students adequate opportunities to develop questions about what they have read, and pose these questions to fellow students?
- Give students adequate time, and practice responding orally?
- Provide practice in summarizing and integrating information from text?

Source: Based on S. Linan-Thompson & S. Vaughn, *Research-Based Methods of Reading Instruction for English Language Learners* (Alexandria, VA: ASCD, 2007). Reprinted with permission.

- *Monitoring comprehension:* Checking for understanding and using fix-up strategies (e.g., rereading, clarifying a concept) to facilitate comprehension.
- *Clarifying:* Clarifying unclear concepts or vocabulary.
- *Using graphic organizers:* Using visual aids that illustrate concepts and relationships among concepts in a text while reading the text.
- *Finding main ideas:* Determining the most important information and explaining this information in one's own words.
- *Summarizing:* Identifying the main ideas, connecting the main ideas, eliminating redundant information, and putting this information in one's own words.
- *Using text structure:* Using knowledge of different text structures (e.g., narrative, expositive) as a framework for comprehension.

In other words, teachers need to teach cognitive strategies that will give students with learning and behavior problems the tools for understanding and constructing meaning from what they are reading.

Knowing what the strategies are is the first step for a teacher; the more difficult one is knowing how to teach them. As is the case with higher-level academic learning, this is particularly challenging because comprehension involves thinking processes that are not nearly as visible as they are in other skills, such as spelling and math calculations. Therefore, instruction in reading comprehension is beneficial when teachers:

- Provide rationales and evidence for the effectiveness of its use.
- Describe and model the strategy using thinking-aloud.
- Provide supported practice and feedback.
- Provide independent practice.
- Teach for generalization (i.e., when and where strategies apply) and maintenance.

Comprehension instruction can be accomplished through more direct explanations and mental modeling associated with cognitive strategy. Based on ideas from schema theories, our instruction assists students in activating their prior knowledge about a topic before they read so that they can apply this knowledge both during and after reading. Students also learn the importance of predicting and questioning as they read.

Effective comprehension instruction encourages students to engage actively not only in discussions related to the content of the text, but also in instructional conversations about the reading process. These discussions can be prompted by the following steps:

1. *Before reading,* the teacher activates the students' background knowledge for the selected passage and/or provides experiences to enrich their backgrounds. The teacher assists students in thinking about how this text may be related to other texts in terms of content, story line, and text structure. The teacher helps students to set purposes for reading by predicting and asking questions about what they are going to read. It is important that teacher support and scaffolding are used in order to prevent students from "guessing" without consideration of relevant text cues. It is also valuable for teachers to preteach proper nouns and to give students key ideas about the text before reading.

2. *During reading,* the teacher encourages students to self-question and monitor their comprehension as they read.

3. *After reading,* the teacher uses follow-up activities such as

   - discussions that focus on the content of the reading as well as evaluation of the content and the writing style

   - discussions that encourage students to generate more questions and ideas for further reading and investigation

   - retellings that assist students in summarizing and organizing what they have read

Explicit instruction in comprehension strategies yields positive learner outcomes, especially for students with reading difficulties (Duke et al., 2011; Klingner et al.,

2007). The idea behind explicit instruction of comprehension is that comprehension can be improved by teaching students to use specific cognitive strategies or to reason strategically when they encounter barriers to comprehension while reading. To see an example of comprehension instruction with middle grade students, go to: www.youtube.com: Reading Comprehension, 3–6, Part 1: Enhancing Explicit Instruction.

The kind of reading involved in constructing a text base is what the recently issued CCSS (www.corestandards.org) for reading refer to when the demand is made to "read closely to determine what the text says explicitly" (p. 10). See Apply the Concept 8-7.

Previewing, Predicting, and Developing Prior Knowledge

Reading comprehension instruction occurs before reading through previewing, predicting, and activating/developing background knowledge. Prereading activities help students prepare to understand and learn from what they read. Taking time to prepare students before they read can pay big dividends in terms of their understanding and finding reading an enjoyable. It's important to note that the CCSS for Reading (www.corestandards.org) indicate that front loading as a means of previewing is not a recommended practice.

> In this **video** , experts explain the importance of developing students' prior knowledge in relation to reading and content area learning. How does prior knowledge influence students' reading fluency and comprehension?

8-7   APPLY THE CONCEPT

Structure of a Concept-Oriented Reading Instruction Lesson

- 10 minutes—Students practice their oral-reading fluency with poetry or informational books (three days per week) or hands-on science activity and/or study of science concepts.

- 10 minutes—The teacher provides a comprehension minilesson on self-monitoring, inferencing, or fix-up strategies, including rereading, chunking, discussing, questioning, visualizing, connecting, looking up, reading ahead, reading aloud, and using knowledge.

- 15 minutes—One of three teacher-led guided reading group uses texts related to the conceptual

theme, during which the teacher models, scaffolds, and provides guided practice in the application of reading comprehension strategies to serve learning related to the conceptual theme.

- 15 minutes—While the teacher is with the second guided reading group, students write about information and concepts learned from the guided reading text or about their responses to a theme-related novel they are reading.

- 15 minutes—While the teacher is with the third guided reading group, students engage in independent reading of novels for which they have book clubs.

Note: Some teachers added up to 5 minutes to each activity for a total of 90 minutes of concept-oriented reading instruction.

Source: Based on "Contributions of Concept-Oriented Reading Instruction to Knowledge About Interventions for Motivations in Reading," by J. T. Guthrie, A. McRae, & S. L. Klauda, 2007, *Educational Psychologist, 42*(4), 237–250.

When teachers "front load" they provide so much information about what students are going to read, it is not necessary to actually read the text. This is substantially different from effective previewing, in which students are provided preparation for reading and learning.

Graves and his colleagues (Graves, Juel, & Graves, 2007) suggest that prereading activities

- Set purposes for reading.
- Motivate students to read.
- Activate and build background knowledge.
- Build knowledge of the text features.
- Relate reading to students' lives.
- Preteach vocabulary and concepts.
- Provide opportunities for prequestioning, predicting, and direction setting.

For students with reading disabilities, it is particularly helpful to preteach proper nouns such as persons names, places, and things. Preteaching these words helps students read more effectively and understand what they read. Remember, prereading activities should be relatively brief and provide students just enough information and connection so that they can read successfully.

What instructional techniques can a teacher use that will help students with learning and behavior problems to activate relevant background knowledge (schema), bridge what they know to what they are reading, motivate them to read, assist them in making predictions about what they are going to be reading, preview the reading, and assist them in becoming familiar with difficult vocabulary? Activating prior knowledge is particularly important for students with learning and behavior problems. As with all learners, their prior knowledge is crucial to the successful construction of meaning. Apply the Concept 8-8 presents ideas for facilitating and teaching comprehension.

One way to promote brainstorming is the use of mind maps, which are really sophisticated graphic organizers.

8-8 APPLY THE CONCEPT

Strategies for Promoting Reading Comprehension for Students Who Are Culturally Diverse and/or English Language Learners

For students from culturally and linguistically diverse backgrounds and for students who are ELLs, a number of strategies can be used to promote reading comprehension.

Making Input More Comprehensible

- Teach new concepts by working from the students' prior knowledge and incorporating the funds of knowledge from the students' communities.
- Use demonstrations and gestures to augment oral and written communication.
- Discuss connections between the concepts being read and the students' home cultures.
- Encourage students to share the new vocabulary in their first language and incorporate the first language into instruction.
- Pair more proficient ELLs with less proficient peers, and encourage students to discuss what they are reading.

- Provide opportunities for students to learn to read and to read in their first language.
- Highlight key words and phrases in text, and incorporate them into semantic maps.
- Teach text structures, and use visual representations of text structures.
- Ask questions or discuss new ideas or vocabulary, slow the pace.
- Repeat key ideas, and write them.
- Use think-alouds to make comprehension strategies more explicit.

Incorporating Multicultural Literature into the Reading Program

- Select literature that reflects various cultures.
- Study authors from various cultures.
- Read literature that incorporates various dialects.
- Select genres that are typical of different cultures.
- Use book lists, directories, Web sites, and textbooks on multicultural education as resources for multicultural literature.
- Provide text written in the students' first languages available to them.

Brainstorming Brainstorming is a teaching strategy that activates the students' relevant prior knowledge, aids the teacher in determining the extent of the students' prior knowledge, and stimulates interest in the topic.

Brainstorming

PROCEDURES: Brainstorming works best with groups of students who are reading the same or related selections. Before beginning the activity, determine the major topic or concept presented in the selection(s). Next decide what to use as a stimulus to represent that topic. It might be a single word or phrase, a picture, a poem, or a short excerpt from the reading passage. Before reading, conduct the brainstorming session:

1. Present the stimulus to the students.

2. Ask the students to list as many words or phrases as they can associate with the stimulus. Encourage them to think about everything they know about the topic or concept. Allow several minutes for the students to think and get ready to report or write their ideas.

3. Record the students' associations on the board. Ask for other associations, and add them to the list. While writing ideas on the board, assist students in making connections among these ideas by talking about how they are related.

4. With the students, categorize the associations. Clarify the ideas and discuss what titles to use for the categories. You may want to organize the ideas into a learning map.

COMMENTS: Brainstorming is a quick and simple way to activate background knowledge. It usually takes 5 to 10 minutes to complete. However, for some students and topic combinations, simple associations without further discussion

> Strategies for organizing story maps are discussed later in this chapter, and strategies for developing content maps are discussed in Chapter 10.

may not provide enough input to activate and build on students' prior knowledge. The next procedure provides additional activities for further activating knowledge.

PreReading Plan The PreReading Plan (PReP) is a three-phase instructional-assessment strategy that builds on the activity of brainstorming. Designed by Langer (1981, 2011), it assists students in accessing knowledge related to the major concepts presented in a reading selection.

PreReading Plan

PROCEDURES: Before beginning the activity, provide a phrase or picture to stimulate group discussion about a key concept in the text. For example, if a science selection is about the types and characteristics of mammals, *mammals* might serve as the stimulus word. After introducing the topic, conduct the following three-phase process:

1. *Initial association with the concept.* Cue students by saying something like, "Say what you think are attributes of mammals." Have the students generate a list of ideas, words, and associations. Record the key ideas on the board, noting the student's name by each association.

2. *Reflections on initial associations.* Now ask the students, "What made you think . . . [the responses given by each of the students during phase 1]?" This phase requires the students to bring to the conscious level their prior knowledge and how it relates to the key concept. It also allows the students to listen to each other's responses.

3. *Reformation of knowledge.* After students have had an opportunity to think and tell about what triggered their ideas, ask, "On the basis of our discussion, do you have any new ideas about mammals?" This question gives the students the opportunity to discuss how they have elaborated or changed their ideas on the basis of the previous discussion. Because the students have had the opportunity to listen to other students, new links between prior knowledge and the key concept are also formed.

On the basis of the information gathered during this three-phase procedure, Langer and Applebee (2007) present a means of assessing prior knowledge into levels to determine whether further concept building will need to be completed before reading. The three levels and their instructional implications are as follows: (1) *Much Knowledge,* including analogies and links to related key ideas and concepts, (2) *Some Knowledge,* including definitions and links to much of the key information needed to comprehend adequately, and (3) *Little Knowledge,* which reflects students who have very little understanding of the key ideas, vocabulary, and concepts and are unlikely to understand what they read without substantive support for building their background knowledge. Remember, depending on the content, students' background knowledge varies.

COMMENTS: The PReP provides a direct means of activating the students' background knowledge. The authors have frequently used both brainstorming and PReP, particularly with upper-elementary and secondary students with learning and behavior problems. We find that taking the extra time to conduct PReP is worthwhile, because it requires students to bring to the conscious level why they made their associations, and it gives them the opportunity to reflect on what they have learned through the discussion. It is a good idea to have students add to and adjust their lists during reading and after they read.

Text Preview Text previews are designed to increase students' prior knowledge, motivate students to read, and provide a scaffold for text comprehension (M. F. Graves et al., 2007). Text previews can be used with students at varying reading and grade levels and with both narrative and expository texts.

Evidence-Based PRACTICE

Text Preview

PROCEDURES: The two major steps in using text previews are preparing the preview and then using it with the students.

1. *Preparation and construction of text previews.* A text preview is a synopsis of a text that is written in an organized framework that enhances student comprehension of the text by bridging it to their real-world experiences. It has three sections: one that piques student interest, a brief discussion of the text's theme (e.g., for stories this could include the setting, character descriptions, and essential story organization), and questions or directions that guide student reading.

2. *Presentation of text previews.* The following steps are suggested for implementing the text preview and should take no longer than 5 to 10 minutes:

- Cue students about the new reading.
- Discuss an interesting aspect of the story or content that will pique motivation.
- Make connections to the students' lives and world knowledge.
- Present the questions or directions that should guide student reading.
- Have students read the text.

Discussing an interesting aspect of the story or content helps students to delve into reading materials, knowing that there will be new knowledge, discoveries, and/or excitement. These motivational activities often involve hands-on experiences and intrigue that are then tied to the story that is being read. For example, a teacher might say, "Feel these fabrics, and tell me what it makes you think about and how it makes you feel. In the story, Robbie has a special blanket made out of these fabrics—satin and flannel. As you read the story think about what is special about this blanket and how it feels." Making connections to the students' lives and their world knowledge also activates background knowledge and creates motivation. Using a connections chart such as the one in

FIGURE 8-9 Connections Chart About Dolphins

Figure 8-9 helps students think about connections they can make to their own lives and to world knowledge they have about a topic. For example, in reading about dolphins, students can list experiences they have had with dolphins as well as facts they know about dolphins before they read and then add to the list after they read.

COMMENTS: Although text previews take time to prepare, students report that previews enable them to understand texts to a fuller extent (Simmons et al., 2010). When using text previews with expository text, the teacher may want to include important points, vocabulary, and big ideas related to the text (Simmons et al., 2010). Additionally, teachers can use text previews as potential writing assignments. Students can be assigned to develop text previews for other students' guided reading. Critical thinking about the ideas presented in a text selection will ensue as students create text previews for one another.

In this **video** ▶, you will see co-teachers use the K-W-L strategy with students to expand their learning about coral reefs. How is this strategy beneficial for students? How can the K-W-L strategy be used in other subject areas?

K-W-L K-W-L is a strategy that is designed to activate students' background knowledge and to assist students in setting purposes for reading expository text (J. Bryant, 1998; Ogle, 1986, 1989, 2009).

Evidence-Based PRACTICE

K-W-L

PROCEDURES: The K-W-L strategy consists of three basic steps representative of the cognitive/metacognitive steps that students employ as they use the strategy:

1. Accessing what I <u>K</u>now
2. Determining what I <u>W</u>ant to learn
3. Recalling what I <u>L</u>earned

To assist the students in using the strategy, Ogle (1986, 1989, 2009) developed a simple worksheet for the

FIGURE 8-10 K-W-L-Q Chart for Pond and Pond Life

What I Know	What I Want to Learn	What I Learned	More Questions I Have
Contains water	How does the pond get its water?	Underground springs and rain	Why do ponds die?
Smaller than a lake	Why are ponds green and muddy?	Algae and other plants make it green	What happens to a pond in winter?
Fish			
Ducks	Does the temperature change?	Like the air but temperature is less affected the deeper you go	How does algae help or hurt a pond?
Frogs			
Muddy	What fish live in the pond?	Blue gill, trout, bass, catfish	
Algae	What insects live in the pond?	Dragonflies, mosquitoes, water fleas	
Insects on top			
Birds eat insects	What plants live in the pond?	Algae, cattails, water lilies	

Source: Based on P. R. Schmidt (1999), KWLQ: Inquiry and literacy learning in science, *The Reading Teachers*, 52, pp. 789–792.

students to complete during the reading–thinking process (see Figure 8-10).

During the *Know* step, the teacher and students engage in a discussion that is designed to assist students in thinking about what they already know about the topic of the text. For this step, the teacher starts by using a brainstorming procedure (see the section on brainstorming). As in the PReP, students are encouraged to discuss where or how they learned the information so as to provide information about the source and substantiveness of their ideas. After brainstorming, the teachers and students discuss the general categories of information that are likely to be encountered when they read, and how their brainstormed ideas could help them determine the categories. For example, a teacher might cue students that when they read they should consider one category that addresses "causes of the war" and a second category that considers "consequences of the war." During the *Want to Learn* step, the teacher and students discuss what they want to learn from reading the text. Although most of this step uses group discussion, before students begin to read, each student writes down the specific questions in which he or she is most interested.

During the *Learned* step, the students write what they learned from reading. They should also check the questions that they generated in the previous step to find out whether they were addressed in the text.

COMMENTS: K-W-L is a strategy for helping students to actively engage in the reading process and for assisting teachers in teaching reading using an interactive model of reading. Informal evaluation of the strategy indicates that students recalled more information in articles when they used K-W-L and that they enjoyed using the strategy and used it independently (Ogle, 1986). Carr and Ogle (1987) added mapping and summarizing activities to K-W-L to gain the advantage of these powerful comprehension tools. Ogle (1989) added a fourth column, "what we still want to learn," and referred to this adaptation as K-W-L Plus. J. Bryant (1998) referred to it as K-W-W-L to

assist students in generating questions and designing scientific experiments, and Schmidt (1999) referred to it as K-W-L-Q, with the *Q* representing more questions. This addition encourages further research and reading.

Questioning Strategies

Asking questions is a major vehicle that teachers use to foster understanding and retention and to check for comprehension. When questions are asked about information in text, that information is remembered better. Asking higher-level questions that require integration of background and text knowledge (see Figure 8-6) will promote deeper processing and therefore more learning (Solis et al., 2012; Vaughn & Edmonds, 2006). Even asking "Why?" and "How?" can significantly increase retention of information.

However, simply asking questions does not ensure that students will develop questioning strategies. Students' answers to questions can give limited insight into their understanding of text. As has already been demonstrated, teacher and student questioning before reading helps to activate prior knowledge and to set purposes for reading. Self-questioning during reading (e.g., Does this make sense? Am I understanding what I am reading? How does this relate to what I already know? What will happen next?) assists students in monitoring comprehension.

The following techniques require teachers to model comprehension questions and comprehension-monitoring questions, teach students to recognize types of questions, and encourage students to self-question before, during, and after they read.

Question Development Learning to ask and answer questions before, during, and after reading is an effective technique associated with improved understanding of text. One of the advantages of this approach is that it can be used in narrative text as well as information text. Also, this practice is particularly useful for students in grades 4 and older with reading disabilities (Solis et al., 2012).

Student Question Generation

The goal is to model question generation through thinking aloud and turn taking. The teacher takes a designated amount of text (with younger students a couple of sentences; with older students a paragraph or more) and reads it first silently and then aloud. She says, "I wonder, _____" and then asks a question about what she has read. She then asks the student to read the same text silently and ask a question. When students become more proficient at asking questions, the teacher's modeling can be reduced.

PROCEDURES: This technique for student question generation relies heavily on modeling, which is a major premise of cognitive strategy instruction. Select materials at the students' instructional to independent reading levels. You can select materials that are more narrative or you can also use information text. You and the students read a sentence or section of the passage and then take turns asking each other questions. Your role is to model good questioning and to provide feedback to students about their questions. In modeling, include higher-level questions that require you to use scriptually and textually implicit information and that require critical and aesthetic reading. Also include monitoring questions (e.g., Does this make sense?).

A YouTube video example shows how a teacher uses sticky notes with students to facilitate their tracking their questions while reading: www.youtube.com: Active Reading-Asking Questions Using Post Its.

There are many procedures for teaching students to generate questions before, during, and after reading. One way is to teach students various question types and to teach them the stems that go with these question types (Swanson, Vaughn et al., 2011).

The procedure itself consists of the following steps:

1. *Silent reading.* You and the students read the sentence or section.

2. *Student questioning.* Close your book while the students ask questions. Model appropriate answers, and reinforce appropriate questioning behavior. The students ask as many questions as possible.

3. *Teacher questioning.* The students close their books, and you ask questions modeling a variety of question types (see Figure 8-6).

4. *Integration of the text.* After completing the procedure with the first sentence or section, repeat the process with subsequent sentences or sections. Integrate the new section with previous sections by asking questions that relate to new and old sections.

5. *Predictive questioning.* When the students have read enough to make a prediction about the rest of the passage, ask predictive questions (e.g., What do you think will happen? Why do you think

so?). If the predictions and verification are reasonable, you and the students move to the next step.

6. *Reading.* You and the students read to the end of the passage to verify and discuss your predictions.

COMMENTS: One important aspect of this strategy is the questions that the teacher models, including:

- *Predictable questions:* The typical *who, what, when, where, why,* and *how* questions

- *Mind-opening questions:* Questions that are designed to help the students understand how written and oral language are used to communicate ideas

- *Introspective questions:* Metacognitive questions that are oriented toward self-monitoring and self-evaluation

- *Ponderable questions:* Questions that stimulate discussion and for which no right or wrong answer is apparent

- *Elaborative knowledge questions:* Questions that require students to integrate their background knowledge with the information given in the text

This procedure can also be used as a game. The students and teacher take turns asking questions and keeping score of appropriate answers. We also recommend that the text be read in longer, more natural segments rather than individual sentences. Some students benefit from having question starters to help them initiate questions. These question starters could be things like, Why did he . . . ? Why do you think the ending . . . ? What would happen if . . . ?

Question–Answer Relationships Strategy The question–answer relationships strategy (QARs; Raphael, 1982, 1984, 1986; Raphael, Highfield, & Au, 2006) is designed to assist students in labeling the types of questions that are asked and to use this information to help guide them as they develop answers. QARs was developed by Raphael and Pearson (1982) to facilitate correct responses to questions. It helps students to realize they need to consider both the text and their prior knowledge when answering questions and to use strategic behavior to adjust the use of each of these sources.

Question–Answer Relationships Strategy

PROCEDURES: QARs was originally taught by Raphael (1984), using the three categories of information suggested in the matrix for reading comprehension (Figure 8-7). The three categories were renamed for use with students:

1. *Right There:* Words used to create the question and words used for the answer are in the same sentence (textually explicit).

2. *Think and Search:* The answer is in the text, but words used to create the question and those used for an appropriate answer would not be in the same sentence (textually implicit).

3. *On My Own:* The answer is not found in the text but in one's head (scripturally implicit).

On the basis of input from teachers, Raphael (1986) modified these categories to include two major categories—*In the Book* and *In My Head*—and then further divided these categories, as shown in Figure 8-11.

Raphael suggests the following procedure for introducing QARs: The first day, introduce the students to the concept of QARs, using the two major categories. Use several short passages (from two to five sentences) to demonstrate the relationships. Provide practice by asking students to identify the type of QAR, the answer to the question, and the strategy they used for finding the answer. The progression for teaching should be from highly supportive to independent:

1. Provide the text, questions, answers, QAR label for each question, and reason why the label was appropriate.

2. Provide the text, questions, answers, and QAR label for each question. Have the students supply the reason for the label.

3. Provide the text, questions, and answers, and have the students supply the QAR labels and reasons for the labels.

FIGURE 8-11 Cue Card for Question–Answer Relationships (QARs)

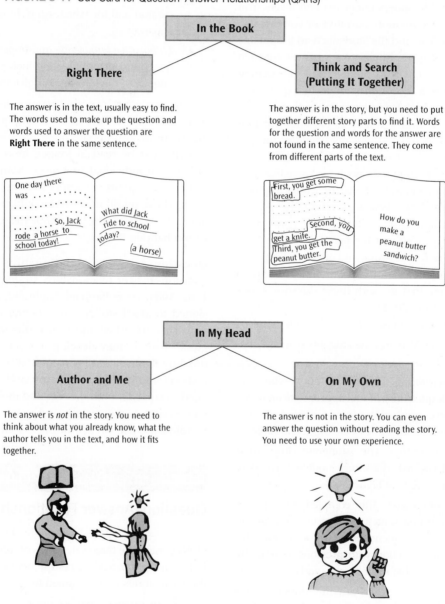

Source: Based on T. E. Raphael (1986), Teaching question–answer relationships, revisited, *The Reading Teacher, 39* (6), pp. 516–523.

4. Provide the text and questions, and have the students supply the answers, QAR labels, and reasons for the labels.

When the students have a clear picture of the difference between *In My Head* and *In the Book*, teach the next level of differentiation for each one of the major categories. First, work on *In the Book*, then go to *In My Head*. When the information must come from the reader but in connection with the information presented by the author, then the QAR is *Author and You*. For example, questions that ask the reader to consider their perceptions or views about an interpretation from the text.

Once the students are effectively using the QARs in short passages, gradually increase the length of the passages and the variety of reading materials. Review the strategy, and model its use on the first question. Have the students then use the strategy to complete the rest of the questions.

COMMENTS: After teaching QARs using the original three categories, Raphael (1984) found that groups of low-, average-, and high-achieving fourth-grade students had higher performance on a comprehension test and gave evidence that the QARs transferred to reading improvement in the content areas. This strategy helped lower achieving students to answer all three types of questions, particularly their performance on textually explicit and implicit questions. Simmonds (1992) taught 24 special education teachers to implement either QARs or selected traditional methods of reading comprehension instruction, including the skills of answering literal questions (recall of factual information and main ideas), locating supportive details, and drawing conclusions. Using a lesson sequence similar to the one just described, they found that students who participated in QARs instruction performed better than other students on tests of comprehension over the social studies text they read. Labeling the types of questions and then using that information to assist in answering questions appear to constitute an effective strategy for students and one that encourages active involvement in the comprehension process. QARs-type approaches have also been used with secondary students with reading disabilities (Klingner et al., 2001).

Self-Questioning Strategies Self-questioning strategies are a good example of how metacognition assists students in reading. These questions typically have the student focus on activating prior knowledge and setting purposes for reading, asking questions to assist the comprehension process, checking understanding during reading, and reviewing after reading to determine understanding. Questions that foster comprehension include:

- What's happening?
- What's the big idea?
- What do you want to know more about?

- Who or what is interesting to you?
- What do you want to find out?
- What's happening so far?
- How well do I understand what I'm reading?
- What would I like to understand better?
- What is the author saying, and what did I think about it?
- What am I learning?

Evidence-Based PRACTICE

Self-Questioning Strategies

PROCEDURES: First, teach the students the concept of a main idea. During this stage, teach them how to identify the main idea(s) in paragraphs.

Teach the students the steps of self-questioning strategy:

1. Why are you studying this passage? (So that you can answer some questions you will be given later.)
2. Find the main idea(s) in the paragraph, and underline it (them).
3. Think of a question about the main idea you have underlined. Remember what a good question should be like. (*Good questions* are those that directly focus on important textual elements. Write the question in the margin.)
4. Learn the answer to your question. (Write the answer in the margin.)
5. Always look back at the previous questions and answers to see how each successive question and answer provides you with more information.

In teaching, model the strategy, and then have the students study the steps in the strategy. Next, have the students practice using this strategy on individual paragraphs, and provide them with immediate corrective feedback. Have the students use a cue card like the one in Figure 8-12 to assist them in remembering the steps in the strategy. When the students succeed, switch to multiple-paragraph passages, and gradually fade the use of the cue cards. Give feedback at the end of each passage. At the end of each lesson, discuss the students' progress and the usefulness of the self-questioning strategy.

COMMENTS: Students with learning disabilities who learned the self-questioning strategy performed significantly higher on comprehension tests than did students who were not taught the strategy (Berkeley et al., 2011; Solis et al., 2012).

Another self-questioning strategy designed specifically for secondary students with reading disabilities, the Kansas University Center for Research on Learning

FIGURE 8-12 Frame for Answering Wh- and How Questions

Student Name: _____

Title: _____

Pages: _____

Date: _____

Who?
What?
Where?
When?
Why?
How?

(KU-CRL) self-questioning strategy, was developed at the KU-CRL (F. L. Clark, Deshler, Shumaker, Alley, & Warner, 1984; Schumaker et al., 2006). This strategy facilitates secondary-level students with learning disabilities in comprehending and remembering the important information presented in content area textbooks. The KU-CRL self-questioning strategy focuses on teaching students how to generate questions about important information in a passage, predict the answers, search for the answers while reading, and talk to themselves about the answers by using the mnemonic ASK IT. The ASK IT steps are as follows:

1. Attend to the clues as you read.
2. Say some questions.
3. Keep predictions in mind.
4. Identify the answer.
5. Talk about the answers.

For self-questioning strategies to be effective for students with reading difficulties, it is important that teachers provide modeling, direct coaching, prompting, and guidance (Swanson, Edmonds, et al., 2011). Teaching students to stop and question themselves before, during, and/or after reading is another key element of success (Edmonds, Vaughn, et al., 2009). Self-questioning practices can also be effective in promoting understanding and interest when reading short stories with older students (Janssen, Braaksma, & Couzijn, 2009).

Questioning the Author Though not technically a practice designed to teach students to ask themselves questions, Questioning the Author (Beck & McKeown, 2006; McKeown, Beck, & Blake, 2009) provides students with well-scaffolded instruction that supports their interactions with texts and eventually with each other as though the author were available for comment and conversation. The idea is to have students actively engage with a text. With Questioning the Author, the teacher gives distinct goals and several queries that assist students in reaching those goals. First, students and teachers require coherent texts so that understanding and engaging in discussion is a possible enterprise. Second, students need to have some background knowledge of the topic so that they can adequately discuss what they are reading; and third, teachers and students require a logical set of questions to better understand text.

Evidence-Based PRACTICE

Questioning the Author

PROCEDURES: First, select text that is coherent. The text type selected may be either narrative or expository. Be sure to consider the background knowledge that students require to understand the text. To the extent possible, identify key ideas and concepts, and preteach them to students before reading the text.

Second, teach students to "grapple" with ideas while they are reading and to consider what the author means and the extent to which the author may not have communicated very well. Meaning is built as students read rather than at the end of the reading. Students share and discuss while reading, enhancing background knowledge and understanding, and increasing understanding of text as they continue reading. The focus is not on the discussion per se but on the understanding of what they are reading.

Third, teachers and students use queries to promote understanding and to place responsibility for understanding text on the students; for example, What is the author trying to tell us? and Why do you think the author is saying this?

Fourth, the teacher establishes the fallibility of the author with the students so that they learn that a text is simply one person's ideas written down and that these ideas should be considered in light of other knowledge and their own experience. This provides students with an engagement with text and the author that is typically not available.

COMMENTS: Several studies document the effectiveness of Questioning the Author in classwide implementation in general education classrooms with at-risk students (for a review, see Beck & McKeown, 2006). Findings have not been conducted separately for students with learning disabilities. Also, studies have been conducted with fourth-grade students.

According to McKeown and Beck (2004), "the development of meaning in [Questioning the Author] focuses on readers' interactions with text as it is being read, situates reader–text interactions in whole-class discussion, and encourages explanatory, evidence-based responses to questions about text" (p. 393). Evidence from their studies in many classrooms suggests that teachers and students who adopted this Questioning the Author perspective also became increasingly engaged with text. In addition, interactions in the classroom changed from the traditional question-and-answer routines, which appear to be much like test questions and answers, to more collaborative discussions that involved both teacher and students in questioning and the development and elaboration of new ideas. You can read more at Reading Rockets.

Text Structure and Summarization Strategies

Text structure refers to the organizational features of text that help readers understand and predict how the text will be organized. For example, text structures around fairy tales and text structures around biographies are different. Understanding how they are different can help you with comprehension. Often, teachers divide text into two major types: narrative and expository. Expository text is also often referred to as information text. *Narrative texts* tell a story and can be organized into components such

as setting, problem statement, goals, event sequences or episodes, and ending. Generally, stories are easier for students to comprehend than expository text because the story structure is more consistent and has a linear orientation, making it more predictable. Carnine, Kame'enui, and Silbert (2005) suggest that teachers use the following four story grammar questions:

1. Who is the story about?
2. What is she or he trying to do?
3. What happens when she or he tries to do it?
4. What happens in the end?

Typical questions that focus on story grammar include:

- Where does the story take place (setting)?
- When does the story take place (setting)?
- Who are the main people in the story (characters)?
- What problems does the main character face (problem)?
- What are the main character's goals (goal)?
- What does the main character want to do to solve the problem (goal)?
- What are the main things that happened in the story to solve the problem (plot)?
- How did each thing work out (plot)?
- Is the problem finally resolved? If so, how (outcome/ending)?

Expository texts are also referred to as *information texts* because they are designed to explain phenomena or provide information. These are the informational texts that students encounter not only in school content area subjects such as social studies, science, math, and vocational education, but also in newspapers and magazines and on the Internet. Expository texts can be more difficult to comprehend because there is more variation in their organization (e.g., describing an object, comparing and contrasting two ideas, explaining a cause–effect relationship), the content may be less familiar, and there may be a high proportion of technical terms. Teaching types of expository texts can help students with comprehension problems to understand the more complex scientific style of thinking that is evident in expository text (Williams, 2005). Figure 8-13 presents six types of expository texts with signal words and cohesive ties that note the relationships and sample frameworks that depict the relationships. These text structures can also guide the types of questions that promote comprehension. For example, here are some questions that can be asked to help students understand the process of "revolution" and how it relates to their lives:

- What motivates individuals to participate in a revolution?

FIGURE 8-13 Types of Expository Texts

Text Type	Cohesive Ties and Signal Words	Sample Frameworks
Descriptive or Enumerative Describes the characteristics, attributes, examples, or a series of facts about a topic	for example, for instance in addition besides to illustrate characteristics are can be described as moreover such as in other words	
Sequential or How To Tell how to do something or a series of events presented in order	first, second, third next last, finally before, after in the past, in the future currently	
Compare–Contrast Two or more topics are compared according to the their likenesses and differences	different from same as, alike however in contrast in comparison, compared to instead of on the other hand whereas similarly	
Cause–Effect Explanation of the reason(s) for something or why something happened and the resulting effect(s)	cause, because therefore, thus as a result of if . . . then consequently for this reason	
Problem–Solution Statement of a problem and possible solutions, sometimes with resulting effects	problem is possible solutions	
Argument or Persuasion Statement of a position on an issue with justification	the point is first, second, next, last reasons major reason consequently therefore	

- What are some revolutions you can think of?
- What conditions are associated with revolution?
- What kinds of things happen to prevent revolution?
- What are examples of people who have participated in revolutions?
- Can you think of examples of situations that would promote your participation in a revolution?

The type of text may vary within an expository passage or paragraph, and thinking about the specific type can facilitate comprehension. As we discussed in the section on question generation, teaching students to generate a range of questions related to the information text they are reading promotes active processing of text and comprehension (Taboada & Guthrie, 2006).

Story-Mapping and Story-Retelling Strategies Story-retelling strategies provide students with a framework for retelling the key points of narrative texts. The strategies can be combined with story maps, which provide students with a visual guide to understanding and retelling stories. Figure 8-14 shows a visual framework for a simple story.

> More techniques related to expository texts are presented in Chapter 10 in the discussion of content area learning.

Teachers have taught students with reading problems how to use story maps and story strategies to aid in comprehending and retelling stories (Bos, 1999; Gardill & Jitendra, 1999) to students with learning disabilities. Bos (1987) used a story-retelling strategy to assist intermediate students with learning and language disabilities in retelling stories. Whereas these two strategies focus on the components of the story, Williams (1998) has developed an instructional lesson to assist students with severe learning disabilities to identify the themes of stories and relate them to their lives.

> In this **video** ▶, a teacher models the story mapping procedure for his students. How do the students respond to the strategy? How does the teacher scaffold their individual and group success?

FIGURE 8-14 Simple Story Map

Name:_____ Date:_____

The Setting
Who   What   Where   When

Trouble
What is the trouble that the main character(s) need to solve?

Order of Action
What action(s) does (do) the main character(s) take to solve the problem?

Resolution
What was the outcome (resolution) for each action? How does (do) the main character(s) react and feel?

End
What happened in the end?

Evidence-Based PRACTICE

Story Mapping

PROCEDURES: Idol (1987b) used the visual in Figure 8-14 and the following procedure to teach story mapping:

1. During the *model* phase, model how to use the story map by reading the story aloud, stopping at points where information pertaining to one of the story components is presented. Ask the students to label the part, and then demonstrate how to write the information on the story map. Have the students copy the information on their own maps. If the information is implicit in the story, model how to generate the inference.

2. During the *lead* phase, have students read the story independently and complete their maps, prompting when necessary. Encourage the students to review their maps after completing the story, adding details that may have been omitted.

3. During the *test* phase, ask students to read a story, generate their maps, and then answer questions such as "Who were the characters?" "Where did the story take place?" and "What was the main character trying to accomplish?"

Bos (1987) used principles based on cognitive strategy instruction to teach a story-retelling strategy. The procedures are as follows:

1. Motivate the students to learn the strategy by demonstrating how it will help them remember what they have read.

2. Describe the components in a story and the steps used to identify and remember the different components:

STORE the Story

Setting: Who, what, when, where

Trouble: What is the trouble that the main character(s) needs (need) to solve?

Order of action: What action(s) does (do) the main character(s) take to solve the problem?

Resolution: What was the outcome (resolution) for each action? How does (do) the main character(s) react and feel?

End: What happened in the end?

Explain how answering these questions will help the students STORE, or remember, the important parts of the story.

3. Practice together reading stories, labeling the components, and retelling the stories. The students can retell their stories to the teacher, retell them to each other, audio record their retellings, or answer questions about the stories.

4. Have the students independently read stories and retell them by using the STORE the Story strategy.

Williams (1998; 2005) developed an instructional program to assist students with learning disabilities to generate themes for stories and relate them to the students' lives. The lesson was organized around a single story and had five parts, as demonstrated for the story "Kate Shelly and the Midnight Limited." This story is about how Kate braved great danger to warn the stationmaster that a railroad bridge had collapsed and thereby averted the wreck of the Midnight Limited. The procedure was as follows:

1. _Prereading discussion about lesson purpose and story topic._ This includes discussion of the importance of identifying and understanding the theme.

2. _Story reading._ The students listen to and/or read the story and discuss the story grammar components and the story (e.g., What do you think will happen next? Do you think Kate was brave? Why?).

3. _Discussion to generate theme._ The teacher and students discuss five questions designed to help generate the theme:

* Who is the main character? (Kate Shelly.)

* What did she do? (She ran more than a mile in a terrible storm to warn the stationmaster about a collapsed railroad bridge; she persevered.)

* What happened? (She reached the station in time to save the train and the passengers.)

* Was this good or bad? (Good.)

* Why was this good or bad? (It was good that Kate persevered because she saved lives.)

4. _Writing the theme._ The teachers and students write the theme using the format "Kate should have persevered. We should persevere."

5. _Generalization to real-life experiences._ Discussion is focused around the following questions: "To whom would this theme apply?" "When would it apply?" "In what situations?"

Williams compared this theme discussion framework to more traditional discussions about stories.

COMMENTS: Students using these story-mapping procedures recalled substantially more relevant information after learning each strategy. They also answered more explicit and implicit comprehension questions about the stories. Students were also more likely to label the parts of the story in their retellings, thereby providing the listener with a framework for listening. Students also generated and applied qualitatively better themes. These same strategies have also been adapted and used to help students plan and write stories.

Emery (1996) suggests using story guides in which the story events are outlined in one column and different characters' perspectives are listed in subsequent columns. This assists the students in seeing how different characters react to different events in the story. Using _why_ questions about the characters during discussions (e.g., Why did the characters act that way? Why did the characters feel that way?) also promotes comprehension.

Paraphrasing Strategy　Getting the main idea(s), paraphrasing, and/or summarizing when reading expository materials are important skills, particularly in content area subjects such as science and social studies. The paraphrasing strategy, developed and validated at KU-CRL (Schumaker, Denton, & Deshler, 1993), instructs students in recalling the main ideas and specific facts of materials they read and has been used successfully with students in elementary (Hagaman, Casey & Reid, 2012), middle school, and adults (Hagaman & Reid, 2008; Hock & Mellard, 2005).

Paraphrasing Strategy

PROCEDURES: The steps in the strategy that the students learn are as follows:

1. *Read a paragraph.* As you silently read, think about what the words mean.

2. *Ask yourself, "What were the main ideas and details of this paragraph?"* This question helps you to think about what you just read. To help you, you may need to look quickly back over the paragraph and find the main idea and the details that are related to the main idea.

3. *Put the main idea and details in your own words.* When you put the information into your own words, it helps you to remember the information. Try to give at least two details related to the main idea.

The acronym for the steps in the strategy is RAP. (Paraphrasing is like rapping or talking to yourself.) Students are also given the following two rules for finding the main idea:

1. Look for it in the first sentence of the paragraph.

2. Look for repetitions of the same word or words in the whole paragraph.

The criteria that are used in generating a paraphrase are that it (1) must contain a complete thought and have a subject and a verb; (2) must be accurate; (3) must make sense; (4) must contain useful information; (5) must be in one's own words; and (6) must have one general statement per paragraph. Specifics for teaching the strategy, including a scripted lesson, cue cards for learning and generalizing the strategy, record and worksheets, and suggested materials for practicing the strategy, are presented in the instructors' guide, *The Paraphrasing Strategy* (*Learning Strategies Curriculum*) (Schumaker et al., 1993).

> Chapter 2 provides a description of cognitive strategy instruction (CSI).

COMMENTS: Students with learning disabilities who learned and used the paraphrasing strategy increased their ability to answer comprehension questions about materials written at their grade level from 48% to 84%, and middle-grade students improved their comprehension (Hagaman & Reid, 2008; Hagaman et al., 2012; Schumaker et al., 1993).

When using this strategy, students talk their paraphrases into an audio recorder rather than write them. This approach seems particularly advantageous for students with learning and behavior problems because many of them also experience writing problems. However, once students have mastered the skill, it may be helpful for them to write their paraphrases. Students can then use the paraphrases as an overview to integrate the information across the entire passage.

We have had students put their paraphrases for each paragraph or section on sticky notes so that they can then arrange the notes to make a summary of the whole reading selection. You and the students may also want to vary the size of the unit that the students paraphrase. For example, for some books, it may work better to paraphrase each section or subsection rather than each paragraph.

Several YouTube videos describe the paraphrasing strategy and paraphrasing strategy notebooks.

Summarization Strategies
Summarization also requires students to generate the main idea and important details from a text. On the basis of analyses of informational or expository texts, Brown and Day (1983) generated five rules for writing summaries:

> In this **video** , you will learn the importance of summarizing information and several strategies to support students' reading and writing skills. What methods do you think best support students' acquisition of these skills?

1. Delete irrelevant or trivial information.

2. Delete redundant information.

3. Select topic sentences.

4. Substitute a superordinate term or event for a list of terms or actions.

5. Invent topic sentences when the author has not provided any.

Summarizing strategies employ many of the principles of cognitive strategy instruction, including explicit explanation of the rules, modeling of the strategy, guided practice in controlled materials, monitoring with corrective feedback, independent practice, and teaching each rule to criterion.

Summarization Strategy

PROCEDURES: To teach the summarization strategy, use sets of short paragraphs, each set highlighting a different rule. In this way, the rules can be explained, modeled, and practiced individually. Then apply the rules to informational passages. As the students learn the rules and their application, give the students more responsibility for practicing the rules and checking that each rule has been applied. Figure 8-15 presents a checklist that students can use to judge the quality of their summaries and teachers can use to monitor student progress.

FIGURE 8-15 Student Checklist for Monitoring Summaries

How Good Is That Summary?

Student: _____   Date: _____

Title: _____

Pages: _____

Summary:

_____

_____

_____

Rating: 3 = Clear, Concise Summary
       2 = Somewhat Clear, Concise Summary
       1 = Several Sentences That Do Not Accurately Summarize Information
       0 = Not Completed

_____ Does the summary state the **main idea**?

_____ Is the **main idea** stated first?

_____ Does the summary give **_only_ the most important information**?

_____ Is the summary brief with **unimportant and redundant information** deleted?

_____ Is the summary written well and clear?

COMMENTS: Reviews of literature on reading comprehension practices for students with reading disabilities at the elementary, middle, and high school level reveal positive outcomes for students when summarization practices for comprehension are taught (Berkeley et al., 2010; Edmonds et al., 2009; Solis et al., 2012). On the whole, students with learning disabilities who were taught the summarization strategy performed better than a comparison group of students with learning disabilities on main idea, inference, and factual questions. Students who participated in the strategy instruction also improved performance on a reading test.

Malone and Mastropieri (1992) taught middle school students with learning disabilities how to summarize and self-question using two questions:

1. Who or what is the passage about?

2. What is happening (to the characters)?

Using principles of direct instruction and explicit teaching of the summarization and self-questioning, they found that these middle school students outperformed students who had received traditional comprehension instruction on recall of the passage content and that the students could generalize the strategy to new texts. Simmons et al. (2010) taught summarization strategies to middle-grade students to improve their reading comprehension during social studies, resulting in overall gains in reading comprehension.

Using Multicomponent Cognitive Strategy Instruction to Teach Comprehension

So far, we have discussed techniques to facilitate the use of specific comprehension skills such as activating prior knowledge, predicting, asking and answering questions, getting the main idea, and summarizing the text. Students with learning and behavior problems often have difficulty with a number of these skills. For example, even when Shamika, an eighth-grade student with decoding and reading comprehension problems, is reading text that is easy for her to decode (about fifth-grade level), she still has difficulty understanding what she reads. Her approach to reading comprehension is to "just begin reading and read to the end." She reads quickly and when finished can answer detailed questions about what she has read if the information is provided in the text. If she is not sure about an idea, Shamika reports, "I usually just skip it." She has difficulty generating a summary and reports that she does not make predictions during reading and does not think about how what she is reading relates to what she already knows. For students like Shamika, it may be more efficient and effective to teach a multicomponent strategy that includes several robust strategies such as predicting, questioning, and summarizing than to teach individual strategies (Klingner et al., 2007; Solis et al., 2012). This section discusses one such multicomponent approach to teaching comprehension—reciprocal teaching (Palincsar & Brown, 1984, 1986; see Rosenshine & Meister, 1994, for a review)—and an adaptation of reciprocal teaching: collaborative strategic reading (CSR; Klingner, Vaughn et al., 2012; Vaughn, Klingner, et al., 2011).

Both reciprocal teaching and CSR are built on ideas associated with metacognition, schema theory, and the sociocultural theory of learning. From metacognition comes the strong emphasis on comprehension monitoring (e.g., checking to determine whether understanding is adequate, given the purposes for reading). From schema theory, these approaches incorporate activities that encourage students to activate and use relevant background knowledge. From sociocultural theory comes scaffolded instruction in which the teacher and students take turns assuming the leader role.

These instructional techniques build on the idea that successful comprehension and learning are based on six activities:

1. Clarifying the purpose of reading (i.e., understanding the task demands, both explicit and implicit)

2. Activating relevant background knowledge

3. Allocating attention to the major content at the expense of trivia

4. Evaluating content for internal consistency and compatibility with prior knowledge and common sense

5. Monitoring ongoing activities to determine whether comprehension is occurring by engaging in such activities as periodic review and self-questioning

6. Drawing and testing inferences including interpretations, predictions, and conclusions

Although both approaches build on these activities, reciprocal teaching was developed first; CSR further elaborates on reciprocal teaching.

Reciprocal Teaching   In the initial research on reciprocal teaching, Palincsar and Brown (Palincsar, 1982; Palincsar & Brown, 1984) chose four comprehension strategies to teach seventh-grade students who had average decoding skills but had significant difficulty with comprehension. The four strategies were as follows:

1. Predicting

2. Clarifying

3. Questioning

4. Summarizing

They used an interactive mode of teaching that emphasized modeling, feedback, and scaffolded instruction.

Evidence-Based PRACTICE

Reciprocal Teaching

PROCEDURES: The procedure used to teach the four strategies was *reciprocal teaching*, a technique in which the teacher and students took turns leading a dialogue that covered sections of the text. Palincsar and Brown (1984) described the teaching procedure as follows:

The basic procedure was that an adult teacher, working individually with a seventh-grade poor reader, assigned a segment of the passage to be read and either indicated

that it was her turn to be the teacher or assigned the student to teach the segment. The adult teacher and the student then read the assigned segment. After reading the text, the teacher (student or adult) for that segment asked a question that a teacher or test might ask on the segment, summarized the content, discussed and clarified any difficulties, and finally made a prediction about future content. All of these activities were embedded in as natural a dialogue as possible, with the teacher and student giving feedback to each other. (pp. 124–125)

The teacher initially modeled the leader role, and as the students assumed the role, the teacher provided feedback by using the following sequence:

1. *Modeling.* "A question I would have asked would be . . ."

2. *Prompting.* "What question do you think might be on a test?"

3. *Instruction.* "Remember, a summary is a short version—it doesn't include details."

4. *Modifying the activity.* "If you can't think of a question right now, go ahead and summarize, and then see if you can think of one."

5. *Praise.* "That was a clear question, because I knew what you wanted." "Excellent prediction—let's see if you're right."

6. *Corrective feedback.* "That was interesting information. It was information I would call a detail. Can you find the most important information?"

To ensure a level of competency, each strategy is introduced individually and in a functional manner (e.g., summarize a television show or movie), and opportunities are provided for the students to practice using the strategy. Palincsar (1988) provides a number of suggestions for teaching each comprehension strategy.

Predicting

• Begin a new passage by having students predict on the basis of the title.

• Encourage students to share information they already know about the topic.

• Refer to, and interweave the text with, their predictions and background knowledge as you read.

• Use headings to help students make predictions.

• Use other opportunities to predict, such as when the author asks questions or gives information about what will be covered next.

• Use predictions in an opportunistic and flexible manner.

Questioning

• Encourage students to ask teacherlike questions.

• Fill-in-the-blank questions should be discouraged.

- If the students cannot think of a question, have the students summarize first.
- Provide prompts if needed (e.g., identify the topic, provide a question word).

Summarizing

- Encourage students to identify the main idea and an example of supportive information.
- Encourage students to attempt their summaries without looking at the passage.
- Remind students of the rules for generating summaries:

  Look for a topic sentence.

  Make up a topic sentence if one is not available.

  Give a name to a list of items.

  Delete what is unimportant or redundant.

Clarifying

- Opportunities for clarifying generally occur when referents (e.g., *you, he, it*) are unclear; difficult or unfamiliar vocabulary is presented; text is disorganized or the information is incomplete; or unusual, idiomatic, or metaphorical expressions are used.
- Clarifying will not always be necessary.
- It may be helpful if students are asked to point out something that may be unclear to a younger student.

COMMENTS: Palincsar and Brown studied the effectiveness of reciprocal teaching with poorly comprehending seventh-grade students who were taught individually or in groups of four to seven students (Palincsar, 1986; Palincsar, 2007; Palincsar & Brown, 1984). Even substantial improvements in standardized reading comprehension scores were reported. Lovett et al. (1996) found that reciprocal teaching resulted in significant improvements in the comprehension skills of seventh- and eighth-grade students with reading disabilities compared to control students. Like Palincsar and Brown (1984), they also found that reciprocal teaching transferred to new texts. Lederer (2000) found that reciprocal teaching improved the ability of fourth through sixth graders with learning disabilities to compose summaries of what they read but not their ability to answer comprehension questions. When three student teachers used reciprocal teaching, they reported that marking children's copies of the text with cue pictures, implementing a reward system to maintain focus, and selecting interesting and challenging literature were important for student success (Speece, MacDonald, Kilsheimer, & Krist, 1997). Reciprocal teaching has been implemented effectively with a range of students including middle school students who are English language learners (ELLs) with learning disabilities, including low

decoders (Klingner & Vaughn, 1996; Vaughn & Klingner, 2004); high school students in remedial classes (Alfassi, 1998), and average and above-average readers at various grade levels (Ahmadi & Ismail, 2012; Rosenshine & Meister, 1994).

Collaborative Strategic Reading   CSR is related to reciprocal teaching, but elaborates on its use by focusing on expository text, specifying use of strategies, engaging students in pairs or cooperative groups, and teaching students to record what they are learning through learning logs (Klingner et al., 2007; Klingner et al., 2012; Klingner, Vaughn, & Schumm, 1998; Vaughn, Denton, et al., 2010; Vaughn, Klingner, & Schumm, 1996).

Evidence-Based PRACTICE

Collaborative Strategic Reading

PROCEDURES: As with reciprocal teaching, students learn four strategies: Previewing (i.e., brainstorming and predicting), Click and Clunk (i.e., comprehension monitoring and clarifying), Get the Gist (i.e., summarization), and Wrap-Up (i.e., self-questioning and summarization). Previewing is used before reading, and Wrap-Up after reading the entire text.

Previewing. The goals of previewing are for students to learn as much about the passage as they can in 2 to 3 minutes, activate their background knowledge about the topic, make predictions about what they will read, and pique their interest in the topic to foster active reading. Using the analogy of a movie preview is a good way to teach previewing. In previewing, students are taught to check out the headings, key words, pictures, tables, graphs, and other key information to identify what they know about the topic and to make predictions. Ms. Royal, who teaches a fifth-grade class that includes a number of students with learning and behavior problems, gives her students 1.5 minutes to write down everything they already know about the topic, 1 minute to share with the group, 1.5 minutes to write down predictions, and 1 minute to share (Klingner & Vaughn, 1998). Figure 8-16 presents the four strategies for CSR with key questions the students can ask as they complete the process.

Click and Clunk. Students "click and clunk" while reading each section of the text. *Clicks* are the portions of the text that make sense, and *clunks* are the portions that aren't clear (e.g., students do not know the meaning of a word). The clicking and clunking strategy is designed to assist students in monitoring their comprehension and to employ fix-up strategies to clarify their understanding. Ms. Royal places the fix-up strategies on clunk cards so that the cooperative groups can use them during reading:

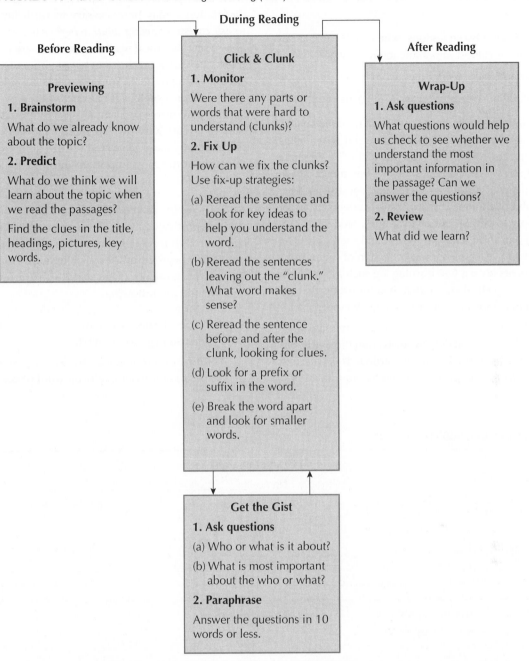

FIGURE 8-16 Plan for Collaborative Strategic Reading (CSR)

During Reading

Before Reading

Previewing

1. Brainstorm

What do we already know about the topic?

2. Predict

What do we think we will learn about the topic when we read the passages?

Find the clues in the title, headings, pictures, key words.

Click & Clunk

1. Monitor

Were there any parts or words that were hard to understand (clunks)?

2. Fix Up

How can we fix the clunks? Use fix-up strategies:

(a) Reread the sentence and look for key ideas to help you understand the word.

(b) Reread the sentences leaving out the "clunk." What word makes sense?

(c) Reread the sentence before and after the clunk, looking for clues.

(d) Look for a prefix or suffix in the word.

(e) Break the word apart and look for smaller words.

After Reading

Wrap-Up

1. Ask questions

What questions would help us check to see whether we understand the most important information in the passage? Can we answer the questions?

2. Review

What did we learn?

Get the Gist

1. Ask questions

(a) Who or what is it about?

(b) What is most important about the who or what?

2. Paraphrase

Answer the questions in 10 words or less.

Source: Based on J. K. Klingner & S. Vaughn (1999), Promoting reading comprehension, content learning, and English acquisition through collaborative strategic reading (CSR), *The Reading Teacher, 52*, pp. 738–747.

- Reread the sentence, and look for ideas that help you to understand the word.
- Reread the sentence leaving out the clunk. What word makes sense?
- Reread the sentences before and after the sentence with the clunk.
- Look for prefixes or suffixes in the word.
- Break the word apart, and look for smaller words you know.

Getting the Gist. Students learn to get the gist by reading each section and then asking themselves the following questions:

- Who or what is it about?
- What is most important about information about the who or what?

The goal is to teach the students to restate in their own words the most important point as a way of making sure they understand what they read (Klingner &

Vaughn, 1998). Students are taught that a "good" gist does the following:

- Answers the two questions: Who or what is it about? and What is most important about the who or what?

- Is paraphrased in your own words

- Contains 10 words or fewer (L. S. Fuchs et al., 1997)

In teaching how to get the gist, we have used the analogy of a sand sieve to demonstrate that the sand (i.e., details) goes through, and all that is left are the rocks (i.e., the main details that answer the two questions). Using the gists from several students or groups to discuss and construct a "best" gist is another technique that can assist students in understanding how to get the gist or main idea. Students repeat the second and third strategies (Clink and Clunk and Getting the Gist) for each paragraph or section of the passage. Having students keep a CSR learning log such as the one in Figure 8-17 can help them to identify information that will assist them in completing the last strategy: Wrap-Up.

Wrap-Up. In the Wrap-Up step, students formulate questions and answers about the key ideas from the entire passage and discuss what they have learned. The goal is to improve their knowledge, understanding, and memory of what they read. For students with learning and language disabilities, it may be necessary to explicitly teach them to ask questions using *what, where, who, when, why,* and *how.* As in reciprocal teaching, students are to think about questions that a teacher might ask. To assist students in generating higher-level questions, it is important to model question stems such as What do you think would happen if . . .? How were _____ and _____ the same? How were they different? Why do you think . . .? Students can use the gists they have generated for the different sections to think about the most important information in the whole passage.

Cooperative Learning Groups. Once they have developed proficiency in applying the comprehension strategies through teacher-led activities, the students learn to use CSR in peer-led cooperative learning groups of about four or five students. Typical roles that are used during CSR include the following:

- *Leader:* Leads group by saying what to read and what strategy to use next.

- *Clunk expert:* Reminds students to use clunk strategies to figure out a difficult word or concept.

FIGURE 8-17 Example of CSR Learning Log

CSR Learning Log

Name: _____

Title: _____   Date: _____
Pages: _____

Preview

What I already know about the topic: _____

_____
What I predict I will learn: _____

_____

Clicks and Clunks

List your clunks and what they mean.

Getting the Gist

Write/tell the gists for the sections you read.

Wrap-Up

What was the most important thing the entire passage was about? _____

_____
Write questions you may have for your classmates. _____
What I learned. _____

_____

- *Announcer:* Calls on different members to read and share ideas.

- *Encourager:* Watches the group, and gives encouragement and feedback.

- *Reporter:* During the whole-class wrap-up, reports to class the important ideas learned and favorite questions.

- *Timekeeper:* Keeps time, and lets the group know when it is time to move on. Students should change roles on a regular basis. After wrapping up in their cooperative groups, a whole-class wrap-up is completed to give the teacher and groups the opportunity to report and to discuss the content.

COMMENTS: CSR has been used by a number of classroom teachers who have students with learning and behavior problems and ELLs included in their classrooms (Klingner & Vaughn, 1996, 2000; Vaughn, Klingner, et al., 2010; Vaughn, Klingner, et al., 2011). For example, seventh- and eighth-grade ELLs with learning disabilities were taught to apply CSR while working on social studies content (Klingner & Vaughn, 1996). Students' reading comprehension scores for the passages they read as well as their scores on standardized tests improved significantly. It has also been a successful practice with upper-elementary and middle school students with reading problems (D. Bryant, Vaughn, et al., 2000; Klingner, Vaughn, & Schumm, 1998; Klingner, Vaughn, Arguelles, Hughes, & Ahwee, 2003). CSR has also been used through technology with middle and high school students with reading difficulties or disabilities (A. Kim, 2002; A. Kim et al., 2003). The computer program Computer-Assisted Collaborative Strategic Reading is designed to provide systematic instruction in comprehension strategies of CSR along with ample practices to apply those strategies. Students' ability to find main ideas and generate comprehension questions improved significantly, and their scores on standardized comprehension tests also improved to a moderate extent (A. Kim et al., 2003). Overall, the results demonstrate the effectiveness of explicit instruction of cognitive strategy training and comprehension monitoring in improving a range of reading comprehension skills.

Special Considerations for Adolescent Readers

All of the approaches to teaching reading comprehension previously discussed are appropriate for older students with reading disabilities. However, in addition to these approaches, several important considerations address the motivation and disposition of older students.

Perhaps one of the most consistent responses of older students with reading difficulties about reading is that they "don't like it." However, it is interesting that although they do not read for pleasure, the majority of adolescents perceive reading as important and as something that they value. Students realize that reading is the key to success in school and to their future success.

1. Remember that all students, even secondary students, want to succeed as readers as long as appropriate and situated instruction is provided.

2. Consider that older students value "choice" about what they read. Even when the topic is restricted to content area learning such as social studies and science, providing choice about text types related to the topic will improve their motivation and interest.

3. Many forms for reading go beyond traditional print. Even poor readers spend time each day searching the Web for information (Klauda & Guthrie, 2012). Consider technology as a source of information and text. What are some of the sources adolescents (even students who are poor readers) read regularly?

   - Text messages
   - TV guides
   - Web sites
   - E-mail

4. With older students, dedication to reading is the best predictor of reading achievement (Klauda & Guthrie, 2012). What is dedication? It refers to the positive valuing of reading, including recognition that reading is important for your future and necessary for school success.

Adapting Approaches to Teaching Reading in Inclusive Classrooms

In this section, we discuss two lesson frameworks or approaches to teaching reading that are often used in general education elementary classrooms and found in basal reading programs. These are approaches that many students with learning and behavior problems encounter; therefore, we present practices for adapting them for effective instruction of these students.

Directed Reading Activity The Directed Reading Activity (DRA), developed by Betts (1946), is the general framework or lesson plan used in many basal readers

(Gunning, 2010a, b; Wilkinson & Anderson, 1995). The DRA is a systematic method for providing instruction in reading, including procedures for teaching word identification as well as comprehension.

Evidence-Based PRACTICE

Directed Reading Activity

PROCEDURES: This general method for teaching reading is designed to be used with students reading at any level who are reading the same selection. The following outline presents the stages that are usually found in a DRA (Betts, 1946):

1. Readiness
   a. Developing conceptual background
   b. Creating interest
   c. Introducing new vocabulary
   d. Establishing purposes for reading

2. Directed silent reading
   a. Constructing meaning
   b. Monitoring comprehension

3. Discussion and comprehension check
   a. Revisiting purposes for reading
   b. Clarifying concepts and vocabulary
   c. Correcting difficulties in applying word identification and comprehension strategies
   d. Evaluating student performance

4. Rereading
   a. Clarifying information
   b. Obtaining additional information
   c. Enhancing appreciation and understanding
   d. Providing opportunities for purposeful oral reading

5. Follow-up activities
   a. Extending skill development
   b. Enriching and generalizing

COMMENTS: Although the DRA is suggested as a framework for teaching in basal readers, modifications are necessary for students who experience reading difficulties. For example, in both the earlier and later elementary grades, many of these students need more systematic, explicit instruction in phonics and decoding strategies than are usually provided. Incorporating fluency building through repeated and partner reading will also assist in providing the needed practice required of these students. The PReP and previewing could be added to the readiness stage of the DRA to activate and build on prior knowledge. Explicit instruction of comprehension and comprehension-monitoring strategies such as self-questioning and summarizing would also support students with reading difficulties. Finally, it is important that reading materials are at the students' instructional level.

One concern about the DRA is that it is teacher dominated and therefore may not facilitate the development of independent reading skills. Encouraging the students to set their own purposes for reading, to self-question as they read, and to generate their own questions and follow-up activities is emphasized in the next framework: the Directed Reading–Thinking Activity (DR–TA).

Directed Reading–Thinking Activity Stauffer (1969, 1970, 1976) developed the DR–TA as a framework for teaching reading that stresses students' abilities to read reflectively and to use prediction and preview strategies to set their own purposes for reading (Gunning, 2010a, b). The purpose of the DR–TA is to provide readers with the ability to do the following:

* Determine purposes for reading.
* Extract, comprehend, and assimilate information.
* Use prediction while reading.
* Suspend judgments.
* Make decisions based on evidence gained from reading.

DR–TA is based on the notion that reading is a thinking process that requires students to relate their own experiences to the author's ideas and thereby construct meaning from the text.

In using this approach, the construction of meaning starts with setting purposes for reading and generating hypotheses about meaning. Constructing meaning from text continues as students acquire more information, confirm or disconfirm hypotheses, and establish new hypotheses. It ends when the hypotheses have been confirmed and the purposes for reading have been met.

Stauffer (1969) describes seven distinguishing features about group DR–TA activities:

1. Students of approximately the same reading level are grouped together.
2. The group size ranges from 2 to 10 students to promote interaction and participation.
3. All students in a group read the same material at the same time. This permits each student to compare

and contrast predictions, justifications for answers, and evaluations with those of his or her peers.

4. Purposes for reading are declared by students; students ask questions to become active readers and thinkers.

5. Answers to questions are validated. Proof is found and tested, and the group judges whether the offered proof is trustworthy.

6. Immediate feedback helps develop integrity and a regard for authenticity.

7. The teacher serves as a facilitator or moderator, and asks provocative questions that require the students to interpret and make inferences from what they have read.

Evidence-Based PRACTICE

DR–TA

PROCEDURES: Adapt the following procedures in using a DR–TA:

1. After each student receives a copy of the material, direct the students to identify a purpose for reading by studying the title, subtitles, pictures, and other elements, to develop a hypothesis about what the passage is about. Following are two questions you might ask to stimulate hypotheses: What do you think a story with this title might be about? What do you think might happen in this story? Have students share these hypotheses, discussing how they arrived at them. Have students use information from their prior knowledge to substantiate their predictions.

2. Once each student has stated his or her hypothesis, encourage the students to adjust their rate of silent reading to their purpose for reading.

3. Teach the students or remind them of the strategies they can use when they come to a word they cannot identify, such as sounding out the word parts and thinking what makes sense and asking for assistance.

4. Select a segment of the text, and direct the students to read it to themselves and check their predictions.

5. When the students have finished reading, have them discuss their predictions. Two target questions to ask are as follows: "Were you correct?" "What do you think now?" Have students reread orally the sections of the text that confirm or contradict their hypotheses. Assist the students in determining whether other source materials may be necessary to clarify meaning, and have the students discuss concepts and vocabulary that are critical to the comprehension process.

6. Repeat the procedure (hypothesis setting, silent reading to validate, oral reading to prove, and discussion) with subsequent segments of the text.

7. Once the passage has been completed, use skill activities to teach skill training (Stauffer, 1969). This entails rereading the story, and reexamining selected words, phrases, pictures, and/or diagrams for the purpose of concurrently developing the students' reading–thinking abilities with the other reading-related skills (Tierney & Readence, 2005). These might include word-attack skills and concept clarification and development.

The processing involved in a DR–TA is summarized as follows:

1. Pupil actions
   a. Predict (set purposes)
   b. Read (process ideas)
   c. Prove (test answers)

2. Teacher actions
   a. What do you think? (activate thought)
   b. Why do you think so? (agitate thought)
   c. Prove it! (require evidence) (Stauffer, 1969)

Stauffer (1969) suggests that once the students are comfortable with the DR–TA process, they should be encouraged to use an individualized DR–TA. In other words, students should use this systematic, predictive process as they read individually. Figure 8-18 presents a sample worksheet that students may use to guide themselves as they complete individual DR–TAs.

COMMENTS: The DR–TA provides teachers with a procedure for teaching students to become active thinkers as they read. This is particularly relevant for students with learning and behavior problems, because it requires that students assume responsibility for the reading–learning process. In comparison to the DRA, in which the teacher sets the purpose for reading and preteaches vocabulary, the DR–TA encourages the students to set their own purposes and decide which vocabulary warrants further development.

Two cautions, however, seem relevant to the DR–TA. First, it requires a great deal of self-directedness in students, particularly when they use the individualized

FIGURE 8-18 Directed Reading–Thinking Activity Individual Prediction Sheet

Name: _____

Passage/Book: _____

Pages	Prediction	Outcome

Summary _____

_____

DR–TA. For students with learning and behavior problems, teachers will need to scaffold instruction so that there is a systematic movement from teacher modeling and control to student control. Second, there is little or no emphasis on teaching word decoding and word identification or fluency-building skills in a direct or systematic manner. Like DRA, providing direct instruction in these areas and having students work in instructional-level materials will be important modifications to make in inclusive classes.

INSTRUCTIONAL ACTIVITIES

This section provides instructional activities that are related to reading comprehension and fluency. Some of the activities teach new skills; others are best suited for practice and reinforcement of already acquired skills. For each activity, the objective, materials, and teaching procedures are described.

Web Resources

Several Web sites provide excellent examples of lesson plans that may assist you in designing effective instruction for your students:

http://www.texasldcenter.org/teachers

(Click on *Teachers,* and you'll be able to locate lessons, professional development, and videos.)

http://www.meadowscenter.org/

(Click on *resources,* and you'll have access to sample lessons and videos.)

http://www.intensiveintervention.org/

(Check out the intensive intervention tools chart and sample lessons.)

Choral Reading

OBJECTIVE: To provide students with opportunities to practice reading aloud rapidly, accurately, and expressively with the teacher

GRADES: Kindergarten through primary

MATERIALS: Reading passages

TEACHING PROCEDURES:

1. Provide each student with a copy of the reading passage.
2. Model fluent reading of the passage by reading aloud. The teacher reads the passage accurately with prosody and sets the pace.
3. Students read along with the teacher the second time the passage is read. This strategy can be implemented individually, in whole groups, or in small groups.

Source: Adapted from University of Texas Center for Reading and Language Arts (2003b).

Partner Reading

OBJECTIVE: To improve students' reading accuracy and rate
GRADES: Elementary through secondary

MATERIALS: Reading passages, graph paper, colored pencils, timer for the teacher

TEACHING PROCEDURES:

1. Pair students, using the following procedure: (a) Rank the students according to reading ability, (b) split the list in half, (c) pair the top-ranked student in the higher performing half (partner 1) with the top-ranked student in the lower performing half (partner 2), and so forth.
2. Give each pair two copies of the reading passage at the instructional level of the less fluent student. (Instructional reading level means that the reader can decode about 90% of the words correctly.)
3. Remind students of the procedures for partner reading: (a) read for 4 minutes each; (b) correct errors (omission/addition of words, stopping more than 3 seconds, etc.); (c) do the best 1-minute reading (while timed); (d) calculate the fluency rate; and (e) graph the fluency rate.
4. Have partner 1 model fluent reading for 4 minutes while partner 2 follows along and identifies and corrects errors. Partner 2 should use the following procedure for error correction:
   a. Say, "Sound it out."
   b. Wait 4 seconds.
   c. If the partner figures out the word, say, "Good. Now reread the sentence."
   d. If the partner doesn't figure out the word, say, "That word is. . . . What word?" Wait for the partner to respond _____. Say, "Good. Now reread the sentence."
5. Have the students reread the passage for 1 minute (best reading), with partner 1 reading first. Partner 2 follows along, marks errors, and marks the last word read at the 1-minute mark.
6. Have the students calculate their fluency during the 1-minute best reading using WCPM. This is found by subtracting the number of errors from the total number of words read: (Total − errors = fluency).
7. Have the students graph their fluency using colored pencils and graph paper, as shown in Figure 8-19.

FIGURE 8-19 Fluency Graph

Source: Based on University of Texas Center for Reading and Language Arts (2001a). Adapted by permission.

Phrase Card Reading

OBJECTIVE: To help students improve their reading rate and accuracy

GRADES: Elementary through intermediate

MATERIALS: Reading passages, index cards, pens

TEACHING PROCEDURES:

1. Pair students, using the procedure described in "Partner Reading."

2. Give each pair two copies of the reading passage at the instructional level of the less fluent student.

3. Have each pair highlight phrases from the passage that include difficult words.

4. Have each pair write these phrases on index cards.

5. Have the more fluent reader in each pair read the phrases from the cards first.

6. Then have the less fluent reader in each pair read the same phrases from the cards. While the less fluent reader reads the phrases, the fluent reader identifies and corrects errors, if any.

Source: Adapted from University of Texas Center for Reading and Language Arts (2002).

Audio-Assisted Reading

OBJECTIVE: To help students improve their reading rate and accuracy

GRADES: Elementary through secondary

MATERIALS: Reading passages, audio player/recorder

TEACHING PROCEDURES:

1. Before the instruction, select a reading passage at each student's instructional or independent reading level. Record the passage. While recording, read with appropriate rate, accuracy, and expression.

2. Tell the students to listen to the passage on their audio player and to follow along by running their fingers under the line of the print. (*Note:* Students should not point to each word.)

3. Have the students read the passage aloud three times along with the audio.

4. Have the students read the passage aloud along with the audio while you listen to identify and correct errors.

5. Have the students read the passage aloud without listening to the audio for 1 minute.

6. Have the students calculate and graph their fluency rate (using the procedure described in "Partner Reading").

Source: Adapted from University of Texas Center for Reading and Language Arts (2002).

Chunk Reading

OBJECTIVE: To help students improve their reading accuracy and rate while reading phrases

GRADES: Elementary

MATERIALS: Reading passages, graph paper, colored pencils, timer for the teacher

TEACHING PROCEDURES:

1. Before the instruction, select a reading passage at an instructional level that is appropriate for the less fluent students. Place slash marks between chunks (i.e., phrases) to mark two- to five-word sentence segments and prepositional phrases in each passage.

2. Pair students using the procedure described in "Partner Reading."

3. Give each pair two copies of the reading passages with chunking marks.

4. Tell the students that connected text is divided into meaningful phrases and that paying attention to these phrases while reading will enhance their fluency and comprehension.

5. Tell the students to pause briefly between phrases, exactly as marked. No pauses should be made except at slash marks.

6. Remind students of the procedure for partner reading: (a) 4-minute reading for each, (b) 1-minute best reading for each, (c) calculating fluency, and (d) graphing.

7. Have partner 1 model fluent reading while partner 2 follows along. Partner 1 emphasizes chunking phrases together for meaning. For instance, read the sentence "One day last week my sister and I drove to the lake" like this: "One day last week / my sister and I / drove to the lake." (A slash indicates a pause.) Then partner 2 reads the passage while partner 1 follows along.

8. Tell the students to reread the passage for 1 minute (best reading), with partner 1 reading first. While partner 1 reads, partner 2 follows along, marks errors, and marks the last word read at the 1-minute mark.

9. Ask the students to calculate the fluency using WCPM (see the procedures in "Partner Reading") and to graph their fluency on the graph paper with colored pencils.

Source: Adapted from University of Texas Center for Reading and Language Arts (2001a).

Dramatic Reading

OBJECTIVE: To help students improve their reading fluency

GRADES: Elementary through secondary

MATERIALS: Copies of a play for each student

TEACHING PROCEDURES:

1. Make groups of four, consisting of two more fluent readers and two less fluent readers.

2. Give a copy of the play to each student, and assign each student a role.

3. Tell students that they will practice the play with other group members and will put on the play for the class.

4. Set a performance day and time.

5. Instruct students to practice the play in their group. Have each student practice reading his or her lines while the other group members listen and provide feedback.

6. Next, have students work together to read their parts as if in a play. Encourage students to provide feedback to each other.

7. On the performance day, have each group put on their play for the class.

Source: Adapted from University of Texas Center for Reading and Language Arts (2002).

Critiquing Oral Reading

OBJECTIVE: To provide students with opportunities to critique their oral reading

GRADES: Primary and intermediate

MATERIALS: Reading passages, tape recorder, a blank tape for each student labeled with the student's name

TEACHING PROCEDURES:

1. Explain that the purpose of the activity is to give the students an opportunity to listen to how they read.

2. Let the students know that they are to listen for things they do well and things they want to improve.

3. Model the process by practicing, recording, listening, and critiquing a passage you read.

4. Before the students read into the tape recorder, have them practice the segment. Each student should practice and then read and record a passage of about 100 to 500 words.

5. After the students record, they should listen to their tapes and finish writing the following statements:

   When I read orally, I do a really good job of _____.

   One thing I could do better when I read out loud is _____.

6. Listen to and discuss each tape, and then ask the students to critique each presentation. Have

the students record their oral reading every 3 to 6 weeks so that they can compare and hear how they are improving.

Adaptations: Each student can record two passages: one that has been practiced and one that is unpracticed.

Previewing

OBJECTIVE: To help students activate their prior knowledge and make predictions about what they are going to learn from the passage

GRADES: Elementary through secondary

MATERIALS: Expository reading passage, copies of a preview log (see Figure 8-20)

TEACHING PROCEDURES:

1. Pass out a preview log to each student.

2. Introduce the topic of the lesson, and ask students to record it at the top of their preview logs.

3. Divide the class into small groups.

4. Give each group 2 minutes to brainstorm what they already know about the topic, and ask them to record their ideas in their preview logs along with how this topic relates to previous lessons.

5. Ask several groups to share their brainstorming ideas.

6. Introduce and discuss three key vocabulary words. Have students record the words along with the definition in their preview logs.

7. Pass out a reading passage to each student.

8. Ask the students to scan the passage, looking for clues or physical features, such as the title, subtitle, headings, subheadings, bolded words, graphics, and/or pictures, that could be used to make predictions about the passage.

9. Ask each group to make two predictions about what they think they are going to learn from the passage. Have students record their predictions in their preview logs.

10. Ask several groups to share their predictions.

11. After the lesson, discuss and check students' predictions to see how close their predictions were to what they actually learned from the text.

Source: Adapted from University of Texas Center for Reading and Language Arts (2001a).

Getting the Gist

OBJECTIVE: To help students identify the main idea of a paragraph

GRADES: Elementary through secondary

FIGURE 8-20 Preview Log

Topic:

What do I already know about the topic?

How does this topic relate to previous lessons?

Key vocabulary and definitions

1._____ : _____
2._____ : _____
3._____ : _____

Predictions

By looking at the   ❑ title   ❑ headings   ❑ pictures   ❑ others: _____
I think that I am going to learn about...

By looking at the   ❑ title   ❑ headings   ❑ pictures   ❑ others: _____
I think that I am going to learn about...

FIGURE 8-21 Gist Log

---

1. Who or what is the paragraph mostly about?

2. What is the most important information about the who or what?

   (Use this information to develop the gist statement.)

3. Write a gist of 10 words or less in a complete sentence.

MATERIALS: Expository reading passage, copies of a gist log (see Figure 8-21)

TEACHING PROCEDURES:

1. Pass out a reading passage and a gist log to each student.

2. Explain to students that a gist statement represents the main idea of a paragraph. The main idea is the most important information in a paragraph.

3. Tell students that there are three steps to getting the gist: (1) naming the *who* or *what* the paragraph is mostly about, (2) telling the most important information about the *who* or *what*, and (3) writing a complete sentence about the gist in 10 words or less.

4. Pair the students, and have them take turns reading with a partner.

5. After each paragraph, each pair identifies who or what the paragraph is mostly about.

6. Next, each pair identifies the most important information about the *who* or *what*.

7. Then each pair puts the two pieces of information together in a complete sentence of 10 words or less.

8. After all pairs complete getting the gist statements, call on several pairs to share their statements with others.

Source: Adapted from Klingner et al. (2001).

Self-Monitoring

OBJECTIVE: To help students monitor their understanding

GRADES: Secondary

MATERIALS: Two different triple-spaced reading passages, two transparencies of both passages, copies of a monitoring symbol cue card, overhead projector, marker

---

Monitoring Symbol Cue Card

✓ = Got it!
? = What Does This Mean?
MBI = Must Be Important
RR = Reread
DW = Difficult Word
LG = Look at Graphs

TEACHING PROCEDURES:

1. Introduce monitoring symbols, and tell students that the use of the symbols will help them to monitor their understanding.

2. Present and describe each symbol.

3. Pass out the first triple-spaced passage.

4. Place the first passage on the overhead projector, and model how to use the symbols while reading.

5. Read the passage aloud, and insert the symbols where appropriate to mirror your self-monitoring strategies. Tell why you insert the symbols.

6. Pass out the second reading passage and a monitoring symbol cue card to each student.

7. Ask the students to insert monitoring symbols as they read.

8. Circulate around the class, and provide additional support if necessary.

9. After the students finish the second passage, place the second passage on the overhead projector. Call on several students to share which symbols they used and why.

10. Answer any questions about the passage or difficult words.

Adaptations: This instructional activity can be used with a Click and Clunk activity. A teacher can ask students to use the Click and Clunk strategy when they come across difficult words.

Source: Adapted from University of Texas Center for Reading and Language Arts (2002).

Generating Questions

See the description of Click and Clunk in the Instructional Activities section entitled Collaborative Strategic Reading, earlier in this chapter.

OBJECTIVE: To help students generate questions about important information after reading

GRADES: Elementary through secondary

MATERIALS: Two different reading passages, overhead projector, marker, transparency

TEACHING PROCEDURES:

1. Pass out the first reading passage to each student.

2. Explain to students that there are three types of questions: "right there" questions (the answer to the question is right in the text); "think and search" questions (the answer to the question is in the text, but students have to read the text and to compose the answer themselves based on what they have read); and "on my own" questions (the answer to the question is not in the text, and students have to integrate their own previous experiences with what they have learned from the text).

3. Read the entire reading passage aloud.

4. Model how to generate questions about the important information by using the key words *how, who, what, when, where,* and *why.*

5. Pass out the second reading passage to each student.

6. Remind students that there are three types of questions.

7. Pair the students, and have them take turns reading with a partner.

8. After reading the entire passage, have each pair generate at least one question for each type.

9. Monitor the students to make sure that they all properly generate questions.

10. After all pairs have finished generating the questions, call on several pairs to share their questions with others.

Source: Adapted from Klingner et al. (2001).

Directed Reading–Thinking Activity (DR–TA)

OBJECTIVE: To help students make and check predictions before, during, and after reading

GRADES: Elementary through secondary

FIGURE 8-22 DR-TA Organizer

Title:_____

Predictions based on the topic:

Predictions based on skimming information such as the title, pictures, etc.:

Predictions after reading the first part of the text: Pages _____ to _____

Predictions after reading the second part of the text: Pages _____ to _____

Predictions after reading the third part of the text: Pages _____ to _____

MATERIALS: Reading passage in which a teacher marks several stop points, copies of a DR–TA organizer (see Figure 8-22)

TEACHING PROCEDURES:

1. Pass out a reading passage and a DR–TA organizer to each student.

2. Before reading, discuss the topic.

3. Show pictures, graphs, headings, or bolded text in the passage, and ask students what they think the passage topic could be.

4. Call on several students to share their predictions about the passage topic. Discuss with students how to generate the best predictions, and record the predictions on the DR–TA organizer. Have students write predictions on their DR–TA organizers.

5. Have students take turns reading the first part of the passage (before the first stop point).

6. Ask the students to think back about predictions they generated and what evidence is presented to either confirm or disprove their predictions.

7. Ask the students to revise or make new predictions if necessary.

8. Call on several students to share their revised and/or new predictions. Discuss with students how to generate the best predictions, and record the predictions on the DR–TA organizer. Have the students write the predictions on their DR–TA organizers.

9. Repeat the same procedure until the entire passage is read.

10. After finishing the entire passage, ask the students to reflect on their predictions.

11. Call on several students to share their reflections.

Source: Adapted from C. Blachowicz and Ogle (2001).

Expository Text Question Cards

OBJECTIVE: To teach students to identify different types of expository text structure and to ask comprehension questions appropriate to each text structure while reading text

GRADE: Secondary

MATERIALS: Expository reading passages (two different passages for each text structure type), expository comprehension cards (one card set for each text structure type; see Figure 8-23)

TEACHING PROCEDURES:

1. Hand out a passage with a concept/definition type to each student.

2. Tell students that the text is the concept/definition type.

3. Provide the students with the card set for the concept/definition type.

4. Model how the students can use the sample questions on the card to ask and answer specific questions about the content.

5. Hand out another passage with the concept/definition type to each student.

6. Have the students take turns reading.

7. During reading, periodically stop the students from reading, and ask several students to use the sample questions on the card to ask and answer specific questions about the content.

8. Use the same procedure for expository reading passages with other text structure types (e.g., cause and effect, compare and contrast).

Source: Adapted from University of Texas Center for Reading and Language Arts (2003a).

FIGURE 8-23 Expository Comprehension Cards

Concept or Definition

1. What topic or concept is described? _____

2. What are some of its characteristics? _____

3. What is its function? _____

4. To what category does it belong? _____

5. What are some related ideas or words? _____

6. What are some examples? _____

7. What do you think is the most unusual or memorable characteristic?

_____

Cause and Effect

1. What happens? _____

2. What causes it to happen? _____

3. What are the important elements or factors that caused it to happen? _____

4. Will the result always happen this way? Why or why not? _____

5. How can elements or factors change? _____

_____

Compare and Contrast

1. What is being compared and contrasted? _____

2. How are things similar? _____

3. How are they different? _____

4. What are the most important qualities that make them the same or different? _____

5. What conclusions can we make? _____

6. How can the things be classified? _____

Position Statement or Support

1. What is the opinion, hypothesis, theory, or argument?

_____

2. Are valid reasons given to accept it? _____

3. Do you agree with the viewpoint, theory, hypothesis presented? Why? Why not? _____

4. What credible evidence and data are presented? ___

_____

Using Narrative Comprehension Cards

OBJECTIVE: To teach students to use narrative comprehension cards while reading text

FIGURE 8-24 Narrative Cards

Green Cards—Use Before Reading
Card 1:   What does the title tell me about this story?
Card 2:   What do the pictures tell me?
Card 3:   What do I already know about?

Yellow Cards—Use During Reading
Card 4:   Who? (Tell who the story is about, or name the characters.)
Card 5:   What? (State the problem.)
Card 6:   When? (Tell the time the story takes place.)
Card 7:   Where? (Tell the place of the story.)
Card 8:   Why? (Explain why something happened.)
Card 9:   How? (Tell how the problem was solved.)
Card 10: What do I think will happen next? (Make predictions.)

Red Cards—Use After Reading
Card 11: Who were the characters?
Card 12: What was the setting? (When and where.)
Card 13: What was the problem?
Card 14: How was the problem solved?
Card 15: Why did . . . ? (Elaborate on why something happened.)

GRADE: Elementary

MATERIALS: Narrative reading passage, narrative comprehension cards (see Figure 8-24), pocket chart

TEACHING PROCEDURES: Before the instruction, set narrative comprehension cards on the left side of the pocket chart in the correct order (1 to 15).

1. Hand out a reading passage to each student.

2. Introduce narrative comprehension cards. Explain to students that each card is color coded. Tell them that green cards are used *before reading*, yellow cards are used *during reading*, and red cards are used *after reading*.

3. Before reading, read the first green card question (card 1) aloud.

4. Call on several students to answer the question. As the first green card question is answered, move the card to the right side of the pocket chart to indicate that the question has been answered.

5. Repeat the same procedure until all green card questions have been answered.

6. Have the students take turns reading.

7. During reading, periodically stop the students from reading, and ask several students to answer the first yellow card question (card 4).

8. As each yellow card question is answered, move the card to the right side of the pocket chart.

9. Repeat the same procedure until all of the yellow card questions have been answered.

10. After reading, ask the students the first red card question.

11. As each red card question is answered, move the card to the right side of the pocket chart.

12. Repeat the same procedure until all red card questions have been answered.

Source: Adapted from University of Texas, Center for Reading and Language Arts (2000a, 2000b).

Story Jumble

OBJECTIVE: To provide students practice in sequencing a story

GRADES: Primary and intermediate

MATERIALS: Short stories that have been cut into story parts (e.g., setting, episodes, endings), paragraphs, or sentences; index cards with the segments of the story mounted onto them

TEACHING PROCEDURES:
1. Present the cards to the students, and have the students read each part and arrange the cards so that the story makes sense.

2. Have students read the story again to determine whether it makes sense. If students disagree about the order, have them explain why they prefer a certain order.

Adaptations: Students can work on this activity in groups of two or three or individually.

Predict the Plot

OBJECTIVE: To provide students with practice in predicting the events and plots in stories.

GRADES: Intermediate and secondary

MATERIALS: Cartoon strips or other picture sequences from books

TEACHING PROCEDURES:
1. Select a cartoon strip or book with pictures, and expose one picture at a time for the students to read.

2. Have students predict the plot by asking such questions as these:
   - What do you think is going to be pictured in the next frame? Why?
   - Of the ideas we have generated, which one do you like best? Why?
   - How do you think the story will end? Why?

3. View the next picture. Discussing the previous predictions and making predictions about the next frame.

4. After the story is completed, have students draw their own pictures, using the characters presented in the strip or creating new characters.

5. Have students share their cartoons with others.

Adaptations: Mystery and adventure stories also lend themselves to this type of plot prediction. Segments of the story could be read, and then predictions could be made. Students could also finish this activity by writing a mystery or adventure story.

WH Game

OBJECTIVE: To provide students with practice in answering *who, what, when, where, why,* and *how* (WH) questions

GRADES: Elementary through secondary

MATERIALS: Generic game board, spinner or die, and markers; WH cards, which are small cards with "WH Game" written on one side and one of the following words written on the other side: Who, What, When, Where, Why, How; sets of Story and Article Cards, which are copies of short stories and articles mounted on cards. There should be one copy for each player. Select topics of interest for the age level of students.

TEACHING PROCEDURES:
1. Explain the game to the students.

2. Have students select a set of Story or Article Cards.

3. Have all students read the story or article and place their cards face down.

4. Have students take a turn by throwing the die or spinning and selecting a WH Card.

5. Have the student make up a question using the Wh- word indicated on the card and answer it correctly in order to move his or her marker.

6. If another player questions the validity of a player's question or answer, the players may look at the story or article card. Otherwise, these cards should remain face down during play.

7. After questions have been asked using one Story or Article Card, another set is selected. The students read this card, and then the game continues.

8. The first player to arrive at the finish wins.

Adaptations: Students may also work in pairs, with one person on the team making up the question and the other person answering it.

Summary

- Fluency is the ability to read a text quickly, accurately, and with expression. The Common Core State Standards emphasize fluency in that they emphasize paying attention to detail and reading clearly and accurately, while the anchor standards include focusing on speaking, listening, and communicating tasks.

- The following techniques have been identified as effective for increasing reading fluency for struggling readers: modeling fluent reading while students' read along, such as repeated reading of a text, choral repeated reading, peer-supported reading, and reading performance; these all allow the teacher to assess and monitor student progress.

- Comprehension is a difficult task to measure quickly, although maze procedures are used to assess reading comprehension for progress-monitoring purposes.

Several standardized and norm-referenced measures take between 25 and 45 minutes to administer (some group administered and some individually administered) and provide reliable and valid information on students' reading comprehension.

- Comprehension instruction should encourage students to engage actively in discussions related to the content of the text and about how to read for meaning. The components of reading comprehension instruction include preview techniques, questioning strategies and comprehension monitoring, and text structure and summarizing strategies.

ASSESSMENT

After completing this chapter, test your knowledge of the concepts by completing the Assessment.

Assessing and Teaching Writing and Spelling

LEARNING OUTCOMES

1. Identify assessment and instructional practices associated with improved writing outcomes for students with learning and behavior problems.

2. Describe the critical features of spelling assessment and instruction for students with learning and behavior problems.

3. Describe the characteristics of students with handwriting problems, and identify the components of effective handwriting and keyboarding programs.

Mike York, a high school teacher of students with learning disabilities (LD), reports, "The adolescents in my program do not want to write. They do not even want to answer questions in writing. Writing a theme for a class is torture." He goes on to describe the students in his class. "The worst thing you can tell them is that you want them to write a long paragraph or theme. I think that for most of these students it is because they really have very poor handwriting skills. If I provide them with a keyboard to compose, they do better. Furthermore, most of them have little experience writing before they get to secondary school. Many were identified as learning disabled in the early elementary grades and then were provided with writing assistance as they went through school. Fortunately, some of the students were provided with instruction in how to use a keyboard and this helps with their writing production. However, production is not the only problem. Quality of writing is also extremely poor. This poor writing influences their success in content area classes. For example, several of my students are very interested in science and work hard to understand and participate in the general education classroom. They also know a lot more about science that they can talk about than that they are able to write about. Unfortunately, almost all assessments in the classroom require students to write their answers. Since my students have writing challenges, they frequently write brief and incomplete answers which give an inaccurate portrait of what they really know. I am now working closely with my students to improve their writing production and quality so that they can be more successful in both general education classrooms as well as the world of work."

Most young children love to scribble. They enjoy writing and drawing on paper, sidewalks, chalkboards, and, unfortunately, even walls. On the first day of school, when first graders are asked whether they know how to write, most of them say yes. What happens to the interest and joy in writing from age 3 to age 13?

Perhaps students would be less reluctant to write if they spent more time writing with feedback from the early grades through secondary grades. Students may also have more positive dispositions about writing if they had improved writing instruction so that their confidence about their writing was higher. Of course, the mechanics related to writing (e.g., spelling and letter formation) also influence their success as writers.

The good news is that we have made considerable progress in how to effectively teach writing to students with disabilities (Mason & Graham, 2008; Mason, Harris, & Graham, 2011). When teachers implement effective intervention approaches that use both the conventions of teaching writing (e.g., capitalization, punctuation, sentence structure) and strategies for improving written expression (e.g., planning, composing the results), the results are quite positive.

The chapter presents background and instructional procedures for using writing strategies and teaching spelling, handwriting, and keyboarding to students who have learning difficulties and disabilities. How to teach writing within content areas and by addressing the Common Core State Standards for writing are also addressed.

Assessing and Teaching the Writing Process

What assessment and instructional practices improve writing outcomes for students with learning and behavior problems? Marynell Schlegel, an elementary resource-room teacher who works with students who have learning and emotional disabilities, realized that her writing instruction needed to be guided by the Common Core State Standards. See Figure 9-1 for a list of the key Common Core State Standards in writing.

Using the CCSS as a guide, Ms. Schlegel decided to read about writing and to change her writing instruction. She decided to implement a process approach to writing that also provided students with specific strategies for improving their writing (Berninger & Wolf, 2009; Foster, 2010; D. Graves, 1983, 1994).

The Writing Process for Students with Learning and Behavior Problems

Ms. Schlegel arranged for students with writing difficulties and students with LD to be in the same classroom so that she could coteach with a general education teacher for three 40-minute periods a week (see Apply the Concept 9-1). During this time, students were to write and participate in skills groups. Initially, instruction included selecting topics of the student's choice, focusing first on the message and then on the mechanics of writing within each written piece. Skills such as organizing ideas and editing for capitalization, punctuation, and spelling were explicitly taught and linked directly to students' writing. Ms. Schlegel knew that to implement the writing process approach in her instruction she would need to consider setting, scheduling and preparing materials, teaching skills, and the teacher's role as a writer. Furthermore, there were many strategic approaches to enhance writing that she wanted to include in her instruction.

Setting The setting should create a working atmosphere promoting independence but in which students can easily interact. For many students, writing requires a quiet area free of interruption, so adequate space designated for quiet writing is needed. But there are also important writing goals that require paired writing, reading, giving feedback to others, and writing conferences with the teacher. So adequate space for interacting with others is also needed. Figure 9-2 depicts how Ms. Schlegel and the classroom teacher arranged the room to create such an atmosphere. Materials and supplies for writing and the students' individual writing folders were stored in specific locations in the room. Students knew where materials could be found, so they did not have to rely on the teacher to get them

FIGURE 9-1 Common Core State Standards for Writing

Text Types and Purposes

1. Write arguments to support claims in an analysis of substantive topics or texts, using valid reasoning and relevant and sufficient evidence.
2. Write informative/explanatory texts to examine and convey complex ideas and information clearly and accurately through the effective selection, organization, and analysis of content.
3. Write narratives to develop real or imagined experiences or events using effective technique, well-chosen details and well-structured event sequences.

Production and Distribution of Writing

1. Produce clear and coherent writing in which the development, organization, and style are appropriate to the task, purpose, and audience.
2. Develop and strengthen writing as needed by planning, revising, editing, rewriting, or trying a new approach.
3. Use technology, including the Internet, to produce and publish writing and to interact and collaborate with others.

Research to Build and Present Knowledge

1. Conduct short as well as more sustained research projects based on focused questions, demonstrating understanding of the subject under investigation.
2. Gather relevant information from multiple print and digital sources, assess the credibility and accuracy of each source, and integrate the information while avoiding plagiarism.
3. Draw evidence from literary or informational texts to support analysis, reflection, and research.

Range of Writing

1. Write routinely over extended time frames (time for research, reflection, and revision) and shorter time frames (a single sitting or a day or two) for a range of tasks, purposes, and audiences.)

Source: Based on © Copyright 2010. National Governors Association Center for Best Practices and Council of Chief State School Officers. All rights reserved.

FIGURE 9-2 Setting the Stage

1. Create a working atmosphere that is similar to a studio.
2. Create an atmosphere in which students can interact easily.
3. Create an atmosphere that encourages independence.

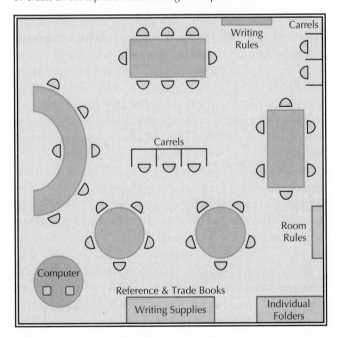

started at the beginning of the writing period. The room arrangement facilitated conferencing between small groups of students, teacher and student, and student and student.

Scheduling and Preparing Materials Ms. Schlegel set up individual writing folders, illustrated in Figure 9-3, where students keep unfinished writing, a list of possible writing topics, a list of selected writing pieces they had completed, a list of writing skills they had mastered, a list of skills and topics in which they had expertise, and dates when conferences with the teacher were held. Students also kept mnemonic cues to assist them in practicing writing strategies that they were learning. A list of the words an individual student was learning to spell, along with a procedure for learning the words and measuring mastery, were also included in the folder (see Figure 9-4).

Ms. Zaragoza is an elementary teacher who organizes skill lessons, 5 to 20 minutes each day, for small groups of students and individual skill lessons for students who have specific difficulties. She also addresses prevailing writing problems by providing approximately 20 minutes of whole-class instruction specifically teaching a target area (e.g., topic sentence, summary) two to three times per week. When she notices that several students are having difficulty with a particular skill (e.g., quotation marks), or thinks that several students are ready to learn a more advanced writing procedure (e.g., the difference between first and third person when writing), she organizes a skill group. She usually teaches one skill group a day and advertises the skill group by writing the name of it on the board. She writes the names of the students whom she has identified as likely to benefit from the skill group on

Knowledge of Writing Strategies

Students who have been identified as having a learning disability (LD) differ from other students in their knowledge of strategies related to writing. They are less aware of steps in the writing process (e.g., think of an idea, decide what the purpose will be, organize the key parts sequentially) and of ideas and procedures for organizing their written text. Students with LD are also more dependent on external cues, such as how much to write, teacher feedback, and mechanical presentation of the paper. They demonstrate significant difficulties in planning, writing, and revising text. Overall, the writing instruction of students with LD improves with well-organized and specific instruction along with ongoing feedback and encouragement to keep writing.

FIGURE 9-3 Individual Writing Folder

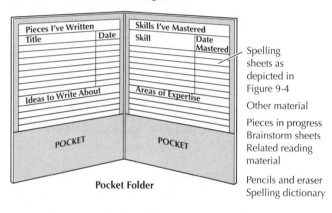

Pocket Folder

Spelling sheets as depicted in Figure 9-4

Other material

Pieces in progress
Brainstorm sheets
Related reading material

Pencils and eraser
Spelling dictionary

FIGURE 9-4 Sample Spelling Form for the Individual Writing Folder

Student: _____

Words I'm Learning to Spell

Date	Word	Written on Card	Practiced Using Strategy	Learned for Test	Learned in Writing	Date Mastered
3/12	1. mystery	✓	✓	✓		
	2. chasing	✓	✓	✓		
	3. haunted	✓	✓	✓		
	4. wouldn't	✓	✓			
	5. elsewhere	✓	✓	✓		
	6. whatever	✓	✓	✓		
	7. their	✓	✓	✓		
	8. there	✓	✓	✓		
	9.					
	10.					

the board but also allows other students to sign up for the skill group. A skill group would last for 1 day or several, depending on the difficulty of the skill. Ms. Zaragoza also teaches daily skill lessons to individual students. Sometimes these skill lessons are responses to a teachable moment—for example, a student might ask how to develop an ending for a story—and at other times are planned and scheduled. Ms. Zaragoza's viewpoint is that practice in writing is essential to enhancing writing skills, but practice alone is insufficient, and skill groups are an essential way to keep students moving and learning as writers.

Teaching Writing Conventions Students with LD display a wide range of abilities in writing (Berninger et al., 2008; Re, Pedron, & Cornoldi, 2007). They are also very different in terms of the writing skills they need to acquire and the ways in which they respond to instruction. Students who are better able to cope with the demands of schooling are better readers and writers over time, so one of the important tasks is to help students cope effectively with their writing difficulties. In designing effective writing skills programs for students with learning problems, variables such as motivation and attitude must be considered, as well as writing conventions.

Ms. Schlegel taught spelling, capitalization, punctuation, and other writing-related skills during each writing period, and then looked for these skills in students' writing, providing feedback and instructional support when they were not well developed. She also had specific time in which she taught "strategies" to facilitate successful writing such as planning practices, revision strategies, and opportunities for students to learn to give appropriate feedback to other students. Much of the time was devoted to small-group instruction and individual writing and conferences with classmates and the teacher. Time for sharing ideas and drafts was often scheduled near the end of the period.

Ms. Schlegel conducted short (5- to 15-minute) skill and strategy lessons with individuals or small groups of students. The topics and groupings for these lessons were based on the students' needs. Skill and strategy lessons were decided on the basis of observations of student writing, requests for help, and data collected from reading students writing. Students were selected to participate in the skill lessons contingent on their abilities and needs. The same topic with different activities was usually covered for four lessons to help provide sufficient practice. She maintained records on each skill area, carefully monitoring students' progress. Ms. Schlegel realized that teaching the elements of writing as well as teaching writing conventions provided her students with the tools they needed to make progress in their writing.

Remember the following critical points about teaching conventions (Fearn & Farnan, 1998):

- Attention to conventions does not disrupt the flow of writing but is part of the discipline of writing.
- Focus on the conventions of writing does not inhibit growth in writing but facilitates it.
- Teach even young children writing conventions. Very young children can learn simple conventions and perform them automatically (see Figure 9-5).
- Reserve about 20% of the instructional time of students with learning and behavior problems for teaching writing conventions.

Perhaps the most important thing to remember about teaching writing to students with learning and behavior problems is that they require adequate time to write—and to receive scaffolded instruction with feedback from the teacher. However, they also require explicit and systematic instruction in the critical elements and skills necessary for effective writing.

FIGURE 9-5 Instructional Timeline: Awareness to Mastery

Instructional Concept	K	1	2	3	4	5	6	7	8
End Punctuation	*	*	*						
Commas in Dates	*	*	*						
Commas in Series	*	*	*	*					
Commas in Addresses	*	*	*	*					
Apostrophes in Contractions		*	*	*	*				
Periods in Abbreviations		*	*	*	*				
Commas in Compound Sentences			*	*	*				
Punctuation in Dialogue			*	*	*	*			
Apostrophes in Possessives			*	*	*	*			
Commas in Complex Sentences				*	*	*			
Quotation Marks and Underlining in Published Titles				*	*	*			
Commas in Series of Adjectives				*	*	*			
Commas to Set Off Appositives				*	*	*	*		
Commas After Introductory Words				*	*	*	*		
Commas After Introductory Phrases				*	*	*	*		
Commas in Compound-Complex Sentences					*	*	*	*	
Commas to Set Off Parenthetical Expressions					*	*	*		
Dashes and Parentheses to Set Off Parenthetical Expressions					*	*	*	*	
Colons in Sentences					*	*	*	*	
Semicolons in Sentences					*	*	*	*	
Capital Letters to Begin Sentences	*	*	*						
Capital Letters in Names	*	*	*						
Capitalizing	*	*	*						
Capital Letters in Days and Months	*	*	*	*					
Capital Letters in Place Names	*	*	*	*					
Capital Letters in Person's Title		*	*	*	*				
Capital Letters in Published Titles		*	*	*	*				
Capital Letters to Show Nationality, Ethnicity, and Language		*	*	*	*				
Capital Letters in Trade Names, Commercial Products, and Company Names			*	*	*	*			
Capital Letters in Names of Institutions, Associations, and Events			*	*	*	*			

Source: L. Fearn & N. Farnan, *Writing Effectively: Helping Children Master the Conventions of Writing* (Boston: Allyn & Bacon, 1998). Copyright © 1998 by Allyn & Bacon. Reprinted by permission.

Monitoring Student Progress

How does a teacher monitor students' progress in writing? When teachers monitor students' progress on critical elements regularly (at least every 2 weeks), students make improved progress (Gunning, 2010a, b). Teachers record students' progress so that they, the students, and parents can see progress, such as the number of words written for younger children and developing a checklist of story elements and their quality for older students.

In this **video** ▶, the teacher frequently monitors her students' writing to help them progress as writers. What methods does the teacher use to assess her students' writing and plan instruction that supports individual student's needs?

Teachers monitor students' progress by noting the following:

- Whether students can complete the written project
- How proficient they are at each element of the writing process (e.g., planning, spelling, handwriting, accuracy of letter formation, composing)
- Whether they can apply the skills and knowledge to other contexts (e.g., during classes other than a writing class)
- How they explain the process they are using
- Which elements of writing are proceeding as expected (e.g., capital letters) and which require additional instruction (e.g., too many run-on sentences).

See Apply the Concept 9-2 for questions concerning progress monitoring.

Monitoring students' progress in writing involves evaluating written products and observing the writing process. Teachers can observe students as they write and use conference times to assess and record their progress. By observing and examining writing processes and products, teachers can plan instruction to meet

---

9-2   APPLY THE CONCEPT

Questions to Consider in Monitoring Student Progress

Assessing Progress

How does the student respond during the activity?

- Can the student complete the task?
- How comfortably and proficiently is the task completed?
- Can the student explain the process used to complete the task?
- Can the student apply the skills and knowledge to other contexts?
- Are there aspects of the task that are causing difficulties?

Adjusting Instruction

Will different approaches, materials, or settings improve student progress?

Different approaches

- Simplify tasks into small steps.
- Do more modeling or demonstration.
- Provide more review.
- Give more guidance.

Different materials

- Decrease difficulty of the material.
- Use different types of writing genres.
- Provide checklists or cue card.

Different settings

- Use peers to assist.
- Change time of day of instruction.
- Change location of task.

Sources: T. G. Gunning, *Assessing and Correcting Reading and Writing Difficulties* (Boston: Allyn & Bacon, 2010); and B. Rosenshine, Advances in research on instruction, in J. W. Lloyd, E. J. Kame'enui, & D. Chard (Eds.), *Issues in Educating Students with* Disabilities (Mahwah, NJ: Erlbaum, 1997).

individual needs. Many teachers keep anecdotal records by creating a record sheet to quickly document students' progress on writing projects. They include a summary of what they observe, the date, and context, and they list skills and writing strategies that need to be taught. Collections of students' written work help teachers, families, and students document growth and development over the school year. Journals and writing folders also provide insight into writing growth. Teachers may periodically review and select representative pieces to show writing development and use progress monitoring to establish writing goals for students.

Determining how the teacher will measure writing progress for each student requires consideration. For example, for young students, the teacher may monitor the number of words written, number of words spelled correctly, and use of capital letters and punctuation. As students mature in their writing, the teacher may decide to monitor use of adjectives and vivid verbs, facility in editing and revising, and overall quality of the writing. Also, these records of progress monitoring may be kept separately for each type of writing. For example, Mr. Dodge, a middle school teacher, expected students to write an "opinion" piece, a "persuasive" piece, an information report, and a narrative story. He kept separate progress-monitoring forms for each of these genres for each student.

It is important to focus on only one or two things at a time. After students demonstrate progress in the target areas, the teacher can add other elements of writing. This way, progress is recorded, but students are not overwhelmed by the number of writing conventions that they need to monitor.

WEB RESOURCES

For a helpful Web site on progress monitoring in writing, see http://www.progressmonitoring.org.

Scoring Progress Monitoring Assessments

In this **video** ▶, students' writing is assessed in several ways. How does the teacher use a rubric to score her students' writing and provide effective feedback to each student?

Teachers value having time to read, review, and give feedback on students' writing. Teachers also value ongoing progress monitoring as a means of guiding instruction and determining progress. How are these writing samples scored?

Teachers can score students' writing in numerous ways, depending on the information teachers need to guide instruction. Several include:

- You can provide students with a writing prompt and a specified amount of time to write. For younger students 3 minutes is often adequate. For students in middle and high school, you might want to provide 7 to 10 minutes. After students write to the prompt, you can score in several ways including: (1) number of words written, (2) number of words spelled correctly, (3) number of thought units, and or overall quality of the writing.

- You can also score writing samples by using a rubric. There are several rubrics that can be designed based on your instructional goals. For example, view the writing rubric.

- You can use an open-ended assessment in which you provide feedback on the target skill, for example, the main idea and a supporting detail.

- You can use a quantitative score such as a number or grade to rate overall quality.

- You can also use the Common Core Standards for the grade you are teaching and develop a checklist to determine whether students are making progress toward standards.

Elements of Writing: Planning, Composing, Revising, Editing, and Publishing

Effective instruction in writing considers preparing students to effectively use each of the elements of writing: prewriting or planning, composing, revising, editing, and publishing. When students learn to write, they do not proceed through the process in a linear fashion. In fact, many authors circle back through previous elements and jump ahead to later ones when they are writing their drafts. Also, not all writing leads to publishing. For example, Steven realized after he read his draft to his friend Jacob that he needed to have more information about what submarines look like on the inside. He returned to the prewriting stage and checked out several books on submarines so that he could complete his story. Furthermore, students must learn to master these elements in a variety of writing styles, including reports, letters, notes, and persuasive writing.

In prewriting, students collect information about a topic through observing, remembering, interviewing, and reading. When composing, students attempt to get ideas on paper in the form of a draft. This process tells students what they know and do not know. During revising, points are explored further, ideas are elaborated, and further connections are made. When students are satisfied with the content, they edit the piece, reviewing it line by line to determine that each word is necessary. Punctuation, spelling, and other mechanical processes are checked. The final element is publication. If the piece is a good one for the student, it is published. Obviously, not all pieces are published.

Many students with LD experience significant problems in editing and writing final copies because they have difficulty with mechanical skills such as spelling, punctuation, and handwriting. These students often produce well-developed stories that are hard to read because of mechanical errors. Other students with LD have difficulty organizing their first drafts and need to rethink sequencing and order during their revisions.

Graham, Harris, and their colleagues (Graham & Harris, 2005; Lane et al., 2008) have successfully taught students with LD and behavior disorders to use self-regulated strategy development when writing:

1. Think: who will read this, and why am I writing it?

2. Plan what to say using TREE:

   T: Topic Sentence

   R: Reasons

   E: Examine reasons

   E: Ending

3. Write and say more.

Prewriting and Planning Many students find the first hurdle of getting started with writing the most difficult. For many students, whether elementary or secondary, it helps to put a topic at the top of the page. This at least helps them stay focused on what they are writing. For younger students, they can write about what they know and have experienced. For older students, topic choice may be within parameters established by the teacher. For example, they may need to write an information report on a country in the world, but they can pick the country and they can pick the topic. This leaves a lot of room for choice, and for some students with LD, a lot of room for indecision. One of the most important roles the teacher can play is to facilitate decision making about topic selection and sticking with the topic.

> In this **video** ▶, the teacher describes how she prepares her students to begin the writing process. What methods does she use to ensure that her students have a clear understanding of the requirements for their writing? What prewriting strategies does she use to prepare them for expository writing in science class?

For younger students, keeping a list of topics so that they are ready to write is a good idea. Students can also share their topics with the class to spark more ideas for others. Teachers can ask for volunteer students to read their topic lists to the entire group. Now ask the students to expand their ideas for writing and to keep their topic lists in their writing folders. Also tell the students that if they think of new topics they want to write about, they may add them to their lists. Finally, ask the students to select a topic and begin writing. Throughout the school, make opportunities for students to identify additional topics for writing. After they become more comfortable writing and more expert in their use of writing conventions, you can work with students to identify, select, and write about an increasing range of genres including information pieces, reports, persuasive writing, and poetry.

Problems in Topic Selection Whether teachers provide guidance about the writing topic or leave the topic open ended, narrowing down the focus of the topic is challenging for many students. Teachers can also facilitate topic selection by presenting a range of writing styles including stories, factual descriptions, mysteries, persuasive writing, writing that involves comparing and contrasting, reporting on topics, and observing. Students often begin writing by telling personal experiences. Through the writing of other authors, students can be introduced to a wide range of categories that can provide exposure to other genres. Figure 9-6 presents a list of suggestions for students when they are stuck about a topic for writing. One of those suggestions, asking a friend to help, is discussed in Apply the Concept 9-3.

Topic selection is difficult for students of all ages. For older students, topic selection is typically broadly defined by the question or assignment posed by the teacher. But students still have to focus and refine the topic for their

FIGURE 9-6 Focusing on a Topic

- Check your folder and reread your idea list.
- Ask a friend to help you brainstorm ideas.
- Listen to others' ideas.
- Write about what you know: your experiences.
- Write a make-believe story.
- Write about a special interest or hobby.
- Write about how to do something.
- Think about how you got your last idea.

A Friend Helps with Topic Selection

Ruth Ann returned with a piece of blank paper, which she handed to Cary. Cary wrote Ruth Ann's name on the paper and underlined it. Then she conducted a rather sophisticated interview.

"Think of three ideas. Want to write about your first day of school?"

"I can't remember. That was 5 years ago," answered Ruth Ann.

"How about the first day in the learning lab?" continued Cary.

"I don't remember that either. It was over a year ago."

Looking at her idea sheet, Cary commented, "I'm writing about a talking dishwasher. Do you want to write about that?"

"Not really," replied Ruth Ann.

"Where do you go on vacations?" asked Cary.

"To Iowa, but I've already written about that."

"Well, have you ever been to a circus?" Cary pursued.

"No."

"How about a zoo?"

"The Los Angeles Zoo," Ruth Ann answered.

"Do you want to write about that?" asked Cary.

"Yeah," remarked Ruth Ann, "that's a good idea."

Cary wrote the number 1 on the paper she had labeled with Ruth Ann's name, and wrote, "las angels zoo" beside it. She remarked, "I don't know how to spell Los Angeles."

"Don't worry," Ruth Ann commented. "I can find that out when I start writing about it."

"OK, let's think up another idea. Have you ever ridden a horse?" asked Cary as she continued the interview.

"No," replied Ruth Ann.

"Do you have any pets?" asked Cary.

"Yeah, I have a cat named Pierre."

"Do you want to write about him?" continued Cary.

"Yes, I could do that," replied Ruth Ann enthusiastically.

Cary wrote the number 2 on the paper and beside it wrote, "writing about your cat."

The conversation continued, with Cary explaining that it is helpful to think up three ideas so that you have some choice when you decide what to write about. After more questioning, Ruth Ann decided that it would be okay to write about a talking shoe, so Cary wrote down Ruth Ann's third idea. Then Cary helped Ruth Ann decide that she was first going to write about her cat. Cary wrote this idea at the bottom of the page and starred it to note that Ruth Ann had selected this topic. Cary ended the interview by saying, "Put this paper in your writing folder so that the next time you have to select a topic, we'll already have two ideas thought up."

writing. In addition to difficulty in thinking of a topic, immature writers often repeat the same topic. Teachers review students' work and determine whether the stories are changing through vocabulary development, concept development, story development, or character development. It could be that the student is learning a great deal about writing even though the story content is changing very little. The teacher can provide specific examples of other genres and instructional procedures for how to write in these genres.

Prewriting Strategies Many students with learning and behavior problems begin writing without much planning about what they are going to write. They find that when they read their drafts aloud, others have difficulty understanding the story or following the sequence. Students with LD often have limited text organization skills because they have difficulty categorizing ideas related to a specific topic, providing advanced organizers for the topic, and relating and extending ideas about the topic. Consequently, we need to teach students prewriting skills so that the writing and rewriting stages will be easier.

In teaching the organization that goes into writing a piece, teachers can model their thinking as they move from topic selection to writing a first draft. Some teachers find it helpful to teach this thinking process by writing their ideas in an organized structure and by asking students to set goals, brainstorm ideas, and sequence their ideas while they are writing (Troia & Graham, 2002). Some teachers use graphic organizers across curriculum areas to organize writing for both narrative and expository texts.

Planning Strategies Graham and colleagues (Graham et al., 2012) have developed and tested several approaches to improving the writing of students with writing difficulties through applying self-regulated strategy development. Teachers use self-regulated strategy development with students to guide their acquisition and use of learning strategies. There are six steps:

1. *Develop background knowledge.* This refers to understanding when and why the strategy might be used.

2. *Discuss the strategy.* This is where the teacher explains the strategy and how it can be beneficial.

3. *Model.* The teacher models the use and application of the strategy.

4. *Memorize.* The student works to remember the key word and the steps that go with the strategy.

5. *Support use of strategy.* The teacher supports the student's use of the strategy, keying them into when to use it and providing feedback.

6. *Independent practice.* Students are expected to use the writing strategy on appropriate tasks and with proficiency.

So what's an example of a "planning" strategy for writing that has been effectively used with students with learning disabilities? A summary of several of these strategies can be viewed in the following articles and are briefly summarized here (Harris et al, 2008; Mason et al., 2011; Mason & Graham, 2008):

POW

1. **P—P**ick my ideas. Students consider what they are going to write about, identify a topic, and then either brainstorm (younger students) or use resources (older students) to gather information.

2. **O—O**rganize my notes. After identifying the key ideas you want to include in your written product, organize them in the desired order and consider details to include.

3. **W—W**rite and say more. Using your organized ideas as a guide, begin writing. After you finish the draft, reread and write additional sentences and expansions.

For older students (middle and high schoolers) who are required to complete more complex writing tasks, consider adding the following two strategies: PLAN and WRITE (Harris et al., 2008; Mason et al., 2011):

PLAN

1. **P—P**ay attention to the prompt.
2. **L—L**ist main ideas to develop your essay.
3. **A—A**dd supporting details.
4. **N—N**umber major points.

WRITE

1. **W—W**ork from your plan to develop a thesis statement.

2. **R—R**emember your goals. As you write and reread your writing, be sure that your big ideas and supporting details relate directly to your goals.

3. **I—I**nclude transition words for each paragraph. Key transition words help the reader understand what you are writing. Examples include *particularly, notably, similarly, equally, besides, such as, for example, indeed, also, further, moreover, actually.*

4. **T—T**ry to use different kinds of sentences. Consider whether you are using comparing and contrasting sentences, sentences that are longer and shorter, and sentences that link and explain.

5. **E—E**xciting words. Writing is more interesting and engaging when you add exciting words such as more interesting verbs, adverbs, and key concept words that relate to your focus.

Several videos demonstrate aspects of prewriting and planning. You can go to youtube and find the Writing Strategies Sample Clip; also consider finding Pre-Writing Strategies as well as The Writing Process: Prewriting Strategies.

Graphic organizers that are used to assist in writing are referred to as *brainstorm sheets* or *structured organizers, semantic maps,* and *story frames* or *maps.* Although these visual organization devices have been used as aids to reading comprehension, they also serve to facilitate the writing process (MacArthur, Graham, & Fitzgerald, 2008; Mason et al., 2011). Ms. Turk, a resource teacher who works with Ms. Schlegel, used a think-aloud technique to model how to use the brainstorm sheet presented in Apply the Concept 9-4. She drew a large brainstorm sheet on the board and then introduced the brainstorming technique to the students.

Ms. Turk began, "I want to write a story about a time when I was really scared. So I decided to write about the time when I was about 10 years old and my dad and I went for a horseback ride. He got hurt, and I wasn't sure we'd get back to the car. There is so much to remember about this story that I am going to jot down a few ideas so that when I begin to write my story, I can remember them all and put them in order. To help me organize my ideas, I'm going to use a brainstorm sheet."

At this point, Ms. Turk explained the brainstorm sheet and the parts of a story. Through class discussion, the students identified a story they had written recently and each part in their story.

Ms. Turk continued modeling, using the brainstorm sheet. "I am going to call my story 'Horseback Ride' for now. I may want to change the name later, since it's easier for me to think of a title after I write the story. Well, it happened when we were on a trip to Mount Graham. So I'm going to write 'Mt. Graham' by 'Where.' I'm not sure how to spell Mt. Graham, but it doesn't matter that I spell it correctly now. I can find out later. Also, since the brainstorm sheet is for me, I don't have to write sentences—just ideas that will help me remember when I'm writing my first draft of the story." Ms. Turk continued to think aloud as she completed the sheet.

Sample Brainstorm Sheet

Name: Ms. Turk
Date: 2/7
Working Title: Horseback Ride
Setting:
Where: Mt. Graham start at trash dump
When: When I was ten years old
Who: Dad and I, also mom and brother

                  Dad and I were riding on trail. Trail
                  got bad.
Action: Dad's horse stumbled on rock. Dad
                  fell off + hurt his arm. Finally he got
                  on horse. I helped. Rode to top of mt.
                  Mom met us. So did brother. Went to
                  hospital.
Ending: Dad was OK.

Ms. Turk demonstrated that the students did not have to fill in the brainstorm sheet in a linear fashion. Sometimes it is easier to fill out the ending first. She also demonstrated how, after she listed all the ideas under the action section, she could go back and number them in the order that made the most sense.

In subsequent lessons, Ms. Turk demonstrated how to write a story from the brainstorm sheet. She also worked individually with students to complete brainstorm sheets and to use them in their writing.

During the year, Ms. Turk used several different brainstorm sheets with her students in her classroom. Figure 9-7 shows a brainstorm sheet that was developed for expository writing (writing that describes the facts or information about a subject area; often associated with social studies and science). However, the students also used this brainstorm sheet for stories. They wrote the title in the center circle, and information related to the setting, problem, action, and ending in the four other circles and their accompanying lines. Students also developed their own brainstorming sheets. For example, Cary combined topic selection and brainstorming, and developed the brainstorm sheet in Figure 9-8. Graphic organizers can assist students in organizing the key ideas in their writing, remembering the steps in completing a well-written piece, and remembering writing strategies that they need to use.

Teaching students to think about what they are going to say before they write is generally a helpful technique. However, completing a visual representation before writing may not facilitate writing for all students (see Apply the Concept 9-5).

Composing Many students with learning and behavior problems begin the writing process here. They think of a topic and, without much planning, begin to write. If the teacher provides a prompt or question requiring a written response, they spend little time planning their response or jotting down key ideas. Instead they write as little as possible. This is probably why secondary teachers value having time to respond to their students' writing but often are frustrated with the minimal impact of their

FIGURE 9-7 Brainstorm Sheet

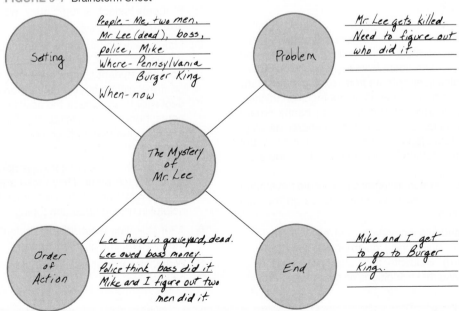

FIGURE 9-8 Cary's Brainstorm Sheet

FIGURE 9-8 Cary's Brainstorm Sheet

feedback on students' progress. Instead, many students with writing difficulties write ideas as they think of them, and each idea they write serves as a stimulus for the next idea. Therefore, effective writing instruction considers providing specific feedback about each element of writing (e.g., composing) and gives students clear strategies for how to successfully compose sentences, paragraphs, and longer essays (Graham et al., 2012).

Some authors suggest using cue cards to assist students in writing better developed stories or essays (De La Paz, 1999). A cue card used by Montague and Leavell (1994) asks students to consider the following elements when composing: where and when, character (have them think and feel just like real people), problem and plan, and story ending. Englert, Raphael, Anderson, Anthony, and Stevens (1991) developed think sheets to assist students in first planning and then organizing their ideas before writing. Figure 9-9 presents the plan think sheet, and Figure 9-10 presents the organization think sheet for the text structure associated with explanations.

> **WEB RESOURCES**
>
> For a helpful Web site on instructional practices in writing for students with LD, see www.ldonline.org.

One of the skills that students must acquire is how to write sentences that are effective and then to organize these effective sentences into meaningful paragraphs. In particular, students with learning problems require instruction in how to

- Add vivid words and lively verbs.
- Combine short and choppy sentences to make more productive sentences.
- Reduce long and run-on sentences.
- Read and revise to add meaning.

9-5 APPLY THE CONCEPT

The Big Picture

A common problem with poor writers is that the surface structure of their writing—the spelling, grammar, and punctuation—prevents them from expressing their ideas in writing and also keeps others from reading them. Many students with learning problems do not focus on thinking about their story. Their stories are often poorly organized, and their ideas are disconnected and/or missing. These same students can *tell* you about the story but have a hard time getting all of the ideas about the story in writing.

Following is the description of a procedure developed by Kucer (1986) to help poor writers focus on the "big picture" of writing:

1. Give students notecards, and allow them to write possible topics on the cards (one topic per card). Students then share ideas about topics and make additions on their topic cards.

2. Students select a topic they want to write about.

3. Major ideas related to the writing topic are written on notecards. The major ideas may come from the student's knowledge and experience or, if the writing is in a content area, the student may need to seek the assistance of class notes, books, and magazines. Major ideas are written as key concepts or thoughts rather than as complete sentences.

4. Students share their major ideas about the topics with each other. They make any additions or comments about the ideas they feel will be helpful in writing about the topics.

5. After selecting major ideas, students organize them in a meaningful sequence.

6. With their cards as a guide, students write their pieces.

FIGURE 9-9 Plan Think Sheet

PLAN

Name _____ Date _____

TOPIC: _____

WHO: Who am I writing for?

_____

_____

WHY: Why am I writing this?

_____

_____

WHAT: What do I know? (Brainstorm)

1. _____
2. _____
3. _____
4. _____
5. _____
6. _____
7. _____
8. _____

HOW: How can I group my ideas?

How will I organize my ideas?

___ Compare/Contrast   ___ Problem/Solution
___ Explanation   ___ Other

Source: C. S. Englert, T. E. Raphael, & L. M. Anderson, *Cognitive Strategy Instruction in Writing Project* (East Lansing, MI: Institute for Research on Teaching, 1989). Reprinted by permission.

FIGURE 9-10 Organization Think Sheet for Text Structure Associated with Explanations

Explanation Organization Form

What is being explained?

Materials/things you need?

Setting?

What are the steps?

First,

Next,

Third,

Then,

Last,

Source: C. S. Englert, T. E. Raphael, & L. M. Anderson, *Cognitive Strategy Instruction in Writing Project* (East Lansing, MI: Institute for Research on Teaching, 1989). Reprinted by permission.

These skills can be taught and practiced separately and then monitored and supported when students write texts. Instructional principles and examples include:

- Teach students to paint a picture with words by using adjectives and adverbs to show readers what they mean. For example, rather than "I ate lunch," the student can write, "I ate my lunch quickly, shoving large bites into my mouth."

- Teach students to avoid using common verbs such as *was, were*, and *said* and instead use more interesting verbs such as *avoided, clamored, quipped, barked, existed,* and *repeated.* In fact, teachers can make lists of words to substitute for more common words and post the lists in the room as a resource. Students can expand the lists themselves by adding more interesting words.

- Teach students to list ideas and then to sequence them (Troia & Graham, 2002).

The Institute for Education Sciences (IES) provides a practice guide for writing instruction with recommendations summarized in Figure 9-11 (Graham et al., 2012).

Revising   Revising is a difficult task for all authors and especially for students with learning problems. Getting the entire message down on paper the first time is difficult enough; making changes so the piece is at its best and can be understood by others is a most formidable task. Many authors need to go back to prewriting and obtain more information, or they spend time conferring with others to find out what parts of their sentences or ideas require additional work. It is also at this stage that some authors abandon the piece. They believe it can never be really good, and so they start again with a new idea.

Most students with learning and behavior problems have difficulty revising and would like to move straight to publication, with little or no revision. Ms. Takamura finds that students will revise their pieces if teachers

FIGURE 9-11 Recommendations from Research on Teaching Writing: IES Practice Guide

---

Recommendation 1
Provide daily time for students to write.

Recommendation 2
Teach students to use the writing process for a variety of purposes.

Recommendation 2a
Teach students the writing process.
1. Teach students strategies for the various components of the writing process.
2. Gradually release writing responsibility.
3. Guide students to select and use appropriate writing strategies.
4. Encourage students to be flexible in their use of the components of the writing process.

Recommendation 2b
Teach students to write for a variety of purposes.
1. Help students understand the different purposes of writing.
2. Expand students' concept of audience.
3. Teach students to emulate the features of good writing.
4. Teach students techniques for writing effectively for different purposes.

Recommendation 3
Teach students to become fluent with handwriting, spelling, sentence construction, typing, and word processing.
1. Teach very young writers how to hold a pencil correctly and form letters fluently and efficiently.
2. Teach students to spell words correctly.
3. Teach students to construct sentences for fluency, meaning, and style.
4. Teach students to type fluently and to use a word processor to compose.

Recommendation 4
Create an engaged community of writers.
1. Teachers should participate as members of the community by writing and sharing their writing.
2. Give students writing choices.
3. Encourage students to collaborate as writers.
4. Provide students with opportunities to give and receive feedback throughout the writing process.
5. Publish students' writing, and extend the community beyond the classroom.

Source: Reprinted with permission from [or Adapted from] Graham, S., Bollinger, A., Booth Olson, C., D'Aoust, C., MacArthur, C., McCutchen, D., & Olinghouse, N. (2012). Teaching Elementary School Students to Be Effective Writers: A Practice Guide (NCEE 2012- 4058). Washington, DC: National Center for Education Evaluation and Regional Assistance, Institute of Education Sciences, U.S. Department of Education. Retrieved from http://ies.ed.gov/ncee/wwc/publications_reviews.aspx#pubsearch.

show them how through the work of other students or the work of professional authors.

Students with LD, particularly adolescents, can learn procedures such as diagnosing, comparing, and operating to assist themselves during the revision process (De La Paz, Swanson, & Graham, 1998). When teachers model, demonstrate, and provide feedback using the Compare and Diagnose procedure, students' revisions and writing improve:

Compare and Diagnose Read your writing and consider the following:

* It ignores the obvious point against my idea.
* There are too few ideas.
* Part of the essay doesn't belong with the rest.
* Part of the essay is not in the right order.

Tactical Operations The listed problems can be fixed by doing the following:

* Rewrite
* Delete
* Add
* Move

Compare Reread the paper, and highlight problems.

Diagnose and Operate Read your writing, and determine whether any of the following apply:

* This doesn't sound right.
* This isn't what I intended to say.
* This is an incomplete idea.
* This part is not clear.
* The problem is _____.

Teachers can show students how to use a "box and explode" strategy as a means for selecting the one sentence in their writing that is the most important but may not be adequately expanded (Block, 1997; Gersten & Baker, 2001; Strickland, Ganske, & Monroe, 2002). Students learn to put this sentence in a box and then to use it as a focus for extending the idea and clarifying story events. Students are taught to "explode" the main idea in the box. For example, suppose a student wrote the following paragraph:

> Julia went to her aunt's house on Sunday. After she got there she saw that her aunt's door was open. She walked in the house and saw her uncle on the floor. She didn't know what to do.

Students would be taught to put a box around the sentence "She walked in the house and saw her uncle on the floor." Then they would work to "explode" that sentence so that the reader would learn more about what happened.

For older students, it is often helpful to occasionally use collaborative writing and revision. This provides students with learning disabilities with a peer to facilitate the process and encourage revising (J. J. Lo, Wang, & Yeh, 2009).

Editing In addition to editing their own work, students serve as editors for the work of their peers. Whereas revision focuses mainly on content, editing focuses mainly on mechanics. After the student and teacher are happy with the content, it is time to make corrections for spelling, capitalizing, punctuation, and language. Students are expected to circle words they are unsure how to spell, put

FIGURE 9-12 Editing Rules

Ⓒircle misspelled words.
Put a box around punctuation.
Underline writing that doesn't sound so good.
Add a ^ to insert a word or phrase.
Add a ^ with a number to insert a sentence.

boxes in places where they are unsure of the punctuation, and underline the sentences about which they feel the language may not be correct. Figure 9-12 provides a poster that can be used in a classroom to remind students of the editing rules. Apply the Concept 9-6 provides guidelines for how teachers and peers might respond to writing.

Although many spelling, punctuation, and language modifications are made during writing and revising, when students edit, they focus solely on mechanical errors. Often, they need to read the text for each type of error. First, they read the text looking for spelling difficulties; next, they read the text looking for punctuation and capitalization difficulties; and finally, they read the text looking for language problems such as noun–verb agreement. Young students may not know what noun–verb agreement

9-6 APPLY THE CONCEPT

Ways for Teachers and Peers to Respond to Writing

Suggestions to Compliment Writing

- I like the way your paper began because . . .
- I like the part where . . .
- I like the way you explained . . .
- I like the order you used in your paper because . . .
- I like the details you used to describe . . .
- I like the way you used dialogue to make your story sound real.
- I like the words you used in your writing, such as . . .
- I like the facts you used, like . . .
- I like the way the paper ended because . . .
- I like the mood of your writing because it made me feel . . .

Questions and Suggestions to Improve Writing

- I got confused in the part about . . .
- Could you add an example to the part about . . . ?
- Could you add more to this _____ part because . . . ?

- Do you think your order would make more sense if you . . . ?
- Do you think you could leave this part out, because . . . ?
- Could you use a different word for _____, because . . . ?
- Is this _____ paragraph on one topic?
- Could you write a beginning sentence to grab your readers?

The following suggestions are designed to assist students in removing the mechanical errors from their writing (Isaacson & Gleason, 1997):

- Have students dictate their story to improve the flow of their writing.
- Provide students with a list of key words and words that are hard to spell to assist with writing and editing.
- Teach students to use a word book.
- Promote peer collaboration in editing.
- Teach students to use technology to support editing and writing.
- Hold students accountable for using the rules of writing they know, such as punctuation, spelling, and other writing conventions that they have been taught.

is, so they should simply look for sentences that do not "sound right" when they read them aloud.

Publishing What does it mean to have a piece published? A piece is prepared in some way that it can be read and shared by others. For younger students this may be in the form of books that have cardboard binding decorated with contact paper, scraps of wallpaper, or clip art. Sometimes these books include a picture of the author, a description of the author, and a list of books published by the author.

Older students who spend more time composing and revising are more likely to "publish" or "publicly share" work that is the result of many weeks of effort and several revisions. Why publish? Publishing is a way of confirming a student's hard work and sharing the piece with others. Writing requires an audience, and periodically we need to share what we write. It is important for all students to publish—not just the best authors. Publishing is a way of involving others in the school and home with the students' writing.

WEB RESOURCES

For additional information on writing and spelling practices for teachers and parents, see http:// k12reader.com.

The Writing Conference Conferring is the heart of the writing process. Experienced writing teachers acknowledge that although conferencing with students about their writing is time consuming, there is simply no better way to be sure that you understand what they are trying to accomplish in their writing and can give the type of feedback to help them with corrections (Kuriloff, 2010).

Successful writing conferences begin with questions from the teacher. Students also know that they will be asked challenging questions about their work. Questions are not asked in a rapid-fire sequence with little time for the student to formulate answers. Instead, questions are carefully selected, and enough time is allowed for the student to respond. Conferences focus on specific areas and are not designed to address all elements of writing. For example, during the conference with the author of the essay shown in Apply the Concept 9-7, "My Best Football Game," the teacher realized that the writing had many problems. She was aware of grammatical, spelling, and punctuation errors. She was also aware that the story rambled, lacked sufficient details, and did not reflect the author's voice. However, she was ecstatic that this 14-year-old student with severe emotional problems had produced a piece of writing that he was excited about. Apply the Concept 9-8 presents the conference the teacher had with the student.

9-7 APPLY THE CONCEPT

Sample Student Writing

"My Best Football Game"

Football is my favorite game I like to play it even when I was little I played for a good team the bandits and one game we played against Macarther school and it started off with us 0 and them 7 and then the game was tied 7 to 7 and then it was time for me to sit on the bench and the score was 7-14 we was winning soon they told me to go back into the game it was getting close to the end and we wanted to win they said it was my turn to run a play and so I ran fast down the feild after the ball was Mike and I look back and see the ball coming right at me and I thought I was going to miss it but I kept looking at it and after I watched it I reached up and pulled the ball down and I kept on running and we won the game 7 to 21.

Some key points about conferring with students follow:

- Do not attempt to get the writer to write about a topic because it is of interest to you or to write the story the way you would write it.

- Ask the student what steps in the writing process the student used to develop this piece.

- If you have taught one of the previously presented strategies (e.g., POW), ask the student to review how he or she applied the strategy.

- Ask questions that teach. (Apply the Concept 9-9 illustrates a conference in which the teacher asks questions that teach.)

- Agree on the steps the student will take to improve the paper, and establish a procedure for checking that these activities occur.

- Conferences should be frequent and brief. Although conferences can range from 30 seconds to 10 minutes, most of them last only 2 to 3 minutes with younger children and longer with older students.

Establishing a Writing Community For students to write well within their classroom, an environment of mutual trust and respect is essential. Establishing a writing community requires that you take the following steps:

1. *Write every day for at least 30 minutes.* Students need time to think, write, discuss, rewrite, confer, revise, talk, read, and write some more. Good writing takes time.

Conferencing with the Author of "My Best Football Game"

Teacher: Mark, this football game was a special one for you. I bet you have a lot of feelings about this game. What are some of your feelings about this game?

Mark: I felt good.

Teacher: Did you feel good like when you remember your homework or was it stronger than that?

Mark: It was stronger. I felt great. Like I was a hero or something.

Teacher: Like a hero?

Mark: Yeah, like in the movies. I really saved the game. Well, I guess not really saved the game because we were already winning. But it was, like, 'cause I made the last touchdown it really said something.

Teacher: What do you think it said?

Mark: It said, hey, watch out 'cause I'm good. Also, that we won and I scored the final points. It was great.

Teacher: What could you do so the reader of your piece would know all of the things you just told me?

Mark: I guess I could include more about how I felt and all.

Teacher: How could you do that? Where would it go?

The teacher decided it was too early to focus on mechanical errors such as spelling and punctuation. Besides being discouraging to Mark, focusing too early on mechanical errors would sidetrack this writer from the story. After the author's story is complete, then work on mechanical errors can begin.

2. *Encourage students to develop areas of expertise.* Younger students write about what they know. However, with encouragement, both younger and older students can become experts in a particular area, subject, or writing form.

3. *Keep students' writing in folders.* Folders should include writing as documentation of what each student knows and has accomplished. Students can refer to their work to illustrate their progress, to indicate skills learned, and to demonstrate range of topic.

4. *Monitor students' progress, establish writing goals, and hold students accountable for learning and practicing what they know.* Together, identify the expected goals for each student, discuss what aspects of these goals are achieved and represented in their writing, and guide rewriting and skills lessons to ensure that these goals are met.

5. *Share writing.* Provide training to students and opportunities for them to share and give feedback to each other.

Conferencing: Following the Lead of the Student

During conferences, the teacher listens to what students say, follows the lead of the students, and asks questions that teach:

Teacher: How's it going, Karin?

Karin: Not very good. I don't know what to write about.

Teacher: You are having trouble with a topic?

Karin: I was going to write about how I want to go and live with my real mom again but I don't know what to say. All I do is write that I want to live with my real mom and then the story is over.

Teacher: It's hard to think of what else might go in the story?

Karin: Well, yeah. I guess I could tell why, but I don't know why, I just want to.

Teacher: Would it be any easier to get started if you told the story as though it were about someone else?

Karin: Like I could tell about a kid who wanted to go and live with her real mom. Then I could tell it like a story.

Teacher: What are some of the things you might write if you told the story this way?

6. *Expand the writing community outside of the classroom.* Place published books by your students in the library for use by other students, and allow students to share their writing with other classes. Encourage authors from other classrooms to visit and read their writings.

7. *Develop students' capacity to evaluate their own work.* Students need to develop their own goals and document their progress toward them.

8. *Facilitate spelling during writing.* Teachers and students can provide instructional feedback to support students in spelling correctly during the writing process. (See Apply the Concept 9-10 for suggestions.)

9. *Assist students who are culturally and linguistically diverse.* With a few adjustments, teachers can create classroom communities that promote their success and learning. See Apply the Concept 9-11 for suggestions.

10. *Remember to teach students specific strategies for writing purposefully* such as compare and contrast, reports, persuasive writing, and interviews.

The writing process approach to instruction of students who have special needs requires time—time to follow the progress of students, confer with students, and teach skills. Most important, it requires time each day for the students to write. (See Apply the Concept 9-12.)

9-10 APPLY THE CONCEPT

Providing Instructional Feedback to Facilitate Spelling Correctly

Prompts to Help Students Notice Errors

- Check to see if that looks/sounds right.
- There is a tricky word on this line.
- You are nearly right.
- Try that again.
- Try it another way.
- You have almost got that. See if you can find what is wrong.

Prompts to Help Students Find Errors

- Find the part that is not right.
- Look carefully to see what's wrong.
- You noticed something was wrong.
- Where is the part that is not right?
- What made you stop?
- Can you find the problem spot?

Prompts to Help Students Fix Errors

- What do you hear first? Next? Last?
- What word starts with those letters?
- Do you think it looks/sounds like?
- What does an *e* do at the end of a word?
- What do you know that might help?
- What could you try?
- You have only one letter to change.
- That sounds right, but does it look right?
- One more letter will make it right.

- It starts like that. Now check the last part.
- Did you write all the sounds you hear?
- Did you write a vowel for each syllable?
- It starts (ends) like _____.
- There is a silent letter in that word.
- You wrote all the sounds you hear. Now look at what you wrote—think!

Prompts of Encouragement

- I like the way you worked that out.
- The results are worth all your hard work.
- You have come a long way with this one.
- That was some quick thinking.
- That looks like an impressive piece of work.
- You are right on target.
- You are on the right track now.
- Now you have figured it out.
- That is quite an improvement.
- That is quite an accomplishment.
- That is coming along.
- You are really settling down to work.
- You have shown a lot of patience with this.
- You have been paying close attention.
- You have put in a full day today.
- I knew you could finish it.
- You make it look so easy.
- You have really tackled that assignment.
- This shows you have been thinking/working.
- It looks like you have put a lot of work into this.

Sources: Adapted from I. C. Fountas & G. S. Pinnell, *Guided Reading: Good First Teaching for All Children* (Portsmouth, NH: Heinemann, 1996); I. C. Fountas & G. S. Pinnell, *Word Matters: Teaching Phonics and Spelling in the Reading/Writing Classroom* (Portsmouth, NH: Heinemann, 1998); and E. B. Fry, J. E. Kress, & D. L. Fountoukidis, *The Reading Teacher's Book of Lists* (New York: Center for Applied Research in Education, 1993).

Considerations for Students Who Are Culturally and Linguistically Diverse

Creating a learning community in the classroom that provides opportunities for all students to succeed is essential to promoting effective written expression. A few guidelines follow:

- Have high expectations for all students. Teachers demonstrate respect and provide opportunities when they treat each student as an able writer and provide the support necessary to ensure their success.

- Allow students to write about topics they know and have experienced. Students with diverse backgrounds and experiences should be viewed as having a rich source of material for writing. Students benefit when they are encouraged to tap into their backgrounds and experiences and to share them with others.

- Allow students to teach all of us about their backgrounds and experiences through their writing.

Students' writing can be viewed as an opportunity for them to better inform us about themselves, their families and communities, and their interpretations of them. Students will want to write when they perceive that their writing has a purpose and is instructive to others.

- Create a classroom setting that is culturally compatible. The social organization of the classroom can facilitate or impair the written expression of students from diverse cultures. Whole-class instructional formats with high expectations for students to volunteer to answer questions may not be compatible with their cultural backgrounds. Read and ask questions about the cultures of the students in your classroom so that you can establish a writing lab that is responsive to their learning styles.

- Use materials, stories, and books that are culturally relevant. Read stories about a range of cultures to students. Encourage students to exchange stories that are culturally familiar. Provide examples of cultures that are similar and different from the ones represented in your classroom.

Using Computers to Facilitate Writing

The use of spell checkers and speech synthesizers to facilitate writing effectiveness for students with LD has been well documented (Graham & Perin, 2007; MacArthur, 1988; McNaughton, Hughes, & Ofiesh, 1997). These tools can be used to assist students whose writing or motor skills interfere with their ability to develop independent writing skills. Displaying writing on a computer monitor facilitates discussion between students and teachers and allows for immediate and easy editing (Zorfass, Corley, & Remz, 1994). When a computer-based speech recognition program was provided to college students with LD, the students performed significantly better on tasks of written expression than did students without the speech recognition program and as well as those who had an assistant (Higgins & Raskind, 1995).

Computers facilitate writing for students with learning problems because they do the following:

- Make revising and editing easier.

- Increase the amount and quality of revision completed.

- Provide spell-checking features.

- Produce neat printed copies that enhance readability.

- Allow for easy error correction (MacArthur et al., 1995).

- Increase the amount of time they spend on the task (Wade-Stein & Kintsch, 2004).

- Improve the quality of writing (Wade-Stein & Kintsch, 2004).

Response to Intervention and Writing

How might response to intervention be used for students with writing difficulties? Students with extreme writing challenges might be provided extra time each day (20 minutes) and extra instruction to determine if their writing improves. Specific research-based strategies might be implemented (Mason et al., 2011). Teachers can maintain copies of students' writing to determine if adequate progress in writing has occurred.

Improving the Writing of Older Students

Most of the practices described in this chapter are designed to be used with a broad range of learners. However, the crisis in the overall poor quality of students' writing has provided a push for improving the writing of older students. Recently, the Carnegie Corporation of New York (Graham & Perin, 2007) issued a report on effective writing practices for older students (grades 4 to 12). They suggest the following research-based practices:

- Teach students writing strategies that include planning, revising, and editing their compositions.

Ten Pointers for Teaching Writing to Students with Special Learning Needs

1. *Allocate adequate time for writing.* Adequate time is a necessary but not sufficient criterion for improving the writing skills of special learners. Students who merely spend 10 to 15 minutes a day practicing the craft of writing are not spending adequate time to improve their skills. Students need a minimum of 30 minutes of time for writing every day.

2. *Provide a range of writing tasks.* Writing about what students know best—self-selected topics—is the first step in writing. After students' skills improve, the range of writing tasks should broaden to include problem solving, writing games, and a variety of writing tasks.

3. *Create a social climate that promotes and encourages writing.* Teachers set the tone through an accepting, encouraging manner. Conferences between students, students and teachers, and students and other persons in the school are conducted to provide constructive feedback on their writing and to provide an audience to share what is written.

4. *Integrate writing with other academic subjects.* Writing can be integrated with almost every subject that is taught. This includes using writing as a means of expression in content area subjects such as social studies and science as well as part of an instructional activity with reading and language arts.

5. *Focus on the processes central to writing.* These processes include prewriting activities, writing, and rewriting activities.

6. *During the writing phase, focus on the higher order task of composing, and attend to the basic elements of spelling and punctuation after the writing is complete.* Some students' mechanics of writing are so poor that they interfere with the students' ability to get ideas down on paper successfully. With these students, focus first on some of the basic elements so that the writing process can be facilitated.

7. *Teach explicit knowledge about characteristics of good writing.* The implicit knowledge about writing needs to be made explicit. For example, different genres and their characteristics need to be discussed and practiced.

8. *Teach skills that aid higher-level composing.* These skills include conferencing with teachers and peers, and strategy instruction. Strategy instruction may provide guidelines for brainstorming, sentence composition, or evaluating the effectiveness of the written piece.

9. *Ask students to identify goals for improving their writing.* Students can set realistic goals regarding their progress in writing. These goals can focus on prewriting, writing, and/or rewriting. Both the students and the teacher can provide feedback as to how successful the students have been in realizing their goals.

10. *Use instructional practices that are associated with improved writing for students.* Several examples of instructional practice not associated with improved writing are grammar instruction, diagramming sentences, and overemphasis on students' errors.

Sources: Adapted from S. Graham & K. Harris (2006), Preventing writing difficulties: Providing additional handwriting and spelling instruction to at-risk students in 1st grade, *Teaching Exceptional Children, 38*(5), pp. 64–66; and S. Graham & K. R. Harris (1988), Instructional recommendations for teaching writing to exceptional students, *Exceptional Children, 54*(6), pp. 506–512.

(Many of the writing strategies discussed previously were developed to meet this recommendation.)

- Help students combine sentences to achieve more complex sentence types and to summarize texts.
- Provide opportunities for students to work together in pairs and groups toward cooperative written products to facilitate quality of composition.
- Establish goals for students' writing to improve outcomes.
- Give students access to and instruction in word processing to facilitate writing.
- Assist students in developing prewriting practices that help generate or organize ideas for writing.
- Use inquiry activities to analyze data related to writing reports.
- Provide extended time for writing and revision.
- Provide students with good models of writing to study and to compare with their own writing.
- Use writing as a tool to enhance content knowledge.

Teaching Writing in the Content Areas

The Common Core State Standards encourage reading and writing of information text. In fact, by fourth grade, half of what students read and write about should include information text. All of the content areas, but particularly social studies, history, and science, provide excellent resources for writing. As students enter high school, they are applying writing increasingly within their academic disciplines (e.g., history), addressing such questions as "What role and influence did Ben Franklin have after the Revolution?" These kinds of questions encourage students to read authentic texts, integrate across texts, and to formulate their own response (Turner & Kearns, 2010).

What are the key common core standards as they relate to promoting writing in history/social studies, science, and technical subjects in grades 6 to 12?

In this **video** ▶, a teacher discusses how she encourages her students to learn the scientific process, use content area vocabulary, and enhance their hypothesis-writing skills in her science class. How can these strategies be used in other content area classes in similar ways?

- Write arguments focused on discipline-specific content. Teachers facilitate students' use of text and other resources to make and justify claims.

- Write informative/explanatory tests, including the narration of historical events, scientific procedures/experiments, or technical processes. Students learn to use discipline-specific constructs and ideas and relate them across resources, providing elaborate descriptions and justifications for their conclusions.

- Produce clear and coherent writing in which the development, organization, and style are appropriate to task, purpose, and audience.

- Develop and strengthen writing in planning, revising, editing, and rewriting for a specific audience and purpose.

- Use technology to produce, publish, and update individual and shared writing, making adjustments as a function of feedback.

- Conduct research projects to address questions (generated by teachers and self-generated), synthesizing findings from multiple sources.

- Gather and use relevant credible information from multiple sources.

- Use evidence from information texts to analyze, reflect, and research.

- Write routinely over extended time frames, including time for reflection and revision for a range of discipline-specific tasks.

As you can see from this summary of the Common Core Standards as they relate to writing in the content area, students with learning and behavior problems will have increased expectations for writing across all of their content areas. For students with writing difficulties, special education teachers will increasingly need to provide instruction and support to ensure that they can meet these demands. What are some of the instructional practices you can implement to facilitate success in writing in the content areas? Some useful practices include the following:

1. Teach students how to determine whether texts and other resources are credible. Identify topics your students are studying, for example, "cells" in biology, or "westward movement" in history. Ask students to search for information on the Web related to these topics. After they identify information, ask them to "rate" on a 1 to 3 scale their confidence in the credibility of the information and how they determined the rating. Provide feedback and guidance until students improve in locating credible resources.

2. Assist students in using more than one resource to formulate a claim. Initially, start with two resources that are rather brief and have similar ideas. Gradually move to showing students more complex and original resources. Ask students to determine their key points, ways they agree and disagree, and how they might use the documents to write and support a claim. Gradually increase in difficulty and reducing support until students can write independent claims.

3. Facilitate assignments that require students to revise and contribute to a long-term written product. Using topics and research reports required in their content area classes, assist students in organizing and writing to develop a research report that depends on sources, responds to ongoing teacher and peer feedback, and develops over a long period (multiple classes and homework assignments).

4. Time spent on writing instruction in the content area facilitates improved writing and improved learning of the content (Klein & Kirkpatrick, 2010). Many teachers worry that additional time spent on writing during content instruction will detract from content learning, but effective instruction of writing within the content area benefits learning as well.

Berninger and Wolf (2009) provide sample lessons on teaching writing in the content area for students with writing difficulties.

See Spotlight on Diversity: Guidelines for Teaching Writing to Students Who Are English-Language Learners.

Spotlight *on Diversity*

Guidelines for Teaching Writing to Students Who Are English Language Learners

Students' writing is influenced by several factors: their knowledge of the English language, English vocabulary development, understanding of word use, and knowledge of the conventions of writing such as noun–verb agreement. Many of the approaches to writing that are discussed in this chapter are highly appropriate for students who are English language learners (ELLs). Teachers should ask themselves the following questions when planning writing instruction for students who are ELLs (Cloud, Genesee, & Hamayan, 2009; Haley & Austin, 2004):

- Do they know what they want to write about?

- Do they feel comfortable using their personal, family, and other relevant experiences in their writing?

- Do they use what they know to support their writing?

- What ways are helpful to get them to start thinking about their composition?

- Do they try to use new words in their writing?

- Do they get suggestions for their writing from family and friends?

- Do they use procedures for deciding what is important and not important in their writing?

- Do they choose different ways to express their ideas and feelings in their writing?

- Do they increasingly use more appropriate and effective language in their writing?

Assessing and Teaching Spelling

What are the critical features of spelling assessment and instruction for students with learning and behavior problems? Most students with learning and behavior disorders need specific instruction in spelling and handwriting, largely as a function of their phonological awareness problems and their inadequate exposure to print. The core phonological deficit is associated with not only reading problems but also spelling problems. Also, students with reading problems read fewer words; therefore, through spelling instruction, they are exposed to the orthography of spelling related to improved spelling.

> Chapter 7 discusses phonological awareness.

Manuel hates spelling and finds it the most frustrating part of writing. He is an eighth-grade student who is adjusting to the transition from a self-contained classroom for students with emotional disabilities to a resource room in a middle school setting. He has learned to use writing to express his feelings, convey information, and create stories. Manuel is proud of the way his writing has improved, and he often shares his stories with others. But he has difficulty with spelling. Manuel has learned to use inventive spelling (spelling words the way they sound or the way he thinks they are spelled) to aid in getting his ideas on paper, but he has difficulty editing because he is unable to detect or correct most of his spelling errors. Like many students with learning and behavior disorders, Manuel needs specialized instruction in spelling to be a successful writer.

Spelling is an important tool in our society. Many people measure one's intelligence or education by their ability to spell. Spelling is particularly difficult in the English language because there is not a one-to-one correspondence between the individual sounds of spoken words and the letters of the written words. Spelling instruction is particularly important for students with reading disabilities because they demonstrate difficulties in spelling long term (Newman Fields, & Wright, 2011). We learn to spell many words by remembering the unique combination or order of letters that produce the correct spelling of that word. We also learn to spell words by being taught the word parts such as blends (/str/, /cl/, /pr/) combinations, as well as silent-letter rules (long vowel with silent e) to help us become better spellers (Moats, 2009).

Spelling facilitates the writing process by freeing the writer to concentrate on content. Although many students with LD have spelling difficulties, spelling is often difficult even for those without an LD. Most beginning writers identify spelling as the key problem they need to solve in writing. Many good readers are poor spellers, and almost all poor readers are poor spellers. The spelling of older students with reading disabilities is similar to the spelling of average readers who are much younger (Bourassa, Treiman, & Kessler, 2006).

Error Analysis

The first step in developing an appropriate spelling program is to determine the type and pattern of the students' spelling errors. After completion of an error analysis, a spelling approach based on students' needs can be implemented.

Error analysis should be done by using both dictated spelling tests and a student's written work. When Manuel and his teacher, Laurie Redwing, attempted to develop Manuel's spelling program, they began by selecting samples of his written work, which included writing he had created and work written from dictation. Ms. Redwing examined these pieces to determine whether there was a pattern to his spelling errors. Ms. Redwing asked herself the following questions about Manuel's spelling:

- Is he applying mistaken rules?
- Is he applying rules that assist him in remembering spellings?
- Is he making careless errors on words he knows how to spell?
- Is he spelling words correctly in isolation but not in context?
- Are there frequently used words that he is consistently misspelling?

After examining the written work and answering these questions, Ms. Redwing discovered the following:

- Manuel did not apply the *-ing* rule appropriately. For example, *run* became *runing*.
- Manuel did not use the spelling rule "*i* before *e* except after *c*." For example, he spelled *believe* as *beleive* and *piece* as *peice*.
- He was inconsistent in spelling words. He would spell them correctly in one piece of written work but not in another.
- He spelled several words correctly on spelling tests but not in context.
- He misspelled many frequently used words, such as *there, was, because, somewhere, very,* and *would*.

After answering the questions, Ms. Redwing examined Manuel's work to look for the following error patterns:

- Additions of unneeded letters (e.g., *boxxes*)
- Omissions of letters (e.g., *som*)
- Reflections of mispronunciations (e.g., *ruf* for *roof*)
- Reflections of dialect (e.g., *sodar* for *soda*)
- Reversals of whole words (e.g., *eno* for *one*)
- Reversals of consonant order (e.g., *cobm* for *comb*)
- Reversals of consonant or vowel directionality (e.g., *Thrusday* for *Thursday*)

- Phonetic spellings of nonphonetic word parts (e.g., *site* for *sight*)
- Neographisms, which are spellings that don't resemble the word (e.g., *sumfin* for *something*)
- Combinations of error patterns

In addition to examining Manuel's work, Ms. Redwing interviewed and observed Manuel to determine what strategies he used when he was unable to spell a word and whether he used any corrective or proofreading strategies after he wrote. Ms. Redwing observed Manuel's writing and then asked him the following two questions:

1. *When you finish writing a piece, what do you do?* (Ms. Redwing was attempting to determine whether Manuel rereads for spelling errors.)
2. *If you are writing and do not know how to spell a word, what do you do?* (Ms. Redwing was attempting to determine what, if any, strategies he used. Did he use invented spelling to facilitate the writing process and underline the word so that he could check the spelling later? Did he stop and try to visualize the word or look for how it was spelled in another location? Did he continue writing and go back later to check the spelling?)

Ms. Redwing discovered that Manuel used few strategies to check or recall spelling when he was writing. In addition to teaching and rehearsing spelling rules, Manuel needed to learn and apply strategies for improving his spelling. After error analysis, intervention included discussing with Manuel the types of errors he was making, teaching him proofreading skills, teaching him techniques for remembering the correct spelling of words, and teaching him one of the spelling approaches discussed in the following subsections. Before looking at specialized approaches to teaching spelling to students with learning and behavior disorders, we will first examine traditional approaches to spelling instruction.

Traditional Spelling Instruction

Spelling is taught in most classrooms through an integrated reading and writing approach. Some classroom teachers prescribe a list of weekly words to be mastered by all students (Fresch, 2007). In the usual procedure, a pretest occurs on Monday, followed on Tuesday by a description of the spelling theme (e.g., long *e* words, homophones, *au* words). Wednesday and Thursday typically involve assignments from the text that students work on independently that involve practice

> In this **video** ▶, observe how the teacher assists her students in learning new spelling words. How does she model the learning process for them? What opportunities do the students have to practice using their new spelling words?

spelling the key words or using them in sentences. These assignments usually include dictionary activities; sentence or paragraph writing using the spelling words; writing the words a designated number of times; and using the words in sentences, stories, or crossword puzzles. Friday is usually designated for the posttest in spelling.

How effective is this procedure for teaching spelling to students with LD? What other procedures might need to be considered in developing effective spelling strategies for these students? The spelling practices used in most classrooms are based more on tradition than on research (Fresch, 2007). For most students with learning difficulties, the introduction of all the words at once, often words that are not in the students' reading vocabularies, and the lack of systematic practice and specific feedback make spelling difficult if not impossible. Students with LD acquire proficiency as spellers when they know the meaning of the word and are asked to learn to spell fewer words at a time.

Phonics Rules for Spelling

How much emphasis should be placed on teaching phonics rules to improve spelling? Evidence suggests that students who are taught spelling alongside code-based (phonics) reading instruction improve in both spelling and word reading (Moats, 2009; O'Connor & Jenkins, 1995). At least for young children, a code-based approach to reading and spelling is likely to be both necessary and helpful. Students with learning problems require systematic and explicit instruction in phonics rules and how these rules relate to writing words. Thus, students need to be taught the clear connection between phonics rules in reading and spelling.

Because there is a lack of consistency in phonics rules, primary emphasis should be given to basic spelling vocabulary with supplemented instruction in basic phonics rules as well as the meanings of word parts and influence of vocabulary. For example, the word parts associated with prefixes and suffixes convey meaning, as do base words such as *friend* (e.g., *friendship, friendly, friendless*). Knowing the meaning of words also helps with spelling. For example, in English many words sound the same but are spelled differently (e.g., *there, their*). The spelling conveys the meaning. Teaching students common *homonyms*—words that sound the same, are spelled differently, and convey different meaning—can help them be better spellers and writers. A sample of common homonyms follows:

> To, too, two
>
> Pain, pane
>
> Whether, weather
>
> Witch, which
>
> Accept, Except
>
> Great, grate

Principles for Teaching Spelling to Students with Learning Difficulties

Several principles should be included in any spelling approach that is used in teaching students who have learning problems.

Teach in Small Units   Teach 3 words a day rather than 4 or 5 (or 15 at the beginning of the week). In a study (N. D. Bryant, Drabin, & Gettinger, 1981) in which the number of spelling words allocated each day to students with LD was controlled, higher performance, less distractibility, and less variance in overall performance were obtained from the group with LD assigned 3 words a day, when compared with groups assigned 4 and 5 words a day.

Teach Spelling Patterns   If the spelling lists each week are based on spelling patterns, students have a better chance of learning and remembering them. Several sample word lists based on patterned spelling follow:

List 1	List 2	List 3	List 4
cat	am	aim	pianos
bat	slam	claim	cellos
rat	clam	chain	patios
fat	tram	rain	sopranos
sat	tam	train	stereos
can	Pam	gain	potatoes
fan	same	regain	studios
ran	fame	brain	ratios
man	tame	pain	volcanoes
tan	blame	afraid	echoes
	flame	braid	
	frame		

You may also want to use contrast words to assist in identifying and teaching spelling patterns. Thus, the spelling patterns in the fourth list provide two contrasting patterns for adding *s* to words that end in *o*.

Provide Sufficient Practice and Feedback   Give students opportunities to practice the words each day and provide feedback. Many teachers do this by having students work with spelling partners who ask them their words and provide immediate feedback. The following method can be used for self-correction and practice. Fold a paper into five columns. Write the correctly spelled words in the first column. The student studies one word, folds the column back, and writes the word in the second column. The student then checks his or her spelling with the correctly spelled word in the first column. After folding the column back, the student writes the word in the third column. The student continues writing the word

Peer Tutoring and Spelling

Use of peer tutors to teach spelling can be helpful in improving spelling for the tutors and the tutees. When a peer-tutoring system was used with students with LD and a good speller from the same classroom, the spelling performance of the student with LD improved and both students rated the peer-tutoring system favorably (Maheady & Gard, 2010; Okilwa & Shelby, 2010). To increase effectiveness, peer tutors should be trained to implement the spelling approach that is most suitable for the target student.

until it has been spelled correctly three times. The student then moves to the next word and continues until the word is spelled correctly three times in a row. This procedure should not be confused with spelling assignments that require the student to write the assigned spelling words a designated number of times. Those procedures are often ineffective because the student does not attend to the details of the spelling word as a whole, often writes the word in segments, and usually copies rather than writing from memory. The student also fails to check words each time after writing, sometimes resulting in words being practiced incorrectly. Adding peer tutoring can help to alleviate these problems (see Apply the Concept 9-13).

Select Appropriate Words   The most important strategy for teaching spelling is that the students can already read the word and know its meaning. Spelling should not focus on teaching the students to read and know the meaning of words. Selection of spelling words should be based on the students' reading and meaning vocabularies. Ideally, high-frequency words should be used.

Teach Spelling Through Direct Instruction   Incidental learning in spelling is reserved primarily for good spellers. Spelling words can be selected from the students' reading or written words or can be part of a programmed text, such as lists provided in basal readers. Direct instruction includes mastery of specific words each day, individualized instruction, and continual review.

Use Instructional Language   The language of instruction, or the dialogue between teachers and students, is critical to success in spelling, particularly for youngsters with learning and behavior problems. Gerber and Hall (1989) indicate that a teacher's language provides a structure that calls attention to critical relationships within and

between words and also isolates critical letter sequences. For example, "You wrote 'nife'; however, the word *knife* starts with a silent letter. It is very unusual, and you just have to remember that it is there. Think about the letter *k* as looking like an open jackknife, and remember that the word *knife* starts with a *k*."

How do you implement peer tutoring for spelling? There are several different approaches (see for review, Maheady & Gard, 2010) but a simple way to get started follows:

1. Arrange for students to work in pairs. Some teachers assign pairs so that a better speller and a poorer speller work together.
2. Provide students with explicit directions for working together. For example, "You will practice 4 words each day until you can spell them without error. You will review the previous words you learned that week to make sure you don't forget them."
3. "Test each other on the words for the day and the previous words for the week. Use the spelling practice strategy if you miss a word."
4. "Provide points to each other based on the number of words spelled correctly at the end of the session."
5. "Provide positive feedback and support to your teammate."

The Classwide-Peer Tutoring Approach.   A teacher's individual help is preferable, but the realities of the classroom frequently make individualized instruction difficult to offer. Structured peer tutoring can be a viable alternative. Delquadri, Greenwood, Stretton, and Hall (1983) have demonstrated the efficacy of the "Peer Tutoring Spelling Game" at all grade levels. The game takes about 15 minutes and includes the following procedures:

1. Tell the students that they will be playing a new game that is like basketball, only it will help them learn to spell words. In this game, they will make "baskets" (2 points) and "foul shots" (1 point).
2. On Monday of each week, teach the list of new words.
3. Assign students to tutor pairs: one is Speller 1 and one is Speller 2.
4. Speller 1 says a word, while speller 2 writes it on his or her paper. Speller 2 then orally spells the written word.
5. If the word is correct, Speller 1 says, "Correct! Give yourself 2 points!" and Speller 2 marks a "2" on his or her list. If the word is incorrect, Speller 1 points to, pronounces, and spells the missed

word orally. Speller 2 then writes the word correctly three times before moving to the next word.

6. When completed, Speller 1 becomes Speller 2 and vice versa.

7. Ask each student report his or her points and record them on the individual score chart.

8. Announce the team winner for the week, and post the winner on the team chart.

Maintain Previously Learned Words For maintenance of spelling words, assign previously learned words as review words and intersperse them with the learning of new spelling words. Students need to review previously learned words frequently to maintain them. After students have mastered spelling words, provide opportunities for students to see and use spelling words in context. Remember, students are more likely to spell words correctly in isolation immediately after preparing for a test than they are to spell the word correctly in context. Providing ongoing review in context for correct spelling is necessary.

Motivate Students to Spell Correctly Using games and activities, selecting meaningful words, and providing examples of the use and need for correct spelling are strategies that help to motivate students and give them a positive attitude about spelling.

Include Dictionary Training As part of the spelling program, dictionary training should be developed, which includes alphabetizing, identifying target words, and locating the correct definition when several are provided. Some students can keep a list of words they frequently misspell.

Spelling Approaches

There are many approaches to teaching spelling, and no single approach has been proven to be superior to others for all students with LD. Some students learn effectively with a multisensory approach, such as the Fernald method; others learn best with a combination of several approaches. A synthesis of spelling interventions (Wanzek, Vaughn, Wexler, Swanson, & Edmonds, 2006) indicated that spelling practices that provide students with spelling strategies or systematic study and word practice methods yield the highest rates of spelling improvement. Other approaches, including sensorimotor activities and technology supports for spelling, resulted in a slight advantage for students over students in comparison conditions. Following are several approaches to teaching spelling, all of which make use of the principles discussed in the previous section.

Test–Study–Test Method This method of learning spelling words is superior to the study–test method (Fitzsimmons & Loomer, 1978; Yee, 1969). In using the test–study–test method, students are first tested on a list of words and then instructed to study the missed words. Strategies are taught for recalling the correct spelling of these words. These strategies often include verbal mediation—saying the word while writing it or spelling it aloud to a partner. After instruction and study, students are then retested. Using this process, students then correct their own spelling test, which is an important factor in learning to spell.

Several word-study techniques that can be applied in using the test–study–test method are presented in Figure 9-13.

Visualization Approach This approach to spelling teaches students to visualize the correct spelling as a means to recall. The visualization approach uses the following procedures:

1. On the board or on a piece of paper, the teacher writes a word that students can read but cannot spell.

2. Students read the word aloud.

3. Students read the letters in the word.

4. Students write the word on paper.

5. The teacher asks the students to look at the word and "take a picture of it" as if the students' eyes were a camera.

6. The teacher asks the students to close their eyes and spell the word aloud, visualizing the letters while spelling it.

7. The teacher asks the students to write the word and check the model for accuracy.

The Five-Step Word-Study Strategy This strategy requires students to learn and rehearse the following five steps and practice them with the teacher and then alone. The steps are as follows:

1. Say the word.

2. Write and say the word.

3. Check the word.

4. Trace and say the word.

5. Write the word from memory and check.

6. Repeat the first five steps.

When students learn this technique, the teacher models the procedure, then the students practice the procedure with assistance from the teacher, and finally the students demonstrate proficiency in the application of the procedure without teacher assistance (Graham & Freeman, 1986).

FIGURE 9-13 Effective Word Study Procedures

Kinesthetic Method (Graham and Freeman, 1986)
1. Say the word.
2. Write and say the word.
3. Check the word and correct if needed.
4. Trace and say the word.
5. Write the word from memory, check it, and correct if needed.
6. Repeat steps one through five.

Copy-Cover-Compare (Murphy et al., 1990)
1. Examine the spelling of the word closely.
2. Copy the word.
3. Cover the word and write from memory.
4. Check the word and correct if needed.
5. If spelled correctly, go to next word.
6. If spelled incorrectly, repeat steps one through four.

Connections Approach (Berninger et al., 1998)
1. Teacher says word, points to each letter, and names it.
2. Child names word and letters.
3. Child shown a copy of the word with the onset and rime printed in different colors.
4. Teacher says the sound and simultaneously points to the onset and rime in order.
5. Child looks at, points to, and says the sound of the onset and rime in order.

Simultaneous Oral Spelling (Bradley, 1981)
1. Teacher reads the word.
2. Child reads the word.
3. Child writes the word saying the name of each letter.
4. Child says word again.
5. Teacher examines correctness of written response; child corrects if needed.
6. Repeat steps one through five two times.

Visual Imagery (Berninger et al., 1995)
1. Look at word and say its name.
2. Close your eyes and imagine the word in your mind's eye.
3. Name letters with your inside voice.
4. Open eyes write word.
5. Check spelling and repeat steps one through four if the word is not spelled correctly.

Source: S. Graham (1999), Handwriting and spelling instruction for students with learning disabilities: A review, *Learning Disability Quarterly, 22* (2), pp. 78–98. Reprinted with permission.

Johnson and Myklebust Technique D. J. Johnson and Myklebust (1967) suggest working from recognition to partial recall to total recall when teaching new spelling words. Recognition can be taught by showing students a word and then writing the word with several unrelated words, asking the students to circle the word they previously saw. The task can gradually be made more difficult by writing distracting words that more closely resemble the target word. In teaching partial recall, the correct word can be written with missing spaces for completing the spelling under it. For example:

with

w _____ th

wit _____

_____ ith

wi _____ _____

w _____ _____ _____

_____ _____ _____ _____

Total recall requires the students to write the word after another person pronounces or to write the word in a sentence. This approach gives repeated practice and focuses students on the relevant details of the word. D. J. Johnson and Myklebust (1967) also suggest that when initial spelling tests are given, the teacher may need to say the word very slowly, emphasizing each syllable. As students learn to spell the words correctly, the teacher gives the test in a normal voice and at a normal rate.

Cloze Spelling Approach The cloze spelling approach is so called because students need to supply missing letters systematically in much the same way that students supply words in the cloze reading procedure. The cloze spelling approach uses a four-step process for teaching students to spell words.

1. *Look–study.* Students are shown the word on a card. Students look at the word and study the letters and their order.
2. *Write missing vowels.* Students are shown the same word on a card with blanks where the vowels usually appear. Students write the entire word, supplying the missing vowel(s).
3. *Write missing consonants.* Students are shown the word with blanks where the consonants usually appear. Students write the entire word, supplying the missing consonant(s).
4. *Write the word.* Students write the word without the model.

Fernald Method Fernald (1943) believed that most spelling approaches were useful for the extremely visual student but not for students who need auditory and kinesthetic input for learning. Because poor spellers are characterized as having poor visual imagery, many may need to be taught through multisensory approaches such as the Fernald method.

According to Fernald (1943), specific school techniques that tend to produce poor spellers include the following:

- Formal spelling periods in which students move through a series of practice lessons, writing and taking dictation with little time to think about how the word is spelled before writing it
- A focus on misspellings and spelling errors, which builds a negative attitude toward spelling

A brief description of the Fernald approach to teaching spelling includes the following procedures:

1. The teacher writes the word to be learned on the chalkboard or paper. The word can be selected from the spelling book or by the student.

2. The teacher pronounces the word clearly. The students repeat the pronunciation of the word while looking at the word. This is done several times for each word.

3. The teacher allows time for students to study the word for later recall. If a student is a kinesthetic learner, the teacher writes the word in crayon and has the student trace the letters of the word with his or her finger. Fernald found that tracing is necessary in learning to spell only when the spelling difficulty is coupled with a reading disability.

4. The teacher removes the word and has the students write it from memory.

5. The students turn the paper over and write the word a second time.

6. The teacher creates opportunities for students to use the word in their writing.

7. The teacher gives written, not oral, spelling drills.

In contrast with Fernald's approach, which recommends not focusing on the student's errors and suggests blocking out errors immediately, other researchers have found some support for a spelling strategy that emphasizes imitation of students' errors plus modeling (J. Kauffman, Hallahan, Haas, Brame, & Boren, 1978; Nulman & Gerber, 1984). Using the imitation plus modeling strategy, the teacher erases the misspelled word and imitates the child's error by writing it on the board. The teacher then writes it correctly with the student and asks the student to compare what he or she wrote with the correct spelling of the word.

Gillingham and Stillman Approach   According to Gillingham and Stillman (1973), spelling is taught by using the following procedures:

1. The teacher says the word very slowly and distinctly, and students repeat the word after the teacher. This is referred to as *echo speech*.

2. Students are asked what sound is heard first. This process continues with all of the letters in the words. This is referred to as *oral spelling*.

3. The students are asked to locate the letter card with the first letter of the word on it and then to write the letter. Students continue with this process until the card for each letter is found, placed in order, and written. This is referred to as *written spelling*.

4. Students read the word.

When writing the word, students orally spell the word letter by letter. This establishes visual-auditory-kinesthetic association.

Correctional procedures in the Gillingham and Stillman approach include the following:

1. Students check their own written words and find errors.

2. If a word is read incorrectly, the students should spell what they said and match it with the original word.

3. If a word is misspelled orally, the teacher writes what the students spelled and asks them to read it, or the teacher may repeat the pronunciation of the original word.

Constant Time-Delay Procedure   The time-delay procedure is designed to reduce errors in instruction. Stevens and Schuster (1987) applied the procedure this way:

1. The verbal cue "Spell _____ (target word)" is immediately followed with a printed model of the target word to be copied by students.

2. After several trials in which there is no time delay between asking students to spell a word and providing a model of the word, a 5-second delay is introduced. This allows students to write the word, or part of the word, if they know it but does not require them to wait very long if they are unable to correctly write the word.

3. The amount of time between the request to spell the word and the presentation of the model can be increased after several more trials.

The time-delay procedure has been effective with students with LD and has several advantages as a spelling instructional method. It is a simple procedure that is easy to implement. Also, it is fun for students because it provides for nearly errorless instruction.

Self-Questioning Strategy for Teaching Spelling   Wong (1986) describes the following self-questioning strategy for teaching spelling:

1. Do I know this word?

2. How many syllables do I hear in this word?

3. Write the word the way I think it is spelled.

4. Do I have the right number of syllables?

5. Underline any part of the word that I am not sure how to spell.

6. Check to see whether it is correct. If it is not correct, underline the part of the word that is not correct, and write it again.

7. When I have finished, tell myself I have been a good worker.

Morphographic Spelling Morphographic spelling provides a highly structured and sequenced approach to teaching remedial spelling (Dixon & Engelmann, 2001). This teacher-directed approach assumes that students have some spelling skills and begins with teaching small units of meaningful writing (morphographs). Students are taught to spell morphographs in isolation, then to combine them to make words. Critical components of this instructional approach to spelling include error correction and feedback (including positive feedback), cumulative review, distributed practice, and highly sequenced lessons.

Several helpful videos provide information about spelling instruction: Go to www.youtube.com and search for several videos such as Teaching Spelling Skills Using Sound and Teaching Spelling in the 21st Century.

WEB RESOURCES
For a helpful Web site on instructional practices related to writing and spelling, see http://www.readingrockets.org.

Instructional Practices in Spelling

Most students with LD have problems with spelling. Yet students with LD have been the focus of relatively few research studies on spelling acquisition. Findings from two syntheses on effective spelling practices for students with LD (Gordon, Vaughn, & Schumm, 1993; Wanzek et al., 2006) yield the following instructional practices:

1. *Providing a weekly list of words.* Students benefit when teachers provide a weekly list of words that are taught. This procedure allows students to practice words throughout the week. Monitoring correct use of these words in writing and then following up on accuracy in spelling with these words is valuable. (See instructional practice 3 in this list for the number of words taught and how they should be distributed.)

2. *Error imitation and modeling.* Students with LD need to compare each of their incorrectly spelled words with the correct spellings. The teacher imitates the students' incorrect spelling and, beside it, writes the word correctly.

The teacher then calls attention to features in the word that will help students remember the correct spelling.

3. *Allocate three spelling words per day.* Students with LD learn to spell fewer words correctly and experience greater frustration when they are required to study a long list of words. Reduce the number of words assigned at any one time to approximately three words per day, and provide effective instruction for those words.

4. *Modality.* It has long been thought that students with LD learn to spell most easily when their modality preferences are considered. Students with LD learn equally well whether spelling by writing the words, arranging and tracing letter shapes or tiles, or typing the words on a computer. However, most students prefer to practice their spelling words on a computer. Because students' preferences are likely to affect their motivation to practice, teachers are wise to consider students' personal preferences.

5. *Computer-assisted instruction.* Computer-assisted instruction (CAI) has been shown to be effective in improving the spelling skills of students with LD. CAI software programs for spelling improvement often incorporate procedures that emphasize awareness of word structure and spelling strategies, and make use of time delay, voice simulation, and sound effects. Such capabilities make the computer an instructional tool with much potential to aid and motivate students with LD in learning to spell.

6. *Peer tutoring.* See the Peer Tutoring Spelling Game (Delquadri et al., 1983), described earlier in the chapter in the section entitled "Principles for Teaching Spelling to Students with Learning Difficulties."

Teaching Handwriting and Keyboarding

What are the characteristics of students with handwriting problems, and what components should be included in an effective handwriting and keyboarding program? Often described as the most poorly taught subject in the elementary curriculum, handwriting is usually thought of as the least important. However, handwriting difficulties create barriers to efficient work production and negatively influence academic success and self-esteem (Feder & Majnemer, 2007). Many students dislike the entire writing process because they find the motor skill involved in handwriting so laborious. *Dysgraphia* refers to students with extreme difficulties with handwriting. Interestingly, drawing performance can serve as a screener for students with handwriting difficulties (Khalid, Yunus, & Adnan, 2010).

Despite the use of word processors, handheld computers, and other devices that can facilitate the writing process, handwriting remains an important skill. Taking notes in class, filling out forms, and success on the job often require legible, fluent writing.

Handwriting Problems

Students with dysgraphia have severe problems learning to write and may exhibit any or all of the following characteristics:

- Poor letter formation
- Letters that are too large, too small, or inconsistent in size
- Incorrect use of capital and lowercase letters
- Letters that are crowded and cramped
- Inconsistent spacing between letters
- Incorrect alignment (letters do not rest on a baseline)
- Incorrect or inconsistent slant of cursive letters
- Lack of fluency in writing
- Incomplete words or missing words
- Slow writing even when asked to write as quickly as possible

Fortunately, with direct instruction and specific practice, many of these problems can be alleviated (Berninger et al., 2006). It is important to alleviate handwriting problems for several reasons: They are associated with reduced interest in writing and thus influence written expression, and students with handwriting difficulties spell worse than those without handwriting problems, even when spelling interventions are provided (Berninger, Abbott, Whitaker, Sylvester, & Nolen, 1995).

Reversals

When 5-year-old Abe signed his name on notes to his grandmother, he often reversed the direction of the *b* in his name. He often wrote other letters backward or upside down. His mother worried that this might be an indication that Abe was dyslexic or having reading problems. Many adults are concerned when youngsters make reversals; however, most children, age 5 and younger, make reversals when writing letters and numbers. Reversals made by students before the age of 6 or 7 are not an indication that the student has LD or is dyslexic and are rarely cause for concern.

Teachers should recognize the following:

- Reversals are common before the age of 6 or 7. Teachers should provide correctional procedures for school-age students who are reversing letters and numbers but should not become overly concerned.
- A few students continue to reverse numbers and letters after the age of 7 and may need direct intervention techniques.

For students who persist in reversing letters and numbers, the following two direct instructional techniques may be helpful:

1. The teacher traces the letter and talks aloud about the characteristics of the letter, asking the students to model the teacher's procedure. For example, while tracing the letter *d*, the teacher says, "First I make a stick starting at the top of the page and going down, and then I put a ball in front of the stick." Students are asked to follow the same procedure and to talk aloud while tracing the letter. Next, the students are asked to do the same procedure, this time drawing the letter. Finally, the students are asked to draw the letter and say the process to themselves.

2. The teacher and students can develop a mnemonic picture device that helps the students recall the direction of the letter. For example, with a student who is reversing the direction of the letter *p*, the teacher might say, "What letter does the word *pie* begin with? That's right, *pie* begins with the letter *p*. Now watch me draw *p*." Drawing the straight line, the teacher says, "This is my straight line before I eat pie, then after I eat pie my stomach swells in front of me. Whenever you make *p* you can think of pie and how your stomach gets big after you eat it, and that will help you make a *p* the right way." This procedure can be repeated several times, with the student drawing the letter and talking through the mnemonic device. Different mnemonic devices can be developed to correspond with the specific letter or number reversal(s) of the child. Berninger et al. (2006) reported that direct instruction with visual cues and memory delays with additional practice checks lead to reduced reversals.

Components of Handwriting

Teaching handwriting requires the teacher to assess, model, and teach letter formation, spacing, and fluency as well as posture, pencil grip, and position of the paper.

Legibility   Legibility is the most important goal of handwriting instruction, and incorrect letter formation is the most frequent interference.

The following six letters account for many of the errors (48%) that students make when forming letters: *q, j, z, u, n,* and *k* (Graham, Berninger, & Weintraub, 1998). Spacing between letters, words, and margins; connecting lines; and closing and crossing of letters (e.g., *t, x*) also influence legibility.

Fluent Writing   How does fluency relate to handwriting? Just as not knowing how to read words fluently impairs reading comprehension, inadequate fluency in writing letters and words impairs written expression and the quality of written responses (Spear-Swerling, 2006). For example, 9-year-old Nguyen's handwriting has improved considerably during the past year. She and her teacher have identified letters that were not formed correctly, and Nguyen has learned to write these letters so that they are legible. Now that her handwriting is easier to read, the teacher realizes that Nguyen has another handwriting problem. In the regular classroom, Nguyen has difficulty taking notes and writing down assignments that are given orally, because she is a very slow writer. She needs to learn writing fluency, which is the ability to write quickly and with ease, without undue attention to letter formation.

Nguyen's teacher decides to teach fluency by gradually increasing expectations about the speed at which letter formation occurs. Nguyen selects two paragraphs and is told to write them as quickly as she can while still maintaining good letter formation. The teacher times her in this procedure. They decide to keep a graph of Nguyen's progress by indicating the time it takes her each day to write the two paragraphs legibly. Nguyen finds that graphing her progress is very reinforcing (see Figure 9-14 and Apply the Concept 9-14). Because Nguyen's fluency problems were not just for

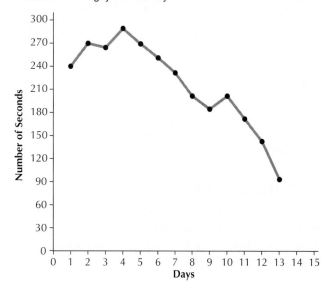

FIGURE 9-14 Nguyen's Fluency

copying but also for writing from dictation, her teacher implemented the same program, this time requiring Nguyen to time herself on oral dictations. Nguyen's time for completion of the passage decreased considerably over a 3-week period.

9-14 APPLY THE CONCEPT

Obtaining a Handwriting Fluency Sample

The following procedures can be used to obtain a fluency sample:

1. Have the student become familiar with the test sentence.
2. Tell the student to write the test sentence a designated number of times at his or her usual rate (2- to 3-minute sample).
3. After the student relaxes, have the student write the sentence as well and as neatly as he or she can.
4. After the student relaxes, have the student write the sentence as quickly and as many times as he or she can in 3 minutes.
5. After the student relaxes, repeat this process with the student with the same sentence.

INSTRUCTIONAL ACTIVITIES

This section provides instructional activities that are related to written expression, including spelling and handwriting. Some of the activities teach new skills; others are best suited for practice and reinforcement of already acquired skills. For each activity, the objective, grades, materials, and teaching procedures are described

Web Resources

For additional information on instruction in writing and spelling, see the International Reading Association and National Council of Teachers of English Web site, http://www.readwritethink.org.

Cubing

OBJECTIVE: To help students develop preliminary ideas about the topic during the prewriting phase

GRADES: Elementary through secondary

MATERIALS: A cube-shaped outline, glue, scissors

TEACHING PROCEDURES:

1. Explain to students that the topic is like a cube that contains different information on each side. Topics can be explored from different angles.

2. Introduce six different ways in which the topic can be explored.
   a. *Describe:* What does it look like?
   b. *Compare:* What is it similar to? What is it different from?
   c. *Associate:* What does it remind you of?
   d. *Analyze:* What are the parts?
   e. *Apply:* What can you do with it?
   f. *Argue for or against:* Take a stand about your topic. Why is it good or why is it not good?

3. Pass out a cube-shaped outline to each student.

4. Have students write their ideas down on the cube-shaped outline. Students work through each side of the cube: describe, compare, associate, analyze, apply, and argue for or against the topic. (Depending on the topic, questions for each dimension will need to be adjusted.)

5. Have the students cut out the outline and glue it together to make a cube.

EXTENDED ACTIVITY: The cube can be used as a resource in writing the essay.

Adapted from University of Texas Center for Reading and Language Arts (2000a, 2000b).

Writing Warm-Up

OBJECTIVE: To help students, especially reluctant writers, gain writing experiences

MATERIALS: Graph paper, colored pencils, timer for the teacher

GRADES: Elementary through secondary

TEACHING PROCEDURES:

1. Explain to students that writing is like exercising. Tell them that writing practice can help them improve their writing and make the writing easier.

2. Choose a topic that will be easy for students to write about. Have students do a writing warm-up once or twice a week.

3. Introduce the day's topic (e.g., homework).

4. Ask students to write as much as they can about the topic for 3 minutes. Tell the students that they do not need to worry about spelling, grammar, or punctuation.

5. Set a timer for 3 minutes. When time is up, have the students put their pencils down and count the number of words they have written.

6. Have students graph the number of words they have written, using colored pencils and graph paper.

7. When students feel comfortable writing their ideas about the topic, introduce the next writing process (e.g, organizing their ideas, revising, editing).

Source: Adapted from University of Texas Center for Reading and Language Arts (2000a, 2000b).

Writing Reports

OBJECTIVE: To help students prepare for a research report by providing guidelines for gathering information necessary for writing a research report

GRADES: Secondary

MATERIALS: Report-planning sheet (see Figure 9-15)

TEACHING PROCEDURES:

1. Explain to students that a report-planning sheet will help them to prepare for writing a research report. After filling out the planning sheet, they can use the information on the planning sheet to write their report.

2. Introduce the day's topic (e.g., volcanoes).

3. Pass out a planning sheet to each student.

4. Have students brainstorm a list of everything they know about the topic and write it down in the first column (i.e., What I Know).

FIGURE 9-15 Report Planning Sheet

Topic: _____

What I Know	What I Want to Find Out	Why I Want to Find Out	How I Will Find Out	What I Learned

5. Have the students examine their brainstorming ideas carefully to identify the areas in need of further research. For instance, if a student knows names of active volcanoes but not much about how a volcano is formed, the student may want to study that. Have students identify what they want to study and write that down in the second column.

6. In the third column, have students write down why they want to study the subtopic they selected.

7. Have students think about a variety of sources where they can find information (e.g., science textbook, Web sites, etc.) on the subtopic and list those sources in the fourth column.

8. Have students conduct their research and write down what they learn in the fifth column.

9. After the students have completed the planning sheet, have them use that information to write the report.

Source: Adapted from Macrorie (1980) and Ogle (1986).

The Use of Graphic Organizers for Writing

OBJECTIVE: To help students organize their ideas when writing first drafts

GRADES: Elementary through secondary

MATERIALS: Copies of a graphic organizer (see Figure 9-16)

TEACHING PROCEDURES:

1. Explain to students that graphic organizers can help them write their draft. (*Note:* Different types of graphic organizers are used depending on type of text.)

2. Model how to use graphic organizers. For instance, write the topic in the center and supporting details on the branches on the graphic organizer. Then

FIGURE 9-16 Graphic Organizer

Topic: _____

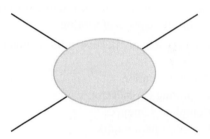

Sentence describing the topic:

1. _____

2. _____

3. _____

create sentences describing the topic by using ideas written on the graphic.

3. Introduce the topic, and pass out copies of a graphic organizer to each student.

4. Have students use the graphic organizer as they write their draft with a partner, in a small group, or independently.

5. After students finish filling out the graphic organizer and creating sentences, call on several students to share their drafts. Provide feedback on their drafts.

Source: Adapted from Nancy and Dill (1997).

Peer Editing

OBJECTIVE: To provide students with opportunities to edit a revised draft as one part of the editing process

FIGURE 9-17 Peer-Editing Checklist

	Yes	No	Edits Made
1. Does each sentence end with a period, question mark, or exclamation point?			
2. Does each sentence start with a capital letter?			
3. Is each sentence a complete sentence?			
4. Is the first sentence of each paragraph indented?			
5. Did my partner check my spelling (by using dictionary and/or thesaurus)?			

GRADES: Elementary

MATERIALS: Student-generated revised draft, peer-editing checklist (see Figure 9-17)

TEACHING PROCEDURES:

1. Explain to students that editing focuses on correcting technical aspects of writing.

2. Introduce each of the five editing points on the checklist:
   a. End punctuation
   b. Beginning capitalization
   c. Complete sentences
   d. Indented paragraphs
   e. Spelling check

3. Pair students, making sure that each pair consists of a good writer and a poor writer.

4. Pass out peer-editing checklists to each pair, and ask students in pairs to exchange their revised drafts.

5. Have the good writer in each pair edit his or her partner's draft by following editing steps, which are outlined on the peer-editing checklist. If a step is followed, a check mark should be placed in the Yes column after that step. If a step is not followed, then a check should be placed in the No column.

6. While the student is completing the checklist, have his or her partner correct errors, if any, and record what corrections were made in the Edits Made column.

7. Repeat the procedure, this time with the poor writer editing his or her partner's draft by following the editing steps.

Source: Adapted from University of Texas Center for Reading and Language Arts (2001b).

Peer Revision

OBJECTIVE: To give students an opportunity to work together in pairs to elaborate on their writing as one part of the revision process

GRADES: Elementary through secondary

MATERIALS: Student-generated rough draft, sticky notes

TEACHING PROCEDURES:

1. Explain to students that good writers get help from their friends and colleagues to improve their writing. One way to do this is to get ideas for elaborating or expanding on what you have already written. Each student needs a rough draft that is ready to be revised (and is neat enough to be read by another student and checked by the teacher).

2. Students work in pairs to complete the following revision steps:
   a. Have a student read his or her rough draft out loud to his or her partner. While the student is reading, he or she may catch a few mistakes. Encourage the student to correct them.
   b. Have the partner read through the rough draft, focusing on the content. The partner makes three sticky-note comments and puts them on the rough draft. One comment is positive (e.g., "I really liked the part where . . ."). The other two comments are helpful (e.g., "Tell me more about . . ." and "I don't understand the part where . . .").
   c. Repeat the process with the second partner.
   d. Have each student work individually to elaborate on his or her draft by addressing the peer sticky-note comments.

Acrostic Writing in the Content Areas

OBJECTIVE: To help students improve their understanding of content through acrostic writing

GRADES: Secondary

MATERIALS: Content area textbook

TEACHING PROCEDURES:

1. Explain to students that they will write a poem about what they have read (e.g., the unit on Native Americans in social studies).

2. Review important information on the previously studied unit (e.g., Native Americans), and create a semantic map by writing the name of the tribe they read about (e.g., Apache) on the blackboard, asking the students to share what they have read about this tribe (prompt the students if necessary), and recording the students' responses on the blackboard.

3. Have students write a poem to describe important characteristics of the Apache by using each letter in it to create one sentence. For instance,

Amazing hunters who once enjoyed a nomadic style of life

Powerful nation of warriors

Adaptable people who learned to tend fields of maize, beans, pumpkins, and watermelons when buffalo became scarce

Courageous Indians known for their resistance to the U.S. government

Hut building, farming, trading, and horse riding were necessary for survival of this proud nation

Epidemics of smallpox and other European diseases almost decimated the once-large tribe

4. Call on several students to share their poems. Provide feedback on their poems in terms of the writing styles and the content.

Source: Adapted from Bromley (1999).

Proofreading with SCOPE

OBJECTIVE: To teach students a mnemonic strategy (SCOPE) to help with proofreading their writing

GRADES: Upper elementary through secondary

MATERIALS: Student-generated writing piece that needs to be edited

TEACHING PROCEDURES:
1. Discuss with students how they can get into difficulty if they are not sufficiently skilled at proofreading their papers before they submit them and therefore get low grades because their papers have many errors.

2. Teach the students SCOPE, a mnemonic strategy that will assist them in proofreading their work before they submit it:
Spelling: Is the spelling correct?

Capitalization: Are the first words of sentences, proper names, and proper nouns capitalized?

Order of words: Is the syntax correct?

Punctuation: Are there appropriate marks for punctuation where necessary?

Express complete thought: Does the sentence contain a noun and a verb, or is it only a phrase?

3. Next, demonstrate using SCOPE with a sample piece of writing on an overhead projector.

4. Give the students ample practice and opportunity to apply SCOPE to their own work.

Interview a Classmate

OBJECTIVE: To give students practice in developing and using questions to obtain more information for the piece they are writing

GRADES: Upper elementary through secondary

MATERIALS: Writing materials and a writing topic, a list of possible questions, an audio recorder (optional)

TEACHING PROCEDURES:
1. Using the format of a radio or television interview, demonstrate and role-play mock interviews with sports, movie, music, and political celebrities. (*Note:* Give students opportunities to play both roles.)

2. Discuss what types of questions allow the interviewee to give elaborate responses (e.g., open questions) and what types of questions do not allow the interviewee to give an expanded answer (e.g., closed questions). Practice asking open questions.

3. Use a piece that you are writing as an example, and discuss whom you might interview to obtain more information. For example, "In writing a piece about what it might have been like to go to the New York World's Fair in 1964, I might interview my grandfather, who was there, to obtain more information."

4. Ask students to select an appropriate person to interview for their writing piece and write possible questions.

5. In pairs, have students refine their questions for the actual interview.

6. Have students then conduct interviews and later discuss how information from the interview assisted them in writing their piece.

What Would You Do If . . . ?

By Alison Gould Boardman

OBJECTIVE: To give students experience developing ideas for narrative writing and following simple story structure

GRADES: Upper elementary and middle school

MATERIALS: Pencil, drawing paper, writing paper

1. Have students fold a piece of drawing paper so that there are four squares.

2. Ask students what they would do if they were invisible for 24 hours. Share ideas, and probe students to add details (e.g., "You would go to the moon. Great, how would you get there? Would you take anyone with you?"). Tell students that now that they have some ideas, they are going to make a rough drawing of four possible things they would do if they were invisible for 24 hours.

3. Students should use pencil or one color to draw pictures of their ideas, one in each quarter of the page. Pictures can be rough drawings or sketches. The purpose of the drawings is to help students generate interest in and remember what they want to write about without the pressure of having to write it down.

4. Begin with the introduction. Students write about how they become invisible. For the body of the story, students choose three of their four ideas to expand on. They use their pictures and build from there. The ending of the story details what happens when they become visible again and concludes their invisible day.

ADAPTATIONS: This assignment can be repeated with topics (from the teacher or students) such as, What would you do if you could fly, run 50 miles an hour, drive a car, etc.? Depending on students' skill levels, the length and content requirements can be adjusted.

Step-by-Step Cartoon Writing

By Alison Gould Boardman

OBJECTIVE: To give beginning or reluctant writers experience sequencing steps, using transition words, and writing a paragraph

GRADES: Elementary

MATERIALS: Index cards without lines, colored pencils, tape, writing materials

TEACHING PROCEDURES:

1. Discuss as a group the types of things students do to get ready for school in the morning.

2. Tell students that they will be drawing a comic strip about what they do when they get up in the morning.

3. Have students draw one event on each index card (e.g., waking up, getting dressed, eating breakfast). Encourage the students to add detail to their pictures to help them remember exactly what happens.

4. Have students put their ideas in order and tape the cards together like a comic strip.

5. Before the students begin writing, have them use their comic strip as a guide to help them tell the story out loud. Encourage students to use transition words such as *first, next, later,* and *finally.* Teachers can post a list of transition words for students to use while telling and writing their paragraphs.

6. Have students write one descriptive sentence about each frame of their comic strip to form a paragraph.

7. Attach the final copy of the paragraph to the comic strip and display in the classroom.

ADAPTATIONS: Students can use this procedure to write any sequenced or how-to paragraph, such as how to bake a cake, make a peanut-butter-and-jelly sandwich, play checkers, or make a bed.

Summary

For many students with learning and behavior problems, writing is one of the most difficult things that they do, asking them to use skills they have not mastered well, such as spelling and handwriting. Teachers need to consider these negative associations when they set up a writing program that encourages students to explore and expand their writing ability while practicing the writing conventions that students will need to express themselves effectively. Assessment practices that include ongoing progress monitoring of the accuracy of letter formation, speed of writing, and quality of writing provide important feedback to teachers as they alter their writing instruction. The physical environment, or setting, is an important feature that sets the tone for writing.

Many students with learning and behavior problems do not benefit from traditional approaches to spelling (e.g., weekly word lists) and need instruction in phonics rules and how these rules relate to writing words. The first step is to conduct a spelling error analysis to identify which spelling patterns students understand and which they misunderstand. Through ongoing instruction in these spelling patterns and progress monitoring to determine learning, teachers can integrate assessment and instruction for improving spelling outcomes for their students. Teachers should teach in small units, and cluster new words according to spelling patterns. They should allow time for students to practice new words, provide feedback, and maintain previously learned words through frequent reviews. Finally, they can motivate students by making spelling fun.

Handwriting difficulties often result in spelling difficulties, low motivation to write as well as poor academic performance, low work production, and reduced self-esteem. Weaknesses in handwriting can be assessed by examining legibility, fluency, and hand position and can usually be remediated with direct instruction and specific practice. Principles of instruction include using a variety of techniques to provide direct instruction that is specific to a student's individual handwriting needs. Provide short, frequent instruction in handwriting skills and many opportunities to practice. Skills should be thoroughly learned in isolation and then applied in the context of the student's writing assignment. Students should evaluate their own handwriting and use the teacher as a model. Handwriting should also be taught as a combined visual–motor task. For each student, teachers assess, model, and teach the needed skills as well as provide opportunities for practice and feedback.

 ASSESSMENT

After completing this chapter, test your knowledge of the concepts by completing this Assessment.

Assessing and Teaching Content Area Learning and Vocabulary

10

LEARNING OUTCOMES

1. Identify specific word instruction and word-learning strategies to teach content area vocabulary.

2. Describe content enhancement, and specify how teachers could use content enhancement to teach content area reading.

3. Describe how teachers adapt textbooks, lectures, assignments, homework, and tests to meet the needs of students with learning and behavior problems.

4. List the three types of study skills, and provide a rationale for why they are important to learning.

When Ms. Cho moved from her position as a special education teacher at the elementary school to one at a high school, her experience and education in teaching reading, writing, and math served her well for part of the school day. However, in addition to the two English periods she teaches daily, she is expected to teach sections of American history and American government to students with learning and behavior problems. Although she minored in political science and history in college, she was concerned that her content knowledge was weak in these areas and that she lacked adequate instructional procedures for teaching content to students with learning and behavior problems. She has also been asked to teach a section of general science; she has chosen to team-teach the class with a science teacher because of her limited content knowledge and her desire to integrate the special education students into general education classes. She also realized that she was responsible for including literacy standards from the Common Core State Standards into her instruction.

Juan, a fourth grader with a reading disability, moved to the United States when he was in the first grade. With the help of his special education teacher, Juan has made considerable progress in reading and understanding texts that have stories. Since entering fourth grade, however, he has been challenged by vocabulary words in expository texts (his math and social studies texts). The vocabulary words that he is encountering in these texts are more complex and abstract than the words in narrative texts, for example, *exponent, ecosystem, matriculate, fibrosis.* As a result, Juan is having significant difficulty understanding what he reads in his math and social studies classes and he is failing to learn the content from these texts.

When Desmond entered Bailey Middle School, he had been receiving help in a special education resource room since second grade. During that time, Ms. Jackson, the resource room teacher, had been working with Desmond on word identification and basic comprehension skills as well as spelling and writing compositions. In elementary school, Desmond went to the resource room for 45 minutes every afternoon. He consistently missed either social studies or science in the general education classroom while he was receiving special assistance in the resource room.

Desmond attends resource English and reading, but he has social studies, science, and home economics classes in general education classes. All of these classes require him to listen to lectures in class and take notes, read textbooks and answer the questions at the end of each section, take timed tests, write reports, and keep track of assignments and turn them in on time. Textbooks for these classes are information driven and contain unfamiliar technical vocabulary. It is challenging for Desmond to learn from textbooks because he does not know the meaning of many of the vocabulary words that are crucial to understanding the content. By the end of the first 9 weeks, Desmond has received failing slips in all three classes. He is frustrated by his classes and is becoming disruptive.

Doreen worked hard in high school and, despite her reading and writing disabilities, is a senior in high school with a high-enough grade-point average to enter college. However, she is feeling overwhelmed by the demands of her classes. Doreen can't seem to get organized. She has difficulty estimating how long it will take her to complete an assignment, and she is unable to keep up with the reading assignments. Doreen is a bright student with good potential to succeed as an architect or engineer, but she may never get through the basic liberal arts courses required for her degree.

Both Desmond and Doreen need strategies to assist them in being more effective learners. They need skills in managing time, organizing notebooks, taking notes, studying for tests, taking tests, reading textbooks, learning new vocabulary, and writing reports and essays. Desmond and Doreen have mastered many of the basics of reading and writing, but they are having difficulty applying them in content area classes.

Many of the reading comprehension and writing strategies highlighted in Chapters 8 and 9 are effective in promoting content area learning and effective studying and learning. In addition, the Strategies Intervention Model (www.ku-crl.org) presented in Chapter 2 can be used to teach many of the study skills and learning strategies suggested in this chapter.

Both Juan and Desmond need systematic vocabulary instruction that introduces important vocabulary words and word-building strategies. Preteaching specific vocabulary words that are crucial to understanding the texts should improve their comprehension. Also, word-building strategies they can apply to figure out the meanings of a variety of words would help improve their vocabulary acquisition.

Ms. Cho, Juan, Desmond, and Doreen are experiencing difficulties functioning in the upper-elementary, secondary, postsecondary school, and professional environments. In these environments, the task demands for teachers and students change dramatically. Special education teachers often coteach, teach content subjects, or need to provide content area teachers with learning and teaching strategies to support students so that they can access the general education curriculum. Students are asked to apply learning strategies and study skills as well as skills in listening, reading, writing, and math to learn content area subjects such as biology, American history, art history, welding, computer programming, and home economics.

Using synonyms, examples, and/or readily understood definitions can be an effective way to enhance students' understanding of a word. First, interact with students to develop a list of synonyms for the new word. Second, teachers can provide examples when few words are available to appropriately define the concept (e.g., *feeling*). Third, teachers can use definitions when introducing new words that are complex. As students progress through the grades and words become more complex, teachers may increasingly use definitions to introduce new words. Teachers should provide student-friendly definitions consisting of words that students know:

- Introduce a vocabulary word—for example, *immigrant*—and ask students to repeat the word so that they know how to pronounce the word.

- Discuss the meaning of the word using synonyms, examples, pictures, and/or definitions. For example, "*Immigrant* means "someone who comes from abroad to live permanently in another country." And, "Most of us have relatives who were immigrants—for example, my grandfather came from Germany and he was an immigrant to the United States."

- Check with students on their understanding of the word by asking students to figure out positive or incorrect examples and to explain them. Positive example of the word *immigrant*: "Tom's grandparents came to the United States from England in 1912. They lived in the United States until they passed away." Ask the students, "Are Tom's grandparents immigrants? Why or why not?" An example of an incorrect use of the word *immigrant*: "Recently, many international students came to the United States to study." Ask the students, "Are the international students immigrants? Why or why not?"

Give students an opportunity to interact with the word either verbally or in writing with either a partner or a group of three. Using the word orally or in writing ensures that the word will retain meaning.

Teaching Vocabulary Through Word-Learning Strategies

In addition to specific word instruction, it is critical to teach students word-learning strategies that are supported by research, including using contextual analysis, morphemic analysis, and dictionaries and other reference aids.

Using Contextual Analysis *Contextual analysis* involves using the context, or text that surrounds an unknown word, to find clues to reveal a word's meaning (C. Blachowicz & Ogle, 2001; Swanson et al., 2011). Contextual analysis may be a useful word-building strategy for students to use during their independent reading. In text, writers often provide the definition, synonym, description, or examples of a word that may be difficult for the reader. Writers provide several types of context clues in their text:

- *Definition.* The word is defined in the sentence. (Example: The *surplus*—that is, an amount left over—was so great that the office was full and desks and chairs were lying on the floor.)

- *Synonym.* The word is compared to another word with a similar meaning. (Example: When Tom went to the parking garage and his car was not there, he was *furious*. Tom was *very mad*.)

- *Description.* The word is described by the context. (Example: After taking a spill on her bike, she was able to stand up, get back on the bike, and pedal away on her own *volition*.)

- *Contrast.* The word is contrasted with some other word, like an antonym. (Example: Kim was *lethargic*, yet her sister was very energetic.)

- *Comparison.* The word is compared with some other word or phrase to illustrate the similarities between them. (Example: John was exhausted after the *interview*, which was more work than mowing grass all day in the neighborhood.)

Regardless of types of context clues, the first step in teaching contextual analysis is to provide explicit modeling in looking at the words surrounding an unknown word and finding possible clues that may help students figure out its meaning. Then a teacher gives students ample opportunities to practice how to use contextual analysis and engage them in lively discussions. Teachers should introduce a few types of context clues (about two) at one time and sequence types of context clues from easy (e.g., definition) to difficult (e.g., comparison).

The following activity helps students understand the supporting role of context in understanding word meanings:

1. Prepare a series of passages in which context is used to define a difficult word.
2. Present the difficult word in isolation.
3. Ask students for the definition of the word.
4. Present the difficult word in context, and point out the word.
5. Have students reread the sentence before, with, and after the one with the difficult word, to look for context clues.

6. Ask students for the definition of the word and how the definition is derived.

7. Have students compare the definition of the word from context with that of the word in isolation.

8. Present other vocabulary words in context. Pair students, and ask them to analyze the context to figure out the meaning of each vocabulary word and record the definition for each word.

9. Have students look up the definitions for the vocabulary words in a dictionary.

It is valuable to prepare students for text that does not provide sufficient information to help them understand words and concepts. They will undoubtedly encounter text in content areas as well as narrative that provides little information or perhaps even misleading information about words and concepts. It is necessary to help students distinguish words that are not defined in text and how to use other resources to gain meaning.

Using Morphemic Analysis   Morphemic analysis in vocabulary instruction involves breaking a word into morphemes, the smallest linguistic units that have meaning, and using their meanings to figure out the meaning of the whole word (Reed, 2008; Reed, Wexler, & Vaughn, 2012). There are two types of morphemes: free, which can stand alone (e.g., *some*), and bound, which must be linked to words or other morphemes (i.e., prefixes and suffixes). Because Greek and Latin morphemes are found commonly in content area textbooks, teaching morphemes and their meanings helps students to independently figure out the meanings of the words. Figure 10-1 provides common Greek and Latin roots and their meanings. Having students break words into small parts based on meaning

FIGURE 10-1 Common Greek and Latin Roots

Root	Meaning	Sample Words
astro	star	astrology, astronaut, asteroid
aud	hear	auditorium, audition
bio	life	biography, biology
dict	speak	dictate, dictator
geo	earth	geography, geology
meter	measure	thermometer
mit, mis	send	transmit, mission, missile
ped	foot	pedal, pedestrian
phon	sound	microphone, phonograph
port	carry	portable, transport
scrib, script	write	manuscript, scribble
spect	see	inspect, spectator
struct	build	construction, destruction

Source: Based on University of Texas Center for Reading and Language Arts (2009). Reprinted by permission.

can help them to figure out the meaning of words on the basis of what they know about the meanings of the smaller parts. For instance, a student can break the word *unchangeable* into the word parts *un, change,* and *able.* If the student knows the meanings of these word parts (*un* meaning "not," *change,* and *able* meaning "able to"), the student can determine that *unchangeable* means "not able to change." Figure 10-2 presents common prefixes and suffixes and their meanings.

Learning prefixes is relatively easy in comparison to learning suffixes (Reed, Wexler & Vaughn, 2012). Prefixes generally have clearer meanings and are spelled more regularly than suffixes. For instance, the prefixes un- and re- have clear meanings of "not" and "again," respectively, and are always spelled as *un* and *re.* In contrast, the suffixes -tion and -ness have more abstract meanings of "the act or process of" and "the state or condition of," respectively. Some suffixes can also be spelled differently depending on the base words (e.g., -tion, -ion, -sion). However, not all suffixes have abstract meanings (e.g., -less meaning "without" and -ful meaning "full of").

Morphemic analysis instruction involves presenting new morphemes and their meanings in several specific steps:

1. Introduce a new morpheme and its meaning.

2. Introduce words containing that morpheme.

3. Provide practice for determining the meaning of words that contain that morpheme.

4. Test students on the meaning of several words that contain that morpheme.

5. Provide practice for the meaning of the new morpheme and previously taught morphemes.

Although morphemic analysis can help students build their vocabulary, several cautions should be considered when planning morphemic analysis instruction. First, this strategy works with a limited set of words; therefore, morphemic analysis instruction should not be too long. Second, only one or two prefixes or suffixes should be introduced at a time, with an emphasis on their applications to unfamiliar words. Teachers can use small groups to promote student discussion of the meanings of word parts and the new words.

FIGURE 10-2 Common Prefixes and Suffixes

Prefix	Meaning	Sample Words	Suffix	Meaning/Function	Sample Words
ante-	before, front	antechamber	-able, -ible	can be done	comfortable, changeable
anti-	against	antislavery, antisocial	-al, -ial	characteristic of	natural, remedial
bi-	two	bicycle	-ance, -ence	state of	importance
co-	with, together	coworker	-ation, -ition,	act, process	tension, attention,
de-	opposite of, down, remove, reduce	deactivate, devalue, dethrone	-tion, -ion, -sion		imagination
			-ant	person connected with	accountant
dis-	not, opposite of	dishonest, disagree	-en	noting action from an adjective made of	harden, loosen, wooden
en-, em-	cause to	enable, embrace			
ex-	out, out of	exterior, exhaust, expose	-er, -or	person connected with	painter, director
fore-	before	foreground	-ful	full of	fearful, beautiful, hopeful
in-	in or into	inside, interior	-fy	make	clarify
in-, im-,	not	inactive, immature,	-ic	having of	poetic
ir-, il-		irregular, illegal	-ish	characteristic of	greenish
inter-	between	international, intersection	-ity, -ty	state of	necessity, honesty
			-ive, -ative,	noting action from an adjective	active, affirmative
intra-	inside	intrastate	-itive		
mid-	middle	midnight	-less	without	fearless, tireless, hopeless
mis-	wrongly	misbehave, mispronounce	-ly	characteristic of	gladly, happily
			-ment	result of an action	entertainment, excitement
non-	not	nonfiction	-ness	state of, condition of	kindness, happiness
over-	too much	overdue, oversleep	-ous, -eous,	having of	joyous, gracious
pre-	before	preheat, preschool	-ious		
re-	again	reread, redo	-y	characterized by	rainy
semi-	half	semicircle			
sub-	under	submarine, subway			
super-	above	supernatural			
trans-	across	transport			
tri-	three	tricycle			
un-	not, opposite of	unable, unchangeable			
under-	too little	underpaid			

Source: Based on University of Texas Center for Reading and Language Arts (2009). Reprinted by permission.

Using Dictionaries and Other Reference Aids It is important for students to learn how to use dictionaries, glossaries, and thesauruses to help broaden and deepen their word knowledge, but it is important to understand that these tools are difficult for most students with learning disabilities to use in order to learn the meaning of words. Using dictionaries and other reference aids can be a difficult task for young students for several reasons:

- Definitions often contain words that students do not understand. Therefore, when possible, teachers should select dictionaries that are written at the appropriate reading level. Second, many words have more than one definition listed in the dictionary (e.g., the word *parcel* can mean something wrapped up or packaged, or a portion or plot of. Teachers should teach students how to determine

the most appropriate meaning. For example, a teacher may present a word having several meanings in sentences. The teacher then asks students to look up the word, examine the definitions listed in the dictionary, read the sentence substituting each definition in the dictionary to see whether it makes sense, and select the definition that is most appropriate for the sentence.

- Although using dictionaries and other reference aids is an important word-building strategy students can use while reading, students should not look up every unknown word. Teachers should encourage students to use contextual analysis and morphemic analysis to assist in determining word meanings. Teachers should encourage students to decide whether a word is important to understanding the passage. When students fail to figure out the meaning of important words through contextual analysis and morphemic analysis, they can look up the word in a dictionary or other reference aid.

Assessing Vocabulary Determining whether students know the meaning of a single word is not difficult. However, knowing how many words students know, which words they know and don't know, and whether they know one or more meanings and can use them orally and in writing—well, that is all more than a little overwhelming. Vocabulary is perhaps one of the most difficult areas of reading and content learning to assess. Vocabulary is also difficult to assess because there are many different levels of knowing what a word means. We can recognize the word when we see or hear it, we can know what the word means when someone else uses it, and/or we can use the word adeptly in conversation and writing. For the purposes of instruction, teachers can monitor the words and concepts related to understanding text or learning from their content area instruction.

Progress Monitoring What can teachers do to monitor their students' vocabulary and concept learning? The first step is to identify the words and concepts that students most need to know and understand for the text or unit to make sense to them. Although it is tempting to select a lot of words for instruction, the most important goal is to select words that have high impact on learning and comprehension. For example, Mr. O'Malley, a middle school social studies teacher, was concerned that many of his students would not understand many of the most important words in his unit on how money works. He realized that he couldn't teach every word at a deep-enough level that students would be able to use them orally and in their writing. He selected eight words for the first week of his unit. He decided to teach two new words each day for the first 4 days and then briefly review the words that he had previously taught. He monitored the progress of students' understanding of these words in two ways. First, he did daily checks with selected students to determine whether they knew what the words meant. Second, he asked students to document in their notebook if they saw or heard any of the key words either during the day at school or at home. Third, he provided a paper-and-pencil assessment of all eight words at the end of the week so that he would know which words required further review during the second week of the unit.

Teaching Content Area Reading

The Common Core State Standards Provide a Framework for Teachers to Guide Their Literacy Instruction in the Content Areas. Thus, social studies, science, and even math teachers are also responsible for ensuring that students have access to high-level texts in their content area and

are prepared to read these texts for understanding. See Figure 10-3 for a list of the Common Core State Standards as they relate to content area reading. For a complete description and analysis including grade-level examples, go to www.commoncore.org.

A summary of the Common Core State Standards for science and technical texts follows (see Figure 10-4). For a complete description and analysis including grade-level examples, go to www.commoncore.org.

Content Enhancement Practices

What is content enhancement, and how can teachers use it to teach content area reading? To teach content area information in any subject, a teacher must teach the important concepts and vocabulary and their relationships. The goal is to enhance the content and teach related vocabulary to help students identify, organize, and comprehend important content information (Bulgren, Marquis, Lenz, Shumaker, & Deshler, 2009). In addition, content enhancements inform students of the purpose of instruction and increase student motivation. Content enhancement routines ensure that students possess the prerequisite background knowledge or provide scaffolded instruction so students can obtain this knowledge; assist students in working with related concepts; and give students the skills to predict, solve problems, infer, and synthesize information in a variety of settings. Several types of content enhancements have been developed and recommended: advance organizers, concept diagrams, comparison tables, semantic feature analysis (SFA), or semantic maps, concept mastery, anchoring, and comparison routines.

What is a concept? A concept is a key word or limited number of words that is essential for understanding content. For example, the following concept might be used in a science course:

> Bacteria are a class of microscopic plants that help people, other animals, and plants; however, bacteria also do things that hurt people, other animals, and plants.

Several related ideas that elaborate on the concept of *bacteria* are as follows:

> Bacteria are small; you use a microscope to see them; bacteria multiply; bacteria live in soil, water, organic matter, plants, or animals; bacteria can make you ill; bacteria can spoil food.

The vocabulary associated with the general concept and its related concepts is the *conceptual vocabulary*.

> In this **video** ⏵, you can observe the strategies used by the teacher to support her students' ability to learn mathematics vocabulary and understand important mathematical concepts. How does she activate and engage their prior knowledge and current understanding?

FIGURE 10-3 Common Core State Standards: Reading in the Content Area

Key Ideas and Details

- Cite specific textual evidence to support analysis of primary and secondary sources.
- Determine the central ideas or information of a primary or secondary source; provide an accurate summary of the source distinct from prior knowledge or opinions.
- Identify key steps in a text's description of a process related to history/social studies (e.g., how a bill becomes law, how interest rates are raised or lowered).

Craft and Structure

- Determine the meaning of words and phrases as they are used in a text, including vocabulary specific to domains related to history/social studies.
- Describe how a text presents information (e.g., sequentially, comparatively, causally).
- Identify aspects of a text that reveal an author's point of view or purpose (e.g., loaded language, inclusion or avoidance of particular facts).

Integration of Knowledge and Ideas

- Integrate visual information (e.g., in charts, graphs, photographs, videos, or maps) with other information in print and digital texts.
- Distinguish among fact, opinion, and reasoned judgment in a text.
- Analyze the relationship between a primary and secondary source on the same topic.

Range of Reading and Level of Text Complexity

- By the end of grade 8, read and comprehend history/social studies texts in the grades 6–8 text complexity band independently and proficiently.

Key Ideas and Details

- Cite specific textual evidence to support analysis of science and technical texts.
- Determine the central ideas or conclusions of a text; provide an accurate summary of the text distinct from prior knowledge or opinions.
- Follow precisely a multistep procedure when carrying out experiments, taking measurements, or performing technical tasks.

Craft and Structure

- Determine the meaning of symbols, key terms, and other domain-specific words and phrases as they are used in a specific scientific or technical context relevant to *grades 6–8 texts and topics*.
- Analyze the structure an author uses to organize a text, including how the major sections contribute to the whole and to an understanding of the topic.
- Analyze the author's purpose in providing an explanation, describing a procedure, or discussing an experiment in a text.

Integration of Knowledge and Ideas

- Integrate quantitative or technical information expressed in words in a text with a version of that information expressed visually (e.g., in a flowchart, diagram, model, graph, or table).
- Distinguish among facts, reasoned judgment based on research findings, and speculation in a text.
- Compare and contrast the information gained from experiments, simulations, video, or multimedia sources with that gained from reading a text on the same topic.

Source:

FIGURE 10-4 Common Core State Standards: Science and Technical Texts

Key Ideas and Details

- Cite specific textual evidence to support analysis of science and technical texts.
- Determine the central ideas or conclusions of a text; provide an accurate summary of the text distinct from prior knowledge or opinions.
- Follow precisely a multistep procedure when carrying out experiments, taking measurements, or performing technical tasks.

Craft and Structure

- Determine the meaning of symbols, key terms, and other domain-specific words and phrases as they are used in a specific scientific or technical context relevant to *grades 6–8 texts and topics*.
- Analyze the structure an author uses to organize a text, including how the major sections contribute to the whole and to an understanding of the topic.

- Analyze the author's purpose in providing an explanation, describing a procedure, or discussing an experiment in a text.

Integration of Knowledge and Ideas

- Integrate quantitative or technical information expressed in words in a text with a version of that information expressed visually (e.g., in a flowchart, diagram, model, graph, or table).
- Distinguish among facts, reasoned judgment based on research findings, and speculation in a text.
- Compare and contrast the information gained from experiments, simulations, video, or multimedia sources with that gained from reading a text on the same topic.

Range of Reading and Level of Text Complexity

- Read and comprehend science/technical texts independently and proficiently.

Source: Common Core State Standards Initiative. Retrieved July 23, 2013 from WWW.CORESTANDARDS.ORG.

These are the words that are necessary for understanding the general idea and are associated with it. Examples of the conceptual vocabulary for a unit on bacteria in a science text are *bacteria, microscope, colony, multiply, reproduce,* and *decay.* These words and their meanings facilitate understanding of the general concept.

A six-step process or teaching routine can be used to teach concepts through content enhancement (Anders, Bos, & Filip, 1984; Lenz & Bulgren, 1995). Admittedly, some concepts and vocabulary are more important than others. Deciding what concepts to teach is a crucial part of content area teaching. The process for teaching concepts is presented in Apply the Concept 10-2 and discussed in more detail in the following sections.

Selecting the Big Idea of Content Learning

Before proceeding with selecting content vocabulary and teaching it, teachers must decide what the "big ideas" are they want every student to learn. One way to do this is for the teacher to ask, "What do I want every student to know about this content unit when I finish teaching it?" The answer to this question provides the big ideas for learning and guides the teacher in selecting key concepts and related vocabulary. A teacher needs to determine the conceptual framework for the unit to present the information in an organized fashion on the basis of this framework. During this step, the teacher should focus on the critical information or knowledge all students need to understand about a particular unit (Bulgren et al., 2007; Vaughn, Martinez et al., 2009).

Selecting Concepts and Related Vocabulary

Selecting the major concepts and related vocabulary to be taught in a unit, a chapter, a section of a book, or a lecture is best completed before students interact with the material.

The process that a teacher uses for determining the major concepts depends on his or her expertise and knowledge in the content area, knowledge of the structure of the textbook information, and knowledge about the students' background for the content and their study/reading skills. A teacher who has specialized in a given content area can probably generate concepts from expert knowledge and experiences and use the assigned textbook along with key resource books and Web sites as the primary resources for verifying the appropriateness of those concepts. A teacher with limited background knowledge could use a variety of resources, such as the assigned textbooks, trade books, state or local curriculum guides, Web sites and other computer-based resources, and other teachers or experts in the field. Some texts—especially those written for students with reading problems—tend to provide too much detail and fail to explain the overall concept or to relate the concepts.

After articulating the major concepts to be learned, the teacher next generates and organizes the related vocabulary. To do this, the teacher studies the assigned text and instructional materials and compiles a list of relevant related words and phrases. In doing this, the teacher might realize that some important vocabulary is missing from the text; if so, it can be added to the list.

To organize the vocabulary list, a teacher can group words that are related and then create a semantic or content map to visually represent the relationships among these terms (Swanson et al., 2011). Figure 10-5 depicts a map that was developed with the conceptual vocabulary a teacher generated from a chapter in a biology text. The map helps to solve an all-too-common problem that confronts content area teachers: deciding what concepts and related vocabulary to teach in a content lesson.

10-2 APPLY THE CONCEPT

Process for Teaching Concepts

The following steps can be used to identify and teach key concepts within content area (e.g., science and social studies) instruction:

1. Identify the "big idea" of what you want students to learn.

2. Decide what concepts and related vocabulary to teach.

3. Evaluate the instructional materials to be used for reader-friendliness or considerateness—alter and supplement as needed.

4. Assess the students on their background knowledge for the concepts and related vocabulary.

5. Use prelearning or prereading activities to facilitate and support learning.

6. Conduct the learning or reading activity.

7. Provide postlearning activities that further reinforce and extend the concepts and information learned.

8. Assess students' learning, and reteach if necessary.

FIGURE 10-5 Map with Conceptual Vocabulary

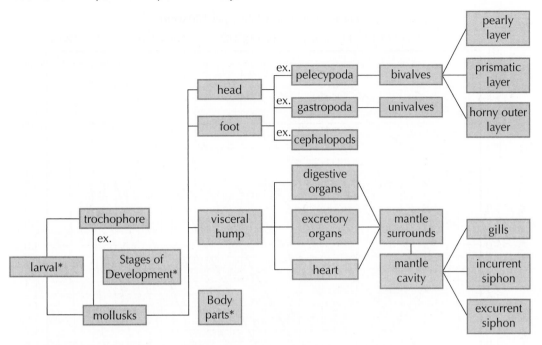

*Note: There seem to be two concepts being developed (apologies to the biologists among us):

1. When classifying animals, biologists look for relationships between animals during the various stages of development from birth to adulthood.

2. Biologists describe the body parts of animals and the functions of each part.

Source: P. L. Anders & C. S. Bos (1984). In the beginning: Vocabulary instruction in content classes. *Topics in Learning and Learning Disabilities, 3*(4), p. 56. Reprinted with permission of PRO-ED.

Evaluating Texts

Before teaching concepts and related vocabulary, teachers need to evaluate the instructional materials and texts they intend to use in teaching the unit so that they are aware of the instruction adaptations needed for students with learning problems. One simple and beneficial way teachers can preview texts is to identify all proper nouns and preteach how to read them and what they mean. Students with reading difficulties who have these proper nouns pretaught read and understand text better (e.g., Fletcher et al., 2006). Some examples of proper nouns include names of cities (e.g., Prague, Beijing, London), states (e.g., Missouri, California), persons (e.g., Mr. Glenview, John Glenshire), and key events (Gettysburg Address).

Although the breadth of instructional materials has increased with the use of the Internet and other media, textbooks still continue to serve as a key resource in instruction. How concepts are presented in a text, whether it is the class textbook, a resource book, or on the Internet, will affect how easily the students comprehend and learn the concepts. The manner in which the text is organized (e.g., use of headings and subheadings, highlighted words, marginal notes) will also affect the comprehensibility of the text.

In this **video** ▶, you will learn how text structure can influence students' comprehension, especially of expository texts. What strategies does the teacher employ to support her eighth-grade students' ability to successfully read their science textbooks?

Readability Traditionally, evaluations of content area texts emphasized readability as determined by readability formulas (e.g., E. Dale & Chall, 1948; Fry, 1977). Most readability formulas, including the Fry readability formula presented in Figure 10-6, are based on two factors: sentence complexity as measured by sentence length, and word difficulty as indexed by word length or frequency. One of the most frequently used procedures for determining the reading level of text is by assessing the Lexile level of the text.

Readability formulas should be used as only one aspect of evaluating a text because they often have a large range of grade levels and do not reveal how difficult the text is for a particular student. For example, a text whose readability formula is predicted to be at grade 7 can range by chance from grade 6.0 to grade 9.0. Readability formulas do not take into account many characteristics of text that are important in comprehension and learning. For example, to reduce the reading level or difficulty as measured by readability formulas, textbooks—particularly adapted

FIGURE 10-6 Fry Readability Graph for Estimating Readability—Extended

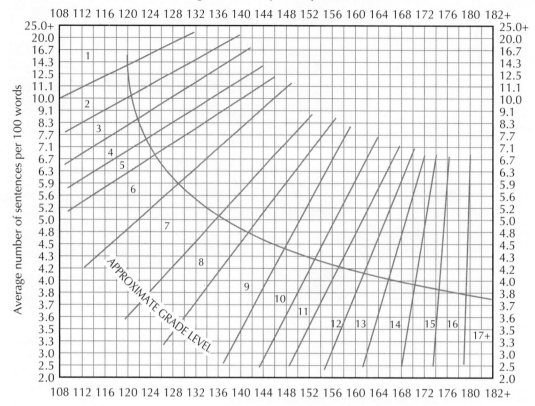

Average number of syllables per 100 words

1. Randomly select three text samples of exactly 100 words, beginning with the beginning of a sentence. Count proper nouns, numerals, and initializations as words.

2. Count the number of sentences in each 100-word sample, estimating the length of the last sentence to the nearest one-tenth.

3. Count the total number of syllables in each 100-word sample. Count one syllable for each numeral or initial or symbol; for example, 1990 is one word and four syllables, LD is one word and two syllables, and "&" is one word and one syllable.

4. Average the number of sentences and number of syllables across the three samples.

5. Enter the average sentence length and average number of syllables on the graph. Put a dot where the two lines intersect. The area in which the dot is plotted will give you an approximate estimated readability.

6. If there is a great deal of variability in the syllable or sentence count across the three samples, more samples can be added.

Source: E. Fry (1977), Fry's readability graph: Clarifications, validity, and extension to level 17, *Journal of Reading, 21,* pp. 242–252.

textbooks that are designed for students with learning and behavior problems—are written in short sentences. Often this means that important relational words such as *and, or, because,* and *if . . . then* have been eliminated to shorten the length of the sentences and thus lower the readability level as predicted by the formula. Although the readability level according to the formula may be lower, the text is actually more difficult to understand. Students' prior knowledge of the content and the concepts and technical vocabulary associated with the content can dramatically affect how easy a text is to comprehend. Last, readability formulas neglect to consider other reader characteristics that affect comprehension, such as interest, purpose, and perseverance.

Another useful tool for determining the complexity of text is coh-metrix. Coh-metrix provides a sophisticated technology for calculating the coherence of text on a wide range of measures. The idea of coh-metrix is to solve many of the problems with readability formulas previously discussed and to help identify text cohesion through the use of a computational tool providing linguistic and discourse representation in text. Figure 10-7 provides a

FIGURE 10-7 Coh-metrix: Computational Tool for Text

> The indices in Coh-Metrix can be categorized into six groups:
>
> 1. General Information and Reference Information
> 2. Readability Indices
> 3. General Word and Text Information
> 4. Syntactic Indices
> 5. Referential and Semantic Indices
> 6. Situational Model Dimensions

brief description of coh-metrix, but a more elaborate one is available on the coh-metrix Web site.

Coh-metrix can be used to analyze text and better understand features of text so that teachers can best align text with student's reading abilities. The coh-metrix site includes a mechanism for calculating the complexity of text on numerous levels.

Considerate, or User-Friendly, Text What characteristics should be considered in evaluating how considerate, or user-friendly, a text is? Criteria for developing considerate text that students can read:

1. *Structure* refers to the manner in which a text is organized and how the text signals its structure. Use of titles, headings, subheadings, introductions, and summary statements; informative and relevant pictures, charts, and graphs; highlighted key concepts; marginal notes; and signaling words (e.g., *first, second, then, therefore*) can facilitate comprehension. In evaluating a text, it is important to check not only whether such structural features are used, but also whether they match the content. For example, sometimes headings will not relate well to the text that follows the headings. In this case, the structural features may serve more as a source of confusion than as an aid. Also, the teacher should check whether the highlighted words in the text represent the important concepts or simply the words that are difficult to decode.

The teacher should also consider whether the format and the table of contents help readers to draw relationships between the various chapters by using such devices as sections and subsections. Do introductions to each section or chapter encourage readers to make connections between previous ideas and concepts already discussed and the new ideas to be presented? Some key features to consider in assessing text structure include:

- The introduction is clearly identified.
- The introduction provides purpose, relevance, and overview.
- Titles, headings, and subheadings reflect main ideas of content.
- Key vocabulary words are highlighted and reflect important concepts.

- Definitions of key terms are provided.
- Signal words or headings are provided.
- Margin notes provide summaries or expand on information.
- Illustrations and pictures enhance important information.
- The summary is clearly identified.
- The summary reviews goals and the most important concepts.
- Review questions require students to think about key concepts and ideas.
- The questions have good balance among main concepts, fact/detail, and critical thinking (application, analysis, reactions).

2. *Coherence* refers to how well the ideas in a text are organized and make sense. Particularly in content area texts, coherence is the way in which the text instructs and makes sense to the reader. With coherent text, the relationships among concepts are clear. Text that is clearer is associated with improved learning, and, importantly, students who are taught to use "self-explanation" while reading text retained the most about what they read (Ainsworth & Burcham, 2007). Coherence is also facilitated by using different kinds of *cohesive ties*—linguistic forms that help to convey meaning across phrase, clause, and sentence boundaries (Rapp et al., 2007).

Examples of cohesive ties are *conjunctions* and *connectives*, *pronoun referents* (using a pronoun to refer to a previously mentioned noun), and *substitutions* (using a word to replace a previously used noun or verb phrase).

3. *Audience appropriateness* refers to how well a textbook is suited to the readers' content knowledge, reading, and study skills. The text needs to provide enough explanation, attributes, examples, and analogies to give readers adequate information to relate to their background knowledge. Superficial mentions of new topics about which the reader has limited background knowledge do little to build understanding. On the other hand, too many or too few technical supporting details can obscure the important concepts.

Another area to consider in relation to the audience is the explicitness of main ideas. Text in which the main ideas are explicit and are regularly placed at the beginning of paragraphs and sections facilitates learning.

Part of the process of preparing to teach content knowledge is evaluating instructional materials for readability and friendliness. By considering the structure, cohesion, and audience appropriateness when evaluating text or other types of

> Chapter 8 discusses how to teach strategies for understanding the main ideas to students with learning and behavior difficulties.

instructional materials (e.g., films, lectures, demonstrations), teachers develop a good idea of how considerate, or user-friendly, the materials are. Based on this evaluation, teachers may decide to modify, augment, or adapt the instructional materials (see the section on adapting textbooks later in this chapter).

Assessing Students' Background Knowledge

Before content area teachers assign a specific chapter or text to read or present a lecture on a topic, they need to assess the students' background knowledge for the concepts and related vocabulary to be covered. Background knowledge plays a critical role in determining how effectively students will comprehend and retain the information and vocabulary to be presented. Semantic mapping (Klingner, Vaughn, & Boardman, 2007) develops background knowledge by using brainstorming ideas about the topic to generate a list of words and phrases related to the key concept. The teacher and students take the ideas given by the students and relate them to the key concept, developing a network that notes the various relationships (e.g., categories, subcategories, definition, class, examples, properties, or characteristics). A semantic map for the concept of *desert* was developed by a group of fifth-grade students with learning disabilities who were preparing to study deserts. The map shown in Figure 10-8, indicates that the students could give examples and characteristics of a desert. However, the students did not produce a class (landform) or a definition ("What is it?"). Additionally, the property and example relations that were generated lacked technical vocabulary, despite further probing on the part of the teacher. The semantic map in Figure 10-8 serves not only as a visual representation of the students' current understanding of the concept of *desert*, but also as

an initial blueprint for teaching (Reyes & Bos, 1998).

Using activities such as semantic mapping and PReP not only provides teachers with valuable information about their students' knowledge, but also activates the students' knowledge. We have found that promoting discussions during these activities and encouraging students to relate first-hand experiences help both students and teachers make connections and clarify concepts.

See Chapter 8 for a review of a technique that assesses background knowledge, the PreReading Plan (PReP).

Using Prelearning Activities

Limited background knowledge signals the teacher that students need more instruction to learn the information that will be presented in a text or lecture. Teachers can present any number of prelearning activities—such as advance organizers, SFA, semantic mapping, and concept diagrams—that students can use before reading an assigned text or listening to a lecture.

Advance Organizers Advance organizers are activities that orient students to the material before reading or class presentation. They provide students with an overview or preview of the content they will be learning. Use of advance organizers is based on the notion that students profit from having a framework for the material to be learned to help them assimilate the new information into their current schemas or cognitive structure. Advance organizers should inform students of the purpose of instruction, identify topics and subtopics, supply background information, introduce new vocabulary, provide an organizational structure, and state the intended student outcomes. Reviews of studies that have explored the effectiveness of

FIGURE 10-8 Concept Map of Fifth-Grade Students' Knowledge of Deserts

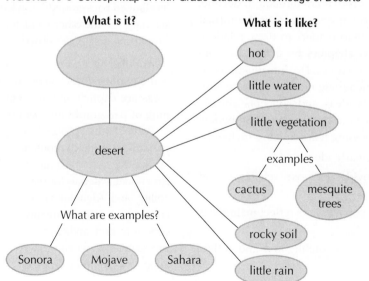

advance organizers on learning have drawn the following conclusions (Corkill, 1992; Preiss & Gayle, 2006):

- Groups that are given advance organizers consistently perform better than control groups that do not receive them. This advantage diminishes when the material is familiar, when the learners have an extensive background of knowledge about the area, when the learners have high IQs, and when tests fail to measure the breadth of transfer ability.
- Advance organizers particularly aid students of lower ability and/or limited background knowledge.
- Advance organizers are more effective when presented before a learning task than when presented after the task.
- Advance organizers that are well structured and detailed are associated with improved learning and retention of learning (Gurlitt, Dummel, Schuster, & Nückles 2012).

Evidence-Based PRACTICE

Advance Organizers

PROCEDURES: Lenz (1983; Lenz et al., 1987, 2005) identified 10 steps for teachers to follow in using an advance organizer (see Apply the Concept 10-3). The resource teacher trained the students in the resource classroom to use advance organizers by giving the students a worksheet with each of the 10 steps as headings. The students then practiced listening to advance organizers given by the resource teacher and completing the worksheets. Next, the students used the advance organizer worksheet in inclusive content area classes, and the resource teacher and students met afterward to discuss the success of the worksheets. They discussed how they could use the advance organizer information to organize notes and how they could modify the worksheet to assist the students to cue in on the most common organizing principles used by particular teachers.

In giving an advance organizer, the teacher provides an organizational framework for the information to be learned (see step 3 in Apply the Concept 10-3). This

In this **video** ▶, a special education teacher supports her students' ability to learn science content through the use of an advance organizer. How does she construct this graphic organizer to scaffold their success? How does she ensure that her students understand the expectations for their participation in the small-group activity? Refer to *Apply the Concept 10-3* for more information about using advance organizers.

10-3 APPLY THE CONCEPT

Steps in Using an Advance Organizer

1. Inform the students of advance organizers.
   a. Announce the advance organizer.
   b. State the benefits of the advance organizer.
   c. Suggest that students take notes on the advance organizer.
2. Clarify the action to be taken.
   a. State the teacher's actions.
   b. State the students' actions.
3. Identify the topics or tasks.
   a. Identify major topics or activities.
   b. Identify subtopics or component activities.
4. Provide background information.
   a. Relate the topic to the course or previous lesson.
   b. Relate the topic to new information.
5. State the concepts to be learned.
   a. State specific concepts/ideas from the lesson.
   b. State general concepts/ideas that are broader than the lesson's content.

6. Clarify the concepts to be learned.
   a. Clarify by examples or analogies.
   b. Clarify by nonexamples.
   c. Caution students of possible misunderstandings.
7. Motivate the students to learn.
   a. Point out the relevance to students.
   b. Be specific, short-term, personalized, and believable.
8. Introduce vocabulary.
   a. Identify the new terms, and define them.
   b. Repeat difficult terms, and define them.
9. Provide an organizational framework.
   a. Present an outline, list, or narrative of the lesson's content.
10. State the general outcome desired.
    a. State the objectives of the instruction/learning.
    b. Relate the outcomes to test performance.

Source: Based on B. K. Lenz (1983), Promoting active learning through effective instruction. *Pointer, 27*(2), p. 12.

framework might be an outline, a diagram in which the parts are labeled, or a picture semantic map, as discussed earlier. The use of visual representations or pictures is particularly salient for students with learning and behavior problems (N. H. Schwartz, Ellsworth, Graham, & Knight, 1998).

COMMENTS: Lenz, Alley, and Schumaker (1987) found that regular content area teachers can implement advance organizers with minimal teacher training (45 minutes). Teachers who used advance organizers expressed satisfaction with the students' response to the instruction as well as the improvement in the overall quality of their own instruction. However, Lenz did find that teacher use of an advance organizer alone was not enough to facilitate student learning. "Learning disabled students had to be made aware that advance organizers were being presented and then had to be trained in the types of information presented in the advance organizer and ways in which that information could be made useful" (Lenz, 1983, p. 12).

Concept Diagrams and Comparison Tables The concept diagram as part of the Concept Mastery Routine (Bulgren et al., 2007; Bulgren, Schumaker, & Deshler, 1988, 1996) is a content enhancement tool that teachers can use to assist students in understanding important key concepts in the reading or lecture; it also works well as a prelearning activity. Research revealed that the Concept Mastery Routine led to gains in students' knowledge in concept and expression of information. The concept diagram is a visual tool that supports students as they delineate a concept by doing the following:

- Exploring their prior knowledge of the concept
- Understanding the relationship of the concept to the overall concept class to which it belongs
- Classifying characteristics of the concept
- Generating examples and nonexamples
- Constructing a content-related definition of the concept

Evidence-Based PRACTICE

Concept Diagrams and Comparison Tables

PROCEDURES: In using a concept diagram (see Figure 10-9), the first step is to prepare the diagram. The teacher identifies major and related concepts of which the students need a deeper or more technical understanding. In a science chapter on fossils, Mr. Bello, the seventh-grade science teacher, felt that it was important that the students develop a more technical understanding of the concept of fossils, so this became the concept to diagram. Second, Mr. Bello used the instructional

materials and his knowledge to list important characteristics of fossils. He also thought about whether each characteristic is "always present," "sometimes present," or "never present." Third, he located examples and nonexamples of the concepts in the instructional materials. In reviewing the chapter he found that nonexamples were not provided, so he decided to show the students fossils and nonfossils to help them to start thinking about examples and nonexamples. Finally, Mr. Bello constructed a definition.

After preparing the concept diagram, the next step is using it with the students to develop their understanding of the concept. After giving an advance organizer to explain its purpose, how the diagram works, and the expectations, the teacher can use the linking steps to teach the concept (Bulgren et al., 1988):

Convey the concept name and why it is the focus of study.

Offer the overall or overarching concept.

Note the key words by having the students brainstorm words related to the concept.

Classify the characteristics by using the key words and other ideas to generate characteristics that are always, sometimes, and never present.

Explore and list examples and nonexamples.

Practice with the examples by having students discuss how the examples relate to the characteristics.

Tie down a definition by generating a content-related definition that includes the concept, the overall concepts, and the characteristics that are always present.

COMMENTS: Concept diagrams help not just students with learning disabilities but all learners in the classroom, making them ideal for inclusion settings. Figure 10-10 presents a sample comparison table and includes the steps that are used in generating the table (see the steps in the upper-right-hand corner, which are the acrostic for COMPARING). An important part of this table and the steps in generating it is outlining the similar and dissimilar characteristics.

Bulgren and her colleagues note that both the concept diagram and the comparison table as shown in Figures 10-9 and 10-10 are "instructional tools developed and researched at the University of Kansas Center for Research on Learning. They represent a number of organizing and teaching devices designed for teachers to use as they teach content information to classes containing diverse student populations. They are data-based teaching instruments that have been found effective when used in instructional routines that combine cues about the instruction, specialized delivery of the content, involvement of the students in the cognitive processes, and

FIGURE 10-9 Concept Diagram

CONCEPT DIAGRAM

Concept	fossils

Overall Concept	past geologic age

Classifying Characteristics

Always Present	Sometimes Present	Never Present
remains or prints	frozen in ice	still alive
plants or animals	trapped in tar	still decaying
thousands of years old	crushed by water	
preserved in the earth	in volcanic ash	

Example:

- tigers in La Brea tar pits
- Siberian mammoth
- petrified forest in Arizona
- fish skeleton in limestone layers

Nonexample:

- your pet cat
- elephant in Africa today
- tree limbs and leaves in your yard
- fish in supermarket

Definition: Fossils are remains or prints of plants or animals who lived thousands of years ago that have been preserved in the earth.

---

a review of the learning process and content materials" (Bulgren, Lenz, Schumaker, & Deshler, 1995).

Semantic Feature Analysis/Relationship Charts Like an advance organizer, SFA is a prelearning activity that serves to organize the major concepts and related vocabulary to be taught in a unit, chapter, or lecture. Whereas the concept diagram can be used to clarify a concept that is difficult for the students, the SFA activity helps students to see the relationships between the major concepts, the related vocabulary, and their current knowledge of the topic. Because knowledge is hierarchically organized, relating the new concepts to students' prior knowledge will help students learn these new concepts. In addition, teaching attributes of a concept as well as teaching examples and nonexamples are important to concept learning, and principles of scaffolded instruction and interactive dialogues will promote learning.

Evidence-Based PRACTICE

Semantic Feature Analysis and Relationship Charts

PROCEDURES: The first step in preparing for an SFA activity is to develop a relationship chart. This chart is based on the idea that ideas or concepts are related to one another in terms of a hierarchy of abstractness. The most inclusive or abstract ideas are called *superordinate concepts;* the most concrete or narrow ideas are identified as *subordinate concepts.* Ideas or concepts that fall in between the superordinate and subordinate concepts are referred to as *coordinate concepts* (Frayer, Frederick, & Klausmeier, 1969). These ideas are then organized into a relationship chart, and the students and teacher discuss the relationship between the various levels of concepts and their own background knowledge. This SFA activity was originally

FIGURE 10-10 Comparison Table for the Concepts of Decimals and Fractions

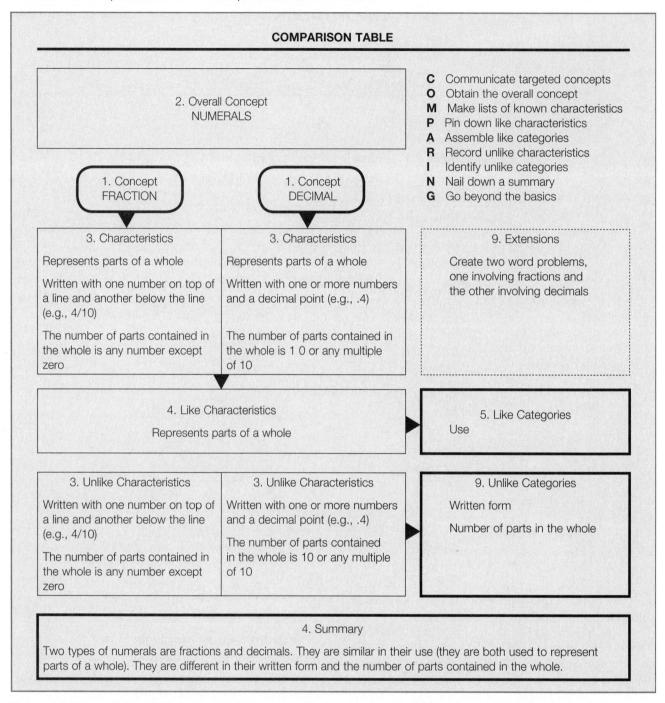

COMPARISON TABLE

2. Overall Concept
NUMERALS

C Communicate targeted concepts
O Obtain the overall concept
M Make lists of known characteristics
P Pin down like characteristics
A Assemble like categories
R Record unlike characteristics
I Identify unlike categories
N Nail down a summary
G Go beyond the basics

1. Concept
FRACTION

1. Concept
DECIMAL

3. Characteristics

Represents parts of a whole

Written with one number on top of a line and another below the line (e.g., 4/10)

The number of parts contained in the whole is any number except zero

3. Characteristics

Represents parts of a whole

Written with one or more numbers and a decimal point (e.g., .4)

The number of parts contained in the whole is 1 0 or any multiple of 10

9. Extensions

Create two word problems, one involving fractions and the other involving decimals

4. Like Characteristics

Represents parts of a whole

5. Like Categories

Use

3. Unlike Characteristics

Written with one number on top of a line and another below the line (e.g., 4/10)

The number of parts contained in the whole is any number except zero

3. Unlike Characteristics

Written with one or more numbers and a decimal point (e.g., .4)

The number of parts contained in the whole is 10 or any multiple of 10

9. Unlike Categories

Written form

Number of parts in the whole

4. Summary

Two types of numerals are fractions and decimals. They are similar in their use (they are both used to represent parts of a whole). They are different in their written form and the number of parts contained in the whole.

Source: J. A. Bulgren, B. Lenz, D. D. Deshler, & J. B. Schumaker, *The Concept Comparison* Routine (Lawrence, KS: Edge Enterprises, Inc., 1995), p. 55. Reprinted with permission.

developed for use in teaching a specific concept, such as is used with concept diagrams (Johnson & Pearson, 1984). In their interactive teaching research, Bos and her colleagues adapted this strategy to text (Bos & Anders, 1992).

When Ms. Cho, the teacher described at the beginning of the chapter, used this technique in her American government class, she first read the assigned American government chapter on contracts. As she read, she listed the important concepts or vocabulary and then arranged them according to superordinate, coordinate, and subordinate concepts. She used words as well as relevant phrases:

contract	counteroffer
promise	holding good
contracting parties	conditions
buyer	acceptance
seller	consideration
written contracts	statute of frauds
verbal contracts	legal obligation
contractual offer	legal action

Next, she organized the vocabulary into a relationship chart (see Figure 10-11). The superordinate concept "Contracts" is used as the name for the chart. The five coordinate concepts (main ideas in the text) serve as the column headings and are listed as the important or major ideas. The related vocabulary or subordinate concepts are listed down the side of the chart. Notice that Ms. Cho left blank spaces for adding important ideas and important vocabulary. She encourages students to add relevant information from their background knowledge.

The relationship chart became Ms. Cho's instructional tool. She made a copy for each student and a transparency so that the class could complete the chart as a group. To do this, she introduced the topic (superordinate concept) of the assignment. The students then discussed what they already knew about contracts. Next, she introduced each coordinate concept (important idea) by assisting the students in generating meanings. During this introduction and throughout the activity, she encouraged students to add their personal experiences or understandings of the terms. For example, when Ms. Cho presented the major idea of *contract,* Joe inquired whether a contract had to be written to be legal. This led to Anya's conveying a first-hand experience of her father's making a verbal contract and having the contract honored in court even though it was not written. The discussion ended with one of the purposes for reading being the clarification of what was needed for a verbal contract to be considered legal.

Following the discussion of the coordinate concepts, Ms. Cho introduced each subordinate concept. Again Ms. Cho and her students predicted what the meanings would be in relation to the topic of contracts. For the more technical vocabulary (e.g., *contractual offer, statute of frauds*), Ms. Cho sometimes provided the meaning, or the students decided to read to clarify the concept. After introducing each concept, she and the students discussed the relationship between each coordinate concept or phrase and each subordinate term or phrase. They used a plus sign (+) to represent a positive relationship,

FIGURE 10-11 Relationship Chart: Contracts

CONTRACTS					Name: _____ Period: _____
	Important Ideas				
	Contract	Promise	Written Contracts	Verbal Contracts	Conditions
Legal action					
Consideration					
Legal obligation					
Holding good					
Contractual offer					
Counteroffer					
Acceptance					
Statute of frauds					
Contracting parties					

+ = positive relationship
− = negative relationship
0 = no relationship
? = unknown relationship

a minus sign (−) to represent a negative relationship, a zero (0) to signify no relationship, and a question mark (?) to indicate that no consensus could be reached without further information.

Ms. Cho found that student involvement during the discussion was important to the success of the SFA strategy. One key to a fruitful discussion was encouraging students to ask each other why they had reached a certain relationship rating. This seemed to encourage students to use their prior knowledge about the topic and seemed to encourage other students to activate what they already knew about the vocabulary.

After completing the relationship chart, Ms. Cho guided the students in setting purposes for reading. These purposes, for the most part, focused on the chart, reading to confirm their predictions and to determine the relationships between the terms for which no agreement could be reached. After completing the reading, Ms. Cho and the students reviewed the relationship chart. They discussed changes to any of the relationships if necessary and reached consensus on those that were previously unknown.

Sometimes when Ms. Cho and her students used a relationship chart, they found that some information was still unclear after reading the text. Then they checked other sources, such as experts in the field, technical and trade books, the Internet, and other media. Ms. Cho also taught the students how to use the relationship chart to study for chapter tests by asking each other questions based on the meanings of the concepts and vocabulary and on their relationships (e.g., What is a contractual offer? What are the conditions necessary to have a contract?). She also taught how the chart could be used to write a report about the concepts.

COMMENTS: Findings from a synthesis on graphic organizers (A. Kim et al., 2004) confirmed that SFA was consistently associated with gains in comprehension. One of the most important questions that is asked during discussion is, Why? (e.g., Why is *evidence* positively related to *evidence in court?*). Students need to justify their reasoning. By answering *why* questions, students think through concepts, reaching a deeper understanding and more effectively relating new information to old.

Semantic and Curriculum Maps Semantic and curriculum maps (Klingner et al., 2007; Lenz, Adams, Bulgren, Pouloit, & Laraux, 2007; Vaughn, Martinez, et al., 2009; Vaughn, Swanson, et al., 2013) are ways of visually representing the concepts and important vocabulary to be taught (refer back to Figure 10-8). These content enhancement devices can be used as prelearning activities that assist students in activating their prior knowledge and in

seeing the relationships between new concepts and related vocabulary.

Semantic Maps

PROCEDURES: In using semantic maps, the teacher can begin by putting the major concept for a lecture or text on the board and then ask students to generate a list of related vocabulary from their background knowledge. However, when presenting more technical vocabulary, the teacher could begin by writing on the board the list of important vocabulary he or she generated in reviewing the text chapter or developing the lecture. After listing the words, the teacher discusses the meanings of the words, using a procedure similar to the one just presented in the section on SFA. Next, the teacher arranges and rearranges the vocabulary with the students until the class has a map that shows the relationships that exist among the ideas.

For example, when presenting the following words for a chapter on fossils, the students and teacher first grouped the animals together.

trilobites	small horses
crinoids	winged insects
ferns	geography of the present
dinosaurs	land masses
lakes	brachiopods
bodies of water	saber-toothed tigers
animals	guide fossils
geography	rivers of the past
trees	plants
oceans	continents

Next, they grouped the plants together. In the case of guide fossils and several other types of fossils with which the students were not familiar (e.g., crinoids, trilobites), they decided to wait until they had read before placing the concepts on the map. Finally, they grouped together the geography terms.

After the map is completed, the teacher instructs the students to refer to the map while reading and/or listening to the lecture. Like the relationship chart, the semantic map can provide a framework for setting purposes for reading. The students read to confirm and clarify their understanding in relation to the map and make changes to it during discussions held as they read or after completing a chapter. The map can also serve as a blueprint for studying and for writing reports.

COMMENTS: A number of researchers have investigated the use of semantic mapping with students who are low

FIGURE 10-12 Visual Display

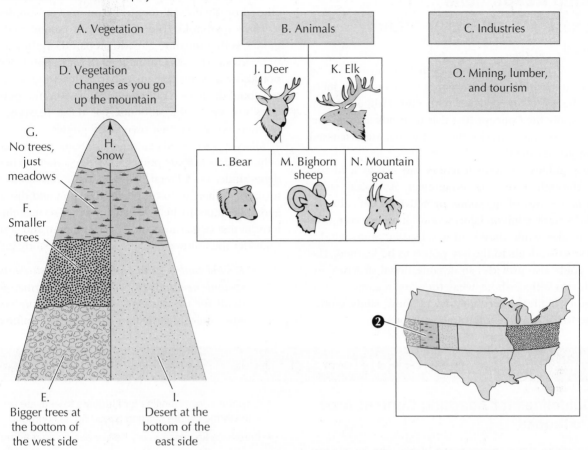

A. Vegetation

D. Vegetation changes as you go up the mountain

G. No trees, just meadows

H. Snow

F. Smaller trees

E. Bigger trees at the bottom of the west side

I. Desert at the bottom of the east side

B. Animals

J. Deer

K. Elk

L. Bear

M. Bighorn sheep

N. Mountain goat

C. Industries

O. Mining, lumber, and tourism

❷

Source: C. Darch & D. Carnine (1986), Teaching content area material to learning disabled students, *Exceptional Children, 53,* p. 243. Copyright © 1986 by the Council for Exceptional Children. Reprinted with permission.

achievers or have learning disabilities (see for review, A. Kim et al., 2004). In some cases, the students generated the maps; in other studies, the teacher had already developed the framework for the map, and the student completed them. Some studies provided a map or visual display (see Figure 10-12) to the students in completed form, and systematic direct instruction (Carnine, 1989) was used to assist the students in learning the information contained in the display (Darch & Carnine, 1986; Bergerud, Lovitt, & Horton, 1988). The research has been consistently encouraging in this area: The use of semantic maps or visual representations of information improves the learning performance of students with learning and behavior problems.

Reinforcing Concept Learning During and After Learning

Whether using an advance organizer, SFA, semantic map, concept diagram, or comparison table, these frameworks can be used to guide students as they read a text or listen to a lecture and as they react to their learning. For example, a semantic map can be used before, during, and after a lesson—students can add new vocabulary to the existing map during the lesson and can revise the map after the lesson. Also, the list of major ideas that is obtained from the advance organizer can serve as the framework in which students can take notes when listening to a lecture. After the lecture, students can meet in small groups and share their notes to create one overview that can serve as a study guide for the test. Students can be instructed on how to develop questions based on a concept diagram or semantic map. These questions can serve as self-questions to be asked when reading and when studying for a test.

Students generally require considerable practice in using these content enhancement devices.

WEB RESOURCES

For helpful Web sites on content area learning, see:

- National Science Teachers Association (NSTA) Web site: http://www.nsta.org.

- National Council for the Social Studies: http://www.socialstudies.org.

Making Adaptations

Textbook Adaptations and Study Guides

Text adaptation is a technique that involves making changes to or adding to an existing text to make it more comprehensible for students with and without special needs. Apply the Concept 10-4 lists textbook adaptations that teachers may consider, three of which are discussed here in greater depth.

Study guides are tools teachers can use to lead students through a reading assignment. A typical study guide is a series of questions or activities that emphasize important content information. Students complete study guides while they read a selection. Study guides help direct students to the key points to be learned. The study guide also provides an organizational structure for students to reflect about what they are reading and to engage in higher order thinking. In short, study guides help to "tutor" a student through a chapter.

Commercially prepared study guides can be purchased or obtained through the Internet as supplements to some textbooks. The advantage of commercial study guides is that they are already prepared, so they are real time-savers. The disadvantage is that the publisher does not know a given teacher's style of teaching, emphasis, or school district's requirements. Moreover, the publisher does not know the students. For these reasons, many teachers construct their own study guides.

Many types of study guides exist. Some are designed to help students activate prior knowledge, others to help students understand literal or inferential information in the textbook, others to foster peer interaction and discussion, and still others to help students recognize meaning patterns in text (e.g., cause and effect, compare and contrast). Consider the following when developing a study guide:

- *Decide how a guide will assist the students with special needs.* Is the textbook information difficult for the students to access and understand? Are there particular sources of information

---

10–4 APPLY THE CONCEPT

Guidelines for Adapting Content Area Textbooks

Substitute the textbook for students who have severe word-recognition problems:

- Audio record textbook content.
- Read textbook aloud to students.
- Pair students to master textbook content.
- Use direct experiences, films, videos, audio recordings, and computer programs as substitutes for textbook reading.
- Work with students individually or in small groups to master textbook material.

Simplify the textbook for students whose reading level is far below that of the textbook used in class:

- Construct abridged versions of the textbook content, or use the publisher's abridged version.
- Provide students with chapter outlines or summaries.
- Use a multilevel, multimaterial approach.

Highlight key concepts for students who have difficulty comprehending textbook material:

- Preview reading assignments with students to orient them to the topic and provide guidelines for budgeting reading and study time.
- Provide students with a purpose for reading.
- Provide an overview of an assignment before reading.

- Structure opportunities for students to activate prior knowledge before starting a reading assignment.
- Introduce key vocabulary before assigning reading.
- Develop a study guide to direct learning.
- Summarize or reduce textbook information to guide classroom discussions and independent reading.
- Color-code or highlight textbooks.
- Reduce the length of assignments.
- Slow down the pace of reading assignments.
- Provide assistance in answering text-based questions.
- Demonstrate or model effective reading strategies.
- Place students in cooperative learning groups to master textbook content.
- Teach comprehension-monitoring techniques to improve ongoing understanding of text material.
- Teach students to use graphic aids to understand textbook information.

Increase idea retention for students who have difficulty with long-term memory:

- Structure postreading activities to improve retention of content.
- Teach reading strategies to improve retention.
- Teach students to record key concepts and terms for study purposes.
- Teach memory strategies to improve retention of text material.

(e.g., graphs and figures) that need to be interpreted? Will students with special needs require support and guidance to get through the chapter and to grasp the most important ideas?

- *Analyze the chapter organization and content.* Can some parts be omitted? Are some parts easier to understand than others? What skills will students need to read and understand this material?

- *Decide how you want to structure your study guide.* Create one that includes the suggested components:

  - Specific information about the reading assignment (page numbers, title)

  - Learning objectives of the assignment

  - Purpose statement for the assignment

  - Introduction of key terms or vocabulary

  - Activities for students to complete

  - Questions for students to answer as they read

  - Sources and Web sites that might provide further information

  - Suggestions about how and when parents and other students can provide assistance

Text Highlighting   Students with comprehension problems have difficulty sifting out important information. Underlining or highlighting key points in textbooks can help students attend to the most salient information. Teachers can highlight the information in a textbook that they think is most important. Then students or adult volunteers can use this book as a guide to highlight the same information in books for students with reading and learning disabilities. Keep in mind that the teacher will also want to teach students this and other textbook study skills (see the section "Study Skills and Learning Strategies").

Using Alternative Reading Materials   For students with very low reading skills who can learn by listening, the teacher can do the following:

- *Audio record textbook chapters.* Some publishers provide Web access of CDs with their textbooks. If the textbook you are using is not accompanied by an audio version, adult and/or student volunteers can read and record the chapters. Students can then listen to the audio at home or in their resource classes.

- *Read text aloud to students.* Encourage students to follow along, reading silently. Pause frequently to assess student learning from the reading.

- *Pair a good reader with a poor reader.* The good reader reads the textbook material aloud and, together, the two students learn the content. Both

students should use self-monitoring comprehension strategies to ensure that both readers comprehend the text.

- *Identify Web sites that teach.* Most students are comfortable using Web sites to acquire information, including video sites.

Sometimes teachers find it necessary to use alternative materials that present similar content, such as films, videos, and trade books. Computer software programs in which the text can be read by the computer, such as encyclopedias on CD-ROM, are other resources.

Teachers may also supplement textbooks with informational trade books (both fiction and nonfiction) and other reading materials (such as magazines and journals). By providing additional reading material that covers similar content to the textbook, teachers enable students who cannot read the textbook to access the content. People today discuss software programs in terms of their user-friendliness. Is the program easy to understand? Does the program use familiar language or at least define unfamiliar terms? Does the program give the user cue words or icons to signal the important ideas and processes? If the user does not understand something, does the program allow the user to ask questions? Does the program have more than one way to explain a difficult concept or process? If the program has these features, then one might consider it user-friendly.

Now take a minute to reread the previous paragraph, but substitute the word *lecture* for the word *program* and the word *listener* for the word *user*. Just as using considerate, or user-friendly, text assists students in learning the critical information, a well-organized lecture makes the students' work easier in that it assists them in seeing relationships among concepts and distinguishing important from supplementary information. It also helps them relate new information to old.

As teachers plan their teaching, the following guidelines can make lectures "listener-friendly":

- Use advance organizers.

- Preteach important vocabulary.

- Use cue words or phrases to let students know what information is important (e.g., "It is important that you know . . .," "The key information to remember is . . .," "In summary . . .").

- Repeat important information.

- Write important information on the board, a transparency, and/or a handout.

- Stress key points by varying the tone and quality of your voice.

- Number ideas or points (e.g., *first, second, next, then, finally*).

- Write technical words or words that are difficult to spell.

- Use a study guide that lists the major concepts, with space for students to add other information.

- Use pictures, concept diagrams, and content maps to show relationships among ideas.

- Provide examples and nonexamples of the concepts you are discussing.

- Ask questions and encourage discussion that requires students to relate the new information to ideas they already know (from their own background or your previous lectures).

- Stop frequently, and have students discuss what they have learned with partners.

- Allow time at the end of a lecture for students to look over their notes, summarize, and ask questions.

Apply the Concept 10-5 provides cues that can assist students in "seeing" the key information. By using these guidelines, teachers will naturally incorporate cues that indicate what information is important.

One technique that has been effective for students with learning and behavior problems in enhancing their understanding and recall of information presented through lectures is the pause procedure (e.g., Dyson, 2008; Hock, 2012; Ruhl, 1996). This procedure consists of pausing during natural breaks in lectures and having students work as partners for about 2 minutes to discuss

10-5 APPLY THE CONCEPT

Cues to Listen and Watch for in Lectures

Type of Cue	Examples
Organizational cues	"Today, we will be discussing . . ."
	"The topic I want to cover today . . ."
	"There are [number] points I want you to be sure to learn . . ."
	"The important relationship is . . ."
	"The main point of this discussion is . . ."
	Any statement that signals a number or position (e.g., *first, last, next, then*).
	"To review/summarize/recap . . ."
Emphasis cues	
Verbal	"You need to know/understand/remember . . ."
	"This is important/key/basic/critical . . ."
	"Let me repeat this . . ."
	"Let me check, now do you understand . . .?"
	Any statement is repeated.
	Words or terms are emphasized.
	Teacher speaks more slowly, more loudly, or with more emphasis.
	Teacher stresses certain words.
	Teacher spells words.
	Teacher asks rhetorical question.
Nonverbal	Information written on overhead/board.
	Information handed out in study guide.
	Teacher emphasizes the point using gestures.

Source: Based on S. K. Suritsky & C. A. Hughes, Note-taking strategy instruction, in D. D. Deshler, E. S. Ellis, & B. K. Lenz, *Teaching Adolescents with Learning Disabilities*, 2nd ed. (Denver, CO: Love, 1996) and Schumaker & Deshler, 2005.

what they are learning and review their notes. Another way to implement the pause procedure is to give students a chance to write one thing they learned and to write one question. At the end of the 2 minutes, the teacher asks students whether they have any questions or concepts that need further discussion or clarification. The teacher then resumes lecturing.

Many content area teachers use Power Points to display critical content information. One procedure that can make learning "less passive" and lead to greater understanding is developing questions about the content that relate to the PowerPoints and promote more interactive and engaged learning (Gier & Kreiner, 2009).

Adapting Class Assignments and Homework

One area in which students with learning and behavior problems often struggle is the completion of assignments and homework. Students with learning disabilities, and particularly students with attention problems, have greater difficulty completing homework assignments (Langberg et al., 2010). Furthermore, students with special learning needs spend more time completing homework assignments than average-achieving students (Harniss, Epstein, Bursuck, Nelson, & Jayanthi, 2001). At the same time, homework has become a significant part of schooling, accounting for a significant amount of time students spend learning. Furthermore, completing homework is associated with both grades, staying in school, and achievement.

> In this **video** ▶, you will learn the importance of adapting and modifying assignments, assessments, and expectations for students with special learning needs such as disabilities or English language learners. How can you accurately assess students' content knowledge if they have limited reading and/or writing skills?

What can teachers do to facilitate homework success for students? Consider that the most common homework and assignment type problems include (Evans et al., 2009; Langberg et al., 2010):

- Problems forgetting to bring materials home and also returning materials to school
- Inaccurately recording homework assignments
- Having unrealistic plans or no plans for completing assignments
- Procrastinating completion of work
- Submitting assignments that are incomplete
- Having disorganized book bags, lockers, and other resources so that organizing and completing assignments is difficult

Teachers can facilitate students' success with assignments and homework by:

- Assisting them in developing a checklist to organize whether they know the assignment, have the materials, and know who to check with for questions
- Keeping a calendar with due dates
- Developing a plan to complete assignments and homework
- Establishing a plan that provides for positive feedback or successfully completing assignments and homework

After conducting a comprehensive review of the literature, H. Cooper and Nye (1994; H. M. Cooper, 2007) concluded that homework assignments for students with disabilities should be brief, focused on reinforcement rather than new material, monitored carefully, and supported through parental involvement. Especially for students with special needs, we do not want homework to result in a "battle" between parents and students. One way to prevent this is to give complete information for assignments. Having complete information helps to motivate students, as does giving them real-life assignments (i.e., assignments that connect homework to events or activities in the home) plus reinforcement, using homework planners, and graphing homework completion. The tips in Apply the Concept 10-6 can help teachers to provide students with a complete set of directions.

Class assignments and homework can be adapted for special learners so that they can experience success without undue attention being brought to their learning difficulties. The key to success is to make assignments appropriate in content, length, time required to complete, and skill level needed to accomplish the task. It is also important to explain the assignments, model several problems if appropriate, and check for understanding (Bender, 2008). Students should know how and where to get help if they get stuck.

Constructing and Adapting Tests

The best way to discover what students have learned is to construct student-friendly tests, adapt test administration and scoring as necessary, consider alternatives to testing (such as assessment portfolios), and teach test-taking skills. Student-friendly tests are considerate to the test taker in both content and format. The content has been covered in class or assigned readings, and students have been told explicitly that they are responsible for learning it. The format is clear and easy to understand.

To construct student-friendly tests, a teacher must first decide what skills and concepts to include. In the test format, directions should be clear and unambiguous, and items should be legible and properly spaced. Attention

Tips for Giving Assignments

1. Explain the purpose of the assignment. Stress what you expect students to learn and why learning the skill or concept is important. Connect the skill or concept to real-life applications.

2. Explain in detail the procedures for completing the assignment. To check for understanding, ask one or two students to summarize the procedures.

3. Get students started by modeling one or two problems or by providing an example.

4. Describe the equipment and materials needed to complete the assignment.

5. Anticipate trouble spots, and ask students how they might tackle difficult parts in the assignment.

6. Explain when the assignment is due.

7. Explain how the assignment will be graded and how it will affect students' grades.

8. Describe appropriate ways to get help or support in completing the assignment.

9. For an in-class assignment, explain your expectations for student behavior while they complete the assignment, and explain what students who finish early should do.

10. Address students' questions.

to format is important for all students, but particularly for those who have difficulty reading and taking tests and who are overly anxious about taking tests. Perhaps one of the most important things to consider with testing is time. Particularly for students with disabilities, most will need additional time to show what they know in a testing situation.

Even with student-friendly tests, students with learning and behavior problems may have difficulty reading tests, working within time constraints, or resisting distractions during a test. Poor or laborious writing can cause them to tire easily and can inhibit performance on a test.

All students tend to perform better on assessments when they are provided accommodations such as more time (Lang et al., 2008; B. J. Lovett, 2010); however, students with disabilities often have differential performance, particularly on reading assessments (Lang et al., 2008). Fortunately, students tend to view accommodations as fair for most students but even more fair for students with disabilities (Lang et al., 2008).

Apply the Concept 10-7 suggests accommodations for test administration and scoring. As teachers decide which, if any, adaptations to use, they should consider

Testing Accommodations

- Read proper nouns to students.
- Read question stems to students.
- Teach students test-taking skills.
- Give frequent quizzes rather than only exams.
- Give take-home tests.
- Test on less content than the rest of the class.
- Change types of questions (e.g., from essay to multiple choice).
- Give extended time to finish tests.
- Read test questions to students.
- Use tests with enlarged print.
- Highlight key words in questions.
- Provide extra space on tests for answering.
- Simplify wording of test questions.
- Allow students to answer fewer questions.
- Give extra help in preparing for tests.
- Give practice questions as a study guide.
- Give open-book and note tests.
- Give tests to small groups.
- Allow the use of learning aids during tests (e.g., calculators).
- Give individual help with directions during tests.
- Allow oral instead of written answers (e.g., audio recording).
- Allow answers in outline format.
- Allow word processors.
- Grade for content, not for spelling and writing mechanics.
- Give feedback to individual students during tests.

Using Portfolios or Work Samples to Monitor Student Progress

Assessment portfolios are collections of work samples that document a student's progress in a content area. You can use portfolios to provide tangible evidence of student performance over a period of time. Portfolios can include writing samples of all stages of the writing process in all genres. Suggestions for developing assessment portfolios include the following:

- Develop a portfolio plan that is consistent with your purposes for the assignment.
- Clarify what work will go into portfolios.
- Start with only a couple of different kinds of entries, and expand gradually.
- Compare notes with other teachers as you experiment with portfolios.
- Make it a long-term goal to include a variety of assessments that address content, process, and attitude goals across the curriculum.
- Make portfolios accessible in the classroom. Students and teachers should be able to add to the collection quickly and easily.
- Develop summary sheets or graphs that help to describe a body of information (e.g., "I can do" lists, lists of books read, or pieces of writing completed). Let students record these data when possible.
- Work with students to choose a few representative samples that demonstrate the student's progress.

- Review portfolios with students periodically (at least four times during the school year). The review should be a time to celebrate progress and to set future goals.
- Encourage students to review portfolios with a classmate before reviewing with the teacher. Students should help to make decisions about what to keep.

Examples of items that can be included in a portfolio are as follows:

- Student assignments and work samples
- Student interviews
- Self-assessments
- Audio recordings
- Videos
- Diagnostic tests
- Achievement tests
- Teacher-made tests
- Pages from writing journals
- Awards
- Personal reading and writing records
- Interest and attitude inventories
- Photographs
- Copies of passages read fluently
- Contributions from parents
- Report cards
- List of accomplishments
- Observation checklists

---

the material to be covered by the test, the test's task requirements (e.g., reading, taking dictation), and the particular needs of special learners.

In addition to or instead of tests, teachers may use portfolios as an assessment tool. Apply the Concept 10-8 presents ideas for developing and using portfolios.

Study Skills and Learning Strategies

What Are the Three Types of Study Skills, and Why Are They Important to Learning? Even when teachers plan user-friendly lectures and make adaptations, students will still need to develop study skills and learning strategies. Particularly as students move into secondary and postsecondary settings, their tasks increasingly require time management, self-monitoring and feedback, listening and note taking, studying from textbooks, and test-taking skills. These study skills are particularly important in

secondary settings because students' grades often depend on written products such as papers, reports, and tests.

Study skills are the competencies associated with acquiring, recording, organizing, synthesizing, remembering, and using information and ideas (Pauk, 2001). Study skills are the key to independent learning, and they help students gain and use information effectively. Study skills are particularly important in postsecondary settings, where students with dyslexia report that their greatest needs are in learning how to organize coursework, learning in lectures, and academic writing (Mortimer & Crozier, 2006).

Students with effective study skills can be characterized as executive learners (Schumm & Post, 1997; Olson, Platt, & Dieker, 2008) in that they

- Are knowledgeable about personal learning strengths and challenges.
- Have a clear understanding about tasks to be accomplished.

- Have a repertoire of learning strategies that can be applied in independent learning situations.
- Have developed a set of help-seeking behaviors to activate when additional assistance is needed.
- Have independent note-taking skills for class lectures as well as for text reading.
- Can organize and plan for the completion of assignments.

Study skills can be divided into three areas:

1. *Personal development skills:* personal discipline, management and organizational skills, self-monitoring and reinforcement, and positive attitudes toward studying
2. *Process skills:* technical methods of studying such as note taking, outlining, learning information from a text, and library reference skills
3. *Expression skills:* retrieval skills, test-taking skills, and using oral and/or written expression to demonstrate understanding

As one would expect, these are the very skills and strategies that students with learning and behavior problems have difficulty developing. This may be because they require explicit and ongoing instruction in how to use study skills practices during class, for independent assignments, and for class planning.

Personal Development Skills

Personal development skills include personal discipline, goal setting, management and organizational skills, self-monitoring and reinforcement, and positive attitudes toward studying. Many of the personal development skills related to school focus on time management, scheduling, organization, self-monitoring, and reinforcement.

Time Management and Scheduling Jon's mother is concerned because Jon, who has learning disabilities, falls asleep while trying to finish book reports the night before they are due. Even if she gets him up early in the morning, there is little chance that he will have time to finish. Even though he knows about the assignments in advance, he waits until they are due to start reading, despite his mom's queries about homework. Granted, it takes Jon longer than the other students to complete assignments, but his teacher gives him the assignments early. He has the skills to get a B or a C if he would just start working on assignments earlier.

Many families and teachers can identify with this scenario. Jon has the skills to complete assignments successfully, but he lacks personal management skills, particularly time management. Teaching a unit on time management at the beginning of the year and then

reinforcing students during the year for the effective use of time can be well worth the effort.

Building a Rationale The first step in getting students to schedule and manage their time is to build a rationale for its importance to success in school and later life. Discuss the following ideas with your students to build a rationale for effective time management:

- Parents/guardians will get off your back when they see that you are getting your work done on time.
- If you write down what you have to do, you don't have to try to remember everything.
- If you set a time to begin, it is easier to get started and not procrastinate.
- When you set a time frame to complete an assignment, it helps you work for a goal and concentrate.
- When you have a schedule, you're less likely to let a short break become a long break.
- Being in control of time makes you feel that you have more control of your life.
- When you get assignments and jobs done on time, then you can really enjoy your free time.
- Scheduling your time helps you to get jobs done and have more time for fun and your friends.

Determining How the Time Is Spent Before students can decide how to schedule their time, they need to determine how they are currently spending it. Using a schedule, have students keep track of their activities for 1 or 2 weeks. Also have them list the school assignments they have for the time period and whether they have "too little," "enough," or "too much" time to complete them.

Estimating Time As part of the time management process, have students determine how long it takes them to complete regularly scheduled tasks such as meals, going to and from school, reading assignments in their various textbooks, writing a paragraph on a topic, and completing a 10-problem math assignment. Although there will probably be considerable variability in the time taken to complete a task, most students with learning and behavior problems underestimate the time it takes. Having students get an idea of the time required can be helpful in planning a schedule. This step will also help students identify and prioritize tasks that need to be completed.

Scheduling If students do not have enough time to get their tasks completed or if they do not have regular times for studying, encourage them to set up a schedule. Some suggestions that students might want to use when setting up their schedules are as follows:

1. Plan regular study times.
2. Plan at least 1-hour blocks of time in which to study.

3. Plan which assignments you are going to work on during study time.

4. Take the first 5 minutes of each study activity to review what you have done already and what you have learned, and to plan what you are going to accomplish today. This helps to promote long-term learning and a sense of accomplishment.

5. When studying longer than 1 hour, plan breaks and stick to the time allowed for the breaks.

6. Use daytime or early evening for study if possible. Most people work less efficiently at night.

7. Work on your most difficult subjects when you are most alert.

8. Distribute your studying for a test over several days rather than cramming the night before the test.

9. Balance your time between studying and other activities. Allow time for recreational activities.

10. Reward yourself by marking through your schedule each time you meet a scheduled commitment and by crossing off items you complete on your to-do list.

The schedule should list not only regular times for studying, but also due dates for assignments and dates for other events so that the schedule serves as a calendar. Students should be encouraged to set aside some time they can use as they please if they accomplish their tasks on schedule during the day or week. This type of self-determined reinforcer can serve as an extra motivation for some students.

Monitoring and Using a To-Do List Setting up a schedule does little good unless students follow and monitor their schedules. Teachers can have students fill in the activities they feel are important to monitor on a weekly schedule. Figure 10-13 presents a schedule and to-do list for Jon. His study time, time spent working out, and recreational time were the most important tasks for him to monitor, so he scheduled them in each week. He also noted when the next book report was due and used his to-do list to schedule other assignments and chores, crossing off tasks as they were accomplished.

Jon developed a contract with himself. If he studied at least 80% of the time he had scheduled during the week, then he could work out at the gym or goof off 2 extra hours on Saturday. In this way, Jon was not only monitoring his schedule, but also setting goals and providing rewards for meeting his goals. After 2 weeks, Jon's teacher encouraged him to review his deadlines and adjust his schedule based on how he had done over the past 2 weeks. While Jon had met his goal of studying 80% of the scheduled time, he still did not complete all his tasks. He had to adjust his goal in order to complete all of this work on time. Although

Jon realized that schedules need to be flexible, he found that planning, even when plans change, helped him to get more work accomplished in a timely manner.

Self-Monitoring and Reinforcement Students with learning and behavior problems have difficulty setting goals and self-monitoring, whether in the areas of attention and memory, reading comprehension, or personal and management skills. Van Reusen and Bos (1990) developed a strategy that students can use to assist them in setting goals and keeping track of their progress. The strategy is the acrostic for MARKER (it gives students a *mark* to work toward and is a *marker* of their progress) and includes the following steps:

Make a list of goals, set the order, set the date.

Arrange a plan for each goal, and predict your success.

Run your plan for each goal, and adjust if necessary.

Keep records of your progress.

Evaluate your progress toward each goal.

Reward yourself when you reach a goal, and set a new goal.

For each goal, students use a goal-planning sheet (see Figure 10-14) to answer the following questions:

- Can I describe my goal?
- What is the reason or purpose for the goal?
- What am I going to do first, second, and third to complete this goal?
- How much time do I have to complete the goal?
- What materials do I need to complete the goal?
- Can I divide the goal into steps or parts? If so, in what order should I complete each step or part?
- How am I going to keep records of my progress?
- How will I reward myself for reaching my goal?

The teacher can use the steps in the Strategies Intervention Model to teach the students the MARKER strategy. After learning the strategy, students usually work on one to three goals at a time, keeping progress data on each goal.

For more on the Strategies Intervention Model, see Chapter 2.

When Van Reusen and Bos (1992) used this strategy with middle and high school students with learning disabilities and behavior disorders, they found that students accomplished more goals and gained a more informed perspective of their educational and personal goals.

Hughes and his colleagues (Hughes, Ruhl, Deshler, & Schumaker, 1995) developed an assignment completion

FIGURE 10-13 Jon's Weekly Schedule and To-Do List

NAME: _Jon_

WEEK OF: _Oct 14_

	MON.	TUES.	WEDS.	THURS.	FRI.	SAT.	SUN.	
6:00 a.m.	get up and eat ——————→							6:00 a.m.
7:00	ride bus	—————————→				sleep	sleep	7:00
8:00	History							8:00
9:00	English					house +		9:00
10:00	PE	same every day				yard	go to	10:00
11:00	Welding					chores	church	11:00
12:00	Lunch						eat	12:00
1:00 p.m.	Algebra					eat	read for fun	1:00 p.m.
2:00	General science					go		2:00
3:00	ride bus					to gym	goof off and	3:00
4:00							eat	4:00
5:00	recreational activity		study		eat have fun	eat and have fun		5:00
6:00	eat ——————————————→							6:00
7:00	study	study	study	study			study	7:00
8:00								8:00
9:00	↓	↓	↓	↓			↓	9:00
10:00	sleep ——————→						sleep	10:00
11:00	↓				sleep ——→		↓	11:00

TO-DO LIST						
history paper due math assign finish book	math assign	math assign book report due	math assign welding project due	science test math test	chores mow grass pull weeds fix cooler	start English paper

strategy for the Strategies Intervention Model that is similar and is the acrostic for PROJECTS. The steps in this learning strategy are as follows:

Psych up. Prepare your assignment-monitoring form and your mind.

Record and ask. Record the assignment, think about it, and ask questions.

Organize. Break the assignment into parts, estimate and schedule the number of study sessions, and organize your materials.

Jump to it. Survey the assignment, and set goals and a reward.

Engage in the work. Follow the instructions, note questions, and get help if you need it.

Check the work. Check for requirements and quality, store the assignment, and reward yourself.

Turn it in. Take it to class, turn it in, record the date, and praise yourself.

Set your course. Record your grade, evaluate your assignment, and think about future assignments.

FIGURE 10-14 Goal-Planning and -Monitoring Sheet

Name: _____ Class: _____ Date: _____

1. Goal: _____

2. Reason(s) for working on goal: _____

3. Goal will be worked on at: _____

4. Date to reach goal (due date): _____

5. Materials needed: _____
_____

6. Steps used to reach the goal: _____
_____
_____

7. Progress toward the goal: Record in each box the date and progress rating.

   3—Goal reached   2—Good progress made   1—Some progress made   0—No progress made

Date / Rating						

8. Reward for reaching goal: _____

Source: Based on A. K. Van Reusen & C. S. Bos, *Use of the Goal-Regulation Strategy to Improve the Goal Attainment of Students with Learning Disabilities* (Final Report) (Tucson: University of Arizona, 1992).

Classroom Participation Students who actively participate in class tend to be more successful academically than their quieter, less attentive peers. Students with learning and behavior problems may benefit from specific strategies to enhance their classroom participation. The SLANT strategy is part of the Strategies Intervention Model and was designed to increase active participation in class. The acrostic for SLANT follows:

        <u>S</u>it up.

        <u>L</u>ean forward.

        <u>A</u>ctivate your thinking.

        <u>N</u>ame key information.

        <u>T</u>rack the talker.

Examples of activating your thinking include asking yourself questions (What is this about? What do I need to remember?), answering your questions (This is about _____. I need to remember _____.) and asking the teacher a question when you do not understand. Examples of naming key information include answering the teacher's questions, sharing your ideas, and additions to others' comments (Ellis, 1991). This general set of activities can be used in any learning situation to improve students' active participation.

An important part of assignment completion and class participation in inclusive classrooms is recruiting positive teacher attention. Students with learning and behavior problems often get the teacher's attention for their negative behaviors rather than their positive behaviors in class. Using instruction, role-play, and reinforcement, one special education teacher taught four middle school students with learning disabilities to recruit positive teacher attention in their general education classrooms (Alber, Heward, & Hippler, 1999). Students were taught to raise their hands and wait quietly to ask such questions as "How am I doing?" or "I don't understand" or "Would you please look at my work?" Observations in the general education classrooms demonstrated that students increased their amount of positive teacher recruiting and teachers increased their rate of student praise. Teaching students strategies for self-monitoring, self-reinforcement, and classroom participation is an important part of the special education curriculum because these skills, like study skills, support student success in the general education classroom and curriculum.

Process Skills

Process skills include the technical methods of studying such as note taking, outlining, learning information from text, and research and library skills.

Listening and Taking Notes In school, students spend more time listening than reading, speaking, or writing. Also, despite all of the advances in technology, the vast majority of students spent most of their time taking notes with pen and paper. Note taking is one of the most efficient ways to record this information and retrieve it in one's own words. It has several important functions:

- Note taking increases students' attention.
- Note taking, as opposed to simply listening, requires a deeper level of cognitive processing

because students must make sense of the information to write the ideas.

- Because the information has been processed more deeply, note taking helps students learn and remember the information more easily.

Even if students do not go back and review their notes, just the act of taking notes results in greater recall of information on tests. Note taking with review practices are associated with substantially higher school learning than not taking notes and reviewing (Kobayashi, 2006). Furthermore, when teachers provide interventions to assist students with note taking and reviewing, students perform better.

Students with learning and behavior problems often have difficulties with listening and taking notes. For some students with severe writing disabilities, it will be important that they have a note taker. Lightweight laptop computers or devices designed specifically for taking notes are also very beneficial if students are instructed in how to use them. Students with learning disabilities may have difficulty with the following:

- Paying attention
- Writing fast and legibly
- Deciding what information to write
- Spelling
- Making sense of notes after the lecture
- Providing a model of what the notes might look like

Given the importance of taking notes and the difficulty some students encounter with this skill, teachers will want to teach students how to take notes, provide an outline so students can take notes within the outline, and consider giving listener-friendly lectures to make note taking easier.

Teaching Students to Take Notes Note taking is a procedure that requires students to listen, interpret, organize, and record information. Therefore, students with limited reading and study skills often feel overwhelmed when they must take notes. Numerous formats for note taking have been suggested (see for review, Kobayashi, 2006). One aspect that these systems have in common is the focus on making note taking and reviewing an interactive learning process. To facilitate this interactive process, two- and three-column note-taking systems have been developed. Figure 10-15 gives an example of each system. Students take class notes in the second column in both systems, using only the front side of the paper. Modified outlining is the format that is most often suggested for taking these notes. In both systems, students note the key concepts in the left-hand

FIGURE 10-15 Formats for Note Taking

Sample Two-Column System

Topic: _____   Date: _____

Triggers or Key Concepts	Class Notes

Sample Three-Column System

Topic: _____   Date: _____

Triggers or Key Concepts	Class Notes	Text Notes

column, sometimes referred to as *triggers,* because they are meant to trigger the ideas noted in the class-notes column. Later, in reviewing, students should be able to cover the second column and use their personal triggers to help them remember the ideas covered in the class notes. In three-column systems, the additional column generally serves as a space to write textbook notes so that they can be integrated with class notes. This is most helpful when the teacher's lectures make frequent, direct ties to the textbook. It is also important to teach some students note-taking subskills such as using abbreviations, diagrams to related ideas, or visual markers and editing notes.

The following list gives several hints for helping students to develop efficient note-taking skills:

- Take notes using a two- or three-column system.
- Take notes on only one side of the paper.
- Date and label the topic of the notes.
- Generally use a modified outline format, indenting subordinate ideas and numbering ideas when possible.
- Skip lines to note changes in ideas.
- Don't worry about punctuation or grammar.
- Write ideas or key phrases, not complete sentences.
- Don't write down every word the teacher says.
- Use pictures and diagrams to relate ideas.
- Use consistent abbreviations (e.g., w/ = with, & = and).
- Put question marks by any points you don't understand. Check them later with the teacher.

- Underline or asterisk information that the lecturer stresses as important.
- Write down information that the lecturer writes on the board or transparency.
- If you miss an idea you want to include, draw a blank (_____) so that you can go back and fill it in.
- If you cannot automatically remember how to spell a word, spell it the way it sounds or the way you think it looks.
- If possible, review the previous sessions' notes right before the lecture.
- If the lecture is about an assigned reading topic, read the information before listening to the lecture.
- As soon as possible after the lecture, go over your notes, filling in the Key Concepts column and listing any questions you still have.
- After going over your notes, try to summarize the major points presented during the lecture.
- Listen actively. In other words, think about what you already know about the topic being presented and how it relates.
- Review your notes before a test.

Direct Instruction in Note Taking Regardless of the note-taking format chosen, a teacher should provide direct instruction in note taking. Direct instruction should include explicit demonstrations of the note-taking process and ample opportunities for students to practice with guidance and feedback. For many students with learning and behavior problems, telling them how to take notes is insufficient; note-taking practice is key. Teachers may want to develop and conduct a unit on listening and note taking. The following is a list of teaching ideas for developing such a unit:

1. *Have students evaluate the effectiveness of their current note-taking skills, and determine whether they will profit from instruction.* Generally, this can be assessed in two ways. First, have students bring to class current examples of notes, and have them evaluate the notes for completeness, format, ease of use for review, and legibility. Apply the Concept 10-9 presents one way that students can evaluate their own notes. Second, present a simulated 10- to 15-minute lecture or a video of a lecture, and ask the students to take notes. Give a test covering the information on the following day. Have the students again evaluate their notes and their test results.

2. *Use video lectures when teaching students to listen effectively and to take notes.* The use of video lectures is particularly helpful because it allows the students to replay the lecture so that they can watch or listen for main ideas. For example, you may be teaching students to watch and listen for cues the lecturer gives to note the important information. After listening to a short segment of video, have the students list the cues and then discuss why they are important. Then replay the segment so that students can verify their list of cues and add other cues.

3. *Control the difficulty of the lectures.* When first introducing new listening or note-taking skills such as listening for cues or using a two-column system, begin with short, well-organized lectures with ample use of advance organizers and visual aids, covering fairly simple, relatively familiar materials. As students reach proficiency, gradually increase the length of the lectures, reduce the use of organizers and visual aids, and increase the difficulty and novelty levels of the materials.

4. *Have students learn how to review their notes for tests.* Although students may learn to take more effective notes, they may fail to use the notes to study for tests. Teach students how to review their notes and ask themselves questions, using the Triggers column to develop questions about the material in the Class Notes column.

5. *Have students monitor the use and effectiveness of note taking in other classes.* To increase the probability that students will generalize their note-taking skills to other classes, have them discuss in which classes the skills would be helpful, and then have them monitor and discuss their effectiveness in those classes.

6. *Have students determine the effects of note taking on learning.* Students need to know that there is a payoff for their increased effort. Have students rate how well they feel they have taken notes over a unit or lecture, and have them monitor their performance on tests of the material. This will aid them in determining whether better note taking leads to better learning.

Overall, note taking and reviewing notes are associated with better performance and more learning (Kobayashi, 2006).

Learning from Text Probably the best known technique for learning information from text is SQ3R, developed by Robinson (1946). This acronym stands for the five steps in this study skill: Survey, Question, Read, Recite, Review. The purpose of this technique is to provide students with a systematic approach to studying text. The following is a brief description of SQ3R:

> *Survey.* Read through the headings quickly to learn what is to be studied.
>
> *Question.* Change each heading into a question (to have in mind what is to be learned from the reading).
>
> *Read.* Read to answer the question.
>
> *Recite.* At the end of each heading, either write brief notes about the highlights of the reading or engage in self-recitation.

Note-Taking Inventory

From time to time, it's smart to check the quality of your notes to see how you're doing. Then you'll know if you need to make any changes or improvements. Use this Note-Taking Inventory whenever you feel the need. Simply check it against that day's class notes.

You'll need a piece of paper and something to write with. Number the paper from 1 to 10. Give yourself 1 point for each item you find in your notes.

1. Date of lecture
2. Title of lecture
3. Writing neat enough for you to read (that's all that counts)
4. No more than one idea per line
5. Plenty of blank space to add extra ideas later
6. All main ideas brought up during class
7. All important details mentioned during class
8. All key terms and definitions given during class
9. Abbreviations used where necessary
10. No unnecessary words

Scoring: Add up your points.

9–10 points: You're a great note taker!

7–8 points: You're a good note taker!

5–6 points: You need to take better notes.

4 points or less: Make a note of this—practice, practice, practice.

Source: J. S. Schumm (2001), *School Power: Study Skill Strategies for Succeeding in School* (Minneapolis, MN: Free Spirit Publishing, Inc.).

Review. After completing these steps on the entire selection, review the main points of the notes by self-recitation. Check to see if the information is correct.

One of the major difficulties associated with the SQ3R method is the complexity of the process, particularly for students who are experiencing reading problems. In content area classes, these students are often attempting to read and learn information from textbooks that are written above their instructional reading levels. A modified version that uses only read, recite, and review has been implemented with effective results with secondary students and may hold promise with older readers (McDaniel, Howard, & Einstein, 2009).

Multipass Schumaker, Deshler, Alley, Warner, and Denton developed a strategy based on SQ3R that incorporates the learning acquisition and generalization stages from the Strategies Intervention Model for students who experience problems learning information from textbooks. This strategy is referred to as Multipass because students make three passes through a text while carrying out the process. Each pass through the text (i.e., Survey, Size-Up, and Sort-Out) entails the use of a different substrategy. Because each substrategy represents a fairly complex set of behaviors, each of the substrategies is taught as a unit, with students reaching proficiency in the first substrategy before learning the next substrategy. Prerequisite skills include the ability to paraphrase and a reading level of fourth grade or above. Research conducted with eight high school students with learning disabilities indicated that the students were able to master the strategy in instructional-level materials and were able to use the strategy in grade-level materials without further training or practice. The students' grade on content tests improved—from barely passing to a grade of C or better.

Evidence-Based PRACTICE

Multipass

PROCEDURES: During the Survey Pass, students become familiar with the main ideas and organization of the chapter (Deshler, Schumaker, & McKnight, 1997; Hock & Mellard, 2005). In completing the Survey Pass, students complete the following steps:

1. *Title.* Read the chapter title. Think about how it fits with what you have already studied. Predict what the chapter will be about.

2. *Introduction.* Read the introduction, and make a statement about the main idea of the chapter. If there is no introduction, read the first paragraph, which is usually the introduction.

3. *Summary.* Turn to the last page of the chapter, read the summary, and make a summary statement. If there is no summary, check the last paragraph to see whether it is a summary. If it is not a summary, make a mental note so that you can summarize later.

4. *Organization.* Look through the chapter to see how the chapter is organized. Use the major

headings to make a written outline. Paraphrase each heading.

5. *Pictures, maps, charts.* Look at the illustrations. Think about why they might have been included.

6. *Table of Contents.* Determine how this chapter fits in with the other information in the book by perusing the table of contents. Decide what relationships this chapter has with the others, especially the chapters immediately preceding and following it. For example, in a history book, chapters are often related because of chronological sequence. Chapters might also have a causal relationship (e.g., perhaps Chapter 6 talks about the causes of the Depression and Chapter 7 talks about its effects). Other types of frequently occurring relationships include general/specific, compare/contrast, and related concepts.

After completing this process, close the book, and think about what the chapter is going to be about and what you already know about the topic.

Using the strategies intervention model, the teacher first describes and then models this survey process. Students should practice with guidance and feedback in materials at their reading instructional level until they are effective and efficient at surveying a chapter.

During the Size-Up Pass, students gain more specific information from the chapter without reading the chapter from beginning to end. Whereas the Survey Pass provides a general framework for the chapter, the Size-Up Pass allows the students to look for the information that fits into that general framework using textual cues. In learning the Size-Up Pass, students complete the following steps:

1. *Illustrations.* Again look over the pictures, maps, and charts, and read the captions. Think about why they are included.

2. *Questions.* Read the questions, including those found at the beginning or interspersed in the chapter. If you can already answer a study question, put a check mark by it.

3. *Words.* Read over the vocabulary words, including any vocabulary list and words highlighted in the chapter.

4. *Headings.* Read a heading. Ask yourself a question that you think will be answered in the section. Scan for the answer. When you find the answer, paraphrase it orally, or state something that you have learned from the information under the heading. Note on your outline what information you have learned from the section.

As with the Survey Pass, the teacher needs to describe the Size-Up process, and the students should practice in instructional-level material until they are proficient.

During the third and final pass, the Sort-Out Pass, students test themselves on the material in the chapter. This pass assists them in determining what they have learned and on what information they should still concentrate. In the final pass, the students read and answer each question at the end of the chapter, using the following process:

1. *Read.* Read the study question at the end of the chapter or each question provided by the teacher.

2. *Answer.* Answer the question if you can.

3. *Mark.* If you can answer a question, put a check by it; if you cannot answer it, put a box in front of it. If you do not know the answer, scan the headings on your outline to determine in which section it most likely will be answered. When you find the likely section, look for the answer. If you find the answer, paraphrase it and check the box. If you do not find the answer, scan the headings a second time for another likely place to find the answer. Again, look for the answer, and paraphrase it if you find it. If you do not find the answer after trying twice, circle the box so that you know you need to come back to it later and possibly get help.

As in the other two steps, the students should practice with materials at their instructional level until they are effective and efficient at answering questions about the material presented in the chapter.

COMMENTS: From the description of Multipass, it should be clear that when students use this strategy, they do not have to read a text in its entirety. Instead, they study the text to determine the main ideas, its overall framework, and related details and to answer the study questions. In this way, students can use this strategy with textbooks that are written above their instructional level. However, several cautionary notes are in order. First, remember to have the students reach proficiency on each substrategy before they begin learning the next substrategy. Second, when the difference between the students' instructional reading level and reading level of the textbook is greater than 1 to 2 years, students may have difficulty moving from instructional-level materials to grade-level materials. Teachers will generally need to provide graduated instructional materials. (For example, Hector's instructional reading level is fifth grade, and he is a ninth grader. Hector will probably need to practice using the strategy in seventh-grade material as an intermediary step.) Third, do not expect students with learning and behavior problems to transfer this study strategy automatically to various content area textbooks. You will need to instruct for generalization.

Most of these materials require professional development training, which can be acquired by contacting: www.ku-crl.org.

Expression Skills: Remembering and Demonstrating Learning

Several skills and processes help us remember and learn new content—an important task related to school success. Remembering and retrieving facts and knowledge, test-taking skills, as well as other oral and/or written expression skills are used to demonstrate understanding and application of knowledge.

Remembering Information Have you ever arrived at the grocery store without your grocery list? What strategies do you use to help you remember what was on the list? Maybe you know how many items were on the list, and now you just need to find out how many of them you can recall. Or maybe you read the list over several times, almost rehearsing it, so it was easier to recall. Or you might use association by thinking of the meals that you were planning for the next few days and trying to associate the needed items with the meals. Or you might visualize your kitchen and quickly think about the refrigerator and each cabinet and the items needed for each. Finally, you might categorize the items on the basis of the sections in the grocery store (e.g., produce, cereal, dairy products, frozen foods). Clearly, there are many strategies for remembering information.

In many ways, remembering information for a test is similar to remembering the items on a grocery list. Often we are asked to remember a list of things (e.g., the major exports of the United Kingdom, the different kinds of flour and their uses, the names of the cranial nerves). During tests, we may be asked to take this information and apply it to specific situations (e.g., to explain why the U.K. economy is struggling), but we still need to remember the basic information.

Students with disabilities often have difficulty memorizing information, whether for tests, presentations, or written work. Sometimes the students do not understand the information to be learned, but in other cases poor performance may be due to difficulties with retrieval of the information, failure to use deliberate memory strategies, and/or poor motivation for school tasks (H. L. Swanson, Howard, & Saez, 2006). Research suggests that these students also have difficulty with metamemory (i.e., awareness of memory strategies and the ability to use and monitor these strategies), because they have trouble with one or more of the following:

- Knowing, selecting, and using appropriate strategies
- Estimating their own memory capacity for specific tasks
- Predicting accuracy on a memory task
- Allotting appropriate time to study
- Deciding when they have studied enough

Consequently, it is important to teach students memory strategies and tricks for remembering. Because teachers regularly ask students to remember information (e.g., for tests, class discussions), it is relatively easy to incorporate teaching memory strategies into the content curriculum. Incorporating the general teaching principles presented in Apply the Concept 10-10 gives principles for making the information more memorable and encouraging learning and remembering the information.

10-10 APPLY THE CONCEPT

General Teaching Principles for Increasing Students' Memory of Information

- Orient student attention before presenting information, and emphasize important vocabulary and concepts when they occur.
- Activate prior knowledge, and help students to make connections between old and new knowledge.
- Use visual aids such as graphic organizers to highlight the important information and make it more memorable.
- Control the amount of information presented; group related ideas.
- Control the rate at which the information is presented.

- Provide time to review, rehearse, and elaborate on the information.
- Teach the students how to use and apply memory strategies and devices.
- Provide time and guidance in developing associations and mnemonics such as acronyms and acrostics.
- Provide opportunities for distributed review of information, and encourage mastery.
- Enhance the meaningfulness of what they are learning.
- Use pictures and very brief videos to illustrate key ideas.
- Increase practice including active manipulation and reasoning.

Many content area learning strategies such as semantic mapping, advance organizers, and SFA can be thought of as teaching procedures that facilitate memory. In addition to these kinds of activities, a number of formal strategies have been deliberately designed to improve memory. These are often referred to as *mnemonics*.

Mnemonics are systematic procedures for enhancing memory. The word *mnemonics* literally means "aids memory." Mnemonics aid memory and retrieval by forming associations between what students need to know and what they currently know. To use mnemonics, the information needs to be distilled so that the students are learning conceptual lists or frameworks. The students then operate on this information by using mnemonics. Mnemonic strategies can be grouped into three types: organization and association, visualization, and verbal rehearsal.

Organization and Association Organizing and associating information refers to arranging the information or associating it with other information in such a way that it is easier to remember. Study the following list of terms in order to remember them:

democracy	mammals
socket wrench	judiciary
biology	anatomy
photosynthesis	drill press
lathe	blowtorch
freedom of speech	constitution

Chances are that you categorized the words according to three superordinate categories, possibly labeled *tools, science concepts,* and *social studies concepts.* Now, instead of learning 12 unrelated words, you are learning three sets of 4 related words. Research shows that the second task is considerably easier. Research and practice have also demonstrated that students experiencing learning problems do not tend to make these associations spontaneously (Mastropieri, Scruggs, & Marshak, 2008). Therefore, one mnemonic strategy to teach students when they are trying to remember lists of information is to associate or categorize related ideas.

Another type of association is the use of acrostics and acronyms. As you saw earlier in this chapter, *acrostics* are groups of sentences whose first words begin with the letters of a significant word. (For examples of acrostics, see SLANT, MARKER, and COMPARING, earlier in this chapter.)

Acronyms are words or abbreviations that are created by joining the first letters of a series of words (or just the major words in a series). Examples are *radar* (radio detecting and ranging), *scuba* (self-contained underwater breathing apparatus), *laser* (light amplification by stimulated emission of radiation); and *FBI* (Federal Bureau of Investigation). If needed, extra letters can be inserted, or the letters can be rearranged. By teaching students to construct acronyms and acrostics, sharing them in class, and then cueing students to use them when they study and take tests, you help them to learn and retrieve information.

The FIRST-letter mnemonic strategy (Nagel, Schumaker, & Deshler, 1994) is one way to help students construct lists of information to memorize and develop an acronym or acrostic for learning and remembering the information. The strategy includes an overall strategy (LISTS) and a substrategy for making the mnemonic device (FIRST). The steps in the overall strategy include the following:

> *Look for clues.* In the class notes and textbooks, look for lists of information that are important to learn. Name or give a heading to each list.
>
> *Investigate the items.* Decide which items should be included in the list.
>
> *Select a mnemonic device, using FIRST.* Use the FIRST substrategy, explained next, to construct a mnemonic.
>
> *Transfer the information to a card.* Write the mnemonic and the list on one side of a card and the name of the list on the other side of the card.
>
> *Self-test.* Study by looking at the heading using the mnemonic to recall the list.

To complete the Select step, students use the FIRST strategy to design an acronym or acrostic:

> *Form a word.* Using uppercase letters, write the first letter of each word in the list; see whether an acronym—a recognizable word or nonsense word—can be made.
>
> *Insert a letter or letters.* Insert one or more letters to see whether a word can be made. (Be sure to use lowercase letters so that you know they do not represent an item on the list—BACk, for example.)
>
> *Rearrange the letters.* Rearrange the letters to see whether a word can be made.
>
> *Shape a sentence.* Using the first letter of each word in the list, try to construct a sentence (an acrostic).
>
> *Try combinations.* Try combinations of these steps to generate the mnemonic.

This strategy is taught by using the Strategies Intervention Model. It can be used with most content but is particularly effective with science and social studies, in which lists of information are to be learned. The strategy provides a systematic method for students to review text and class notes, construct lists, and develop acronyms and acrostics that help them to remember and retrieve information.

Visualization and Key-Word Method Another strategy that is helpful in remembering information is visualization. Visualization is making a mental image of what you want to remember. Sometimes the visual image is simply the information that needs to be remembered. For example, it is not unusual to notice students closing their eyes when they are trying to remember how to spell a word. They may be using visualization to recall "what the word looks like."

If the information is complex, however, it may be helpful for the students to change the image of what they want to remember into a picture that will trigger or cue the information. One strategy used to do this is the *key-word method* (e.g., Mastropieri, Sweda, & Scruggs, 2000; Scruggs, Mastropieri, Berkeley, & Graetz, 2009). Using this visualization strategy, students construct a picture that represents an interactive relationship between a concept and its definition. Figure 10-16 shows a key-word picture generated for the concept of *allegro* and its definition (i.e., to move quickly). This picture is used to link the vocabulary word with the definition using key words that together sound like the vocabulary word. In Figure 10-16, *leg* and *row* are the key words used to construct a picture that triggers the definition of *allegro*.

The following steps are suggested for creating the key-word picture (King-Sears, Mercer, & Sindelar, 1992) and are the acrostic for IT FITS:

> Identify the word or term.

> Tell the definition or answer information.

> Find a key word that sounds like the new word or the word you need to remember.

FIGURE 10-16 Key-Word Picture Generated for the Concept *Allegro*

Source: C. A. Hughes, Memory and test-taking strategies, in D. D. Deshler, E. S. Ellis, & B. K. Lenz, *Teaching Adolescents with Learning Disabilities,* 2nd ed. (Denver, CO: Love, 1996), p. 223. Reprinted with permission.

Imagine an interaction, that is, something that the key word and the answer information can do together. If you draw a sketch of the interaction, you may review it later for improved memory.

Think about the key word and the interaction.

Study your vocabulary and the information, using your key word to help you remember. Review by asking for each item: What was my key word for [word]? What was happening in my picture [or image]? What is the information I am supposed to remember?

The key-word method is most effective in increasing the recall of information by students with learning disabilities when the key-word relationships are presented to the students rather than having individual students generate them (Fulk, Mastropieri, & Scruggs, 1992). Students should have ample opportunities to create key-word associations as a class or in cooperative groups before having students work individually.

Verbal Rehearsal Repeating the information aloud or to yourself can help to facilitate memory. Verbal rehearsal is the major cognitive strategy that is used to enhance short-term memory (Hughes, 1996; Loomes, Rasmussen, Pei, Manji, & Andrew, 2008). Rehearsal is most effective if there is limited interference between the time of the rehearsal and the time of recall, the number of items to be remembered is limited, and the information is clustered or chunked.

General Memory Strategies Often several mnemonics are used simultaneously. For example, after you have categorized the words in a list, you can use acronyms and acrostics within each category to help you remember the specific words and then use rehearsal to practice, review, and test your memory. Teaching students with learning and behavior problems which strategies to use for which types of information and how to combine strategies is generally necessary. In addition to teaching students how to use the various memory strategies, it is also important to teach students to use periodic review to minimize forgetting.

Studying and Taking Tests Studying and taking tests are important aspects of secondary schools. Tests are the primary means that teachers use to determine whether students have learned new concepts and can apply them. In a 9-week grading period, students were expected to take an average of 11 tests in each content area. On the average, teachers used scores on tests to determine approximately half of a grade for a course. Although a great deal of effort is placed on tests to measure learning, teachers often do not teach test-taking strategies.

Studying for Tests Studying for tests means that students should be reviewing information on a regular basis so they are not left cramming the day before the test. To help promote positive study habits, Teri Martinez, a middle school resource social studies teacher, taught the following guidelines for studying:

1. *Manage your study time.* Keep up with assignments, and do daily and weekly reviews. Ms. Martinez planned 5 minutes each day at the end of her social studies class for students to review the material. On Monday, she took an extra 5 minutes and had the students review the previous week's work. She used individual, small-group, and whole-class discussion to review.

2. *Create study aids.* Create a semantic map or other graphic organizer to help students remember key information. Ms. Martinez often used an ongoing map during review sessions, and the students added to the map each day. Ms. Martinez also taught the students how to create and use flash cards for key concepts and vocabulary. She taught the students the following procedures:

- When learning vocabulary, put the word on one side and the definition and an example on the other side.

- When learning other information, put the question on one side and the answer on the other side.

- When learning a formula, put the formula on one side and examples of how it is used on the other side.

- Review the flash cards in random order or after sorting the cards into categories or making a semantic map.

- Keep index cards in notebooks and on desks during class.

- Make a card when learning about a key concept or idea.

3. *Learn about the test.* The more information students learn about the format, type, and time allotted for the test, the more effectively they can prepare for it. Rather than telling the students about the test, Ms. Martinez would start the discussion by saying, "Let's talk about the test. What do you want to ask me?" She used the following checklist to guide the students' questioning:

- Format of test, types of questions

- How much test is worth

- Date of test

- Time allotted for test

- Whether books or notes are allowed

- Information covered

- Teacher recommendations for how to study

- Teacher recommendations for what to study

4. *Predict questions.* Ms. Martinez also demonstrated how the students can predict the questions that will be asked. The students can use what they know about the teacher's testing style, their class notes, their maps, and other study aids to predict questions. Two days before a test, Ms. Martinez had the students work in cooperative groups and write what they thought would be the most important questions on the test and then answer them.

5. *Think positive.* An important part of doing well on a test is having a positive attitude and believing that one is going to do well. Ms. Martinez finds that she enjoys working with the students on having positive attitudes. Each day during their review, she asks the students about the following:

- What they learned today

- How it relates to what they already know

- What they will be working on tomorrow

- How well they have learned the information

She also has them rate how well they think they will do on the test and think about what they could do to improve their ratings. Just before a test, Ms. Martinez takes several minutes to review test-taking strategies and to have the students visualize themselves being successful as they take the test.

Test-Taking Strategies In a 2005 study, Carter and colleagues taught 38 high school students with disabilities the following test-taking strategies in a series of six lessons:

- Bubble-sheet completion and pacing

- Sorting problems: identifying which items are the easiest and solving those problems first

- Estimating: solving math problems by rounding

- Substitution and back-solving: substituting the given answers in a multiple-choice test into the question to find the correct answer

- Recopying problems: rewriting problems in a more familiar form

- Underlining and reading all answers

- Elimination of redundant or off-the-wall answers

While students in the study did demonstrate small increases in their test scores after learning the strategies, Carter and coworkers (2005) report that students with disabilities need to learn test-taking strategies within the content instruction. In other words, to best prepare students with disabilities to take multiple-choice tests, you should integrate test-taking instruction into content instruction on a regular basis.

Other test-taking strategies and hints that can help students perform better on tests include:

- Survey the test.
- Read the directions carefully. Underline key words in the directions that tell you what to do.
- Be sure you understand the scoring system (e.g., is guessing penalized?).
- If you have memorized specific outlines, formulas, mnemonics, and the like, write down that information before you forget it.
- When answering questions, place a mark in the margin for those questions about which you are unsure and/or want to review.
- Place the questions in the context of what has been discussed in class and what you have read.
- Avoid changing answers arbitrarily.
- Review your answers.

Taking Objective Tests For students with learning and behavior problems, it may be beneficial to teach specific test-taking strategies. The PIRATES strategy can be used for taking objective tests (Hughes, Ruhl, Schumaker, & Deshler, 2002) and uses the Strategies Intervention Model. Research indicates that students with learning disabilities can increase their performance by 20 to 40 percentage points by learning and applying this strategy. The steps in the strategy are as follows:

<u>P</u>repare to succeed.

- Put your name and PIRATES on the test.
- Allot time, and order the sections.
- Say affirmations.
- Start within 2 minutes.

<u>I</u>nspect the instructions.

- Read instructions carefully.
- Underline what to do and where to respond.
- Notice special requirements.

<u>R</u>ead, remember, reduce.

- Read the whole question.
- Remember what you studied.
- Reduce your choices.

<u>A</u>nswer or abandon.

- Answer the question.
- Abandon the question for the moment.

<u>T</u>urn back.

<u>E</u>stimate your answer.

- Avoid absolutes.
- Choose the longest or most detailed choice.
- Eliminate similar choices.

<u>S</u>urvey.

- Survey to ensure that all questions have been answered.
- Switch an answer only if you are sure.

When using this strategy, a student repeats, for each section of the test, the second, third, and fourth steps (i.e., inspect the instructions; read, remember, reduce; answer or abandon).

In addition to this strategy, there are a number of hints for taking objective tests. Apply the Concept 10-11 presents information that is helpful in answering objective questions (e.g., true–false, multiple-choice, matching, and completion).

Taking Essay Tests Essays tests are not used as frequently as objective tests, but when essay questions are incorporated into a test, they make up a sizable portion of the test grade. This type of test can be particularly difficult for students with disabilities. Not only do the test takers have to recall information, they have to write clearly in terms of organization, legibility, spelling, and grammar. Students with difficulties in written expression may be able to orally express the answer to the question, but their writing skills may make it difficult for them to communicate that knowledge. You may want to audio record the student's answers. For some students, it may be advantageous to teach a strategy for answering essay questions so that the students organize the information and communicate it effectively. One strategy that has been developed to assist students in organizing better responses to essay questions is called ANSWER (Hughes, Schumaker, & Deshler, 2001). The steps include the following:

<u>A</u>nalyze the situation.

- Read the question carefully.
- Underline key words.
- Gauge the time you need.

<u>N</u>otice requirements.

- Scan for and mark the parts of the question.
- Ask and say what is required.
- Tell yourself that you will write a high-quality answer.

Tips for Answering Objective Questions

True–False Questions

- Remember, *everything* in a true statement must be true. One false detail makes it false.
- Look for qualifying words that tend to make statements false, such as *all, always, everyone, everybody, never, no, none, no one, only*.
- Look for qualifying words that tend to make statements true, such as *generally, most, often, probably, some, sometimes, usually*.
- Simplify questions that contain double negatives by crossing out both negatives and then determining whether the statement is true or false.
- Don't change an answer unless you have a good reason to. Usually, your first impression is correct.

Matching Questions

- Read directions carefully. Determine whether each column contains an equal number of items and whether items can be used more than once.
- Read both columns before you start matching, to get a sense of the items.
- Focus on each item in one column, and look for its match in the other column.
- If you can use items only once, cross out each item as you use it.

Multiple-Choice Questions

- Determine whether you are penalized for guessing.
- Answer the questions you know, putting a check mark in the margin next to items you want to return to later.

- Read all possible options, even when you are pretty sure of the right answer.
- See whether multiple options are available (e.g., c. A and B; d. All of the above).
- Minimize the risk of guessing by reading the stem with each option to see which option is most logical.
- Use a process of elimination, crossing out options you know are wrong.
- When you do not know the answer and you are not penalized for guessing, use the following signals to help you select the right option:

    The longest option is often correct.

    The most complete answer is often correct.

    The first time the option "all of the above" or "none of the above" is used, it is usually correct.

    The option in the middle, particularly if it is the longest, is often correct.

    Answers with qualifiers such as *generally, probably, sometimes,* and *usually* are frequently correct.

Completion Questions

- Determine whether more than one word can be put in one blank.
- If blanks are of different lengths, use length as a clue for the length of the answer.
- Read the question to yourself so that you can hear what is being asked.
- If more than one answer comes to mind, write them down; then reread the question with each answer to see which one fits best.
- Make sure that the answer you provide fits grammatically and logically.

Source: Selected ideas based on J. Langan, *Reading and Study Skills,* 8th ed. (New York: McGraw-Hill, 2007).

Set up an outline.

- Set up the main ideas.
- Assess whether they match the question.
- Make changes if necessary.

Work in details.

- Remember what you learned.
- Add details to the main ideas using abbreviations.
- Indicate the order.
- Decide whether you are ready to write.

Engineer your answer.

- Write an introductory paragraph.
- Refer to your outline.
- Include topic sentences.
- Tell about details for each topic sentence.
- Use examples.

Review your answer.

- Look to see whether you answered all parts of the question.

- Inspect to see whether you included all main ideas and details.
- Touch up your answer.

In her social studies class, Ms. Martinez taught the ANSWER strategy because essay questions were one format she used in her tests. She also gave students a list of direction words for essay questions (see Figure 10-17). She demonstrated how taking one concept such as *democracy* and using different direction words would change the response. In her daily reviews, she frequently discussed one of the cue words in relation to the content that had been covered that day. She provided examples of how to write an answer to a question using that cue word.

Providing appropriate content instruction for students with special needs in general education classrooms is challenging but potentially beneficial to all learners. Effective teachers implement the following practices associated with improved outcomes in content area learning (Scruggs et al., 2009):

- Hands-on activities
- Computer-assisted learning
- Peer mediation
- Spatial or graphic organization
- Study aids
- Classroom learning strategies
- Mnemonic strategies
- Explicit instruction

FIGURE 10-17 Direction Words for Answering Essay Questions

Cue	Meaning	Cue	Meaning
Analyze	Break into parts, and examine each part.	Interpret	Explain, and share your own judgment.
Apply	Discuss how the principles would apply to a situation.	Justify	Provide reasons for your statements or conclusion.
		List	Provide a numbered list of items or points.
Compare	Discuss differences and similarities.	Outline	Organize your answer into main points and supporting details. If appropriate, use outline format.
Contrast	Discuss differences and similarities, stressing the differences.		
		Prove	Provide factual evidence to support your logic or position.
Critique	Analyze and evaluate, using criteria.		
Define	Provide a clear, concise statement that explains the concept.	Relate	Show the connection among ideas.
		Review	Provide a critical summary in which you summarize and present your comments.
Describe	Give a detailed account, listing characteristics, qualities, and components as appropriate.		
		State	Explain precisely.
Diagram	Provide a drawing.	Summarize	Provide a synopsis that does not include your comments.
Discuss	Provide an in-depth explanation. Be analytical.		
Explain	Give a logical development that discusses reasons or causes.	Trace	Describe the development or progress of the idea.
Illustrate	Use examples or, when appropriate, provide a diagram or picture.		

Add your own direction words and definitions!

INSTRUCTIONAL ACTIVITIES

This section provides instructional activities that are related to content area learning and study skills. Some of the activities teach new skills; others are best suited for practice and reinforcement of already acquired skills. For each activity, the objective, materials, and teaching procedures are described.

Word Association Map

OBJECTIVES: To teach students a strategy for learning vocabulary words

GRADES: Secondary

MATERIALS: Textbook chapter, word association map worksheet (see Figure 10-18)

TEACHING PROCEDURES:

1. Introduce a key vocabulary word (e.g., *wicked*), and write it on the map.

2. Ask students to brainstorm what the word means.

3. With student input, come up with a good definition, and write it on the map. If necessary, provide examples to help students understand the meaning of the word.

4. Test students on several examples and nonexamples (e.g., example: "The witch in the children's story is mean for no reason and is wicked"; nonexample: "Diana is a considerate boss who is always willing to listen").

5. Ask the students to identify synonyms and antonyms of the word and write them on their word maps (e.g., synonyms: *unkind, bad;* antonyms: *good, considerate*).

6. Finally, ask the students to create their own personal sentences with the word.

Source: Adapted from University of Texas Center for Reading and Language Arts (2001a).

Add-a-Part: Prefixes and Suffixes

OBJECTIVE: To give students practice in creating words with prefixes and suffixes

GRADES: Fourth through secondary

MATERIALS: Cards with prefixes (e.g., *dis-*), cards with suffixes (e.g., *-able*), cards with root words (e.g., *honest, comfort*) that can be combined with these prefixes and suffixes, two plastic bags

TEACHING PROCEDURES:

1. Have students sit in a circle.

2. Place the plastic bag of cards with prefixes and suffixes and the other bag with root words in the middle of the circle within reach of everyone.

3. Model playing the "add-a-part" game by drawing one card out of each bag, saying the affix (e.g., *-less*) and the root word (e.g., *care*) on the cards, and creating a new word with the affix (e.g., *careless*). Say the new word and its meaning, and tell whether the word is real or not.

4. Have the students take turns playing the game.

Source: Adapted from University of Texas Center for Reading and Language Arts (2001b).

VOCAB

OBJECTIVE: To teach students the VOCAB strategy and enhance their vocabulary

GRADES: Secondary

FIGURE 10-18 Word Association Map Worksheet

MATERIALS: A list of vocabulary terms that are generally related (e.g., federal government, legislative branch, executive branch, judicial branch); index cards or pieces of paper

TEACHING PROCEDURES:

1. Discuss the components of the VOCAB strategy, and introduce the strategy step by step:

   <u>V</u>erify the key vocabulary terms and concepts to be learned, and put them on individual vocabulary cards or pieces of paper.

   <u>O</u>rganize the vocabulary word cards into a diagram that shows the relationship of the words to each other as you understand them in the context of what is being learned.

   <u>C</u>ommunicate your reasoning, and share your diagram with a partner and vice versa.

   <u>A</u>ssess the diagrams, discuss similarities and differences, and adjust your diagram with helpful ideas from your partner.

   <u>B</u>uild your understanding with self-testing.

2. Identify and provide for students a list of vocabulary words.

3. Have the students write one of the words on each of the index cards or pieces of paper.

4. Ask the students to organize the words in any way that they think shows the correct relationships among the words.

5. Have the students explain how and why they organized the words the way they did.

6. On the basis of the discussion, have the students reorganize their words if they think they have a different understanding of the meaning of the words.

7. Circulate among the pairs, and monitor students' discussions to make sure that they are building their understanding of the words through self-testing.

8. As a whole class, have several pairs of students share how and why they arranged their words.

Source: Adapted from University of Texas Center for Reading and Language Arts (1999).

Click and Clunk

OBJECTIVE: To help students monitor their understanding as they read and apply fix-up strategies to determine the meanings of unfamiliar words

GRADES: Elementary through secondary

MATERIALS: Reading passage, clunk cards, paper

TEACHING PROCEDURES:

1. Introduce clunk cards. Explain to students that *click* means words or ideas they understand and *clunk* means the words or ideas that they do not know. The students continue to read until they have a clunk. Tell the students that they can use the clunk cards when they have a clunk to figure out the meaning of a word.

2. Model each of the fix-up strategies on the clunk cue cards.

3. Provide opportunities for guided practice, followed by independent practice in which students apply these strategies as they read.

4. Pair students, and ask them to read each paragraph of the passage.

5. After reading each paragraph, have the students find clunks and write them on the paper. Then, have the students use the fix-up strategies on the clunk cards to figure out what the clunks mean. Provide supports if necessary.

6. Have the students record the definition of the clunk on the paper.

7. Repeat the same procedure until the students have read the entire selection.

8. When they have read the entire selection, have several pairs of students share their clunks and the fix-up strategies they used to help them determine meaning.

Source: Adapted from Klingner, Vaughn, Dimino, Schumm, and Bryant (2001).

Contextual Searching

OBJECTIVE: To help students use various context clues to identify the meaning of the words

Clunk Card 1
Reread the sentence with the clunk, and look for key ideas.

Clunk Card 2
Reread the sentence before and after the clunk to look for clues.

Clunk Card 3
Look for a prefix and suffix in the word.

Clunk Card 4
Break the word into smaller words that you know.

GRADES: Secondary

MATERIALS: Ten vocabulary words; contextual sentences for each vocabulary word using the five types of context clues (i.e., definition, description, contrast, comparison, synonym), sentence strips, list of possible definitions; dictionary

TEACHING PROCEDURES: Before the instruction,

1. Identify 10 vocabulary words.

2. Develop one context clue for each word. Be sure to use different types of context clues.

3. Write a sentence with a vocabulary word containing one context-clue type (definition, description, contrast, comparison, or synonym) on each sentence strip.

During the instruction,

4. Present the first five vocabulary words in isolation (e.g., *cilia, volition, lethargic, inquisition,* and *literally*).

5. Ask the students for definitions of the words.

6. Write the words and the students' definitions on the chalkboard or overhead.

7. Present the vocabulary words in context.

8. Model how to use the type of context clue to figure out the meaning of the unfamiliar words (see Figure 10-19).

9. Have the students compare the definitions from context to their definitions in isolation.

10. Present the other five vocabulary words in isolation.

11. Ask the students for definitions of the words.

12. Write the words and the students' definitions on the chalkboard or overhead.

13. Present the vocabulary words in context.

14. Pair students, and ask them to analyze the context to figure out the meaning of each vocabulary word and record their definitions for each word.

15. Ask the students to identify which type of context clue they used for each vocabulary word.

16. Ask the students to compare their definitions from context clues to their definitions in isolation.

17. Have students look up the definitions for the vocabulary words in the dictionary.

18. Call on several pairs of students to share how the dictionary definition fits with their definition from context clues.

Source: Adapted from University of Texas Center for Reading and Language Arts (2002).

WEB RESOURCES

For further description of content enhancement routines and a video discussing them, see www.ku-crl.org.

Jeopardy!

OBJECTIVE: To give students practice in using reference and trade books to obtain information and to generate questions

GRADES: Secondary

MATERIALS: Reference and trade books, Jeopardy! board with four categories and five answers per category, index cards to fit in the Jeopardy! board

TEACHING PROCEDURES:

1. Divide the students into three teams of two to four students. Explain that each team is going to make a Jeopardy!-style game for the other students to play.

2. To make the game, each team needs to select four categories. Then have the students use reference books, trade books, and other sources to generate

FIGURE 10-19 Using Context Clues

Context Clue Type	Example
Definition: The word is defined in the sentence.	If disease reaches your bronchial tubes, *cilia*—tiny hairlike structures—are another barrier to prevent infection.
Description: The word is described by the context.	After taking a spill on her bike, she was able to stand up, get back on the bike, and pedal away on her own *volition*.
Contrast: The word is compared with some other word as an antonym.	Kim was *lethargic,* yet her sister was very energetic.
Comparison: The word is compared with some other word or phrase to illustrate the similarities between them.	Birgit was exhausted after the *inquisition*, which was like being in a boat on rough seas.
Synonym: The word is compared to another word with a similar meaning.	Tom interpreted the message *literally*; that is, he believed the message as though every word were real.

JEOPARDY!

Pop Music	Presidents	Football	Southwest
20	20	20	20
40	40	40	40
60	60	60	60
80	80	80	80
100	100	100	100

five questions and answers for each category that other students could possibly answer. Have them write the questions and answers on separate index cards and order the questions and answers from easy to difficult.

3. Each team then takes a turn directing its Jeopardy! game. First, the team inserts their category names and answer cards into the Jeopardy! board. Then they direct the game as the two other teams compete against each other. To direct the game, one student should serve as master of ceremonies, another as timekeeper, and the rest as judges.

4. To play, each team takes a turn selecting a category and a level underneath the category. The answer is then exposed, and the team members have 15 seconds to give the question. If the question is correct, they get the number of points indicated and are allowed to make another selection. If the answer is incorrect, the other team has 15 seconds to give an answer.

Study Groups

OBJECTIVE: To provide students with the opportunity to work in groups when studying a textbook for a test

GRADES: Secondary

MATERIALS: Content area textbook chapter or sections on which the students are going to be tested, index cards

TEACHING PROCEDURES:

1. Have students who are studying for tests that cover the same material work in groups of two to three students. (*Note:* When students first do this activity, the teacher will generally need to demonstrate and guide the students through the process.)

2. Have the students read the assigned materials together, stopping at the end of each paragraph or section to discuss the main ideas and the important vocabulary. Each main idea and important vocabulary for each section should be written on an index card.

3. After the students finish reading the assignment using this technique, they should take all the main idea cards and arrange them in logical groupings or in a logical order.

4. Have the students take each important vocabulary card and write a simple definition that makes sense according to the text. Then have them arrange the important vocabulary next to the related main idea.

5. Next, have each student copy onto paper the arrangement that was organized for the main ideas and vocabulary (with definitions).

6. Finally, the students should study the paper and then take turns quizzing each other on the information.

Learn Those Words!

OBJECTIVE: To teach students a simple strategy for memorizing vocabulary words—either English words or those of a foreign language

GRADES: Fifth through secondary

MATERIALS: Index cards used whole or cut in half or in thirds, a pen, a paper cutter or scissors

TEACHING PROCEDURES:

1. Have students write a word on one side of an index card and its definition or translation on the reverse side.

2. Have students study the words and then test themselves. Have them form two piles of cards as they work: a pile for the words they know and another for those they do not know. Students continue to study the words they don't know until there are no more cards in the unknown pile.

3. Tell the students that they should always keep a set of words with them. While they are waiting in line or waiting for class to begin, they can test themselves on their words.

4. Have students make new sets of words and continuously review the old sets.

In specific word instruction, teachers select a few vocabulary words that are critical for understanding a text and are difficult for students. Words can be selected from a text that the teacher will read aloud or from a text that students will read themselves. Teachers can highlight selected words after reading or preteach the vocabulary words. Students also need word-learning strategies that they can use independently while reading. Effective word-learning strategies include using contextual analysis, morphemic analysis, and reference aids.

Content enhancement is used to help students identify, organize, and comprehend important content. First, teachers select important concepts and related vocabulary. Next, teachers evaluate materials. Reviewing texts before reading helps teachers to identify the difficulty of the ideas or concepts. Teachers then assess students' prior knowledge through the use of activities. Next, teachers can implement appropriate prelearning activities that students can use before reading an assigned text or listening to a lecture. Finally, the semantic map, concept diagram, or other activity becomes a learning tool that students can use as a guide during and after reading.

Text adaptation involves changing an existing text to make it more comprehensible for students. Methods for adapting textbooks include using study guides, highlighting important points, or using alternatives to reading such as audio recording text chapters or reading aloud. Lectures can be adapted by making their organization and key points clear to students through aids such as advance organizers, vocal cues, or visual aids. Teachers who are aware of students' abilities and needs construct assignments and homework that are appropriate in content, length, time required to complete, and skill level. Teachers should always communicate why an assignment is important, when it is due, what support is available, and what steps are involved. Teachers should tell students explicitly what they will be responsible for knowing, should design tests that are clear and easy to understand, and should provide accommodations during testing situations.

Personal development skills, process skills, and expression skills are the three types of study skills. They are important because they help students to manage their time; use strategies to organize, synthesize, and remember new information; and communicate what they have learned to others. Study skills are critical to independent and efficient learning.

After completing this chapter, test your knowledge of the concepts by completing this Assessment.

Assessing and Teaching Mathematics* 11

*Contributions by Terry L. Weaver, Union University

LEARNING OUTCOMES

1. Identify factors that influence math success.
2. Describe progress monitoring and assessment practices in mathematics.
3. Explain prenumber skills.
4. Describe the numeration concepts students need to progress in arithmetic.
5. List factors contributing to difficulties with problem solving, and describe how teachers can assist students in learning problem-solving strategies.
6. Articulate how math interventions can be used to improve students' performance.

Sanjay, a third-grade student who has behavior disorders, spends most of his day in the general education third-grade classroom. He is in the top math group and is proud of this achievement. His special education teacher is pleased that he is fulfilling his behavior contract and has not had any serious disturbances since he has been included in the general education classroom.

Claudia, a seventh-grade student who spends part of her day in a classroom for students with learning disabilities, is not nearly as successful in math. In fact, when asked what her favorite academic time is during the day, she says, "I love to write. In fact, I think I will be an author. I have already written several books for the classroom, and one was even selected for the library." When asked what she thinks of math, she looks away and says, "No way! Don't even mention it. I can't do math. We don't get along."

Claudia has had difficulty with mathematics since she was in the primary grades. Her first-grade teacher thought that she simply was not interested in math and suggested that her parents obtain special tutoring help during the following summer. Her parents found that the special help did little good, and when Claudia continued to have serious difficulty with math in second grade, the teacher referred her for assessment for possible learning disabilities. The assessment results suggested that she had difficulty with spatial relations and using memory to recall rote math facts. She has received special help in math for the past 4 years, and though she seems to have made progress, her math skills are still her weakest academic area.

Some students with learning and behavior problems have difficulty with language arts (reading, writing, and spelling), some have difficulty with mathematics, and some have difficulty with both. Compared with students who only have math problems, students who have both math and reading problems are far more likely to continue to have math problems in later grades (Jordan & Hanich, 2003). With an increased need for students to understand problem solving for success in the workplace, the need for all students to demonstrate proficient math skills is high.

Factors Influencing Math Success

Math success can be influenced by several factors including teacher preparation and knowledge of math instruction, school curriculum and materials, as well as students' characteristics that influence their understanding and retention of math. Let's consider each of these and what you might do to address them in your educational setting.

One consideration for effective math instruction is teachers who are knowledgeable about math concepts and recognize the prerequisite skills for constructs they are teaching as well as how the constructs they are teaching relate to subsequent knowledge and skills. For example, if students are having difficulty with division, it is often because they lack the prerequisite skills related to multiplication or because they have difficulty understanding the construct of dividing into groups. Teachers who have the mathematical facility to identify key components that students need to know to successfully complete mathematics problems are more effective. Thus, teachers' knowledge and understanding of mathematic influence their instruction.

School curriculum and materials also influence students' performance in mathematics. Schools that have a well-conceptualized math curriculum with the necessary materials and resources for teachers are more likely to develop successful math instruction.

The third factor, and perhaps the one that you can most influence, is the learning characteristics of students and how instruction can be modified to support their acquisition of mathematics knowledge and skills. What are some of the students' characteristics that influence math acquisition? These vary somewhat for students who have significant reading disabilities, but typically these students display the following deficits (Geary, 2010; Vukovic & Siegel, 2010):

1. *Cognitive factors* such as distractibility and cognitive learning strategies

2. *Education factors* such as the quality and amount of instructional intervention across the range of areas of mathematics (e.g., computation, measurement, time, and problem solving)

3. *Self-regulations factors* such as persistence, attitudes toward mathematics, and math anxiety

4. *Neuropsychological patterns* such as perception and visual spatial skills.

Considering these factors, it is not surprising that many students with learning and behavior problems have difficulty in math. Interestingly, although students with learning disabilities demonstrate significant difficulties with math, they do not report lower self-perceptions of their math skills than those of average-achieving students (Montague & van Garderen, 2003). Because much of their educational intervention has focused on computation, they often have limited exposure to other elements of math, including measurement, time, and practical problem solving. Many students with learning and behavior problems struggle with applying computation skills to everyday math problems. Persistence and motivation to succeed are associated with good math performance, and many students with learning and behavior problems lack these qualities. The fourth factor that was identified, unique neuropsychological patterns, characterizes many students with learning and behavior problems.

Language development also plays an important role in learning mathematics. Reduced vocabulary levels and difficulties with reasoning and conceptual abstractions interfere with learning. The language of teacher directions, curricular materials, and mathematics does not aid students with learning and behavior problems to understand and learn the concepts and skills they need in order to succeed in mathematics. This is especially applicable to students with lower cognitive abilities and those with difficulties in understanding English (i.e., English-language learners; ELLs). Teachers can simplify the vocabulary they use within a lesson because students with lower cognitive abilities and who are ELLs may have difficulty understanding oral and written concepts (Tucker, Singleton, & Weaver, 2006). The teacher can use the more readily understood vocabulary and follow it with a less complex term meaning the same thing (e.g., "Show me the fraction that equals one half" becomes "Show me the fraction or part that equals or is the same as one half"). The teacher can also use an example that is visually easy to image (e.g., "parallel lines" or "like railroad tracks running side by side"). Teachers can make revisions to the directions provided in texts, thereby allowing better understanding. However, if a difficult word is essential, then a marginal note (a simpler word written in the margin and tied to the difficult word by a line) can be provided to increase understanding.

Moreover, students can benefit from developmental activities wherein students are provided opportunities to develop mathematical experiences that will become the basis for generalizations of mathematical concepts and skills. These activities provide opportunities for students to develop connections to what they already know and can more readily help students "to see" how new learning is related to learning that is already understood (Tucker et al., 2006). Mental imagery is built by developmental activities allowing the student to have a better picture of what the teacher is saying (they can see that the real world is this way). As a teacher builds mental imagery, concrete thinking is facilitated. The use of developmental activities increases memory of skills learning and reduces the amount of practice required, allowing learning to occur (Tucker et al., 2006).

Barnes et al. (2006) reported that students with math disabilities are likely to have problems with both math facts and math procedures. Also, in a study by Badian and Ghublikian (1983), students with significantly lower math than reading skills (low math) were compared with two other groups: students with significantly higher math skills than reading skills and students who had similar math and reading skills. The results indicated that the low-skill math group demonstrated lower scores overall on the following abilities:

- Paying sustained attention
- Working in a careful and organized manner
- Accepting responsibility

These findings partially explain why students with learning and behavior problems have difficulty with mathematics. Students with learning disabilities often have difficulty applying learning strategies and are frequently characterized as having perceptual and neurological complications. Students with emotional disturbances may have greater difficulties with mathematics than with other subjects because it requires persistence and concentration. Students with math difficulties frequently display:

- Number deficts
- Problems with retrieving math facts
- Conceptual misunderstandings of math

Remember that students with math disabilities, besides having difficulties within the area of mathematics, often have other related difficulties that cause interference in learning mathematics. Students with math disabilities only are less at risk than are students with both math and reading disabilities. Yet, math disabilities, as with any disability, demonstrate wide diversity among students. This requires much attention to and development of instructional interventions to meet specific needs.

Teaching Considerations

Teachers need to consider a number of factors when developing math programs for students with special needs, regardless of the students' ages or the curricular program being used.

Comprehensive Programming Mr. Noppe was not happy with his math program. He taught students in special education at an elementary school, and 90% of his math program consisted of teaching math computation. In discussing his math program with a coteacher, he said, "I know I need to include more than just computation, but I'm not sure what else I should be teaching. I guess I should ask the students to apply some of their math computation. Next year, I want to concentrate on my math program and make it more comprehensive."

Students need to be taught and be involved in a full range of mathematics skills, including basic facts, operations, algebra, word problems, mathematical reasoning, time, measurement, fractions, and math application. Teachers should not focus their entire mathematics program on math facts and the four basic operations of addition, subtraction, multiplication, and division. The Common Core Math Standards provide guidelines for math instruction content and processes. These standards (listed in Apply the Concept 11-1) can be useful to teachers as they design curriculum and instruction for students with special needs. Having students work on the developmental and conceptual foundations of mathematics will aid them in understanding the big ideas underlying mathematics (e.g., the use of like units in their computations and problem solving) that they will need in learning and practicing new skills. Building the foundational scaffold onto which learners can fuse new skills and concepts is a key element to success in mathematics learning.

Remember that a relevant feature of a comprehensive math program is to teach concepts and vocabulary—to make sure that students understand the language of mathematics. Students with disabilities are less likely to know the relevant concepts and specific vocabulary related to mathematics learning. Thus, when they participate in problem solving in real-life contexts, they may not understand key words such as *perimeter* or *diameter;* younger students may not understand words such as *minus, half,* or *percentage.* Pairing the difficult concept with lots of examples and nonexamples and the difficult vocabulary with simpler words aids in understanding.

Common Core Math Standards

Instructional programs from prekindergarten through grade 12 in the following areas should enable all students to use the following concepts (www.core-standards.org/math):

1. Counting and Cardinality
2. Operations and Algebraic Thinking
3. Number and Operations in Base Ten
4. Number and Operations—Fractions
5. Measurement and Data
6. Geometry
7. Ratios and Proportional Relationship
8. The Number System
9. Expressions and Equations
10. Functions
11. Statistics and Probability

In addition to the above identified Content Areas, mathematic success is set to rest on the following processes and proficiencies:

- Make sense of problems, and persevere in solving them.
- Reason abstractly and quantitatively.
- Construct viable arguments, and critique the reasoning of others.
- Model with mathematics.
- Use appropriate tools strategically.
- Attend to precision.
- Look for and make use of structure.
- Look for and express regularity in repeated reasoning.

Individualization Sanjay and Claudia, the two students described at the beginning of this chapter, have very different needs in math. Individualization in math programming refers not just to the task but also to the way in which the task is presented. Some students learn math facts through rote drill, whereas other students learn math facts by associating them with known facts. We often assume that an individualized program means that a student works alone; but individualization actually means that the program is designed to meet the individual needs of the student. It is often beneficial for the students to work in small groups to explore and develop patterns and relationships, and hypothesize and test those hypotheses in the process of learning new skills and rehearsing and practicing problems. In addition, small groups that focus on solving the same problem can include students of different abilities, particularly when the teacher creates a cooperative environment for solving the problems and allowing the students to learn from each other.

Correction and Feedback Receiving immediate feedback about performance is particularly important in mathematics. If students are performing an operation incorrectly, they should be told which parts are correct and which parts are incorrect. Showing students patterns in their errors is an important source of feedback. Students also need to learn to check their own work and monitor their errors. Working in pairs can help in this process of checking and monitoring because students benefit from a peer's help when they may not from the teacher.

Remember, feedback includes pointing out improvements as well as needed changes.

Students in Ms. Wong's math class were given a worksheet to practice their new skill of using dollar signs and decimal points in their subtraction problems. Ms. Wong told the students to do only the first problem. After they completed the problem, they were to check it and make any necessary changes. If they thought that their answer to the problem was correct, they were to write a small c next to their answer; if not, they were to write a small i for incorrect next to the answer. They were also to indicate with a check mark where they thought they had made a mistake. Ms. Wong moved quickly from student to student, checking their work. Students who had the first problem correct were given task-specific praise and directions for the rest of the problems: "Good for you. You got the first problem correct, and you had the confidence, after checking it, to call it correct. I see you remembered to use the dollar sign and decimal points where they were needed. After you finish the first row, including checking your problems, meet with another student to see how your answers compare. Do you know what to do if there is a discrepancy in your answers? That's right. You'll need to check each other's problem to locate the error." For the students who had solved the problem incorrectly, Ms. Wong stopped by each student's desk and said, "Tell aloud how you did this. Start from the beginning, and as you think of what you're doing, say it aloud so I can follow." Ms. Wong finds that students often notice their own errors, or she will identify some faulty thinking by the students that keeps them from correctly solving the problem. Once the error has been found and corrected, Ms. Wong asks the student to do the next problem, again saying what is being done aloud. If correct, Ms. Wong gives task-specific praise and directions for the rest of the problems.

Alternative Approaches to Instruction If a student is not succeeding with one instructional approach or program, the teacher should not hesitate to make a change. Most students learn best when they are provided prerequisite skills to support the math processes and opportunities to practice with feedback. Consider changing resources if students are having difficulty including adjusting textbooks, workbooks, math stations, and manipulatives.

Applied Mathematics Concrete and representational materials and real-life applications of math problems make math relevant and increase the likelihood that students will transfer skills to applied settings such as home and work. Students can continue to make progress in mathematics throughout their school years when they have the underlying foundational scaffold from which to build their skills and problem solving. The emphasis needs to be on problem solving rather than on rote drill and practice activities.

The term *situated cognition* refers to the principle that students will learn complex ideas and concepts in the contexts in which they occur in day-to-day life (real-world application). Students need many opportunities to practice what they learn in the ways in which they will eventually use what they learn. This is a critical way to promote the generalization of mathematical skills. For example, when teaching measurement, a teacher can give students real-world application opportunities to use the mathematics they are learning, such as measuring rooms for carpet, determining the mileage to specific locations, and so on.

When Ms. Wong's students successfully used dollar signs and decimals in subtraction, she gave each of them a mock checkbook, which included checks and a ledger for keeping the balance. In each of their checkbooks, she wrote the amount of $100.00. During math class for the rest of the month, she gave students "money" for their checkbook when their assignments were completed and their behavior was appropriate. She asked them to write her checks when they wanted supplies (pencils, erasers, chalk) or privileges (going to the bathroom, free time, meeting briefly with a friend). Students were asked to maintain the balances in their checkbooks. Students were penalized $5.00 for each mistake the "bank" located in the checkbook ledgers at the end of the week, much like a charge a real bank would make for an overdrawn account.

Generalization Generalization, or transfer of learning, needs to be taught. As most experienced teachers know,

students often can perform skills in the special education room but cannot perform them in a regular classroom. To facilitate the transfer of learning between settings, teachers must provide opportunities to practice skills by using a wide range of materials such as textbooks, workbooks, manipulatives (e.g., blocks, rods, tokens, real money), and word problems. For example, the teacher could have students measure different objects with things (unsharpened pencils, sheets of construction paper, or newspaper pages) rather than rulers or yardsticks. Teachers also need to systematically reduce the amount of help they provide students in solving problems. When students are first learning a math concept or operation, teachers provide a lot of assistance in performing it correctly. As students become more skillful, they need less assistance. Teachers must remember that generalization or transfer of learning must be planned for rather than "teach and hope" that it will occur.

When Ms. Wong's students correctly applied subtraction with dollars and decimals in their checkbooks, she asked them to perform similar problems for homework. Ms. Wong realized that before she could be satisfied that the students had mastered the skill, they needed to perform it outside of her classroom and without her assistance.

Participation in Goal Selection Allowing students to participate in setting their own goals for mathematics is likely to increase their commitment to achieving goals. Students who selected their own mathematics goals improved their performance on math tasks over time more than did those students whose mathematics goals were assigned to them by a teacher (L. S. Fuchs, Bahr, & Rieth, 1989). Even very young children can participate in selecting their overall mathematics goals and can keep progress charts on how well they are performing.

Instructional Approaches Students in the United States have scored well below others (Taiwan, South Korea, Singapore, Hong Kong, Japan) in mathematics proficiency in grades 4 and 8 on the international assessment of mathematics, Trends in International Mathematics and Science Study (TIMSS; National Center for Educational Statistics, 2007). We need to examine how we teach. It may be advantageous for math teachers to consider focusing instruction on the development of fewer mathematical topics that are the more ones so that students become truly proficient. This approach is used in many other countries that have demonstrated successful outcomes in mathematics (Ginsburg, Cooke, Leinwand, Noell, & Pollock, 2005).

The National Research Council (NRC, 2001) indicates that "mathematical proficiency" is the essential goal of instruction. What is mathematical proficiency? It is what any student needs in order to acquire mathematical understanding. The NRC describes five interwoven strands that compose proficiency. Consider how you are integrating these strands into your instruction. Also consider how you might determine whether the students you teach are making progress along each of these strands.

1. *Conceptual understanding* refers to understanding mathematic concepts and operations.

2. *Procedural fluency* is the ability to accurately and efficiently conduct operations and mathematics practices.

3. *Strategic competence* is the ability to formulate and conduct mathematical problems.

4. *Adaptive reasoning* refers to thinking about, explaining, and justifying mathematical work.

5. *Productive disposition* is appreciating the useful and positive influences of understanding mathematics and how one's disposition toward mathematics influences success.

See Apply the Concept 11-2 for suggested instructional practices.

It is particularly important for teachers to design mathematics programs that enhance learning for all students, especially those with diverse cultural or linguistic backgrounds. See the next section for suggestions on how to do this.

Considerations for Students Who Are Culturally and Linguistically Diverse: Enhancing Skills in Mathematics

An essential part of successful mathematics learning is to provide instructional practices and assignments that facilitate the learning of mathematics for all students. An important caution when dealing with students with diverse backgrounds is that their prior experiences will also be

---

11-2 APPLY THE CONCEPT

Instructional Practices for Mathematics

On the basis of several syntheses of mathematics instruction for students with learning and behavior problems (Baker, Gersten, & Lee, 2002; Gersten et al., 2009), we recommend the following 10 instructional practices:

1. *Use data to make decisions about instruction and progress.* Teachers and/or students should use data to determine if instructional changes are needed. The links to changes in instruction are central to the use of data-based decision making.

2. *Involve peers* in working together to develop understandings and a foundational scaffold from which to engage the learning of mathematics skills and practice computation and word problems. In addition to developing a foundational scaffold, practicing computations, and problem solving, peers can provide support by teaching each other self-monitoring, correcting answers, and charting data for progress monitoring.

3. *Inform parents* about students' progress and success in mathematics *and involve parents in their student's learning* so that they can enhance interest and practice of mathematics at home. Provide parents with information about students' success in mathematics so that they can recognize those accomplishments at home. Have students demonstrate (teach) the mathematics that they are learning at school to their parents rather than having parents just help with homework. Many times, the parents' mathematics knowledge is based on rote memorization that is not helpful to their child's learning and understanding.

4. *Use instructional routines* that focus on developmental and cognitive behavioral techniques that benefit students with learning and behavior problems and engage them in the learning process.

5. *Instructional design features* are effective ways to achieve the following: teach students to develop a foundational scaffold to support additional learning, differentiate problem types, use a wide range of examples, separate confusing elements, and provide opportunities for students to reach performance levels before introducing more new principles.

6. *Teach students the principles of mathematics to mastery* and then move to more advanced principles. Many students with special needs are given the same instructional mathematics curriculum (e.g., subtraction with regrouping) from second through ninth grades. Upper-level students need to learn mathematics at levels beyond this, including prealgebra and algebra. Some may need to focus on functional mathematics.

7. *Establish realistic goals* for progress in mathematics with students by providing information to students about their present performance and what they need to learn and how to learn best (e.g., paired with peers, or use of manipulatives, number lines, or calculators).

8. *Monitor progress* on a weekly basis through graphing or visual display so that students can chart and see how they are performing. Make adjustments in teaching, materials, grouping, or other features of instruction if students are not making adequate progress.

9. *Provide evidence* that hard work and effort yield good outcomes and progress. Students can also learn to reinforce themselves for setting and meeting goals in mathematics.

10. *Use computer-assisted instruction* as an effective way to learn and practice arithmetic computation and mathematical problem solving.

---

diverse (Tucker, Singleton, & Weaver, 2006). To build on particular prior experiences, you must ensure that all students have had those same experiences. To take for granted that they have them is a common error of many teachers. To accomplish successful learning, one must consider the needs of students from diverse cultures and language backgrounds; suggestions to consider include:

- Assign individuals from different backgrounds to work in pairs or small groups, providing opportunities in mathematical problem solving that will ensure similarity of prior learning experiences and social interaction, with infrequent failure.

- Use manipulatives to provide common first-hand experiences to concretely explore the meaning of mathematical symbols and problems. Manipulatives enhance learning, increase social interaction, and provide an easy means of crossing potential language barriers.

- Model an enthusiastic and positive attitude about appreciating and learning more about the cultures and languages of other groups.

- Consider ways to infuse aspects of the various cultures of the students in your classroom and of students not represented into the mathematics curriculum provided by your school. Students will appreciate the inclusiveness you develop, feel accepted, be more engaged, and learn a great deal about each other and other cultures when cultural diversity is a part of their daily learning routines.

- Infuse aspects of mathematics and story problems that reflect names and events from diverse cultures. Encourage students to design mathematics and story problems that are reflective of other cultures. Books and newspaper or magazine articles or stories about individuals, families, groups, and data from other cultures can be incorporated to design mathematically based story problems.

- Link students' accomplishments to their hard work and effort. Remind students that they performed a task well because they worked hard, persisted, reread, rethought, revisualized, modeled, and so forth.

- Use culturally relevant materials as a springboard for mathematics learning. The ways in which mathematics is practiced in various cultures, the mathematical games that are played, and the use of mathematics cross-culturally can be embedded into mathematics instruction.

- Use the students' languages within the instruction. Ask students to provide the mathematical word that means the same as "_____" in their home language, and then use both words when referring to the term. Encourage all students in the room to learn the term and to use and apply the terms that represent the languages of the students in the class. Communicate to students that you value their home language and culture.

- Use technology to enhance learning and understanding of mathematical principles. Computers provide language that typically is available to most students. Encourage expertise on the computer, and provide multiple opportunities to practice skills. MathPad Plus is designed for students in kindergarten through grade 8 to enable learners to do arithmetic directly on the computer. This program is ideal for learners who need help organizing or navigating through math problems or who have difficulty using a pencil and paper with math.

Assessing and Progress Monitoring Mathematics Performance

How is mathematics performance assessed, and how is progress monitored? Mr. Sebeny is a first-year special education teacher. He is fortunate to work in a middle school with three other special education teachers who have been at the school for several years and are used to team teaching. They've asked Mr. Sebeny whether he would be comfortable teaching mathematics to all of the special education students. He quickly realized that his first task would be to determine the mathematics performance level of all of his students. Mr. Sebeny knows that he needs to select a measure that will tell him what students know and don't know and how they compare with other students in their grade.

> In this video ●, the teacher uses a variety of methods to assess her students' math skills. How does she assess individual students and provide feedback to them when they are each at different stages in their group projects?

There are many ways in which Mr. Sebeny could obtain the information he needs to develop instructional programs for his students. One of the first questions Mr. Sebeny needs to address is whether he has the time to use an individually administered assessment or whether he needs to use a group-administered measure. For students with special needs, individually administered measures yield the most information.

Second, Mr. Sebeny needs to determine whether the measure is designed for students in the age range of the students he is teaching. Figure 11-1 provides a list of mathematics measures, states whether they are administered to groups or individuals, and lists the age range for which they are appropriate. Figure 11-2 provides a list of progress-monitoring measures for math.

FIGURE 11-1 Measures to Assess Mathematics Performance Progress Monitoring

Test Name	How Administered	Age/Grade Appropriate	Other Information
Comprehensive Math Assessment	Group	Grades 2–8	Based largely on the NCTM'S critical elements in mathematics instruction
Diagnostic Achievement Battery	Individual	Most grade levels	Provides normative data on student performance but not specific information for designing strengths and weaknesses
Wide Range Achievement Test	Individual or group	Most grade levels	Provides normative data on student performance but difficult to identify students' needs for instruction
Woodcock Johnson III Tests of Achievement	Individual	Most grade levels	Provides normative data on student performance but may not provide adequate information for designing instruction
Test of Early Mathematics Ability	Individual	Ages 3–9	Provides information to assist with designing and monitoring instruction
BRIGANCE Diagnostic Comprehensive Inventory of Basic Skills—Revised	Individual	Prekindergarten–grade 9	Provides information to assist with designing and monitoring instruction
Comprehensive Mathematical Ability Test	Individual	Grades 1–12	Provides information to assist with designing instruction
Key Math—Revised	Individual	Grades 1–12	Provides information to assist with designing instruction
Test of Mathematical Abilities	Individual	Grades 3–12	Provides information to assist with designing instruction
Math—Level Indicator: A Quick Group Math Placement Test	Group	Grades 4–12	Takes approximately 30 minutes, and because it is group administered, it quickly determines the performance levels of a large group of students. The problems are based on the NCTM standards.

How can teachers best make decisions about whether students are learning mathematics effectively? How can teachers monitor the progress of their students so that they can document the rate of progress they are making in mathematics? Considerable and growing evidence indicates that when teachers use curriculum-based measurement (CBM) to monitor their students' progress and to adjust their instruction accordingly, students make gains at much more rapid rates than when CBM is not used (Shapiro, Keller, Lutz, Santoro & Hintze, 2006).

What is CBM for math? Simply stated, it is a way of documenting the extent to which the student is learning the critical elements in the curriculum that you have targeted. To illustrate, let's consider the case of Ricky, a fifth-grade boy with learning and attention problems, who has been struggling with math. His goals for the next 10 weeks are to know all subtraction facts up to 100 automatically and quickly, to be able to do addition with regrouping word problems, and to be able to appropriately use basic

measurement terms such as *inches, feet,* and *yards.* Here is how Ricky and his teacher use CBM.

Ricky's teacher pretested on all 100 subtraction facts in random order, timing him while he completed the worksheet. She then showed Ricky how to graph his performance in two ways: by graphing how long it took him to complete the worksheet and by graphing the number of correct problems. Together, they agreed that Ricky would take a version of this test once every week to determine whether he could decrease the amount of time he needed to complete the test and increase the number of problems he got correct. Together, they established a schedule of work assignments and practice sessions. Figure 11-3 shows the graph that Ricky kept.

Ricky's teacher followed a similar procedure with measurement and problem solving to determine what Ricky knew and what he needed to know. Then the teacher established a simple graph that Ricky could complete to monitor his progress. Ricky and his teacher frequently

FIGURE 11-2 Progress-Monitoring Measures for Math

Test Name	Concepts Addressed	Grade	Website	Forms
Monitoring Basic Skills Progress	Math computation Math concepts	Grade 1 and above	http://www.proedinc.com	30 forms per grade
PASeries Math	Numbers Operations Geometry Algebra Data analysis Measurement	Grades 3–12	http://www.paseries.com	6 forms per grade
Star Math	Computation Application Concepts	Grades 1–12	http://www.renlearn.com	Unlimited forms
Yearly ProgressPro	Curriculum-based measurement	Grade 1 and above	http://Mhdigitallearning.com	13 forms per grade
AIMSweb Systems	Oral counting Number identification Quantity discrimination Missing number Basic skill areas	Grades K–8	http://www.aimsweb.com	33–50 forms for each construct

FIGURE 11-3 Ricky's Progress-Monitoring Chart

discussed Ricky's progress and modified assignments and instruction to facilitate his learning.

Computerized applications of CBM procedures are available for mathematics as well as spelling and reading (L. S. Fuchs, Hamlett, & Fuchs, 1990; Gersten et al., 2009). One Web resource for math activities that is loaded with explanations, interactive practice, games, and teacher resources is AAA Math.

Assessing Number Sense

Assessing number sense can be an effective way to monitor the progress of young children in mathematics and to determine who has mathematics difficulties. *Number sense* refers to whether a student's understanding of a number and of its use and meaning is flexible and fully developed. One definition of number sense is "a child's fluidity and flexibility with numbers, the sense of what numbers mean, and an ability to perform mental mathematics and to look at the world and make comparisons" (Gersten & Chard, 1999, p. 19). In terms of assessment, number sense is particularly important because it assists teachers in determining which students currently have mathematical difficulty and even serves as a predictor for students who may have learning difficulties in the future (Geary, 2010).

Measures that can be used to quickly determine students' understanding of number sense are available (L.S. Fuchs et al., 2007; Gersten et al., 2012). Each of these measures can easily be constructed and changed by the teacher to determine what a student knows. These include the following five:

1. *Number identification.* In this task, students must orally identify numbers between 0 and 20 when these are presented randomly on a piece of paper.

2. *Number writing.* Students are asked to write the number when given a number orally between 1 and 20.

3. *Quantity discrimination.* This task requires students to name which of two numbers is the larger (or smaller).

4. *Missing number.* Students are provided with a string of numbers and are asked to identify which number is missing.

5. *Computation.* Students are asked to complete computations that are representative of their grade level. Students have 2 minutes to complete as many problems as possible.

In addition, several counting measures can be used as effective screening tools for students with mathematical difficulties or to monitor students' progress in this area (Clarke & Shinn, 2004):

1. *Count to 20.* This is a beginning-level skill requiring students to count to 20 while the teacher records the correct and incorrect numbers in the sequence.

2. *Count by 3 and 6.* This skill requires students to count from a predetermined number, such as from 5, in increments of 3 or 6. The teacher records the accuracy and speed with which the students perform this task.

3. *Count by 2, 5, or 10.* This skill requires student to count by the designated number—2, 5, or 10—in increments up to a specified number, such as 20 for 2s, 50 for 5s, or 100 for 10s. The teacher records the accuracy with which students perform this task.

How Effective Are Test Accommodations in Mathematics for Students with Disabilities?

Assessment is an important part of the instructional routine. Teachers use assessment to assist them in determining what students know and can do and what they need to know and do. Appropriate assessments allow teachers to monitor students' progress and to make effective instructional decisions that will improve the students' performances. Having the results of daily, weekly, and monthly progress assessments long with more long-term assessments (e.g., state-mandated tests) makes planning effective instruction easier. Assessments can also tell teachers how students compare to others at their same age or grade level.

The idea behind test accommodations is that they are more responsive to the individual needs of students with disabilities. Elbaum (2007) reports that when mathematics tests are read aloud to students with disabilities and their performance on these tests is compared with students without disabilities, the read-aloud condition is more helpful to elementary students with disabilities than elementary students without disabilities. However, the reverse is true for secondary students with disabilities; their improved performance with accommodations is overall lower than for students without disabilities. Keep in mind that a teacher is bound by the student's individualized education program (IEP) to make the accommodations and modifications that are stated in the document. Many times the accommodation is extended time (1.5 or 2 times the normal time allotted), having the mathematics assessment read to the student, and spreading the assessment over several days.

Response to Intervention and Math

Response to intervention (RTI) is a way to more quickly identify students who need additional instruction and to provide the necessary instructional intervention within the classroom to help ensure mastery. RTI has been applied most frequently to the academic area of early reading. However, there are currently schools and districts using RTI in mathematics at both the elementary and middle school levels. How can RTI be used in math? You can learn more about RTI and mathematics by exploring this IRIS module. Initially, many of the same principles that applied to the use of RTI in reading also can be applied to math. These include:

• *Screening.* Students can be screened to determine if they have math problems in numeracy, math calculations, and/or problem solving.

• *Evidence-based math.* Schools and districts can ensure that math instruction for all students is based on the best research available.

• *Interventions.* When students have difficulties that are not adequately addressed through the evidence-based math program in the classroom, additional instruction through short-term interventions (10 to 20 weeks) can be implemented.

• *Progress monitoring.* Students' progress in the classroom and in interventions can be documented to ensure that they are staying on track and meeting curriculum benchmarks.

More recently, Gersten et al. (2009) provided a set of recommendations to aid teachers, principals, and others in their use of RTI for early identification of students who need help in mathematics and for focused mathematics intervention in elementary and middle schools. These recommendations include:

1. Screen all students to identify those at risk for potential mathematics difficulties and to provide interventions to students identified as at risk.

2. Focus instructional materials for students receiving interventions on in-depth treatment of whole numbers in kindergarten through grade 5 and on rational numbers in grades 4 through 8.

3. Provide explicit and systematic instruction during intervention. This includes providing models of proficient problem solving, verbalization of thought processes, guided practice, corrective feedback, and frequent cumulative review.

4. Provide instruction on solving word problems that is based on common underlying structures.

5. Include opportunities for students to work with visual representations of mathematical ideas.

6. Devote about 10 minutes in each session to building fluent retrieval of basic arithmetic facts.

7. Monitor the progress of students receiving supplemental instruction and other students who are at risk.

8. Include motivational strategies in Tier II and Tier III interventions.

Key principles for secondary intervention include:

- Instructional explicitness
- Instructional design that minimizes the learning challenge
- Strong conceptual basis for procedures taught
- Emphasis on drill and practice
- Cumulative review as part of drill and practice
- Motivators to help students regulate their attention and behavior and to work hard

Prenumber Skills

What are the prenumber skills students need to progress in arithmetic? Many students come to school with few experiences that allow them to develop important prenumber skills, such as one-to-one correspondence, classification, and seriation. These skills are essential to success in learning other mathematics concepts and skills.

One-to-One Correspondence

Matching one object with another is a core skill in any mathematics curriculum. It eventually leads the student to a better understanding of numeration and representation. One-to-one correspondence is used in life when we set a table, one place setting for each person; go to the theater, one ticket and seat for each person; and distribute paper in the classroom, one piece for each student. Activities for teaching one-to-one correspondence include the following:

- Use every opportunity to teach students the relationship between number words (e.g., *one, two, three, four*) and objects. For example, "Here are two paintbrushes: one for you and one for Madju." "There are five students in our group, and we need one chair for each student."

- Use familiar objects such as toy cars or blocks, and give a designated number (e.g., three) to each student. Pointing to the objects, ask students to place one block next to each of the objects. "You have one block here, and you placed one block next to it. You have a second block here, and you placed a block next to it. And you have a third block here, and you placed a block next to it."

- Give the student a set of cards with numbers that the student recognizes. Ask the student to put the correct number of blocks on top of each number card. Reverse the task by giving objects to students and asking them to put the correct number card next to the objects.

Classification

Classification is the ability to group or sort objects on the basis of one or more common properties. For example, classification can be done by size, color, shape, texture, or design. Classification is an important prenumber skill because it focuses on common properties of objects and requires students to reduce large numbers of objects to smaller groups. Most students are naturally interested in sorting, ordering, and classifying. Activities for teaching classification include the following:

- Ask students to sort different-colored, -shaped, and -sized objects into groups. Ask them which rule they used for sorting their objects.

- Give each student an empty egg carton and a box of small objects. Ask the students to sort the objects according to one property (e.g., color). Now ask them to think of another way in which they can sort the objects (e.g., size, texture).
- Using an assortment of objects, ask a student to classify several of the objects into one group. Other students then try to guess the property or properties that qualify the objects for the group.
- Students can use pictures for sorting tasks. Animals, foods, plants, toys, and people can all be sorted by different properties.
- Board games and bingo games can be played by sorting or classifying shapes, colors, or pictures.

Seriation

Seriation is similar to classification in its dependence on the recognition of common attributes or properties of objects. With seriation, ordering depends on the degree to which the object possesses the attribute. For example, seriation can occur by length, height, color, or weight. Activities for teaching seriation include the following:

- Give students some objects of varied length, like sharpened pencils or used crayons, and ask the students to put the objects in order from shortest to longest.
- Ask students to stack their books from largest, on the bottom, to smallest, on the top.
- Using a peg and some rings of varied sizes, ask students to put the rings on the peg, from largest to smallest.
- Fill jars of the same size with varied amounts of sand, rice, water, or marbles, and ask students to put them in order.

Algebraic Principles

Most teachers think that algebra is a subject taught in secondary schools. Yet the Common Core Standards indicate that all students should understand the foundations of algebra. Students should understand mathematical patterns, relationships, and functions. Students should also be able to view mathematical structures and situations and represent and analyze them using algebraic symbols. Moreover, students should be able to represent and understand quantitative relationships through the use of mathematical models in their problem solving. The foundations of algebra and its basic principles can be learned at many different ages and within many math topics.

You might not point out to young students that they are solving algebraic problems when they are presented with fill-in the symbol that completes a pattern (e.g., XX OO XX O_) or provide a number that creates an equality (e.g., 2 + [_] = 3). However, just thinking that they can do algebra could be that great motivator that jumpstarts their learning of more mathematics.

Math Concepts and Computation
Numeration and Place Value

What are several numeration concepts? Teachers and parents often assume that children understand numbers because they can count or name them. Understanding numbers is an essential basic concept; many children who have trouble with computation and word problems are missing numeral concepts. For example, Nadia's beginning experiences with math were positive. She had learned to read and write numbers and even to perform basic addition and subtraction facts. However, when Nadia was asked to perform problems that involved addition with regrouping, she demonstrated that she had very little knowledge of numbers and their meaning (her errors are shown here) and thus quickly fell behind her peers in math.

$$
\begin{array}{r} 48 \\ +26 \\ \hline 614 \end{array} \quad
\begin{array}{r} 37 \\ +55 \\ \hline 812 \end{array} \quad
\begin{array}{r} 68 \\ +17 \\ \hline 715 \end{array}
$$

Her computations are correct, but she lacks the understanding of the concepts *numeration* and *place value* and what to do when the result exceeds the place value (tens and ones). The use of manipulatives would aid her understanding. She could use bundled and loose sticks to represent the problem; she could take 10 of the 14 (8 + 6) loose sticks and make a new bundle of ten to be placed with the other bundled tens (4 and 2). This would aid her in her understanding of numeration and place value.

Understanding numeration and place value is necessary in the following areas of mathematics:

- *Progress in computation.* Like Nadia, many students fail to make adequate progress in math because they lack understanding of numbers and place value.
- *Estimation* (i.e., "number sense"). Many students with learning difficulties in math do not have a sense of how much $1.00 is, what it means to have 35 eggs, or "about" how much 24 plus 35 equals. They cannot check their answers by looking at problems and determining which answers could not be correct because the answer doesn't make "sense."
- *Reducing conceptual errors.* Students who understand the meaning of the numbers 43 and 25 would be less likely to make the following error:

$$
\begin{array}{r} 43 \\ -25 \\ \hline 22 \end{array}
$$

- *Understanding place value.* Students who know the meaning of the number 28 are going to have far less difficulty understanding the value of the 2 and the 8. Students need to understand that the 2 in 28 represents two 10s and the 8 represents eight 1s.

- *Understanding regrouping.* Regrouping errors, such as those following, are less likely to occur if a student understands numeration.

$$\begin{array}{r} 39 \\ +27 \\ \hline 516 \end{array} \qquad \begin{array}{r} 56 \\ -18 \\ \hline 42 \end{array} \qquad \begin{array}{r} 41 \\ -24 \\ \hline 23 \end{array}$$

- *Application of math computation to everyday problems.* Students who do not understand the real meaning of numbers have difficulty applying computation to everyday problems.

- *Understanding zero.* Students need to understand that 0 (zero) has more meaning than just "nothing." For example, in the number 40, they need to understand the meaning of the 0 as a placeholder (zero ones).

Readiness for Numeration: Eighteen Concepts Engelhardt, Ashlock, and Wiebe (1984) identified 18 numeration readiness concepts that can be assessed through paper-and-pencil assessment and interview. A list of the behaviors that correspond to each concept, along with examples of how the concept can be assessed, follows each concept.

Concept 1: Cardinality The face value of each of the 10 digits (0 through 9) tells how many. It is a good idea to get students to learn that zero is a number and is the empty set.

1. Identify sets with like numerousness (1 through 9). "Circle the groups with the same number of *x*s."

2. Represent and name the numerousness of the empty set (zero). "The box has 2 hats in it. Make 0 hats in the circle." Zero can be illustrated as [ ] or the empty set.

3. Identify, write, and name the numeral that corresponds to the numerousness of a set (1 through 9). "Circle the numeral showing how many mice there are. How many mice are there?"

3　　2　　6　　4　　9

4. Construct sets with a given numerousness (1 through 9). "Draw five dots." Remember to include zero set in these examples.

5. Recognize sets of one to five without counting. Place from one to five objects behind a book. Say to the students, "As soon as I move this book, I want you to tell me how many objects there are." Without counting, the students should tell you how many objects are in the group. Remember to include the zero set in these examples.

Concept 2: Grouping Pattern When representing quantity, objects are grouped into sets of a specified size (base) and sets of sets.

1. Form sets of 10 from a random set of objects or marks. "Circle the *x*s to make as many groups of 10 as possible. Now circle the *o*s, *A*s, and the ***s to make as many groups of 10 as possible."

```
XXXXXXXXXXXX    XXXXX    XXXXXX
OOOOOOOOOOOO    OOOOO    OOOOOOOO
AAAAAAAAAA      AAAAA    AAAAAA
***************  ******  *********
```

2. Construct appropriate groups to show how many. Give students about 125 Popsicle® sticks and rubber bands. Say, "Bundle these sticks so that it will be easy to tell how many there are." Ask the students what was the basis (the number in each set) they used for their bundling the sticks together.

Concept 3: Place Value The position of a digit in a multidigit number determines its value (places are assigned values).

1. Given two multidigit numbers with the same digits but in different orders, identify the position of the digits as distinguishing the two numbers. "How are 145 and 154 alike? How are they different?"

2. Explain that the value of a digit in a multidigit number is dependent on its position. Using the numeral 5, place it in each column, and ask, "How does the number change? How much is it worth?" Repeat with several other numerals

(e.g., 3, 8) and then with other multidigit numbers (e.g., 125, 372).

100s	10s	1s

Concept 4: Place Value (Base 10) A power of 10 is assigned to each position or place (the place values). It is a good idea to provide the position or place names: thousands, hundreds, tens, and ones. Furthermore, it is a good idea to build from single-digit numbers to double-, then triple-, and four-digit numbers. With middle school students who have mastery of the base 10 concept, other base numbers (e.g., base 5 or 2) can be introduced.

1. Identify, name, and show the values for each place in a multidigit number. Show the number 1,829, and say, "What is the name of the place the numeral 8 is in?"

2. Select the place having a given value. Show the number 6,243, and say, "Circle or point to the numeral in the thousands place."

Concept 5: One Digit per Place Only one digit is written in a position or place.

1. Identify and name which numerals (digits) can be assigned to a place. Say to the students, "Tell me the numerals that can be written in the tens place."

2. State that no more than one digit should be written in a place or position. Then ask, "What's wrong with these problems?"

$$
\begin{array}{ccc}
85 & 27 & 13 \\
+39 & +35 & +48 \\
\hline
1114 & 512 & 511
\end{array}
$$

3. Rewrite or restate a nonstandard multidigit numeral (or its representation) as a numeral with only one digit in each place or position. Say to the students, "Write the numeral for this:"

10s	1s
5	4
7	8

Bundled and loose straws or 10 blocks and unit blocks could also be used to help gain this understanding of one digit per place.

Concept 6: Places—Linear/Ordered The places (and their values) in a multidigit (whole-number) number are linearly arranged and ordered from right to left.

1. Identify the smaller-to-larger ordering of place values in a multidigit number. Show the number 6,666 to the students, and say, "Underline the 6 that is worth the most, and circle the 6 that is worth the least."

2. Describe how the place values are ordered. Show the number 8,888 to the students, and say, "Point to the 8 that is 8 hundreds; point to the 8 that is 8 tens." Then ask, "Which of these 8s is worth more?"

3. State or demonstrate that the places in a multidigit number are linearly arranged. Say to the students, "Rewrite this problem correctly."

$$
\begin{array}{cccc}
  & 7 &   & 1 \\
  &   & 2 & 4 \\
  & 6 & 3 & 8 \\
+ &   &   & 0 \\
\hline
\end{array}
$$

Concept 7: Decimal Point The decimal point in a decimal fraction indicates the location of the units (ones) and tenths and hundredths places. Use the table to illustrate where this occurs in order to make a link to prior knowledge. Have the students place the numerals in the correct place. Start with the number 13, then 13.5, and several more numbers with tenths; once the tenths are understood, use numbers with hundredths, like 26.34, 57.92, and 10.01. Ask the students to tell you the value of different numbers.

1. Given a decimal fraction, identify the digit in the units (ones) place. Show the number 29.64 to the students, and say, "Circle the numeral in the ones place." Repeat this with several other numbers like 45.72, 26.89, and 19.03.

10s	1s	tenths	hundredths

2. Given juxtaposed digits and a digit's value, identify and place the decimal point to show the appropriate multidigit number. Show the number 284 to the students, and say, "Place the decimal in the correct place to show 2 tens, 8 ones, and 4 tenths." After tenths, you can use numbers that include hundredths. As students become more proficient,

you can show a number like 3201 and say, "Place the decimal in the correct place to show 3 tens, 2 ones, and 1 hundredth."

3. State the meaning (function) of the decimal point.

Concept 8: Place Relation/Regrouping Each place in a multidigit number has a value 10 times greater than that of the place to its right and one-tenth the value of the place to its left (place relationships and regrouping).

1. Describe the relationships between the values of two adjacent places in a multidigit number. Show the number 222 to the students, and say, "How does the first 2 in the number compare with the second 2?"

2. Express the value of a multidigit number in several ways. Give the following problem to the students: 1 hundred, 8 tens, and 6 ones can also be expressed as _____ tens and _____ ones.

Concept 9: Implied Zeros All numbers have an infinite number of juxtaposed places, each occupied by an expressed or implied digit. In places to the left of nonzero digits in whole numbers written as numerals, zeros are understood; in places to the right of nonzero digits and the decimal point in decimal fractions, zeros are understood.

1. Name the digit in any given place for any multidigit number. Tell the students to rewrite each number and show a digit in each place.

1000s	100s	10s	1s	tenths	Hundredths
683					
27					
79					
4.3					
351.84					

2. Rewrite a given number with as few digits as needed. Tell the students to cross out the zeros that are not needed.

0301	004	01.30
1010	105	0246.080

3. State a rule for writing zeros in a multidigit number. Ask the students, "When do we need to write zeros in a number?"

Concept 10: Face Times Place The value of any digit in a multidigit number is determined by the product of its face and place values (implied multiplication).

1. Show, name, and identify the value of a specified digit within a multidigit number. Show the number 1,468 to the students, and ask, "How much is the 6 worth: 0, 6, 10, 60, or 16?" Ask, "What is the 4 worth: 4, 40, 400, or 4,000?" Then use more examples. Also, include a decimal number, like 25.79, and ask, "How much is the 7 worth: 70, 7, 7 tenths, or 7 hundredths?

2. Name and identify the operation that is used to determine the value of a digit in a multidigit number. Ask the students, "In 1,468 how do we find that 6 is worth 60? Do we add, subtract, multiply, or divide?"

3. State a rule for finding the value of a specified digit in a multidigit number. Ask the students, "How do you know that 6 is worth 60 in the number 1,468?"

Concept 11: Implied Addition The value of a multidigit number is determined by the sum of the values of each digit (implied addition).

1. Express any multidigit number as the sum of the values of each digit.

   294 = _____ ones + _____ tens + _____ hundreds
   Also use a decimal number, like 38.4. 38.4 = _____ tenths + _____ ones + _____ tens.

2. Express the sum of digit values as a multidigit number.
   4 ones + 3 tens + 6 hundreds = _____
   Also use a decimal number, 2 tenths, 4 ones, 5 tens, _____ (remind students who may forget the decimal point).

3. Identify the operation that is used to determine the value of a multidigit number. Ask the students, "To know the value of 287, do we add, subtract, multiply, or divide the value of each numeral?"

Concept 12: Order Multidigit numbers are ordered.

1. Order multidigit numbers. Say to the students, "Put these numbers in the correct order from smallest to largest: 1689, 1001, 421, 1421." Remember to use multidigit decimal numbers too (e.g., 32.4, 101.45, 7.1, 78.23, 45.34, 45.23, 45.31, 45.07).

2. Describe a procedure for determining which of two unequal multidigit numbers is larger. Show the numbers 984 and 849 to the students, and ask, "How do you know which is larger?" Also use unequal multidigit decimal numbers such as 3.45 and 3.06, and ask, "How do you know which is larger?"

Concept 13: Verbal Names (0 through 9) In English, the verbal names for the numbers 0 through 9 are unique.

1. Identify the oral/written names of the 10 digits. Ask the students to write the name next to each digit:

   0 _____   4 _____   7 _____

   1 _____   5 _____   8 _____

   2 _____   6 _____   9 _____

   3 _____

2. State the names for the 10 digits.

Concept 14: Verbal Names with Places In English, the verbal names for multidigit numbers (except 10 through 12) are closely associated with the written numbers (i.e., combining face and place names).

1. Give a multidigit number. Identify the verbal name for one of the digits that includes both a face and place name. Show the number 2,847, and ask the students, "How is the 8 read?"

   a. eight

   b. eight hundred

   c. eighty

   d. eighteen

2. Identify the digit in a multidigit number that is stated first in giving the verbal name. Say to the students, "Write the numeral that is said first in reading the number."

   44 _____   6,186 _____

   284 _____   37 _____

3. Select two-digit numbers whose naming pattern is different from most. Ask the students to circle the numbers that when read aloud are different from the others: 17, 43, 126, 11, 281.

Concept 15: Periods and Names Beginning with the ones place, clusters of three (whole numbers) adjacent places are called *periods* and are named by the place value of the rightmost member of the number triad (e.g., ones, thousands, millions).

1. Given a multidigit number, insert commas to form periods. Ask the students to put commas in the correct places: 28146, 682, 7810, 192642.

2. Name the periods of a given multidigit number. Ask the students, "Which number represents the periods?"

   284,000,163_____

   (ones, hundreds, thousands, millions)

Concept 16: Naming in the Ones Period Numerals in the ones period are named by stating, from left to right, each digit's name (except zero) followed by its place name (ones being omitted; special rules exist for naming tens).

1. Name three-digit numbers (tens digit not being a 1 or 0). Tell the students to write the name for 683.

2. Name three-digit numbers (tens digit being 1). Tell the students to write the name for 718.

3. Name three-digit numbers (tens digit being 0). Tell the students to write the name for 502.

Concept 17: Naming Multidigit Numbers In naming a multidigit number, the digits in each period are read as if they were in the ones period, followed by the period name (ones period name being omitted).

1. Name multidigit numbers up to six digits. Tell the students to write the name for 284,163.

2. Name multidigit numbers over six digits. Ask the students to read the following numbers:

   1,846,283   27,219,143

   103,600,101   3,078,420

Concept 18: Decimal Places and Their Verbal Names Beginning with the decimal, the first place to the right is the tenths place. The adjacent places (to the right) are hundredths, thousandths, ten thousandths, hundred thousandths. In reading the decimal numbers, they are named by the place value of the rightmost member of the decimal number (e.g., 25.6 is twenty-five and six tenths; 65.39 is sixty-five and thirty-nine hundredths).

1. Give a decimal number, identify the verbal name for the decimal digits place. Show the number 43.7, and ask the students, "How is the 7 read?"

   a. seven hundredths

   b. seven tenths

   c. seventy

   d. seventeen

2. Identify the decimal digit name in a multidigit decimal number that is stated by giving the verbal name. Say to the students, "Write the decimal verbal name that is said in reading the number."

   4.63 _____   6.18 _____

   28.41 _____   1.373 _____

Teaching Place Value Place value is directly related to the students' understanding of numeration. Students need to be able to do the following:

- *Group by ones and tens.* Using manipulatives, pictures, and then numerals, students need practice and instruction in grouping by ones and tens. Students can sort manipulatives such as buttons or sticks in groups of 10. Students can also use a table grid to record their answers.

Tens	Ones	Answer
2	3	23
6	2	62
4	7	47

Source: J. M. Engelhardt, R. B. Ashlock, & J. H. G. Wiebe, *Helping Children Understand and Use Numerals* (Boston: Allyn & Bacon, 1984), pp. 89–149. Copyright 1984 by Allyn & Bacon. Adapted by permission.

Use "tens blocks" and "single blocks" to represent numbers. For example, 24 can be represented as follows:

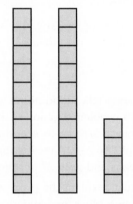

Flannel boards can also be used to group tens and ones.

- *Naming tens.* Teach students to identify numbers by the number of tens. For example, 6 tens is 60, 4 tens is 40, 8 tens is 80, and so on. Give students opportunities to count by tens and then name the number. For example, "Count by tens 3 times." "Ten, twenty, thirty." "Count by tens 7 times." "Ten, twenty, thirty, forty, fifty, sixty, seventy." Also give students opportunities to draw picture diagrams that represent the place values of tens and ones and to identify the number from diagrams.

- *Place value beyond two digits.* Once students can accurately group and identify numbers at the two-digit level, introduce them to three- and four-digit numbers. It is a good idea to be certain students have mastered the concept of *two-digit place value* before introducing numbers and place values greater than two digits. Many of the principles that students have learned in terms of two-digit place value will generalize to three digits and beyond. Give students plenty of opportunity to group, orally name, and sequence three- and four-digit place values.

- *Place value with older students.* Because place value is a concept that is taught during the primary

grades, students who have not adequately learned the skill will likely have problems with computation and word problems. Students need opportunities to learn place value. Many of the games and activities that have been designed to teach place value focus on young children and are less appropriate for older students. Following are five sources of numbers that may be useful for teaching place value to older students:

1. An odometer

2. Numbers from students' science or social studies texts

3. Numbers from the population of your school (e.g., number of freshmen, sophomores, juniors, seniors)

4. Population data from your town, county, state, or country

5. The financial data page from a newspaper

Addition, Subtraction, Multiplication, and Division

Most of students' time in math instruction is spent on computation: memorizing facts and practicing addition, subtraction, multiplication, and division problems; and completing math sheets, workbook pages, and problems copied from books that require the continued practice and application of math computation principles. It is probably for this reason that many students find math boring and miss its applicability to everyday life. Providing appropriate instruction and instructional activities is important to turning the learning of computation into a more desirable process for students.

Teachers can help to make computation exercises and fact learning more engaging by using computer-assisted instruction, which is equally effective for teaching basic arithmetic facts as the conventional drill and practice (Okolo, 1992). Students are likely to be more persistent in solving math problems and have a better attitude toward math when they participate in computer-assisted instruction (Cawley, Foley, & Doan, 2003).

Teachers can also improve students' understanding of computation as they improve students' conceptual knowledge and understanding of mathematics. One intervention for third-grade students with math disabilities addressed conceptual knowledge (Kaufmann, Handl, & Thony, 2003). Students were taught counting principles, the use of arithmetic symbols, memorization of numerals that equaled 10, strategies for memorizing facts, complex multistep calculations, and procedural language for using memorized facts. Students who participated in the intervention made significant gains.

Computing math problems is much easier for students if they understand numeration and place value and if they are given frequent practical application of the math problems. When students are having difficulty performing math computation, it may be for the following three reasons:

1. They do not have an understanding of numeration and/or place value.

2. They do not understand the operation they are performing.

3. They do not know basic math facts and their application to more complicated computation. Students with attention deficit disorder often demonstrate difficulty in computation because they fail to automatize computational skills at an appropriate age (Ackerman, Anhalt, & Dykman, 1986). By *automatize*, we mean learning computational facts so that they are automatic, quickly done in one's head. Students with attention deficit disorder require more time for computation.

Understanding the Operation Students should be able to demonstrate their understanding of an operation by drawing picture diagrams and illustrating it with manipulatives. For example, Sara was able to write the correct answer to the multiplication fact $3 \times 2 = 6$. However, when asked to draw a picture to represent the problem, she drew three flowers and two flowers. She seemed totally undisturbed that the number of flowers she drew was different from the answer she wrote. When asked why she had drawn the number of flowers she did, Sara said, "I drew three flowers for the 3 and two flowers for the 2." When the teacher questioned her further, she discovered

that Sara had no understanding of multiplication. By rote, she had memorized the answers to some of the elementary multiplication facts. The teacher used manipulatives such as chips and interlocking cubes to illustrate multiplication.

The following activities can be helpful in teaching students to understand mathematical operations:

- The following drawing illustrates how chips in rows can be used to illustrate multiplication. For example, ask, "How many 4s make 20? Fours are placed on the board _____ times."

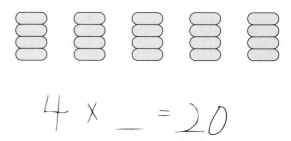

- Have students talk aloud about what is involved in solving a problem. Do not let them merely *read* the problem; ask them to *explain* what it means. For example, "63 − 27 means that someone had 63 jelly beans and gave 27 of them to a friend."

- Have students explain the process to another student by using block manipulatives. For example, "24 + 31 is the same as adding 4 one-block pieces to 1 one-block piece and 2 ten-block pieces to 3 ten-block pieces."

- Have students close their eyes and use noises to illustrate operations. For example, to illustrate multiplication, the teacher can tap in groups of six and ask, "How many times did I tap a group of 6?"

> tap-tap-tap-tap-tap-tap
> tap-tap-tap-tap-tap-tap
> tap-tap-tap-tap-tap-tap

"Yes, I tapped a group of 6 three times. Now I am going to tap a group of 6 three times again, and I want you to tell me how many taps there are altogether. Yes, when you tap a group of 6 three times there are 18 total taps." This same process can be used for addition and subtraction (Bley & Thornton, 1981).

In addition, for a student who is more visual in his or her learning or has a hearing impairment, you could show the 3 rows of 6 stars and ask similar questions. "How many rows of 6 stars are there? Now count the rows by sixes. Six, twelve, eighteen; that is correct." For the more kinesthetic learners, the teacher could have the students stand in three groups of six students each, and ask the questions and count off.

Knowing Basic Math Facts Two of the reasons students may have difficulty with computation have been discussed: They do not understand numeration and/or place value, and they do not understand the computation process. A third reason students may have difficulty with computation is they do not know basic math facts. A common instructional misconception is that if students learn basic arithmetic facts they will no longer have difficulties with other arithmetic operations and problems. Arithmetic facts do not help students in analyzing or understanding the application of arithmetic operations; however, they do aid in the acquisition and speed of performing arithmetic operations. Students who do not know basic math facts are going to be considerably slower and less accurate in math computation and less likely to solve problems effectively. It is difficult for students to understand the math process because so much of their attention is focused on computing one small segment of problems. This is not unlike the student who when reading spends so much time decoding an unknown word that comprehension suffers.

Using thinking strategies assists in the acquisition and retention of basic math facts (Thornton & Toohey, 1985). Without direct instruction, students with learning disabilities often do not discover and use these strategies and relationships for learning and retaining math facts (Thornton, 1978). Some thinking strategies that are used by students who are successful at solving basic math facts (Thornton & Toohey, 1985; Thornton, Tucker, Dossey, & Bazik, 1983) can be taught to students who are having difficulties:

- *Using doubles.* Students can learn to use doubles to solve basic math facts. If a student knows 6 + 6 = 12, then the student can easily compute 6 + 7.
- *Counting-on.* Students do not need to resort to counting from one to solve math facts. They can learn to count on from the largest number in an addition fact. For example:

$$7 + 2 = \rule{2cm}{0.4pt}$$

The student counts on two more from 7: "seven, eight, nine." Students can use this same principle when subtracting, only they count backward. For example:

$$7 - 2 = \rule{2cm}{0.4pt}$$

The student counts backward two from 7: "seven, six, five." Students can be taught counting-on before operations, and then they will only need to learn to apply the principle.

- *Using the commutative idea.* The commutative property means that adding or multiplying any two numbers always yields the same answer

regardless of their order. Students can be taught that with addition and multiplication, if they know it one way, they know it the other. For example:

$$3 + 5 = 8$$
$$5 + 3 = 8$$
$$2 \times 9 = 18$$
$$9 \times 2 = 18$$

- *Thinking one more or less than a known fact.* Rasheed knew most of the easy math facts and several of the basic math facts but had trouble with the more difficult ones. When his teacher taught him how to use the math facts he knew to solve the more difficult ones, his math performance improved. For example, Rasheed knew 5 + 5 = 10, but when he was presented with 5 + 6, he began counting on his fingers. His teacher taught him to think of 5 + 6 as one more than 5 + 5, and 5 + 4 as one less than 5 + 5. Pictures such as the following can help to illustrate the principle:

5 + 5 = 10	** ** *	+	** ** *	=
5 + 6 =	** *	+	** **	=
5 + 4 =	** ** *	+	** ** *	=

- *Using tens.* Students can learn that 10 + any single-digit number merely changes the 0 in the 10 to the number they are adding to it.
- *Using nines.* There are two strategies that students can apply to addition facts that involve nines. First, they can think of the 9 as a 10 and then subtract 1 from the answer. As illustrated here, the student is taught to think of the 9 as a 10:

- *Counting by twos, threes, and fours.* Being able to count by multiples helps in addition, multiplication, and division. Multiplication facts can be taught by interpreting 3 × 4 as counting by threes 4 times. Division facts, such as 8 / 2, can be

FIGURE 11-4 Relationships between Addition and Subtraction; Multiplication and Division

Known Addition Facts	Made-Up Subtraction Facts
5 + 5 = 10	$10 - 5 = 5$
3 + 2 = 5	_____
8 + 8 = 16	_____
6 + 4 = 10	_____

Known Multiplication Facts	Made-Up Division Facts
7 × 4 = 28	$28 \div 4 = 7$
8 × 8 = 64	_____
5 × 9 = 45	_____
5 × 10 = 50	_____

interpreted as, "How many times do you count by twos before you reach 8?"

- *Relationships between addition and subtraction, between multiplication and division.* After students learn addition facts, you can show them the relationship between the addition fact and subtraction. For example, if students know 7 + 6 = 13, they can learn the relationships between the known addition fact and the subtraction fact, 13 − 7 = _____. Whenever possible, reinforce this principle as students are working, "You know 8 + 4 = 12, so 12 − 4 = must be _____." Give students known addition facts, and ask them to form subtraction problems. These sample relationships can be used to teach multiplication and division facts (see Figure 11-4).

Van Luit and Naglieri (1999) have been successful in teaching students to compute multiplication and division by ensuring that they learn the following six concepts:

1. Multiplication is repeated addition.
2. Reversibility means that 4 × 7 is the same as 7 × 4.
3. The need to memorize the basic multiplication facts below 100.
4. Division is repeated subtraction.
5. The need to memorize the basic division facts below 100.
6. Ways to apply multiplication and division in real-life problems.

If you think these strategies for assisting students in learning math facts seem logical and automatic, you are right. For most students, they are. However, students with learning difficulties in math do not automatically use these strategies, and this prevents them from acquiring the math facts they need for accurate and speedy computation.

When these strategies are taught directly, students' math performance improves. When Ms. Pappas taught strategies to students who were having difficulty in addition, she used the strategies summarized in Apply the Concept 11-3, and she enlisted the help of other students who were performing the math skill accurately. She interviewed students who knew how to perform the skill and asked them to talk aloud while they solved the problems so that she could learn what strategies they used. She then taught these strategies to students who were having problems.

Peer-Assisted Instructional Practices Perhaps one of the most effective procedures for teaching math facts to students with learning and behavior problems is the use of cross-age tutors. Cross-age tutors are older students, often students who do not have learning or behavior problems, who serve as tutors for younger students with learning difficulties. Cross-age tutors are particularly effective in teaching math facts because the skills they need to be effective can be acquired quickly, in as little as two 45-minute periods. In a study that successfully used cross-age tutors to teach addition facts to students with learning disabilities (Beirne-Smith, 1991), tutors were trained to do the following:

- Use contingent reinforcement.
- Use task and error correction procedures.
- Use procedures for counting-on.
- Use procedures for rote memorization of facts.
- Repeat skills and instruction until mastery.

Cooperative learning groups, usually small groups of students (three to five per group), can be used to have students work together to solve problems. Maheady, Harper, and Sacca (1988) conducted a cooperative learning math instruction program for ninth- and tenth-grade students with mild disabilities. Students who participated in the cooperative teams performed better in mathematics and received higher grades than those who did not.

Constant Time-Delay Procedure Constant time delay is a procedure for teaching math facts that provides for systematic assistance from the teacher through near errorless control of the prompt to ensure the successful performance of the student (Gast, Ault, Wolery, Doyle, & Belanger, 1988; Schuster, Stevens, & Doak, 1990; Stevens & Schuster, 1988; Wolery, Cybriwsky, Gast, & Boyle-Gast, 1991). Students are presented with a math problem and are allowed a specific amount of time to give the correct answer. If students do not respond within the allotted time, a controlling prompt (typically, the teacher modeling the correct response) is provided. Students then repeat the model. Correct responses before and after the prompt are reinforced; however, only

Strategies for Teaching Addition Facts

Addition Facts Groups by Strategy for Recall			
	Fact Group	**Examples**	**Most Popular Strategy for Working Out Unknown Answers**
No fingers needed!	Count-Ons Zero Facts Doubles 10 Sums	(+1, +2, +3, facts) (6 + 0, 0 + 4) (4 + 4, 7 + 7) (especially 6 + 4)	"Feel" the count Show it Use pictures (e.g., 7 + 7 is the 2-week fact; 7 + 7 = 14) Use 10-frame
	9s Near Doubles Four Last Facts	(4 + 9, 9 + 6) (4 + 5, 7 + 8) (7 + 5, 8 + 4, 8 + 5, 8 + 6)	Use pattern Relate to doubles (via pictures) Make 10, add extra

Note: Turnarounds (commutatives of facts within each group) would be learned before moving to a different group of facts.

Verbal Prompts Used in the Addition Program			
Fact Group	**Sample**	**Facts**	**Sentence Patterns (Verbal Prompts)**
Count-Ons	8 +2	3 +7	Start BIG and count on.
Zeros	6 +0	0 +3	Plus zero stays the same.
Doubles	5 +5	7 +7	Think of the picture.
Near Doubles	5 +6	7 +8	Think doubles to help.
9s	4 +9	9 +7	What's the pattern?
Near 10s	7	6	Use 10 to help.

Source: C. A. Thornton & M. A. Toohey (1985), Basic math facts: Guidelines for teaching and learning, *Learning Disabilities Focus, 1*(1), pp. 50, 51. Reprinted with permission of the Division for Learning Disabilities.

correct responses that are provided before the prompt are counted toward criterion.

Math Computation Errors How could students make the errors in Figure 11-5? It appears as though all the students did was guess. Yet each of the students who computed the problems can tell you what he or she did to get the answer. Most errors that students make are rule governed. Although the rule they are applying is not always obvious, the students are using some rule to tell them how to compute a problem. In problem A in Figure 11-5, Erika said, "I took 1 away from 7 to get 6 and took 0 away from 5 to get 5." In problem B, Jeff added across, adding the 3 and 1 to get 4 and adding the 2 and 3 to get 5. In problem C, Yolanda said, "I knew this wasn't right, but it was the best I knew how to do. I multiplied 3 × 4 to get 12, and then 6 × 4 to get 24." In problem D, Shawn knew that 7 plus 7 plus 7 was 21, but he was operating under the faulty rule that you always carry the smaller number, so he wrote the 2 in the ones column and carried the 1. In problem E, Jae said, "I added 4 plus 1 because it was easier than adding 4 plus 3." When given several similar

FIGURE 11-5 Math Computational Errors

(A)	15 − 7 —— 65	(B)	15 + 23 —— 45	(C)	63 × 23 —— 2412
		(D)	37 27 17 —— 72	(E)	13 + 4 —— 53

problems, she had no concerns about placing the number in the ones or tens column, depending on where it was easier for her to add. All of these students applied faulty rules as they performed math computations. Once the teacher discovered the faulty rules they were applying, she was able to teach them the underlying concepts and the correct rule for completing computations.

Teachers can learn a great deal about students' thinking in mathematics through an oral diagnostic interview (Lankford, 1974). Such an interview will provide information about what each student is doing and why he or she is doing it that way. For the diagnostic interview to yield accurate, helpful information, the teacher must ask the student questions about math computation in a nonthreatening way. For example, "I am interested in learning what you say to yourself while you do this problem. Say aloud what you are thinking." It is often most effective to use a problem that is different from the one the

student has performed incorrectly. The assumption behind this interview is that there is an underlying reason behind the mistakes, and understanding why a student is making errors provides valuable diagnostic information that leads directly to instruction. Roberts (1968) identified four common failure strategies in computation, which are summarized in Apply the Concept 11-4.

Students with learning problems are slower but not necessarily less accurate when it comes to doing computation and learning math facts. When teaching mathematics in your classroom, teachers should consider that students with learning problems may need additional practice to learn math facts and more time to perform mathematics computations because they often lack the skill in automatization to perform math computation effectively and efficiently.

Language of Math Computation "What do you mean by 'find the difference'?" a student might ask. "Am I supposed to add or subtract? Why don't you just say it in plain English?" Many students with learning and behavior problems have difficulty with the language of computation. However, understanding the vocabulary is important for success in the regular classroom, application to math story problems, and communication with others. Understanding the terminology of the four basic operations as well as the symbols associated with the processes is important. Students also need to understand the vocabulary that is associated with the answer derived from each of these processes. Table 11-1 illustrates the relationship between the process, symbol, answer, and problem.

11-4 APPLY THE CONCEPT

Errors in Computation

1. *Wrong operation.* The student attempts to solve the problem by using the wrong process. In this example the student subtracted instead of adding.

$$\begin{array}{r} 24 \\ +11 \\ \hline 13 \end{array}$$

2. *Computational error.* The student uses the correct operation but makes an error recalling a basic number fact.

$$\begin{array}{r} 24 \\ +11 \\ \hline 58 \end{array}$$

3. *Defective algorithm.* The student attempts to use the correct operation but uses a wrong procedure for solving the problem. The error is not due to computation.

$$\begin{array}{r} 24 \\ -17 \\ \hline 13 \end{array}$$

4. *Random response.* The student has little or no idea how to solve the problem, and writes numbers randomly.

$$\begin{array}{r} 304 \\ -196 \\ \hline 396 \end{array}$$

Source: Based on G. H. Roberts (1968), The failure strategies of third-grade arithmetic pupils, *The Arithmetic Teacher, 15,* pp. 442–446.

TABLE 11-1 Relationship of Process, Symbol, Answer, and Problem

Process	Symbol	Answer	Problem
Addition	+	Sum	6 + 4 =
Subtraction	−	Difference	5 − 3 =
Multiplication	×	Product	8 × 5 =
Division	÷	Quotient	12 ÷ 6 =

After teaching the information on the chart, the teacher can use the following three activities:

1. Cover one column (e.g., the symbols), and ask the student to write the answer.
2. Place each of the symbols, answers, and problems on a separate index card, and ask the student to sort them by process.
3. Play concentration with two columns. Two columns of index cards (e.g., the symbol cards and answer cards) are laid answer down, and the students take turns searching for matching pairs by selecting two cards. When a student picks up a corresponding pair, he or she keeps the pair and takes another turn.

Use of Calculators Many students with learning and behavior problems let computation interfere with their ability to learn problem solving. They spend so much time learning to compute the problem accurately that they miss the more important aspects of mathematics, such as concept development and practical application.

Many teachers do not use calculators because they believe that the use of calculators threatens the acquisition of basic skills. Mr. Coffland, a third-grade teacher, put it this way: "If I let my students use calculators to solve problems, they will not have adequate practice in basic skills. They will become too dependent on using the calculator." Research suggests that Mr. Coffland has little to fear. The results of a summary of 79 studies (Hembree, 1986) on the use of calculators suggest the following:

- The use of calculators does not interfere with basic mathematics skill acquisition. In fact, calculator use can improve skill acquisition.
- Only in fourth grade does sustained calculator use interfere with skill development.
- The use of calculators in testing situations results in much higher achievement scores, particularly when students are low in problem-solving ability.
- The use of calculators improves students' attitudes toward mathematics.
- Calculators can be introduced at the same time that paper-and-pencil practice exercises are introduced.

- Students can use calculators to solve complex problems that they construct. This also provides support for improved self-concept with math skills.

In summary, as long as students get basic skills instruction, the use of calculators is a positive aid to mathematics instruction. There are several ways in which students who are having difficulty with mathematics instruction can use calculators:

1. *To develop a positive attitude.* Using a calculator removes the drudgery associated with solving computations and makes problem solving fun.

2. *To improve self-concept.* Being able to compute extremely complex problems on a calculator gives students confidence in their mathematics abilities.

3. *To improve practice in problem solving.* Students are willing to tackle difficult problem-solving tasks when they have a calculator to help solve the problem. Students still have to decide what numbers are used, what operation is involved, and whether additional operations are necessary. Using a calculator can free students from the burden of computation and allow more focus on thinking about the problem.

4. *To develop their own problems.* Using a calculator lets students develop their own problems. They can then exchange their problems with each other and use their calculators to solve them.

Fractions

The National Mathematics Advisory Panel (2008) states that a conceptual understanding of fractions and decimals, as with learning whole numbers, and the operational procedures for using them are mutually reinforcing; however, the concept of fractions is one of the most difficult math concepts for children and adults (Hecht, Vagi, & Torgeson, 2007). Moreover, the difficulties with fractions (including decimals and percents) is a great obstacle to further progress in mathematics (National Mathematics Advisory Panel, 2008). Teachers, through the use of their instructional materials, ensure the learning of conceptual and procedural knowledge of fractions and of proportional reasoning. Even though many teachers think the concept of fractions is difficult to teach, the concept of a fraction can be introduced before the actual fractions are

> In this **video** ▶, you will watch students use manipulatives to learn about equivalent fractions. What strategies does the teacher use to support her students' ability to calculate fractions? What other strategies can also be used?

FIGURE 11-6 Unit Representation of Fractions

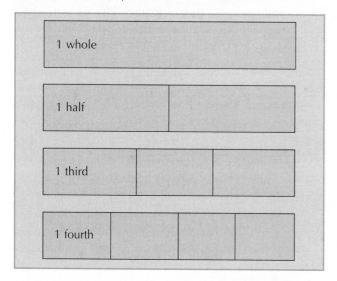

rods, cardboard strips and squares, blocks, fractional circle wheels, cooking utensils such as measuring cups, and any unit dividers such as egg cartons and muffin pans.

Teaching fractions, like teaching most concepts, proceeds from concrete to abstract. Apply the Concept 11-5 demonstrates the teaching sequence.

However, the use of intuitive procedures for the acquisition of knowledge in fractions is unlikely to be successful with low achievers (Kelly, Gersten, & Carnine, 1990). Success in understanding fractions is likely to occur when the following three variables are presented (Kelly et al., 1990):

1. *Systematic practice in discriminating among different problem types.* Students with learning and behavior problems often confuse algorithms when computing fractions. For example, they learn to compute denominators and then use this procedure when adding, subtracting, multiplying, and dividing.

2. *Separation of confusing elements and terminology.* Much of the language of learning fractions is unfamiliar and confusing to youngsters. If the language is well explained and the concepts are well illustrated, students are more likely to be successful in learning fractions.

3. *Use a wide range of examples to illustrate each concept.* Students have a difficult time generalizing beyond the number of examples provided by the teacher; a wide range and large number of examples facilitate understanding.

The Institute for Education Sciences issued a practice guide on research-based practices for teaching fractions (Siegler et al., 2010). They provide the following guidance for instruction in fractions.

even discussed. For example, Figure 11-6 shows the relationship between common fractional terminology and represented units. Moreover, through the availability of calculators, teachers can now place less emphasis on being able to compute fractions and more emphasis on understanding the meaning and use of fractions.

Children as young as 3, 4, and 5 are introduced to the concept of fractions as they receive halves or quarters of apples as part of lunch. They also help a parent in food preparation and cooking. "We use one cup of milk and one-half cup of flour." "You'll need to share the cookie with your brother. You each may have half of the cookie." When children enter school, teachers often use cooking activities to enhance students' understanding of fractions. Many manipulative aids can be used to teach fractions: colored

11–5 APPLY THE CONCEPT

Sequence for Teaching Fractional Concepts

The student

1. Manipulates concrete models (e.g., manipulating fractional blocks and pegs).

2. matches fractional models (e.g., matching halves, thirds, fourths).

3. Points to fractional model when name is stated by another (e.g., the teacher says "half," and the student selects a model of "half" from several distractors).

4. Names fractional units when selected by another (e.g., the teacher points to a fractional unit such as a "fourth," and the student names it).

5. Draws diagrams or uses manipulatives to represent fractional units (e.g., the teacher says or writes fractional units such as "whole," "half," and "third," and the student uses manipulatives or drawings to represent these units).

6. Writes fraction names when given fractional drawings (e.g., next to the drawing, the student writes "half").

7. Uses fractions to solve problems (e.g., place 1½ cups of sugar in a bowl).

8. Uses the concept of like units to help solve computations with fractions.

Recommendation 1   Build on students' informal understanding of sharing and proportionality to develop initial fraction concepts.

- Use equal-sharing activities to introduce the concept of fractions. Use sharing activities that involve dividing sets of objects as well as single whole objects.
- Extend equal-sharing activities to develop students' understanding of ordering and equivalence of fractions.
- Build on students' informal understanding to develop more advanced understanding of proportional reasoning concepts. Begin with activities that involve similar proportions, and progress to activities that involve ordering different proportions.

Recommendation 2   Help students recognize that fractions are numbers and that they expand the number system beyond whole numbers. Use number lines as a central representational tool in teaching this and other fraction concepts from the early grades onward.

- Use measurement activities and number lines to help students understand that fractions are numbers, with all the properties that numbers share.
- Provide opportunities for students to locate and compare fractions on number lines.
- Use number lines to improve students' understanding of fraction equivalence, fraction density (the concept that there are an infinite number of fractions between any two fractions), and negative fractions.
- Help students understand that fractions can be represented as common fractions, decimals, and percentages, and develop students' ability to translate among these forms.

Recommendation 3   Help students understand why procedures for computations with fractions make sense.

- Use area models, number lines, and other visual representations to improve students' understanding of formal computational procedures.
- Provide opportunities for students to use estimation to predict or judge the reasonableness of answers to problems involving computation with fractions.
- Address common misconceptions regarding computational procedures with fractions.
- Present real-world contexts with plausible numbers for problems that involve computing with fractions.

Recommendation 4   Develop students' conceptual understanding of strategies for solving ratio, rate, and proportion problems before exposing them to cross-multiplication as a procedure to use to solve such problems.

- Develop students' understanding of proportional relations before teaching computational procedures that are conceptually difficult to understand (e.g., cross-multiplication). Build on students' developing strategies for solving ratio, rate, and proportion problems.
- Encourage students to use visual representations to solve ratio, rate, and proportion problems.
- Provide opportunities for students to use and discuss alternative strategies for solving ratio, rate, and proportion problems.

Recommendation 5   Professional development programs should place a high priority on improving teachers' understanding of fractions and of how to teach them.

- Build teachers' depth of understanding of fractions and computational procedures involving fractions.
- Prepare teachers to use varied pictorial and concrete representations of fractions and fraction operations.
- Develop teachers' ability to assess students' understandings and misunderstandings of fractions.

Measurement

Measurement includes weight, distance, quantity, length, money, and time. Measurement can be taught almost entirely with applied problems. For example, students learn time by using the clock in the classroom or by manipulating a toy clock; they learn money by making purchases with real or toy money; and they learn measures such as pint, liter, and teaspoon through following recipes. With each measurement unit that is taught (e.g., weight, distance, money), students need to learn the vocabulary and concepts for that unit. Only after students understand the terminology and concepts and have had experience applying the concepts in real measurement problems should they be exposed to measurement instruction through the use of less applied procedures such as textbooks and worksheets.

In addition, an instructional activity has been provided for you to help illustrate the use of a real-world problem to help in the teaching of the concept of fractions (see Cake for Four—No, Make that Six! in the "Instructional Activities" section later in the chapter). Another instructional activity has been provided for you to help illustrate the use of lots of examples to teach the concept of use of like units with fractions (see Finding Like Units in the "Instructional Activities" section later in the chapter).

Time Even before coming to school, most children can tell time by the hour or know when the clock says that it is time to go to bed or time for dinner. The following teaching sequence assists students in understanding time:

1. *Teach students to sequence events.* Younger students can sequence the normal routine of the school day. For instance, "First we have a group story, then reading, then we go to recess." Additional practice in sequencing events can occur with story cards, events that occur at home, field trips, and so on.

2. *Ask students to identify which events take longer.* Name two events (e.g., math time and lining up for recess), and ask students to identify which event takes longer. Name several events, and ask students to put them in order from the event that takes the longest to the one that is quickest to complete.

1:25

one twenty-five

A scope-and-sequence list of skills for teaching time is presented in Apply the Concept 11-6.

Money Students with learning disabilities often have difficulty applying money concepts because they have not mastered many of the earlier concepts, such as the value of coins, how coins compare (e.g., a quarter is more than two times as much as a dime), and how the value of the coins relates to what can be purchased. One parent reported that her child was frequently taken advantage of because he would trade coins of high value for coins of less value. Students with learning difficulties often do not know the price of common goods. Although they may not need to know the exact price of a loaf of bread or a television set, they should be able to estimate what these items cost.

When initially teaching students to identify money, start with real coins. After they learn to recognize real coins, switch to play money and then to representations of money on workbook pages. The following sequence is useful in teaching money identification:

1. *Teach students to match the same coins.* Give students several different coins, and ask them to place all of the same coins in the same group.

2. *Ask students to point to the coin when you name it.* Depending on the students' skill level, you may want to start with two coins (e.g., a penny and a nickel) and then progress to three and four. At this point, students do not need to be able to tell the name of the coin; they merely need to be able to locate it when it is named.

3. *Students name the coin.* At this level, the students tell the name of the coin.

When students can accurately identify the name of the coins, the value of the coins is discussed. Coins and dollars are discussed in terms of both their purchase power and how they relate to each other. Activities and problems that require students to use money and make change assure students that they can apply what they have learned about money. For example, students can learn to keep and balance a checkbook and to give change when role-playing a clerk in a store.

A scope-and-sequence list for teaching money is presented in Apply the Concept 11-7.

11-6 APPLY THE CONCEPT

Time: Scope and Sequence of Skills

The student

- Sequences events—first, and then next.
- Identifies duration of events—what takes longer and what is quicker to do.
- Tells time to the hour.
- Tells time to the half hour.
- Knows the days of the week.
- Knows the names of the months.
- Tells time to the quarter hour.
- Knows the number of days in a week.
- Knows the number of months in a year.
- Can use a calendar to answer questions about the date, the day, and the month.
- Writes time to the hour.
- Writes time to the half hour.
- Writes time using 5-minute increments.
- Writes time accurately.
- Can solve story problems using time.

Money: Scope and Sequence of Skills

The student

- Correctly identifies penny, nickel, dime, and quarter.
- Knows how many cents are in a penny, nickel, dime, and quarter.
- Can add to the correct amount when shown combinations of pennies, nickels, dimes, and quarters.
- Can describe items that can be purchased with combinations of pennies, nickels, dimes, and quarters.

- Can solve simple word problems involving pennies, nickels, dimes, and quarters.
- Can identify a dollar bill, a $5 bill, a $10 bill, and a $20 bill.
- Can identify the value of combinations of coins and various dollar bills.
- Can solve verbal math problems involving combinations of coins and various dollar bills.

Problem Solving

What factors contribute to difficulties with problem solving, and how can teachers assist students in learning problem-solving strategies? Many students with learning problems have trouble with traditional story problems in mathematics because their difficulty in reading makes understanding the math problem almost impossible. In addition, students with learning problems often have difficulty with logical reasoning, which is the basis of many story problems. It is also common that their mathematics education has focused primarily on operations and not on understanding the reasons for operations or even a thorough understanding of the numbers that are involved in operations. Because of their difficulties with reading and logical reasoning and perhaps because of insufficient instruction in mathematics, students with learning problems often find problem solving the most difficult aspect of mathematics.

Despite its difficulties, problem solving may be the most important skill we teach students who have learning and behavior problems. Whereas most other students can apply the operations they learn to real-life problems with little direct instruction, students with learning problems will be less able to apply these skills without instruction, rehearsal, and practice. Students with learning disabilities lack metacognitive knowledge about strategies for math problem solving. Poor math performance is not solely a function of math computation difficulties (Montague et al., 2011; Vukovic & Siegel, 2010). Students who are taught strategies for problem solving are more likely to be successful than are students who are taught the sequence for solving problems (Montague et al., 2011; Powell et al., 2009).

Students need to know when and how to add, subtract, multiply, and divide. Knowing *when* involves understanding the operation and applying it in the appropriate situation. Knowing *how* is the accurate performance of the operation. Most students are better at *how* than at *when*; problem solving gives students practice at these skills.

Factors Affecting Successful Verbal Problem Solving

Teachers need to consider the factors that affect successful story problem solving when writing and selecting story problems and instructing students. Use the following strategies:

In this **video** ⏵, a student demonstrates her ability to use verbal and visual problem-solving skills to manipulate fractions and solve a word problem. However, as she miscalculates the solution, how does the teacher scaffold and guide her toward the correct solution?

- *Teach big ideas.* When students understand the big idea or principle, all of the subordinate concepts around that big idea make more sense and are easier to learn and remember (Carnine, 1997). An example of a big idea is volume. You can teach students the principle of volume and then provide examples of real-life problems that students can solve by applying the big-idea principles they learn about volume.

- *Sameness analysis.* Carnine and colleagues determined the importance of sameness in mathematical problem solving through a series of research investigations (Engelmann, Carnine, & Steely, 1991). The idea is to connect math concepts so that students see the ways in which aspects of mathematical problem solving are the same. Identify types of word problems, and then explicitly teach students the ways in which these word problems are alike.

- *Cue words.* The presence or absence of cue words can significantly affect students' abilities to solve verbal word problems. The cue word *altogether* is illustrated in the following example: "Maria has 4 erasers. Joe has 7 erasers. How many erasers do they have *altogether?*" The cue word *left* is illustrated in the following example: "Jasmine has 9 pieces of candy. She gave 3 pieces to Lin. How many does she have *left?*" Students need to be taught to look for cue words that will guide them in solving problems.

- *Reasoning*. Ask students to think about the idea behind the story problem. Does it appear that the person in the problem will get more or less? Why? What operation will help to solve this? What numbers in the story do we have to use? Are there numbers that we do not have and need to compute? Ask students to explain the way in which they set up and calculated the problem so that they can justify what they've done and why they've done it that way.

- *Syntactic complexity*. The sentence structure within the story problem needs to be kept simple. The sentence length and vocabulary can also affect verbal problem solving.

- *Extraneous information*. Extraneous information in word problems causes difficulties because the majority of students attempt to use all of the information in solving the problem. For example: "Mary's mother baked 10 cookies. Mary's sister baked 8 cookies. Mary's brother baked 3 cupcakes. How many *cookies* were baked?" The information regarding Mary's brother baking three cupcakes is extraneous, yet many students will use the information in attempting to solve the problem. Extraneous information in story problems is associated with decreases in accuracy and computation speed with students. Students will construct the problem using the numbers available in the story problem, disregarding the question and the content available in the story problem. When students can complete story problems successfully without extraneous information, teach them to complete story problems with extraneous information.

- *Content load*. The *content load* refers to the number of ideas contained within a story problem. The story problem should not be overloaded with concepts. Students need to be taught to discriminate between relevant and irrelevant concepts.

- *Suitable content*. Story problems should contain content that is interesting and appealing to students and relevant to the types of real problems that students have or are likely to encounter.

- *Monitor progress*. Use weekly tests of word problem solving to monitor study progress on each type of word problem students have mastered and/or are learning. Reteach when necessary.

- *Provide guided practice*. Use diagrams to demonstrate how to solve the problem, and guide students through the development and use of these diagrams. As students demonstrate increasing proficiency with independent use of diagrams and strategies for effective problem solving, reduce the amount of support provided.

- *Use computer-assisted instruction*. Computer-assisted instruction gives students opportunities to practice computation and problem solving independently and provides correction and feedback. Many students prefer to do mathematics with the computer. *My Math* (Cawley, 2002) is an example of a computer software program that incorporates three mathematical components: computation problems, arithmetic word problems, and arithmetic story problems.

WEB RESOURCES

For students who want to get online and work on mathematics, there is a Web site that provides games, flash cards, homework help, and worksheets along with options to purchase software for use at home. This Web site is located at http://www.aplusmath.com/. You may find it worth a look and possibly send your students to it during class time or for use at home.

Methods of Teaching Story Problem Solving

Students also need to learn specific strategies that will assist them in using a successful process for mastering story problems in class and applying those principles to the mathematics of everyday life. The Institute for Education Sciences provides a guide for how to teach problem solving in mathematics based on current research (Woodward et al., 2012), and the recommendations from this brief follow.

Recommendation 1 Prepare problems and use them in whole-class instruction.

1. Include both routine and nonroutine problems in problem-solving activities.

2. Ensure that students will understand the problem by addressing issues students might encounter with the problem's context or language.

3. Consider students' knowledge of mathematical content when planning lessons.

Recommendation 2 Assist students in monitoring and reflecting on the problem-solving process.

1. Provide students with a list of prompts to help them monitor and reflect during the problem-solving process.
2. Model how to monitor and reflect on the problem-solving process.
3. Use student thinking about a problem to develop students' ability to monitor and reflect.

Recommendation 3 Teach students how to use visual representations.

1. Select visual representations that are appropriate for students and the problems they are solving.
2. Use think-alouds and discussions to teach students how to represent problems visually.
3. Show students how to convert the visually represented information into mathematical notation.

Recommendation 4 Expose students to multiple problem-solving strategies.

1. Provide instruction in multiple strategies.
2. Provide opportunities for students to compare multiple strategies in worked examples.
3. Ask students to generate and share multiple strategies for solving a problem.

Recommendation 5 Help students recognize and articulate mathematical concepts and notation.

1. Describe relevant mathematical concepts and notation, and relate them to the problem-solving activity.
2. Ask students to explain each step used to solve a problem in a worked example.
3. Help students make sense of algebraic notation.

A step-by-step strategy for teaching sixth-grade students to solve story problems is illustrated in Apply the Concept 11-8 (E. M. Smith & Alley, 1981). Students first need to learn the strategies, then practice them with support from a teacher, and finally practice them independently until they can apply the principles with success. After continued success, students make adaptations in or condense the steps they use.

Montague and colleagues (1986a, 1986b) demonstrated the efficacy of the learning strategy approach described in Apply the Concept 11-9, with secondary adolescents with learning disabilities.

In summary, when teaching story problems to students with learning and behavior problems, teachers should keep the following guidelines in mind:

- Be certain the students can perform the arithmetic computation before introducing the computation in story problems.
- Develop a range of story problems that contain the type of problem you want students to learn to solve.
- Instruct with one type of problem until mastery is attained.
- Teach the students to read through a word problem and visualize the situation. Ask them to read the story aloud and tell what it is about.
- Ask the students to reread the story—this time to get the facts.
- Identify the key question. In the beginning stages of problem solving, the students should write the key question so that they can refer to it when the computation is complete.
- Identify extraneous information.

11-8 APPLY THE CONCEPT

Steps for Teaching Students to Solve Story Problems

Story Problem: Mark had $1.47 to spend. He spent $0.34 on gum. How much money does he have left?

   I. Read the problem.
      A. Find unknown words.
      B. Find cue words (e.g., left).
  II. Reread the problem.
      A. Identify what is given.
         1. Is renaming needed?
         2. Are there unit changes?

      B. Decide what is asked for.
         1. What process is needed?
         2. What unit or category is asked for? (e.g., seconds, pounds, money)
 III. Use objects to show the problem
      A. Decide what operation to use.
 IV. Write the problem.
  V. Work the problem.

- Reread the story problem, and attempt to state the situation in a mathematical sentence. The teacher plays an important role in this step by asking the students questions and guiding them in formulating the arithmetic problem.

- Tell the students to write the arithmetic problem and compute the answer. (Students can compute some problems in their heads without completing this step.)

- Tell the students to reread the key question and be sure that they have completed the problem correctly.

- Ask the students whether their answer is likely, based on their estimate.

Teaching math story problems does not have to be limited to the content area of math and can be integrated into reading comprehension instruction. For example, a story about a mother duck and her babies was part of a student's reading lesson. During mathematics, the teacher made minor changes in the story and used it for instruction in story problems in mathematics (see Figure 11-7).

This same procedure can be used with junior high and high school students' content area textbooks. Math story problems can be taken from social studies and science tests; Cawley and Miller (1986) refer to these as knowledge-based problems. Usually, these problems require specific knowledge in the content area. Cawley (1984) identifies the integration of math into other

11-9 APPLY THE CONCEPT

Teaching Adolescents to Solve Story Problems

The eight steps in the verbal math problem-solving strategy are directed to the student and are described below:

1. **Read the problem aloud.** Ask the teacher to pronounce or define any word you do not know. (The teacher pronounces and provides meanings for any words if the student asks.)

   Example: In a high school there are 2,878 male and 1,943 female students enrolled. By how many students must the enrollment increase to make the enrollment 5,000?

2. **Paraphrase the problem aloud.** State important information, giving close attention to the numbers in the problem. Repeat the question part aloud. A self-questioning technique such as "What is asked?" or "What am I looking for?" can help you provide focus on developing the solution.

   Example: Altogether there are a certain number of kids in high school. There are 2,878 boys and 1,943 girls. The question is by how many students must the enrollment increase to make the total enrollment 5,000. What is asked? How many more students are needed to total 5,000 in the school?

3. **Visualize.** Graphically display the information. Draw a representation of the problem.

4. **State the problem.** Complete the following statements aloud: "I have . . ." "I want to find . . ." Underline the important information in the problem.

   Example: I have the number of boys and the number of girls who go to the school now.

I want to find how many more kids are needed to total 5,000.

5. **Hypothesize.** Complete the following statements aloud: "If I . . ." "Then . . ." "How many steps will I use to find the answer?" Write the operation signs.

   Example: If I add 2,878 boys and 1,943 girls, I'll get the number of kids now. Then I must subtract that number from 5,000 to find out how many more must enroll. First add, then subtract. + −. This is a two-step problem.

6. **Estimate.** Write the estimate. My answer should be around . . . or about . . . Underline the estimate.

   Example: 2,800 and 2,000 are 4,800. 4,800 from 5,000 is 200. My answer should be around 200.

7. **Calculate.** Show the calculation and label the answer. Circle the answer. Use a self-questioning technique such as, "Is this answer in the correct form?" Correct labels for the problems should be reinforced.

   Example:

$$
\begin{array}{r}
2{,}878 \\
+\,1{,}943 \\
\hline
4{,}821
\end{array}
\qquad
\begin{array}{r}
5{,}000 \\
-\,4{,}821 \\
\hline
179\ \text{students}
\end{array}
$$

8. **Self-check.** Refer to the problem, and check every step to determine accuracy of operation(s) selected and correctness of response and solution. Check computation for accuracy. Use the self-questioning technique by asking whether the answer makes sense.

Source: M. Montague & C. S. Bos (1986), The effect of cognitive strategy training on verbal math problem-solving performance of learning disabled adolescents, *Journal of Learning Disabilities, 19,* pp. 26–33. Copyright © 1986 by PRO-ED, Inc. Reprinted by permission.

FIGURE 11-7 Example of Teacher-Altered Story for Use in Story-Problem Instruction

The mother duck went to the pond with her *eight* babies. They looked for their new friend. *Two* more baby ducks joined them. How many baby ducks were there?

content areas as an important means of promoting generalization of math concepts.

Pictures can be used to facilitate processing information in solving mathematical word problems. For example, using Figure 11-8, a teacher could say, "The small monkeys have four bananas, and the large monkeys have six bananas. How many bananas would they have if they put them all together?"

Instructional manipulatives can also be used to assist students with learning problems in solving mathematical word problems. Cuisenaire rods, base 10 blocks, fraction strips, and multilink cubes can be used to represent the numerical values in the problem and to assist students in better understanding and solving mathematical word problems (Van de Walle & Lovin, 2005).

Improving Math Performance

How can math interventions be used to improve math performance? One way to conceptualize developing and implementing effective interventions for students with math disabilities is to consider approaches that include cognitive, behavioral, and alternative instructional delivery systems, which includes cooperative learning, computer-assisted instruction, and interactive video games.

FIGURE 11-8 Pictures Help to Solve Math Story Problems

Cognitive Approaches

Cognitive behavior modification can be used with instructional procedures in mathematics. CBM often takes the form of self-instruction, which relies on using internalized language to facilitate the problem-solving process. When self-talk is said aloud, these verbalizations are beneficial to the arithmetic process. For example, teachers can model math procedures by thinking aloud and describing their steps in solving the problem.

$$8 + 17 = \underline{\hspace{1cm}}$$

"The first thing I notice is that the sign is a plus sign, which means that I'm going to add the two numbers together. I know that my answer is going to be larger than 17 because that's the bigger of the two numbers. I'm going to start with 17 and count up, making a slash for each number until I have 8 slashes. That will be my answer."

Using these types of think alouds with students and then demonstrating how to proceed will help them to develop procedures for solving problems.

Leon and Pepe (1983) taught a five-step self-instructional sequence to special education teachers. Students receiving arithmetic instruction from these teachers who were trained in the sequence improved greatly both in arithmetic computation and in generalizing the skills they acquired. Second-grade students with learning disabilities became more proficient at learning addition through strategy instruction than through drill and practice. This study demonstrated that even very young children with learning disabilities can benefit from cognitive approaches to math instruction (Tournaki, 2003). The following sequence for using self-instruction in mathematics is a modification of the approach used by Leon and Pepe (1983):

1. *Modeling.* The teacher demonstrates how to compute a problem by using overt self-instruction. This overt self-instruction, or talking aloud about the process, assists students who have learning problems in knowing what they should say to themselves and what questions they should ask to keep themselves focused on the process.

2. *Coparticipation.* The teacher and students compute the problem together by using overt self-instruction. This step helps the students to put the procedure in their own words, yet supplies the support of the teacher while the students are still learning the process.

3. *Student demonstration.* The students compute the problem alone by using overt self-instruction, and the teacher monitors the students' performance. The students are more independent in this step; however, the teacher is still available to give correction and feedback.

4. *Fading overt self-instruction.* The students continue to demonstrate the computation of the problem with internal self-instruction. Often students have a check sheet of symbols or key words to cue them to the key points.

5. *Feedback.* The students complete the problem independently by using covert self-instruction and providing self-reinforcement for a job well done.

Behavioral Approaches

Cues Behavioral techniques are also available to improve students' math performance. As you know, stimulus cues precede responses and often control or provide information to control responses. In arithmetic instruction, teachers need to identify relevant cues and determine whether the students are aware of these cues and are using them appropriately. In Figure 11-9, three different problems are presented; there are many different cues that a student must understand and attend to before accurately performing these problems. For example, in problem 1 of Figure 11-9, the student must know what "+" means, what the numbers represent, and what procedure to follow to perform the problem. In problem 2, the student must know what the picture represents, the difference between the short and long hands of the clock, and what each of the numbers represents. Problem 3 requires the student to understand the cue *long* and to know what type of tool is needed to address the problem. Math provides many stimulus cues, and teachers need to be certain that students recognize and understand the cues and attend to them.

Teachers can also provide cues to assist students in learning new skills. For example, the following list illustrates cues a teacher provided when students were first learning long division:

÷ (divide) $6\sqrt{478}$ $8\sqrt{521}$
× (multiply)
− (subtract)
↓ (bring down)

FIGURE 11-9 Math Problems Enlisting Various Cues

(1)   37
       24
     + 89

(2)

What time is it?_____

(3) How long is this line?_____

Corrective Feedback Providing corrective feedback reinforces student performance. Corrective feedback involves telling the students what they are doing well, including procedures, accuracy of responses, and work style. It also involves identifying areas in which a student needs further assistance. Corrective feedback should be given frequently. Teachers should not wait until students have completed tasks but should give feedback while they are working on the task. Feedback should also be precise. Rather than saying, "You are doing a good job," a teacher should say, "You remembered to carry. All of the answers in the first row are correct. Good job."

Task Analysis Task analysis is a process of specifying the behaviors needed for a particular task that can help to shape student responses. Students are taught behaviors from the simple to the more complex until they can perform the target behavior. For example, a teacher's goal may be for a student to complete two-place addition with carrying by solving a verbal math problem. The student's present level of performance is knowledge of math facts when adding numbers between 0 and 9. Through task analysis, the teacher identifies the prerequisite concepts that need to be known and the many problem-solving skills that need to be shaped through instruction and practice before the student is performing the target behavior, in this case a verbal math problem with two-place addition:

- Number concepts for 0–9
- Number concepts for 10–100
- Place value
- Simple oral word problems, requiring addition knowledge for 0–9
- Simple written word problems, requiring addition knowledge for 0–9
- Two-place addition problems
- Oral-addition word problems requiring knowledge of two-place addition
- Written-addition word problems requiring knowledge of two-place addition

The teacher decided that it would take approximately 3 months to reach the goal. He knew that his mathematics program would focus on other skills during that period (e.g., time, measurements, and graphs). Apply the Concept 11-10 lists several things teachers can do to improve their students' math performance.

Focus on Real-World Mathematics

Many students with learning and behavior problems manage to graduate despite having only a minimal

Improving Math Performance

Baker, Gersten, and Lee (2002) conducted a synthesis of all of the empirical research on teaching mathematics to students with math difficulties. They reported several themes from these studies that teachers should consider in their instructional routines:

- Use ongoing progress-monitoring data in mathematics. These data allow teachers to determine how students are progressing, adjust instruction, and give feedback to students on their performance.
- Use peer-assisted learning to provide support for mathematical learning. When peers work together on organized practices of computing and problem solving, both peers benefit.
- Use explicit and systematic instruction in the elements of mathematics, which is associated with improved outcomes in math for students. This type of instruction guides students through problems and calculations rather than relying on students to figure it out independently.
- Provide families with information on how their students are performing, and engage families as the supporters and motivators for their children's progress in mathematics.

---

understanding of mathematics skills. Many, relieved to escape formal education in mathematics, have the unfortunate misconception that they are finished with mathematics. Soon they find that functioning as an adult requires managing money, interest on loans, and credit cards as well as filing taxes, completing employment forms for deductions, and using basic math skills in their jobs.

In this **video** ▶, teachers plan and implement a variety of strategies to integrate real-world mathematics applications in their lessons. What other ways can you integrate math across the curriculum and make it relevant to students' experiences?

Many of the skills that are most important for students with learning disabilities are not part of general mathematics curricula because they do not need to be taught through direct instruction to non-learning-disabled students. What are some of the real-world issues that need to be part of the math curriculum for most students with learning and behavior problems? Start with topics that are of high importance to them. For example, ask students to identify three things they would like to buy. Ask them to determine how much they cost at several different stores. Be sure to consider extras like whether tax and shipping apply.

As students move through the grades, providing them with many opportunities to practice real-world mathematics is essential. Start with asking them to estimate how much their "take-home" pay would be based on an hourly rate and 40 hours per week of employment. Ask them to identify the monthly prices of apartments in an area where they would like to live. Now compute how much they would have left if they rented an apartment in that area. These types of real-world issues are prevalent and prepare students for thinking about in everyday life.

Math instruction for students with disabilities requires teachers to consider the functional math skills that students need. Apply the Concept 11-11 presents an outline of content for teaching functional math.

Curricula and Materials

Traditional math curricula have provided problems for students with learning disabilities. What are some of the typical problems with math curricula and how might you address these issues?

- The text is challenging to read and understand. You can interpret the text with students and provide concrete examples.
- The sequencing of math procedures and the approaches are poor. Teach the math procedures in a sequence that allows for maximizing learning and retention.
- The reading vocabulary is difficult, and the reading level is too high.
- The sequencing of material presented is poor, multiple concepts are introduced, and the focus skips from one concept to another.
- An insufficient number of problems covers each concept.
- Insufficient opportunities and problems focus on application.
- The page formatting is too varied.
- Students often do not have the prerequisite skills that the text assumes they possess.

Content for Teaching Functional Math

Consumer Skills

Using computer to enhance life skills and access to banking and other personal decision making

Making change

Determining cost of sale items using percentages (e.g., "25% off")

Determining tax amounts

Doing cost comparisons

Buying "on time"

Balancing a checkbook

Determining total cost of purchases

Homemaking Skills

Measuring ingredients

Budgeting for household expenses

Calculating length of cooking and baking time when there are options (e.g., for a cake using two 9" round pans vs. two 8" round pans)

Measuring material for clothing construction

Doing cost comparisons

Health Care

Weighing oneself and others

Calculating caloric intake

Determining when to take medication

Auto Care

Calculating cost of auto parts

Measuring spark plug gaps

Determining if tire pressure is correct

Figuring gas mileage

Home Care

Determining amount of supplies (paint, rug shampoo) to buy

Determining time needed to do projects

Measuring rods and drapes

Finding cost of supplies

Finding cost of repairs

Vocational Needs

Calculating payroll deductions

Determining money owed

Knowing when to be at work

Doing actual math for various jobs

Leisure Activities

Comparing travel expenses

Magazine and newspaper costs

Membership fees

Entertainment: movies, video rentals, sporting and artistic events

Home Management

Determining where to live

Moving expenses

Move-in expenses

Utilities

Insurance

Furniture

Additional expense

Transportation

Public or automobile

Maintenance

Insurance

Sources: Adapted from J. R. Patton, M. E. Cronin, D. S. Bassett, & A. E. Koppel (1997), A life skills approach to mathematics instruction: Preparing students with learning disabilities for the real-life demands of adulthood, *Journal of Learning Disabilities, 30*(2), pp. 178–187; and S. E. Schwartz & D. Budd (1981), Mathematics for handicapped learners: A functional approach for adolescents, *Focus on Exceptional Children, 13*(7), pp. 7–8. Reproduced by permission of Love Publishing Company.

Teachers who attempt to use traditional curricula with students who have learning difficulties will need to control for these factors in their teaching. This means that the teacher may have to carefully and thoughtfully select the concepts, skills, and problems as well as the instructional explanations from the traditional math curricula materials or choose alternative math materials.

A number of curricula have been developed that focus on teaching math skills to students with learning difficulties. Some of these curricula are described in Apply the Concept 11-12.

Sources of Curricula and Materials

- *Connecting Math Concepts* (Bernadette, Carnine, Engelmann, & Engelmann, 2003) is designed to provide explicit instruction and explanations of basic math concepts and the relationships between concepts for students in grades kindergarten through 8. Mastered concepts are then used to build problem-solving skills. The lessons proceed in small, incremental steps with continuous review. Materials include teacher's guides, student textbooks and workbooks, and fact and independent worksheets for additional practice. All lessons are scripted for teachers and provide systematic instruction in story problems.

- *Math Exploration and Applications*, developed by Bereiter, Hilton, Rubinstein, and Willoughby (1998), provides instruction, games, and manipulatives for building fluency in math skills. It is also available in Spanish.

- *The Corrective Mathematics Program,* by Engelmann, Carnine, and Steely (2005), provides remedial basic math for students in grades 3 through 12, addressing seven areas: addition, subtraction, multiplication, division, basic fractions, decimals and percentages, and rational numbers and equations.

- *Structural Arithmetic,* by Stern, Stern, and Gould (1998), involves students in prekindergarten through third grade in making, discovering, and learning math concepts and facts. Colorful blocks are used to assist students in discovering math concepts.

- *Cuisenaire rods,* developed by M. Georges Cuisenaire, help impart conceptual knowledge of the basic structure of mathematics.

- *Real-Life Math* (Ellen McPeek Glisam) provides an imaginary town (Willow, USA) where students learn math by learning to live on a paycheck. Students learn to budget money and pay expenses. Activity book and materials are available from Pro-Ed publishers (http://www.proedinc.com).

- *Key Math Teach and Practice*, by Connolly (1988), was developed to provide diagnosis of math difficulties and remedial practice. Materials include a teacher's guide, student progress charts, and sequence charts. Activities and worksheets are also provided.

- *Saxon Math* for kindergarten through secondary grades was developed to provide math instruction that continuously builds on previous instruction while increasing the complexity to learn math concepts in depth. Math concepts, problem solving, and applications are sequential.

INSTRUCTIONAL ACTIVITIES

This section provides instructional activities related to mathematics. Some of the activities teach new skills; others are best suited for practice and reinforcement of already acquired skills. For each activity, the objective, materials, and teaching procedures are described.

Two-Digit Numbers: Focus on Reversals

OBJECTIVE: To help students understand and use two-digit numbers successfully (for use with students who write 23 for 32, 41 for 14, etc.)

GRADES: Primary

MATERIALS: Objects that can be grouped by tens (e.g., pencils, paper, chips, sticks)

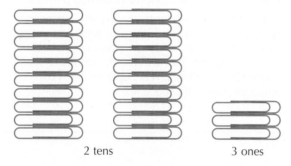

2 tens   3 ones

TEACHING PROCEDURES: Four steps are recommended: First, tell the students to group objects such as Popsicle sticks or chips in tens, and then ask them to say the number of tens and the number of ones left over. Next, the students count orally by tens and use objects to show the count (e.g., 2 tens is 20, 6 tens is 60, and so on). When multiples of ten are established, extra ones are included (e.g., 2 tens and 3 is 23). Because of naming irregularities, teens are dealt with last.

The students then group objects by tens and write to describe the grouping. The tens–ones labels, used in early stages, are gradually eliminated. On separate sheets of paper, the students write the number that corresponds with the grouping. The children use objects (tens and ones) to help compare and sequence numbers.

Two Up

OBJECTIVE: To practice multiplication facts by rehearsing counting by twos, threes, fours, and so on

GRADES: Primary through intermediate

PREREQUISITE BEHAVIORS: Counting by twos, threes, and so on

MATERIALS: A set of 48 cards made by printing the multiples of 2 from 1 to 12, using a different color of pen for each set (e.g., 2, 4, . . . 12 in red, blue, green, and brown)

TEACHING PROCEDURES: Directions for playing the game are as follows: The cards are shuffled and dealt, giving an equal number of cards to each player. The player who has the red 2 starts the game by placing the red 2 in the middle of the table. The next player must place a red 4 on top of the red 2 or pass. Next a red 6 is needed, and so on. Each of the players plays in a similar manner. A player can play only one card each turn.

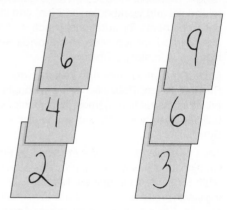

The object of the game is to play the cards from 2 on up. The first player to play all of his or her cards is the winner.

ADAPTATIONS: This game can be played with decks of threes, fours, sixes, and so on, called "Three Up," "Four Up," and so on. A different deck of cards must be made for each multiple.

Clock-Reading Bingo

OBJECTIVE: To give students practice in associating the time on a clock face to its written and spoken form

GRADES: Primary

MATERIALS: Cards that show times on a standard clock, large game boards with 16 squares and with times written at the bottom of each square, 16 "clock" chips (made by placing gummed labels on cardboard chips and drawing a clock on the face of the label), markers

TEACHING PROCEDURES: A caller holds up a clock face. The players must decide whether the time shown by that clock is on their game board. If it is, the player places a marker in the square that contains the written form. The winner is the first person who correctly completes a row in any direction and reads the time in each winning square.

three o'clock	seven o'clock	fifteen minutes after four	twenty minutes after twelve
fifteen minutes after six	twenty minutes after twelve	twenty minutes to eleven	twenty minutes after eleven
five minutes after five	fifteen minutes after ten	twenty-five minutes after one	twenty-five minutes to eleven
nine thirty	five minutes to seven	twenty-five minutes after twelve	ten o'clock

Coin Concentration

OBJECTIVE: To practice reading money amounts in four different notations and to reinforce coin recognition

GRADES: Primary, intermediate to high school (see "Adaptations" for older students)

PREREQUISITE BEHAVIORS: Coin value, value placement, coin recognition of dollars and cents

MATERIALS: Money picture card, money word card, money decimal card, money cents card

TEACHING PROCEDURES: The game of Coin Concentration can be played at several levels of difficulty, with varying skill emphasis depending on specific classroom needs. At the simplest level, use only one kind of money card. (Make two copies of the card, and cut it apart on the solid lines so students play with a total of 20 cards.) Decide on the number and type of cards to be used, and place them face down on the table.

The first player turns over two cards, one at a time, trying to match values. If the cards match, the player keeps them. If not, the player turns them back over on the table in their original location. Then the next player tries to make a match by turning over two more cards and so on, until all the cards are matched with their pair.

The winner is the player with the most matched cards. For variety, ask the students to add the total value of their cards, and the player with the highest value wins. To add variety and increase difficulty, put different type cards down, and players can match 4¢ to $.04 or to *four cents*.

ADAPTATIONS: This activity can be used with older students by increasing the difficulty of the coin values represented and by adding a fifth card. On the fifth card is the name of an object that costs the corresponding amount. For example, if the money value is $329.00, the fifth card may have an MP3 written on it.

Shopping Spree

OBJECTIVE: To give students practice using money and understanding the concept of addition and subtraction with money

GRADES: Elementary-age students who are having difficulty with the money concepts (see "Adaptations" for use with older students)

MATERIALS: Coins (and dollar bills when teaching the more advanced concepts), pictures of items

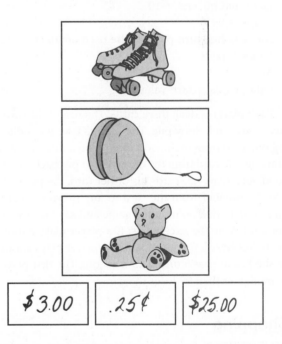

TEACHING PROCEDURES: Cut out magazine pictures of things children would like to buy, and put a price on each picture. Start with easy amounts, such as 5¢, 10¢, 25¢; then in future lessons, increase the complexity of the amounts to such things as 63¢ and 51¢. For higher grades, use dollar amounts. Have the class divide into two groups, with half the students serving as store clerks and the other half as shoppers. The shoppers buy picture items from the clerks. The shoppers are responsible for giving the correct amount of money. The clerks are responsible for giving the correct change. Then have students trade roles.

At a later date, distribute specific amounts of money, and ask students to select several items without going over their designated amount. Or, ask students to show two or three different items and tell which item they can afford with their amount of money.

ADAPTATIONS: For older students, you can distribute pretend checkbooks. Each student gets a specified amount in his or her checkbook and must make appropriate deductions as he or she makes purchases.

99

OBJECTIVE: To generalize and practice adding numbers in one's head or on paper

GRADES: Intermediate to high school

MATERIALS: Playing cards, paper, and pencils

TEACHING PROCEDURES: Explain that the objective of this game is to add cards up to a score of 99. Establish the following rules:

Jacks and queens = 10
Kings = 99
Nines = free-turn pass—to be used anytime
Fours = pass
Aces = 1
Other cards = face value

Each player is dealt three cards. The rest of the cards go face down on a draw pile. The players take turns discarding one card from their hand face up on a discard pile and drawing one card from the draw pile to put back into their hand. As a player discards his or her card, the player must add the number from the card to any previous score acquired up to that point in the game and say the new score out loud. Note the exceptions: If a player plays a nine, he or she receives a free-turn pass. If a player plays a four, he or she has to pass a turn with no score. The first player to score higher than 99 loses the game.

Shopping

OBJECTIVE: To provide practice in addition, subtraction, and comparing prices (problem solving)

GRADES: Junior high

MATERIALS: Supermarket sale ads that include the price per item (optionally mounted individually on cardboard and covered with clear plastic), made-up shopping lists to hand out to the class, pencil, and paper

TEACHING PROCEDURES: Divide the class into small groups. Tell the students that their shopping list contains the items that they will need this week. Assign each group a designated amount for groceries (e.g.,

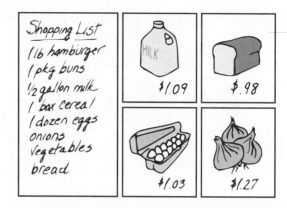

$30.00). The object is to buy everything on the list while spending the least amount of money. Place on each desk the supermarket sale ads, each with the name of its store. After students buy an item, they record its price and the store where they bought it. (It's easier if one student in each group buys the meats, one buys the dairy products, and so on.) When the students have bought all the items on the list, tell them to total their bills and be ready to present the results.

Cake for Four—No, Make That Six!

By Sandra Stroud

OBJECTIVE: Developing students' concept of fractions by having them partition an object into equal parts

GRADES: Second through fourth grades (possibly higher)

MATERIALS: For each student, a 6-inch paper circle; five strips construction paper, 1 inch wide by 8 inches long, in a color contrasting to that of the paper circle; eight small cookies, placed in a small sandwich bag

TEACHING PROCEDURES: Students move desks together so that each student has a partner with whom to compare his or her work. Materials are distributed. The teacher introduces the lesson by telling the students that they are going to take part in a "Let's Pretend" activity that will help them to learn that when they eat a piece of cake that has been divided into equal parts, they are actually eating a fraction of that cake.

The students are asked to imagine that they have just helped to bake a cake. It is their favorite kind of cake, and because there are four people in their pretend family, they are planning to divide it into four equal pieces. They are asked to think of the paper circle on their desk as the top of the cake and to show the teacher—and their partners—how they would use the strips of paper to divide the cake into four equal parts. When each child has successfully demonstrated this first partitioning task, they are asked what fraction of the whole cake each piece is and how that fraction is written.

Next, they are asked to imagine that their grandmother and grandfather have arrived unexpectedly and that the grandparents have accepted the family's invitation to stay for supper. The family certainly wants to share the cake with their grandparents, so into how many pieces will they now divide their cake? The teacher makes sure that each student shows six equal portions and that they understand that each piece of cake is now 1/6 of the whole—just enough for the six people at the dinner table. However, before that cake is served, Uncle Bob and Aunt Doris arrive! Now the cake will be divided into how many equal pieces? Finally, the time comes to decorate the cake with the cookies and to cut and serve the cake. (As a reward for all their good thinking, the students now get to eat the decorations—1/8 at a time!)

Students enjoy the story associated with this activity, and they enjoy comparing their partitioned cakes with those of their peers. This is a good example of cooperative learning. Students especially enjoy eating their cookies at the end of this activity.

The Values of Coins

By Ae-hwa Kim

OBJECTIVE: To help students learn the relative values of coins (e.g., students will determine that a quarter is worth 25 times as much as one cent)

GRADES: Primary

MATERIALS: Models with real coins for each step

TEACHING PROCEDURES: For the initial instruction, the teacher shows all models and coins and addresses the objective of the lesson. During the lesson, the teacher models and verbally explains each step, provides students with guided and independent practice, and gives them feedback.

1. Show students proportionate models to represent the values of coins.

1	1	1	1	1	1	1	1	1	1
1	1	1	1	1	1	1	1	1	1
1	1	1	1	1	1	1	1	1	1
1	1	1	1	1	1	1	1	1	1
1	1	1	1	1	1	1	1	1	1
1	1	1	1	1	1	1	1	1	1
1	1	1	1	1	1	1	1	1	1
1	1	1	1	1	1	1	1	1	1
1	1	1	1	1	1	1	1	1	1
1	1	1	1	1	1	1	1	1	1

2. Teach the values of coins and their relative values with models, which visually represent the values of coins and their relative worth. For example, one nickel is worth five pennies and so takes up the space of five pennies.

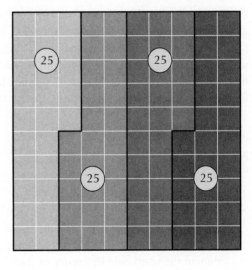

3. Teach the value of a set of coins with models, which visually represent the value of a set of coins.

4. Teach the students to compare the values of sets of coins with models.

5. Teach the students to use models to create a set of coins with a given value. Allow the students to use different combinations of coins to make the given value.

6. Teach the students to create a set of coins with a given value by using the fewest coins with models.

Source: Based on an activity by R. L. Drum & W. G. Petty (1997), Teaching the value of coins, *Teaching Children Mathematics, 5*(5), pp. 264–268.

Learning Addition

By Ae-hwa Kim

OBJECTIVE: To help students understand how to do addition with three-digit numbers and to provide practice in addition through activities

GRADES: Primary

MATERIALS: Pictures of three different types of animals; three lengths of bricks (short, medium, and long); scratch paper

TEACHING PROCEDURES:

1. Seat three volunteer "animals" (e.g., zebra, giraffe, and deer) on chairs side by side in front of a chalkboard. Hang a sign with a picture of each animal around the neck of the student who acts as that animal. The sign on the right (deer) also has the word *ones* or *1s*, signifying the units place of the number. The middle sign (giraffe) shows the word *tens* or *10s*, signifying the tens place of the number. The sign on the left (zebra) has the word *hundreds* or *100s*, signifying the hundreds place of the number. Throughout the activity, the place-value words are visible.

2. Give each animal a supply of bricks. Long bricks signify hundreds; medium bricks signify tens; and short bricks signify single units. Give two long bricks to the hundreds zebra, five medium bricks to the tens giraffe, and eight short bricks to the ones deer. (First number = 258.)

3. Ask each animal to tell what he or she has been given as the teacher writes the combined number on the chalkboard.

4. Teach students the rules to this activity:

   - All business exchanges begin with the ones deer, then the tens giraffe, and finally the hundreds zebra. The animals receive their shipments in turn and take inventory of their bricks as they are received.

   - The inventory process ensures that the ones deer never has 10 ones bricks (short), the tens giraffe never has 10 tens bricks (medium), and the hundreds zebra never has 10 hundreds bricks (i.e., each animal's total is nine or less). If any animal has more than 10 bricks, he or she must trade 10 bricks for 1 brick of the next greater value.

5. The brick suppliers will arrive to deliver more bricks to each animal. For example, the supplier may bring 4 hundreds bricks, 7 tens bricks, and 3 ones bricks. (Second number = 473.)

6. When the ones deer inventories 11 bricks, a teacher reminds him or her of the rules and establishes that the ones deer must deliver a stack of 10 short bricks back to the supplier in exchange for 1 medium brick, which must then be given to the tens giraffe. The single short brick that remains is recorded on the chalkboard. When the 7 newly delivered medium bricks are added to the original 5 medium bricks and the medium brick is passed from the ones deer, the tens giraffe then has 13 medium bricks. Therefore, he or she delivers one set of 10 bricks to the supplier in exchange for 1 long brick, which is then given to the hundreds zebra. The tens giraffe then reports an inventory of 3 medium bricks remaining. Our hundreds zebra then reports a total inventory of 7 long bricks, or hundreds. (Final answer: 258 + 473 = 731.)

Source: Based on an activity by M. M. Bartek (1997), Hands-on addition and subtraction with the Three Pigs, (2), pp. 68–71.

Addition and America

By Ae-hwa Kim

OBJECTIVE: To motivate students to solve addition problems as well as to increase their accuracy of solving problems

GRADES: Second through fourth grades (possibly higher)

MATERIALS: Map of the United States, tickets made of cards on which math addition facts are printed

TEACHING PROCEDURES:

1. Show students the map of the United States to get their attention.

2. Explain the rules of game:

   - The students try to move from their home state to another state across the nation.

   - Students have to have their ticket to travel from state to state.

   - Students must solve the addition problem printed on the ticket and read the name of the state. (The name of the state will be printed on the map, so students just need to read the word.)

   - Only when students get the right answer are they allowed to move to the next state. If students miss the problem, they have to stay in their current state until their next trial time.

3. Let the students play a game. During the game, the teacher assists them and also records the speed and accuracy of their answers.

Note: This game can be extended to subtraction, multiplication, and division.

Source: Based on an activity by D. E. Miller (1997), Math across America, *Teaching Exceptional Children, 24*(2), pp. 47–49.

The Value of Numbers

By Ae-hwa Kim

OBJECTIVE: To help students understand the value of numbers (ones value, tens value, and hundreds value)

GRADES: Primary

MATERIALS: Popsicle sticks; rubber bands to group the Popsicle sticks; a sign; number cards; three boxes to hold ones, tens, and hundreds of Popsicle sticks

TEACHING PROCEDURES:

Practice

1. Count the number of Popsicle sticks.

2. Model putting a rubber band around a group of 10 sticks; then ask students to put a rubber band around each new group of 10 sticks.

3. Model putting 1s in the ones box, 10s in the tens box, and so on. Ask students to put 1s in the ones box, 10s in the tens box, and so on.

Activity

1. Show the students a sign that says "Thank you for the _____ Popsicle sticks" (e.g., 157).

2. Model putting that number of Popsicle sticks in the boxes; then ask students to put the number of Popsicle sticks in the boxes.

3. Change the numbers on the sign repeatedly, and allow students to practice grouping Popsicle sticks according to the sign.

Source: Based on an activity by C. Paddock (1997). Ice cream stick math. *Teaching Exceptional Children, 24*(2), pp. 50–51.

Finding Like Units

OBJECTIVE: To help students understand the need to use like units in working with fractions (common denominator for addition, subtraction, multiplication, and division of fractions)

GRADES: Middle and upper grades

MATERIALS: Whiteboard (chalkboard), dry-erase markers (chalk), overhead projector (document camera/projector), and transparencies

TEACHING PROCEDURES:

1. Write on the whiteboard the terms "8 feet" and "98 inches." Then below those write "12 yards" and "24 yards." Point to the top two lengths, and ask, "Which is longer?" Then point to the bottom two lengths, and repeat the question, "Which is longer?" Ask, "Why was the second group easier to compare?" Students should indicate that the same units were used.

2. Now write "48 eggs" and "60 eggs" on the whiteboard. Next, below that write "51 eggs" and

"5 dozen eggs," and then point to top two amounts, and ask, "Which is more?" Now point to the bottom amounts, and ask, "Which is more?" Ask, "Why are the first two egg amounts easier to compare?" Students should indicate that the same units were used. Next, explain that when comparing quantities, it is always easier when like units are compared.

3. Write two fractions on the whiteboard (e.g., 4/7 and 2/7). Below these write two other fractions with different denominators (e.g., 1/3 and 3/8). Point to the top pair of fractions, and ask, "Which is greater?" Then point to the bottom pair of fractions, and ask, "Which is greater?" Ask why the first pair of fractions is easier to compare. Students should indicate that the same units were used. Repeat to the students, "It is always easier to compare quantities if the units are the same."

4. Next, write "13 inches" and "1 foot" on the whiteboard. Ask the students, "How many inches are there in a foot?" Next mark out the "1 foot," and write "12 inches" above it. Tell the students how much easier it is to compare two lengths when we rewrite them using the same units.

5. Write the fractions "2/3" and "3/4" on the whiteboard. Tell the students that you are going to show them how to rewrite these two fractions so that they will have the same units. Next, get two transparencies. One should be lined horizontally with four equal segments, and the other should be lined with three equal segments that look like the following illustration:

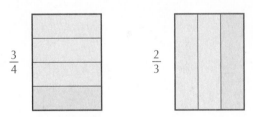

6. Next, tell the students that you want them to cut the pieces so that you will have the same size pieces in both of the fractions. Show them that you can cut the first fraction vertically into three equal parts, and then you can cut the second fraction horizontally into four equal parts. Do this with each transparency (see the following illustration). After doing this, write the new names for each of the fractions.

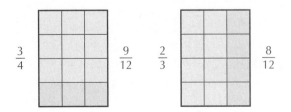

Now ask the students to look at the new fractions' names and decide which is greater.

[The students should say 3/4 is greater than 2/3 because 9/12 is greater than 8/12.]

7. Now show the students that in a multiplication problem involving two fractions they can get the new names for the two fractions by multiplying the numerator and the denominator by the other fraction's denominator.

$$\frac{3 \times 3}{4 \times 3} = \frac{9}{12} \qquad \frac{2 \times 4}{3 \times 4} = \frac{8}{12}$$

ACTIVITY

1. Show the students two new fractions, and ask them which is greater. Then give two more new ones, and ask which is the lesser one.

2. Pair the students, and have them create two fractions for each other, and have them ask which one is greater or lesser.

3. Have the students generate multiplication of two fractions for each to solve using multiplication of the numerator and the denominator by the other fraction's denominator.

Source: Based on an activity by B. F. Tucker, A. H. Singleton, & T. L. Weaver (2006), *Teaching Mathematics to All Children: Designing and Adapting Instruction to Meet the Needs of Diverse Learners* (Upper Saddle River, NJ: Pearson Education, Inc.).

- Factors influencing math success include cognitive, educational, self-regulation, and/or neurological factors that may manifest in difficulties understanding math concepts and vocabulary; reasoning, or dealing with abstract concepts that prevail in math; poor memory, making it difficult to remember new concepts; and symbolism difficulties, interfering with learning what symbols refer to. Many students with learning disabilities and behavior problems also have difficulty in sustaining attention, working carefully, and accepting responsibility. Furthermore, because of their difficulty with math, many of these students have received an overabundance of instruction in basic skills but have not been exposed to essential math concepts and problem-solving strategies. In planning curricula for these students, teachers should consider such factors as comprehensive yet individualized programming, providing correction and feedback, generalizing examples to real-life situations, allowing students to participate in goal selection, and using discovery instead of didactic instruction.

- Assessment helps teachers determine what students know and need to know as well as how students compare to others of the same age or grade level. In addition, appropriate assessments allow teachers to monitor students' progress and make effective instructional decisions based on the information they have gathered. When curriculum-based measurement is used to monitor students' progress and adjust instruction accordingly, students make gains at much more rapid rates. Assessments that measure number sense include counting measures, number identification measures, and number writing.

- Prenumber skills that facilitate students' growth in math include one-to-one correspondence, classification, and seriation.

- Math concepts and computation include the numeration concepts of cardinality; grouping patterns; place value; one digit per place; linear order; decimal point; place relation; implied zeros; implied addition; order; name of numbers; periods and names; and understanding "zero."

- Mathematical problem solving can be affected by reading problems, poorly developed logical reasoning skills, and instruction that focuses primarily on computation. Teachers can increase students' problem-solving abilities by teaching big ideas, using sameness analysis, teaching cue words, teaching reasoning strategies, simplifying the sentence structure of word problems, eliminating extraneous information, and monitoring the number of concepts presented as well as the interest level. Computer-assisted instruction is a motivational way to provide practice in problem solving and feedback on performance.

- Teachers can best improve students' math performance by combining a variety of techniques that are appropriate for individual students and the skills they need to develop. Cognitive approaches to math instruction rely on verbalizing or making explicit steps or strategies in solving math problems. Behavioral approaches use the idea of stimulus–response learning to focus on the cues that students need to know in order to succeed in math. Alternative ways to deliver math instruction include cooperative learning, computer-assisted instruction, and interactive video. New curricula have been developed specifically for teaching math skills to students with learning and behavior problems.

After completing this chapter, test your knowledge of the concepts by completing this Assessment.

Abudarham, S. (2002). Assessment and appraisal of communication needs. In S. Abudarham and A. Hurd (Eds.), *Management of communication needs in people with learning disability* (pp. 33–81). London: Whurr.

Ackerman, P. T., Anhalt, J. M., and Dykman, R. A. (1986). Arithmetic automatization failure in children with attention and reading disorders: Associations and sequelae. *Journal of Learning Disabilities, 19,* 222–232.

Ainsworth, S., and Burcham, S. (2007). The impact of text coherence on learning by self-explanation. *Learning and Instruction, 17*(3), 286–303.

Alber, S. R., Heward, W. L., and Hippler, B. J. (1999). Teaching middle school students with learning disabilities to recruit positive teacher attention. *Exceptional Children, 65,* 253–270.

Alfassi, M. (1998). Reading for meaning: The efficacy of reciprocal teaching in fostering reading comprehension in high school students in remedial classes. *American Educational Research Journal, 35*(2), 309–332.

Allen, R. V. (1976). *Language experiences in communication.* Boston: Houghton Mifflin.

Allen, R. V., and Allen, C. (1966–68). *Language experiences in reading* (Levels I, II, and III). Chicago: Encyclopedia Britannica.

Allen, R. V., and Allen, C. (1982). *Language experience activities* (2nd ed.). Boston: Houghton Mifflin.

Alley, G. R., and Deshler, D. D. (1979). *Teaching the learning disabled adolescent: Strategies and methods.* Denver: Love.

American Academy of Child and Adolescent Psychology. (2009). *FAQs on child and adolescent depression.* Retrieved from http://www.aacap.org/cs/child_and_adolescent_depression_resource_center/faqs

American Foundation for Suicide Prevention. (2009). *Warning signs of suicide.* Retrieved from http://www.afsp.org/index.cfm?/page_id50519EC1A-D73A-8D90-7D2E9E2456182D66

Amish, P. L., Gesten, E. L., Smith, J. K., Clark, H. B., and Stark, C. (1988). Social problem-solving training for severely emotionally and behaviorally disturbed children. *Behavioral Disorders, 13*(3), 175–186.

Anders, P. L., and Bos, C. S. (1984). In the beginning: Vocabulary instruction in content classroom. *Topics in Learning and Learning Disabilities, 3*(4), 53–65.

Anderson, D. H., Fisher, A., Marchant, M., Young, K. R., and Smith, J. A. (2006). The cool card intervention: A positive support strategy for managing anger. *Beyond Behavior, 16,* 3–5.

Arguelles, M. E., Vaughn, S., and Schumm, J. S. (1996). *Executive summaries of 69 schools throughout the state of Florida participating in the ESE/FEFP 1995–1996 pilot program.*

Arndt, S. A., Konrad, M., and Test, D. W. (2006). Effects of the self-directed IEP on student participation in planning meetings. *Remedial and Special Education, 27*(4), 194–207.

Ashbaker, B. Y., and Morgan, J. (2005). *Paraprofessionals in the classroom.* Boston: Pearson.

Ashton-Warner, S. (1958). *Spinster.* New York: Simon and Schuster.

Ashton-Warner, S. (1963). *Teacher.* New York: Simon and Schuster.

Ashton-Warner, S. (1972). *Spearpoint.* New York: Knopf.

August, D., Branum-Martin, L., Cardenas-Hagan, E., and Francis, D. J. (2009). The impact of an instructional intervention on the science and language learning of middle grade English language learners. *Journal for Research on Educational Effectiveness, 2*(4), 345–376.

August, D., and Shanahan, T. (2006). *Developing literacy in second-language learners: Report of the National Literacy Panel on language-minority children and youth.* Mahwah, NJ: Erlbaum.

Axelrod, S. (1998). *How to use group contingencies.* Austin, TX: PRO-ED.

Badian, N. A., and Ghublikian, M. (1983). The personal-social characteristics of children with poor mathematical computation skills. *Journal of Learning Disabilities, 16*(3), 154–157.

Baker, S., Gersten, R., and Lee, D. (2002). A synthesis of empirical research on teaching mathematics to low-achieving students. *The Elementary School Journal, 103*(1), 51–73.

Bandura, A. (1977). *Social learning theory.* Englewood Cliffs, NJ: Prentice Hall.

Bandura, A. (1986). *Social foundations of thought and action: A social cognitive theory.* Englewood Cliffs, NJ: Prentice Hall.

Barnes, M. A., Wilkinson, M., Khemani, E., Boudousquie, A., Dennis, M., and Fletcher, J. M. (2006). Arithmetic processing in children with spina bifida: Calculation accuracy, strategy use, and fact retrieval fluency. *Journal of Learning Disabilities, 39,* 174–187.

Batsche, G., Elliott J., Graden, J. L., Grimes, J., Kovaleski. J. F., Prasse, D., et al. (2005). *Response to intervention: Policy considerations and implementation.* Alexandria, VA: National Association of State Directors of Special Education.

Beck, I. L. (2006). *Making sense of phonics.* New York: Guilford.

Beck, I. L., and McKeown, M. G. (2006). *Improving comprehension with questioning the author.* New York: Scholastic.

Beck, I. L., McKeown, M. G., and Kucan, L. (2002). *Bringing words to life: Robust vocabulary instruction.* New York: Guilford.

Beirne-Smith, M. (1991). Peer tutoring in arithmetic for children with learning disabilities. *Exceptional Children, 57,* 330–337.

Bell, A. C., and D'Zurilla, T. J. (2009). Problem-solving therapy for depression: A meta-analysis. *Clinical Psychology Review, 29*(4), 348–353.

Bender, W. N. (2008). *Differentiating instruction for students with learning disabilities: Best teaching practices for general and special educators* (2nd ed.). Thousand Oaks, CA: Corwin Press.

Bereiter, C., Hilton, P., Rubinstein, J., and Willoughby, S. (1998). *Math exploration and applications.* Chicago: Science Research Associates.

Bergerud, D., Lovitt, T. C., and Horton, S. (1988). The effectiveness of textbook adaptations in life science for high school students with learning disabilities. *Journal of Learning Disabilities, 21,* 70–76.

Berkeley, S., Bender, W. N., Peaster, L. G., and Saunders, L. (2009). Implementation of response to intervention. *Journal of Learning Disabilities, 42*(1), 85–95.

Bernadette, K., Carnine, D., Engelmann, S., and Engelmann, O. (2003). *Connecting math concepts.* Chicago: Science Research Associates.

Berninger, V. W., Abbott, R. D., Whitaker, D., Sylvester, L., and Nolen, S. B. (1995). Integrating low- and high-level skills in instructional protocols for writing disabilities. *Learning Disability Quarterly, 18,* 293–310.

Berninger, V. W., Nielsen, K. H., Abbott, R. D., Wijsman, E., and Raskind, W. (2008). Writing problems in developmental dyslexia: Under-recognized and under-treated. *Journal of School Psychology, 46*(1), 1–21.

Berninger, V. W., Rutberg, J. E., Abbott, R. D., Noelia, G., Anderson-Youngstrom, M., Brooks, A., et al. (2006). Tier 1 and Tier 2 early intervention for handwriting and composing. *Journal of School Psychology, 44*(1), 3–30.

Berres, F., and Eyer, J. T. (1970). In A. J. Harris (Ed.), *Casebook on reading disability* (pp. 25–47). New York: David McKay.

Betts, E. A. (1946). *Foundations of reading instruction.* New York: American Book.

Blachman, B. A. (2000). Phonological awareness. In M. L. Kamil, P. B. Mosenthal, P. D. Pearson, and R. Barr (Eds.), *Handbook of reading research.* (Vol. 3, pp. 483–502). Mahwah, NJ: Erlbaum.

Blachowicz, C., and Ogle, D. (2001). *Reading comprehension: Strategies for independent learners.* New York: Guilford.

Blachowicz, D. O., and Ogle, D. (2008). *Reading comprehension: Strategies for independent learners.* New York: Guilford.

Blair, K. S. (1996). *Context-based functional assessment and intervention for preschool age children with problem behaviors in childcare.* Unpublished dissertation, University of Arizona, Tucson.

Bley, N. S., and Thornton, C. A. (1981). *Teaching mathematics to the learning disabled.* Rockville, MD: Aspen.

Block, C. C. (1997). *Literacy difficulties: Diagnosis and instruction.* Orlando, FL: Harcourt Brace.

Block, C. C., Morrow, L. M., and Parris, S. R. (2008). *Comprehension instruction: research-based best practices.* New York: Guilford.

Bos, C. S. (1987, October). *Promoting story comprehension using a story retelling strategy.* Paper presented at the Teachers Applying Whole Language Conference, Tucson, AZ.

Bos, C. S. (1999). Informed, flexible teaching: Promoting student advocacy and action. In P. Westwood and W. Scott (Eds.), *Learning disabilities: Advocacy and action* (pp. 9–19). Melbourne: Australian Resource Educators Association.

Bos, C. S., and Anders, P. L. (1992). A theory-driven interactive instructional model for text comprehension and content learning. In B. Y. L. Wong (Ed.), *Contemporary intervention research in learning disabilities: An international perspective* (pp. 81–95). New York: Springer-Verlag.

Bos, C. S., and Filip, D. (1984). Comprehension monitoring in learning disabled and average students. *Journal of Learning Disabilities, 17*(4), 229–233.

Bourassa, D. C., Treiman, R., and Kessler, B. (2006). Use of morphology in spelling by children with dyslexia and typically developing children. *Memory and Cognition, 34*(3), 703–714.

Bradley, J. M. (1975). *Sight word association procedure.* Unpublished manuscript, College of Education, University of Arizona, Tucson.

Bradley, L. (1981). The organization of motor patterns for spelling: An effective remedial strategy for backward readers. *Developmental Medicine and Child Neurology, 23,* 83–91.

Bradley, R., Danielson, L., and Hallahan, D. P. (2002). *Identification of learning disabilities: Research to practice.* Mahwah, NJ: Erlbaum.

Briggs, A., Austin, R., and Underwood, G. (1984). Phonological coding in good and poor readers. *Reading Research Quarterly, 20,* 54–66.

Bromley, K. (1999). Key components of sound writing instruction. In L. B. Gambrell, L. M. Morrow, S. B. Neuman, and M. Pressley (Eds.), *Best practices in literacy instruction* (pp. 152–174). New York: Guilford.

Brown, A. L., and Day, J. D. (1983). Macrorules for summarizing texts: The development of expertise. *Journal of Verbal Learning and Verbal Behavior, 22,* 1–14.

Bryant, D., Vaughn S., Linan-Thompson, S., Ugel, N., Hamff, A., and Hougen, M. (2000). Reading outcomes for students with and without reading disabilities in general education middle school content area classes. *Learning Disability Quarterly, 23,* 238–252.

Bryant, J. (1998). K-W-W-L: Questioning the known. *The Reading Teacher, 51,* 618–620.

Bryant, N. D., Drabin, I. R., and Gettinger, M. (1981). Effects of varying unit size on spelling achievement in learning disabled children. *Journal of Learning Disabilities, 14*(4), 200–203.

Bryant, D. P., Smith, D. D., and Bryant, B. R. (2008). *Teaching students with special needs in inclusive classrooms.* New York: Pearson Education, Inc.

Bulgren, J., Deshler, D. D., and Lenz, B. K. (2007). Engaging adolescents with LD in higher order thinking about history concepts using integrated content enhancement routines. *Journal of Learning Disabilities, 40*(2), 121–133.

Bulgren, J., Schumaker, J. B., and Deshler, D. D. (1988). Effectiveness of a concept teaching routine in enhancing the performance of LD students in secondary-level mainstream classes. *Learning Disability Quarterly, 11,* 3–17.

Bulgren, J., Schumaker, J. B., and Deshler, D. D. (1996). *The content enhancement series: The concept mastery routine.* Lawrence, KS: Edge Enterprises.

Bulgren, J. A., Lenz, B. K., Schumaker, J. B., and Deshler, D. D. (1995). *The content enhancement series: The concept comparison routine.* Lawrence, KS: Edge Enterprises.

Bulgren, J. A., Marquis, J. G., Lenz, B. K., Shumaker, J. B., and Deshler, D. D. (2009). Effectiveness of question exploration to enhance students' written expression of content knowledge and comprehension. *Reading and Writing Quarterly, 25*(4), 271–289.

Burns, M. K., Griffiths, A., Parson, L. B., Tilly, W. D., and VanDerHayden, A. (2007). Response to intervention: Research for practice. *Alexandria, VA: National Association of State Directors of Special Education.*

Calhoon, M. B., and Fuchs, L. S. (2003). The effects of peer-assisted learning strategies and curriculum-based measurement on the mathematics performance of secondary students with disabilities. *Remedial and Special Education, 24*(4), 235–245.

Canter, A. (2006). Problem solving and RTI: New roles for school psychologists. NASP *Communiqué, 34*(5). Retrieved December 14, 2007, from http://www.nasponline.org/publications/cq/cq345rti.aspx

Carnine, D. (1989). Teaching complex content to learning disabled students: The role of technology. *Exceptional Children, 55,* 524–533.

Carnine, D., Silbert, J., and Kame'enui, E. J. (1997). *Direct instruction reading* (3rd ed.). Columbus, OH: Merrill.

Carr, E., and Ogle, D. (1987). K-W-L plus: A strategy for comprehension and summarization. *Journal of Reading, 30,* 626–631.

Carr, E. G., Dunlap, G., Horner, R. H., Koegel, R. L., Turnbull, A. P., Sailor, W., et al. (2002). Positive behavior support: Evolution of an applied science. *Journal of Positive Behavior Interventions, 4,* 4–16.

Carter, E. W., and Kennedy, C. H. (2006). Promoting access to the general curriculum using peer support strategies. *Research and Practice for Persons with Severe Disabilities, 31,* 284–292.

Carter, E. W., Wehby, J., Hughes, C., Johnson, S. M., Plank, D. R., Barton-Arwood, S. M., and Lunsford, L. B. (2005). Preparing adolescents with high-incidence disabilities for high-stakes testing with strategy instruction. *Preventing School Failure, 49*(2), 55–62.

Catts, H., and Kahmi, A. (Eds.). (2005). *The connection between language and reading disabilities.* Mahwah, NJ: Erlbaum.

Cawley, J. (2002). My Math [Unpublished computer software]. Storrs, CT.

Cawley, J. F. (1984). An integrative approach to needs of learning disabled children: Expanded use of mathematics. In J. F. Cawley (Ed.), *Developmental teaching of mathematics for the learning disabled.* Rockville, MD: Aspen.

Cawley, J. F., Foley, T. F., and Doan, T. (2003). Giving students a voice in selecting arithmetical context. *Teaching Exceptional Children, 36,* 8–17.

Cawley, J. F., and Miller, J. H. (1986). Selected views on metacognition, arithmetic problem solving, and learning disabilities. *Learning Disabilities Focus, 2*(1), 36–48.

Chard, D. J., Ketterlin-Geller, L. R., Baker, S. K., Doabler, C., and Apichatabutra, C. (2009). Repeated reading intervention for students with learning disabilities: Status for the evidence. *Exceptional Children, 75*(3), 263–281.

Chard, D. J., Vaughn, S., and Tyler, B. (2002). A synthesis of research on effective intervention for building reading fluency with elementary students with learning disabilities. *Journal of Learning Disabilities, 35*(5), 386–406.

Christ, T. J., and Ardoin, S. P. (2009). Curriculum-based measurement of oral reading: Passage equivalence and probe-set development. *Journal of School Psychology, 47*(1), 55–75.

Christ, T. J., Burns, M. K., and Ysseldyke, J. E. (2005). Conceptual confusion within response-to-intervention vernacular: Clarifying meaningful differences. NASP *Communiqué, 34*(3). Retrieved December 14, 2007, from http://www.nasponline.org/publications/cq/cq343rti.aspx

Clark, F. L., Deshler, D. D., Schumaker, J. B., Alley, G. R., and Warner, M. M. (1984). Visual imagery and self-questioning: Strategies to improve comprehension of written materials. *Journal of Learning Disabilities, 17*(3), 145–149.

Clarke, B., and Shinn, M. R. (2004). A preliminary investigation into the identification and development of early mathematics curriculum-based measurement. *School Psychology Review, 33*(2), 234–248.

Conderman, G., Bresnahan, V., and Pedersen, T. (2009). *Purposeful co-teaching: Real cases and effective strategies.* Thousand Oaks, CA: Corwin Press.

Connolly, A. J. (1998). *Key math-revised: A diagnostic inventory of essential mathematics.* Circle Pines, MN: American Guidance Service.

Cooper, H., and Nye, B. (1994). Homework for students with learning disabilities: The implications of research for policy and practice. *Journal of Learning Disabilities, 27,* 470–479.

Cooper, H. M. (2007). *The battle over homework: Common ground for administrators, teachers, and parents* (3rd ed.). Thousand Oaks, CA: Corwin Press.

Cooper, P., and Bilton, K. M. (2002). *Attention deficit/hyperactivity disorder: A practical guide for teachers* (2nd ed.). Great Britain: David Fulton Publishers Ltd.

Corkill, A. J. (1992). Advance organizers: Facilitators of recall. *Educational Psychology Review, 4,* 33–67.

Cortiella, C. (2006). *A parent's guide to response to intervention.* National Center for Learning Disabilities. Retrieved December 14, 2007, from www.ncld.org/images/stories/downloads/parent_center/rti_final.pdf

Coterell, G. (1972). A case of severe learning disability. *Remedial Education, 7,* 5–9.

Cox, A. R. (1992). *Foundations for literacy: Structures and techniques for multisensory teaching of basic written English language skills (Alphabetic phonics).* Cambridge, MA: Educators Publishing Service.

Cummins, J. (1981). *Bilingualism and minority language children.* Ontario: Ontario Institute for Students in Education.

Cunningham, P. M. (2008). *Phonics they use: Words for reading and writing as an author.* Boston: Allyn & Bacon.

Cunningham, P. M., and Hall, D. P. (1994a). *Making words.* Parsippany, NJ: Good Apple.

Cunningham, P. M., and Hall, D. P. (1994b). *Making big words.* Parsippany, NJ: Good Apple.

Dale, E., and Chall, J. S. (1948). A formula for predicting readability. *Educational Research Bulletin, 27,* 37–54.

Daniel, S. S., Walsh, A. K., Goldston, D. B., Arnold, E. M., Reboussin, B. A., and Wood, F. B. (2007). Suicidality, school dropout, and reading problems among adolescents. *Journal of Learning Disabilities, 39*(6), 507–514.

Darch, C., and Carnine, D. (1986). Approaches to teaching learning-disabled students literal comprehension during content area instruction. *Exceptional Children, 53*(3), 240–246.

De La Paz, S. (1999). Teaching writing strategies and self-regulation procedures to middle school students with learning disabilities. *Focus on Exceptional Children, 31*(5), 1–16.

De La Paz, S., Swanson, P., and Graham, S. (1998). Contribution of executive control to the revising problems of students with writing and learning difficulties. *Journal of Educational Psychology, 90,* 448–460.

Delquadri, J. C., Greenwood, C. R., Stretton, K., and Hall, R. V. (1983). The peer tutoring spelling game: A classroom procedure for increasing opportunity to respond and spelling performance. *Education and Treatment of Children, 6*(3), 225–239.

Dembinski, R. J., and Mauser, A. J. (1977). What parents of the learning disabled really want from professionals. *Journal of Learning Disabilities, 10,* 578–584.

Denton, C. A., Anthony, J. L., Parker, R., and Hasbrouck, J. (2004). The effects of two tutoring programs on the English reading development of Spanish-English bilingual students. *The Elementary School Journal, 104,* 289–305.

Deshler, D. D., Ellis, E. S., and Lenz, B. K. (1996). *Teaching adolescents with learning disabilities: Strategies and methods* (2nd ed.). Denver: Love.

Deshler, D. D., Schumaker, J. B., and McKnight, P. C. (1997). *The survey routine.* Lawrence: University of Kansas Press.

Dettmer, P., Thurston, L. P., and Selberg, N. J. (2004). *Consultation, collaboration, and teamwork for students with special needs* (5th ed.). Boston: Allyn & Bacon.

Dieker, L. A. (2001). What are the characteristics of "effective" middle and high school co-taught teams for students with disabilities? *Preventing School Failure, 48*(1), 14–23.

Dixon, R. C., and Engelmann, S. (2001). *Spelling through morphographs.* Columbus, OH: SRA/McGraw-Hill.

Donovan, M. S., and Cross, C. T. (2002). *Minority students in special and gifted education.* Washington, DC: National Academy Press.

Duffy, G., Lanier, J. E., and Roehler, L. R. (1980). *On the need to consider instructional practice when looking for instruction implications.* Paper presented at the Reading Expository Materials. University of Wisconsin–Madison.

Duling, W. P. (1999). Literacy development of second language learners with technology and LEA. In O. G. Nelson and W. M. Linek (Eds.), *Practical classroom applications of language experience: Looking back, looking forward* (pp. 248–256). Boston: Allyn & Bacon.

Durkin, D. D. (1978–79). What classroom observations reveal about reading comprehension instruction. *Reading Research Quarterly, 14*(4), 481–533.

Dweck, C. S., and Kamins, M. L. (1999). Person versus process praise and criticism: Implications for contingent self-worth and coping. *Developmental Psychology, 35*(3), 835–847.

Dyson, B. J. (2008). Assessing small-scale interventions in large-scale teaching: A general methodology and preliminary data. *Active Learning in Higher Education, 9*(3), 265–282.

Edmonds, M. S., Vaughn, S., Wexler, J., Reutebuch, C. K., Cable, A., Tackett, K., et. al. (2009). A synthesis of reading interventions and effects on reading outcomes for older struggling readers. *Review of Educational Research, 79,* 262–300.

Ehren, B. J., Montgomery, J., Rudebusch, J., and Whitmire, K. (2006). *Responsiveness to intervention: New roles for speech-language pathologists.* Retrieved from http://www.asha.org/members/slp/schools/prof-consult/NewRolesSLP.htm

Ehri, L. (2004). Teaching phonemic awareness and phonics: An explanation of the National Reading Panel Meta-Analyses. In P. McCardle and V. Chhabra (Eds.), *The voice of evidence in reading research* (pp. 153–186). Baltimore: Paul H. Brookes.

Elbaum, B. (2007). Effects of an oral testing accommodation on the mathematics performance of secondary students with and without learning disabilities. *Journal of Special Education, 40*(4), 218–229.

Elbaum, B., Vaughn, S., Hughes, M., and Moody, S. W. (1999). Grouping practices and reading outcomes for students with disabilities. *Exceptional Children, 65*(3), 399–415.

Elkonin, D. B. (1973). U.S.S.R. In J. Downing (Ed.), *Comparative reading* (pp. 551–579). New York: Macmillan.

Ellis, E. (1991). *SLANT: A starter strategy for participation.* Lawrence, KS: Edge Enterprises.

Emery, D. W. (1996). Helping readers comprehend stories from the characters' perspectives. *The Reading Teacher, 49,* 534–541.

Engelhardt, J. M., Ashlock, R. B., and Wiebe, J. H. (1984). *Helping children understand and use numerals* (pp. 89–149). Boston: Allyn & Bacon.

Engelmann, S., Bruner, E. C., Hanner, S., Osborn, J., Osborn, S., and Zoref, L. (1995). *Reading mastery: Rainbow edition.* Columbus, OH: SRA/McGraw-Hill.

Engelmann, S., Meyer, L., Carnine, L., Becker, W., Eisele, J., and Johnson, G. (1999). *Corrective reading program.* Columbus, OH: SRA/McGraw-Hill.

Englert, C. S., Raphael, T. E., Anderson, L. M., Anthony, H. M., and Stevens, D. D. (1991). Making strategies and self-talk visible: Writing instruction in regular and special education classrooms. *American Educational Research Journal, 23,* 337–372.

Espin, C., Wallace, T., Campbell, H., Lembke, E., Long, J. D., and Ticha, R. (2008). Curriculum-based measurement in writing: Predicting the success of high-school students on state standards tests. *Exceptional Children, 74*(2), 174–193.

Exceptional Parent. (1984, March). Parent advocacy. *Exceptional Parent, 14*(2), 41–45.

Fairbanks, S., Sugai, G., Guardino, D., and Lathrop, M. (2007). Response to intervention: Examining classroom behavior support in second grade. *Exceptional Children, 73*(3), 288–310.

Fearn, L., and Farnan, N. (1998). *Writing effectively: Helping children master the conventions of writing.* Boston: Allyn & Bacon.

Ferguson, P. M. (2002). A place in the family: An historical interpretation of research on parental reactions to having a child with a disability. *The Journal of Special Education, 36,* 124–130.

Fernald, G. M. (1943). *Remedial techniques in basic school subjects.* New York: McGraw-Hill.

Fernald, G. M. (1988). *Remedial techniques in basic school subjects.* (L. Idol, Ed.). Austin, TX: PRO-ED (original edition 1943).

Fielding, L., and Roller, C. (1992). Making difficult books accessible and easy books acceptable. *The Reading Teacher, 45,* 678–682.

Fitzsimmons, R. J., and Loomer, B. M. (1978). *Spelling: Learning and instruction.* (Report No. CS 205 117). Des Moines: Iowa State Department of Public Instruction. (ERIC Document Reproduction Service No. ED 176 285).

Flavell, J. H. (1976). Metacognitive aspects of problem solving. In L. B. Resnick (Ed.), *The nature of intelligence.* Hillsdale, NJ: Erlbaum.

Fletcher, J. M., Lyon, G. R., Fuchs, L. S, and Barnes, M. A. (2007). *Learning Disabilities.* New York: Guilford.

Foorman, B. R., and Ciancio, D. J. (2005). Screening for secondary intervention: Concept and context. *Journal of Learning Disabilities, 38*(6), 494–499.

Francis, D. J., Rivera, M., Rivera, H., Lesaux, N., and Kieffer, M. (2006). Research-based recommendations for instruction and academic interventions. Retrieved from Center on Instruction Web site: http://www.centeroninstruction.org

Frayer, D. A., Frederick, W. C., and Klausmeier, H. J. (1969). *A schema for testing the level of concept mastery* (Working Paper No. 16). Madison: University of Wisconsin, Wisconsin Research and Development Center for Cognitive Learning.

Frederickson, N., and Turner, J. (2003). Utilizing the classroom peer group to address children's social needs: An evaluation of the Circle of Friends intervention approach. *Journal of Special Education, 36,* 234–246.

Fresch, M. J. (2007). Teachers' concerns about spelling instruction: A national survey. *Reading Psychology, 28*(4), 301–330.

Fricke, S., Bowyer-Crane, C., Haley, A. J., Hulme, C., and Snowling, M. J. (2012). Efficacy of language intervention in early years. *Journal of Child Psychology and Psychiatry, and Allied Disiplines, 54*(3), 280–290. doi: 10.1111/jcpp.12010

Friend, M. (2000). Perspectives: Collaboration in the twenty-first century. *Remedial and Special Education, 20,* 130–132, 160.

Fry, E. B. (1977). Fry's readability graph: Clarifications, validity, and extension to level 17. *Journal of Reading, 21,* 242–252.

Fry, E. B., Fountoukidis, D. L., and Polk, J. K. (1985). *The new reading teacher's book of lists.* Englewood Cliffs, NJ: Prentice Hall.

Fuchs, D., Fuchs, L. S., and Burish, P. (2000). Peer-assisted learning strategies: An evidence-based practice to promote reading achievement. *Learning Disabilities Research and Practice, 15,* 85–91.

Fuchs, D., Fuchs, L. S., Mathes, P. G., and Simmons, D. C. (1997). Peer-assisted learning strategies: Making classrooms more responsive to diversity. *American Educational Research Journal, 34,* 174–206.

Fuchs, D., Fuchs, L. S., Thompson, A., Al Otaiba, S., Yen, L., Yang, N. J., et al. (2003). Exploring the importance of reading programs for kindergartners with disabilities in mainstream classrooms. *Exceptional Children, 68,* 295–311.

Fuchs, L. S., Fuchs, D., Compton, D. L., Bryant, J. D., Hamlett, C. L., and Seethaler, P. M. (2007). Mathematics screening and progress monitoring at first grade: Implications for responsiveness to intervention. *Exceptional Children, 73(3)*, 311–330.

Fuchs, L. S., Fuchs, D., and Hamlett, C. L. (1989). Effects of instrumental use of curriculum-based measurement to enhance instructional programs. *Remedial and Special Education 10(2)*, 43–52.

Fuchs, L. S., Fuchs, D., Hamlett, C. L., Phillips, N. B., and Karns, K. (1995). General educators' specialized adaptation for students with learning disabilities. *Exceptional Children, 61(5)*, 440–459.

Fuchs, L. S., Fuchs, D., Hamlett, C. L., Phillips, N. B., Karns, K., and Dutka, S. (1997). Enhancing students' helping behavior during peer-mediated instruction with conceptual mathematical explanations. *The Elementary School Journal, 97*, 223–249.

Fuchs, L. S., Fuchs, D., and Speece, D. L. (2002). Treatment validity as a unifying construct for identifying learning disabilities. *Learning Disability Quarterly, 25*, 33–45.

Fuchs, L. S., Hamlett, C., and Fuchs, D. (1990). *Monitoring basic skills progress: Basic math.* Austin, TX: PRO-ED.

Fujiki, M., Brinton, B., and Todd, C. M. (1996). Social skills of children with specific language impairment. *Language, Speech, and Hearing Services in Schools, 27*, 195–202.

Fulk, B. J. M., Mastropieri, M. A., and Scruggs, T. E. (1992). Mnemonic generalization training with learning disabled adolescents. *Learning Disabilities Research and Practice, 7*, 2–10.

Gallagher, P. A., Powell, T. H., and Rhodes, C. A. (2006). *Brothers & sisters: A special part of exceptional families.* Baltimore: Brookes.

Ganske, K. (2000). *Word journeys: Assessment-guided phonics, spelling, and vocabulary instruction.* New York: Guilford Press.

Gast, D., Ault, M., Wolery, M., Doyle, P., and Belanger, S. (1988). Comparison of constant time delay and the system of least prompts in teaching sight word reading to students with moderate retardation. *Education and Training in Mental Retardation, 23*, 117–128.

Gerber, M. M., and Hall, R. J. (1989). Cognitive-behavioral training in spelling for learning handicapped students. *Learning Disabilities Quarterly, 12*, 159–171.

Gersten, R., and Baker, S. (2001). Teaching expressive writing to students with learning disabilities: A meta-analysis. *Elementary School Journal, 101(3)*, 251–272.

Gersten, R., Beckmann, S., Clarke, B., Foegen, A., Marsh, L., Star, J. R., and Witzel, B. (2009). *Assisting students struggling with mathematics: Response to Intervention (RtI) for elementary and middle schools* (NCEE 2009-4060). Washington, DC: National Center for Education Evaluation and Regional Assistance, Institute of Education Sciences, U.S. Department of Education. Retrieved from http://ies.ed.gov/ncee/wwc/publications/practiceguides/

Gersten, R., and Chard, D. (1999). Number sense: Rethinking arithmetic instruction for students with mathematical disabilities. *Journal of Special Education, 33(1)*, 18–28.

Gibb, G. S., and Dyches, T. T. (2000). *Guide to writing quality individualized educational programs: What's best for students with disabilities?* Boston: Allyn & Bacon.

Gillingham, A., and Stillman, B. W. (1973). *Remedial training for children with specific disability in reading, spelling, and penmanship.* Cambridge, MA: Educators Publishing Service.

Ginsburg, A., Cooke, G., Leinwand, S., Noell, J., and Pollock, E. (2005). *Reassessing U.S. international mathematics performance: New findings from the 2003 TIMSS and PISA.* Washington, DC: American Institutes for Research.

Ginsburg-Block, M. D., Rohrbeck, C. A., and Fantuzzo, J. W. (2006). A meta-analytic review of social, self-concept, and behavioral outcomes of peer-assisted learning. *Journal of Educational Psychology, 98(4)*, 732–749.

Glover, T. A., and Vaughn, S. (2010). *The promise of response to intervention: Evaluating current science and practice.* New York: Guilford.

Goldenberg, C. (2008). Teaching English language learners: What the teacher does—and does not—say. *American Educator, 32(2)*, 1–19.

Goldstein, A. P., Sprafkin, R. P., Gershaw, N. J., and Klein, P. (1980). *Skillstreaming the adolescent.* Champaign, IL: Research Press.

Good, R. H., Bank, J., and Watson, J. (2004). *IDEL: Indicadores dinámicos del éxito en la lectura.* Longmont, CO: Sopris West.

Gordon, J., Vaughn, S., and Schumm, J. S. (1993). Spelling intervention: A review of literature and implications for instruction for students with learning disabilities. *Learning Disabilities Research and Practice, 8*, 175–181.

Graham, S. (1999). Handwriting and spelling instruction for students with learning disabilities: A review. *Learning Disability Quarterly, 22*(2), 78–98.

Graham, S., Berninger, V., and Weintraub, N. (1998). The relationship between handwriting style and speed and legibility. *Journal of Educational Research, 91,* 290–297.

Graham, S., and Freeman, S. (1986). Strategy training and teacher- vs. student-controlled study conditions: Effects on LD students' spelling performance. *Learning Disability Quarterly, 9,* 15–22.

Graham, S., and Harris, K. (2005). *Writing better: Effective strategies for teaching students with learning difficulties.* Baltimore: Brookes.

Graham, S., and Perin, D. (2007). *Writing next: Effective strategies to improve writing of adolescents in middle and high schools: A report to Carnegie Corporation of New York.* Washington, DC: Alliance for Excellent Education.

Graves, D. (1994). *A fresh look at writing.* Portsmouth, NH: Heinemann.

Graves, D. H. (1983). *Writing: Teachers and children at work.* Portsmouth, NH: Heinemann.

Graves, A. W., Gersten, R., and Haager, D. (2004). Literacy instruction in multiple-language first-grade classrooms: Linking student outcomes to observed instructional practice. *Learning Disabilities Research & Practice, 19*(4), 262–272.

Graves, M. F. (2006). *The vocabulary book: Learning and instruction.* New York: Teachers College Press.

Graves, M. F. (2009). *Essential readings on vocabulary instruction.* Newark, DE: International Reading Association.

Gunn, B., Biglan, A., Smolkowski, K., and Ary, D. (2000). The efficacy of supplemental instruction in decoding skills for Hispanic and non-Hispanic students in early elementary school. *Journal of Special Education, 34*(2), 90–103.

Gunning, T. G. (2010a). *Assessing and correcting reading and writing difficulties* (4th ed.). Boston, MA: Allyn & Bacon.

Gunning, T. G. (2010b). *Creating literacy instruction for all students* (7th ed.). Boston: Allyn & Bacon.

Guszak, F. J. (1972). *Diagnostic reading instruction in the elementary school.* New York: Harper & Row.

Haager, D., Gersten, R., Baker, S., and Graves, A. (2003). The English-language learner classroom observation instrument: Observations of beginning reading instruction in urban schools. *Reading in the classroom: Systems for observing teaching and learning,* 111–144.

Haager, D., and Mahdavi, J. (2007). Teacher roles in implementing intervention (pp. 245–264). In D. Haager, J. Klingner, and S. Vaughn (Eds.), *Evidence-based reading practices for response to intervention.* Baltimore: Brookes.

Hagaman, J. L., and Reid, R. (2008). The effects of the paraphrasing strategy on the reading comprehension of middle school students at risk for failure in reading. *Remedial and Special Education, 29*(4), 222–234.

Haley, M. H., and Austin, T. Y. (2004). *Content-based second language teaching and learning: An interactive approach.* Boston: Allyn & Bacon.

Hall, R. V., and Hall, M. L. (1998). *How to use planned ignoring (Extinction)* (2nd ed.). Austin, TX: PRO-ED.

Harbort, G., Gunter, P. L., Hull, K., Brown, Q., Venn, M. L., Wiley, L. P., et al. (2007). Behaviors of teachers in co-taught classes in a secondary school. *Teacher Education and Special Education, 30*(1), 13–23.

Harniss, M. K., Epstein, M. H., Bursuck, W. D., Nelson, J., and Jayanthi, M. (2001). Resolving homework-related communication problems: Recommendations of parents of children with and without disabilities. *Reading & Writing Quarterly, 17,* 205–225.

Harris, K. R., Graham, S., Mason, L. H., and Friedlander, B. (2008). *Powerful writing strategies for all students.* Baltimore, MD: Brookes.

Harry, B. (2008). Collaboration with culturally and linguistically diverse families: Ideal versus reality. *Exceptional Children, 74*(3), 372–388.

Hastings, R. P., Daley, D., Burns, C., and Beck, A. (2006). Maternal distress and expressed emotion: Cross-sectional and longitudinal relationships with behavior problems of children with intellectual disabilities. *American Journal on Mental Retardation, 111*(1), 48–61.

Hazel, J. S., Schumaker, J. B., Sherman, J. A., and Sheldon, J. (1982). Application of a group training program in social skills and problem solving to learning disabled and non-learning disabled youth. *Learning Disability Quarterly, 5,* 398–409.

Hazel, J. S., Schumaker, J. B., Sherman, J. A., and Sheldon-Wildgen, J. (1981). *ASSET: A social skills program for adolescents.* Champaign, IL: Research Press.

Hecht, S. A., Vagi, K. J., and Torgesen, J. K. (2007). Fraction skills and proportional reasoning. In D. B. Berch and M. M. M. Mazzocco (Eds.), *Why is math so hard for some children? The nature and origins of mathematical learning difficulties and disabilities* (pp. 121–132). Baltimore: Brookes.

Hembree, R. (1986). Research gives calculators a green light. *Arithmetic Teacher, 34*(1), 18–21.

Herzog, P. R. (1998). *PhonicsQ: The complete cueing system.* Available from http://www.phonicsq.com

Hickman, P., Pollard-Durodola, S., and Vaughn, S. (2004). Storybook reading: Improving vocabulary and comprehension for English language learners. *The Reading Teacher, 57*(8), 720.

Higgins, E. L., and Raskind, M. H. (1995). An investigation of the compensatory effectiveness of speech recognition on the written composition performance of postsecondary students with learning disabilities. *Learning Disability Quarterly, 18,* 159–174.

Hock, M., and Mellard, D. (2005). Reading comprehension strategies for adult literacy outcomes. *Journal of Adolescent and Adult Literacy, 49*(3), 192–200.

Hoover, J., and Stenhjem, P. (2003). Bullying and teasing of youth with disabilities: Creating positive school environments for effective inclusion. *Issue Brief: Examining current challenges in secondary education and transition, 2*(3), 1–6.

Hoover, J. H., and Salk, J. (2003). *Bullying: Bigger concerns.* St. Cloud, MN: St. Cloud State University, Department of Special Education.

Hoover, J. J., and Patton, J. R. (2008). The role of special educators in a multitiered instructional system. *Intervention in School and Clinic, 43*(4), 195–202.

Howard, K. A., and Tryon, G. S. (2002). Depressive symptoms in and type of classroom placement for adolescents with LD. *Journal of Learning Disabilities, 35*(2), 185–190.

Hughes, C. A. (1996). Memory and test-taking strategies. In D. D. Deshler, E. S. Ellis, and B. K. Lenz (Eds.), *Teaching adolescents with learning disabilities: Strategies and methods* (2nd ed., pp. 209–266). Denver: Love.

Hughes, C. A., Ruhl, K. L., Deshler, D. D., and Schumaker, J. B. (1995). *The assignment completion strategy.* Lawrence, KS: Edge Enterprises.

Hughes, C. A., Schumaker, J. B., and Deshler, D. D. (2001). *The essay test-taking strategy.* Lawrence, KS: Edge Enterprises.

Hughes, C. A., Schumaker, J. B., Deshler, D. D., and Mercer, C. D. (1993). *The test-taking strategy* (Rev. ed.). Lawrence, KS: Edge Enterprises.

Idol, L. (1987b). Group story mapping: A comprehension strategy for both skilled and unskilled readers. *Journal of Learning Disabilities, 20*(4), 196–205.

Idol, L., Nevin, A., and Paolucci-Whitcomb, P. (2000). *Collaborative consultation* (3rd ed.). Austin, TX: PRO-ED.

Isaacson, S., and Gleason, M. M. (1997). Mechanical obstacles to writing: What can teachers do to help students with learning problems? *Learning Disabilities Research Practice, 12*(3), 188–194.

Isherwood, R. S., and Barger-Anderson, R. (2007). Factors affecting the adoption of co-teaching models in inclusive classrooms: One school's journey from mainstreaming to inclusion. *Journal of Ethnographic & Qualitative Research, 2,* 121–128.

Janney, R., and Snell, M. E. (2000). *Behavioral support.* Baltimore: Brookes.

Janney, R. E., and Snell, M. E. (2006). Modifying schoolwork in inclusive classrooms. *Theory into practice, 45*(3), 215–223.

Johnson, D. D., and Pearson, P. D. (1984). *Teaching reading vocabulary* (2nd ed.). New York: Holt, Rinehart and Winston.

Johnson, D. J., and Myklebust, H. R. (1967). *Learning disabilities: Educational principles and practices.* New York: Grune & Stratton.

Johnson, D. W., Johnson, R. T., and Smith, K. (2007). The state of cooperative learning in postsecondary and professional settings. *Educational Psychology Review, 19*(1), 15–29.

Johnson, R. T., and Johnson, D. W. (1986). Action research: Cooperative learning in the science classroom. *Science and Children, 24,* 31–32.

Jordan, N. C., and Hanich, L. B. (2003). Characteristics of children with moderate mathematics deficiencies: A longitudinal perspective. *Learning Disabilities Research and Practice, 18*(4), 213–221.

Kame'enui, E. J., and Carnine, D. W. (1998). *Effective teaching strategies that accommodate diverse learners.* Upper Saddle River, NJ: Prentice Hall.

Kauffman, J., Hallahan, D., Haas, K., Brame, T., and Boren, R. (1978). Imitating children's errors to improve spelling performance. *Journal of Learning Disabilities, 11,* 33–38.

Kaufmann, L., Handl, P., and Thony, B. (2003). Evaluation of a numeracy intervention program focusing on basic numerical knowledge and conceptual knowledge: A pilot study. *Journal of Learning Disabilities, 36,* 564–573.

Keller-Marulis, M. A., Shapiro, E. S., and Hintze, J. M. (2008). Long-term diagnostic accuracy of curriculum-based measures in reading and mathematics. *School Psychology Review, 37*(3), 374–390.

Kelly, B., Gersten, R., and Carnine, D. (1990). Student error patterns as a function of curriculum design: Teaching fractions to remedial high school students and high school students with learning disabilities. *Journal of Learning Disabilities, 23,* 23–29.

Kim, A. (2002). *Effects of Computer-Assisted Collaborative Strategic Reading (CACSR) on reading comprehension for students with learning disabilities.* Unpublished doctoral dissertation, University of Texas, Austin.

Kim, A., Vaughn, S., Klingner, J. K., Woodruff, A. L., Klein, C., and Kouzekanani, K. (2003). *Improving the reading comprehension of middle school students with reading disabilities through Computer-Assisted Collaborative Strategic Reading.* Manuscript submitted for publication.

Kim, A., Vaughn, S., Wanzek, J., and Wei, S. (2004). Graphic organizers and their effects on the reading comprehension of students with LD: A synthesis of research. *Journal of Learning Disabilities, 37*(2), 105–118.

King-Sears, M. E., Mercer, C. D., and Sindelar, P. T. (1992). Toward independence with key word mnemonics: A strategy for science vocabulary instruction. *Remedial and Special Education, 13*(5), 22–33.

Kirk, S. A., Kirk, W. D., and Minskoff, E. H. (1985). *Phonic remedial reading lessons.* Novato, CA: Academic Therapy Publications.

Klingner, J. K., and Edwards, P. (2006). Cultural considerations with response-to-intervention models. *Reading Research Quarterly, 41,* 108–117.

Klingner, J. K., and Solano-Flores, G. (2007). Cultural responsiveness in response-to-intervention models. In *Accommodating students with disabilities: What works?* Educational Testing Service.

Klingner, J. K., and Vaughn, S. (1996). Reciprocal teaching of reading comprehension strategies for students with learning disabilities who use English as a second language. *Elementary School Journal, 96,* 275–293.

Klingner, J. K., and Vaughn, S. (1998). Using collaborative strategic reading. *Teaching Exceptional Children, 30*(6), 32–37.

Klingner, J. K., and Vaughn, S. (1999a). Promoting reading comprehension, content learning, and English acquisition through collaborative strategic reading (CSR). *The Reading Teacher, 52*(7), 738–747.

Klingner, J. K., and Vaughn, S. (2000). The helping behaviors of fifth graders while using collaborative strategic reading during ESL content classes. *TESOL Quarterly, 34*(1), 69–98.

Klingner, J. K., and Vaughn, S. (2002). Joyce: The changing roles and responsibilities of an LD specialist. *Learning Disability Quarterly, 25,* 19–32.

Klingner, J. K., Vaughn, S., Argüelles, M. E., Hughes, M. T., and Ahwee, S. (2003). Collaborative strategic reading: "Real world" lessons from classroom teachers. *Remedial and Special Education.*

Klingner, J. K., Vaughn, S., and Boardman, A. (2007). *Teaching reading comprehension to students with learning difficulties.* New York: Guilford.

Klingner, J. K., Vaughn, S., Dimino, J., Schumm, J. S., and Bryant, D.P. (2001). *From clunk to click: Collaborative strategic reading.* Longmont, CO: Sopris West.

Klingner, J. K., Vaughn, S., and Schumm, J. S. (1998). Collaborative strategic reading during social studies in heterogeneous fourth-grade classrooms. *Elementary School Journal, 99,* 3–22.

Klingner, J. K., Vaughn, S., Schumm, J. S., Cohen, P., and Forgan, J. W. (1998). Inclusion or pull-out: Which do students prefer? *Journal of Learning Disabilities, 32*(2), 148–158.

Kloo, A., and Zigmond, N. (2008). Co-teaching revisited: Redrawing the blueprint. *Preventing School Failure, 52*(2), 12–20.

Kloomok, S., and Cosden, M. (1994). Self-concept in children with learning disabilities: The relationship between global self-concept, academic discounting, nonacademic self-concept, and perceived social support. *Learning Disability Quarterly, 17*(2), 140–153.

Kobayashi, K. (2006). Combined effects of note-taking/-reviewing on learning and the enhancement through interventions: A meta-analytic review. *Educational Psychology, 26*(3), 459–477.

Kress, R. A., and Johnson, M. S. (1970). Martin. In A. J. Harris (Ed.), *Casebook on reading disability* (pp. 1–24). New York: David McKay.

Kucer, S. B. (1986). Helping writers get the "big picture." *Journal of Reading, 30*(1), 18–25.

Kuhn, M. R., and Stahl, S. (2003). Fluency: A review of developmental and remedial practices. *Journal of Educational Psychology, 95,* 3–21.

Lancelotta, G. X., and Vaughn, S. (1989). Relation between types of aggression and sociometric status: Peer and teacher perceptions. *Journal of Educational Psychology, 81*(1), 86–90. In W. R. Borg. *Applying educational research.* New York: Longman.

Lane, K. L, Harris, K. R., Graham, S., Weisenbach, J. L., Brindle, M., and Morphy, P. (2008). The effects of self-regulated strategy development on the writing performance of second-grade students with behavioral and writing difficulties. *The Journal of Special Education, 41*(4), 234–253.

Langer, J. A. (1981). From theory to practice: A prereading plan. *Journal of Reading, 25*(2), 152–156.

Lankford, F. G. (1974). *Some computational strategies in seventh grade pupils.* Unpublished manuscript, University of Virginia.

Lardieri, L. A., Blacher, J., and Swanson, H. L. (2000). Sibling relationships and parent stress in families of children with and without learning disabilities. *Learning Disability Quarterly, 23*(2), 105–116.

Leadholm, B., and Miller, J. (1992). *Language sample analysis: The Wisconsin guide.* Madison, WI: Bureau for Exceptional Children, Wisconsin Department of Public Education.

Lederer, J. M. (2000). Reciprocal teaching of social studies in inclusive elementary classrooms. *Journal of Learning Disabilities, 33,* 51–106.

Lenz, B. K. (1983). Promoting active learning through effective instruction: Using advance organizers. *Pointer, 27*(2), 11–13.

Lenz, B. K., Adams, G. L., Bulgren, J. A., Pouloit, N., and Laraux, M. (2007). Effects of curriculum maps and guiding questions on the test performance of adolescents with learning disabilities. *Learning Disability Quarterly, 30*(4), 235–244.

Lenz, B. K., Alley, G. R., and Schumaker, J. B. (1987). Activating the inactive learner: Advance organizers in the secondary content classroom. *Learning Disability Quarterly, 10*(10), 53–67.

Lenz, B. K., and Bulgren, J. A. (1995). Promoting learning in content classes. In P. A. Cegleka and W. H. Berdine (Eds.), *Effective instruction for students with learning problems* (pp. 385–417). Boston: Allyn & Bacon.

Lenz, B. K., Schumaker, J., Deshler, D., and Beals, V. (1993). *The word identification strategy.* Lawrence: University of Kansas.

Leon, J. A., and Pepe, H. J. (1983). Self-instructional training: Cognitive behavior modification for remediating arithmetic deficits. *Exceptional Children, 50*(1), 54–60.

Lessenbery, B. M., and Rehfeldt, R. A. (2004). Evaluating stress levels of parents with disabilities. *Exceptional Children, 70*(2), 231–233.

Linan-Thompson, S., and Vaughn, S. (2007). *Research-based methods of reading instruction for English language learners.* Alexandria, VA: ASCD.

Linan-Thompson, S., Vaughn, S., Hickman-Davis, P., and Kouzekanani, K. (2003). Effectiveness of supplemental reading instruction for second-grade English language learners with reading difficulties. *Elementary School Journal, 103*(3), 221–238.

Loomes, C., Rasmussen, C., Pei, J., Manji, S., and Andrew, G. (2008). The effect of rehearsal training on working memory span of children with fetal alcohol spectrum disorder. *Research in Developmental Disabilities, 29*(2), 113–124.

Lovett, M. W., Borden, S. L., Warren-Chaplin, P. M., Lacerenza, L., DeLuca, T., and Giovinazzo, R. (1996). Text comprehension training for disabled readers: An evaluation of reciprocal teaching and text analysis training programs. *Brain and Language, 54,* 477–480.

Lyerla, K. D., Schumaker, J. B., and Deshler, D. D. (1994). *The paragraph writing strategy* (Rev. ed.). Lawrence, KS: Edge Enterprises.

MacArthur, C., Graham, S., Schwartz, S., and Schafer, W. D. (1995). Evaluation of a writing instruction model that integrated a process approach, strategy instruction, and word processing. *Learning Disability Quarterly, 18,* 278–291.

MacArthur, C. A. (Winter 1988). Computers and writing instruction. *Teaching Exceptional Children,* 37–39.

MacArthur, C. A., Graham, S., and Fitzgerald, J. (2008). *Handbook of writing research.* New York: Guilford.

Macrorie, K. (1980). *The I search paper.* Portsmouth, NH: Heinemann.

Maheady, L., Harper, G. F., and Mallette, B. (2001). Peer-mediated instruction and interventions and students with mild disabilities. *Remedial and Special Education, 22,* 4–14.

Maheady, L., Harper, G. F., and Sacca, M. K. (1988). Peer mediated instruction: A promising approach to meeting the needs of learning disabled adolescents. *Learning Disability Quarterly, 11,* 108–113.

Malone, L. D., and Mastropieri, M. A. (1992). Reading comprehension instruction: Summarization and self-monitoring training for students with learning disabilities. *Exceptional Children, 58,* 270–279.

Marston, D., Muyskens, P., Lau, M., and Canter, H. (2003). Problem solving model for decision-making with high-incidence disabilities: The Minneapolis experience. *Learning Disabilities Research and Practice, 18*(3), 187–200.

Martin, J. H., and Friedberg, A. (1986). *Writing to read. A parent's guide to the new, early learning program for young children.* New York: Warner.

Martinez, M., and Teale, W. H. (February 1988). Reading in a kindergarten classroom library. *The Reading Teacher, 568–572.*

Mastropieri, M., Scruggs, T. E., and Marshak, L. (2008). Training teachers, parents, and peers to implement effective teaching strategies for content area learning. In T. E. Scruggs and M. A. Mastropieri (Eds.), *Personnel preparation: Advances in learning and behavioral disabilities* (Vol. 21, pp. 309–327). Bingley, UK: Emerald.

Mastropieri, M. A., and Scruggs, T. E. (1998). Constructing more meaningful relationships in the classroom: Mnemonic research into practice. *Learning Disabilities Research and Practice, 13*(3), 138–145.

Mastropieri, M. A., Scruggs, T. E., Spencer, V., and Fontana, J. (2003). Promoting success in high school world history: Peer tutoring versus guided notes. *Learning Disabilities Research and Practice, 19*(1), 52–65.

Mastropieri, M. A., Sweda, J., and Scruggs, T. E. (2000). Putting mnemonic strategies to work in an inclusive classroom. *Learning Disabilities Research and Practice, 15*(2), 69–74.

Mathes, P. G., Torgesen, J. K., and Howard, A. J. (2001). The effects of peer-assisted literacy strategies for first-grade readers with and without additional computer-assisted instruction in phonological awareness. *American Educational Research Journal, 38*(2), 371–410.

Matuszny, R. M., Banda, D. R., and Coleman, T. J. (2007, Mar./Apr.). A progressive plan for building collaborative relationships with parents from diverse backgrounds. *Teaching Exceptional Children, 24–31.*

McDaniel, M. A., Howard, D. C., and Einstein, G. O. (2009). The read-recite-review study strategy: Effective and portable. *Psychological Science, 20*(4), 516–522.

McGinnis, E., and Goldstein, A. (2003). *Skillstreaming in early childhood: New strategies and perspectives for teaching prosocial skills.* Champaign, IL: Research Press.

McIntosh, R., Vaughn, S., Schumm, J., Haager, D., and Lee, O. (1993). Observations of students with learning disabilities in general education classrooms: You don't bother me and I won't bother you. *Exceptional Children, 60,* 249–261.

McIntyre, C. W., and Pickering, J. S. (1995). *Clinical studies of multisensory structured language education for students with dyslexia and related disorders.* Poughkeepsie, NY: Hamco.

McKeown, M. G., and Beck, I. L. (2004). Transforming knowledge into professional development resources: Six teachers implement a model of teaching for understanding text. *Elementary School Journal, 104,* 391–408.

McNaughton, D., Hughes, C., and Ofiesh, N. (1997). Proofreading for students with learning disabilities: Integrating computer and strategy use. *Learning Disabilities Research and Practice, 12*(1), 16–28.

Meichenbaum, D. (1977). *Cognitive-behavior modification: An integrative approach.* New York: Plenum.

Mercer, C. D., Mercer, A. R., and Bott, D. A. (1984). *Self-correcting learning materials for the classroom.* Columbus, OH: Merrill.

Michaelsen, L. K., and Sweet, M. (2008). The essential elements of team-based learning. *New Directions for Teaching and Learning, 2008*(116), 7–27.

Moats, L. C. (2000). *Speech to print: Language essentials for teachers.* Baltimore: Brookes.

Montague, M., and Bos, C. S. (1986a). The effect of cognitive strategy training on verbal math problem-solving performance of learning-disabled adolescents. *Journal of Learning Disabilities, 19,* 26–33.

Montague, M., and Bos, C. S. (1986b). Verbal math problem solving and learning disabilities: A review. *Focus on Learning Problems in Math, 8*(2), 7–21.

Montague, M., and Leavell, A. G. (1994). Improving the narrative writing of students with learning disabilities. *Remedial and Special Education, 15,* 21–33.

Montague, M., and van Garderen, D. (2003). A cross-sectional study of mathematics achievement, estimation skills, and academic self-perception in students of varying ability. *Journal of Learning Disabilities, 36,* 437–447.

Mortimore, T., and Crozier, W. R. (2006). Dyslexia and difficulties with study skills in higher education. *Studies in Higher Education, 31*(2), 235–251.

Murphy, J., Hern, C., Williams, R., and McLaughlin, T. (1990). The effects of the copy, cover, compare approach in increasing spelling accuracy with learning disabled students. *Contemporary Educational Psychology, 15,* 378–386.

Nagel, B. R., Schumaker, J. B., and Deshler, D. D. (1994). *The FIRST-letter mnemonic strategy* (Rev. ed.). Lawrence, KS: Edge Enterprises.

Nancy, A., and Dill, M. (1997). *Let's write.* New York: Scholastic.

National Association of State Directors of Special Education. (2006). *Response to intervention: Policy considerations and implementation.* Retrieved from http://www.nasdse.org

National Center for Educational Statistics. *Trends in International Mathematics and Science Study (TIMSS)* (2007 Results). Retrieved June 1, 2009, from http://nces.ed.gov/timss/figure07_2.asp

National Mathematics Advisory Panel. (2008). *Foundations for success: The final report of the national mathematics advisory panel.* Washington, DC: U.S. Department of Education.

National Mental Health Association. (2003). *Adolescent depression: Helping depressed teens.* Washington, DC: Author.

National Reading Panel. (2000). *Teaching children to read: An evidence-based assessment of the scientific research literature on reading and its implications for reading instruction.* Bethesda, MD: National Institute of Child Health and Human Development, National Institutes of Health.

National Research Council. (2001). *Adding it up: Helping children learn mathematics.* Washington, DC: National Academy Press.

Nelson, A. (1998). *A long hard day on the ranch.* Buffalo, NY: Firefly Books Limited.

Nelson, N. W. (1998). *Childhood language disorders in context: Infancy through adolescence* (2nd ed.). Boston: Allyn & Bacon.

Niemi, P., Poskiparta, E., Vauras, M., and Mäki, H. (1998). Reading and writing difficulties do not always occur as the researcher expects. *Scandinavian Journal of Psychology, 39*(3), 159–169.

Nippold, M. A. (1998). *Later language development: The school-age and adolescent years.* Austin, TX: PRO-ED.

Nippold, M. A., and Sun, L. (2008). Knowledge of morphologicaly complex words: A developmental study of older children and young adolescents. *Language, Speech, and Hearing Services in Schools, 39*(3), 365–373.

Nulman, J. H., and Gerber, M. M. (1984). Improving spelling performance by imitating a child's errors. *Journal of Learning Disabilities, 17,* 328–333.

O'Connor, R. E., and Jenkins, J. R. (1995). Improving the generalization of sound/symbol knowledge: Teaching spelling to kindergarten children with disabilities. *Journal of Special Education, 29,* 255–275.

Ogle, D. M. (1986). K-W-L: A teaching model that develops active reading of expository text. *The Reading Teacher, 39,* 564–570.

Ogle, D. M. (1989). The know, want to know, learn strategy. In K. D. Muth (Ed.), *Children's comprehension of text: Research into practice* (pp. 205–233). Newark, DE: International Reading Association.

Okilwa, N. S., and Shelby, L. (2010). The effects of peer tutoring on academic performance of students with disabilities in graded 6 through 12: A synthesis of the literature. *Remedial and Special Education, 31*(6), 450–463.

Okolo, C. M. (1992). The effects of computer-based attribution retraining on the attributions, persistence, and mathematics computation of students with learning disabilities. *Journal of Learning Disabilities, 25,* 327–334.

Okrainec, J. A., and Hughes, M. J. (1996, July). *Conversational interactions between intellectually disabled and normal progress adolescents during a problem-solving task.* Paper presented at the meeting of the World Congress of IASSD, Helsinki, Finland.

Olson, J. L., Platt, J. M., and Dieker, L. (2008). *Teaching children and adolescents with special needs.* Upper Saddle River, NJ: Prentice Hall.

Olweus, D. (1993). *Bullying at school: What we know and what we can do.* Cambridge, MA: Blackwell.

Orsmond, G. I., Seltzer, M. M., Greenberg, J. S., and Krauss, M. W. (2006). Mother-child relationship quality among adolescents and adults with autism. *American Journal on Mental Retardation, 111*(2), 121–137.

Orton, S. T. (1937). *Reading, writing, and speech problems in children.* New York: W. W. Norton.

OSEP Technical Assistance Center on Positive Behavioral Interventions and Supports. (2009). Reducing behavior problems in the elementary school. Retrieved from http://www.pbis.org/

Owens, R. E. (2010). *Language disorders: A functional approach to assessment and intervention* (5th ed.). Boston: Pearson/Allyn & Bacon.

Palincsar, A. S. (1982). *Improving the reading comprehension of junior high students through the reciprocal teaching of comprehension-monitoring.* Unpublished doctoral dissertation, University of Illinois, Urbana.

Palincsar, A. S. (1986). The role of dialogue in providing scaffolded instruction. *Educational Psychologist, 21*(1–2), 73–98.

Palincsar, A. S. (1988). *Reciprocal teaching instructional materials packet.* East Lansing: Michigan State University.

Palincsar, A. S. (2007). Reciprocal teaching 1982 to 2006: The role of research, theory, and representation in the transformation of instructional research. In D. W. Rowe and R. T. Jimenez (Eds.), *56th Yearbook of the national reading conference* (pp. 38–49). Oak Creek, WI: National Reading Conference.

Palincsar, A. S., and Brown, A. L. (1984). Reciprocal teaching of comprehension fostering and comprehension monitoring activities. *Cognition and Instruction, 1*(2), 117–175.

Palincsar, A. S., and Brown, A. L. (1986). Interactive teaching to promote independent learning from text. *The Reading Teacher, 39*(8), 771–777.

Palincsar, A. S., and Duke, N. K. (2004). The role of text and text-reader interactions in young children's reading development and achievement. *The Elementary School Journal, 105*(2), 183–197.

Patton, J. R., Cronin, M. E., Bassett, D. S., and Koppel, A. E. (1997). A life skills approach to mathematics instruction: Preparing students with learning disabilities for the real-life math demands of adulthood. *Journal of Learning Disabilities, 30*(2), 178–187.

Pauk, W. (2001). *Essential study strategies.* Columbus, OH: Prentice Hall.

Pfeffer, C. R. (1986). *The suicidal child.* New York: Guilford Press.

Preiss, R. W., and Gayle, B. M. (2006). A meta-analysis of the educational benefits of employing advanced organizers. In B. M. Gayle, R. W. Preiss, N. Burrell, and M. Allen (Eds.), *Classroom communication and instructional processes: Advances through meta-analysis* (pp. 329–344). Mahwah, NJ: Lawrence Erlbaum Associates.

Premack, D. (1959). Toward empirical behavior laws. *Psychological Review, 66*(4), 219–233.

President's Commission on Excellence in Special Education. (2002). *A new era: Revitalizing special education.* Washington, DC: U.S. Department of Education.

RAND Reading Study Group (2002). *Reading for Understanding: Toward an R&D Program in Reading Comprehension.* Washington, DC: RAND.

Raphael, T. E. (1982). Question-answering strategies for children. *The Reading Teacher, 36,* 188.

Raphael, T. E. (1984). Teaching learners about sources of information for answering comprehension questions. *Journal of Reading, 27,* 303–311.

Raphael, T. E. (1986). Teaching question-answer relationships revisited. *The Reading Teacher, 39*(6), 516–523.

Raphael, T. E., and Pearson, P. D. (1982). *The effect of metacognitive awareness training on children's*

question-answering behavior. (Tech. Rep. No. 238). Urbana: University of Illinois, Center for Study of Reading.

Rashotte, C. A., and Torgesen, J. K. (1985). Repeated reading and reading fluency in learning disabled children. *Reading Research Quarterly, 20*(2), 180–188.

Rathvon, N. (2004). *Early reading assessment: A practitioner's handbook.* New York: Guilford.

Re, A. M., Pedron, M., and Cornoldi, C. (2007). Expressive writing difficulties in children described as exhibiting ADHD symptoms. *Journal of Learning Disabilities, 40*(3), 244–255.

Reed, Deborah K. (2008). A synthesis of morphology interventions and effects on reading outcomes for students in grades K–12. *Learning Disabilities Research and Practice, 23*(1), 36–49.

Reutzel, D. R., Jones, C. D., Fawson, P. C., and Smith, J. A. (2008). Scaffolded silent reading: A complement to guided repeated oral reading that works! *The Reading Teacher, 62*(3), 194–207.

Reyes, E. I., and Bos, C. S. (1998). Interactive semantic mapping and charting: Enhancing content area learning for language minority students. In R. Gersten and R. Jimenez (Eds.), *Innovative practices for language minority students* (pp. 133–150). Pacific Grove, CA: Brooks/Cole.

Ritchey, K. D., and Goeke, J. L. (2006). Orton-Gillingham and Orton-Gillinham-based reading instruction: A review of the literature. *Journal of Special Education, 40*(3), 171–183.

Rivera, D. P., and Smith, D. D. (1997). *Teaching students with learning and behavior problems* (3rd ed.). Boston: Allyn & Bacon.

Rivera, D. P., Smith, R. G., Goodwin, M. W., and Bryant, D. P. (1998). Mathematical word problem solving: A synthesis of intervention research for students with learning disabilities. In T. E. Scruggs and M. A. Mastropieri (Eds.), *Advances in learning and behavioral disabilities* (vol. 12, pp. 245–285). Greenwich, CT: JAI Press.

Roberts, G. H. (1968). The failure strategies of third grade arithmetic pupils. *The Arithmetic Teacher, 15,* 442–446.

Robertson, H. M. (1999). LEA and students with special needs. In O. G. Nelson and W. M. Linek (Eds.), *Practical classroom applications of language experience: Looking back, looking forward* (pp. 221–223). Boston: Allyn & Bacon.

Robinson, F. P. (1946). *Effective study.* New York: Harper and Brothers.

Rose, T. L. (1984). The effect of two prepractice procedures on oral reading. *Journal of Learning Disabilities, 17,* 544–548.

Rose, T. L., and Beattie, J. R. (1986). Relative effects of teacher-directed and taped previewing on oral reading. *Learning Disability Quarterly, 9,* 193–199.

Rosenshine, B. (1997). Advances in research in instruction. In J. W. Lloyd, E. J. Kame'enui, and D. Chard (Eds.), *Issues in educating students with disabilities.* Mahwah, NJ: Erlbaum.

Rosenshine, B., and Meister, C. (1994). Reciprocal teaching: A review of the research. *Review of Education Research, 64,* 479–530.

Ruhl, K. L. (1996). Does nature of student activity during lecture pauses affect notes and immediate recall of college students with learning disabilities? *Journal of Postsecondary Education and Disability, 12*(2), 16–27.

Rupley, W. H., Logan, J. W., and Nichols, W. D. (1998). Vocabulary instruction in a balanced reading program. *The Reading Teacher, 52,* 338–346.

Saenz, L. M., Fuchs, L. S., and Fuchs, D. (2005). Peer-assisted learning strategies for English language learners with learning disabilities. *Exceptional Children, 71,* 231–247.

Salend, S. J., and Nowak, M. R. (1988). Effects of peer-previewing on LD students' oral reading skills. *Learning Disability Quarterly, 11,* 47–53.

Samuels, S. J. (1997). The method of repeated reading. *The Reading Teacher, 50,* 376–381. Originally published in The Reading Teacher in January 1979 (vol. 32).

Santoro, L., Chard, D. J., Howard, L., and Baker, S. K. (2008). Making the very most of classroom read-alouds to promote comprehension and vocabulary. *The Reading Teacher, 61*(5), 396–408.

Schmidt, P. R. (1999). KWLQ: Inquiry and literacy learning in science. *The Reading Teacher, 52,* 789–792.

Schumaker, J. B., Denton, P. H., and Deshler, D. D. (1993). *The paraphrasing strategy* (Rev. ed.) (Learning Strategies Curriculum). Lawrence: University of Kansas.

Schumaker, J. B., Deshler, D. D., Alley, G. R., Warner, M. M., and Denton, P. H. (1982). Multipass: A learning strategy for improving reading comprehension. *Learning Disability Quarterly, 5*(3), 295–304.

Schumaker, J. B., Nolan, S. M., and Deshler, D. D. (1994). *The error monitoring strategy* (Rev. ed.). Lawrence: Center for Research on Learning Disabilities, University of Kansas.

Schumm, J. S. (2001). *School power: Study skill strategies for succeeding in school.* Minneapolis, MN: Free Spirit.

Schumm, J. S., and Mangrum, C. T. (1991). FLIP: A framework for textbook thinking. *Journal of Reading, 35,* 120–124.

Schumm, J. S., and Post, S. A. (1997). *Executive learning: Successful strategies for college reading and studying.* Columbus, OH: Prentice Hall.

Schumm, J. S., and Vaughn, S. (1995). *Using Making Words in heterogeneous classrooms.* Unpublished manuscript, University of Miami (FL), School Based Research.

Schumm, J. S., Vaughn, S., Haager, D., McDowell, J., Rothlein, L., and Saumell, L. (1995a). General education teacher planning: What can students with learning disabilities expect? *Exceptional Children, 61*(4), 335–352.

Schumm, J. S., Vaughn, S., Haager, D., McDowell, J., Rothlein, L., and Saumell, L. (1995b). Teacher planning for individual student needs: What can mainstreamed special education students expect? *Exceptional Children, 61,* 335–352.

Schumm, J. S., Vaughn, S., and Harris, J. (1997). Pyramid power for collaborative planning. *Teaching Exceptional Children, 29*(6), 62–66.

Schuster, J. W., Stevens, K. B., and Doak, P. K. (1990). Using constant time delay to teach word definitions. *Journal of Special Education, 24,* 306–318.

Schwartz, N. H., Ellsworth, L. S., Graham, L., and Knight, B. (1998). Assessing prior knowledge to remember text: A comparison of advance organizers and maps. *Contemporary Educational Psychology, 23*(1), 65–89.

Schwartz, S. E., and Budd, D. (1981). Mathematics for handicapped learners: A functional approach for adolescents. *Focus on Exceptional Children, 13*(7), 1–12.

Scruggs, T. E., Mastropieri, M. A., Berkeley, S., and Graetz, J. E. (2009). Do special education interventions improve learning of secondary content? A meta-analysis. *Remedial and Special Education.* Retrieved from http://rse.sagepub.com/content/early/2009/02/27/0741932508327465.

Scruggs, T. E., Mastropieri, M. A., and McDuffie, K. A. (2007). Co-teaching in inclusive classrooms: A metasynthesis of qualitative research. *Exceptional Children, 73*(4), 392–416.

Seidel, J. F., and Vaughn, S. (1991). Social alienation and the LD school dropout. *Learning Disabilities Research and Practice, 6*(3), 152–157.

Seligman, M., and Darling, R. B. (2007). *Ordinary families, special children* (3rd ed.). New York: Guilford.

Seymour, P. H. K., Aro, M., and Erskine, J. (2003). Foundation literacy acquisition in European orthographies. *British Journal of Psychology, 94,* 143–174.

Shanahan, T., and Beck, I. L. (2006). Effective literacy teaching for English-language learners. In D. August & T. Shanahan (Eds.), *Developing a literacy in a second language: Report of the national literacy panel* (pp. 415–488). Mahway, NJ: Erlbaum.

Shapiro, E. S., Keller, M. A., Lutz, G. J., Santoro, L. E., and Hintze, J. M. (2006). Curriculum-based measures and peformance on state assessment and standarized tests: Reading and math performance in Pennsylvania. *Journal of psychoeducational assessment, 24*(1), 19–35. doi: 10.1177/0734282905285237

Share, D. L., and Stanovich, K. E. (1995). Cognitive processes in early reading development: A model of acquisition and individual differences. *Issues in Education: Contributions from Education Psychology, 1,* 1–57.

Shaywitz, S. E., Morris, R., and Shaywitz, B. A. (2008). The education of dyslexic children from childhood to young adulthood. *Annual Review of Psychology, 59,* 451–475.

Sheras, P. L. (1983). Suicide in adolescence. In E. Walker and M. Roberts (Eds.), *Handbook of clinical child psychology.* New York: Wiley.

Shippen, M. E., Simpson, R. G., and Crites, S. A. (2003). A practical guide to functional behavioral assessment. *Teaching Exceptional Children, 35,* 36–44.

Shore, K. (2003). *Elementary teacher's discipline problem solver: A practical A–Z guide for managing classroom behavior problems.* San Francisco: Jossey-Bass.

Simmons, D., Hairrell, A., Edmonds, M., Vaughn, S., Larsen, R. Willson, V., et al. (2010). A comparison of multiple-strategy methods: Effects on fourth-grade students' general and content-specific reading comprehension and vocabulary development. *Journal of Research on Educational Effectiveness, 3*(2), 121–156.

Smith, E. M., and Alley, G. R. (1981). *The effect of teaching sixth graders with learning difficulties a strategy for solving verbal math problems* (Research Report No. 39). Institute for Research in Learning Disabilities.

Smith, T. J., and Adams, G. (2006). The effect of comorbid AD/HD and learning disabilities on parent-reported behavioral and academic outcomes of children. *Learning Disability Quarterly, 29,* 101–112.

Spear-Swerling, L. (2006). *The importance of teaching handwriting.* Retrieved August 10, 2006, from http://www.ldonline.org/spearswerling/10521

Speece, D. L., MacDonald, V., Kilsheimer, L., and Krist, J. (1997). Research to practice: Preservice teachers reflect on reciprocal teaching. *Learning Disabilities Research and Practice, 12,* 177–187.

Stahl, S. A. (2004). What do we know about fluency? In P. McCardle and V. Chhabra, *The voice of evidence in reading research* (pp. 187–211). Baltimore: Brookes.

Stauffer, R. G. (1969). *Directing reading maturity as a cognitive process.* New York: Harper & Row.

Stauffer, R. G. (1970). *The language-experience approach to the teaching of reading.* New York: Harper & Row.

Stauffer, R. G. (1976). *Teaching reading as a thinking process.* New York: Harper & Row.

Stern, C., Stern, M. B., and Gould, T. S. (1998). *Structural arithmetic.* Cambridge, MA: Educators Publishing Service.

Stevens, K. B., and Schuster, J. W. (1987). Effects of a constant time delay procedure on the written spelling performance of a learning disabled student. *Learning Disability Quarterly, 10,* 9–16.

Stevens, K. B., and Schuster, J. W. (1988). Time delay: Systematic instruction for academic tasks. *Remedial and Special Education, 9*(5), 16–21.

Stivers, J. (2008). Strengthen your coteaching relationship. *Intervention in School and Clinic, 44*(2), 121–125.

Stratton, B. D., Grindler, M. C., and Postell, C. M. (1992). Discovering oneself. *Middle School Journal, 24,* 42–43.

Strickland, D. S., Ganske, K., and Monroe, J. (2002). *Supporting struggling readers and writers: Strategies for classroom intervention, 3–6.* Portland, ME: Stenhouse.

Strickland, D. S., and Schickedanz, J. A. (2009). *Learning about print in preschool: Working with letters, words, and beginning links with phonemic awareness.* Newark, DE: International Reading Association.

Stuart, M. (1999). Getting ready for reading: Early phoneme awareness and phonics training improves reading and spelling in inner-city second language learners. *British Journal of Educational Psychology, 69*(4), 587–605.

Stuebing, K. K., Fletcher, J. M., LeDoux, J. M., Lyon, G. R., Shaywitz, S. E., and Shaywitz, B. A. (2002). Validity of IQ-discrepancy classifications of reading difficulties: A meta-analysis. *American Educational Research Journal, 39,* 469–518.

Sugai, G., Horner, R., and Gresham, F. M. (2002). Behaviorally effective school environments. In M. Shinn, H. Walker, and G. Stoner (Eds.), *Interventions for achievement and be-havior problems II: Preventive and remedial approaches* (pp. 315–350). Bethesda, MD: National Association of School Psychologists. (ERIC Document Reproduction Service No. ED 462 655).

Suritsky, S. K., and Hughes, C. A. (1996). Notetaking strategy instruction. In D. D. Deshler, E. S. Ellis, and B. K. Lenz (Eds.), *Teaching adolescents with learning disabilities* (2nd ed., pp. 267–312). Denver: Love.

Swanson, H. L. (1999a). Reading research for students with LD: A meta-analysis of intervention outcomes. *Journal of Learning Disabilities, 32,* 504–532.

Swanson, H. L. (1999b). Instructional components that predict treatment outcomes for students with learning disabilities: Support for a combined strategy and direct instruction model. *Learning Disabilities Research and Practice, 14*(3), 129–140.

Swanson, H. L., Howard, C. B., and Saez, L. (2006). Do different components of working memory underlie different subgroups of reading disabilities? *Journal of Learning Disabilities, 39*(3), 252–269.

Tackett, K. K., Roberts, G., Baker, S., and Scammacca, N. K. (2009). *Implementing response to intervention: Practices and perspectives from five schools - Frequently asked questions.* Portsmouth, NH: Center on Instruction.

Thornton, C. A. (1978). Emphasizing thinking strategies in basic fact instruction. *Journal for Research in Mathematics Education,* 215–227.

Thornton, C. A., and Toohey, M. A. (1985). Basic math facts: Guidelines for teaching and learning. *Learning Disabilities Focus, 1*(1), 44–57.

Thornton, C. A., Tucker, B. F., Dossey, J. A., and Bazik, E. F. (1983). *Teaching mathematics to children with special needs.* Menlo Park, CA: Addison-Wesley.

Thorpe, H. W., and Borden, K. F. (1985). The effect of multisensory instruction upon the on-task behavior and word reading accuracy of learning disabled students. *Journal of Learning Disabilities, 18,* 279–286.

Tierney, R. J., and Readence, J. E. (2005). *Reading strategies and practices: A compendium* (6th ed.). Boston: Allyn & Bacon.

Toolan, J. M. (1981). Depression and suicide in children: An overview. *American Journal of Psychotherapy, 35*(3), 311–323.

Torgesen, J. K. (1999). Assessment and instruction for phonemic awareness and word recognition skills. In H. W. Catts and A. G. Kamhi (Eds.), *Language and reading disabilities* (pp. 128–153). Boston: Allyn & Bacon.

Torgesen, J. K. (2000). Individual differences in response to early interventions in reading: The lingering problem of treatment resisters. *Learning Disabilities Research and Practice, 15,* 55–64.

Torgesen, J. K., Wagner, R. K., and Rahsotte, C. A. (1994). Longitudinal studies of phonological processing and reading. *Journal of Learning Disabilities 19,* 623–630.

Tournaki, N. (2003). The differential effects of teaching addition through strategy instruction versus drill and practice to students with and without learning disabilities. *Journal of Learning Disabilities, 36,* 449–458.

Trelease, J. (2006). *The read-aloud handbook* (6th ed.). New York: Penguin.

Troia, G. A., and Graham, S. (2002). The effectiveness of a highly explicit, teacher-directed strategy instruction routine: Changing the writing performance of students with learning disabilities. *Journal of Learning Disabilities, 35,* 290–305.

Tucker, B. F., Singleton, A. H., and Weaver, T. L. (2006). *Teaching mathematics to all children: Designing and adapting instruction to meet the needs of diverse learners.* Upper Saddle River, NJ: Pearson.

U.S. Department of Education. (2006a). "Assistance to states for the education of children with disabilities and preschool grants for children with disabilities: Final rule," 34 CRF Parts 300 and 301, *Federal Register* 71: 156 (Aug. 14, 2006): 46540–46845. Retrieved February 14, 2007, from www.idea.ed.gov/download/final-regulations.pdr

U.S. Department of Education. (2006b, April). *Twenty-sixth annual report to congress on the implementation of the Individuals with Disabilities Education Act.* Washington, DC: U.S. Department of Education.

Ulanoff, S. H., and Pucci, S. L. (1999). Learning words from books: The effects of read aloud on second language vocabulary acquisition. *Bilingual Research Journal, 23,* 319–332.

University of Texas Center for Reading and Language Arts. (1999). *Enhancing vocabulary instruction for secondary students.* Austin, TX: UT System/Texas Education Agency.

University of Texas Center for Reading and Language Arts. (2000a). *Establishing an intensive reading and writing program for secondary students.* Austin, TX: UT System/Texas Education Agency.

University of Texas Center for Reading and Language Arts. (2000b). *First grade teacher reading academy.* Austin, TX: UT System/Texas Education Agency.

University of Texas Center for Reading and Language Arts. (2001a). *Effective instruction for elementary struggling readers: Research-based practices.* Austin, TX: UT System/Texas Education Agency.

University of Texas Center for Reading and Language Arts. (2001b). *Second grade teacher reading academy.* Austin, TX: UT System/Texas Education Agency.

University of Texas Center for Reading and Language Arts. (2002). *Effective instruction for secondary struggling readers: Research-based practices.* Austin, TX: UT System/Texas Education Agency.

University of Texas Center for Reading and Language Arts. (2003a). *Fourth grade teacher reading academy.* Austin, TX: UT System/Texas Education Agency.

University of Texas Center for Reading and Language Arts. (2003b). *Third grade teacher reading academy.* Austin, TX: UT System/Texas Education Agency.

Vadasy, P. F., and Sanders, E. A. (2008). Repeated reading intervention: Outcomes and interactions with readers' skills and classroom instruction. *Journal of Educational Psychology, 100*(2), 272–290.

Van Luit, J. E. H., and Naglieri, J. A. (1999). Effectiveness of the MASTER program for teaching children multiplication and division. *Journal of Learning Disabilities, 32,* 98–107.

Van Reusen, A. K., and Bos, C. S. (1990). I PLAN: Helping students communicate in planning conferences. *Teaching Exceptional Children, 22,* 30–32.

Vaughn, S., Cirino, P. T., Linan-Thompson, S., Mathes, P. G., Carlson, C. D., Cardenas-Hagan, E., et al. (2006). Effectiveness of a Spanish intervention and an English intervention for English language learners at risk for reading problems. *American Educational Research Journal, 43*(3), 449–487.

Vaughn, S., and Fuchs, L. S. (2006). A response to "Competing views: A dialogue on response to intervention": Why response to intervention is necessary but not sufficient for identifying students with learning disabilities. *Assessment for Effective Intervention, 32*(1), 58–61.

Vaughn, S., Gersten, R., and Chard, D. J. (2000). The underlying message in LD intervention research: Findings from research syntheses. *Exceptional Children, 67*(1), 99–114.

Vaughn, S., Hogan, A., Kouzekanani, K., and Shapiro, S. (1990). Peer acceptance, self-perceptions, and social skills of LD students prior to identification. *Journal of Educational Psychology, 82*(1), 1–6.

Vaughn, S., and Klingner, J. K. (2004). Teaching reading comprehension to students with learning disabilities. In K. Apel, B. J. Ehren, E. R. Silliman, and C. A. Stone (Series Eds.); C. A. Stone, E. R. Silliman, B. J. Ehren, and K. Apel (Vol. Eds.), *Challenges in language and literacy; Handbook of language and literacy: Development and disorders* (pp. 541–555). New York: Guilford Press.

Vaughn, S., and Klingner, J. K. (2007). Response to Intervention (RtI): A new era in identifying students with learning disabilities. In D. Haager, J. Klingner, and S. Vaughn (Eds.), *Validated reading practices for three tiers of intervention* (pp. 3–9). Baltimore: Brookes.

Vaughn, S., Klingner, J. K., and Schumm, J. S. (1996). *Collaborative strategic reading.* Miami, FL: School-Based Research, University of Miami.

Vaughn, S., and Lancelotta, G. X. (1990). Teaching interpersonal skills to poorly accepted students: Peer-pairing versus non-peer-pairing. *Journal of School Psychology, 28,* 181–188.

Vaughn, S., Lancelotta, G. X., and Minnis, S. (1988). Social strategy training and peer involvement: Increasing peer acceptance of a female LD student. *Learning Disabilities Focus, 4*(1), 32–37.

Vaughn, S., and Linan-Thompson, S. (2003). What is special about special education for students with learning disabilities? *Journal of Special Education, 37,* 140–147.

Vaughn, S., and Linan-Thompson, S. (2004). *Research-based methods of reading instruction.* Alexandria, VA: ASCD.

Vaughn, S., Linan-Thompson, S., and Hickman, P. (2003). Response to instruction as a means of identifying students with reading/learning disabilities. *Exceptional Children, 69*(4), 391–409.

Vaughn, S., Linan-Thompson, S., Mathes, P. G., Cirino, P. T., Carlson, C. D., Pollard-Durodola, S. D., et al. (2006). Effectiveness of Spanish intervention for first-grade English language learners at risk for reading difficulties. *Journal of Learning Disabilities, 39*(1), 56–73.

Vaughn, S., Martinez, L. R., Linan-Thompson, S., Reutebuch, C. K., Carlson, C. D., and Francis, D. J. (2009). Enhancing social studies vocabulary and comprehension for seventh-grade English language learners: Findings from two experimental studies. *Journal of Research on Educational Effectiveness, 2*(4), 297–324.

Vaughn, S., Mathes, P. G., Linan-Thompson, S., Cirino, P. T., Carlson, C. D., Pollard-Durodola, S. D., et al. (2006). First-grade English language learners at-risk for reading problems: Effectiveness of an English intervention. *Elementary School Journal, 107*(2), 153–180.

Vaughn, S., McIntosh, R., Schumm, J. S., Haager, D., and Callwood, D. (1993). Social status and peer acceptance revisited. *Learning Disabilities Research and Practice, 8,* 82–88.

Vaughn, S., McIntosh, R., and Spencer-Rowe, J. (1991). Peer rejection is a stubborn thing: Increasing peer acceptance of rejected students with learning disabilities. *Learning Disabilities Research and Practice, 6*(2), 83–88, 152–157.

Vaughn, S., Schumm, J. S., and Arguelles, M. E. (1997). The ABCDE's of co-teaching. *Teaching Exceptional Children, 30*(2), 4–10.

Vaughn, S., Swanson, E. A., Roberts, G., Wanzek, J., Stillman-Spisak, S. J., Solis, M., and Simmons, D. (2013). Improving reading comprehension and social studies knowledge in middle school. *Reading Research Quarterly, 48*(1), 77–93.

Villa, R. A., Thousand, J. S., and Nevin, A. I. (2008). *A guide to co-teaching: Practical tips for facilitating student learning* (2nd ed.). Thousand Oaks, CA: Corwin Press.

Vygotsky, L. S. (1978). *Mind in society: The development of higher psychological processes.* Cambridge, MA: Harvard University Press.

Wade-Stein, D., and Kintsch, E. (2004). Summary street: Interactive computer support for writing. *Cognition and Instruction, 22*(3), 333–362.

Wallace, T., Shin, J., Bartholomay, T., and Stahl, B. J. (2001). Knowledge and skills for teachers supervising the work of paraprofessionals. *Exceptional Children, 67,* 520–534.

Wanzek, J., and Vaughn, S. (2009). Students demonstrating persistent low response to reading intervention: Three case studies. *Learning Disabilities Research and Practice, 24*(3), 151–163.

Wanzek, J., Vaughn, S., Wexler, J., Swanson, E. A., and Edmonds, M. (2006). A synthesis of spelling and reading outcomes for students with learning disabilities. *Journal of Learning Disabilities, 39*(6), 528–543.

Weiss, M. P., and Lloyd, J. (2003). Conditions for co-teaching: Lessons from a case study. *Teacher Education and Special Education, 26*(1), 27–41.

Weiss, M. P., and Lloyd, J. W. (2002). Congruence between roles and actions of secondary special educators in co-taught and special education settings. *Journal of Special Education, 36,* 58–68.

Wexler, J., Vaughn, S., Edmonds, M., and Reutebuch, C. K. (2008). A synthesis of fluency interventions for secondary struggling readers. *Reading and Writing: An Interdisciplinary Journal, 21*(4), 317–347.

Wexler, J., Vaughn, S., Roberts, G., and Denton, C. A. (2010). The efficacy of repeated reading and wide reading practice for high school students with severe reading disabilities. *Learning Disabilities Research and Practice, 25*(1), 2–10.

White, T. G., Sowell, J., and Yanagihara A. (1989). Teaching elementary students to use word-part clues. *The Reading Teacher, 42*(4), 302–308.

Whitehurst, G. J., and Lonigan, C. J. (2001). Emergent literacy: Development from pre-readers. In S. B. Neuman and D. K. Dickinson (Eds.), *Handbook of early literacy research* (pp. 11–29). New York: Guilford Press.

Wiig, E. H., and Semel, E. M. (1984). *Language assessment and intervention for the learning disabled* (2nd ed.). Columbus, OH: Merrill.

Wilkinson, I. A. G., and Anderson, R. C. (1995). Sociocognitive processes in guided silent reading: A microanalysis of small-group lessons. *Reading Research Quarterly, 30*(4), 710–740.

Williams, J. P. (1998). Improving the comprehension of disabled readers. *Annals of Dyslexia, 48,* 213–238.

Williams, J. P. (2005). Instruction in reading comprehension for primary-grade students. *Journal of Special Education, 39*(1), 6–18.

Wolery, M., Cybriwsky, C. A., Gast, D. L., and Boyle-Gast, K. (1991). Use of constant time delay and attentional responses with adolescents. *Exceptional Children, 57,* 462–474.

Wong, B. Y. L. (1986). A cognitive approach to teaching spelling. *Exceptional Children, 53,* 169–173.

Worthy, J. (1996). A matter of interest: Literature that hooks reluctant readers and keeps them reading. *The Reading Teacher, 50,* 204–212.

Wylie, R. E., and Durrell, D. D. (1970). Teaching vowels through phonograms. *Elementary English, 47,* 787–791.

Yee, A. (1969). Is the phonetic generalization hypothesis in spelling valid? *Journal of Experimental Education, 37,* 82–91.

Yopp, H. K., and Yopp, R. H. (2009). Phonological awareness is child's play. *Young, 64,* 1–9. Retrieved from http://www.naeyc.org/files/yc/file/200901/BTJPhonologicalAwareness.pdf

Zeno, S. M., Ivens, S. H., Millard, R. T., and Duvvuri, R. (1995). *The educator's word frequency guide.* Brewster, NY: Touchstone Applied Science Associates.

Zigmond, N. (2001). Special education at a crossroads. *Preventing School Failure, 45*(2), 70–74.

Zigmond, N. (2003). Where should students with disabilities receive special education services? Is one place better than another? *Journal of Special Education, 37,* 193–199.

Zorfass, J., Corley, P., and Remz, A. (1994). Helping students with disabilities become writers. *Educational Leadership, 51*(5), 62–66.

Name Index

A

Abbott, R. D., 304
Abruzzini, D., 167
Abudarham, S., 83
Ackerman, P. T., 378
Adams, G. L., 84, 332
Adams, M. J., 182
Adlof, S. M., 178
Adnan, R., 303
Ahmadi, M. R., 258
Ahwee, S., 261
Ainsworth, S., 325
Alber, S. R., 343
Alberto, P. A., 78
Alfassi, M., 258
Alfieri, L., 21
Allen, C., 208
Allen, R. V., 208
Alley, G. R., 40, 250, 328, 389
American Academy of Child and
    Adolescent Psychology, 88
American Foundation for Suicide
    Prevention, 88
American Speech-Language-Hearing
    Association (ASHA), 158
Amish, P. L., 89
Anders, P. L., 322, 323, 330
Anderson, D. H., 38
Anderson, L. M., 286, 287
Anderson, R. C., 262
Andrew, G., 350
Anhalt, J. M., 378
Anthony, H. M., 286
Apichataburtra, C., 226
Applebee, A. N., 244
Archer, A., 41
Ardoin, S. P., 20
Arguelles, M. E., 117, 123, 261
Arndt, E. J., 144
Arndt, S. A., 12
Aro, M., 237
Ashbaker, B. Y., 129
Ashlock, R. B., 373
Ashton-Warner, S., 209
Au, K. H., 247
August, D., 160, 238

Ault, M., 380
Austin, R., 197
Austin, T. Y., 296
Axelrod, S., 32

B

Badian, N. A., 363
Bahr, C. M., 365
Baker, S. K., 226, 227, 288, 366
Ball, E. W., 182
Beck, I.L., 204
Banda, D. R., 131
Bandura, A., 36
Banis, C. J., 167
Bank, J., 224
Baratz, J. C., 162
Barger-Anderson, R., 115, 122
Barnes, M. A., 177
Barnhart, R. K., 200
Bartek, M. M., 400
Bartholomay, T., 129
Bassett, D. S., 394
Batsche, G., 60
Bauman, J. F., 193, 316
Baumeister, J., 38
Bazik, E. F., 379
Beals, V., 40
Bear, D. R., 207, 208
Beattie, J. R., 226
Beck, A., 136
Beck, I. L., 198, 250, 251, 316
Beeler, T., 182
Beirne-Smith, 1991, 380
Beishuizen, J., 42
Belanger, S., 380
Bell, A. C., 89
Bender, W. N., 17, 53, 121, 337
Bereiter, C., 395
Bergerud, D., 333
Berkeley, S., 17, 53, 121, 230, 231, 249,
    256, 350
Bernadette, K., 395
Bernarding, M. B., 167
Berninger, V. W., 276, 278, 295, 301, 304
Berres, F., 213
Bertin, P., 200

Betts, E. A., 261, 262
Bilton, K. M., 82
Birsh, J. R., 205
Blacher, J., 136
Blachman, B. A., 144, 180, 182
Blachowicz, C., 270, 317
Blachowicz, D. O., 239
Black, R., 182
Blair, K. S., 28, 79
Blake, R. G., 250
Bley, N. S., 378
Block, C. C., 240, 288
Bloom, F., 205
Bloomfield, L., 200
Boardman, A. G., 238, 309, 310, 326
Boegler, S., 167
Bollinger, A., 288
Booth Olson, C., 288
Borden, K. F., 213
Boren, R., 302
Bos, C. S., 42, 44, 51, 75, 118, 130, 133, 179,
    195, 253, 254, 322, 323, 326, 330,
    341, 343, 390
Bott, D. A., 102
Bourassa, D. C., 296
Bowers, L., 166, 167
Bowers, R., 167
Boyle-Gast, K., 380
Braaksma, M., 250
Bradley, J. M., 213
Bradley, L., 301
Bradley, R., 6, 50
Brame, T., 302
Branum-Martin, L., 6, 238
Bresnahan, V., 123
Bridges, M. S., 146, 150
Briggs, A., 197
Bromley, K., 309
Brown-Chidsey, R., 48
Brown, A. L., 41, 255, 256, 257, 258
Bruner, E. C., 203
Bryant, B. R., 35, 182
Bryant, D. P., 35, 261, 356
Bryant, J., 245, 246
Bryant, N. D., 298
Buchanan, C., 200
Budd, D., 394

425

Jones, C. D., 231
Jordan, N. C., 362
Ju, S., 85
Juel, C., 243

K

Kahmi, A., 146
Kame'enui, E. J., 22, 193, 251, 280, 316
Kamins, M. L., 86
Kaplan, P., 32, 33
Kärnä, A., 84
Karns, K., 20
Katsiyannis, A., 78, 85
Kauffman, J., 302
Kaufmann, L., 377
Kearns, J., 295
Keen, D., 136
Keller-Margulis, M. A., 20, 368
Kelly, B., 384
Kennedy, C. H., 99
Kessler, B., 296
Ketterlin-Geller, L. R., 226
Khalid, P. I., 303
Kieffer, M., 229
Kilsheimer, L., 258
Kim, A., 261, 332, 333
Kim, A. H., 398, 400, 401
Kim, J. S., 230
Kim, Y. S., 222
King-Sears, M. E., 350
Kintsch, E., 293
Kirk, S. A., 182, 203, 204
Kirk, W. D., 182, 204
Kirkpatrick, L. C., 295
Klauda, S. L., 242, 261
Klausmeier, H. J., 329
Klein, P., 92
Klein, P. D., 295
Klingner, J. K., 49, 50, 51, 67, 120, 128, 238, 239, 240, 242, 249, 256, 258, 259, 261, 269, 326, 332, 356
Kloo, A., 119
Kloomok, S., 85
Knight, B., 328
Kobayashi, K., 344, 345
Kohfeldt, J., 32, 33
Konrad, M., 12
Koppel, A. E., 394
Kouzekanani, K., 204
Kratoville, B. L., 166
Krauss, M. W., 136
Kreiner, D. S., 337
Kress, J. E., 292
Kress, R. A., 213
Krist, J., 258
Kucer, S. B., 286
Kuhn, M. R., 230

Kukan, L., 316
Kuriloff, P. C., 290

L

Lancelotta, G. X., 83, 90
Landis, D., 210
Lane, H. B., 182
Lane, K. L., 282
Lang, S. C., 338
Langan, J., 353
Langberg, J. M., 337
Langer, J. A., 244
Lanier, J. E., 240
Lankford, F. G., 382
Laraux, M., 332
Lardieri, L. A., 136
Lathrop, M., 79
Lau, M., 60
Lazzari, A. M., 166
Leavell, A. G., 286
Lechner, O., 182
Lederer, J. M., 258
Lee, D., 366
Lee, I. S., 79
Lee, O., 74
Leinwand, S., 365
Lenz, B. K., 40, 320, 322, 327, 328, 329, 330, 332, 336, 350
Leon, J. A., 391
Lesaux, N., 229
Lessenberry, B. M., 136
Lieberman, R., 88
Lin, D. M.-Y., 193
Linan-Thompson, S., 60, 65, 204, 235, 237, 241
Lindamood, P. A., 182, 205
Lindsay, G., 63
Little, T. D., 146
Lloyd, J. W., 123, 280
Lo, J. J., 289
Lo, L., 12
Loban, W., 149
Lobel, A., 199
Loeb, D. F., 153
Logan, J. W., 315
LoGiudice, C., 166, 167
LoGiudice, M., 167
Lonigan, C. J., 226
Loomer, B. M., 300
Loomes, C., 350
Lovett, B. J., 338
Lovett, M. W., 258
Lovin, L. H., 391
Lovitt, T. C., 333
Lundberg, I., 182
Lutz, J. G., 368
Lyerla, K. D., 40

Lyon, G. R., 177
Lyons, T. S., 166

M

MacArthur, C. A., 284, 288, 293
MacDonald, V., 258
Macrorie, K., 307
Maddox, M., 149
Mahdavi, J., 118
Maheady, L., 99, 299, 380
Mallette, B., 99
Malone, K., 166
Malone, L. D., 256
Mancha, S., 210
Manji, S., 350
Marchant, M., 38
Marquis, J. G., 320
Marshak, L., 349
Marston, D., 60
Martin, J. E., 12
Martin, J. H., 210
Martinez, L. R., 151, 238, 316, 322, 332
Martinez, M., 226
Mason, L. H., 39, 276, 284, 293
Mastropieri, M. A., 99, 122, 213, 256, 349, 350
Mather, N., 195, 235
Mathes, P. G., 98, 182, 187, 203, 204, 231
Matuszny, R. M., 131
Mauser, A. J., 137
McConnell, S. R., 99
McCurdy, B. L., 76
McCutchen, D., 288
McDaniel, M. A., 346
McDuffie, K. A., 122
McGinnis, E., 92
McGovern, K. I., 199
McIntosh, R., 74, 94, 116
McIntyre, C. W., 207
McKenna, J. W., 66
McKeown, M. G., 250, 251, 316
McKnight, P. C., 346
McMaster, K. L., 99
McNaughton, D., 293
McPeek Glisam, E., 395
McRae, A., 242
Meichenbaum, D., 36
Meister, C., 256, 258
Mellard, D., 254, 346
Mercer, A. R., 102
Mercer, C. D., 40, 102, 350
Metsala, J. L., 177
Michaelsen, L. K., 97
Millard, R. T., 194, 196
Miller, D. E., 400
Miller, J. H., 390

Subject Index

A

AAA Math, 369

Abstract language, 146–147

Academic performance, common behaviors, 2

Academic vocabulary, 315

Acceptance, 131–132

Accommodations
collaboration, issues with, 119–120
IEP elements, 11
inclusion with peers, 6
math tests, 370
need for, 3
second-language acquisition, 162–163

Achievement tests, identifying needs, 6–7

Acquisition stage, learning, 35–36, 36f

Acronyms, memory skills, 349–350

Acrostics, 308–309, 349–350

Adaptations
class assignments and homework, 337
coteaching and, 125–128
instructional design, 21
math curricula and materials, 393–395
tests, 337–339
textbook adaptations, 334–337

Add-a-Part: Prefixes and Suffixes, 355

Adding sounds, 179

Addition and America activity, 400

Addition fact groups strategy, 381

Addition skills, 377–383, 380f, 382f, 383t

Administrative support, 118

Adolescents
math story problems, 390
reading skills, special consideration, 261
social difficulties, 85–89

Advanced organizers, 283, 326–328

Aesthetic reading, 240, 240f

Affixes, 144, 145f

African American English, 161f–162f

Aggressive behavior, 3, 83–84

AIMweb Systems, 183

Algebraic principles, 372

Alliteration skills, 179–182, 180t

Alphabetic principle
explicit instruction, 198–208, 200f, 202f, 203f, 204f, 205f

letter-sound correspondence, 184–188, 185f, 186f, 187f, 188f
multisensory structured language instruction, 205
phonological awareness, teaching of, 180–182, 180t, 181f, 182f
reading instruction components, 178

Analytic phonics, 192

ANSWER, essay test strategies, 352–354, 354f

Antecedents, manipulating, 28–29

Antecedents, target behaviors, 77

Antonyms, 157

A Parent's Guide to Response to Intervention (RTI), 67

Application stage, learning, 35–36, 36f

Applied behavior analysis
decreasing undesirable behavior, 33–35
increasing desirable behavior, 29–33, 32f, 33f
learning stages, 35–36, 36f
manipulating antecedents, 28–29
positive behavioral support, 75–79

Applied mathematics, 365

Apply the Concept
33 ways to say "very good," 31
adaptations by general education teachers, 116
advance organizers, 327–328
ASSET, 92
bullying, prevention of, 84
cognitive strategy instruction, 40–41
collaboration, benefits and misuse of, 119
communication with families, 133
comprehension, concept-oriented lessons, 242
comprehension, cultural diversity and, 243
comprehension, English language learners, 241, 243
comprehension monitoring, 44
conversations, learning and, 152
cooperative learning, 98
coteaching, 122, 125
decoding unknown words, 190
English language learners with disabilities, 24
evaluating instruction, 23
families, needs of, 137

FAST, activity sheet for, 91

feedback, providing, 64

fluency, 224, 225, 227, 228, 229

functional math, 394

generalizing, 36

handwriting fluency, 305

intensive interventions, 66

language intervention strategies, 153

language skills, teaching guidelines, 151

listen and watch cues, lectures, 336

math skills, common core, 364

math skills, curricula and materials, 395

math skills, fractions, 384

math skills, problem solving, 389, 390

math skills, teaching of, 381, 382, 393

memory skills, improving, 348

nonresponse to instruction, 62

paraprofessional collaboration, 130

phonological skills, 179

prefixes, suffixes and inflectional endings, 194

progress monitoring, 55, 57

reinforcers, 30

RTI (response to intervention), 8, 61, 65, 67, 139

scaffolding, 22

self-regulation, promoting, 86

spelling, peer tutoring and, 299

strategy effectiveness, assessing, 39

teaching concepts, 322

testing accommodations, 338

test taking strategies, 353

textbook adaptations, 334

text types and learning to read, 198–199

time, measurement skills, 386

time-out, 35

transition planning, 14

word bank cards, 211

writing, big picture focus, 286

writing, responses to, 289, 291–292

writing, special learning needs students, 294

writing, teaching strategies, 278

writing, topic selection, 283

Arguments, text structure, 252f

ASK IT, 250, 250f

Coh-metrix, 324–325, 325*f*
Coin Concentration activity, 397
Collaboration, students
cooperative learning, 93, 97–98
Collaboration, teachers
benefits and misuse of, 119
communication skills, 132–135
coplanning, 125–128, 126*f*, 127*f*
coteaching, overview of, 121–129, 121*f*, 126*f*, 127*f*
families, working with, 130–131, 135–139
issues and dilemmas, 118–121
overview of, 116–117
paraprofessionals, collaboration with, 129–130
resources for, 118
RTI and, 63, 67–68, 117–118, 135
Collaborative strategic reading (CSR), 256–261, 259*f*, 260*f*
Common Core State Standards
content area reading, 320, 321*f*
language standards, 142–143, 143*f*
math skills, 363–364
reading fluency and comprehension, 220–222, 221*f*
writing across content areas, 294–295
writing standards, 277*f*
Communication, student skills. *See also* Oral language skills
language development and difficulties, 146–150, 148*f*, 149*f*
pragmatics, 144, 146
social disabilities and, 83
speech-language therapy, 164
Communication, with families
IEPs, 12
progress monitoring, 17
Communication, with professionals
coteaching and, 125
with general education teachers, 134–135
interviewing skills, 132–134
principles of, 131–132
RTI model for collaboration, 135
Compare and Diagnose, writing revisions, 288
Compare-contrast texts, structure of, 252*f*
Comparison tables, 328–329, 329*f*, 330*f*
Completion questions, test strategies, 353
Compliments, phrases for, 31
Composing, writing process, 285–287, 287*f*
Compound Concentration game, 216
Compound words, decoding, 192–193
Comprehension. *See* Reading fluency and comprehension
Comprehensive Test of Phonological Processing (CTOPP), 184
Computational skills, 377–383, 380*f*, 382*f*, 383*t*

Computer-assisted instruction
reading practice, 228
spelling, 303
writing, 293
Concept Builders, 166
Concept diagrams, 328–329, 329*f*, 330*f*
Concepts, teaching of
assignments and homework adaptations, 337, 338
conceptual vocabulary, 322
prelearning activities, 326–333
reinforcing concepts, 333
selecting concepts and vocabulary, 322, 323*f*
student background knowledge, 326, 326*f*
superordinate, subordinate, and coordinate concepts, 329–330
test adaptations, 337–339
textbook adaptations, 334–337
texts, evaluation of, 323–326, 324*f*, 325*f*
Conceptual vocabulary, defined, 320, 322
Conferences with family, 137–139
Connect-A-Card, 167
Connections approach, spelling, 301*f*
Consequences, use of, 29–35, 32*f*, 33*f*, 74–75
Considerate texts, 325–326
Consonant-le (C+le) syllables, 195*t*
Consonant sounds, 185–186, 185*f*, 186*f*
Consonant-vowel-consonant-e (CVCe) syllables, 195*t*
Constant time-delay procedure, math skills, 380–381
Constant time-delay procedure, spelling, 302
Consultant teaching, defined, 117
Consultation, overview of, 116–117
Content, language skills, 143–144, 143*f*, 208–213, 209*f*, 212*f*
Content areas, writing across, 294–295
Content area vocabulary
assignments and homework adaptations, 337, 338
common core reading standards, 320, 321*f*
example scenario, 313–314
instructional activities, 355–358
math skills, 362–363, 382–383, 384
oral and reading vocabularies, 315–316
prelearning activities, 326–333
reinforcing concepts, 333
selecting concepts and vocabulary, 322, 323*f*
student background knowledge, 326, 326*f*
test adaptations, 337–339
textbook adaptations, 334–337
texts, evaluation of, 323–326, 324*f*, 325*f*
word-learning strategies, 317–320, 318*f*, 319*f*
Context, language skills, 150, 190, 196–197

Context, teaching-learning process, 14–16, 15*f*, 44
Contextual analysis, vocabulary skills, 317–318
Contextual Searching activity, 356–357, 357*f*
Contingency contracting, 33, 33*f*
Contingent restraint, 35
Continuants, letter sounds, 185
Conventions, writing skills, 278–279
Conversations, learning and, 41–44, 43*f*, 151, 152, 159
Conversations: A Framework for Language Intervention, 167
Cooperative learning, 93, 97–98, 124, 260–261
Coordinate concepts, 329–332
Coordination of paraprofessionals, 117
Coplanning, 125–128, 126*f*, 127*f*
Copy-cover-compare method, spelling, 301*f*
Correction, math instruction, 364–365, 392
Corrective reading, 201–203, 201*f*, 202*f*, 203*f*
Coteaching
communication skills, 132–135
coplanning, 125–128, 126*f*, 127*f*
models for, 123–124
overview of, 117, 121–129, 121*f*, 126*f*, 127*f*
roles and challenges, 115–116
secondary students, 124–125
Council for Exceptional Children, 67, 129
Counseling, support services, 4–5
Counting skills, 179, 369–370, 379–380
Create a Comic, 172
Creature from Outer Space, 165, 168
Critical reading, skills involved, 239–240, 240*f*
Cubing, 306
Cue cards, writing process, 286
Cues
essay tests, 354*f*
lectures, 336
math instruction, 392
Culturally diverse students
comprehension skills, 243
family considerations, 138
language skills, 159–160
mathematics instruction, 366–367
RTI and, 67
special education and, 51
writing, teaching tips, 293
Curriculum-based measurement (CBM), progress, 17, 20, 183–184, 367
Curriculum maps, 332–333

D

Date by Telephone activity, 108
Daydream Chair, 169–170
Decision-making team, RTI approaches, 61
Decodable text, 198, 199

Decoding, 177–178, 189–197, 190*f*, 191*f*, 192*f*, 193*f*, 195*f*, 196*f*
Deleting sounds, 179
Demonstrating, study skills, 348–354, 354*f*
Descriptive texts, structure of, 251–253, 252*f*
Diagnostic assessments, phonics skills, 183–184
Dialogue, learning and, 41–44, 43*f*
Dialogue journals, progress monitoring, 17
DIBELS progress monitoring, 17
Dictionaries, vocabulary instruction, 319
Differential reinforcement, 33–34
Digital recorders, 100
Digraph, consonants, 185–186, 186*f*
Directed Reading Activity (DRA), 261–263
Directed reading-thinking activity (DR-TA), 263–264, 269–270
Direct teaching approach, vocabulary, 316
Discrimination skills, 179
Division, math skills, 377–383, 380*f*, 382*f*, 383*t*
Dramatic reading activities, 266–267
Duration sampling, 77
Dysgraphia, 303–305
Dyslexia, 205, 207

E

Early intervention services (EIS), 51
Easy reader text, 199
E-books, use for repeated readings, 228
Editing, writing process, 287–290, 289*f*
Effective instruction, 16–17
Eighteen Concepts, math skills, 372–376
Elaboration, language skills, 153, 157
Elaborative knowledge questions, 247
Elkonin procedure (boxes), 181–182, 181*f*, 182*f*
Emotional disabilities, students with, 5–6, 12–13
English language learners (ELLs)
    collaborative strategic reading, 258–261, 259*f*, 260*f*
    comprehension skills, 243
    designing instruction for, 24
    family considerations, 138
    idioms, 146–147
    math instruction, 362–363, 366–367
    modified language experience approach, 208–211, 209*f*
    needs identification, 51
    phonemic remedial reading lessons, 203–205, 204*f*, 205*f*
    reading instruction, tips for, 237
    repeated reading, 229
    RTI, use of, 61, 67
    second-language acquisition, 160–163, 160*f*, 161*f*, 162*f*
    web resources, 163
    writing, teaching tips, 293, 296

Entry stage, learning, 35–36, 36*f*
Environment, learning. *See* Classroom environment and management
Equipment, selection and use, 100–104, 101*f*, 102*f*, 103*f*
Error analysis, spelling, 297
Error Monitoring Strategy, 40
Essay tests, strategies for, 352–353
Ethics, paraprofessional collaborations, 129–130
Evaluation of instruction, 23, 128–129
Event sampling, 77
Evidence-based instruction
    advance organizers, 327–328
    ASSET, 90–91, 92
    brainstorming, 244
    choral repeated reading, 229–230
    concept diagrams and comparison tables, 328–329, 329*f*, 330*f*
    Directed Reading Activity (DRA), 261–263
    directed reading-thinking activity (DR-TA), 263–264
    FAST, 90, 90*f*, 91
    Fernald method (VAKT), 211–213, 212*f*
    fluency, peer-supported reading, 230–231, 231*f*
    fluency, reading performance, 232, 232*f*
    fluency, repeated reading, 227–228
    K-W-L strategy, 245–246, 246*f*
    modified language experience approach, 208–211, 209*f*
    Multipass strategy, 346–347
    multisensory structured language instruction, 207
    onset-rime and word families, 200–201, 201*f*
    phonemic remedial reading lessons, 203–205, 204*f*, 205*f*
    phonic generalizations, 206–207
    questioning strategies, comprehension, 247–251, 248*f*, 250*f*
    reading mastery and corrective reading, 201–203, 201*f*, 202*f*, 203*f*
    relationship charts, 329–332
    scaffolded sustained silent reading, 231
    semantic and curriculum maps, 332–333
    semantic feature analysis, 329–332
    sight words, techniques for building, 213–214, 214*f*
    special education, features of, 4
    story mapping, 253–254, 253*f*
    summarization strategy, 255–256, 256*f*
    text preview, 245
    word study, 207–208
Examples, language skills and, 154
Executive function, 42
Expansion, language skills, 153
Expectations, classroom behavior, 72–75, 75*f*
Explicit instruction, 21, 198–208, 200*f*, 202*f*, 203*f*, 204*f*, 205*f*

Exploring Pragmatic Language, 167
Expository text question cards, 270–271*f*
Expository texts, structure of, 251–253, 252*f*
Externalizing behaviors, 82
Extinction, 33, 77
Extracurricular activities, 85

F

Families
    adjustments by, 136–139
    beginning reading participation, 188–189
    collaboration with, 130–131
    cultural or linguistical diversity, 138
    experiences of, 113–114
    homework, 337, 338
    IEP team members, 5, 7–8, 12
    language skill development, 163
    math instruction, 366
    positive behavioral support, 79
    reading fluency improvement, 234
    Response to Intervention (RTI), role in, 50, 67–68
    severity of problem, input from, 3
    transition planning, 13–14
FAST, 90, 90*f*, 91
Feedback
    classroom management and, 74
    instruction delivery and, 24
    language skills, 154
    large and small group instruction, 95, 96
    math instruction, 364–365, 392
    peer teaching, 98–99
    providing of, 64
    social skills, teaching principles, 93–94
    spelling, teaching of, 297, 298–299
    writing, revising and editing, 287–290, 289*f*, 292
Fernald method (VAKT), 211–213, 212*f*
Fernald method, spelling, 301–302
Fighting. *See* Aggressive behavior
Figurative language, 146–147
Figurative Language: A Comprehensive Program, 154
Finding Like Units activity, 401–402
Find the Way, 170
First Grade PALS, 233*f*
FIRST-letter mnemonic strategy, 40, 349–350
Five-step word strategy, spelling, 300–301
Flannel boards, 377
Flexible grouping, instructional design, 20–21. *See also* Groups
Fluency, handwriting, 304–305
Fluency, number sense, 369–370
Fluency, reading. *See* Reading fluency and comprehension
Form, language, 144, 147–148, 148*f*, 158
Fractions, math skills, 383–385, 384*f*
Friendships, 94. *See also* Peer interactions

Fry readability formula, 323–324, 324*f*
Functional behavioral assessment (FBA), 79–82, 80*f*, 81*f*
Functional math skills, 394
Fun with Figurative Language, 172–173

G

Games, instructional, 102–103, 103*f*, 155–157
General education teachers. *See* Teachers
Generalization stage, learning, 35–36, 36*f*, 365
Getting the gist, 259–260, 267–269
Gillingham and Stillman approach, spelling, 302
Gist, getting the, 259–260, 267–269
Goals
    behavior change, 77
    designing instruction, 20–23
    fluency goals, 224–225, 224*f*
    IEP elements, 8, 10–11, 11*f*
    interpersonal problem solving, 89–93, 90*f*
    language, common core standards, 142–143, 143*f*
    performance record, 19–20, 19*f*
    planning, coteaching and, 125–128, 126*f*, 127*f*
    school-wide, 79
    self-regulation, 37–38
    SMART guideline, 11
    time management skills, 340–343, 342*f*, 343*f*
    transition planning, 13–14
Go Fish for Rimes, 216
Grading, coteaching and, 128
Grammar Scramble: A Grammar and Sentence-Building Game, 167
Gram's Cracker: A Grammar Game, 167
Graphemes, 180–182, 180*t*, 181*f*, 182*f*
Graphic organizers, 241, 284, 307
Graphs, progress monitoring, 17–18, 18*f*
Great Leaps, 233*f*
Greek roots, vocabulary, 318
Greetings, by teacher, 93
Groups
    collaborative strategic reading (CSR), 258–261, 259*f*, 260*f*
    cooperative learning, 93, 97–98
    coteaching and, 121*f*
    group contingencies, 32
    instructional design and, 20–21
    instructional environment, 95–99
    instruction delivery, 24
    large group instruction, 95
    math skill practice, 380
    mixed-ability groups, 123
    multiple groups, coteaching, 124
    RTI interventions, 65
    RTI tiers of response, 57–58, 58*f*

same-ability groups, 124
small-group instruction, 95–96
study groups, content area vocabulary and, 358
Guardians. *See* Families
Guided oral reading, 226–227

H

Handwriting, 303–305
HELP, 166
High-frequency words, 194–196, 196*f*
High-utility words, 316
Homework, adapting, 337
Homogeneous groups, 121*f*
Homonyms, 298
How to texts, structure of, 252*f*
Hyperactivity
    classroom management and, 84–85
    common behaviors, 2

I

IDEA. *See* Individuals with Disabilities Education Act (IDEA)
Identifying Feelings activity, 109
Idioms, 146–147, 156–157
IEP. *See* Individual Education Plan (IEP)
IFSP (Individualized Family Service Plan), 138
Imagery, math skills and, 363
I'm in My Own Little House activity, 109–110
I'm New Here activity, 109
Implicit code instruction, 208–213, 209*f*, 212*f*
Inclusion with peers. *See also* Peer interactions
    challenges of, 115–116
    class participation, 343
    decisions about, 5–6
Independent learning, 96–97
Indirect teaching approach, vocabulary, 316
Individual Education Plan (IEP)
    committee for, 5
    coteaching, models for, 123
    family involvement, 12, 136–137
    inclusion with peers, decisions about, 5–6
    as performance record, 19–20, 19*f*
    special education, features of, 4
    student involvement, 12–13
    team members, 7–8
    transition planning, 13–14
    writing of, 7–11, 9*f*, 10*f*, 11*f*
Individualized Family Service Plan (IFSP), 138
Individuals with Disabilities Education Act (IDEA)
    family involvement and, 139

functional behavioral assessment, 79–82, 80*f*, 81*f*
    IEP guidelines, 7–8, 10, 12
    inclusion with peers, 5–6
    Response to Intervention (RTI), 48
    student placement, 5
    transition planning, 13–14
Individuals with Disabilities Education Improvement Act (IDEIA), 51, 51*f*
Individual transition plan (ITP), 13–14
Inflectional endings, word sounds, 144, 145*f*, 192–193, 194
Information texts, structure of, 251–253, 252*f*
Inquiry-based learning, 41–42
Institute for Education Sciences (IES)
    writing instruction guidelines, 287, 288*f*
Instructional activities. *See also* Evidence-based instruction
    audio-assisted reading, 266
    choral reading, 265
    chunk reading, 266
    content area vocabulary, 355–358
    directed reading-thinking activity (DR-TA), 269–270
    dramatic reading, 266–267
    expository text question cards, 270–271*f*
    generating questions, 269
    getting the gist, 267–269
    language skills, 165–172
    mathematics skills, 396–402
    narrative comprehension card activity, 271–272, 271*f*
    oral reading critiques, 267
    partner reading, 265
    phonological awareness, 215–216
    phrase card reading, 266
    predict the plot, 272
    previewing, 267
    reading fluidity and comprehension, 265–272
    self-monitoring, 269
    story jumble, 272
    WH game, 272
    writing skills, 305–310
Instructional arrangement, classroom, 95–99
Instructional content
    antecedents, 28
    delivery of, 23–24
    severity of problem, determining, 3
Instructional cycle, 15*f*, 16
Instructional design, 20–23, 24
Instructional games, 102–103, 103*f*
Instructional goals. *See* Goals
Instructional materials, selection of, 100–104, 101*f*, 102*f*, 103*f*
Instructional modifications. *See* Accommodations
Instructional time, RTI, 57–58, 58*f*
Interactive dialogue, learning and, 41–44, 43*f*
Internalizing behaviors, 82

International Dyslexia Association, 6

International Multisensory Language Education (IMSLEC), 207

Interpersonal problem solving (ISP), 89–93, 90f

Interval sampling, 77

Interventions. *See* Response to intervention (RTI)

Interviewing skills, 132–134, 309

Intrinsic reinforcers, 30–31

Introducing People activity, 110

Introspective questions, 247

Invitation to Play activity, 110

In Your Shoes activity, 110

IQ tests, identifying student needs, 6–7

IRIS module, math skills, 370–371

Irregular verbs, 149f

I Spy, 170–171

IT FITS, 350

ITP (Individual transition plan), 13–14

It's For Sale!, 169

J

Jeopardy, 357–358, 358f

Johnson and Myklebust technique, spelling, 301

Journals, 19–20, 19f

K

Keyboarding skills, 303–305

Key-word method, memory skills, 350

Kinesthetic method, spelling, 301f

K-W-L strategy, 245–246, 246f

L

Language. *See* English language learners (ELLs); Oral language skills

Language for Learning, 154

Language Lessons in the Classroom, 166

Large group instruction, 95

Latin roots, vocabulary, 318

LCD projectors, 101

Learning, stages of, 35–36, 36f

Learning Addition activity, 400

Learning centers, 124

Learning disabilities. *See also* Individual Education Plan (IEP)

communication disabilities and, 83

identifying student needs, 6–7, 50, 63–64

prevalence of, 50

Learning environment. *See* Classroom environment and management

Learning logs, 17

Learning strategies. *See* Study skills

Learning Strategies Curriculum, 40–41, 42

Learn Those Words!, 358–359

Least restrictive environment, 5–6

Legal issues. *See also* Individuals with Disabilities Education Act (IDEA)

contingent restraint, 35

time-out, 35

Legibility, handwriting, 304

Letter-sound correspondence

consonant sounds, 185–186, 186f

explicit instruction, 198–208, 200f, 202f, 203f, 204f, 205f

implicit code instruction, 208–213, 209f, 212f

instructional activities, 215–216

multisensory structured language instruction, 205

overview of, 179–180

phonic generalizations, 206–207

resources of, 187

sight words, techniques for building, 213–214, 214f

teaching of, 180–182, 180t, 181f, 182f, 184–188, 185f, 186f, 187f, 188f

vowel sounds, 187–188, 187f, 188f

Lexile level of a text, 323–324, 324f

Library of Vocabulary Photographs, 166

Linguistically diverse students. *See also* English language learners (ELLs)

family considerations, 138

mathematics instruction, 366–367

RTI and, 67

second-language acquisition, 160–163, 160f, 161f, 162f

special education needs, 51

writing, teaching tips, 293

Linguistic reading programs, 200–201, 201f

Linkage goals, transition planning, 13–14

Listening skills

common core standards, 221f

communication principles, 132

lecture cues, 336

study skills, 343–345, 344f

Listen My Children, and You Shall Hear, 166

LISTS strategy, 349–350

Long vowels, 187–188, 187f, 188f, 193f

M

Maintenance stage, learning, 35–36, 36f

Making and Keeping Friends activity, 109

Making words, 207–208

Manipulation of phonemes, 179, 180–182, 180t, 181f, 182f

Manipulatives, math instruction, 367, 383–384

Many Meanings activity, 170

Marblesoft Simtech, 58

MARKER strategy, 341

Matching tests, strategy for, 353

Mathematics skills

accommodations, 370

assessment and progress monitoring, 367–371, 368f, 369f

calculators, use of, 383

Common Core State Standards, 363–364

computation skills, 377–383, 380f, 382f, 383t

curricula and materials, suggestions for, 393–395

curriculum-based measurement, performance, 20

diverse students, 366–367

factors influencing, 362–367

fractions, 383–385, 384f

functional math, 394

identifying student needs, 6–7

instructional activities, 102–103, 103f, 396–402

instructional practices, 363–366

math facts, learning of, 379

measurement, 385–387

number sense, 369–370

numeration and place value, 372–377

performance improvement, approaches to, 391–395

prenumber skills, 371–372

problem solving, 387–391, 391f

response to intervention, 370–371

RTI interventions, 65

support services, 4–5

universal screening, 54–55

vocabulary and, 382–383, 384

MathPadPlus, 367

Meaning, words

decoding, structural analysis, 192–193

decoding, syntax and semantics, 196–197

implicit code instruction, 208–213, 209f, 212f

language development and difficulties, 146–150, 148f, 149f

pragmatics, 144–145

Measurement, math skills, 385–387

Measures of Academic Progress (MAPS), 58

Memory

common difficulties, 2

executive function, 42

reading and, 178

skills, tips for improving, 348–354, 354f

Mental imagery, math skills and, 363

Metacognition, 42, 178, 256–257

Metaphors, 146–147, 156–157

Mind-opening questions, 247

Mixed-ability groups, 123

Mnemonics, use of, 349–350

Modeling

cognitive strategy instruction (CSI), 37

comprehension, teaching guidelines, 241–242

Phonological awareness (*cont.*)
    English language learners, instructional tips, 237
    evidence-based practice, onset rimes and word families, 200–201, 201*f*
    explicit instruction, 198–208, 200*f*, 202*f*, 203*f*, 204*f*, 205*f*
    Fernald method (VAKT), 211–213, 212*f*
    implicit code instruction, 208–213, 209*f*, 212*f*
    instructional activities, 215–216
    letter-sound correspondence, 184–188, 185*f*, 186*f*, 187*f*, 188*f*
    modified language experience approach, 208–211, 209*f*
    multisensory structured language instruction, 205, 207
    phonemic remedial reading lessons, 203–205, 204*f*, 205*f*
    phonic generalizations, 206–207
    reading mastery and corrective reading, 201–203, 201*f*, 202*f*, 203*f*
    resources for, 187
    response to intervention and progress monitoring, 182–184
    sight words, techniques for building, 213–214, 214*f*
    spelling, teaching of, 296–303, 301*f*
    targeted instruction, example of, 175–177
    teaching of, 180–182, 180*t*, 181*f*, 182*f*
    vowel sounds, 187–188, 187*f*, 188*f*
    word study, 207–208
Phonology, 143*f*, 144, 160*f*
Phrase card reading, 266
Physical restraint, 35
Picture association, sight words, 213–214, 214*f*
Pictures, language skill development, 159
PIRATES strategy, 352
Place value, math skills, 372–377
PLAN, prewriting strategy, 284
Planning, teachers. *See also* Individual Education Plan (IEP)
    coplanning, 125–128, 126*f*, 127*f*
    families, role of, 136–137
    problem-solving model, RTI, 60–61
Planning skills, students
    language instruction, 154
    writing assignments, 281–285, 285*f*, 286*f*, 287*f*, 307*f*
Play the Part, 172
Please Help activity, 108
Ponderable questions, 247
Portfolios, 17, 339
Positive behavioral intervention and supports (PBIS), 75–79
Positive behavioral support (PBS), 75–79
Positive reinforcement, 29–31, 74
Postsecondary settings, transition planning, 13–14

POW, prewriting strategy, 284
Pragmatic Activities for Language Intervention, 167
Pragmatic communication, 83
Pragmatics, 144, 146, 148–150, 149*f*, 158–159
Praise, 31, 86
Predictable language, text types, 198
Predictions, reading and, 178
Predictive questions, 247
Predict the plot activity, 272
Prefixes
    decoding, 192–193
    language, morphology, 144, 145*f*
    list of common prefixes, 145*f*, 319*f*
    sight words and, 189
    vocabulary instruction, 318, 319*f*
Prelearning activities, content vocabulary, 326–333
Premack principle, 31–32
Prenumber skills, 371–372
PreReading Plan (PReP), 244–245, 326
President's Commission on Excellence in Special Education, 2002, 50
Preteaching vocabulary, 316–317
Previewing books, comprehension and, 240–246, 246*f*, 258
    instructional activities, 267
    PreReading Plan (PReP), 244–245
Previewing books, fluency and, 226–227
Prewriting activities, 281–285, 285*f*, 286*f*, 287*f*
Prior knowledge
    brainstorming, 244
    PreReading Plan (PReP), 244–245
    previewing, predicting, and developing, 242–246, 246*f*
    reading and, 178
    text preview, 245
Privileges, as reward, 74, 75*f*
Problem box activity, 108
Problem-solution texts, structure of, 252*f*
Problem solving
    applied mathematics, 365
    interpersonal problem solving, 89–93, 90*f*
    scaffolded instruction, 41–42
Problem-solving model, RTI, 60–61
Problem-solving model, teacher collaboration, 120–121
Procedures, classroom, 72–75, 75*f*. *See also* Classroom environment and management
Process skills, 343–347, 344*f*
Professional development, 50
Proficiency stage, learning, 35–36, 36*f*
Progress graphs and charts, 17–19, 18*f*, 19*f*
Progress journal, 19–20, 19*f*
Progress monitoring
    comprehension, 234–236, 235*f*
    consequences, use of, 29

    evaluation measures, 17–20, 18*f*, 19*f*
    math skills, 364–365, 367–371, 368*f*, 369*g*
    phonological awareness and phonics, 182–184
    portfolios and work samples, 339
    reading fluency, 222–224, 222*t*
    Response to Intervention (RTI), 48, 49–50, 52–54, 53*f*, 57
    self-regulation, 37–38
    vocabulary skills, 320
    Web Resources, 120
    writing skills, 280–281, 291
PROJECTS, time management, 342–343
Proofreading with SCOPE, 309
Proverbs, 146–147, 156–157
Psychologist, role of, 64
Punctuation errors, writing revision, 289
Punishment, 34, 77

Q

Question-answer relationships (QAR) strategy, 247–249, 248*f*
Questioning skills, interviews, 132–134
Questioning skills, teachers, 132
Questioning strategies, comprehension skills, 246–251, 248*f*, 250*f*
Questioning the Author, comprehension skills, 250–251
Questions, activities for generating, 269–272, 271*f*
Questions, test-taking strategies, 353
Quick pacing, 23
QuickReads, 233*f*

R

R-controlled syllables, 195*t*
Readability of texts, 323–325, 324*f*, 325*f*
Readers' theater, 232, 232*f*
Reading
    common core content area standards, 320, 321*f*
    culturally and linguistically diverse students, 51
    curriculum-based measurement, performance, 20
    digital recorders, 100
    executive function, 42
    identifying student needs, 6–7
    instructional games, 102–103, 103*f*
    language development and difficulties, 146–150, 148*f*, 149*f*
    RTI interventions, 65
    scaffolding and, 21–22
    support services, 4–5
    universal screening, 54–55, 56*f*